Microsoft® Office XP

Illustrated Introductory, Enhanced Edition

Microsoft® Office ᴾ

Illustrated Introductory, Enhanced Edition

Beskeen/Duffy/Friedrichsen/Reding

Approved
Courseware
CORE
(1 of 2)

Australia • Canada • Mexico • Singapore • Spain • United Kingdom • United States

THOMSON

COURSE TECHNOLOGY

Microsoft Office ᵡᴾ - Illustrated Introductory, Enhanced Edition
Beskeen/Duffy/Friedrichsen/Reding

Managing Editor:
Nicole Jones Pinard

Production Editor:
Catherine G. DiMassa

QA Manuscript Reviewers:
John Freitas, Ashlee Welz, Alex
White, Harris Bierhoff, Serge
Palladino, Holly Schabowski, Jeff
Schwartz

Product Managers:
Jennifer T. Campbell, Christina
Kling Garrett

Developmental Editors:
Katherine T. Pinard, Rachel
Biheller Bunin, Barbara Clemens,
Pamela Conrad

Text Designer:
Joseph Lee, Black Fish Design

Editorial Assistant:
Elizabeth M. Harris

Composition House:
GEX Publishing Services

Contributing Authors:
Ann Fisher, Rachel Biheller Bunin,
Carol Cram

The Illustrated Series Vision

Teaching and writing about computer applications can be extremely rewarding and challenging. How do we engage students and keep their interest? How do we teach them skills that they can easily apply on the job? As we set out to write this book, our goals were to develop a textbook that:

▶ works for a beginning student

▶ provides varied, flexible and meaningful exercises and projects to reinforce the skills

▶ serves as a reference tool

▶ makes your job as an educator easier, by providing resources above and beyond the textbook to help you teach your course

Our popular, streamlined format is based on advice from instructional designers and customers. This flexible design presents each lesson on a two-page spread, with step-by-step instructions on the left, and screen illustrations on the right. This signature style, coupled with high-caliber content, provides a comprehensive yet manageable introduction to Microsoft Office XP - it is a teaching package for the instructor and a learning experience for the student.

AUTHOR ACKNOWLEDGMENTS

David Beskeen It has, once again, been a pleasure working with all the talented people at Course Technology. I would like to especially thank Katherine Pinard who has worked hard on my chapters to make them better and easier to understand. I would also like to thank my family, Karen and the three J's, for being so understanding during the long hours of writing.

Jennifer Duffy I wish to express particular thanks to Pam Conrad for her tireless help and keen editorial sensibilities. I am also deeply grateful for the support of my husband, Fred Eliot, and our daughter, Isabella, who patiently waited to be born until this book was nearly finished.

Ann Fisher I would like to thank Nicole Pinard for giving me this opportunity to write about Outlook and Internet Explorer, Rachel Bunin, my developmental editor, for her creative suggestions, and Emily Heberlein, my product manager, for her support and encouragement.

Lisa Friedrichsen The Access portion is dedicated to my students, and all who are using this book to teach and learn about Access. Thank you. Also, thank you to all of the professionals who helped me create this book.

Elizabeth Eisner Reding Creating a book of this magnitude is a team effort: I would like to thank my husband, Michael, for putting up with my ridiculous mood swings, Emily Heberlein, the project manager, and my development editors, Barbara Clemens and Kitty Pinard, for their insightful suggestions and corrections. I would also like to thank the production and editorial staff for all their hard work that made this project a reality.

Thanks to all the reviewers who provided invaluable feedback and ideas to us: Diane Blaney, Anne Burchardt, Janis Cox, Stephanie Hazen, Judy Irvine, Brenda Jacobsen, Joe LaMontagne, Dr. Dominic Ligori, Glenn Rogers (Western Nevada Community College), and Rick Sheridan.

Preface

Welcome to *Microsoft Office^XP–Illustrated Introductory, Enhanced Edition.* Each lesson in this book contains elements pictured to the right.

▶ How is the book organized?

The book is organized into sections, by application, illustrated by the brightly colored tabs on the sides of the pages: Windows 2000, Introducing Office XP, Internet Explorer, Word, Excel, Access, PowerPoint, and Outlook. Four Integration units follow the Excel, Access, and PowerPoint sections.

• Bonus Exercises! We have included 40 pages of Bonus Exercises located at the back of the book to provide extra reinforcement for Word, Excel, Access, PowerPoint, Outlook, and Office Integration.

• Windows Training! Included in the back of the book is a trial version of the TOM Windows training module which includes tutorials of Windows 2000 and Windows XP.

• Updated Instructor's Resource CD! PowerPoint Presentations have been added for every unit and are located on the Instructor's Resource CD.

▶ What kinds of assignments are included in the book? At what level of difficulty?

The lessons use MediaLoft, a fictional chain of bookstores, as the case study. The assignments on the blue pages at the end of each unit increase in difficulty. Project files and case studies, with many international examples, provide a great variety of interesting and relevant business applications for skills. Assignments include:

• **Concepts Reviews** include multiple choice, matching, and screen identification questions.

• **Skills Reviews** provide additional hands-on, step-by-step reinforcement.

• **Independent Challenges** are case projects requiring critical thinking and application of the unit skills. The Independent Challenges increase in difficulty, with the first one in each

---

Each 2-page spread focuses on a single skill.

Concise text that introduces the basic principles in the lesson and integrates the brief case study (indicated by the paintbrush icon).

Unit D — Word 2002

Editing Headers and Footers

To change header and footer text or to alter the formatting of headers and footers you must first open the Header and Footer areas. You can open headers and footers using the Header and Footer command on the View menu, or by double-clicking a header or footer in Print Layout view. Alice modifies the header by adding a small circle symbol between "Buzz" and the date. She also adds a border under the header text to set it off from the rest of the page. Finally, she removes the header and footer text from the first page of the document.

Steps

Trouble?
If the Header and Footer toolbar is in the way, click its title bar and drag it to a new location.

1. Place the insertion point at the top of page 2, position the ⬚ pointer over the header text at the top of page 2, then double-click
   The Header and Footer areas open.

2. Place the insertion point between the two spaces after Buzz, click **Insert** on the menu bar, then click **Symbol**
   The Symbol dialog box opens and is similar to Figure D-13. **Symbols** are special characters, such as graphics, shapes, and foreign language characters, that you can insert into a document. The symbols shown in Figure D-13 are the symbols included with the (normal text) font. You can use the Font list arrow on the Symbols tab to view the symbols included with each font on your computer.

3. Scroll the list of symbols if necessary to locate the black circle symbol shown in Figure D-13, select the **black circle symbol**, click **Insert**, then click **Close**
   A circle symbol is added at the location of the insertion point.

QuickTip
You can enter different text in the First Page Header and First Page Footer areas.

4. With the insertion point in the header text, click **Format** on the menu bar, then click **Borders and Shading**
   The Borders and Shading dialog box opens.

TABLE D-3: Buttons on the Header and Footer toolbar

button	function
Insert AutoText ▼	Inserts an AutoText entry, such as a field for the filename, or the author's name
Insert Page Number	Inserts a field for the page number so that the pages are numbered automatically
Insert Number of Pages	Inserts a field for the total number of pages in the document
Format Page Number	Opens the Page Number Format dialog box; use to change the numbering format or to begin automatic page numbering with a specific number
Insert Date	Inserts a field for the current date
Insert Time	Inserts a field for the current time
Page Setup	Opens the Page Setup dialog box
Switch Between Header and Footer	Moves the insertion point between the Header and Footer areas

▶ WORD D-12 **FORMATTING DOCUMENTS**

Hints as well as troubleshooting advice, right where you need it — next to the step itself.

Quickly accessible summaries of key terms, toolbar buttons, or keyboard alternatives connected with the lesson material. Students can refer easily to this information when working on their own projects at a later time.

Every lesson features large, full-color representations of what the screen should look like as students complete the numbered steps.

Brightly colored tabs indicate which section of the book you are in.

unit being the easiest (most step-by-step with detailed instructions). Independent Challenges 2 and 3 become increasingly open-ended, requiring more independent problem solving.

- **E-Quest Independent Challenges** are case projects with a Web focus. E-Quests require the use of the World Wide Web to conduct research to complete the project.

- **Visual Workshops** show a completed file and require that the file be created without any step-by-step guidance, involving independent problem solving.

▶ Is this book Certified?

When used in conjunction with *Microsoft Office XP – Illustrated Second Course,* this book covers the Microsoft Office Specialist Core objectives for Word, Excel and Access, and the Comprehensive objectives for PowerPoint. See the inside front cover for more information on other Illustrated titles meeting Microsoft Office Specialist certification.

Please note that Microsoft no longer refers to this program by the MOUS acronym. The first page of each unit includes ⌐MOUS⌐ symbols to indicate which skills covered in the unit are Microsoft Office Specialist skills. A grid in the back of the book lists all the exam objectives and cross-references them with the lessons and excercises.

▶ What online content solutions are available to accompany this book?

Visit www.course.com for more information on our online content for Illustrated titles. Options include **MyCourse 2.0**, **WebCT**, and **Blackboard**.

FIGURE D-13: Symbol dialog box

Black circle symbol is selected

Name of selected symbol

Inserts selected symbol at location of insertion point

The subset changes as you scroll the list of symbols

Available symbols (yours might differ)

Character code for selected symbol

FIGURE D-14: Symbol and border added to header

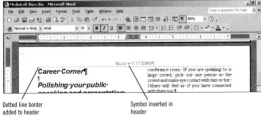

Dotted line border added to header

Symbol inserted in header

Inserting and creating AutoText entries

In addition to inserting AutoText entries into headers and footers, you can use the AutoText command on the Insert menu to insert AutoText entries into any part of a document. Word includes a number of built-in AutoText entries, including salutations and closings for letters, as well as information for headers and footers. To insert a built-in AutoText entry at the location of the insertion point, point to AutoText on the Insert menu, point to a category on the AutoText menu, then click the AutoText entry you want to insert. You can also use the Insert AutoText button on the Header and Footer toolbar to insert an AutoText entry from the Header/Footer category into a header or footer.

Word's AutoText feature also allows you to store text and graphics that you use frequently so that you can easily insert them in a document. To create a custom AutoText entry, enter the text or graphic you want to store—such as a company name or logo—in a document, select it, point to AutoText on the Insert menu, and then click New. In the Create AutoText dialog box, type a name for your AutoText entry, then click OK. The text or graphic is saved as a custom AutoText entry. To insert a custom AutoText entry in a document, point to AutoText on the Insert menu, click AutoText, select the entry name on the AutoText tab in the AutoCorrect dialog box, click Insert, then click OK.

FORMATTING DOCUMENTS WORD D-13 ◀

Clues to Use boxes provide concise information that either expands on the major lesson skill or describes an independent task that in some way relates to the major lesson skill.

The pages are numbered according to section and unit. Word indicates the section, D indicates the unit, 13 indicates the page.

Instructor's Resources

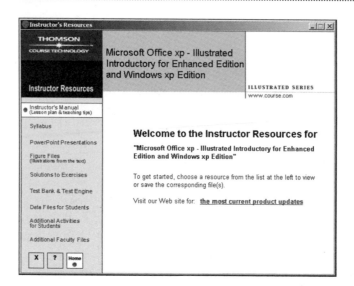

The Instructor's Resources CD is Course Technology's way of putting the resources and information needed to teach and learn effectively into your hands. We believe this CD represents the highest quality and most cutting edge resources available to instructors today. Many of these resources are available at **www.course.com**. The resources available with this book are:

Instructor's Manual Available as an electronic file, the Instructor's Manual is quality-assurance tested and includes unit overviews, file listings, and detailed lecture topics with teaching tips for each unit. The Instructor's Manual is available on the Instructor's Resources CD-ROM or you can download it from **www.course.com**.

Syllabus Prepare and customize your course easily using this sample course outline.

PowerPoint Presentations Each unit has a corresponding PowerPoint presentation that you can use in lecture, distribute to your students, or customize to suit your course.

Figure Files The figures in the text are provided on the Instructor's Resources CD to help you illustrate key topics or concepts. You can create traditional overhead transparencies by printing the figure files. Or you can create electronic slide shows by using the figures in a presentation program such as PowerPoint.

Solutions to Exercises Solutions to Exercises contain every file students are asked to create or modify in the lessons and End-of-Unit material. A Help file on the Instructor's Resources CD includes information for using the Solution Files. There is also a document outlining the solutions for the End-of-Unit Concepts Review, Skills Review, and Independent Challenges.

ExamView Test Bank and Test Engine This textbook is accompanied by ExamView, a powerful testing software package that allows instructors to create and administer printed, computer (LAN-based), and Internet exams. ExamView includes hundreds of questions that correspond to the topics covered in this text, enabling students to generate detailed study guides that include page references for further review. The computer-based and Internet testing components allow students to take exams at their computers, and also save the instructor time by grading each exam automatically.

Data Files for Students Data Files contain all of the data that students will use to complete the lessons and End-of-Unit material. A Readme file includes instructions for using the files. Adopters of this text are granted the right to install the Data Files on any standalone computer or network. The Data Files are available on the Instructor's Resources CD-ROM, the Review Pack, and can also be downloaded from **www.course.com**.

Additional Activities for Students Additional Activities for Students contains Extra Independent Challenges.

SAM, Skills Assessment Manager for Microsoft Office XP SAM is the most powerful Office XP assessment and reporting tool that will help instructors gain a true understanding of your students' proficiency in Microsoft Word, Excel, Access, and PowerPoint 2002.

TOM, Training Online Manager for Microsoft Office XP TOM is Course Techology's Microsoft Office Specialist approved training tool for Microsoft Office XP. Students will watch and listen as each task is performed. Next, they practice it with step-by-step help. Finally, they will try it on their own. Students gain confidence in their newfound skills as they work in a safe, simulated environment.

Brief Contents

Contents

Windows 2000

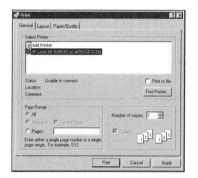

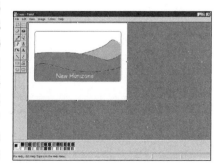

Contents

Office XP

Introducing Microsoft Office XP

Internet

Getting Started with Internet Explorer

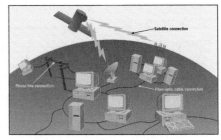

Word 2002

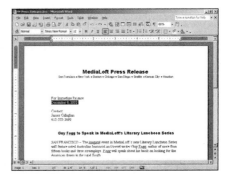

Contents

Formatting Documents   WORD D-1

Excel 2002

Getting Started with Excel 2002   EXCEL A-1

Building and Editing Worksheets — EXCEL B-1

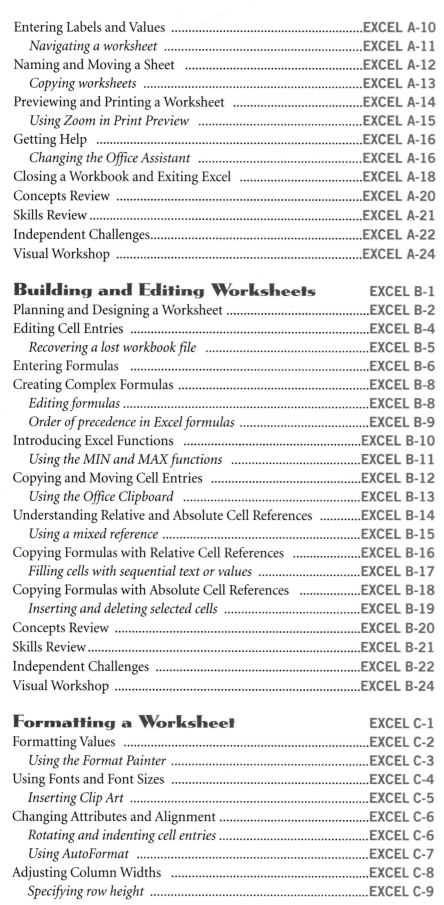

Formatting a Worksheet — EXCEL C-1

Contents

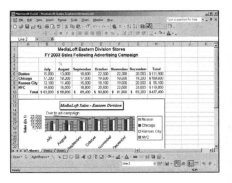

Integration

Integrating Word and Excel — INTEGRATION A-1

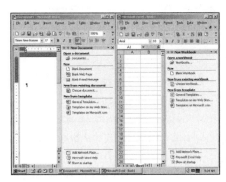

Access 2002

Contents

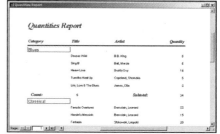

Integration

PowerPoint 2002

Getting Started with PowerPoint 2002

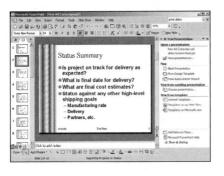

Creating a Presentation

Contents

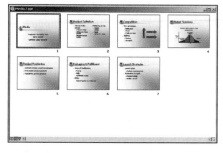

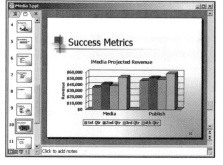

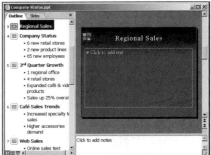

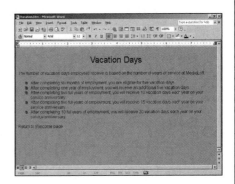

Contents

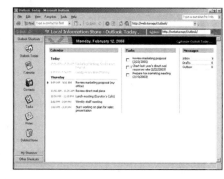

Appendix: Beyond E-mail: Understanding Additional Outlook Features

Windows 2000 Appendix A

Appendix A: Formatting a Disk

Windows 98 Appendix A

Appendix A: Formatting a Disk

Bonus Exercises

Bonus Exercises for Office XP

Read This Before You Begin

Software Information and Required Installation

This book was written and tested using Microsoft Office XP - Professional Edition, with a typical installation on Microsoft Windows 2000, with Internet Explorer 5.0 or higher. There are several instances where, in order to cover a software feature clearly, an additional feature not part of the typical installation is referenced. To insure that all the steps and exercises can be completed as written, make sure the following features are available before beginning these units:

- Excel Unit A (page A-8): Using Excel Templates (Clues to Use)
- PowerPoint Unit A (page A-9): Using AutoContent Wizards (Clues to Use)
- PowerPoint Unit B (page B-5): Using Speech Recognition (Clues to Use)
- PowerPoint Unit C (page C-14) and Integration Unit C (page C-4): Converter feature to import text from Word into PowerPoint
- Integration Unit D: Depending on your Office installation, the templates and themes available to you may differ. Tips are included in the lessons and Instructor's Manual for this situation.

Tips for Students

What are Project Files?

To complete many of the units in this book, you need to use Project Files. You use a Project File, which contains a partially completed document used in an exercise, so you don't have to type in all the information you need in the document. Your instructor will either provide you with a copy of the Project Files or ask you to make your own copy. Detailed instructions on how to organize your files, as well as a complete listing of all the files you'll need and will create, can be found in the back of the book (look for the yellow pages) in the Project Files List.

Why is my screen different from the book?

1. Your Desktop components and some dialog box options might be different if you are using an operating system other than Windows 2000.

2. Depending on your computer hardware capabilities and the Windows Display settings on your computer, you may notice the following differences:
   - Your screen may look larger or smaller because of your screen resolution (the height and width of your screen)
   - The colors of the title bar in your screen may be a solid blue, and the cells in Excel may appear different from the purple and gray because of your color settings

3. Depending on your Office settings, your toolbars may display on a single row and your menus may display with a shortened list of frequently used commands. Office menus and toolbars can modify themselves to your working style by displaying only the most frequently used buttons and menu commands, as shown here.

Toolbars on one row

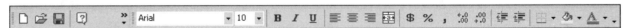

To view buttons not currently displayed, click a Toolbar Options button  at the end of either the Standard or Formatting toolbar. To view the full list of menu commands, click the double arrow at the bottom of the menu.

In order to have your toolbars display on two rows, showing all buttons, and to have the full menus display, you must turn off the personalized menus and toolbars feature. Click Tools on the menu bar, Click Customize, select the show Standard and Formatting toolbars on two rows and Always show full menus check boxes on the Options tab, then click Close. This book assumes you are displaying toolbars on two rows and full menus.

Toolbars on two rows

Read This Before You Begin

Important Information for Access Units if you are using floppy disks

Compact on Close?

If you are storing your Access databases on floppy disks, you should NOT use the Compact on Close option (available from the Tools menu). While the Compact on Close feature works well if your database is stored on your hard drive or on another large storage device, it can cause problems if your database is stored on a floppy when the size of your database is greater than the available free space on the floppy. Here's why: When you close a database with the Compact on Close feature turned on, the process creates a temporary file that is just as large as the original database file. In a successful compact process, this temporary file is deleted after the compact procedure is completed. But if there is not enough available space on your floppy to create this temporary file, the compact process never finishes, which means that your original database is never closed properly. And if you do not close an Access database properly before attempting to use it again, you can easily corrupt it beyond repair. *Therefore, if you use floppies to complete these exercises, please follow the guidelines on how to organize your databases on floppies in the **Project Files List** so that you do not run out of room on a floppy. Also, please **do not use the Compact on Close feature for databases stored on floppies**.*

Closing a Database Properly

It is extremely important to close your databases properly before copying, moving, e-mailing the database file, or before ejecting the Project Files floppy disk from the disk drive. Access database files are inherently multi-user, which means that multiple people can work on the same database file at the same time. To accomplish this capability, Access creates temporary files to keep track of which record you are working on while the database is open. These temporary files must be closed properly before you attempt to copy, move, or e-mail the database. They must also be closed before you eject a floppy that contains the database. If these temporary files do not get closed properly, the database can easily be corrupted beyond repair. Fortunately, Access closes these temporary files automatically when you close the Access application window. So to be sure that you have properly closed a database that is stored on a floppy, *close not only the database window, but also **close the Access application** window before copying, moving, or e-mailing a database file, as well as before ejecting a floppy that stores the database.*

2000 vs. 2002 File Format

New databases created in Access 2002 default to an Access 2000 file format. That's why "Access 2000 file format" is shown in the database window title bar for the figures in this book. This also means that Access databases now support seamless backward compatibility with the prior version of Access like other products in the Microsoft Office suite such as Word and Excel.

But while the Project Files for this book could be opened and used in Access 2000, the figures in this book present the Access 2002 application, use the Access 2002 menus and toolbars, and highlight the new features of Access 2002 including new task panes, new quick keystrokes, PivotTables, PivotCharts, and improved dynamic Web pages.

Getting
Started with Windows 2000

Objectives

- ► **Start Windows and view the Active Desktop**
- ► **Use the mouse**
- ► **Start a program**
- ► **Move and resize windows**
- ► **Use menus, keyboard shortcuts, and toolbars**
- ► **Use dialog boxes**
- ► **Use scroll bars**
- ► **Use Windows Help**
- ► **Close a program and shut down Windows**

Microsoft Windows 2000 is an **operating system**, a computer **program**, or set of instructions, that controls how the computer carries out basic tasks such as displaying information on your computer screen and running programs. Windows 2000 helps you save and organize the results of your work as **files**, which are electronic collections of data. Windows 2000 also coordinates the flow of information among the programs, printers, storage devices, and other components of your computer system, as well as among other computers on a network. When you work with Windows 2000, you will notice many **icons**, small pictures intended to be meaningful symbols of the items they represent. You will also notice rectangular-shaped work areas known as **windows**, thus the name of the operating system. These icons, windows, and various other words and symbols create what is referred to as a **graphical user interface** (**GUI**, pronounced "gooey"), through which you interact with the computer. ◢ This unit introduces you to basic skills that you can use in all Windows programs.

Starting Windows and Viewing the Active Desktop

When you turn on your computer, Windows 2000 automatically starts and the Active Desktop appears. The **Active Desktop**, shown in Figure A-1, is where you organize all the information and tools you need to accomplish your computer tasks. You can access, store, share, and explore information seamlessly, whether it resides on your computer, a network, or the **Internet**, a worldwide collection of over 40 million computers linked together to share information. The desktop is called "active" because it offers an interactive link between your computer and the Internet, so that Internet content displayed on your desktop, such as stock prices or weather information, is always up to date. When you start Windows for the first time, the desktop appears with the **default** settings, those preset by the operating system. For example, the default color of the desktop is blue. If any of the default settings have been changed on your computer, your desktop will look different than the one in the figures, but you should be able to locate all the items you need. The bar at the bottom of your screen is called the **taskbar**, which shows what programs are currently running. You use the Start menu, accessed by clicking the **Start button** at the left end of the taskbar, to perform such tasks as starting programs, finding and opening files, and accessing Windows Help. The **Quick Launch toolbar** is next to the Start button; it contains several buttons you can click to start Internet-related programs quickly, and another that you can click to show the desktop when it is not currently visible. Table A-1 identifies the icons and other elements you see on your desktop. If Windows 2000 is not currently running, follow the steps below to start it now.

Trouble?

If you don't know your password, see your instructor or technical support person.

1. Turn on your computer and monitor

You might see a "Please select the operating system to start" prompt. Don't worry about selecting one of the options; Microsoft Windows 2000 Professional automatically starts after 30 seconds. When Windows starts and the desktop appears, you may see a Log On to Windows dialog box. If so, continue to Step 2. If not, view Figure A-1, then continue on to the next lesson.

Trouble?

If the Getting Started with Windows 2000 dialog box opens, move your mouse pointer over the Exit button in the lower-right corner of the dialog box and press the left mouse button once to close the dialog box.

2. Enter the correct user name, type your password, then press **[Enter]**

Once the password is accepted, the Windows desktop appears on your screen. See Figure A-1.

Accessing the Internet from the Active Desktop

Windows 2000 provides a seamless connection between your desktop and the Internet with Internet Explorer. Internet Explorer is an example of a **browser,** a program designed to access the **World Wide Web** (also known as the **WWW,** or simply the **Web**). Internet Explorer is integrated with the Windows 2000 operating system. You can access it by clicking its icon on the desktop or on the Quick Launch toolbar. You can access Web pages, and place Web content such as weather or stock updates on the desktop for instant viewing. This information is updated automatically whenever you connect to the Internet, making your desktop truly active. You can also communicate electronically with other Internet users, using the Windows e-mail and newsreader program, Outlook Express.

FIGURE A-1: Windows Active Desktop

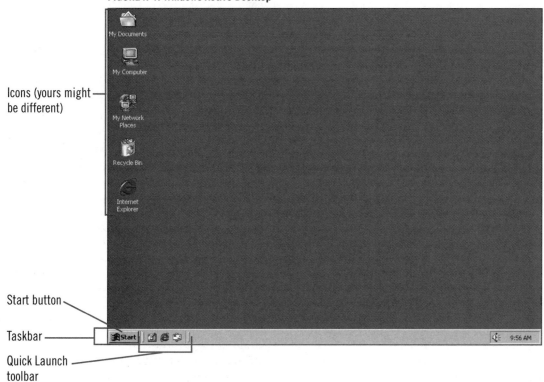

Icons (yours might be different)

Start button

Taskbar

Quick Launch toolbar

TABLE A-1: Elements of the Windows desktop

desktop element	icon	allows you to
My Documents folder		Store programs, documents, graphics, or other files
My Computer		Work with different disk drives and printers on your computer
My Network Places		Open files and folders on other computers and install network printers
Recycle Bin		Delete and restore files
Internet Explorer		Start Internet Explorer to access the Internet
Connect to the Internet		Set up Internet access
Start button	Start	Start programs, open documents, search for files, and more
Taskbar		Start programs and switch among open programs
Quick Launch toolbar		Start Internet Explorer, start Outlook Express, and display the desktop

Windows 2000

Using the Mouse

A **mouse** is a hand-held **input or pointing device** that you use to interact with your computer. Input or pointing devices come in many shapes and sizes; some, like a mouse, are directly attached to your computer with a cable; others function like a TV remote control and allow you to access your computer without being right next to it. Figure A-2 shows examples of common pointing devices. Because the most common pointing device is a mouse, this book uses that term. If you are using a different pointing device, substitute that device whenever you see the term "mouse." When you move the mouse, the **mouse pointer** on the screen moves in the same direction. The **mouse buttons** are used to select icons and commands, which is how you communicate with the computer. Table A-2 shows some common mouse pointer shapes that indicate different activities. Table A-3 lists the five basic mouse actions. ✐ Begin by experimenting with the mouse now.

Steps 1 2 3 4

1. **Locate the mouse pointer on the desktop, then move the mouse across your desk or mousepad**
   Watch how the mouse pointer moves on the desktop in response to your movements; practice moving the mouse pointer in circles, then back and forth in straight lines.

Trouble?

If the My Computer window opens during this step, your mouse isn't set with the Windows 2000 default mouse settings. See your instructor or technical support person for assistance. This book assumes your computer is set to all Windows 2000 default settings.

2. **Position the mouse pointer over the My Computer icon**
   Positioning the mouse pointer over an item is called **pointing**.

3. **With the pointer over the My Computer icon, press and release the left mouse button**
   Pressing and releasing the left mouse button is called **clicking** (or single-clicking, to distinguish it from double-clicking, which you'll do in Step 7). When you position the mouse pointer over an icon or any item and click, you select that item. When an item is **selected**, it is **highlighted** (shaded differently from other items), and the next action you take will be performed on that item.

4. **With the My computer icon selected, press and hold down the left mouse button, then move the mouse down and to the right and release the mouse button**
   The icon becomes dimmed and moves with the mouse pointer; this is called **dragging**, which you do to move icons and other Windows elements. When you release the mouse button, the item is positioned at the new location.

5. **Position the mouse pointer over the My Computer icon, then press and release the right mouse button**
   Clicking the right mouse button is known as **right-clicking**. Right-clicking an item on the desktop produces a **pop-up menu**, as shown in Figure A-3. This menu lists the commands most commonly used for the item you have clicked. A **command** is a directive that provides access to a program's features.

QuickTip

When a step tells you to "click," use the left mouse button. If it says "right-click," use the right mouse button.

6. **Click anywhere outside the menu to close the pop-up menu**

7. **Position the mouse pointer over the My Computer icon, then quickly press and release the left mouse button twice**
   Clicking the mouse button twice quickly is known as **double-clicking**, which, in this case, opens the My Computer window. The **My Computer** window contains additional icons that represent the drives and system components that are installed on your computer.

8. **Click the Close button ▣ in the upper-right corner of the My Computer window**

TABLE A-2: **Common mouse pointer shapes**

shape	used to
↖	Select items, choose commands, start programs, and work in programs
I	Position mouse pointer for editing or inserting text; called the insertion point
⧗	Indicate Windows is busy processing a command
↔	Change the size of a window; appears when mouse pointer is on the border of a window
☝	Select and open Web-based data

FIGURE A-2: Common pointing devices

Trackball

Trackpoint

Right mouse button

Left mouse button

Intellimouse

Mouse

FIGURE A-3: Displaying a pop-up menu

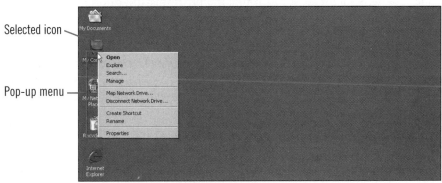

Selected icon

Pop-up menu

CLUES TO USE

More about the mouse: Classic style and Internet style

Because Windows 2000 integrates the use of the Internet with its other functions, it allows you to extend the way you click in a Web browser program on the Internet to the way you click in other computer programs. With the default Windows 2000 settings, you click an item to select it and double-click an item to open it. In a Web browser program, however, you point to an item to select it and single-click to open it. Windows 2000 gives you two choices for clicking: with the **Classic style**, you double-click to open items, and with the **Internet style**, you single-click to open items. To switch between styles, double-click the My Computer Icon (or click if you are currently using the Internet style), click Tools on the menu bar, click Folder Options, click the General tab if necessary, click the Single-click to Open an Item option or the Double-click to Open an Item option in the Click items as follows section, and then click OK.

TABLE A-3: Basic mouse techniques

technique	what to do
Pointing	Move the mouse to position the mouse pointer over an item on the desktop
Clicking	Press and release the left mouse button
Double-clicking	Press and release the left mouse button twice quickly
Dragging	Point to an item, press and hold the left mouse button, move the mouse to a new location, then release the mouse button
Right-clicking	Point to an item, then press and release the right mouse button

Windows 2000

Starting a Program

Clicking the Start button on the taskbar opens the Start menu, which lists submenus for a variety of tasks described in Table A-4. As you become familiar with Windows, you might want to customize the Start menu to include additional items that you use most often. Windows 2000 comes with several built-in programs, called **accessories**. Although not as feature-rich as many programs sold separately, Windows accessories are useful for completing basic tasks. In this lesson, you start a Windows accessory called **WordPad**, which is a word-processing program you can use to create and edit simple documents.

Steps

1. Click the **Start button** on the taskbar
The Start menu opens.

2. Point to **Programs**
The Programs submenu opens, listing the programs and categories for programs installed on your computer. WordPad is in the category called Accessories.

QuickTip

Windows 2000 features personalized menus, which list only the commands you've most recently used. Whenever you want to view other commands available on the menu, rest the mouse pointer over the double arrows ⚟ at the bottom of the menu.

3. Point to **Accessories**
The Accessories menu, shown in Figure A-4, contains several programs to help you complete common tasks. You want to start WordPad. If you do not see WordPad, rest the mouse pointer over the double arrows at the bottom of Programs submenu and wait. The full menu will open after a few seconds.

4. Click **WordPad**
WordPad opens with a blank document window open, as shown in Figure A-5. Don't worry if your window does not fill the screen; you'll learn how to maximize it in the next lesson. Note that a **program button** appears on the taskbar and is highlighted, indicating that WordPad is open.

TABLE A-4: Start menu categories

category	description
Windows Update	Connects to a Microsoft Web site and updates your Windows 2000 files as necessary
Programs	Displays a menu of programs included on the Start menu
Documents	Displays a menu of the most recently opened and recently saved documents
Settings	Displays a menu of tools for selecting settings for your system
Search	Locates programs, files, folders, people, or computers on your computer network, or finds information and people on the Internet
Help	Provides Windows Help information by topic, alphabetical index, or search criteria
Run	Opens a program or file based on a location and filename that you type or select
Shut Down	Provides options to log off, shut down, or restart the computer

FIGURE A-4: Cascading menus

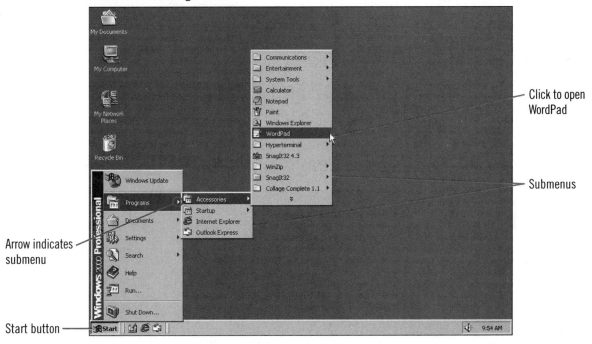

Click to open
WordPad

Submenus

Arrow indicates
submenu

Start button

FIGURE A-5: WordPad program window

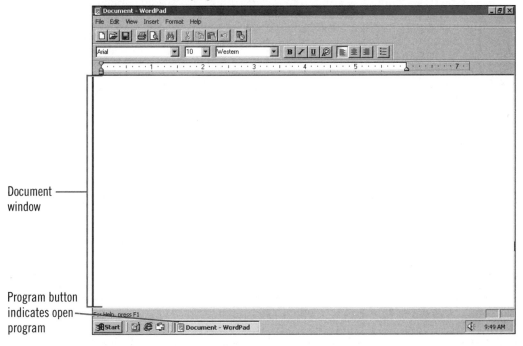

Document
window

Program button
indicates open
program

The Startup Folder

You can specify one or more programs to open each time you start Windows 2000 by placing shortcuts in the Startup Folder. This might be useful if you know you will be working in the same programs first thing every day. To place a program in the Startup Folder, click the Start button, point to Settings, then click

Taskbar & Start Menu. Click the Advanced tab of the Taskbar and Start Menu Properties dialog box, click Advanced, and then, in the Start Menu folder, locate the shortcut to the program you want to specify, and drag it to the Startup folder.

Moving and Resizing Windows

One of the powerful features of Windows is the ability to open more than one window or program at once. This means, however, that the desktop can get cluttered with the various programs and files you are using. You can keep your desktop organized by changing the size of a window or moving it. You can do this by clicking the sizing buttons in the upper-right corner of any window and dragging a corner or border of any window that does not completely fill the screen. Practice sizing and moving the WordPad window now.

Steps

1. If the WordPad window does not already fill the screen, click the **Maximize button** in the WordPad window

When a window is **maximized**, it takes up the whole screen.

2. Click the **Restore button** in the WordPad window

To **restore** a window is to return it to its previous size, as shown in Figure A-6. The Restore button only appears when a window is maximized.

3. Position the pointer on the right edge of the WordPad window until the pointer changes to ↔, then drag the border to the right

The width of the window increases. You can size the height or width of a window by dragging any of the four sides individually.

QuickTip

You can resize windows by dragging any corner. You can also drag any border to make the window taller, shorter, wider, or narrower.

4. Position the pointer in the lower-right corner of the WordPad window until the pointer changes to ↖, as shown in Figure A-6, then drag down and to the right

The height and width of the window increase proportionally when you drag a corner instead of a side. You can also position a restored window wherever you wish on the desktop by dragging its title bar. The **title bar** is the area along the top of the window that displays the file name and program used to create it.

5. Drag the **title bar** on the WordPad window up and to the left, as shown in Figure A-6

The window is repositioned on the desktop. At times, you might wish to close a program window, yet keep the program running and easily accessible. You can accomplish this by minimizing a window.

QuickTip

If you have more than one window open and you want to quickly access something on the desktop, you can click the Show Desktop button on the Quick Launch toolbar. All open windows are minimized so the desktop is visible.

6. In the WordPad window, click the **Minimize button**

When you **minimize** a window, it shrinks to a program button on the taskbar, as shown in Figure A-7. WordPad is still running, but it is out of your way.

7. Click the **WordPad program button** on the taskbar to reopen the window

The WordPad program window reopens.

8. Click the **Maximize button** in the upper-right corner of the WordPad window

The window fills the screen.

FIGURE A-6: **Restored program window**

Title bar

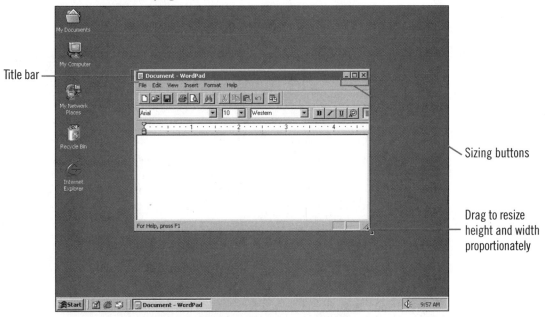

Sizing buttons

Drag to resize
height and width
proportionately

FIGURE A-7: **Minimized program window**

Indicates program
is running but not
in use

More about sizing windows

Keep in mind that many programs contain two sets of sizing buttons: one that controls the program window itself and another that controls the window for the file with which you are working. The program sizing buttons are located in the title bar and the file sizing buttons are located below them. See Figure A-8. When you minimize a file window within a program, the file window is reduced to an icon in the lower-left corner of the program window, but the size of the program window remains intact.

FIGURE A-8: **Program and file sizing buttons**

Program window
sizing buttons

File window sizing
buttons

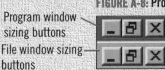

Windows 2000

Using Menus, Keyboard Shortcuts, and Toolbars

A **menu** is a list of commands that you use to accomplish certain tasks. You've already used the Start menu to start WordPad. Each Windows program also has its own set of menus, which are located on the **menu bar** under the title bar. The menus organize commands into groups of related operations. See Table A-5 for a description of items on a typical menu. **Toolbar buttons** offer another method for executing menu commands; instead of clicking the menu and then the menu command, you simply click the button for the command. A **toolbar** is a set of buttons usually positioned below the menu bar in a Windows program. In Windows 2000, you can customize a toolbar by adding buttons to or removing buttons from toolbars to suit your preferences. You will open the Control Panel, then use a menu and toolbar button to change how the contents of the window appear, and then add and remove a toolbar button.

Steps

QuickTip

You now have two windows open: WordPad and the Control Panel. The Control Panel is the active window (or active program) because it is the one with which you are currently working. WordPad is inactive because it is open but you are not working with it. Working with more than one window at a time is called multitasking.

1. **Click the Start button on the taskbar, point to Settings, then click Control Panel**
   The Control Panel window opens over the WordPad window. The **Control Panel** contains icons for various programs that allow you to specify how your computer looks and performs.

2. **Click View on the menu bar**
   The View menu appears, listing the View commands, as shown in Figure A-9. On a menu, a **check mark** identifies a feature that is currently enabled or "on." To disable or turn "off" the feature, you click the command again to remove the check mark. A **bullet mark** can also indicate that an option is enabled. To disable a bulleted option, you must select another option in its place.

3. **Click Small Icons**
   The icons are now smaller than they were before, taking up less room in the window.

4. **Press [Alt][V] to open the View menu, then press [T] to execute the Toolbars command**
   The View menu appears again, and then the Toolbars submenu appears, with checkmarks next to the commands that are currently selected. You opened these menus using the keyboard. Notice that a letter in each command on the View menu is underlined. These are **keyboard navigation indicators**, indicating that you can press the underlined letter, known as a **keyboard shortcut**, instead of clicking to execute the command.

5. **Press [C] to execute the Customize command**
   The Customize Toolbar dialog box opens. A dialog box is a window in which you make specifications for how you want a task performed; you'll learn more about working in a dialog box shortly. In the Customize Toolbar dialog box, you can add toolbar buttons to the current toolbar, or remove buttons already on the toolbar. The list on the right shows which buttons are currently on the toolbar, and the list on the left shows which buttons are available to add.

6. **Click the Favorites button in the Available toolbar buttons section, then click the Add button**
   As shown in Figure A-10, the Favorites button is added to the Standard toolbar of the Control Panel window.

7. **Click Favorites in the Current toolbar buttons section, click the Remove button, then click Close on the Customize Toolbar dialog box**
   The Favorites button disappears from the Standard toolbar, and the Customize Toolbar dialog box closes.

QuickTip

When you rest the pointer over a button without clicking, a Screentip appears, telling you the name of the button.

8. **On the Control Panel toolbar, click the Views button list arrow** 🔲▾
   Some toolbar buttons have an arrow, which indicates the button contains several choices. Clicking the button shows the choices.

9. **In the list of View choices, click Details**
   The Details view includes a description of each program in the Control Panel.

Check mark

FIGURE A-9: **Opening a menu**

Menu bar

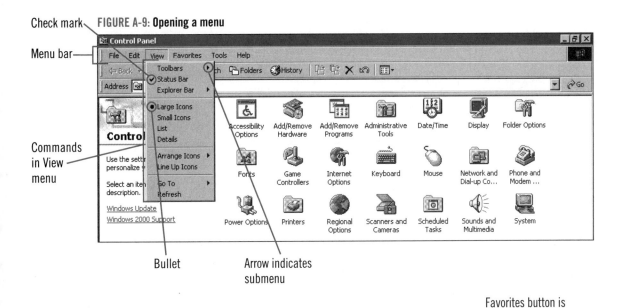

Commands
in View
menu

Bullet

Arrow indicates
submenu

Favorites button is
added to the toolbar

FIGURE A-10: **Customize Toolbar dialog box**

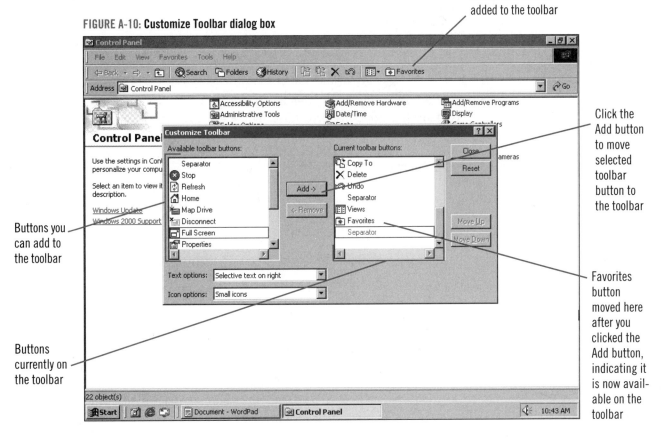

Click the
Add button
to move
selected
toolbar
button to
the toolbar

Buttons you
can add to
the toolbar

Buttons
currently on
the toolbar

Favorites
button
moved here
after you
clicked the
Add button,
indicating it
is now avail-
able on the
toolbar

TABLE A-5: **Typical items on a menu**

item	description	example
Dimmed command	Indicates the menu command is not currently available	Undo Ctrl+Z
Ellipsis	Opens a dialog box that allows you to select different or additional options	Save As...
Triangle	Opens a cascading menu containing an additional list of commands	Zoom ▶
Keyboard shortcut	Executes a command using the keyboard instead of the mouse	Paste Ctrl+V
Underlined letter	Indicates the letter to press for the keyboard shortcut	Print Preview

Using Dialog Boxes

A **dialog box** is a window that opens when you choose a menu command that is followed by an ellipsis (...), or any command that needs more information before the program can carry out the command you selected. Dialog boxes open in other situations as well, such as when you open a program in the Control Panel. See Figure A-11 and Table A-6 for some of the typical elements of a dialog box. Practice using a dialog box to control your mouse settings.

Steps 1 2 3 4

Trouble?

If you can't see the Mouse icon, resize the Control Panel window.

1. In the Control Panel window, double-click the **Mouse icon**

The Mouse Properties dialog box opens, as shown in Figure A-12. **Properties** are characteristics of a specific computer element (in this case, the mouse) that you can customize. The options in this dialog box allow you to control the way the mouse buttons are configured, select the types of pointers that appear, choose the speed of the mouse movement on the screen, and specify what type of mouse you are using. **Tabs** at the top of the dialog box separate these options into related categories.

2. Click the **Motion tab** if necessary to make it the front-most tab

This tab contains three options for controlling the way your mouse moves. Under Speed, you can set how fast the pointer moves on the screen in relation to how you move the mouse. You drag a **slider** to specify how fast the pointer moves. Under Acceleration, you can click an **option button** to adjust how much your pointer accelerates as you move it faster. When choosing among option buttons, you can select only one at a time. Under Snap to default, there is a **check box**, which is a toggle for turning a feature on or off—in this case, for setting whether or not you want your mouse pointer to move to the default button in dialog boxes.

3. Under Speed, drag the **slider** all the way to the left for Slow, then move the mouse pointer across your screen

Notice how slowly the mouse pointer moves. After you select the options you want in a dialog box, you need to select a **command button**, which carries out the options you've selected. The two most common command buttons are OK and Cancel. Clicking OK accepts your changes and closes the dialog box; clicking Cancel leaves the original settings intact and closes the dialog box. The third command button in this dialog box is Apply. Clicking the Apply button accepts the changes you've made and keeps the dialog box open so that you can select additional options. Because you might share this computer with others, it's important to return the dialog box options back to the original settings.

QuickTip

You can also use the keyboard to carry out commands in a dialog box. Pressing [Enter] is the same as clicking OK; pressing [Esc] is the same as clicking Cancel.

4. Click **Cancel**

The original settings remain intact and the dialog box closes.

FIGURE A-11: **Elements of a typical dialog box**

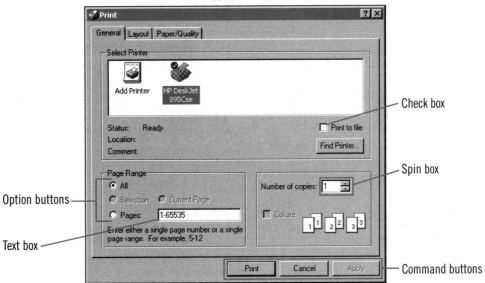

Check box

Spin box

Option buttons

Text box

Command buttons

FIGURE A-12: **Mouse Properties dialog box**

Tabs

Slider

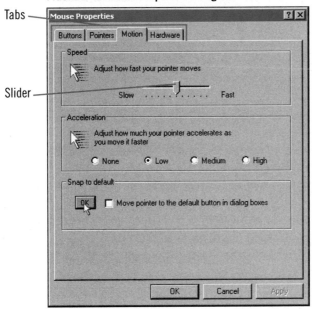

TABLE A-6: **Typical items in a dialog box**

item	description	item	description
Check box	A box that turns an option on (when the box is checked) and off (when it is unchecked)	**List box**	A box containing a list of items; to choose an item, click the list arrow, then click the desired item
Text box	A box in which you type text	**Spin box**	A box with two arrows and a text box; allows you to scroll in numerical increments or type a number
Option button	A small circle that you click to select a single dialog box option; you cannot check more than one option button in a list	**Slider**	A shape that you drag to set the degree to which an option is in effect
Command button	A rectangular button in a dialog box with the name of the command on it	**Tab**	A place in a dialog box where related commands and options are organized

Using Scroll Bars

When you cannot see all of the items available in a window, scroll bars appear on the right and/or bottom edges of the window. **Scroll bars** allow you to view the additional contents of the window. There are several ways you can scroll in a window. When you need to scroll only a short distance, you can use the scroll arrows. To scroll the window in larger increments, click in the scroll bar above or below the scroll box. Dragging the scroll box moves you quickly to a new part of the window. See Table A-7 for a summary of the different ways to use scroll bars. With the Control Panel window in Details view, you can use the scroll bars to view all of the items in this window.

Steps

1. In the Control Panel window, drag the **lower-right corner** of the dialog box up toward the upper-left corner until the scroll bars appear, as shown in Figure A-13
   Scroll bars appear only when the window is not large enough to include all the information. After you resize the dialog box, they appear along the bottom and right side of the dialog box. You may have to size your window smaller than the one in the figure for your scroll bars to appear.

2. Click the **down scroll arrow**, as shown in Figure A-13
   Clicking this arrow moves the view down one line.

3. Click the **up scroll arrow** in the vertical scroll bar
   Clicking this arrow moves the view up one line.

4. Click anywhere in the area below the scroll box in the vertical scroll bar
   The view moves down one window's height. Similarly, you can click in the scroll bar above the scroll box to move up one window's height.

5. Drag the **scroll box** all the way down to the bottom of the vertical scrollbar
   The view now includes the items that appear at the very bottom of the window.

6. Drag the **scroll box** all the way up to the top of the vertical scroll bar
   This view shows the items that appear at the top of the window.

7. Click the area to the right of the scroll box in the horizontal scroll bar
   The far right edge of the window comes into view. The horizontal scroll bar works the same as the vertical scroll bar.

8. Click the area to the left of the scroll box in the horizontal scroll bar
   You should return the Control Panel to its original settings.

9. Maximize the Control Panel window, click the **Views button list arrow** ▦▾ on the Control Panel toolbar, then click **Large Icons**

QuickTip

The size of the scroll box changes to reflect how much information does not fit in the window. A larger scroll box indicates that a relatively small amount of the window's contents is not currently visible; you need to scroll only a short distance to see the remaining items. A smaller scroll box indicates that a relatively large amount of information is currently not visible.

FIGURE A-13: Scroll bars

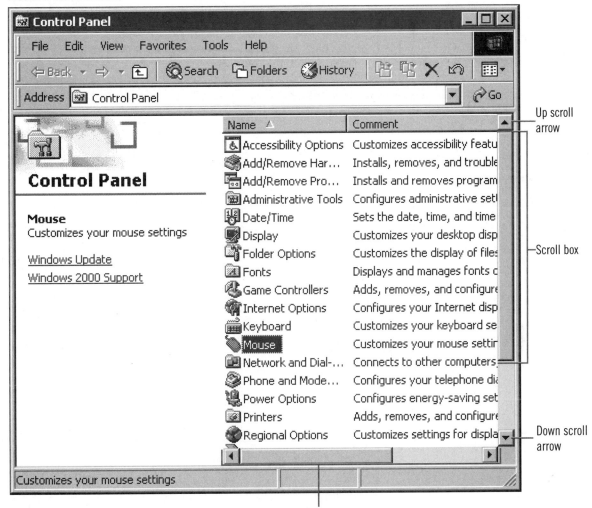

Up scroll arrow

Scroll box

Down scroll arrow

Horizontal scroll bar

TABLE A-7: Using scroll bars in a window

to	do this
Move down one line	Click the down arrow at the bottom of the vertical scroll bar
Move up one line	Click the up arrow at the top of the vertical scroll bar
Move down one window height	Click in the area below the scroll box in the vertical scroll bar
Move up one window height	Click in the area above the scroll box in the vertical scroll bar
Move up a large distance in the window	Drag the scroll box up in the vertical scroll bar
Move down a large distance in the window	Drag the scroll box down in the vertical scroll bar
Move a short distance side-to-side in a window	Click the left or right arrows in the horizontal scroll bar
Move to the right one window width	Click in the area to the right of the scroll box in the horizontal scroll bar
Move to the left one window width	Click in the area to the left of the scroll box in the horizontal scroll bar
Move left or right a large distance in the window	Drag the scroll box in the horizontal scroll bar

Steps

Using Windows Help

When you have a question about how to do something in Windows 2000, you can usually find the answer with a few clicks of your mouse. **Windows Help** works like a book stored on your computer, with a table of contents and an index to make finding information easier. Help provides guidance on many Windows features, including detailed steps for completing procedures, definitions of terms, lists of related topics, and search capabilities. You can browse or search for information in the Help window, or you can connect to a Microsoft Web site on the Internet for the latest technical support on Windows 2000. You can also access **context-sensitive help**, help specifically related to what you are doing, using a variety of methods such as right-clicking an object or using the question mark button in a dialog box. In this lesson, you get Help on starting a program. You also get information on the taskbar.

1. Click the **Start button** on the taskbar, then click **Help**

The Windows Help window opens with the Contents tab in front, as shown in Figure A-14. The Contents tab provides you with a list of Help categories. Each category contains two or more topics that you can see by clicking the book or the category next to it.

2. Click the **Contents tab** if it isn't the front-most tab, click **Working with Programs**, then view the Help categories that are displayed

The Help window contains a selection of topics related to working with programs.

3. Click **Start a Program**

Help information for this topic appears in the right pane, as shown in Figure A-15. **Panes** divide a window into two or more sections. At the bottom of the text in the right pane, you can click Related Topics to view a list of topics that may also be of interest to you. Some Help topics also allow you to view additional information about important words; these words are underlined, indicating that you can click them to display a pop-up window with the additional information.

4. Click the underlined word **taskbar**, read the definition, then press **[Enter]** or click anywhere outside the pop-up window to close it

5. In the left pane, click the **Index tab**

The Index tab provides an alphabetical list of all the available Help topics, like an index at the end of a book. You can type a topic in the text box at the top of the pane. As you type, the list of topics automatically scrolls to try to match the word or phrase you type. You can also scroll down to the topic. In either case, the topic appears in the right pane.

6. In the left pane, click the **Search tab**

You can use the Search tab to locate a Help topic using keywords. You enter a word or phrase in the text box and click List Topics; a list of matching topics appears below the text box. To view a topic, double-click it or select the topic, then click Display.

7. In the left pane, click the **Favorites tab**

You can add the To Start a Program topic, or any other displayed topic, to the Favorites tab of the Help window by simply clicking the Favorites tab, then clicking the Add button.

8. Click the **Web Help button** on the toolbar

Information on the Web site for Windows 2000 Help appears in the right pane (a **Web site** is a document or related documents that contain highlighted words, phrases, and graphics that link to other sites on the Internet). To access online support or information, click one of the available options.

9. Click the **Close button** in the upper-right corner of the Windows Help window

The Help window closes.

FIGURE A-14: Windows Help window

Help toolbar

Help tabs

Click to view
alphabetical
list of Help
topics

Click to search
for words and
phrases in
Help topics

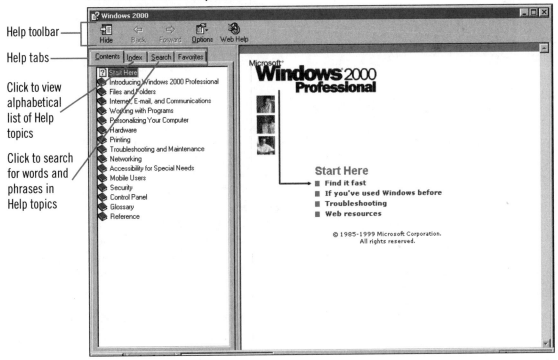

FIGURE A-15: Viewing a Help topic

Help topic

Pointer
changes to
hand pointer
when a topic
is selected

Left pane
contains Help
categories
and topics

Right pane
contains help
on the topic
you select

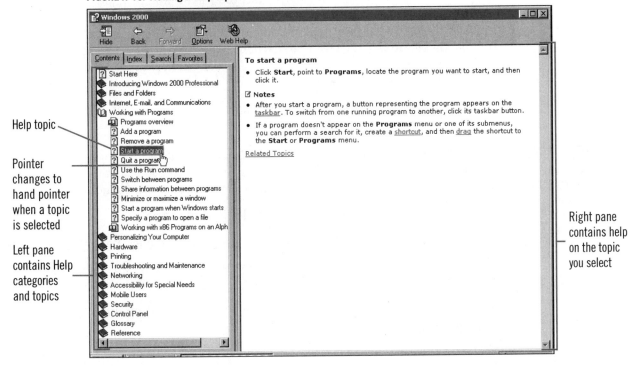

Context-sensitive help

To receive help in a dialog box, click the Help button in the upper-right corner of the dialog box; the mouse pointer changes to ▷?. Click the Help pointer on the item for which you need additional information. A pop-up window provides a brief explanation of the selected feature. You can also right-click the button on an item in a dialog box, then click the What's This? button to view the Help explanation.

Closing a Program and Shutting Down Windows

When you are finished working on your computer, you need to make sure you shut it down properly. This involves several steps: saving and closing all open files, closing all the open programs and windows, shutting down Windows, and finally, turning off the computer. If you turn off the computer while Windows is running, you could lose important data. To **close** programs, you can click the Close button in the window's upper-right corner or click File on the menu bar and choose either Close or Exit. To shut down Windows after all your files and programs are closed, click Shut Down from the Start menu, then select the desired option from the Shut Down dialog box, shown in Figure A-16. See Table A-8 for a description of shut down options. Close all your open files, windows, and programs, then exit Windows.

1. In the Control Panel window, click the **Close button** ☒ in the upper-right corner of the window

   The Control Panel window closes.

2. Click **File** on the WordPad menu bar, then click **Exit**

   If you have made any changes to the open file, you will be prompted to save your changes before the program quits. Some programs also give you the option of choosing the Close command on the File menu in order to close the active file but leave the program open, so you can continue to work in it with a different file. Also, if there is a second set of sizing buttons in the window, the Close button on the menu bar will close the active file only, leaving the program open for continued use.

3. If you see a message asking you to save changes to the document, click **No**

   WordPad closes and you return to the desktop.

QuickTip

Complete the remaining steps to shut down Windows and your computer only if you have been told to do so by your instructor or technical support person.

4. Click the **Start Button** on the taskbar, then click **Shut Down**

   The Shut Down Windows dialog box opens, as shown in Figure A-16. In this dialog box, you have the option to log off, shut down the computer, or restart the computer.

5. Click the **What do you want the computer to do? list arrow**

6. If you are working in a lab, click the **list arrow** again and click **Cancel** to leave the computer running; if you are working on your own machine or if your instructor told you to shut down Windows, click **Shut down**, then click **OK**

7. If you see the message "It is now safe to turn off your computer," turn off your computer and monitor

   On some computers, the power shuts off automatically, so you may not see this message.

FIGURE A-16: Shut Down Windows dialog box

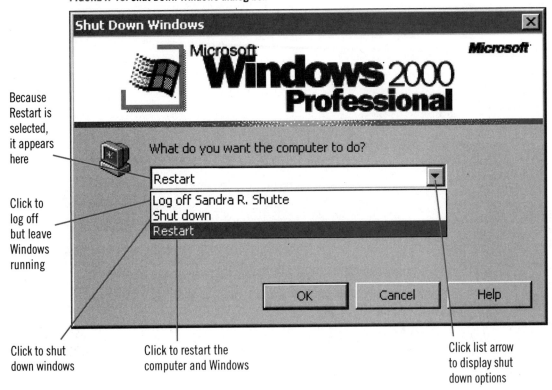

Because Restart is selected, it appears here

Click to log off but leave Windows running

Click to shut down windows

Click to restart the computer and Windows

Click list arrow to display shut down options

CLUES TO USE

The Log Off command

To change users on the same computer quickly, you can choose the Log Off command from the Shut Down Windows dialog box. When you choose this command, the current user is logged off and Windows 2000 shuts down and automatically restarts, stopping at the point where you need to enter a password. When the new user enters a user name and password, Windows restarts and the desktop appears as usual.

TABLE A-8: Shut down options

shut down option	function	when to use it
Shut down	Prepares the computer to be turned off	When you are finished working with Windows and you want to shut off your computer
Restart	Restarts the computer and reloads Windows	When you want to restart the computer and begin working with Windows again (your programs might have frozen or stopped working)
Log off	Ends your session, then reloads Windows for another user	When you want to end your session but leave the computer running for another user

Practice

▶ Concepts Review

Identify each of the items labeled in Figure A-17.

FIGURE A-17

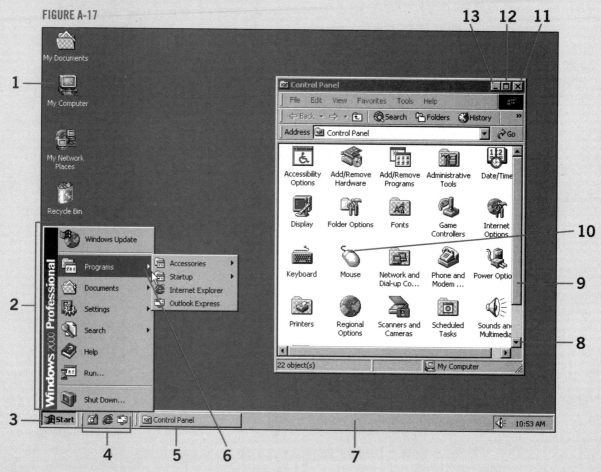

Match each of the statements with the term it describes.

14. Shrinks a window to a button on the taskbar
15. Shows the name of the window or program
16. The taskbar item you first click to start a program
17. Requests more information that you supply before carrying out command
18. Shows the Start button, Quick Launch toolbar, and any currently open programs
19. An input device that lets you point to and make selections
20. Graphic representation of program

a. Taskbar
b. Dialog box
c. Start button
d. Mouse
e. Title bar
f. Minimize button
g. Icon

Select the best answer from the list of choices.

21. The acronym GUI stands for
   a. Grayed user information.
   b. Group user icons.
   c. Graphical user interface.
   d. Group user interconnect.

22. **Which of the following is NOT provided by Windows 2000?**
    a. The ability to organize files
    b. Instructions to coordinate the flow of information among the programs, files, printers, storage devices, and other components of your computer system
    c. Programs that allow you to specify the operation of the mouse
    d. Spell checker for your documents

23. **All of the following are examples of using a mouse, EXCEPT**
    a. clicking the Maximize button.
    b. pressing [Enter].
    c. double-clicking to start a program.
    d. dragging the My Computer icon.

24. **The term for moving an item to a new location on the desktop is**
    a. pointing.
    b. clicking.
    c. dragging.
    d. restoring.

25. **The Maximize button is used to**
    a. return a window to its previous size.
    b. expand a window to fill the computer screen.
    c. scroll slowly through a window.
    d. run programs from the Start menu.

26. **What appears if a window contains more information than can be viewed in the window?**
    a. Program icon
    b. Cascading menu
    c. Scroll bars
    d. Check boxes

27. **A window is active when**
    a. you can only see its program button on the taskbar.
    b. its title bar is dimmed.
    c. it is open and you are currently using it.
    d. it is listed in the Programs submenu.

28. **You can exit Windows by**
    a. double-clicking the Control Panel application.
    b. double-clicking the Program Manager control menu box.
    c. clicking File, then clicking Exit.
    d. selecting the Shut Down command from the Start menu.

► Skills Review

1. **Start Windows and view the Active Desktop.**
   a. Turn on the computer, if necessary.
   b. After Windows starts, identify as many items on the desktop as you can, without referring to the lesson material.
   c. Compare your results to Figure A-1.

2. **Use the mouse.**
   a. Double-click the Recycle Bin icon.
   b. Drag the Recycle Bin window to the upper-right corner of the desktop.
   c. Right-click the title bar of the Recycle Bin, then click Close.

3. **Start a program.**
   a. Click the Start button on the taskbar, then point to Programs.
   b. Point to Accessories, then click Calculator (rest your pointer on the double arrows to display more menu commands if necessary).
   c. Minimize the Calculator window.

4. **Move and resize windows.**
   a. Drag the Recycle Bin icon to the bottom of the desktop.
   b. Double-click the My Computer icon to open the My Computer window.
   c. Maximize the window, if it is not already maximized.

d. Restore the window to its previous size.

e. Resize the window until you see the vertical scroll bar.

f. Minimize the My Computer window.

g. Drag the Recycle Bin back to the top of the desktop.

5. Use menus, keyboard shortcuts, and toolbars.

a. Click the Start button on the taskbar, point to Settings, then click Control Panel.

b. Click View on the menu bar, point to Toolbars, then click Standard Buttons to deselect the option and hide the toolbar.

c. Redisplay the toolbar.

d. Press [Alt][V] to display the View menu, then press [L] to view the Control Panel as a list.

e. Note the change, then use keyboard shortcuts to change the view back.

f. Click the Up One Level button to view My Computer.

g. Click the Back button to return to the Control Panel.

h. Click View, click Toolbars, then click Customize.

i. Add a button to the toolbar, remove it, then close the Customize the Toolbar dialog box.

j. Click the Restore button on the Control panel window.

6. Use dialog boxes.

a. Double-click the Display icon, then click the Screen Saver tab.

b. Click the Screen Saver list arrow, click any screen saver in the list, then view it in the Preview box above the list.

c. Click the Effects tab.

d. In the Visual effects section, click the Use large icons check box to select it, then click Apply.

e. Note the change in the icons on the desktop and in the Control Panel window.

f. Click the Use large icons check box to deselect it, click the Screen Saver tab, return the screen saver to its original setting, then click Apply.

g. Click the Close button in the Display Properties dialog box, but leave the Control Panel open.

7. Use scroll bars.

a. Click View on the Control Panel toolbar, then click Details.

b. Resize the Control Panel window, if necessary, so that both scroll bars are visible.

c. Drag the vertical scroll box down all the way.

d. Click anywhere in the area above the vertical scroll box.

e. Click the down scroll arrow until the scroll box is back at the bottom of the scroll bar.

f. Drag the horizontal scroll box so you can read the descriptions for the icons.

8. Get Help.

a. Click the Start button on the taskbar, then click Help.

b. Click the Contents tab, then click Introducing Windows 2000 Professional.

c. Click Tips for New Users, click the Use the Personalized Menus feature, then click Overview of Personalized Menus.

d. Read the topic contents, then click Related Topics.

9. Close a program and shut down Windows.

a. Click the Close button to close the Help topic window.

b. Click File on the menu bar, then click Close to close the Control Panel window.

c. Click the Calculator program button on the taskbar to restore the window.

d. Click the Close button in the Calculator window to close the Calculator program.

e. Click the My Computer program button on the taskbar, then click the Close button to close the window.

f. If you are instructed to do so, shut down your computer.

► Independent Challenges

1. Windows 2000 has an extensive help system. In this independent challenge, you will use Help to learn about more Windows 2000 features and explore the help that's available on the Internet.

  a. Open Windows Help and locate help topics on adjusting the double-click speed of your mouse and displaying Web content on your desktop.

If you have a printer, print a Help topic for each subject. If you do not have a printer, write a summary of each topic.

  b. Follow these steps below to access help on the Internet. If you don't have Internet access, you can't do this step.

  i. Click the Web Help button on the toolbar.

  ii. Click the link <u>Windows 2000 home page</u>. A browser opens and prompts you to connect to the Internet if you are not already connected.

  iii. Write a summary of what you find.

  iv. Click the Close button in the title bar of your browser, then disconnect from the Internet and close Windows Help.

2. You may need to change the format of the clock and date on your computer. For example, if you work with international clients it might be easier to show the time in military (24-hour) time and the date with the day before the month. You can also change the actual time and date on your computer, to accomodate such things as time zone changes.

  a. Open the Control Panel window, then double-click the Regional Options icon.

  b. Click the Time tab to change the time to show a 24-hour clock rather than a 12-hour clock.

  c. Click the Date tab to change the Short date format to show the date, followed by the month, followed by the year (e.g., 30/3/01).

  d. Change the time to one hour later using the Date/Time icon in the Control Panel window.

  e. Return the settings to the original time and format, then close all open windows.

3. Calculator is a Windows program on the Accessories menu that you can use for calculations you need to perform while using the computer. Follow these guidelines to explore the Calculator and the Help that comes with it:

  a. Start the Calculator from the Accessories menu.

  b. Click Help on the menu bar, then click Help Topics. The Calculator Help window opens, showing several help topics.

  c. View the help topic on how to perform simple calculations, then print it if you have a printer connected.

  d. Open the Perform a scientific calculation category, then view the definition of a number system.

  e. Determine how many months you have to work to earn an additional week of vacation if you work for a company that provides one additional day of paid vacation for every 560 hours you work. (*Hint:* Divide 560 by the number of hours you work per month.)

  f. Close all open windows.

4. You can customize many Windows features to suit your needs and preferences. One way you do this is to change the appearance of the taskbar on the desktop. In this challenge, try the guidelines described to explore the different ways you can customize the appearance of the taskbar.

  a. Position the pointer over the top border of the taskbar. When the pointer changes shape, drag up an inch.

  b. Resize the taskbar back to its original size.

  c. Click the Start button on the taskbar, point to Settings, then click Taskbar & Start Menu.

  d. In the upper-right corner of the General tab, click the Help button, then click the first check box to view the pop-up window describing it. Repeat this for each check box.

  e. Click each check box and observe the effect in the preview area. (*Note:* Do not click OK.)

  f. Click Cancel.

▶ Visual Workshop

Use the skills you have learned in this unit to customize your desktop so it looks like the one in Figure A-18. Make sure you include the following:

- Calculator program minimized
- Vertical scroll bar in Control Panel window
- Large icons view in Control Panel window
- Rearranged icons on desktop; your icons may be different (*Hint:* If the icons *snap* back to where they were, they are set to be automatically arranged. Right-click a blank area of the desktop, point to Arrange Icons, then click Auto Arrange to deselect this option.)

Use the Print Screen key to make a copy of the screen, then print it from the Paint program. (To print from the Paint program, click the Start button on the taskbar, point to Programs, point to Accessories, then click Paint; in the Paint program window, click Edit on the menu bar, then click Paste; click Yes to fit the image on the bitmap, click the Print button on the toolbar, then click Print in the Print dialog box. See your instructor or technical support person for assistance.)

When you have completed this exercise, be sure to return your settings and desktop back to their original arrangement.

FIGURE A-18

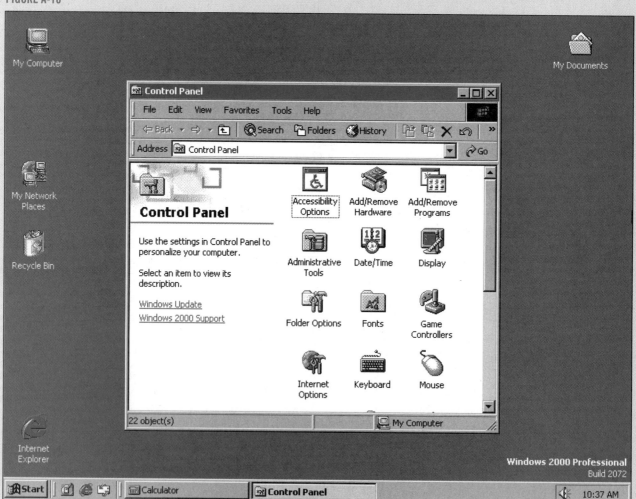

Working

with Programs, Files, and Folders

Objectives

► **Create and save a WordPad document**
► **Open, edit, and save an existing Paint file**
► **Work with multiple programs**
► **Understand file management**
► **View files and create folders with My Computer**
► **Move and copy files with My Computer**
► **Manage files with Windows Explorer**
► **Delete and restore files**
► **Create a shortcut on the desktop**

Most of your work on a computer involves using programs to create files. For example, you might use WordPad to create a resumé or Microsoft Excel to create a budget. The resumé and the budget are examples of **files**, electronic collections of data that you create and save on a disk. In this unit, you learn how to work with files and the programs you use to create them. You create new files, open and edit an existing file, and use the Clipboard to copy and paste data from one file to another. You also explore the file management features of Windows 2000, using My Computer and Windows Explorer. Finally, you learn how to work more efficiently by managing files directly on your desktop.

Creating and Saving a WordPad Document

Windows 2000

As with most programs, when you start WordPad a new, blank **document** (or file) opens. To create a new file, such as a memo, you simply begin typing. Your work is automatically stored in your computer's **random access memory (RAM)** until you turn off your computer, at which point anything stored in the computer's RAM is erased. To store your work permanently, you must save your work as a file on a disk. You can save files either on an internal **hard disk**, which is built into your computer, usually the C: drive, or on a removable 3.5" or 5.25" **floppy disk**, which you insert into a drive on your computer, usually the A: or B: drive. Before you can save a file on a floppy disk, the disk must be formatted. (See the Appendix, "Formatting a Disk," or your instructor or technical support person for more information.) When you name a file, you can use up to 255 characters including spaces and punctuation in the File Name box, using either upper- or lowercase letters. ⬤━ In this lesson, you start WordPad and create a file that contains the text shown in Figure B-1. Then you save the file to Project Disk 1.

1. Click the **Start button** on the taskbar, point to **Programs**, point to **Accessories**, click **WordPad**, then click the **Maximize button** if the window does not fill your screen
   The WordPad program window opens with a new, blank document in the document window. The blinking insertion point I indicates where the text you type will appear.

Trouble?

If you make a mistake, press [Backspace] to delete the character to the left of the insertion point.

2. Type **Memo**, then press **[Enter]**
   Pressing [Enter] inserts a new line and moves the insertion point to the next line.

3. Press **[Enter]** again, then type the remaining text shown in Figure B-1, pressing **[Enter]** at the end of each line
   Now that the text is entered, you can format it. **Formatting** changes the appearance of text to make it more readable or attractive.

QuickTip

Double-click to select a word or triple-click to select a paragraph.

4. Click to the left of the word **Memo**, drag the mouse to the right to highlight the word, then release the mouse button
   The text is now **selected** and any action you make will be performed on the text.

5. Click the **Center button** 🔳 on the Formatting toolbar, then click the **Bold button** on the Formatting toolbar
   The text is centered and bold.

6. Click the **Font Size list arrow** 🔟 ▾, then click **16** in the list
   A **font** is a particular shape and size of type. The text is enlarged to 16 point. One **point** is 1/72 of an inch in height. Now that your memo is complete, you are ready to save it to your Project Disk.

7. Click **File** on the menu bar, then click **Save As**
   The Save As dialog box opens, as shown in Figure B-2. In this dialog box, you specify where you want your file saved and also give your document a name.

Trouble?

This unit assumes that the Project Disk is in the A: drive. If not, substitute the correct drive any time you are instructed to use the 3½ Floppy (A:) drive. See your instructor or technical support person for help.

8. Click the **Save in list arrow**, and then click **3½ Floppy (A:)**, or whichever drive contains your Project Disk 1
   The drive containing your Project Disk is now active, meaning that any files currently on the disk appear in the list of folders and files and that the file you save now will be saved on the disk in this drive.

9. Click the **text** in the File name text box, type **Memo**, then click **Save**
   Your memo is now saved as a WordPad file with the name "Memo" on your Project Disk. Notice that the WordPad title bar contains the name of the file.

FIGURE B-1: **Text to enter in WordPad**

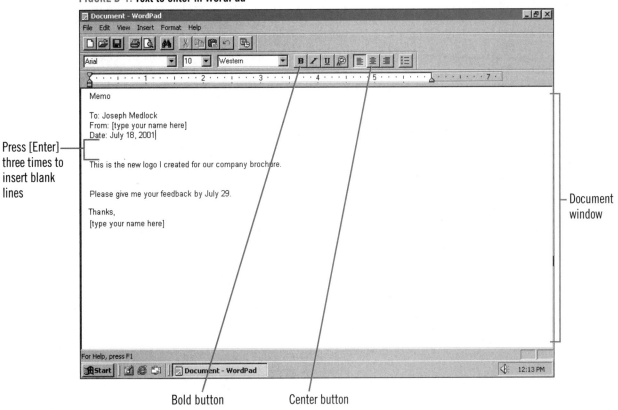

Press [Enter] three times to insert blank lines

Bold button   Center button

FIGURE B-2: **Save As dialog box**

Type new filename here

Click to select the location in which to save file

Creating a new document

When you want to create a new document in WordPad once the program is already open and another document is active, you can click the New button ☐ on the Standard toolbar. A dialog box opens from which you can choose to create a new Rich Text, Word 6, Text, or Unicode Text document. **Rich Text** documents, the WordPad default document format, can include text formatting and tabs, and be available for use in a variety

of other word-processing programs; **Word 6** documents can be opened, edited, and enhanced in Microsoft Word version 6.0 or later without conversion; **Text** documents can be used in numerous other programs because they contain no formatting; and **Unicode Text** documents can contain text from any of the world's writing systems, such as Roman, Greek, and Chinese. You select one of the options by clicking it, and then clicking OK.

Opening, Editing, and Saving an Existing Paint File

Sometimes you create files from scratch, but often you may want to use a file you or someone else has already created; to do so, you need to **open** the file. Once you open a file, you can **edit** it, or make changes to it, such as adding or deleting text. After editing a file, you can save it with the same filename, which means that you no longer will have the file in its original form, or you can save it with a different filename, so that the original file remains unchanged. In this lesson, you use **Paint**, a drawing program that comes with Windows 2000, to open a file, edit it by changing a color, then save the file with a new filename to leave the original file unchanged.

Steps

1. Click the **Start button** on the taskbar, point to **Programs**, point to **Accessories**, click **Paint**, then click the **Maximize button** if the window doesn't fill the screen
   The Paint program opens with a blank work area. If you wanted to create a file from scratch, you would begin working now.

2. Click **File** on the menu bar, then click **Open**
   The Open dialog box works similarly to the Save As dialog box.

3. Click the **Look in list arrow**, then click **3½ Floppy (A:)**
   The Paint files on your Project Disk 1 are listed in the Open dialog box, as shown in Figure B-3.

> **QuickTip**
> You can also open a file by double-clicking it in the Open dialog box.

4. Click **Win B-1** in the list of files, and then click **Open**
   The Open dialog box closes and the file named Win B-1 opens. Before you make any changes to a file, you should save it with a new filename, so that the original file is unchanged.

5. Click **File** on the menu bar, then click **Save As**

6. Make sure **3½ Floppy (A:)** appears in the Save in text box, select the text **Win B-1** in the File name text box if necessary, type **Logo**, then click **Save**
   The Logo file appears in the Paint window, as shown in Figure B-4. Because you saved the file with a new name, you can edit it without changing the original file. You will now use buttons in the **Tool Box**, a toolbar of illustration tools available in Windows Paint, and the **Color Box**, a palette of colors from which you can choose, to modify the graphic.

7. Click the **Fill With Color button** in the Tool Box, then click the **Blue color box**, which is the fourth from the right in the first row
   Notice how clicking a button in the Tool Box changes the mouse pointer. Now when you click an area in the image, it will be filled with the color you selected in the Color Box. See Table B-1 for a description of the tools in the Tool Box.

8. Move the pointer into the **white area that represents the sky** until the pointer changes to , then click
   The sky is now blue.

9. Click **File** on the menu bar, then click **Save**
   The change you made is saved to disk.

FIGURE B-3: Open dialog box

List of files

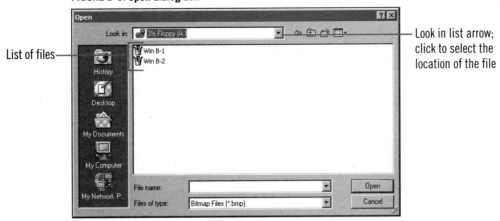

Look in list arrow;
click to select the
location of the file

FIGURE B-4: Paint file saved with new filename

Name of file
appears in
title bar

Tool Box

Choose this
blue color

Color box

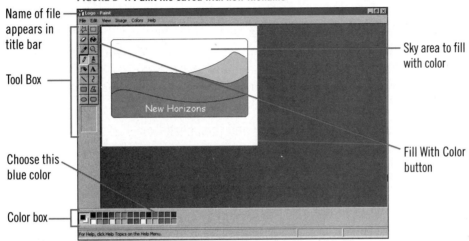

Sky area to fill
with color

Fill With Color
button

TABLE B-1: Paint Tool Box buttons

tool	description	tool	description
Free-Form Select button	Selects a free-form section of the picture to move, copy, or edit	Airbrush button	Produces a circular spray of dots
Select button	Selects a rectangular section of the picture to move, copy, or edit	Text button	Inserts text into the picture
Eraser button	Erases a portion of the picture using the selected eraser size and foreground color	Line button	Draws a straight line with the selected width and foreground color
Fill With Color button	Fills closed shape or area with the current drawing color	Curve button	Draws a wavy line with the selected width and foreground color
Pick Color button	Picks up a color off the picture to use for drawing	Rectangle button	Draws a rectangle with the selected fill style; also used to draw squares by holding down [Shift] while drawing
Magnifier button	Changes the magnification; lists magnifications under the toolbar	Polygon button	Draws polygons from connected straight-line segments
Pencil button	Draws a free-form line one pixel wide	Ellipse button	Draws an ellipse with the selected fill style; also used to draw circles by holding down [Shift] while drawing
Brush button	Draws using a brush with the selected shape and size	Rounded Rectangle button	Draws rectangles with rounded corners using the selected fill style; also used to draw rounded squares by holding down [Shift] while drawing

Working with Multiple Programs

A powerful feature of Windows is its capability to run more than one program at a time. For example, you might be working with a document in WordPad and want to search the Internet to find the answer to a question. You can start your browser, a program designed to access information on the Internet, without closing WordPad. When you find the information, you can leave your browser open and switch back to WordPad. Each open program is represented by a program button on the taskbar that you click to switch between programs. You can also copy data from one file to another, (whether the files were created with the same Windows program or not), using the **Clipboard**, a temporary area in your computer's memory, and the Cut, Copy, and Paste commands. See Table B-2 for a description of these commands. In this lesson, you copy the logo graphic you worked with in the previous lesson into the memo you created in WordPad.

Trouble?

If some parts of the image or text are outside the dotted rectangle, click anywhere outside the image, then select the image again, making sure you include everything.

1. Click the **Select button** ⬚ on the Tool Box, and then drag a rectangle around the entire **graphic**

When you release the mouse button, the dotted rectangle surrounds the selected area, as shown in Figure B-5. Make sure the entire image is inside the rectangle. The next action you take affects the entire selection.

2. Click **Edit** on the menu bar, and then click **Copy**

The logo is copied to the Clipboard. When you **copy** an object onto the Clipboard, the object remains in its original location and is also available to be pasted into another location.

QuickTip

To switch between programs using the keyboard, press and hold down [Alt], press [Tab] until the program you want is selected, then release [Alt].

3. Click the **WordPad program button** on the taskbar

WordPad becomes the active program.

4. Click in the **first line below the line that ends "for our company brochure."**

The insertion point indicates where the logo will be pasted.

5. Click the **Paste button** 📋 on the WordPad toolbar

The contents of the Clipboard, in this case the logo, are pasted into the WordPad file, as shown in Figure B-6.

6. Click the **Save button** 💾 on the toolbar

The Memo file is saved with the logo inserted.

7. Click the WordPad **Close button**

Your WordPad document and the WordPad program close. Paint is now the active program.

8. Click the Paint **Close button**; if you are prompted to save changes, click **Yes**

Your Paint document and the Paint program close. You return to the desktop.

TABLE B-2: **Overview of cutting, copying and pasting**

Toolbar button	function	keyboard shortcut
✂ **Cut**	Removes selected information from a file and places it on the Clipboard	[Ctrl][X]
📋 **Copy**	Places a copy of selected information on the Clipboard, leaving the file intact	[Ctrl][C]
📋 **Paste**	Inserts whatever is currently on the Clipboard into another location within the same file, or in a different file	[Ctrl][V]

FIGURE B-5: Selecting the logo to copy and paste into the Memo file

Select button —

Dotted line
indicates
selected
area

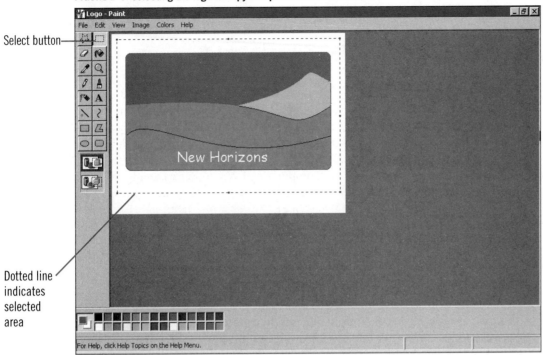

FIGURE B-6: Memo with pasted logo

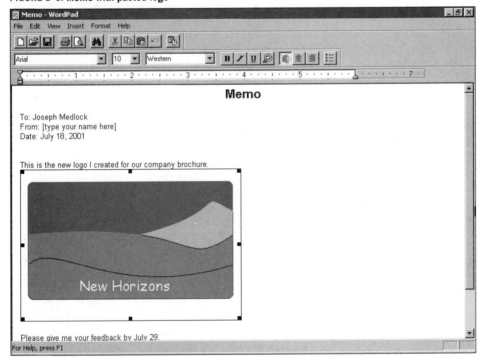

Understanding File Management

After you have created and saved numerous files using various programs, **file management**, the process of organizing and keeping track of all of your files, can be a challenge. Fortunately, Windows 2000 provides tools to keep everything organized so you can easily locate the files you need, move files to new locations, and delete files you no longer need. There are two main tools for managing your files: My Computer and Windows Explorer. In this lesson, you preview the ways you can use My Computer and Windows Explorer to manage your files.

Windows 2000 gives you the ability to:

Create folders in which you can save your files

Folders are areas on a floppy disk or hard disk in which you can store files. For example, you might create a folder for your documents and another folder for your graphic files. Folders can also contain additional folders, which creates a more complex structure of folders and files, called a **file hierarchy**. See Figure B-7 for an example of how files can be organized.

QuickTip

To browse My Computer using multiple windows, click Tools on the menu bar, and then click Folder Options. In the Folder Options dialog box, click the General tab, and then under Browse Folders, click the Open each folder in its own window option button. Each time you open a new folder, a new window opens, leaving the previous folder's window open so that you can view both at the same time.

Examine and organize the hierarchy of files and folders

You can use either My Computer or Windows Explorer to see the overall structure of your files and folders. By examining your file hierarchy with these tools, you can better organize the contents of your computer and adjust the hierarchy to meet your needs. Figures B-8 and B-9 illustrate how My Computer and Windows Explorer list folders and files.

Copy, move, and rename files and folders

If you decide that a file belongs in a different folder, you can move it to another folder. You can also rename a file if you decide a different name is more descriptive. If you want to keep a copy of a file in more than one folder, you can copy it to new folders.

Delete files and folders you no longer need, as well as restore files you delete accidentally

Deleting files and folders you are sure you don't need frees up disk space and keeps your file hierarchy more organized. The **Recycle Bin**, a space on your computer's hard disk that stores deleted files, allows you to restore files you deleted by accident. To free up disk space, you should occasionally empty the Recycle Bin by deleting the files permanently from your hard drive.

Locate files quickly with the Windows 2000 Search feature

As you create more files and folders, you may forget where you placed a certain file or you may forget what name you used when you saved a file. With Search, you can locate files by providing only partial names or other factors, such as the file type (for example, a WordPad document or a Paint graphic) or the date the file was created or modified.

Use shortcuts

If a file or folder you use often is located several levels down in your file hierarchy (in a folder within a folder, within a folder), it might take you several steps to access it. To save time accessing the files and programs you use frequently, you can create shortcuts to them. A **shortcut** is a link that gives you quick access to a particular file, folder, or program.

FIGURE B-7: Sample file hierarchy

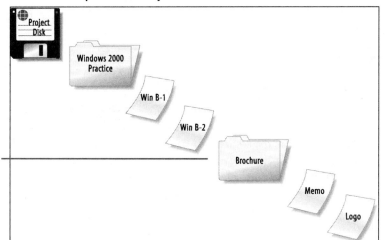

In this hierarchy, Brochure folder is a subfolder of Windows 2000 Practice folder

FIGURE B-8: Brochure folder shown in My Computer

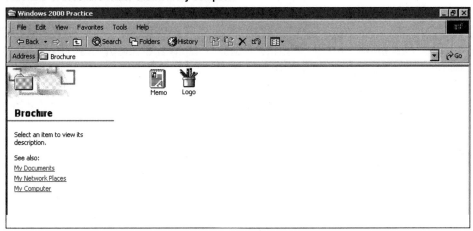

FIGURE B-9: Brochure folder shown in Windows Explorer

Windows 2000 allows you to see the file hierarchy as well as the selected folder's contents

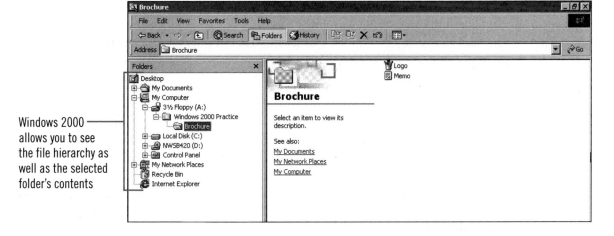

Viewing Files and Creating Folders with My Computer

My Computer shows the contents of your computer, including files, folders, programs, disk drives, and printers. You can click the icons representing these various parts of your computer to view their contents or properties. You can manage your files using the My Computer menu bar and toolbar. See Table B-3 for a description of the toolbar buttons. ✒️ In this lesson, you begin by using My Computer to move around in your computer's file hierarchy, then you create two new folders on your Project Disk 1 for the files you created.

Steps

Trouble?

If you do not see the toolbar, click View on the menu bar, point to Toolbars, and then click Standard Buttons. If you do not see the Address Bar, click View, point to Toolbar, and then click Address Bar.

1. Double-click the My Computer icon on your desktop, then click the Maximize button if the My Computer window does not fill the screen

My Computer opens and displays the contents of your computer, as shown in Figure B-10. Your window may contain icons for different folders, drives, and printers.

2. Make sure your Project Disk 1 is in the floppy disk drive, then double-click the 3½ Floppy (A:) icon

The contents of your Project Disk 1 appear in the window. These are the project files and the files you created using WordPad and Paint. Each file is represented by an icon, which indicates the program that was used to create the file. If Microsoft Word is installed on your computer, the Word icon appears for the WordPad files; if not, the WordPad icon appears.

Trouble?

This book assumes that your hard drive is the C: drive. If yours differs, substitute the appropriate drive for the C: drive wherever it is referenced. See your instructor or technical support person for assistance.

3. Click the Address list arrow on the Address Bar, as shown in Figure B-10, then click Local Disk (C:) or the letter for the main hard drive on your computer

The window changes to show the contents of your hard drive. The Address Bar allows you to open and view a drive, folder, or even a Web page. You can also type in the Address Bar to go to a different drive, folder, or Web page. For example, typing "C:\" will display drive C:; typing "E:\Personal Letters" will display the Personal Letters folder on the E: drive, and typing "http://www.microsoft.com" opens Microsoft's Web site if your computer is connected to the Internet.

4. Click the Back button on the toolbar

The Back button displays the previous location, in this case, your Project Disk.

5. Click the Views button 🔲▾ on the toolbar, then click Details

Details view shows not only the files and folders, but also the sizes of the files, the types of files, folders, or drives and the date the files were last modified.

6. Click 🔲▾, then click Thumbnails

This view offers less information but provides a preview of graphics and a clear view of the contents of the disk.

7. Click File on the menu bar, point to New, then click Folder

A new folder is created on your Project Disk 1, as shown in Figure B-11. The folder is called "New Folder" by default. It is selected and ready to be renamed. You can also create a new folder by right-clicking in the blank area of the My Computer window, clicking New, then clicking Folder.

QuickTip

To rename a folder, click the folder to select it, click the folder name so it is surrounded by a rectangle, type the new folder name, then press [Enter].

8. Type Windows 2000 Practice, then press [Enter]

Choosing descriptive names for your folders helps you remember their contents.

9. Double-click the Windows 2000 Practice folder, repeat Step 7 to create a new folder in the Windows 2000 Practice folder, type Brochure for the folder name, then press [Enter]

10. Click the Up button 🔲 to return to your Project Disk 1

WORKING WITH PROGRAMS, FILES, AND FOLDERS

FIGURE B-10: My Computer window

Menu bar

Toolbar

Address bar

Address list arrow

Your icon list may differ

Status bar

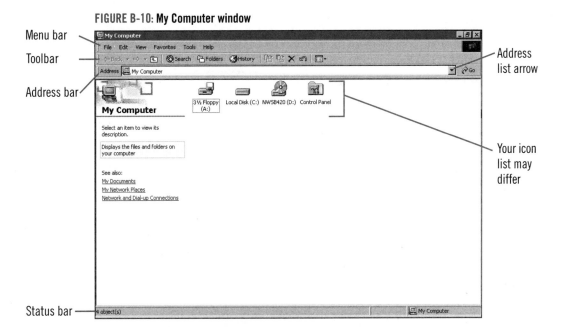

FIGURE B-11: Creating a new folder

Back button

Folder is located on disk in the A: drive

Type new name here

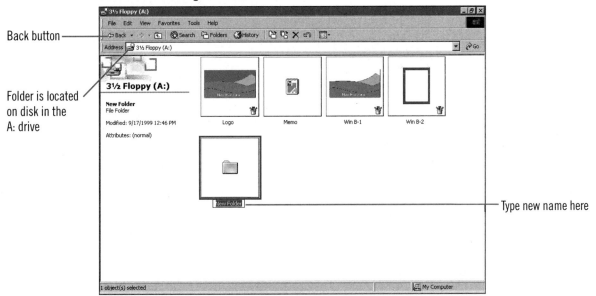

TABLE B-3: Buttons on the My Computer toolbar

button	function
⇐	Moves back to the previous location you have already visited
⇒	Moves forward to the previous location you have already visited
🗀	Moves up one level in the file hierarchy
🗀	Opens the Browse For Folder dialog box, to move the selected file to a new location
🗀	Opens the Browse For Folder dialog box, to copy the selected file to a new location
↺	Undoes the most recent My Computer operation
✕	Deletes a folder or file permanently
▦▾	Lists the contents of My Computer using different views

WORKING WITH PROGRAMS, FILES, AND FOLDERS

Moving and Copying Files with My Computer

You can move a file or folder from one location to another using a variety of methods in My Computer or Windows Explorer. If the file or folder and the location to which you want to move it are both visible on the desktop, you can simply drag the item from one location to the other. You can also use the cut, copy, and paste commands on the Edit menu or the corresponding buttons on the toolbar. Finally you can right-click the file or folder and choose the Send to command to "send" it to another location—most often a floppy disk for **backing up** files. Backup copies are made in case you have computer trouble, which may cause you to lose files. In this lesson, you move your files into the folder you created in the last lesson.

1. Click **View**, point to **Arrange Icons**, then click **by Name**
   In this view, folders are listed first in alphabetical order, followed by files, also in alphabetical order.

2. Click the **Win B-1 file**, hold down the mouse button and drag the file onto the **Windows 2000 Practice folder**, as shown in Figure B-12, then release the mouse button
   Win B-1 is moved into the Windows 2000 Practice folder.

3. Double-click the **Windows 2000 Practice folder** and confirm that it contains the Win B-1 file as well as the Brochure folder

4. Click the **Up button** 🔼 on the My Computer toolbar, as shown in Figure B-12
   You return to your Project Disk. The Up button shows the next level up in the folder hierarchy.

5. Click the **Logo file**, press and hold down **[Shift]**, then click the **Memo file**
   Both files are selected. Table B-4 describes methods for selecting multiple objects.

6. Click the **Move To button** 📋 on the 3½ Floppy (A:) toolbar
   The filenames turn gray, and the Browse For Folder dialog box opens, as shown in Figure B-13.

7. Click the **plus sign** ➕ next to My Computer if you do not see 3½ Floppy (A:) listed, double-click the 3½ **Floppy (A:) drive**, double-click the **Windows 2000 Practice folder**, double-click the **Brochure folder**, then click **OK**
   The two files are moved to the Brochure folder. Only the Windows 2000 Practice folder and the Win B-2 file remain.

8. Click the **Close button** in the 3½ Floppy (A:) window

QuickTip

It is easy to confuse the Back button with the Up button. The Back button returns you to the last location you visited, no matter where it is in your folder hierarchy. The Up button displays the next level up in the folder hierarchy, no matter where you last visited.

FIGURE B-12: Dragging a file from one folder to another

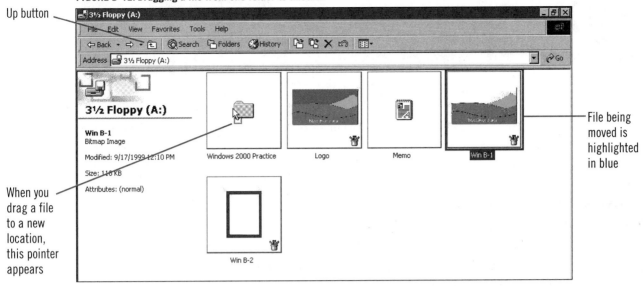

Up button

When you drag a file to a new location, this pointer appears

File being moved is highlighted in blue

FIGURE B-13: Moving files

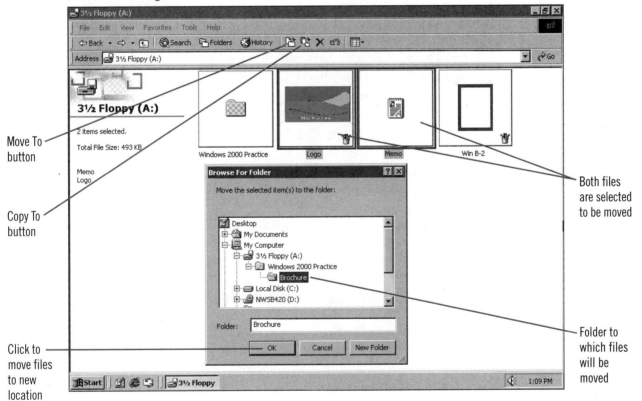

Move To button

Copy To button

Click to move files to new location

Both files are selected to be moved

Folder to which files will be moved

TABLE B-4: Techniques for selecting multiple files and folders

to select	do this
Individual objects not grouped together	Click the first object you want to select, then press and hold down [Ctrl] as you click each additional object you want to add to the selection
Objects grouped together	Click the first object you want to select, then press and hold down [Shift] as you click the last object in the list of objects you want to select; all the objects listed between the first and last objects are selected

Windows 2000

Managing Files with Windows Explorer

As with My Computer, you can use Windows Explorer to copy, move, delete, and rename files and folders. However, **Windows Explorer** is more powerful than My Computer: it allows you to see the overall structure of the contents of your computer or network, (the file hierarchy), while you work with individual files and folders within that structure. This means you can work with more than one computer, folder, or file at once. ➤ In this lesson, you copy a folder from your Project Disk 1 onto the hard drive and then rename the folder.

Steps

Trouble?

If you do not see the toolbar, click View on the menu bar, point to Toolbars, then click Standard Buttons. If you do not see the Address Bar, click View, point to Toolbars, then click Address Bar.

1. **Click the Start button, point to Programs, point to Accessories, click Windows Explorer, then click the Maximize button if the Windows Explorer window doesn't already fill the screen**
   Windows Explorer opens, as shown in Figure B-14. The window is divided into two areas called **panes**. The left pane, called the **Explorer Bar**, displays the drives and folders on your computer in a hierarchy. The right pane displays the contents of whatever drive or folder is currently selected in the left pane. Each pane has its own set of scroll bars, so that changing what you can see in one pane won't affect what you can see in the other. Like My Computer, Windows Explorer has a menu bar, toolbar, and Address Bar.

2. **Click View on the menu bar, then click Details if it is not already selected**
   Remember that a bullet point next to a command on the menu bar indicates that it's selected.

Trouble?

If you cannot see the A: drive, you may have to click the plus sign (+) next to My Computer to view the available drives on your computer.

3. **In the left pane, scroll to and click 3½ Floppy (A:)**
   The contents of your Project Disk 1 appear in the right pane.

4. **In the left pane, click the plus sign (+) next to 3½ Floppy (A:)**
   You can click the plus sign (+) or minus sign (-) next to any item in the left pane to show or hide the different levels of the file hierarchy, so that you don't always have to look at the entire structure of your computer or network. A plus sign (+) next to a computer, drive, or folder indicates there are additional folders within that object. A minus sign (-) indicates that all the folders of the next level of hierarchy are shown. Clicking the + displays (or "expands") the next level; clicking the – hides (or "collapses") them.

QuickTip

When neither a + nor a – appears next to an icon, it means that the item does not have any folders in it, although it may have files, which you can see listed in the right pane by clicking the icon.

5. **In the left pane, double-click the Windows 2000 Practice folder**
   The contents of the Windows 2000 Practice folder appear in the right pane of Windows Explorer, as shown in Figure B-15. Double-clicking an item in the left pane that has a + next to it displays its contents in the right pane and also expands the next level in the hierarchy in the left pane.

Trouble?

If you are working in a lab setting, you may not be able to add items to your hard drive. Skip Steps 6, 7, and 8 if you are unable to complete them.

6. **In the left pane, drag the Windows 2000 Practice folder on top of the C: drive icon, then release the mouse button**
   When you drag files or folders to a different drive, they are copied rather than moved. The Windows 2000 Practice folder and the files in it are copied to the hard disk.

7. **In the left pane, click the C: drive icon**
   The Windows 2000 Practice folder should now appear in the list of folders in the right pane. You may have to scroll to see it. Now you should rename the folder so you can distinguish the original folder from the copy.

QuickTip

You can also rename a selected file by pressing [F2], or using the Rename command on the File menu.

8. **Right-click the Windows 2000 Practice folder in the right pane, click Rename in the pop-up menu, type Practice Copy, then press [Enter]**

FIGURE B-14: Windows Explorer window

Left pane, also known as Explorer Bar

Contents of the C: drive

Your list of folders and files will vary

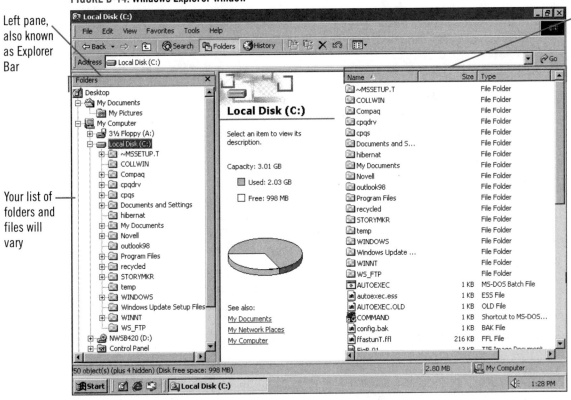

FIGURE B-15: Contents of Windows 2000 Practice folder

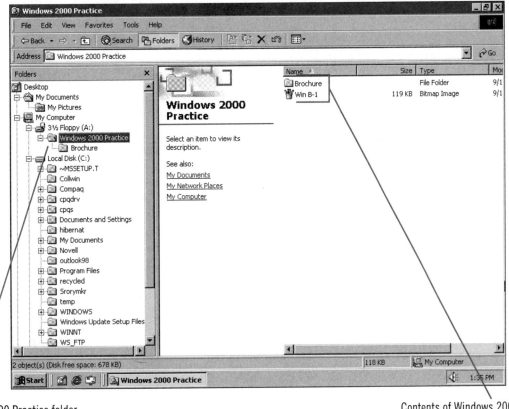

Windows 2000 Practice folder selected in left pane

Contents of Windows 2000 Practice folder appear in right pane

Windows 2000

Deleting and Restoring Files

To save disk space and manage your files more effectively, you should **delete** (or remove) files you no longer need. Because files deleted from your hard drive are stored in the Recycle Bin until you remove them permanently by emptying the Recycle Bin, you can restore any files you might have deleted accidentally. However, if you delete a file from your floppy disk it will not be stored in the Recycle Bin—it will be permanently deleted. See Table B-5 for an overview of deleting and restoring files. There are many ways to delete files and folders from the My Computer and Windows Explorer windows, as well as from the Windows 2000 desktop. In this lesson, you delete a file by dragging it to the Recycle Bin, restore it, and delete a folder by using the Delete command in Windows Explorer.

Steps

1. Click the **Restore button** 🗗 on the Windows Explorer title bar
You should be able to see the Recycle Bin icon on your desktop. If you can't see it, resize or move the Windows Explorer window until it is visible. See Figure B-16.

2. If necessary, scroll until you see the Practice Copy folder in the right pane of Windows Explorer

QuickTip

If you are unable to delete the file, it might be because your Recycle Bin is full, or too small, or the properties have been changed so that files are not stored in the Recycle Bin but are deleted instead. See your instructor or technical support person for assistance.

3. Drag the **Practice Copy folder** from the right pane to the **Recycle Bin** on the desktop, as shown in Figure B-16, then click **Yes** to confirm the deletion if necessary
The folder no longer appears in Windows Explorer because you have moved it to the Recycle Bin.

4. Double-click the **Recycle Bin icon** on the desktop
The Recycle Bin window opens, as shown in Figure B-17. Depending on the number of files already deleted on your computer, your window might look different. Use the scroll bar if you can't see the files.

5. Click **Edit** on the Recycle Bin menu bar, then click **Undo Delete**
The Practice Copy folder is restored and should now appear in the Windows Explorer window. You might need to minimize your Recycle Bin window if it blocks your view of Windows Explorer, and you might need to scroll to the bottom of the right pane to find the restored folder.

6. Click the **Practice Copy folder** in the right pane, click the **Delete button** ✕ on the Windows Explorer toolbar (resize the window as necessary to see the button), then click **Yes**
When you are sure you no longer need files you've moved into the Recycle Bin, you can empty the Recycle Bin. You won't do this now, in case you are working on a computer that you share with other people. But, when you're working on your own machine, simply right-click the Recycle Bin icon, then click Empty Recycle Bin in the pop-up menu.

7. Close the Recycle Bin
If you minimized the Recycle Bin in Step 4, click its program button to open the Recycle Bin window, and then click the Close button.

FIGURE B-16: **Dragging a folder to delete it**

Drag the folder here

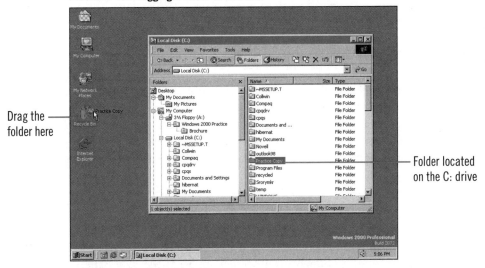

Folder located on the C: drive

FIGURE B-17: **Recycle Bin window**

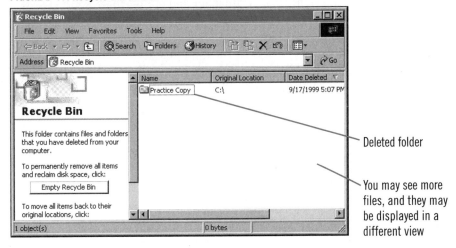

Deleted folder

You may see more files, and they may be displayed in a different view

TABLE B-5: **Methods for deleting and restoring files**

ways to delete a file	ways to restore a file from the Recycle Bin
Select the file, then click the Delete button on the toolbar	Click the Undo button on the toolbar
Select the file, then press [Delete]	Select the file, click File, then click Restore
Right-click the file, then click Delete on the pop-up menu	Right-click the file, then click Restore
Drag the file to the Recycle Bin	Drag the file from the Recycle Bin to any other location

CLUES TO USE

Customizing your Recycle Bin

You can set your Recycle Bin according to how you like to delete and restore files. For example, if you do not want files to go to the Recycle Bin but rather want them to be immediately and permanently deleted, right-click the Recycle Bin, click Properties, then click the Do Not Move Files to the Recycle Bin check box. If you find that the Recycle Bin fills up too fast and you are not ready to delete the files permanently, you can increase the amount of disk space devoted to the Recycle Bin by moving the Maximum Size of Recycle Bin slider to the right. This, of course, reduces the amount of disk space you have available for other things. Also, you can choose not to have the Confirm File Delete dialog box open when you send files to the Recycle Bin. See your instructor or technical support person before changing any of the Recycle Bin settings.

Creating a Shortcut on the Desktop

When you frequently use a file, folder, or program that is located several levels down in the file hierarchy, you may want to create a shortcut to the object. You can place the shortcut on the desktop or in any other location, such as a folder, that you find convenient. To open the file, folder, or program using the shortcut, double-click the icon. In this lesson, you use Windows Explorer to create a shortcut on your desktop to the Memo file.

Steps

1. **In the left pane of the Windows Explorer window, click the Brochure folder**
   The contents of the Brochure folder appear in the right pane.

2. **In the right pane, right-click the Memo file**
   A pop-up menu appears, as shown in Figure B-18.

3. **Click Create Shortcut in the pop-up menu**
   The file named Shortcut to Memo file appears in the right pane. Now you need to move it to the desktop so that it will be accessible whenever you need it.

Trouble?

Make sure to use the right mouse button in Step 4. If you used the left mouse button by accident, right-click the Shortcut to Memo file in the right pane of Windows Explorer, click Delete, and repeat Step 4.

4. **Click the Shortcut to Memo file with the right-mouse button, then drag the shortcut to an empty area of the desktop**
   Dragging an icon using the left mouse button copies it. Dragging an icon using the right mouse button gives you the option to copy it, move it, or create a shortcut to it. When you release the mouse button a pop-up menu appears.

5. **Click Move Here in the pop-up menu**
   A shortcut to the Memo file now appears on the desktop, as shown in Figure B-19. You might have to move or resize the Windows Explorer window to see it.

6. **Double-click the Shortcut to Memo file icon**
   WordPad starts and the Memo file opens (if you have Microsoft Word installed on your computer, it will start and open the file instead). Using a shortcut eliminates the many steps involved in starting a program and locating and opening a file.

7. **Click the Close button in the WordPad or Word title bar**
   Now you should delete the shortcut icon in case you are working in a lab and share the computer with others.

QuickTip

Deleting a shortcut deletes only the link; it does not delete the original file or folder to which it points.

8. **On the desktop, click the Shortcut to Memo file, press [Delete], then click Yes to confirm the deletion**
   The shortcut is removed from the desktop and is now in the Recycle Bin.

9. **Close all windows, then shut down Windows**

FIGURE B-18: Creating a shortcut

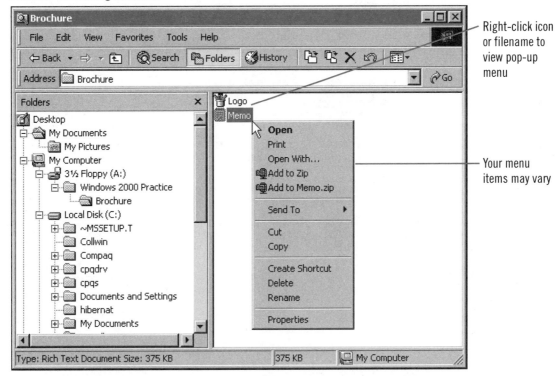

Right-click icon or filename to view pop-up menu

Your menu items may vary

FIGURE B-19: Shortcut on desktop

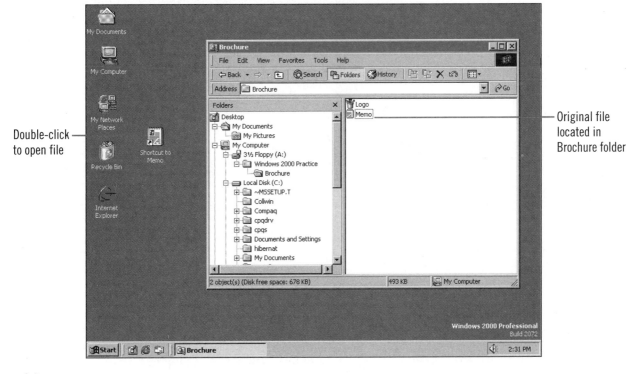

Double-click to open file

Original file located in Brochure folder

Adding shortcuts to the Start menu

If you do not want your desktop to get cluttered with icons but you would still like easy access to certain files, programs, and folders, you can create a shortcut on the Start menu. Drag the file, program, or folder that you want to add to the Start menu from the Windows Explorer window to the Start button. The file, program, or folder will appear on the first level of the Start menu.

Practice

► Concepts Review

Label each of the elements of the Windows Explorer window shown in Figure B-20.

FIGURE B-20

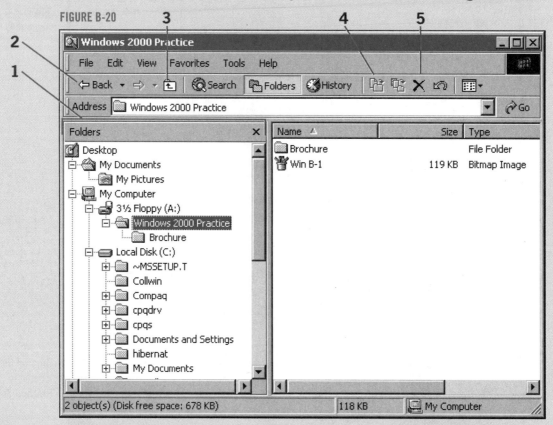

Match each of the statements with the term it describes.

6. Electronic collections of data   a. **RAM**
7. Your computer's temporary storage area   b. **Folders**
8. Temporary location of information you wish to paste into another program   c. **Files**
9. Storage areas on your hard drive for files, folders, and programs   d. **File hierarchy**
10. Structure of files and folders   e. **Clipboard**

Select the best answer from the list of choices.

11. **To prepare a floppy disk to save your files, you must first do which of the following?**
    a. Copy work files to the disk   c. Erase all the files that might be on the disk
    b. Format the disk   d. Place the files on the Clipboard
12. **You can use My Computer to**
    a. create a drawing of your computer.   c. change the appearance of your desktop.
    b. view the contents of a folder.   d. add text to a WordPad file.
13. **Which of the following best describes WordPad?**
    a. A program for organizing files   c. A program for creating basic text documents
    b. A program for performing financial analysis   d. A program for creating graphics

14. **Which of the following is NOT a way to move files from one folder to another?**
   a. Open the file and use the Save As command to save the file in a new location
   b. In My Computer or the Windows Explorer, drag the selected file to the new folder
   c. Use the Move To button on the Standard toolbar in the My Computer or the Windows Explorer window
   d. Use the [Ctrl][X] and [Ctrl][V] keyboard shortcuts while in the My Computer or the Windows Explorer window

15. **In which of the following can you view the hierarchy of drives, folders, and files in a split pane window?**
   a. Windows Explorer
   b. Programs
   c. My Computer
   d. WordPad

16. **To restore files that you have sent to the Recycle Bin,**
   a. click File, then click Empty Recycle Bin.
   b. click Edit, then click Undo Delete.
   c. click File, then click Undo.
   d. You cannot retrieve files sent to the Recycle Bin.

17. **To select files that are not grouped together, select the first file, then**
   a. press [Shift] while selecting the second file.
   b. press [Alt] while selecting the second file.
   c. press [Ctrl] while selecting the second file.
   d. click on the second file.

18. **Pressing [Backspace]**
   a. deletes the character to the right of the cursor.
   b. deletes the character to the left of the cursor.
   c. moves the insertion point one character to the right.
   d. deletes all text to the left of the cursor.

19. **The size of a font is measured in**
   a. centimeters.
   b. points.
   c. places.
   d. millimeters.

20. **The Back button on the My Computer toolbar**
   a. starts the last program you used.
   b. displays the next level of the file hierarchy.
   c. backs up the currently selected file.
   d. displays the last location you visited.

▶ Skills Review

Use Project Disk 2 to complete the exercises in this section.
1. **Create and save a WordPad file.**
   a. Start Windows, then start WordPad.
   b. Type **My Drawing Ability**.
   c. Press [Enter] three times.
   d. Save the document as *Drawing Ability* to your Project Disk 2.
2. **Open, edit, and save an existing Paint file.**
   a. Start Paint and open the file Win B-2 on your Project Disk 2.
   b. Inside the picture frame, use the ellipses tool to create a circle filled with purple and then use the rectangle tool to place a square filled with yellow inside the circle.
   c. Save the picture as *First Unique Art* to your Project Disk 2.
3. **Work with multiple programs.**
   a. Select the entire graphic and copy it to the Clipboard, then switch to WordPad.
   b. Place the insertion point in the last blank line, paste the graphic into your document, then deselect the graphic.
   c. Save the changes to your WordPad document.
   d. Switch to Paint.
   e. Using the Fill With Color button, change the color of a filled area of your graphic.
   f. Save the revised graphic with the new name *Second Unique Art* to Project Disk 2.
   g. Select the entire graphic and copy it to the Clipboard.
   h. Switch to WordPad, move the insertion point to the line below the graphic by clicking below the graphic and press [Enter], type **This is another version of my graphic.** below the first picture, then press [Enter].

   i. Paste the second graphic under the text you just typed.

   j. Save the changed WordPad document as *Two Drawing Examples* to your Project Disk 2.

   k. Exit Paint and WordPad.

4. View files and create folders with My Computer.

   a. Open My Computer.

   b. Double-click the drive that contains your Project Disk 2.

   c. Create a new folder on your Project Disk 2 by clicking File, New, then Folder, and name the new folder *Review*.

   d. Open the folder to display its contents (it is empty).

   e. Use the Address Bar to view your hard drive, usually (C:).

   f. Create a folder on the hard drive called *Temporary*, then use the Back button to view the Review folder.

   g. Create two new folders in it, one named *Documents* and the other named *Artwork*.

   h. Click the Forward button as many times as necessary to move up in the file hierarchy and view the contents of the hard drive.

   i. Change the view to Details.

5. Move and copy files with My Computer.

   a. Use the Address Bar to view your Project Disk 2.

   b. Use the [Shift] key to select *First Unique Art* and *Second Unique Art*, then cut and paste them into the Artwork folder.

   c. Use the Back button as many times as necessary to view the contents of Project Disk 2.

   d. Select the two WordPad files, *Drawing Ability* and *Two Drawing Examples*, then move them into the Review folder.

   e. Open the Review folder, select the two WordPad files again, then drag them into the Documents folder.

6. Manage files with Windows Explorer.

   a. Open Windows Explorer and view the contents of the Artwork folder in the right pane.

   b. Select the two Paint files.

   c. Drag the two Paint files from the Artwork folder to the Temporary folder on the hard drive to copy them.

   d. View the contents of the Documents folder in the right pane.

   e. Select the two WordPad files.

   f. Repeat Step c to copy the files to the Temporary folder on the hard drive.

   g. View the contents of the Temporary folder in the right pane to verify that the four files are there.

7. Delete and restore files and folders.

   a. Resize the Windows Explorer window so you can see the Recycle Bin icon on the desktop, then scroll in Windows Explorer so you can see the Temporary folder in the left pane.

   b. Delete the Temporary folder from the hard drive by dragging it to the Recycle Bin.

   c. Click Yes if necessary to confirm the deletion.

   d. Open the Recycle Bin, restore the Temporary folder and its files to your hard disk, and then close the Recycle Bin. (*Note:* If your Recycle Bin is empty, your computer is set to automatically delete items in the Recycle Bin.)

   e. Delete the Temporary folder again by pressing [Delete]. Click Yes if necessary to confirm the deletion.

8. Create a shortcut on the desktop.

   a. Use the left pane of Windows Explorer to locate the Windows folder on your hard drive. Select the folder to view its contents in the right pane. (*Note:* If you are in a lab setting, you may not have access to the Windows folder.)

   b. In the right pane, scroll through the list of objects until you see a file called Explorer.

   c. Drag the Explorer file with the right mouse button to the desktop to create a shortcut.

   d. Close Windows Explorer.

   e. Double-click the new shortcut to make sure it starts Windows Explorer. Then close Windows Explorer again.

   f. Delete the shortcut for Windows Explorer and exit Windows.

► Independent Challenges

If you are doing all of the Independent Challenges, you may need to use additional floppy disks. Label the first new disk Project Disk 3, and the next Project Disk 4.

1. You have decided to start a bakery business and you want to use Windows 2000 to organize the files for the business.

a. Create two new folders on your Project Disk 3, one named *Advertising* and one named *Customers*.

b. Use WordPad to create a letter inviting new customers to the open house for the new bakery, then save it as *Open House Letter* and place it in the Customers folder.

c. Use WordPad to create a list of five tasks that need to get done before the business opens (such as purchasing equipment, decorating the interior, and ordering supplies), then save it as *Business Plan* to your Project Disk 3, but don't place it in a folder.

d. Use Paint to create a simple logo for the bakery, save it as *Bakery Logo*, and then place it in the Advertising folder.

e. Print the file Bakery Logo, then delete it from your Project Disk 3.

FIGURE B-21

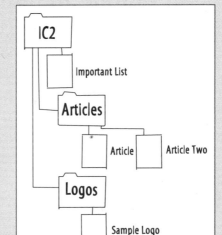

2. On your computer's hard drive, create a folder called *IC2*. Follow the guidelines listed here to create the file hierarchy shown in Figure B-21.

a. Start WordPad, create a new file that contains a list. Save the file as *To Do List* to your Project Disk 3 (Project Disk 4 if you are out of space on Project Disk 3).

b. Start My Computer and copy the Open House Letter file on your Project Disk 3 to the IC2 folder. Rename the file *Article*.

c. Copy the Memo file again to the IC2 folder on your hard drive and rename the second copy of the file *Article Two*.

d. Use My Computer to copy any Paint file to the IC2 folder and rename the file *Sample Logo*, then delete the Sample Logo file.

e. Copy the To Do List from your Project Disk 3 to the IC2 folder and rename the file *Important List*.

f. Move the files into the folders shown in Figure B-21.

g. Copy the IC2 folder to your Project Disk 3. Then delete the IC2 folder on your hard drive. Using the Recycle Bin, restore the file called IC2. To remove all your work on the hard drive, delete this folder again.

3. With Windows 2000, you can access the Web from My Computer and Windows Explorer, allowing you to search for information located not only on your computer or network, but also on any computer on the Internet.

a. Start Windows Explorer, then click in the Address Bar so the current location (probably your hard drive) is selected, type **www.microsoft.com**, then press [Enter].

b. Connect to the Internet if necessary. The Microsoft Web page appears in the right pane of Windows Explorer.

c. Click in the Address Bar, then type **www.course.com**, press [Enter], and then wait a moment while the Course Technology Web page opens.

d. Make sure your Project Disk is in the floppy disk drive, then click 3½ Floppy (A:) in the left pane.

e. Click the Back button list arrow, then click Welcome to Microsoft's Homepage.

f. Capture a picture of your desktop by pressing [Print Screen] located on the upper-right side of your keyboard. (This stores the picture on the Clipboard.) Open the Paint program, paste the contents of the Clipboard into the drawing window, then print it.

g. Close Paint without saving your changes.

h. Close Windows Explorer and disconnect from the Internet.

4. Create a shortcut to the drive that contains your Project Disk 3. Then capture a picture of your desktop showing the new shortcut by pressing [Print Screen], located on the upper-right side of your keyboard. The picture is stored temporarily on the Clipboard. Then open the Paint program and paste the contents of the Clipboard into the drawing window. Click No when asked to enlarge the Bitmap. Print the screen, close Paint without saving your changes, then delete the shortcut when you are finished.

► Visual Workshop

Recreate the screen shown in Figure B-22, which contains the Brochure window in My Computer, two shortcuts on the desktop, and two open files. Press [Print Screen] to make a copy of the screen, (a copy of the screen is placed on the Clipboard), open Paint, click Paste to paste the screen picture into Paint, then print the Paint file.

FIGURE B-22

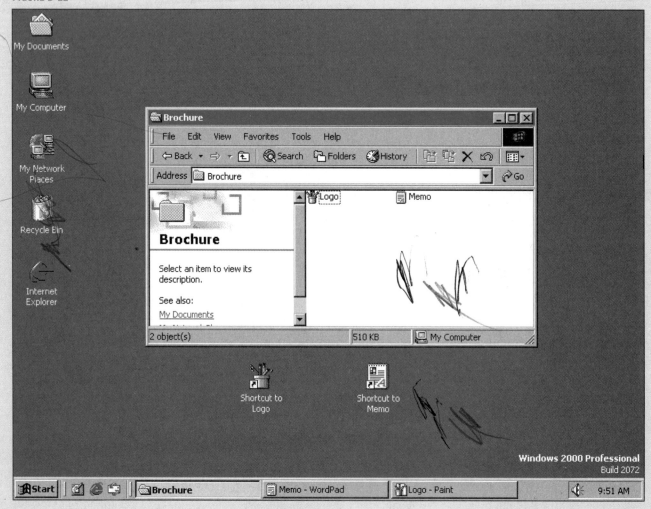

Introducing
Microsoft Office XP

Objectives

► **Define the Office XP Suite**
► **Create a document with Word 2002**
► **Build a worksheet with Excel 2002**
► **Manage data with Access 2002**
► **Create a presentation with PowerPoint 2002**
► **Browse the World Wide Web with Internet Explorer**
► **Integrate Office information**
► **Manage office tasks with Outlook 2002**

Microsoft Office XP is a collection of software programs designed to help you accomplish tasks quickly and efficiently. Each Office program is designed to complete specific tasks and has similar buttons and commands to make switching among the programs easy and seamless. The Microsoft Office programs are supplied together in a group called a **suite** (although you can also purchase them separately). Suite programs are designed so that you can easily transfer information among them. This unit introduces you to the Microsoft Office suite programs, as well as to MediaLoft, a nationwide chain of bookstore cafés that sells books, CDs, DVDs, and videos. By exploring how MediaLoft uses Microsoft Office components, you will learn how each program can be used in a business environment.

Defining the Office XP Suite

Microsoft Office XP is a collection of software programs known as **business productivity software** because it helps business people work efficiently. Office is available in several configurations, and the most commonly used programs are Word, Excel, Access, PowerPoint, and Outlook. Internet Explorer is a Web browser that comes with Windows and can be downloaded from the Web. The Office programs have a similar "look and feel," and are designed to exchange information seamlessly. All MediaLoft employees use Office programs to create business documents, communicate with associates, and access the Internet. See Figure A-1 for an overview of MediaLoft's stores and Figure A-2 for sample Office documents.

Details

▶ **The basic tools: Microsoft Office XP Suite components**

The Office suite components work individually and with each other to help people accomplish tasks and work together. **Microsoft Word** lets you create powerful text documents. Isaac Robinson, the marketing director of the MediaLoft Chicago store, uses Word to create letters, reports, faxes, and flyers. You can automatically calculate and analyze data with **Microsoft Excel**. Jim Fernandez, MediaLoft's office manager, uses Excel to create budgets, financial statements, and payroll summaries. **Microsoft Access** lets you organize, track, and update complex data. Kelsey Lang, a MediaLoft marketing manager, uses Access to create and maintain a customer information database. You can create powerful visual presentations using **Microsoft PowerPoint**. Maria Abbott, MediaLoft's general sales manager, uses PowerPoint to create a slide show summarizing the company's performance; she will show it at an annual meeting of store managers. You can easily track contacts, appointments, and e-mail with **Microsoft Outlook**. Marketing manager Alice Wegman uses Outlook to stay in touch with MediaLoft employees around the world.

Internet Explorer lets you stay in touch with information on the Internet and World Wide Web. Alice Wegman, a MediaLoft marketing manager, uses Internet Explorer to find out about competitors in geographic areas the company is considering as sites for expansion.

▶ **Working together: Program compatibility and integration**

Because the Office suite programs have a similar "look and feel," you can use your knowledge of one program's tools in other suite programs. For example, you can use the same commands and icons for common tasks such as printing and saving. Office documents are **compatible** with one another, meaning that you can easily place, or **integrate**, an Excel chart into a PowerPoint slide, or you can insert an Access table into a Word document. You can specify that information in one file be automatically updated whenever information in another file changes. The Office programs also share a common dictionary, so that special words you use often can be used consistently across all of your Office documents. And you can use the Office Clipboard to easily transfer up to 24 entries between any Office programs.

▶ **Supporting collaboration and teamwork: The new business model**

Office supports the way people do business today, which emphasizes communication and knowledge sharing within companies and across the globe via company intranets and the Internet. All Office programs include the ability to share information over the Internet—called **online collaboration**. Employees can share documents, schedule online meetings, and have discussions over the World Wide Web. Office supports teamwork by allowing people to share documents and team members' feedback that can all be incorporated in one place.

FIGURE A-1: MediaLoft stores

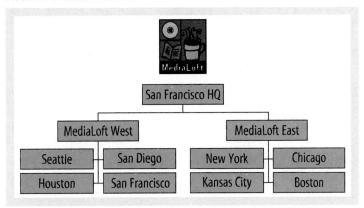

FIGURE A-2: Office documents created by MediaLoft employees

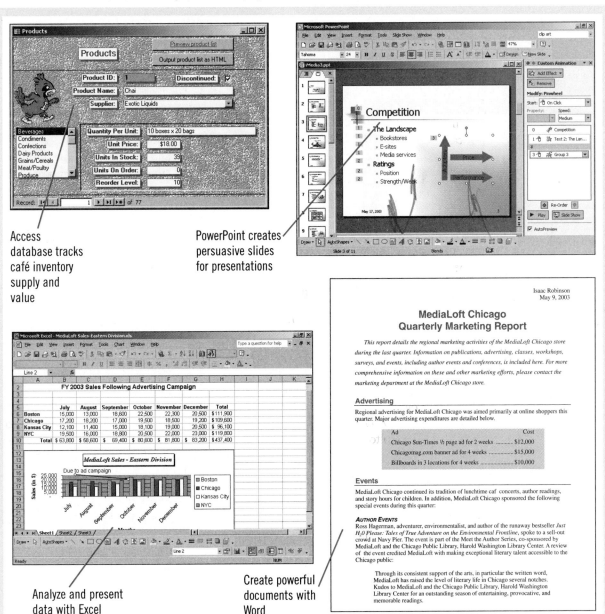

Access database tracks café inventory supply and value

PowerPoint creates persuasive slides for presentations

Analyze and present data with Excel

Create powerful documents with Word

Creating a Document with Word 2002

Microsoft Word 2002 is a **word processing** program that allows you to create and edit text documents. You can also format text with characteristics such as bold and italics to make text information easier to understand and to make important information stand out. You can use a word processor to create reports, memos, or letters that contain text, tables, and graphics. Sophisticated text-handling tools, such as an electronic thesaurus, indexes, and footnotes make Word ideal for long and complex text documents such as books. MediaLoft employees use Word to create documents for the company's Annual Report. The memo requesting information for the report is shown in Figure A-3. The memo contains the kinds of elements that make a document readable and professional looking.

The following are some of the benefits of using Word:

▶ **Enter text quickly and easily**
Word makes it easy to enter and edit text. Rather than having to retype a document, you can rearrange and revise the text on-screen. Bullets or numbers can make lists more attractive and easier to understand. When you move items in a numbered list, Word automatically corrects the numbers to reflect the new order.

▶ **Organize information in a table to make it easier to read**
Some information is easier to read in rows and columns, and it's easy to create and modify a table in Word. Once you create a table, you can edit its contents and modify its appearance using your own formatting or predesigned formats. You can always sort table data without any additional typing.

▶ **Create error-free copy**
You can use the Word spelling checker after you finish typing to help you create error-free documents. It compares each word in a document to a built-in dictionary and notifies you if it does not recognize a word. The Word AutoCorrect feature can automatically correct misspelled words as you type them. Word provides entries for commonly misspelled words, and you can also add your own.

▶ **Combine text and graphics**
Using Word, you can combine text and graphics easily in the same document.

▶ **Communicate with others**
You can use special Word features to communicate with teammates. For example, you can insert **comments** within a document that coworkers can see. You can use the **tracking** feature to keep a record of edits and view edits others make in a document. Figure A-3 shows a Word document containing tracked changes, text, and graphics as they look on the screen; Figure A-4 shows the printed memo.

▶ **Add special effects**
Word lets you create columns of text, drop caps (capital letters that take up two or three lines), and WordArt (customized text with a three-dimensional or shadowed appearance), adding a polished quality to your documents.

FIGURE A-3: Memo created in Word

Tracking changes

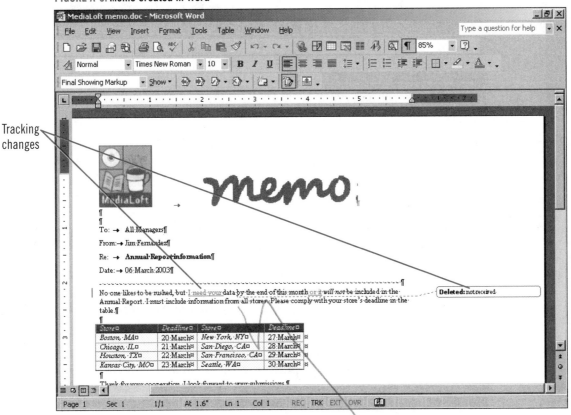

FIGURE A-4: Printout of completed memo

Graphic containing company logo

Graphic created in an art program

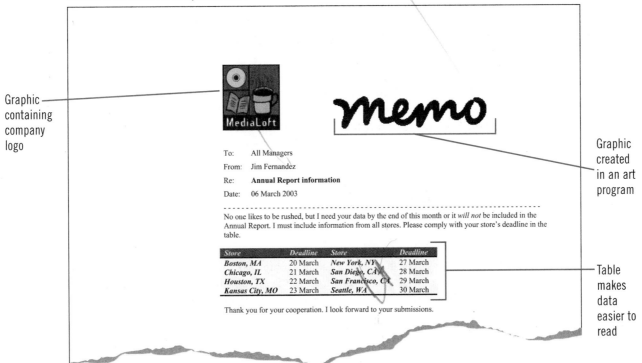

Table makes data easier to read

Building a Worksheet with Excel 2002

Microsoft Excel 2002 is a **spreadsheet** program you can use to analyze data, perform calculations, and create charts. Excel performs numeric calculations rapidly and accurately. Like traditional paper-based spreadsheets, this electronic spreadsheet contains a **worksheet** area that is divided into columns and rows that form individual cells. **Cells** can contain text, numbers, formulas, or a combination of all three. MediaLoft employees use Excel to store and analyze sales data as well as other numeric information they have collected. They can then format the data for insertion into the Annual Report.

The following are some of the benefits of using Excel:

► **Calculate results quickly and accurately**

With Excel, you can enter data quickly and accurately using formulas. Excel then calculates the results.

► **Recalculate easily**

Excel recalculates data easily by updating information automatically when you change or correct an entry.

► **Perform what-if analysis**

Because Excel automatically recalculates formulas when data changes, you can ask "what-if?" and create a variety of business scenarios, such as, "What if the interest rate on a corporate credit card changes?" Anticipating possible outcomes helps you make better business decisions.

► **Complete complex mathematical formulas**

Using Excel, you can easily complete complicated mathematical computations by using built-in formulas. The program tells you what data to enter, then you fill in the blanks, saving you valuable time.

► **Communicate with others**

In today's offices it is common for a group of people to review the same document. Readers can use the Comments feature to attach explanatory comments to worksheet cells. You can also keep track of changes others make to your worksheets by using powerful change-tracking tools.

► **Create charts**

Excel makes it easy to create charts based on worksheet information. With Excel, charts are automatically updated as worksheet data changes. The worksheet in Figure A-5 shows a bar chart that illustrates sales revenue for the eight MediaLoft stores over a three-year period.

► **Analyze worksheet data**

Worksheets containing data in a long list are easy to summarize and analyze quickly using the PivotTable feature. Once you create a PivotTable, you can chart its output. Without the PivotTable feature, it would be very difficult to analyze lengthy Excel data.

► **Create attractive output**

You can enhance the overall appearance of numeric data by using charts, graphics, and text formatting, as shown in Figure A-5. Figure A-6 shows the printed worksheet.

FIGURE A-5: Worksheet created in Excel

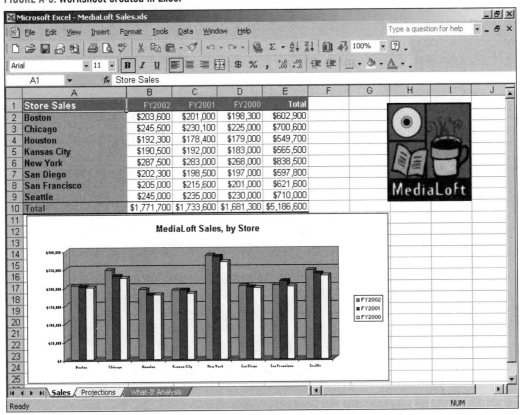

FIGURE A-6: Printout of annual revenue data with corresponding chart

Company
logo
graphic
inserted

Sales Summary

Store Sales	FY2002	FY2001	FY2000	Total
Boston	$203,600	$201,000	$198,300	$602,900
Chicago	$245,500	$230,100	$225,000	$700,600
Houston	$192,300	$178,400	$179,000	$549,700
Kansas City	$190,500	$192,000	$183,000	$565,500
New York	$287,500	$283,000	$268,000	$838,500
San Diego	$202,300	$198,500	$197,000	$597,800
San Francisco	$205,000	$215,600	$201,000	$621,600
Seattle	$245,000	$235,000	$230,000	$710,000
Total	$1,771,700	$1,733,600	$1,681,300	$5,186,600

Formatting
makes data
easier to
read

Corresponds
to FY 2002
sales for
Boston

MediaLoft Sales, by Store

Legend
identifies
colors
used in
chart

Managing Data with Access 2002

Microsoft Access 2002 is a database management system. A **database** is a collection of related information such as a list of employees, their Social Security numbers, salaries, and vacation time. A **database management system** organizes databases and allows you to link multiple groups of information. With Access, you can arrange and analyze large amounts of data in grids called **tables**, such as an inventory of products, or the members of a sales department. The tables in a database are related to one another by a common piece of information, such as a product number, which makes the database a powerful information retrieval tool. You can rearrange and combine the information in the tables in a variety of ways. For example, an inventory database might be listed alphabetically, by stocking location, or by the number of units on order. You might use a salesperson's name from a Sales Rep table and a product description from a Products table to create a sales report. A powerful database program like Access lets you use your data in a wide variety of ways. MediaLoft stores use Access databases to keep track of inventory. Information from these databases is used to generate inventory lists and data for the Annual Report.

The following are some of the benefits of using Access:

▶ **Enter data easily**

Employees can enter data in an existing table as the database grows or changes. Because Access organizes the data for you, the order in which you enter items is not a concern.

▶ **Retrieve data easily**

Access makes it easy for you to specify **criteria**, or conditions, and then produce a list of all data that conforms to those criteria. You might want to see a list of products by supplier or a list of discontinued products. Figure A-7 shows an inventory table containing music sold at MediaLoft's stores.

▶ **Create professional forms**

You can enter data into an on-screen form that you create in Access. Using a form makes entering data more efficient, and you'll be less prone to making errors. Figure A-8 shows a screen form that the MediaLoft music department uses for data entry.

▶ **Create flexible, professional reports**

You can create a report that summarizes any or all of the information in an Access table. You can create your own layout, and add summaries of data within the report. For example, a MediaLoft inventory report could include all the information in the Music Inventory table, then be subtotaled by music category.

▶ **Add graphics to printed screen forms and reports**

Forms and reports can contain graphic images, text formatting, and special effects, such as WordArt, to make them look more professional.

FIGURE A-7: List of inventory items in Access

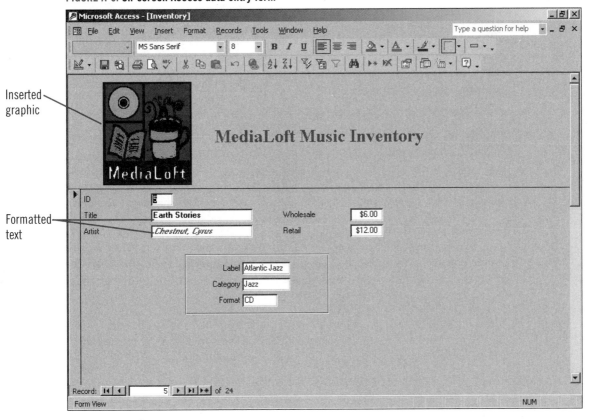

Microsoft Access

File Edit View Insert Format Records Tools Window Help

Inventory : Table

ID	Artist	Title	Label	Category	Format	Wholesale	Retail
1	Cook, Jesse	Gravity	Columbia	New Age	CD	$5.00	$10.00
2	Adams, Oleta	Come Walk with Me	CBS Records	Gospel	CD	$6.00	$12.00
3	Winans, BeBe & CeCe	Greatest Hits	Benson	Gospel	Vinyl	$4.00	$8.00
4	Yanni	Tribute	MCA	New Age	CD	$5.00	$10.00
5	Chestnut, Cyrus	Earth Stories	Atlantic Jazz	Jazz	CD	$6.00	$12.00
6	Yanni	If I Could Tell You	Virgin Records	New Age	CD	$5.00	$10.00
7	Tree Frogs	World Café	New Stuff	Rap	CD	$3.00	$6.00
8	Winans, BeBe & CeCe	Relationships	Capitol	Gospel	CD	$6.00	$12.00
9	Brickman, Jim	No Words	Windham Hill	New Age	Cassette	$5.00	$10.00
10	Nu Nation	God's Property	B-Rite Music	Rap	CD	$7.00	$14.00
11	4 Him	Message	Benson	Gospel	CD	$7.00	$14.00
12	Lantz, David	Sacred Road	Narada	New Age	Cassette	$6.00	$12.00
13	Carey, Mariah	Mariah Carey	Columbia	Rock	CD	$5.00	$10.00
14	Tesh, John	Ironman Triathlon	GTS Records	New Age	Cassette	$5.00	$10.00
15	Carey, Mariah	Daydream	Columbia	Rock	CD	$6.00	$12.00
16	Lantz, David	Heartsounds	Narada	New Age	CD	$7.00	$14.00
17	Roches, The	The Roches	Warner Bros. Records	Folk	Cassette	$6.00	$12.00
18	Roches, The	Can We Go Home Now	Ryko	Folk	CD	$6.00	$12.00
19	Tesh, John	Live at the Red Rocks	GTS Records	New Age	CD	$7.00	$14.00
20	Smith, Michael	I'll Lead You Home	Reunion	Gospel	CD	$7.00	$14.00
21	Tesh, John	Winter Song	GTS Records	New Age	CD	$5.00	$10.00
22	Winston, George	December	Windham Hill	New Age	CD	$5.00	$10.00
23	Bolton, Michael	Time, Love & Tenderness	Sony Music	Rock	CD	$6.00	$12.00
24	Winston, George	Autumn	Windham Hill	New Age	CD	$5.00	$10.00

Record: 1 of 24

Datasheet View · NUM

FIGURE A-8: On-screen Access data entry form

Microsoft Access - [Inventory]

File Edit View Insert Format Records Tools Window Help

MS Sans Serif   8   B I U

Inserted graphic

MediaLoft Music Inventory

MediaLoft

ID	5

Formatted text

| Title | Earth Stories | Wholesale | $6.00 |
| Artist | *Chestnut, Cyrus* | Retail | $12.00 |

Label Atlantic Jazz
Category Jazz
Format CD

Record: 5 of 24

Form View · NUM

Creating a Presentation with PowerPoint 2002

Microsoft PowerPoint 2002 is a **presentation graphics** program you can use to develop slides and handouts for visual presentations. In PowerPoint, a **slide** is a "page" in an on-screen display called a **slide show**, in which consecutive images appear on a computer screen. The computer can be connected to a projector so a roomful of people can see the presentation. You can then use your on-screen slide content to create handouts, outlines, notes and 35-mm slides. Store managers present highlights of the Annual Report to MediaLoft executives using a slide show and notes created in PowerPoint.

The following are some of the benefits of using PowerPoint:

▶ **Create and edit slides easily**

You can enter text directly on a PowerPoint slide, enabling you to see how your slide will look. After you have learned how to edit text in Word, you can use the same techniques in PowerPoint. You can cut, copy, paste, and move slide text quickly and easily.

▶ **Combine information from Office programs**

You can use data you create in Word, Excel, Access, and other Office programs in your PowerPoint slides. This means that you can easily insert a worksheet you created in Excel, for example, without having to retype the information.

▶ **Add graphics**

Predesigned images called **clip art**, an Excel chart, or a corporate logo can further enhance any presentation. PowerPoint comes with many clip art images and accepts the most commonly available graphic file formats. PowerPoint also allows you to create your own shapes and enhance text with special effects using WordArt. Figure A-9 shows a slide containing a chart created in Excel and a graphic image of a corporate logo.

▶ **Print a variety of presentation materials**

In addition to being able to print out a slide, you can also create many other types of printed materials. Notes printed with each slide can contain hints and reminders for the speaker or for the audience members, who might receive printed copies of the presentation slides. Figure A-10 shows notes in PowerPoint. You can also print other types of handouts for presentation attendees that contain a reduced image of each slide and a place for handwritten notes.

▶ **Communicate with others**

In many businesses, employees share information and often contribute to others' work. You can use the Comments feature to insert explanatory comments on a slide. This makes communication more efficient, because co-workers can point out areas that are unclear or particularly effective.

▶ **Add special effects**

You can create slides that use special transitions from one slide to the next. Animation effects allow you to determine how and when slide elements appear on the screen and which sound effects accompany them. You can add audio and video clips to make your presentation look professional.

FIGURE A-9: Slide created in PowerPoint

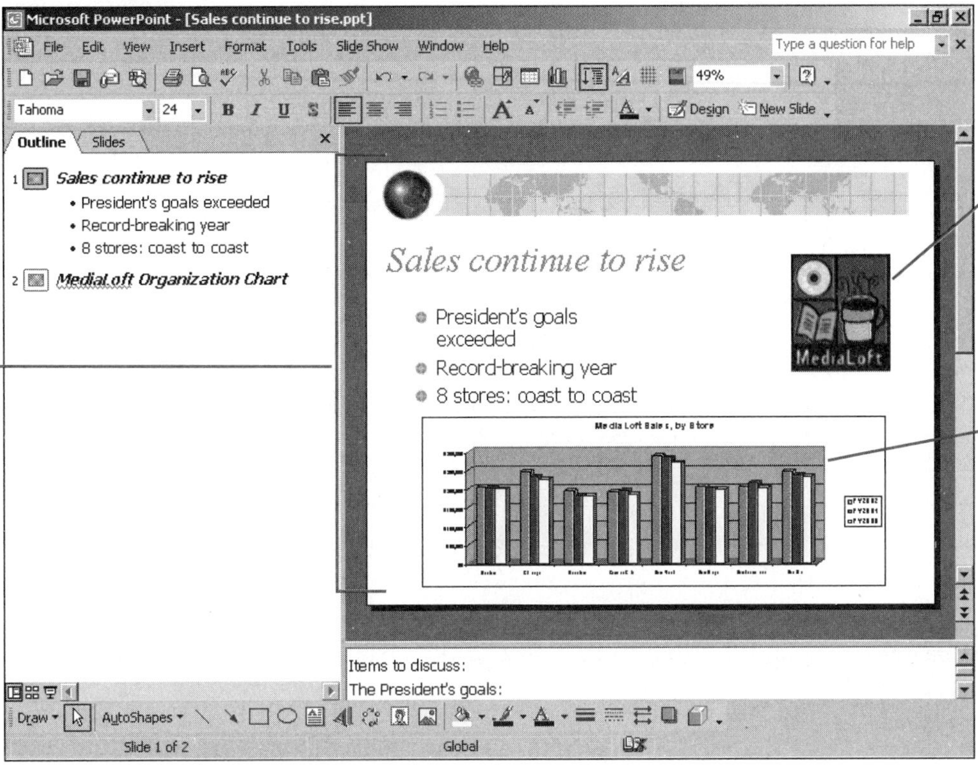

Corporate logo as a graphic image

Background layout created using PowerPoint template

Excel chart as a graphic image

FIGURE A-10: Notes created in PowerPoint

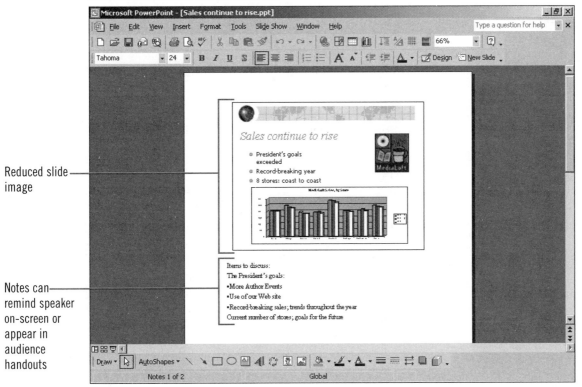

Reduced slide image

Notes can remind speaker on-screen or appear in audience handouts

Office XP

Browsing the World Wide Web with Internet Explorer

The **World Wide Web**—also known as the **Web**—is the part of the Internet that brings text, graphics, and multimedia information to your desktop. Internet Explorer is a **browser,** a program designed to help you view the graphic images and multimedia data on the Web. Many Web sites let you move to other sites with the click of your mouse using **links,** special areas that take you to different Web site addresses.  MediaLoft employees keep informed on the latest trends and research competitors by using Internet Explorer.

Details

The following are some of the benefits of using Internet Explorer:

► **Display Web sites**
Once you're connected to the Internet, you can view interesting and informative Web sites from all around the globe.

► **Move from one Web site to another**
Web page links let you effortlessly move from site to site. You can easily find information related to the topic in which you're interested.

► **Save your favorite Web site locations**
Once you've located interesting Web sites, such as the one shown in Figure A-11, you can save their Web site addresses so you can return to them later without performing another search. Internet Explorer makes it easy to compile a list of your favorite locations.

► **Use multimedia**
Web pages frequently contain video and audio clips. Internet Explorer allows you to experience the multimedia capabilities of the Web.

► **Communicate with others**
You can use your browser to participate in online discussions with other users.

► **Incorporate Web information**
Internet Explorer makes it easy to combine the immediacy of the Web with the power of Office suite programs: import data—whether it is text, graphics, or numbers—from the Web and edit it in the Office program you select, such as Word or Excel.

► **Print Web pages**
As you travel the Web, you may want to print the information you find. You can easily print an active Web page—including its text and graphics.

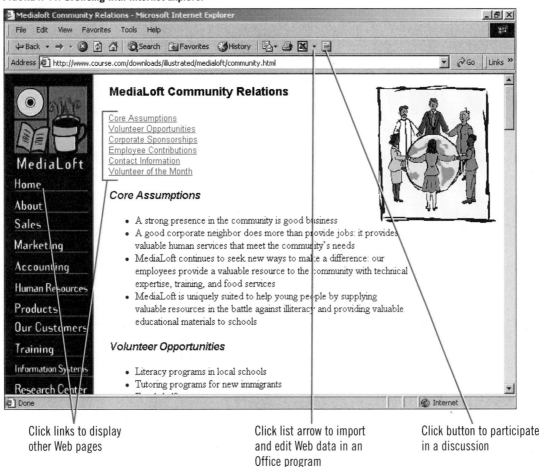

Click links to display
other Web pages

Click list arrow to import
and edit Web data in an
Office program

Click button to participate
in a discussion

Integrating Office Information

Information created in one Office program can be used in another. This means that a chart created in Excel can be used in Word without having to be retyped or reentered. Information in an Access table can be exported to Excel and analyzed, or pasted into a Word document. An outline created in Word can be imported into PowerPoint, saving you time and allowing you to work more efficiently. Using Office, integrating information is easy and can be accomplished in many ways. MediaLoft employees use integration as a means of working efficiently.

The following are some of the benefits of using integration:

► **Create information once**

It is not necessary to retype information each time you want to use it in another document or program. For example, an Excel chart can be pasted into a Word document and a PowerPoint slide, as shown in Figure A-12. Because you can copy information into the Office Clipboard, it is easy to paste it into any other Office program. Data can also be linked, so that when the original document is changed, the pasted data is changed too.

► **Merge data**

In addition to simple copy-and-paste techniques, Office programs offer more sophisticated processes, such as merging Access data with Word. This feature makes it possible to combine information in a database with text in a letter. The result is that you can easily create form letters with the click of a few buttons.

► **Export data**

Data in an Access table can be exported to Excel. Once in Excel, the data can be further analyzed and charted. Or, a PowerPoint presentation can be exported to Word, where you can save and edit the document to create special handouts to accompany the presentation. See Figure A-13.

► **Create hyperlinks**

With so many interrelated documents being used in business, it's helpful to know that Office lets you link on-screen documents. You can click on specially formatted text or graphics called **hyperlinks** and automatically be transferred to another area of your current document, or to another document entirely.

FIGURE A-12: **Excel chart used in Word document and PowerPoint slide**

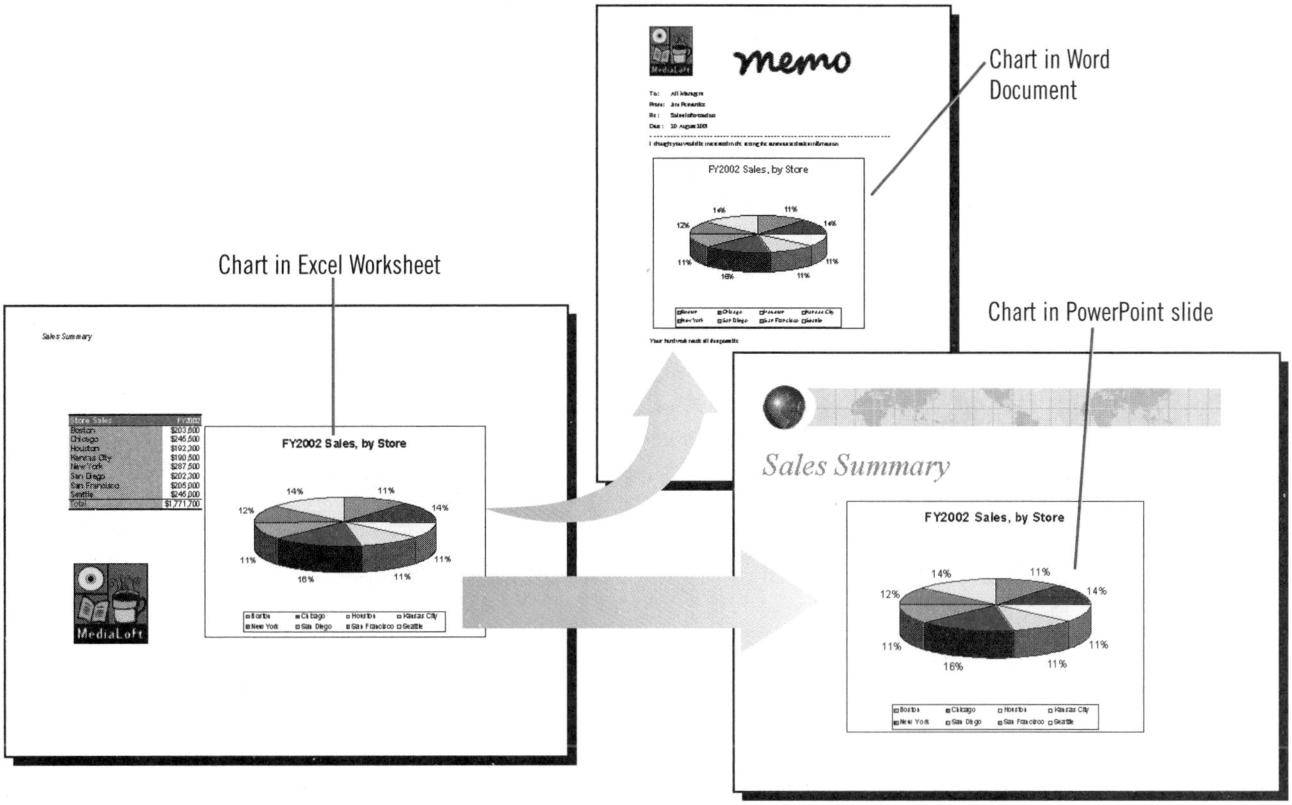

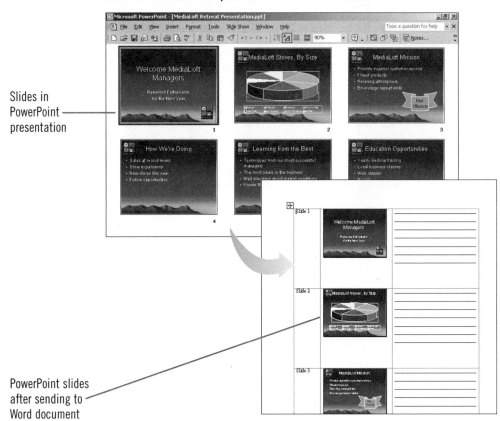

Chart in Excel Worksheet

Chart in Word Document

Chart in PowerPoint slide

FIGURE A-13: **PowerPoint presentation in a Word document**

Slides in PowerPoint presentation

PowerPoint slides after sending to Word document

Managing Office Tasks with Outlook 2002

There's more to office work than creating documents, worksheets, databases, and presentations. Microsoft Outlook 2002 is an electronic **personal information manager** that helps you manage a typical business day. You can use it to schedule appointments, keep track of contacts, and send e-mail and files to people on your local network or intranet, as well as across the Internet to anyone with an Internet address. For example, using the Inbox, you can send electronic mail messages—or **e-mail**—to anyone with an e-mail address. Table A-1 describes tasks you can perform with Outlook.  MediaLoft employees work more efficiently by using Outlook to send messages between stores, schedule appointments, and keep track of deadlines.

The following are some of the benefits of using Outlook:

► Process mail

Use the Inbox to read, forward, reply to, and create e-mail. The Inbox displays unread messages in bold text, so you can tell which messages still need to be read.

► Create an address book

Keep track of e-mail addresses in an address book so that you don't have to type an e-mail address each time you create a new message. You can also create distribution lists so that you can easily send messages to a group of people with whom you communicate frequently, without having to enter each e-mail address over and over.

► Send attachments

In addition to the actual content of a message, you can attach individual files to an e-mail message. This means you can send a colleague a spreadsheet created in Excel, for example, along with an explanatory message.

TABLE A-1: Additional Outlook tasks

task	description
Manage appointments	Use Calendar to make appointments, plan meetings, and keep track of events
Manage tasks	Use Tasks to keep track of pending jobs, set priorities, assign due dates, and express completion expectations for tasks
Track contacts	Use Contacts to record information such as names, addresses, phone numbers, and e-mail addresses for business and personal associates
Maintain a journal of your activities	Use Journal to track project phases, record activities, and manage your time
Create reminders	Use Notes—an electronic equivalent of yellow sticky notes—to leave reminders for yourself

Getting

Started with Internet Explorer

Objectives

► **Understand Web browsers**
► **Start Internet Explorer**
► **Explore the browser window**
► **Open and save a URL**
► **Navigate Web pages**
► **Get Help**
► **Print a Web page**
► **Search for information on the Internet**
► **Exit Internet Explorer**

In this unit you will learn about the basic features of Internet Explorer, use the World Wide Web to find information, and navigate to new locations on the Web, or to other Web pages in a Web site. You need to connect to the Internet to complete this unit. MediaLoft is a chain of café bookstores founded in 1988. MediaLoft stores offer customers the opportunity to purchase books, music, and videotapes while enjoying a variety of exotic coffees, teas, and freshly baked desserts. Alice Wegman is a marketing manager at MediaLoft. Alice wants to start selling trendy gift items that would appeal to young adults between the ages of 18 and 35. She decides to hire a marketing consultant to help her choose the right items to sell to this target audience.

Understanding Web Browsers

A **computer network** consists of two or more computers that can share information and resources. An **intranet** is a computer network that connects computers in a local area only, such as computers in a company's office. Users can dial into intranets from remote locations to share company information and resources. The **Internet** is a network of connected computers and computer networks located around the world. There are over 200 million users worldwide in more than 100 countries currently connected to the Internet through telephone lines, cables, satellites, and other telecommunications media, as illustrated in Figure A-1. Through the Internet, these computers can share many types of information, including text, graphics, sound, video, and computer programs. Anyone who has access to a computer and a connection to the Internet through a computer network or modem can use this rich information source. The **World Wide Web** (the **Web** or **WWW**) is a part of the Internet containing linked Web pages. Web pages contain highlighted words, phrases, or graphics called **hyperlinks**, or simply **links**, that open other Web pages when you click them. Figure A-2 shows a sample Web page. A page's links can also open graphics files or play sound or video files. **Web browsers** are software programs used to access and display Web pages. Web browsers, such as Microsoft Internet Explorer and Netscape Navigator, make navigating the Web easy by providing a graphical, point-and-click environment. This unit features **Internet Explorer**, a popular browser. ✏ Alice uses Internet Explorer and the Web to find a company that will assist her in hiring a marketing consultant.

Using Internet Explorer, Alice can:

► **Display Web pages**

Alice can access Web pages from all over the world for many business purposes. Alice can find potential marketing consultants on Web sites that offer employment services. She can also check the pages of competing retailers to see what type of trendy gifts they sell.

► **Use links to move from one Web page to another**

Alice can use the hyperlinks on competing retailers' Web pages to get more specific information about their operations.

► **Play audio and video clips**

A Web browser can play audio and video clips if it has been configured to do so and your computer has the appropriate hardware, such as speakers. Alice might find some Web sites that include video clips of focus groups, interviews in which consumers are videotaped while discussing their opinions of various products and services.

► **Search the Web for information**

Alice can take advantage of various search engines in her Web browser to look for companies that specialize in employment services.

► **Save a list of favorite Web pages**

Alice can use Internet Explorer to save a list of Web pages that she might need to visit again, such as a page for a competing retailer. By adding a Web page to her list of favorites, it is easy for her to return to the page later.

► **Print or save the text and graphics on Web pages**

If Alice wants to keep a hard copy of the information or images she finds, she can easily print the entire Web page, including any graphics. She can also save the text or graphics on a Web page, or copy this information temporarily to the Clipboard, where it is available for pasting into other programs.

FIGURE A-1: Internet structure

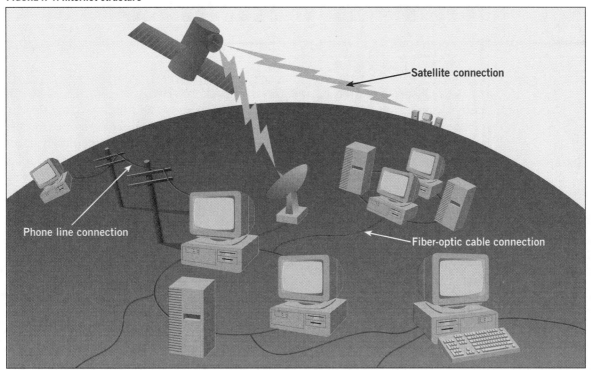

Satellite connection

Phone line connection

Fiber-optic cable connection

FIGURE A-2: Sample Web page

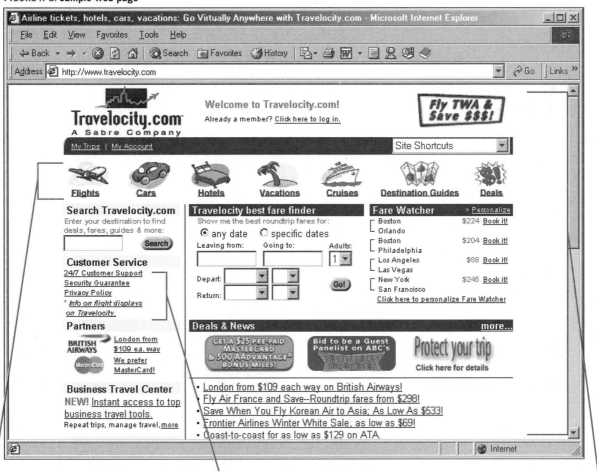

Graphic hyperlinks

Text hyperlinks

Web page

Internet

Starting Internet Explorer

Internet Explorer is a Web browser that connects your computer to the Web using an Internet connection. You can start Internet Explorer by clicking Start on the taskbar, pointing to Programs, then clicking Internet Explorer. After Internet Explorer is installed, its icon appears on your Windows desktop, and you can click it to start Internet Explorer. You can also start Internet Explorer by clicking the Internet Explorer icon on the Quick Launch toolbar. ◢◣ Before Alice can take advantage of the Web's many features to start her search for a marketing consultant, she must start Internet Explorer.

Trouble?

If an Internet Connection Wizard dialog box opens at any point, you will either need to connect to the Internet or enter your Internet settings. Ask your technical support person for assistance.

Trouble?

If the icon is not on your desktop, click the Start button on the taskbar, point to Programs on the Start menu, and then click Internet Explorer. Skip Step 3.

1. **If you connect to the Internet using a modem and a telephone, follow your normal procedure to establish your connection**

2. **Locate the Internet Explorer icon on your Windows desktop**
   The icon should appear on the left side of your screen, as shown in Figure A-3. The exact location of the Internet Explorer icon might vary on different computers. Ask your instructor or technical support person for assistance if you are unable to locate the Internet Explorer icon.

3. **Double-click the Internet Explorer icon on the Windows desktop**
   Internet Explorer opens and displays your home page, which may look similar to the one shown in Figure A-4. A **home page** is the first page that opens every time you start Internet Explorer. Your home page might be one for your school, one for your employer, or one that you specify. Because the Internet is an active environment, many of the Web pages shown in the figures will have changed since this book was written.

4. **If necessary, click the Maximize button on the Internet Explorer title bar to maximize the program window**

CLUES TO USE

History of the Internet and the World Wide Web

The Internet has its roots in the United States Department of Defense Advanced Research Projects Agency Network (ARPANET), which began in 1969. In 1986 the National Science Foundation formed NSFNET, which replaced ARPANET. NSFNET expanded the foundation of the U.S. portion of the Internet with high-speed, long-distance lines. In 1991, the U.S. Congress further expanded the Internet's capacity and speed and opened it to commercial use.

Over 200 countries now have Internet access.

The World Wide Web was created in Switzerland in 1991 to allow links between documents on the Internet. Software programs designed to access the Web (called Web browsers) use common "point-and-click" interfaces. The first graphical Web browser, Mosaic, was introduced at the University of Illinois in 1993. Microsoft Internet Explorer and Netscape Navigator are two current, popular Web browsers.

FIGURE A-3: Internet Explorer icon on the desktop

Your icons might differ

Internet Explorer icon on desktop

Internet Explorer icon on Quick Launch toolbar

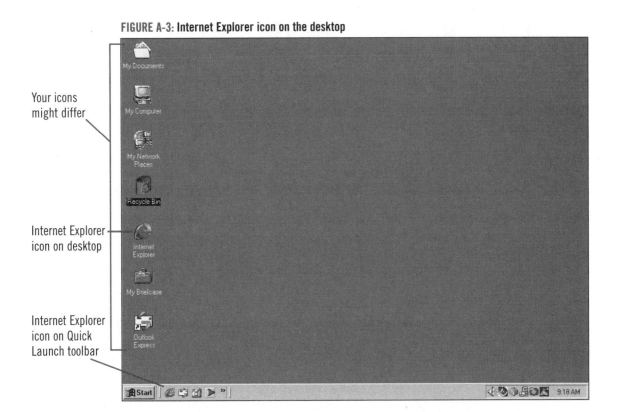

FIGURE A-4: Home page for Microsoft Network

Current Web page displayed (yours will differ)

Internet Explorer Browser window

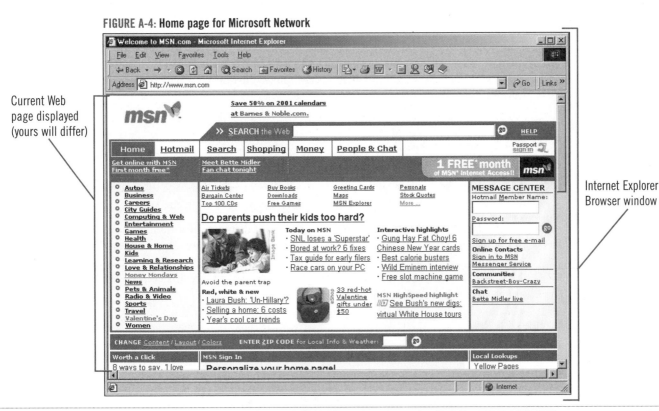

Internet

Exploring the Browser Window

The elements of the Internet Explorer browser window let you view, print, and search for information on the Web. You can customize elements of the window, such as the toolbar and Address bar. For example, you can choose to view the buttons on the toolbar with or without their corresponding text labels. ✎ Before using, or **surfing**, the Web, Alice needs to become more familiar with the components of the Internet Explorer browser window. Find and compare the elements below, using Figure A-5 as a guide.

Details

▶ The **title bar** at the top of the page usually contains the name of the Web page currently displayed in the Web browser window.

▶ The **menu bar** provides access to most of the browser's features through a variety of commands.

▶ The Standard Buttons **toolbar** provides buttons for many options, such as stopping the transfer of a Web page, moving from one Web page to another, printing Web pages, and searching for information on the Internet. Table A-1 explains these buttons. The toolbars can show large or small icons and have different text settings. The default setting for toolbars is "Selective text on right." Many commonly used commands available on menus are more readily accessed using the toolbar buttons. Depending on the programs installed on your computer, you may have additional buttons.

▶ The **Address bar** displays the address of the Web page currently opened. The **Uniform Resource Locator (URL)**, or the Web page's address, appears in the Address bar after you open (or load) the page. If you click the Address bar list arrow, you will see a list of addresses you have recently visited in the Address bar.

QuickTip

You can resize the Links bar to view more links by placing your mouse pointer to the left of the word Links on the Links bar and dragging to the left.

▶ The **Links bar** is a convenient place to store links to Web pages that you use often. You can add a link to the Links bar by dragging the Internet Explorer icon 🖭 that precedes the URL in the Address bar to the Links bar. Links placed in the Links bar are also found in the Links folder under the Favorites menu.

▶ The **Go button** is used along with the Address bar to help you search for Web sites about a particular topic. You can enter a keyword or words in the Address bar, then click the Go button to activate the search. When the search is complete, a list of related Web sites will open in a search results Web page.

▶ The **status indicator** is animated while a new Web page loads.

▶ The **browser window** is the specific area where the current Web page appears. You might need to scroll down the page to view its entire contents.

▶ The **vertical scroll bar** allows you to move the current Web page up or down in the browser window. The **scroll box** indicates your relative position within the Web page.

▶ The **status bar** performs three main functions: 1) displays information about your connection progress whenever you open a new Web page, 2) notifies you when you connect to another Web site, and 3) identifies the percentage of information transferred from the Web server to your browser. The status bar also displays the Web addresses of any links on the Web page when you move your mouse pointer over them.

FIGURE A-5: Elements of the Internet Explorer window

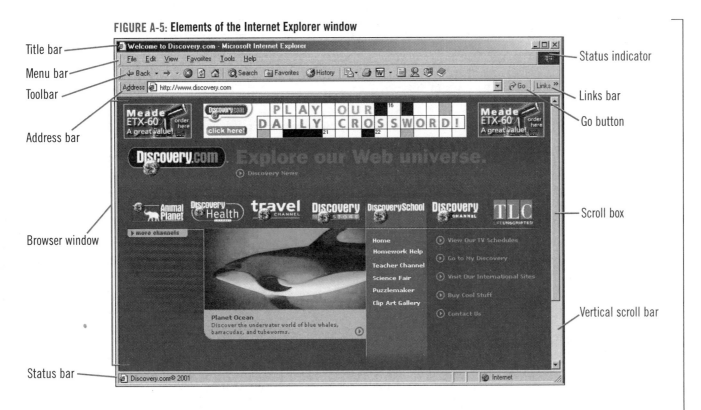

Title bar
Menu bar
Toolbar
Address bar
Browser window
Status bar

Status indicator
Links bar
Go button
Scroll box
Vertical scroll bar

TABLE A-1: Toolbar buttons

button name	button	description
Back		Opens the previous page
Forward		Opens the next page
Stop		Stops loading the page
Refresh		Refreshes the contents of the current page
Home		Opens the home page
Search		Opens the Search Assistant in the Explorer Search bar
Favorites		Opens the Explorer Favorites bar
History		Opens the Explorer History bar
Mail		Displays options for working with mail and news
Print		Prints the current Web page
Edit		Transfers the currently displayed Web page to Microsoft FrontPage or Microsoft Word for editing. The Edit icon in your browser window depends on which text editing software programs you have installed on your computer.
Discuss		Lets you add or edit discussion servers and open the Discussion bar

Internet

Opening and Saving a URL

As you learned in the previous lesson, the address for a Web page is also called a URL. Each Web page has a unique URL beginning with "http" (which stands for Hypertext Transfer Protocol) followed by a colon, two forward slashes, www (which identifies the page on the World Wide Web), and the Web site's name. After the name of the Web site, another slash and one or more folder names and a filename might appear. For example, in the address http://www.course.com/downloads/illustrated/medialoft/community.html, the name of the Web site is *www.course.com*; folders at that site are *downloads* and *illustrated*; and within the downloads/illustrated/medialoft folder is a file named *community.html*. The **Favorites menu** allows you to create your own list of frequently visited Web pages that you can then access without having to type a URL. After you add a Web page to your Favorites list, you can automatically access that page by clicking the Favorites button on the toolbar and then clicking its name, or by clicking the favorite's name on the Favorites menu. ◄━━━ Alice wants to investigate how to post a job opening on the Monster.com Web site. Because she plans to return to this site often as she completes her research, she adds it to her Favorites list.

1. **Click anywhere in the Address bar**
   The current address is highlighted; any text you type replaces it.

Trouble?

The Internet is an active environment. Web sites and contents are constantly changing so the Web pages and addresses printed in this book may differ from those you see when you complete the lessons.

2. **Type www.monster.com**
   Internet Explorer will automatically add the http:// protocol to the beginning of the address you type, after you press [Enter]. If you have typed a specific address in the Address bar previously, the AutoComplete feature will recognize the first few characters you type, then complete the name of the address for you.

3. **Press [Enter]**
   The status bar displays the connection process. After a few seconds, the Monster.com home page opens in the browser window, as shown in Figure A-6.

4. **Click Favorites on the menu bar, then click Add to Favorites**
   The Add Favorite dialog box opens as shown in Figure A-7. Favorites can be placed in folders or can be listed as menu items under the Favorites menu.

5. **Click Create in to open the Create in list (if necessary)**
   The Add Favorite dialog box expands to show the folders in which you can place the URL for the Monster.com page. The title of the Web page appears in the Name text box and the Favorites folder is selected by default. If the default name is unclear, you can change the favorite's default page name by typing a new name in the Name text box.

Trouble?

If a message appears saying the name for the shortcut already exists on your Favorites menu, click Yes to overwrite it.

6. **Click OK**
   The name and URL for Monster.com are added to your Favorites list.

7. **Click the Back button ◄ on the Standard Buttons toolbar**
   The previous Web page appears in the Web page area.

8. **Click Favorites on the menu bar, then click Monster.com – Work. Life. Possibilities.**
   The Monster.com home page opens in the Web page area.

FIGURE A-6: Home page for Monster.com

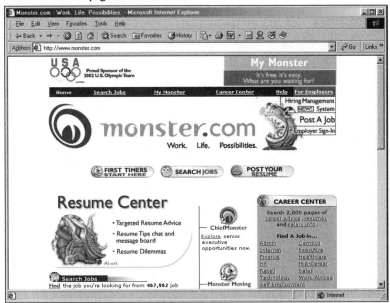

FIGURE A-7: Add Favorite dialog box

Name of Web page

Click to display folders

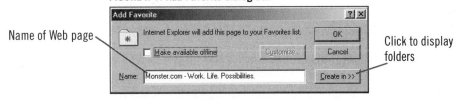

FIGURE A-8: Organize Favorites dialog box

Click to create a new folder for favorites

Select a favorite from the list, then click the Move to Folder button to specify in which folder to place it

Folders

Favorites

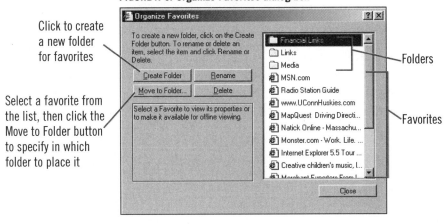

CLUES TO USE

Creating and organizing favorites

Once you add a Web page to your Favorites menu, returning to that page is much easier. To keep your Favorites menu manageable, only add pages that you expect to visit again. You can organize your list of favorites by placing them into folders by category. For example, you may want to create folders according to your interests, such as Sports, Cooking, and Travel. You may want to create folders in which each member of the household can place their favorites. To add a folder to your Favorites list, click Favorites on the menu bar, then click Organize Favorites. The Organize Favorites dialog box opens, as shown in Figure A-8. Click the Create Folder button to add a new folder to the list of folders and favorites. You can add a favorite to a specific folder by clicking the favorite, then clicking the Move to Folder button. You can also drag and drop a favorite into a folder. To see the contents of a folder, simply click the folder to open it, then click it again to close it.

Internet

Navigating Web Pages

Hyperlinks enable you to navigate to, or open, another location on the same Web page or to jump to an entirely different Web page. You can follow these links to obtain more information about a topic by clicking the highlighted word or phrase. If you change your mind or if a page takes too long to load, you can click the Stop button on the toolbar. 🖋️ Before she posts her job description on Monster.com, Alice decides to investigate a few other employment-related Web sites for comparison.

Steps

Steps 1234

Trouble?

If the URL is no longer active, type "jobs" in the Address bar, then press [Enter].

1. Click the **Address bar**, type **www.careerbuilder.com**, then press **[Enter]**

The home page for CareerBuilder opens. You want to see what other job-seeking sites are available.

2. Type **www.headhunter.net** in the Address bar, press **[Enter]**, view the Web page, type **www.hotjobs.com** in the Address bar, then press **[Enter]**

These are all good sites, but you decide to go back to Monster.com.

QuickTip

If you want to cancel loading the page, click the Stop button 🛑 on the toolbar.

3. Click the **Back button** ← on the toolbar as many times as necessary to return to Monster.com

The Web page for Monster.com opens in the browser window.

4. Place your mouse pointer on the **Post A Job** link

The mouse pointer changes to 👆 when you place it over an active link, as shown in Figure A-9.

Trouble?

If a Security Alert dialog box opens, click OK, if you receive an error message, click a different link on the page.

5. Click **Post A Job**

The status indicator is animated while the new Web page loads. The Post a Job Web page opens in your Web browser window, as shown in Figure A-10.

6. Click the **Home button** 🏠 on the Standard Buttons toolbar

The home page that opens when you start Internet Explorer reappears in your Web browser window.

FIGURE A-9: Hyperlinks on Monster.com home page

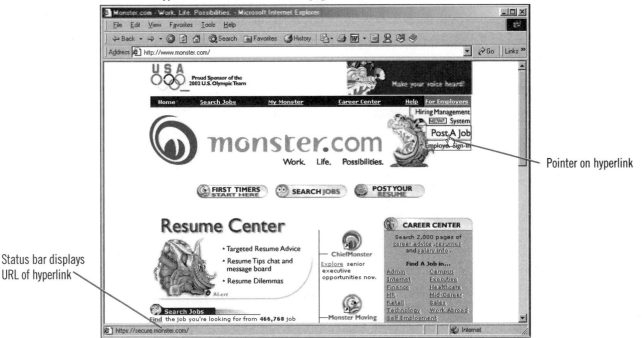

Status bar displays
URL of hyperlink

Pointer on hyperlink

FIGURE A-10: Post A Job Web page

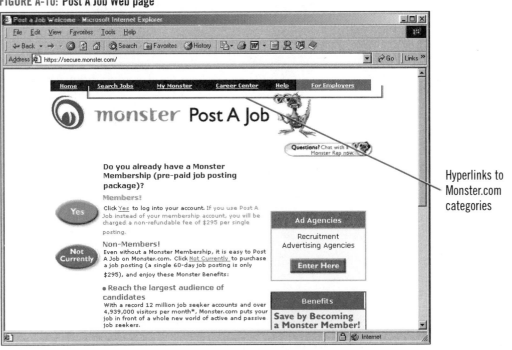

Hyperlinks to
Monster.com
categories

CLUES TO USE

Selecting a home page

When you click 🏠 on the toolbar, the page that is specified as the home page opens in your Web browser window. Each time you start Internet Explorer, the first page that appears is your home page. When you install Internet Explorer, the default home page is the Welcome to MSN.com home page at the MSN Web site. You can easily select a different home page to open each time you start Internet Explorer. Simply go to the page that you want to be your home page in your Web browser window, click Tools on the menu bar, click Internet Options, click the General tab, click Use Current in the Home page area, then click OK to specify the current page as your home page.

Internet

Getting Help

Internet Explorer provides a Help system with information and instructions on various features and commands.  While exploring pages in the Monster.com Web site, Alice viewed a page that uses a font she finds difficult to read. Because that page contains information that she needs, she decides to access the Help system to find out if she can change the font used on a Web page.

Steps

1. **Click Help on the menu bar**
   The Help menu opens.

2. **Click Contents and Index**
   The Microsoft Internet Explorer Help window opens.

3. **Click the Contents tab**
   The Contents tab works like a table of contents in a book. Your screen should look like Figure A-11. Table A-2 explains how each of the three tabs provides a different way to access Help information.

4. **Click the Search tab**
   The Search tab allows you to search for a specific word or phrase.

QuickTip

You can also press [Enter] instead of clicking List Topics to display the relevant topics.

5. **Type fonts in the Type in the keyword to find text box, then click List Topics**
   As shown in Figure A-12, a list of relevant topics appears in the Select Topic to display list box.

6. **Double-click Display text in a different font in the Select Topic to display list box**
   As shown in Figure A-13, the text in the right pane of the Microsoft Internet Explorer Help window provides information on how to change the font. The word font is highlighted because it was your keyword in the search.

7. **Click the Close button in the upper-right corner of the Microsoft Internet Explorer Help window**
   The Help window closes.

TABLE A-2: Help options

tab	function
Contents	Lists the categories available in Help
Index	Lists available Help topics in alphabetical order, and lets you locate specific topics
Search	Locates the desired Help topic based on the keyword or phrase you enter

CLUES TO USE

Viewing sites in other languages

The Web is an international forum; as you surf the Web, you may find sites that display text in the native language of the country where the site originates. If you are a native English-speaking person, most Web sites have an English link somewhere on the site's home page that you can click to display the site in English.

FIGURE A-11: Microsoft Internet Explorer Help window

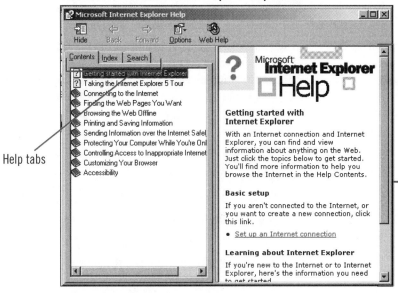

Help tabs

Description of selected Help featues

FIGURE A-12: Search tab

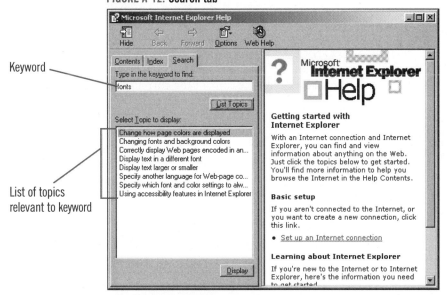

Keyword

List of topics relevant to keyword

FIGURE A-13: Help information

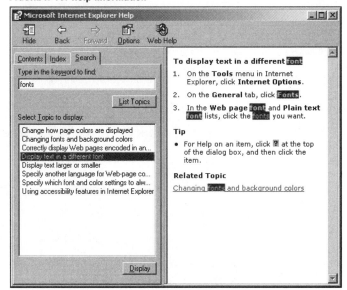

Internet

Internet

Printing a Web Page

You can quickly print the Web page that appears in the browser window by clicking the Print button on the toolbar. When you click File on the menu bar, then click Print, the options in the Print dialog box allow you to specify print parameters such as the number of copies and the page range. When you print a Web page, its text and any graphics will appear on your hard copy. Table A-4 explains printing options in more detail. Alice decides to print a copy of the Post A Job Web page for her files.

Steps 1234

1. **Click the Back button ↵ on the Standard Buttons toolbar**
   You return to the Monster.com Post A Job page, as shown in Figure A-14.

QuickTip

To print a Web page without changing any settings, click on the toolbar.

2. **Click File on the menu bar, then click Print**
   The Print dialog box opens.

3. **Make sure 1 appears in the Number of copies text box, and that the All option button is selected in the Page Range area**
   One copy of all the pages for that Web page will be printed.

4. **Make sure your computer is connected to a printer, that it is turned on, and that it contains paper**

Trouble?

If your computer is not connected to a printer or if an error message appears, ask your technical support person for assistance.

5. **Click Print**
   The Print dialog box closes, and one copy of the current Web page prints.

TABLE A-3: Printing options

option	tab	description
Select Printer	General	Displays information about the name, status, type, and location of the active printer
Print range	General	Allows you to choose to print all pages, a range of pages, or a selection on a page
Copies	General	Indicates the number of copies of each page to print and their sequence
Print all linked documents	Options	Opens and prints each document referenced by a link on the current page
Print Frames	Options	Allows you to print only the current frame or all frames, separately or together
Print table of links	Options	Prints links in a table at the end of the document
Orientation	Layout	Allows you to specify landscape or portrait painting
Page Order	Layout	Whether Page order is Front to Back or Back to Front
Pages per sheet	Layout	How many pages print on each sheet of paper
Paper Source	Paper/Quality	Allows you to specify where paper is feeding from; whether automatically selected, first available tray, or from a manual paper feed

FIGURE A-14: Post A Job Web page

Copying information from a Web page

You can select text on a Web page and use the Copy and Paste commands to use the same information in another program, such as Microsoft Word or other Office programs. You can also save a graphic image from a Web page by right-clicking the image, clicking Save Picture As on the shortcut menu, and then specifying where to save the image. If you just need to copy an image, click the Copy command on the shortcut menu. Using the Copy command saves the text or image to the Clipboard.

Keep in mind that the same laws that protect printed works generally protect information and graphics published on a Web page. Do not use material on a Web page without citing its source and checking the site carefully for any usage restrictions.

Internet

Searching for Information on the Internet

A large and ever-increasing number of Web pages and other information sources are available through the Internet. At times, finding the information you want may seem like looking for the proverbial needle in the haystack. Luckily, you can use Web **search engines** to help you locate the information you need. You simply enter a relevant keyword or phrase describing the information you want to find, and the search engine provides you with a list of related Web sites. Each of these Web sites is listed as a hyperlink, so you can quickly and easily go to the site and see if it has the information you are seeking. You can click View on the menu bar, point to Explorer Bar, then click Search to open the Explorer Search bar. ✎ Alice posted her job description on Monster.com. While she waits for responses from potential candidates, she decides to review some interviewing methods. It has been a long time since she has interviewed anyone. She decides to search the Internet for interviewing information. She uses the Internet Explorer built-in shortcuts to start her search.

Trouble?
If you do not see the same Search bar as shown in Figure A-15, click the Customize button at the top of the Search task pane, click the Use the Search Assistant for the smart searching option button in the Customize Search Settings dialog box, then click OK.

QuickTip
You can choose one search engine for each time you search the Web by clicking the Customize button on the Explorer Search bar, clicking the Use one search service for all searches option button, clicking the name of a search engine in the Choose the search service list, then clicking OK.

1. **Click the Search button ▣ on the Standard Buttons toolbar**
   As shown in Figure A-15, the browser window splits into two panes. The **Explorer Search bar** opens and contains the Search Assistant, which displays a list of search categories so you can quickly find Web pages, people, businesses, previous searches, or maps. If you click the More link, you will see options for looking up a word, and finding a picture. The right pane shows the Web page you were viewing before beginning your search.

2. **Make sure the Find a Web page option button is selected in the Search bar, click the Find a Web page containing text box, then type Interviewing Techniques**
   Now that you've specified your search keywords, you can initiate the search.

3. **Click Search**
   Your search results appear as a list of related Web sites called **hits**. See Figure A-16. Some search engines list hits by category or topic, whereas others list Web page names. You can click any hyperlink to open the Web page or a list of Web pages for a category.

4. **Examine the hit list in the Search bar by scrolling up or down, then click a hyperlink of your choice**
   The related page containing information about interviewing opens in the browser window. When you finish exploring the hyperlinked site, you can continue or end your search.

5. **Click ▣ to close the Search bar**

6. **Click the Home button ▣ on the Standard Buttons toolbar**
   Your home page appears in the browser window.

FIGURE A-15: Search task pane

Search button

Customize button

Explorer Search bar

Enter search keyword(s) here

Search category options

FIGURE A-16: Search results

Your search engine might differ

Click to open this category (or Web site)

Your results might differ

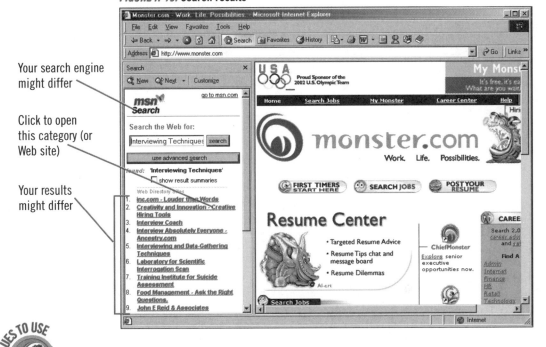

CLUES TO USE

Search engines

Many search engines, such as Yahoo!, Google, Infoseek, Lycos, WebCrawler, and Excite, can help you locate information on the Internet. These search engines routinely use software programs to methodically catalog, or crawl, through the entire Internet and create huge databases with links to Web pages and their URLs. When you enter a keyword or phrase, the search engine examines its database index for relevant information and displays a list of Web sites.

Each search engine differs slightly in the way it formats information, the way it records the number of Internet sites in the database, and how often it updates the database. If you don't find what you need using one search engine, try running the same search using a different search engine or search phrase, until you find what you need. Most people develop personal favorites and learn which engine works best in various situations.

Internet

Exiting Internet Explorer

When you are ready to exit Internet Explorer, you can click the Close button in the upper-right corner of the browser window or click Close on the File menu. You do not need to save files before you exit. However you may want to clear out your Favorites folder. Alice has completed her research on the Web and is ready to exit Internet Explorer.

Steps

1. Click **Favorites** on the menu bar, click **Organize Favorites**, select the Favorites that you created in this unit, click **Delete**, click **Yes** in the Confirm File Delete dialog box, then click **Close** to close the Organize Favorites dialog box

2. Click **File** on the menu bar
   The File menu opens, as shown in Figure A-17.

3. Click **Close**
   The Internet Explorer browser window closes.

4. If you connected to the Internet by telephone, follow your normal procedure to close your connection

QuickTip

You can also exit from Internet Explorer by clicking the Close button in the upper-right corner of the browser window.

 CLUES TO USE

Saving or sending a Web page

Before exiting from Internet Explorer, you may want to save a copy of the current page or send someone a copy. By selecting Save As on the File menu, you can choose to save the complete Web page, including any graphics—or just the text from the page—in a file on your computer. If you want to send the complete page to someone, click File on the menu bar, point to Send, click Page By Email, and then use your e-mail program to address and send the message to the intended recipient. If you want to send the Link only, not the whole page, click File on the menu bar, point to Send, click Link by Email.

FIGURE A-17: Internet Explorer with File menu open

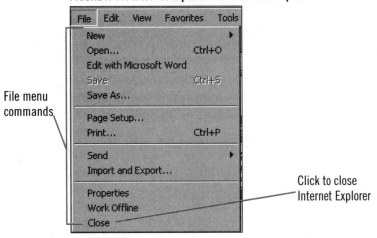

FIGURE A-17: Internet Explorer with File menu open

File menu commands

Click to close Internet Explorer

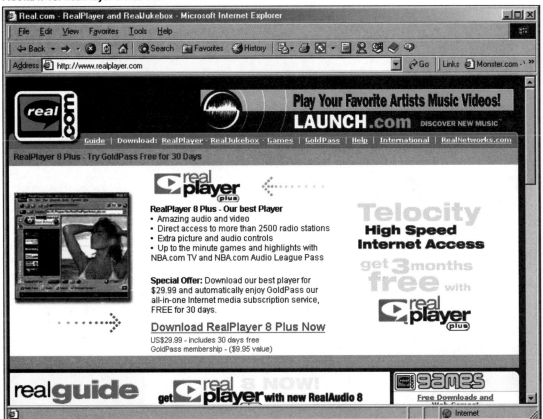

FIGURE A-18: RealPlayer's Web site

Using RealPlayer

As you surf the Web, you may encounter a Web site with links to video or audio clips. Without the proper "player" software, your computer will be unable to play the clips. You can download a free copy of RealPlayer 8 Basic from www.realplayer.com. Most Web sites will direct you to the RealPlayer Web site, if you try to play a video clip unsuccessfully. RealPlayer 8 Basic allows you to play audio and video clips and listen to your favorite radio stations. RealPlayer includes Real.com Guide, which tells you about some of the most popular and unusual Web sites to visit. You can also watch channels, such as CNN, Comedy Central, and Disney using RealPlayer. Before you download any new software to any computer, be sure you have permission to do so for the computer on which you are working.

Internet

Practice

► Concepts Review

Label each element of the Internet Explorer browser window shown in Figure A-19.

FIGURE A-19

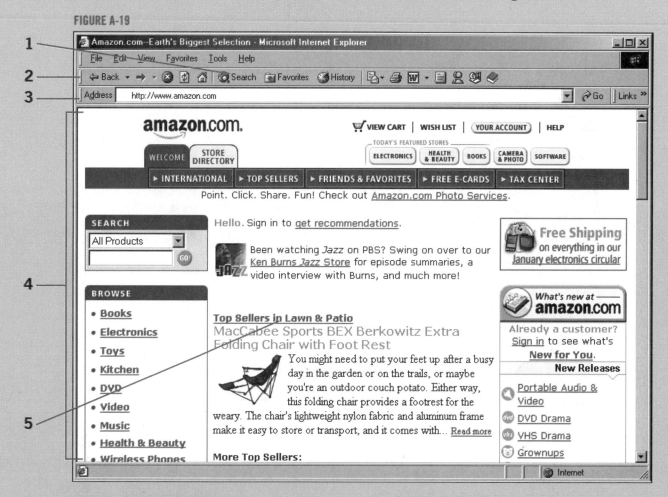

Match each term with the statement that describes it.

6. Address bar
7. Toolbar
8. Favorites button
9. Status indicator
10. Back button

a. Is animated while Internet Explorer loads a page
b. Displays the URL for the currently displayed page
c. Includes buttons for options on the menu bar
d. Displays a list of saved Web pages
e. Displays the previously viewed page

Select the best answer from the list of choices.

11. **Software programs used to access and display Web pages are called:**
    a. Web sites.
    b. Web windows.
    c. Web documents.
    d. Web browsers.

12. **If you want to save the name and URL of a Web page and return to it later, you can add it to:**
    a. Favorites.
    b. Bookmarks.
    c. Home pages.
    d. Preferences.

13. **An international telecommunications network that consists of hyperlinked documents is called:**
    a. NSFNET.
    b. Netscape Navigator.
    c. Internet Explorer.
    d. the World Wide Web.

14. **The _____ has buttons used to perform many common functions, such as printing Web pages and returning to the home page.**
    a. Address bar
    b. Toolbar
    c. Status bar
    d. Menu bar

15. **You can search for Web sites by category by entering a keyword in the Address bar, then clicking the:**
    a. Search button.
    b. Home button.
    c. Go button.
    d. Link button.

16. **Which of the following URLs is valid?**
    a. http://www.usf.edu
    b. htp://www.usf.edu
    c. http:www.usf.edu
    d. http//www.usf.edu

17. **Which button should you click if you want to stop a Web page that is currently loading on your computer?**
    a.
    b.
    c.
    d.

18. **Highlighted or underlined words that allow you to navigate to another Web page location are called:**
    a. Explorers.
    b. Favorites.
    c. Web browsers.
    d. Hyperlinks.

19. **The URL of the Web page currently displayed in your Web browser window appears in the**
    a. Title bar.
    b. Browser window.
    c. Address bar.
    d. Status bar.

20. **To locate information on a specific topic on the Internet, you can use a:**
    a. URL locator.
    b. Web browser.
    c. Favorites list.
    d. Search engine.

▶ Skills Review

1. **Start Internet Explorer.**
   a. Make sure your computer is connected to the Internet.
   b. Start Internet Explorer.

2. **Explore the browser window.**
   a. Identify the toolbar, menu bar, Address bar, Go button, Links bar, status bar, status indicator, URL, browser window, and scroll bars.
   b. Identify the toolbar buttons for printing, searching, viewing favorites, and returning to the home page.
   c. Identify the complete URL of the current Web page.

3. **Open and save a URL.**
   a. Open the Web page www.nationalgeographic.com using the Address bar.
   b. Explore the site by using the scroll bars, toolbar, and hyperlinks.

   c. Open the Web page www.caribbean.com using the Address bar.

   d. Add the current Web page to your Favorites list.

   e. Click the Home button.

   f. Click the Favorites button.

   g. Click Welcome to Caribbean Online on the Favorites menu to return to that page.

   h. Close the Explorer Favorites bar.

4. **Navigate Web pages.**

   a. Open the Web page www.usps.com using the Address bar.

   b. Follow the links to investigate the content.

   c. Click the Home button.

5. **Get Help.**

   a. Open Microsoft Internet Explorer Help, then click the Contents tab.

   b. Click Browsing the Web Offline.

   c. Click Making pages available offline.

   d. Read about making pages available offline.

   e. Close the Microsoft Internet Explorer Help window.

6. **Print a Web page.**

   a. Open the Web page www.mapquest.com using the Address bar.

   b. Print one copy of the first page only.

7. **Search for information on the Internet.**

   a. Open the Search bar.

   b. Type any keyword or phrase for which you would like to find information, then execute the search.

   c. Explore some of the hyperlinks you find and some of the pages that open.

   d. When you finish reviewing the Web sites you find, close the Search bar.

8. **Exit Internet Explorer.**

   a. Delete any Favorites you created using the Organize Favorites dialog box.

   b. Exit Internet Explorer.

 # Independent Challenge 1

You have an upcoming interview at an advertising agency for a position in the Creative Department. To prepare for your interview, you feel the need to read about what is happening in the world of advertising. You use the Web to brush up on your advertising knowledge.

   a. Start Internet Explorer.

   b. Research an article about a popular advertising campaign from one of the sites listed below:

• Adweek	www.adweek.com
• Advertising Age	www.adage.com
• Advertising Age Global	www.adageglobal.com
• American Advertising Federation	www.aaf.org

   c. Click the Print button to print one page.

   d. Exit Internet Explorer.

Independent Challenge 2

You leave tomorrow for a business trip to Gibraltar. You want to be sure that you take the right clothes for the weather and decide that the best place to check weather conditions is the Web.

a. Start Internet Explorer.

b. Go to www.travel.com, then search the site to find out about Gibraltar.

c. Open two of the following weather sites to determine the weather in Gibraltar at this time of the year.

- The Weather Channel   www.weather.com
- CNN Weather   www.cnn.com/WEATHER
- Yahoo! Weather   weather.yahoo.com

d. Use the Print command to print the weather report for Gibraltar from two sites.

e. Exit Internet Explorer.

Independent Challenge 3

As a visiting nurse who makes house calls, you need to buy a new car that you can rely on to get you to your daily appointments. You decide to use the Web to compare some car models that you have in mind.

a. Start Internet Explorer, then access the following automobile Web sites:

- Ford   www.ford.com
- Honda   www.honda.com
- Kia   www.kia.com
- Cars.com   www.cars.com

b. Print a page from a Web site that offers a reliable, compact car under $25,000. See Figure A-20 as an example.

c. Exit Internet Explorer.

FIGURE A-20: Cars.com

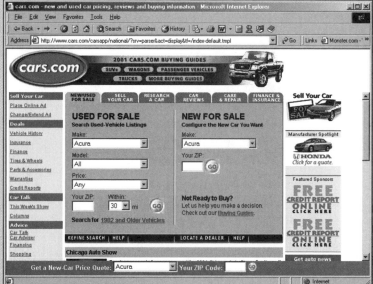

Independent Challenge 4

You would like to customize your Web browser so that it always uses the same search engine. You decide to compare two that have been recommended to you and determine which one you like the most.

a. Start Internet Explorer. Using the two search engines listed below, type **paint your own pottery** in the Search text box.

- Go.com   www.go.com
- MSN Search   www.msn.com

b. On a piece of paper, list the name of each search engine and the number of hits it produced.

c. Indicate which search engine you think is better and why. Write down a few reasons for your preference.

d. Click the Search button on the toolbar, click the Customize button on the Explorer Search bar, click the search service you like, then click OK.

e. Open the Customize Search Settings dialog box and click Reset.

f. Exit Internet Explorer.

Internet

► # Visual Workshop

Use the Search Assistant to find and print a Web page showing a map of London's Heathrow airport, similar to the one shown in Figure A-21. The map can come from any one of several Web pages identified in your Search results. Be sure to identify the Web site on which the map was located.

FIGURE A-21

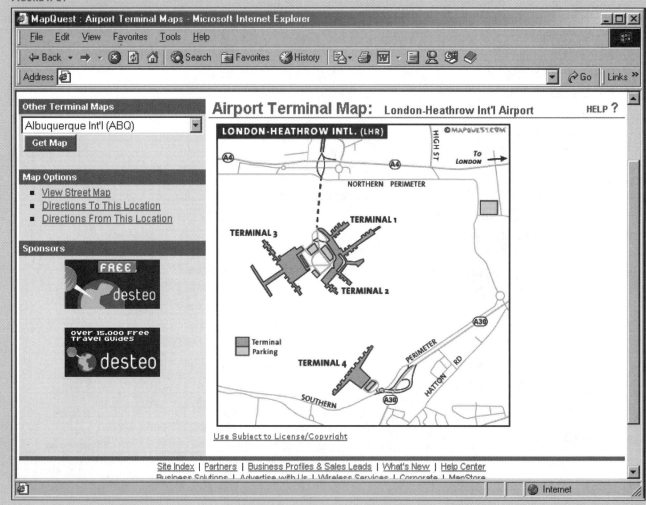

Getting
Started with Word 2002

![Objectives]

Objectives

- ► **Understand word processing software**
- ► **Start Word 2002**
- ► **Explore the Word program window**
- ► **Start a document**
- ► **Save a document**
- ► **Print a document**
- ► **Use the Help system**
- ► **Close a document and exit Word**

Microsoft Word 2002 is a word processing program that makes it easy to create a variety of professional-looking documents, from simple letters and memos to newsletters, research papers, Web pages, business cards, resumes, financial reports, and other documents that include multiple pages of text and sophisticated formatting. In this unit, you will explore Word's editing and formatting features and learn how to start Word and create a document. Alice Wegman is the marketing manager at MediaLoft, a chain of bookstore cafés that sells books, music, and videos. Alice familiarizes herself with Word and uses it to create a memo to the marketing staff. You will work with Alice as she creates her memo.

Understanding Word Processing Software

A **word processing program** is a software program that includes tools for entering, editing, and formatting text and graphics. Microsoft Word is a powerful word processing program that allows you to create and enhance a wide range of documents quickly and easily. Figure A-1 shows the first page of a report created using Word and illustrates some of the Word features you can use to enhance your documents. The electronic files you create using Word are called **documents**. One of the benefits of using Word is that document files are stored on a disk, making them easy to transport and revise. Alice needs to write a memo to the marketing staff to inform them of an upcoming meeting. Before beginning her memo, she explores Word's editing and formatting capabilities.

You can use Word to accomplish the following tasks:

▶ **Type and edit text**

Word's editing tools make it simple to insert and delete text in a document. You can add text to the middle of an existing paragraph, replace text with other text, undo an editing change, and correct typing, spelling, and grammatical errors with ease.

▶ **Copy and move text from one location to another**

Using Word's more advanced editing features you can copy or move text from one location and insert it in a different location in a document. You also can copy and move text between documents. Being able to copy and move text means you don't have to retype text that is already entered in a document.

▶ **Format text and paragraphs with fonts, colors, and other elements**

Word's sophisticated formatting tools allow you to make the text in your documents come alive. You can change the size, style, and color of text, add lines and shading to paragraphs, and enhance lists with bullets and numbers. Using text-formatting features creatively helps you highlight important ideas in your documents.

▶ **Format and design pages**

Word's page-formatting features give you power to design attractive newsletters, create powerful resumes, and produce documents such as business cards, CD labels, and books. You can change the paper size and orientation of your documents, add headers and footers to pages, organize text in columns, and control the layout of text and graphics on each page of a document.

▶ **Enhance documents with tables, charts, diagrams, and graphics**

Using Word's powerful graphic tools you can spice up your documents with pictures, photographs, lines, shapes, and diagrams. You also can illustrate your documents with tables and charts to help convey your message in a visually interesting way.

▶ **Create Web pages**

Word's Web page design tools allow you to create documents that others can read over the Internet or an intranet. You can enhance Web pages with themes and graphics, add hyperlinks, create online forms, and preview Web pages in your Web browser.

▶ **Use Mail Merge to create form letters and mailing labels**

The Word Mail Merge feature allows you to easily send personalized form letters to many different people. You can also use Mail Merge to create mailing labels, directories, e-mail messages, and many other types of documents.

Format the size and appearance of text

Insert graphics

Create columns of text

Add bullets to lists

Create tables

MediaLoft Marketing Report, April 2003

Add headers to every page

MediaLoft Book Buyer Survey

In an effort to develop an economic profile of the MediaLoft book buyers, the marketing department hired the market research firm Takeshita Consultants, Inc. to create and administer a survey of the MediaLoft customer base. A secondary goal of the survey was to identify the areas in which MediaLoft can improve its service and products in the book department. Over 20,000 people completed the survey, which was distributed at MediaLoft stores, the Chicago Book Fair, the Modern Language Association annual meeting, the San Diego Literary Festival, and other events.

Align text in paragraphs evenly

Book-buyer Profile

A typical MediaLoft book-buyer is a 42-year-old professional with an annual household income between $40,000 and $60,000. He or she has graduated from college and has one child. The typical book-buyer works in the city and owns a home in an urban or suburban area.

- 42% graduated from college.
- 32% have a graduate level degree.
- 26% have completed high school.
- 60% earn more than $40,000 per year.
- 8% earn more than $70,000 per year.
- 60% are employed as professionals.
- 20% work in clerical/service industries.
- 20% work in trades.

Survey Methods

The survey was distributed to purchasing and non-purchasing customers at MediaLoft stores during January and February 2003. Surveys were distributed at other events as they were held. The table below shows the distribution of surveys by location and by sex. Roughly equal numbers of surveys were completed at the eight MediaLoft stores.

Survey Location	Male	Female
MediaLoft stores	6,657	7,801
Chicago Book Fair	1,567	1,238
MLA annual meeting	563	442
SD Literary Festival	398	487
Other	865	622
Total	**10,050**	**10,590**
	Grand Total	**20,640**

Purchasing Habits

Respondents report they purchase one or two books a month. 80% purchase books online, but 68% prefer to shop for reading material in bookstores.

Add lines

Preferred Genres

14% 25%
18%
16%
19% 8%

■ Fiction ■ Non-Fiction
■ Biography/Memoir ■ Technical
■ Professional ■ Children's

Create charts

Customer Satisfaction

On the whole, MediaLoft book customers gave the book department a favorable review. Customers rated the quality of book offerings as excellent, the quantity of titles as very good, and the subject coverage as excellent. Equally favorable ratings were given to the sales staff and the physical appearance of MediaLoft stores. Book-buyers did express interest in seeing a wider selection of non-fiction titles and deeper discounts for computer and professional titles. The organization and variety of titles in the children's and juvenile departments could also be improved.

1►

Add page numbers

CLUES TO USE

Planning a document

Before you create a new document, it's a good idea to spend time planning it. Identify the message you want to convey, the audience for your document, and the elements, such as tables or charts, you want to include. You should also think about how you want your document to sound and look—is it a business letter, which should be written in a pleasant, but serious tone and have a formal appearance, or are you creating a flyer that must be colorful, eye-catching, and fun to read?

The purpose and audience for your document will determine the appropriate design. Planning the layout and design of a document involves deciding how to organize the text, selecting the fonts to use, identifying the graphics to include, and selecting the formatting elements that will enhance its message and appeal. For longer documents, such as newsletters, it can be useful to sketch the layout and design of each page before you begin.

Word 2002

Word 2002

Starting Word 2002

Before starting Word, you must start Windows by turning on your computer. Once Windows is running, you can start Word or any other application by using the Start button on the Windows taskbar. You can also start Word by clicking the Word icon on the Windows desktop or the Word icon on the Microsoft Office Shortcut bar, if those items are available on your computer. Alice uses the Start button to start Word so she can familiarize herself with its features.

1. Click the **Start button** ![Start] on the Windows taskbar
The Start menu opens on the desktop.

2. Point to **Programs** on the Start menu
The Programs menu opens, as shown in Figure A-2. The Programs menu displays the list of programs installed on your computer. If you are using personalized menus in Windows, your Programs menu might display only the most frequently used programs; click the double arrow at the bottom of the Programs menu to expand the menu and display the complete list of programs.

Trouble?

If Microsoft Word is not on your Programs menu, ask your technical support person for assistance.

3. Click **Microsoft Word** on the Programs menu
The **Word program window** opens and displays a blank document and the New Document task pane, as shown in Figure A-3. The blank document opens in the most recently used view. **Views** are different ways of displaying a document in the document window. Figure A-3 shows a blank document in Print Layout view. The lessons in this unit will use Print Layout view.

4. Click the **Print Layout View button** ![icon] as shown in Figure A-3
If your blank document opened in a different view, the view changes to Print Layout view.

Trouble?

If your toolbars are on one row, click the Toolbar Options button ![icon] at the end of the Formatting toolbar, then click Show Buttons on Two Rows.

5. Click the **Zoom list arrow** on the Standard toolbar as shown in Figure A-3, then click **Page Width**
The blank document fills the document window. Your screen should now match Figure A-3. The blinking vertical line in the upper-left corner of the document window is the **insertion point**. It indicates where text will appear when you type.

6. Move the mouse pointer around in the Word program window
The mouse pointer changes shape depending on where it is in the Word program window. In the document window in Print Layout view, the mouse pointer changes to an **I-beam pointer** I or a **click and type pointer** I⁼. You use these pointers to move the insertion point in the document or to select text to edit. Table A-1 describes common mouse pointers.

7. Place the mouse pointer over a toolbar button
When you place the pointer over a button or some other element of the Word program window, a ScreenTip appears. A **ScreenTip** is a label that identifies the name of the button or feature.

TABLE A-1: Common Word pointers

pointer	use to
I	Move the insertion point in a document or to select text
I⁼ or I	Move the insertion point in a blank area of a document in Print Layout or Web Layout view; automatically applies the paragraph formatting required to position text at that location in the document
↖	Click a button, menu command, or other element of the Word program window; appears when you point to elements of the Word program window
⬈	Select a line or lines of text; appears when you point to the left edge of a line of text in the document window
↜	Open a hyperlink; appears when you point to a hyperlink in the task pane or a document

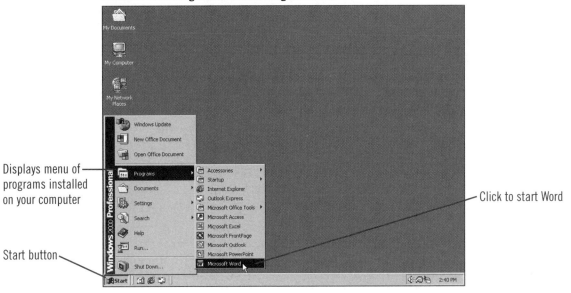

FIGURE A-2: Starting Word from the Programs menu

Displays menu of programs installed on your computer

Start button

Click to start Word

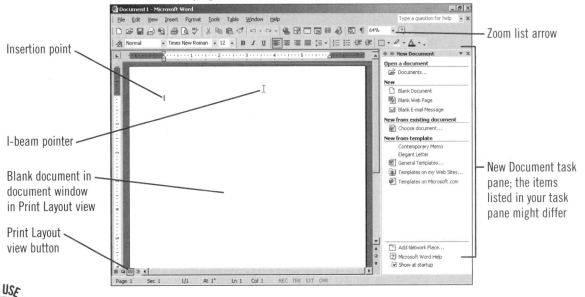

FIGURE A-3: Word program window in Print Layout view

Insertion point

I-beam pointer

Blank document in document window in Print Layout view

Print Layout view button

Zoom list arrow

New Document task pane; the items listed in your task pane might differ

CLUES TO USE

Using Word document views

Each Word view provides features that are useful for working on different types of documents. The default view, **Print Layout view**, displays a document as it will look on a printed page. Print Layout view is helpful for formatting text and pages, including adjusting document margins, creating columns of text, inserting graphics, and formatting headers and footers. Also useful is **Normal view**, which shows a simplified layout of a document, without margins, headers and footers, or graphics. When you want to quickly type, edit, and format text, it's often easiest to work in Normal view. **Web Layout view** allows you to accurately format Web pages or documents that will be viewed on a computer screen. In Web Layout view, a document appears just as it will when viewed with a Web browser. Finally, **Outline view** is useful for editing and formatting longer documents that include multiple headings. Outline view allows you to reorganize text by moving the headings.

You switch between views by clicking the view buttons on the horizontal scroll bar or by using the commands on the View menu. Changing views does not affect how the printed document will appear. It simply changes the way you view the document in the document window.

Exploring the Word Program Window

Word 2002

When you start Word, a blank document appears in the document window and the New Document task pane appears.  Alice examines the elements of the Word program window.

Using Figure A-4 as a guide, find the elements described below in your program window.

► The **title bar** displays the name of the document and the name of the program. Until you give a new document a different name, its temporary name is Document1. The title bar also contains resizing buttons and the program Close button, common to all Windows programs.

► The **menu bar** contains the names of the Word menus. Clicking a menu name opens a list of commands from which you can choose. The menu bar also contains the Ask a Question box and the Close Window button. You use the **Ask a Question box** to access the Word Help system.

► The **toolbars** contain buttons for the most commonly used commands. The **Standard toolbar** contains buttons for frequently used operating and editing commands, such as saving a document, printing a document, and cutting, copying, and pasting text. The **Formatting toolbar** contains buttons for commonly used formatting commands, such as changing font type and size, applying bold to text, and changing paragraph alignment. The Clues to Use in this lesson provides more information about working with Word's toolbars.

► The **New Document task pane** contains shortcuts for opening a document and for creating new documents. The blue words in the New Document task pane are **hyperlinks** that provide quick access to existing documents, document templates, and dialog boxes used for creating and opening documents. As you learn more about Word, you will work with other task panes that provide shortcuts to Word formatting and editing features. Clicking a hyperlink in a task pane can be quicker than using menu commands and toolbar buttons to accomplish a task.

► The **document window** displays the current document. You enter text and format your document in the document window.

► The horizontal and vertical rulers appear in the document window in Print Layout view. The **horizontal ruler** displays left and right document margins as well as the tab settings and paragraph indents, if any, for the paragraph in which the insertion point is located. The **vertical ruler** displays the top and bottom document margins.

► The **vertical and horizontal scroll bars** are used to display different parts of the document in the document window. The scroll bars include **scroll boxes** and **scroll arrows**, which you can use to easily move through a document.

► The **view buttons** at the left end of the horizontal scroll bar allow you to display the document in Normal, Web Layout, Print Layout, or Outline view.

► The **status bar** displays the page number and section number of the current page, the total number of pages in the document, and the position of the insertion point in inches, lines, and characters. The status bar also indicates the on/off status of several Word features, including tracking changes, overtype mode, and spelling and grammar checking.

FIGURE A-4: Elements of the Word program window

Title bar
Menu bar
Standard toolbar
Formatting toolbar
Horizontal ruler
Document window
Vertical ruler
View buttons
Status bar
Horizontal scroll bar

Ask a Question box
New Document task pane
Hyperlink
Scroll box
Vertical scroll bar
Scroll arrow

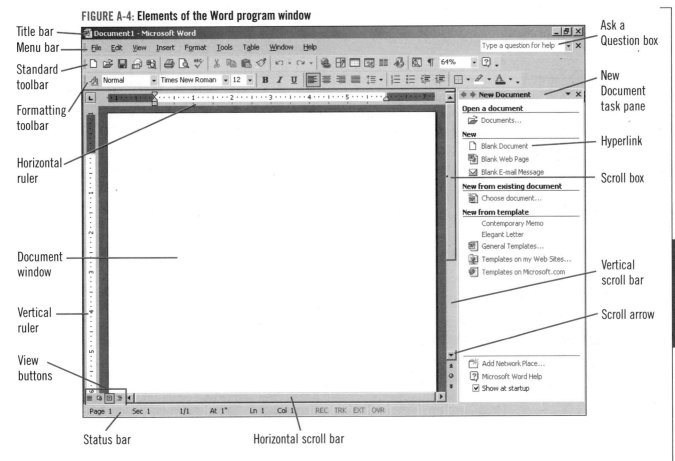

Word 2002

Working with toolbars and menus in Word 2002

The lessons in this book assume you are working with full menus and toolbars visible, which means the Standard and Formatting toolbars appear on two rows and display all the buttons, and the menus display the complete list of menu commands.

You can also set Word to use personalized toolbars and menus that modify themselves to your working style. When you use personalized toolbars, the Standard and Formatting toolbars appear on the same row and display only the most frequently used buttons. To use a button that is not visible on a toolbar, click the Toolbar Options button ⁑ at the end of the toolbar, and then click the button you want on the Toolbar Options list. As you work, Word adds the

buttons you use to the visible toolbars, and moves the buttons you haven't used recently to the Toolbar Options list. Similarly, Word menus adjust to your work habits, so that the commands you use most often appear on shortened menus. You click the double arrow at the bottom of a menu to view additional menu commands.

To work with full toolbars and menus visible, you must turn off the personalized toolbars and menus features. To turn off personalized toolbars and menus, click Tools on the menu bar, click Customize, select the Show Standard and Formatting toolbars on two rows and Always show full menus check boxes on the Options tab, and then click Close.

Word 2002

Starting a Document

You begin a new document by simply typing text in a blank document in the document window. Typing with a word processor is easy because word processors include a **word-wrap** feature, which means as you reach the edge of the page when you type, Word automatically moves the insertion point to the next line of the document. You need only press [Enter] when you want to start a new paragraph or insert a blank line. Also, you can easily edit text in a document by inserting new text or by deleting existing text. Alice types a quick memo to the marketing staff to inform them of the agenda and schedule for the next marketing meeting.

1. Click the **Close button** in the New Document task pane
The task pane closes and the blank document fills the screen.

2. Type **Memorandum**, then press **[Enter]** four times
Each time you press [Enter] the insertion point moves to the start of the next line.

3. Type **DATE:**, then press **[Tab]** twice
Pressing [Tab] moves the insertion point several spaces to the right. You can use the [Tab] key to align the text in a memo header or to indent the first line of a paragraph.

4. Type **April 21, 2003**, then press **[Enter]**
When you press [Enter], a purple dotted line appears under the date. This dotted underline is a **smart tag**. It indicates that Word recognizes the text as a date. If you move the mouse pointer over the smart tag, a **Smart Tag Actions button** ⓘ appears above the date. Smart tags are just one of many automatic features you will encounter as you type. Table A-2 describes other automatic features available in Word. You can ignore the smart tags in your memo.

5. Type: **TO: [Tab] [Tab] Marketing Staff [Enter]**
            FROM: [Tab] Your Name [Enter]
            RE: [Tab] [Tab] Marketing Meeting [Enter] [Enter]
Red or green wavy lines may appear under the words you typed. A red, wavy line means the word is not in Word's dictionary and might be misspelled. A green, wavy line indicates a possible grammar error. You can correct any typing errors you make later.

6. Type **The next marketing meeting will be held May 6th at 10 a.m. in the Bloomsbury room on the ground floor.**
As you type, notice that the insertion point moves automatically to the next line of the document. You also might notice that Word corrects typing errors or makes typographical adjustments as you type. This feature is called **AutoCorrect**. AutoCorrect automatically detects and adjusts typos, certain misspelled words (such as "taht" for "that"), and incorrect capitalization as you type. For example, in the memo, Word automatically changed "6th" to "6th."

7. Type **Heading the agenda will be a discussion of our new cafe music series, scheduled for August. Please bring ideas for promoting this exciting new series to the meeting.**
When you type the first few characters of "August," Word's AutoComplete feature displays the complete word in a ScreenTip. **AutoComplete** suggests text to insert quickly into your documents. You can ignore AutoComplete for now. Your memo should resemble Figure A-5.

8. Position the pointer I after **for** (but before the space) in the second sentence, then click
Clicking moves the insertion point after "for."

9. Press **[Backspace]** three times, then type **to debut in**
Pressing [Backspace] removes the character before the insertion point.

10. Move the insertion point before **marketing** in the first sentence, then press **[Delete]** ten times to remove the word marketing and the space after it
Pressing [Delete] removes the character after the insertion point. Figure A-6 shows the revised memo.

FIGURE A-5: Memo text in the document window

Blank lines between paragraphs

Purple dotted underline indicates a smart tag

Red, wavy underline indicates a possible misspelled word (your memo will show your name)

Text wraps to the next line (yours might differ)

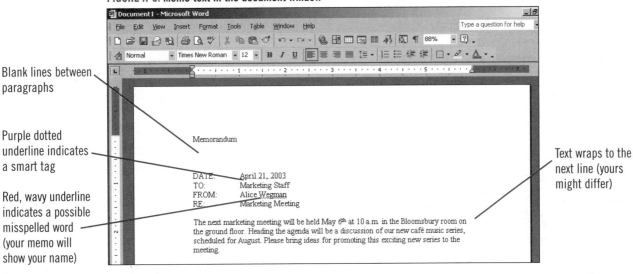

FIGURE A-6: Edited memo text

Text inserted in the memo

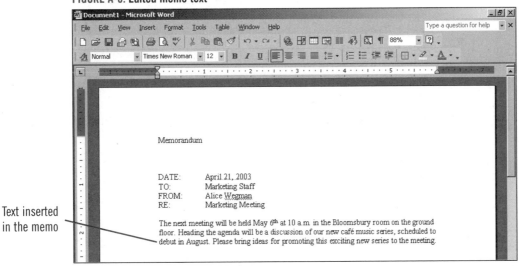

TABLE A-2: Word's automatic features

feature	what appears	to use
AutoComplete	A ScreenTip suggesting text to insert appears as you type	Press [Enter] to insert the text suggested by the ScreenTip; continue typing to reject the suggestion
Spelling and grammar	A red, wavy line under a word indicates a possible misspelling; a green wavy line under text indicates a possible grammatical error	Right-click red- or green-underlined text to display a shortcut menu of correction options; click a correction to accept it and remove the wavy underline
AutoCorrect	A small blue box appears when you place the pointer under text corrected by AutoCorrect; an AutoCorrect Options button appears when you point to the corrected text	Word automatically corrects typos, minor spelling errors, and capitalization, and adds typographical symbols (such as © and ™) as you type; to reverse an AutoCorrect adjustment, click the AutoCorrect Options button, then click Undo
Smart tag	A purple dotted line appears under text Word recognizes as a date, name, address, or place; a Smart Tag Actions button appears when you point to a smart tag	Click the Smart Tag Actions button to display a shortcut menu of options (such as adding a name to your address book in Outlook or opening your Outlook calendar to a date); to remove a smart tag, click Remove this Smart Tag on the shortcut menu

Saving a Document

To store a document permanently so you can open and edit it in the future, you must save a document as a **file** on your computer. When you **save** a document you give it a name, called a **filename**, and indicate the location where you want to store the file. Files can be saved to your computer's internal hard disk, to a floppy disk, or to a variety of other locations. You can save a document using the Save button on the Standard toolbar or the Save command on the File menu. Once you have saved a document for the first time, you should save it again every few minutes and always before printing so that the saved file is updated to reflect your latest changes. ✐━━ Alice saves her memo with the filename Marketing Memo.

Steps 1 2 3 4

Trouble?

If you don't see the extension .doc on the filenames in the Save As dialog box, don't worry. Windows can be set to display or not to display the file extensions.

1. Click the **Save button** 🖫 on the Standard toolbar

The first time you save a document, the Save As dialog box opens, as shown in Figure A-7. The default filename, Memorandum, appears in the File name text box. The default filename is based on the first few words of the document. The ".doc" extension is assigned automatically to all Word documents to distinguish them from files created in other software programs. To save the document with a different filename, type a new filename in the File name text box, and use the Save in list arrow to select where you want to store the document file. You do not need to type .doc when you type a new filename. Table A-3 describes the functions of the buttons in the Save As dialog box.

2. Type **Marketing Memo** in the File name text box

The new filename replaces the default filename. It's a good idea to give your documents brief filenames that describe the contents.

Trouble?

This book assumes your Project Files are stored in drive A. Substitute the correct drive or folder if this is not the case.

3. Click the **Save in list arrow**, then navigate to the drive or folder where your Project Files are located

The drive or folder where your Project Files are located appears in the Save in list box. Your Save As dialog box should resemble Figure A-8.

4. Click **Save**

The document is saved to the location you specified in the Save As dialog box, and the title bar displays the new filename, "Marketing Memo."

5. Place the insertion point before **August** in the second sentence, type **early**, then press **[Spacebar]**

You can continue to work on a document after you have saved it with a new filename.

6. Click 🖫

Your change to the memo is saved. Saving a document after you give it a filename saves the changes you make to a document. You also can click File on the menu bar, and then click Save to save a document.

CLUES TO USE

Recovering lost document files

Sometimes while you are working on a document, Word might freeze, making it impossible to continue working, or you might experience a power failure that shuts down your computer. Should this occur, Word has a built-in recovery feature that allows you to open and save the files that were open during the interruption. When you restart Word after an interruption, the Document Recovery task pane opens on the left side of your screen and lists both the original and the recovered versions of the Word files. If you're not sure which file to open (original or recovered), it's usually better to open the recovered file because it includes your latest changes to the document. You can, however, open and review all the versions of the file that were recovered and select the best one to save. Each file listed in the Document Recovery task pane has a list arrow with options that allow you to open the file, save the file, delete the file, or show repairs made to the file.

FIGURE A-7: Save As dialog box

Active folder or drive

Folders and files in the active folder or drive (yours will differ)

Default filename and file extension are selected

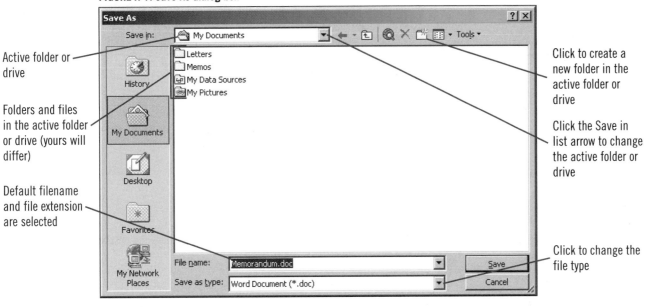

Click to create a new folder in the active folder or drive

Click the Save in list arrow to change the active folder or drive

Click to change the file type

FIGURE A-8: File to be saved to drive A

Location of Project Files (yours might differ)

New filename

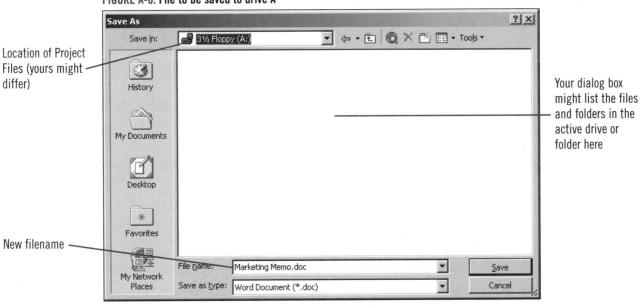

Your dialog box might list the files and folders in the active drive or folder here

TABLE A-3: Save As dialog box buttons

button	use to
⇐ Back	Navigate to the drive or folder previously shown in the Save in list box; click the Back list arrow to navigate to a recently displayed drive or folder
🔁 Up One Level	Navigate to the next highest level in the folder hierarchy (to the drive or folder that contains the current folder)
🔍 Search the Web	Connect to the World Wide Web to locate a folder or file
✕ Delete	Delete the selected folder or file
📁 Create New Folder	Create a new folder in the current folder or drive
⊞ ▾ Views	Change the way folder and file information is shown in the Save As dialog box
Tools ▾ Tools	Open a menu of commands related to the selected drive, folder, or file

Word 2002

Printing a Document

Before you print a document, it's a good habit to examine it in Print Preview to see what it will look like when printed. When you are ready, you can print a document using the Print button on the Standard toolbar or the Print command on the File menu. When you use the Print button, the document prints using the default print settings. If you want to print more than one copy of a document or select other printing options, you must use the Print command. ✒ Alice displays her memo in Print Preview and then prints a copy.

Steps

1. **Click the Print Preview button** 🔍 **on the Standard toolbar**
   The document appears in Print Preview. It is useful to examine a document carefully in Print Preview so that you can correct any problems before printing it.

QuickTip

You can also use the Zoom list arrow on the Print Preview toolbar to change the magnification in the Print Preview window.

2. **Move the pointer over the memo text until it changes to** 🔍, **then click the memo**
   Clicking with the ⊕ pointer magnifies the document in the Print Preview window and changes the pointer to 🔍. The memo appears in the Print Preview window exactly as it will look when printed, as shown in Figure A-9. Clicking with 🔍 reduces the size of the document in the Print Preview window.

3. **Click the Magnifier button** 🔍 **on the Print Preview toolbar**
   Clicking the Magnifier button turns off the magnification feature and allows you to edit the document in Print Preview. In edit mode, the pointer changes to I. The Magnifier button is a **toggle button**, which means you can use it to switch back and forth between magnification mode and edit mode.

4. **Compare the text on your screen with the text in Figure A-9, examine your memo carefully for typing or spelling errors, correct any mistakes, then click the Close Preview button** Close **on the Print Preview toolbar**
   Print Preview closes and the memo appears in the document window.

5. **Click the Save button** 💾 **on the Standard toolbar**
   If you made any changes to the document since you last saved it, the changes are saved.

6. **Click File on the menu bar, then click Print**
   The Print dialog box opens, as shown in Figure A-10. Depending on the printer installed on your computer, your print settings might differ slightly from those in the figure. You can use the Print dialog box to change the current printer, change the number of copies to print, select what pages of a document to print, and modify other printing options.

7. **Click OK**
   The dialog box closes and a copy of the memo prints using the default print settings. You can also click the Print button 🖨 on the Standard toolbar or the Print Preview toolbar to print a document using the default print settings.

FIGURE A-9: Memo in the Print Preview window

Magnifier button

Close Preview button

Marketing Memo.doc (Preview) - Microsoft Word

File Edit View Insert Format Tools Table Window Help

Type a question for help

100% Close

Memorandum

DATE: April 21, 2003
TO: Marketing Staff
FROM: Alice Wegman
RE: Marketing Meeting

The next meeting will be held May 6th at 10 a.m. in the Bloomsbury room on the ground floor. Heading the agenda will be a discussion of our new café music series, scheduled to debut in early August. Please bring ideas for promoting this exciting new series to the meeting.

Page 1   Sec 1   1/1   At 3.1"   Ln 12   Col 16   REC TRK EXT OVR

FIGURE A-10: Print dialog box

Default printer (yours might differ)

Select the pages to print

Select the aspects of the document to print

Change printer properties, such as paper size

Change the number of copies to print

Change the number of pages to print on a sheet of paper

Print using current settings

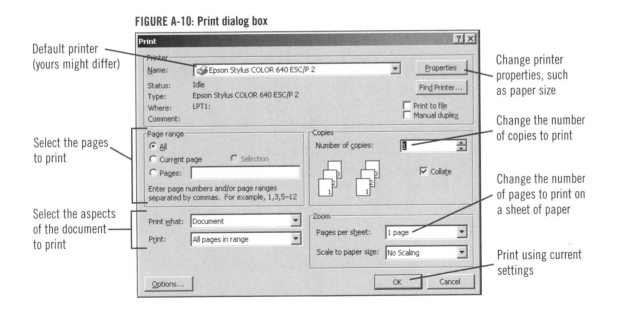

Print

Printer
Name: Epson Stylus COLOR 640 ESC/P 2   Properties
Status: Idle   Find Printer...
Type: Epson Stylus COLOR 640 ESC/P 2
Where: LPT1:   ☐ Print to file
Comment: ☐ Manual duplex

Page range   Copies
⦿ All   Number of copies: 1
○ Current page   ○ Selection
○ Pages: ☑ Collate
Enter page numbers and/or page ranges
separated by commas. For example, 1,3,5-12

Print what: Document   Zoom
Print: All pages in range   Pages per sheet: 1 page
                                     Scale to paper size: No Scaling

Options...   OK   Cancel

Word 2002

Using the Help System

Word includes an extensive Help system that provides immediate access to definitions, instructions, and useful tips for working with Word. You can quickly access the Help system by typing a question in the Ask a Question box on the menu bar, or by clicking the Microsoft Word Help button on the Standard toolbar. Table A-4 describes the many ways to get help while using Word. ✐ Alice is curious to learn more about typing with AutoCorrect and viewing a document in Print Preview. She searches the Word Help system to discover more about these features.

Steps 1234

1. **Type AutoCorrect in the Ask a Question box on the menu bar, then press [Enter]**
   A drop-down menu of help topics related to AutoCorrect opens. You can select a topic from this menu or click See more... to view additional help topics related to your query.

QuickTip

Click the Print button 🖨 on the Help window toolbar to print the current help topic.

2. **Click About automatic corrections on the drop-down menu**
   The Microsoft Word Help window opens, as shown in Figure A-11. The left pane of the Help window contains the Contents, Answer Wizard, and Index tabs, which you can use to search for and display information on help topics. The right pane of the Help window displays the "About automatic corrections" help topic you selected. The blue text in the Help window indicates a link to a definition or to more information about the topic. Notice that the pointer changes to 🖑 when you move it over the blue text.

3. **Read the information in the Help window, then click the blue text hyperlinks**
   Clicking the link expands the help topic to display more detailed information. A definition of "hyperlink" appears in green text in the Help window.

4. **Read the definition, then click hyperlinks again to close the definition**

5. **Click Using AutoCorrect to correct errors as you type, then read the expanded information, clicking the down scroll arrow as necessary to read the entire help topic**
   Clicking the up or down scroll arrow allows you to navigate through the help topic when all the text does not fit in the Help window. You can also **scroll** by clicking the scroll bar above and below the scroll box, or by dragging the scroll box up or down in the scroll bar.

QuickTip

Click the Back ⬅ and Forward ➡ buttons on the Help window toolbar to navigate between the help topics you have viewed.

6. **Click the Answer Wizard tab in the left pane if necessary, type print a document in the What would you like to do? text box, then click Search**
   When you click Search, a list of help topics related to your query appears in the Select topic to display box on the Answer Wizard tab, as shown in Figure A-12. The active help topic—the topic selected in the Select topic to display box—appears in the right pane.

7. **Click the Index tab, type print preview in the Type keywords text box, then click Search**
   As you type, notice that Word automatically supplies possible keywords in the Type keywords box. When you click Search, a list of help topics related to Print Preview appears in the Choose a topic box. You can use the Index tab to narrow the scope of the help topics related to your query by searching for topics related to specific words or phrases.

8. **Click Edit text in print preview in the Choose a topic box**
   The help topic appears in the right pane of the Help window.

9. **Click the Close button on the Help window title bar to close Help**

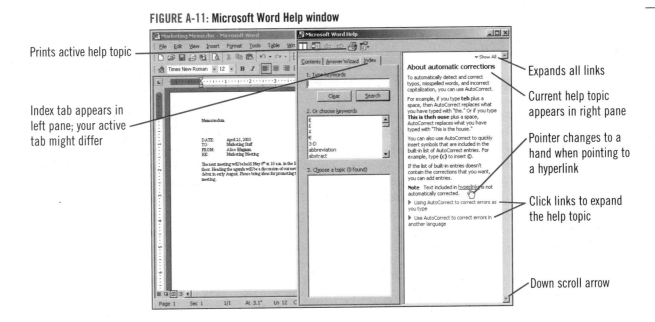

FIGURE A-11: Microsoft Word Help window

Prints active help topic

Index tab appears in left pane; your active tab might differ

Expands all links

Current help topic appears in right pane

Pointer changes to a hand when pointing to a hyperlink

Click links to expand the help topic

Down scroll arrow

FIGURE A-12: Answer Wizard tab in the Microsoft Word Help window

Query used to search for topic

List of help topics related to query

Close button

Active help topic

TABLE A-4: Word resources for getting Help

resource	function	to use
Ask a Question box	Provides quick access to the Help system	Type a word or question in the Ask a Question box, then press [Enter]
Office Assistant	Displays tips and Help topics related to your current task and provides access to the Help system	Press [F1] or click the Microsoft Word Help button [?] on the Standard toolbar, select a Help topic or type a word or question in the Office Assistant dialog box, then click Search
Microsoft Word Help window	Catalogs and displays the detailed Help topics included in the Help system	Browse the table of contents on the Contents tab, type a question in the text box on the Answer Wizard tab, or search for topics related to a keyword on the Index tab
What's This?	Displays information about elements of the Word program window in ScreenTips	Press [Shift][F1] or click the What's This? command on the Help menu, then use the ⬛? pointer to click the element for which you want help
Help on the World Wide Web	Connects to the Microsoft Office Web site, where you can search for information on a topic	Click the Office on the Web command on the Help menu

Closing a Document and Exiting Word

When you finish working on a document and have saved your changes, you can close the document using the Close Window button on the menu bar or the Close command on the File menu. Closing a document closes the document only, it does not close the Word program window. To close the Word program window and exit Word, you can use the Close button on the title bar or the Exit command on the File menu. Using the Exit command closes all open documents. It's good practice to save and close your documents before exiting Word. Figure A-14 shows the Close buttons on the title bar and menu bar. Alice closes the memo and exits Word.

1. **Click File on the menu bar, then click Close**
   If you saved your changes to the document before closing it, the document closes. If you did not save your changes, an alert box opens asking if you want to save the changes.

QuickTip

Click the New Blank Document button ⬜ on the Standard toolbar to create a new blank document.

2. **Click Yes if necessary**
   The document closes, but the Word program window remains open, as shown in Figure A-15. You can create or open another document, access Help, or close the Word program window.

3. **Click File on the menu bar, then click Exit**
   The Word program window closes. If any Word documents were still open when you exited Word, Word would close all open documents, prompting you to save changes to those documents if necessary.

CLUES TO USE

Using the Office Assistant to get Help

The Office Assistant, shown in Figure A-13, is an animated character that appears on your screen to provide tips while you work. For example, when you begin typing a letter, the Office Assistant anticipates what you are doing and opens to offer help writing a letter. You can accept this help or continue working on your own. The Office Assistant also appears when you use the Microsoft Word Help button ? to access the Word Help system. In this case, the Office Assistant displays a list of help topics related to tasks you have recently completed and provides space for you to search for information on other topics. Selecting a help topic in the Office Assistant displays that topic in the Microsoft Help window. When you finish working with the Office Assistant, right-click it and then click Hide to close it. You also can turn off the Office Assistant: right-click it, click Options, deselect the Use the Office Assistant check box on the Options tab in the Office Assistant dialog box, and then click OK. To turn it on again, click Show Office Assistant on the Help menu.

FIGURE A-13: Office Assistant

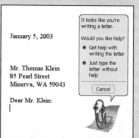

FIGURE A-14: Close and Close Window buttons

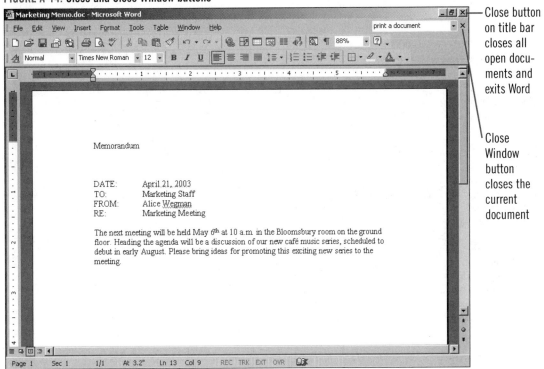

Close button on title bar closes all open documents and exits Word

Close Window button closes the current document

FIGURE A-15: Word program window with no documents open

New Blank Document button

Practice

► Concepts Review

Label the elements of the Word program window shown in Figure A-16.

FIGURE A-16

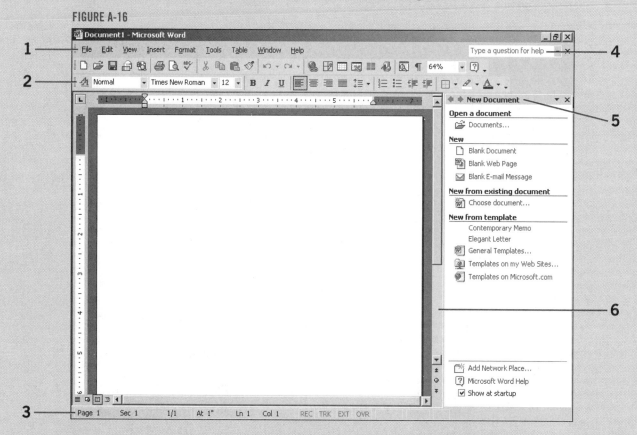

Match each term with the statement that best describes it.

7. Print Preview
8. Office Assistant
9. Status bar
10. Menu bar
11. AutoComplete
12. Horizontal ruler
13. AutoCorrect
14. Normal view

a. Suggests text to insert into a document
b. Provides access to Word commands
c. Displays the document exactly as it will look when printed
d. Provides tips on using Word and displays Help topics
e. Fixes certain errors as you type
f. Displays the number of pages in the current document
g. Displays a simple layout view of a document
h. Displays tab settings and document margins

Select the best answer from the list of choices.

15. Which element of the Word program window contains hyperlinks to help you quickly accomplish a task?
   a. Formatting toolbar
   b. Menu bar
   c. New Document task pane
   d. Status bar

16. Which button is found on the Formatting toolbar?
   a. Underline button
   b. Drawing button
   c. Format Painter button
   d. Tables and Borders button

17. What is the function of the Exit command on the File menu?
   a. To save changes to and close the current document
   b. To close the current document without saving changes
   c. To close all open documents and the Word program window
   d. To close all open programs

18. Which view would you use if you want to adjust the margins in a document?
   a. Outline view
   b. Print Layout view
   c. Normal view
   d. Web Layout view

19. Which of the following does *not* appear on the status bar?
   a. The current page number
   b. The current line number
   c. The Overtype mode status
   d. The current tab settings

20. Which of the following is *not* used to access Word Help topics?
   a. The Ask a Question box
   b. The Search task pane
   c. The Office Assistant
   d. The Answer Wizard

▶ Skills Review

1. Start Word 2002.
   a. Start Word using the Programs menu.
   b. Switch to Print Layout view if necessary.
   c. Change the zoom level to Page Width if necessary.

2. Explore the Word program window.
   a. Identify as many elements of the Word program window as you can without referring to the unit material.
   b. Click each menu name on the menu bar and drag the pointer through the menu commands.
   c. Point to each button on the Standard and Formatting toolbars and read the ScreenTips.
   d. Point to each hyperlink in the New Document task pane.
   e. Click the view buttons to view the blank document in Normal, Web Layout, Print Layout, and Outline view.
   f. Return to Print Layout view.

3. Start a document.
   a. Close the New Document task pane.
   b. In a new blank document, begin typing a fax to one of your customers at Plateau Tours and Travel in Montreal.
   c. Type FAX at the top of the page, then press [Enter] four times.

d. Type the following, pressing [Tab] as indicated and pressing [Enter] at the end of each line:

To: [Tab] **Dr. Monique Lacasse**
From: [Tab] **Your Name**
Date: [Tab] **Today's Date**
Re: [Tab] **Travel arrangements**
Pages: [Tab] **1**
Fax: [Tab] **(514) 555-3948**

e. Press [Enter], then type **I have reserved a space for you on the February 4-18 Costa Rica Explorer tour. You are scheduled to depart Montreal's Dorval Airport on Plateau Tours and Travel charter flight 234 at 7:45 a.m. on February 4th, arriving in San Jose at 4:30 p.m. local time.**

f. Press [Enter] twice, then type **Please call me at (514) 555-4983 or stop by our offices on rue St-Denis.**

g. Insert this sentence at the beginning of the second paragraph: **I must receive full payment within 48 hours to hold your reservation.**

h. Using the [Backspace] key, delete **Travel** in the Re: line, then type **Costa Rica tour.**

i. Using the [Delete] key, delete **48** in the last sentence, then type **72.**

4. Save a document.

a. Click File on the menu bar, then click Save.

b. Save the document as **Lacasse Fax** to the drive and folder where your Project Files are located.

c. After your name, type a comma, a space, and then type **Plateau Tours and Travel**.

d. Click the Save button to save your changes to the document.

5. Print a document.

a. Click the Print Preview button to view the document in Print Preview.

b. Click the word FAX to zoom in on the document, then proofread the fax.

c. Click the Magnifier button to switch to edit mode, then correct any typing errors in your document.

d. Close Print Preview, then save your changes to the document.

e. Print the fax using the default print settings.

6. Use the Help system.

a. Click the Microsoft Word Help button to open the Office Assistant. (*Hint*: If the Help window opens instead of the Office Assistant, close the Help window, click Help on the menu bar, click Show the Office Assistant, then click the Microsoft Word Help button again.)

b. Type **save a document** in the Office Assistant text box, then click Search.

c. Click the topic Save a document.

d. Read about saving documents in Word by clicking the links to expand the help topic.

e. Click the Contents tab, then double-click the topic Viewing and Navigating Documents.

f. Click the topic Zoom in on or out of a document, then read the help topic.

g. Close the Microsoft Word Help window.

7. Close a document and exit Word.

a. Close the Lacasse Fax document, saving your changes if necessary.

b. Exit Word.

▶ Independent Challenge 1

You are a performance artist, well known for your innovative work with computers. The Missoula Arts Council president, Jeb Zobel, has asked you to be the keynote speaker at an upcoming conference in Missoula, Montana, on the role of technology in the arts. You are pleased at the invitation, and write a letter to Mr. Zobel accepting the invitation and confirming the details. Your letter to Mr. Zobel should reference the following information:

- The conference will be held October 10–12, 2003 at the civic center in Missoula.
- You have been asked to speak for one hour on Saturday, October 11, followed by a half hour for questions.
- Mr. Zobel suggested the lecture topic "Technology's Effect on Art and Culture."
- Your talk will include a 20-minute slide presentation.
- The Missoula Arts Council will make your travel arrangements.
- Your preference is to arrive in Missoula on Friday, October 10, and depart on Sunday, October 12.
- You want to fly in and out of the airport closest to your home.

a. Start Word.

b. Save a new blank document as **Zobel Letter** to the drive and folder where your Project Files are located.

c. Model your letter to Mr. Zobel after the sample business letter shown in Figure A-17: there are 3 blank lines after the date, 1 blank line after the inside address, 1 blank line after the salutation, 1 blank line after each body paragraph, and 3 blank lines between the closing and your typed name.

d. Begin the letter by typing today's date.

e. Type the inside address. Be sure to include Mr. Zobel's title and the name of the organization. Make up a street address.

f. Type a salutation.

g. Using the information listed above, type the body of the letter:
- In the first paragraph, accept the invitation to speak and confirm the important conference details.
- In the second paragraph, confirm your lecture topic and provide any relevant details.
- In the third paragraph, state your travel preferences.
- Type a short final paragraph.

h. Type a closing, then include your name in the signature block.

i. Save your changes.

j. Preview and print the letter, then close the document and exit Word.

FIGURE A-17

July 8, 2003

Dr. Amanda Russell
Department of Literature and Creative Writing
Nashua State College
Nashua, NH 03285

Dear Dr. Russell:

Thank you for the invitation to speak at your upcoming seminar on "The Literature of Place." I will be happy to do so. I understand that the seminar will be held from 2:30 p.m. to 4:30 p.m. on September 17 in the Sanders Auditorium. As you suggested, I will address the topic "Writers of the Monadonock Region."

I appreciate your invitation and I look forward to working with you on September 17.

Sincerely,

Jessica Grange

► Independent Challenge 2

Your company has recently installed Word 2002 on its company network. As the training manager it's your responsibility to teach employees how to use the new software productively. Since installing Word 2002, several employees have asked you about smart tags. In response to their queries, you decide to write a memo to all employees and explain how to use the smart tag feature. You know that smart tags are designed to help users perform tasks in Word that normally would require opening a different program, such as Microsoft Outlook (a desktop information-management program that includes e-mail, calendar, and address book features). Before writing your memo, you'll learn more about smart tags by searching the Word Help system.

FIGURE A-18

> WORD TRAINING MEMORANDUM
>
>
> To: All employees
> From: Your Name, Training Manager
> Date: Today's date
> Re: Smart tags in Word 2002

a. Start Word and save a new blank document as **Smart Tags Memo** to the drive and folder where your Project Files are located.

b. Type **WORD TRAINING MEMORANDUM** at the top of the document, press [Enter] four times, then type the memo heading information shown in Figure A-18. Make sure to include your name in the From line and the current date in the Date line.

c. Press [Enter] twice to place the insertion point where you will begin typing the body of your memo.

d. Search the Word Help system for information on working with smart tags.

e. Type your memo after completing your research. In your memo, define smart tags, then explain what they look like, how to use smart tags, and how to remove smart tags from a document.

f. Save your changes, preview and print the memo, then close the document and exit Word.

► Independent Challenge 3

Yesterday you interviewed for a job as marketing director at Komata Web Designs. You spoke with several people at Komata, including Hiro Kobayashi, Director of Operations, whose business card is shown in Figure A-19. You need to write a follow-up letter to Mr. Kobayashi, thanking him for the interview and expressing your interest in the company and the position. He also asked you to send him some samples of your marketing work, which you will enclose with the letter.

FIGURE A-19

a. Start Word and save a new blank document as **Komata Letter** to the drive and folder where your Project Files are located.

b. Begin the letter by typing today's date.

c. Four lines below the date, type the inside address, referring to Figure A-19 for the address information. Be sure to include the recipient's title, company name, and full mailing address in the inside address. (*Hint*: When typing a foreign address, type the name of the country in capital letters by itself on the last line.)

d. Two lines below the inside address, type the salutation.

e. Two lines below the salutation, type the body of the letter according to the following guidelines:

- In the first paragraph, thank him for the interview. Then restate your interest in the position and express your desire to work for the company. Add any specific details you think will enhance the power of your letter.

- In the second paragraph, note that you are enclosing three samples of your work and explain something about the samples you are enclosing.
- Type a short final paragraph.

f. Two lines below the last body paragraph, type a closing, then four lines below the closing, type the signature block. Be sure to include your name in the signature block.

g. Two lines below the signature block, type an enclosure notation. (*Hint*: An enclosure notation usually includes the word "Enclosures" or the abbreviation "Enc." followed by the number of enclosures in parentheses.)

h. Save your changes.

i. Preview and print the letter, then close the document and exit Word.

 # Independent Challenge 4

Unlike personal letters or many e-mail messages, business letters are formal in tone and format. The World Wide Web is one source for information on writing styles, proper document formatting, and other business etiquette issues. In this independent challenge, you will research guidelines and tips for writing effective and professional business letters. Your online research should seek answers to the following questions: What is important to keep in mind when writing a business letter? What are the parts of a business letter? What are some examples of types of business letters? What are some useful tips for writing business letters?

a. Use your favorite search engine to search the Web for information on writing and formatting business letters. Use the keywords **business letters** to conduct your search. If your search does not result in links to information on business letters, try looking at the following Web sites: www.eHow.com, www.business-letters.com, or www.about.com.

b. Review the Web sites you find. Print at least two Web pages that offer useful guidelines for writing business letters.

c. Start Word and save a new blank document as **Business Letters** to the drive and folder where your Project Files are located.

d. Type your name at the top of the document, then press [Enter] twice.

e. Type a brief report on the results of your research. Your report should answer the following questions:
- What are the URLs of the Web sites you visited to research guidelines for writing a business letter? (*Hint*: A URL is a Web page's address. An example of a URL is www.eHow.com.)
- What is important to keep in mind when writing a business letter?
- What are the parts of a business letter?
- In what situations do people write business letters? Provide as many examples as you can think of.

f. Save your changes to the document, preview and print it, then close the document and exit Word.

▶ **Visual Workshop**

Create the cover letter shown in Figure A-20. Since you plan to print the letter on your letterhead, you do not need to include your return address. Save the document with the name **Publishing Cover Letter** to the drive and folder where your Project Files are stored, print a copy of the letter, then close the document and exit Word.

FIGURE A-20

June 16, 2003

Ms. Olivia Johansen
Managing Editor
Conway Press
483 Grove Street
Wellesley, MA 02181

Dear Ms. Johansen:

I read of the opening for an editorial assistant on the June 15 edition of Boston.com, and I would like to be considered for the position. A recent graduate of Whitfield College, I am interested in pursuing a career in publishing.

My desire for a publishing career springs from my interest in writing and editing. At Whitfield College, I was a frequent contributor to the student newspaper and was involved in creating a Web site for student poetry and short fiction.

I have a wealth of experience using Microsoft Word in professional settings. For the past several summers I worked as an office assistant for Packer Investment Consultants, where I used Word to create newsletters and financial reports for clients. During the school year, I also worked part-time in the Whitfield College admissions office. Here I used Word's mail merge feature to create form letters and mailing labels.

My enclosed resume details my talents and experience. I would welcome the opportunity to discuss the position and my qualifications with you. I can be reached at 617-555-3849.

Sincerely,

Your Name

Enc.

Editing

Documents

Objectives

- MOUS ► **Open a document**
- MOUS ► **Select text**
- MOUS ► **Cut and paste text**
- MOUS ► **Copy and paste text**
- MOUS ► **Use the Office Clipboard**
- MOUS ► **Use the Spelling and Grammar checker and the Thesaurus**
- MOUS ► **Find and Replace text**
- MOUS ► **Use wizards and templates**

Word's sophisticated editing features make it easy to revise and polish your documents. In this unit, you learn how to open an existing file, revise it by replacing, copying, and moving text, and then save the document as a new file. You also learn to perfect your documents using Word's proofing tools, and to quickly create attractive, professionally designed documents using wizards and templates. Alice Wegman needs to create a press release about a new MediaLoft lecture series in New York. The press release should provide information about the series so that newspapers, radio stations, and other media outlets can announce it to the public. Alice also needs to create a fax coversheet to use when she faxes the press release to her list of press contacts. You will work with Alice as she creates these documents.

Word 2002

Opening a Document

Sometimes the easiest way to create a document is to edit an existing document and save it with a new filename. To modify a document, you must first **open** it so that it displays in the document window. Word offers several methods for opening documents, described in Table B-1. Once you have opened a file, you can use the Save As command to create a new file that is a copy of the original. You can then edit the new file without making changes to the original. ✍️ Rather than write her press release from scratch, Alice decides to modify a press release written for a similar event. She begins by opening the press release document and saving it with a new filename.

Steps 1234

Trouble?

If the New Document task pane is not open, click File on the menu bar, then click New.

QuickTip

You also can use the Open button 📂 on the Standard toolbar or the Open command on the File menu to open the Open dialog box.

QuickTip

You also can double-click a filename in the Open dialog box to open the file.

1. Start Word

Word opens and a blank document and the New Document task pane appear in the program window, as shown in Figure B-1. The New Document task pane contains links for opening existing documents and for creating new documents.

2. Click the Documents or More Documents hyperlink under Open a document in the New Document task pane

The Open dialog box opens. You use the Open dialog box to locate and select the file you want to open. The Look in list box displays the current drive or folder.

3. Click the Look in list arrow, then click the drive containing your Project Files

A list of Project Files appears in the Open dialog box, as shown in Figure B-2. If your Project Files are located in a folder, double-click the folder to display its contents.

4. Click the filename WD B-1 in the Open dialog box, then click Open

The document opens. Notice that the filename WD B-1 appears in the title bar. Once you have opened a file, you can edit it and use the Save or the Save As command to save your changes. You use the **Save** command when you want to save the changes you make to a file, overwriting the file that is stored on a disk. You use the **Save As** command when you want to create a new file with a different filename, leaving the original file intact.

5. Click File on the menu bar, then click Save As

The Save As dialog box opens. By saving a file with a new filename, you create a document that is identical to the original document. The original filename is selected (highlighted) in the File name text box. Any text you type will replace the selected text.

6. Type NY Press Release in the File name text box, then click Save

The original file closes and the NY Press Release file is displayed in the document window. Notice the new filename in the title bar. You can now make changes to the press release file without affecting the original file.

TABLE B-1: Methods for opening documents

use	to	if you want to
The Open button 📂 **on the Standard toolbar, Open command on the File menu, or [Ctrl][O]**	Open the Open dialog box	Open an existing file; a fast way to open a document when the New Document task pane is not displayed
The Documents or More Documents hyperlink in the New Document task pane	Open the Open dialog box	Open an existing file; a fast way to open a document when the New Document task pane is displayed
A filename hyperlink in the New Document task pane	Open the file in the document window	Open the file; a fast way to open a file that was recently opened on your computer
The Choose a document hyperlink in the New Document task pane	Open the New From Existing Document dialog box	Create a copy of an existing file; a fast way to open a document you intend to save with a new filename

FIGURE B-1: New Document task pane

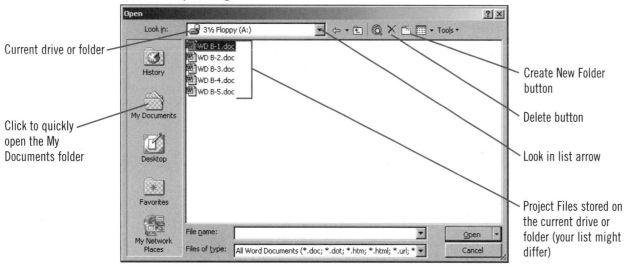

Open button

Your task pane might also include hyperlinks to recently opened files here

Documents hyperlink (yours might be the More Documents hyperlink)

Click to open an existing file as a new file

FIGURE B-2: Open dialog box

Current drive or folder

Click to quickly open the My Documents folder

Create New Folder button

Delete button

Look in list arrow

Project Files stored on the current drive or folder (your list might differ)

Managing files and folders

The Open and Save As dialog boxes include powerful tools for navigating, creating, and deleting files and folders on your computer, a network, or the Web. By selecting a file or folder and clicking the Delete button ☒, you can delete the item and send it to the Recycle Bin. You can also create a new folder for storing files by clicking the Create New Folder button ☐ and typing a name for the folder. The new folder is created in the current folder.

Using the Save As dialog box, you can also create new files that are based on existing files. You can create a new file by saving an existing file with a different filename or by saving it in a different location on your system. You also can save a file in a different file format so that it can be opened in a different software program. To save a file in a different format, click the Files of type list arrow, then click the type of file you want to create. For example, you can save a Word document (which has a .doc file extension) as a plain text file (.txt), as a Web page file (.htm), or in a variety of other file formats.

Selecting Text

Before deleting, editing, or formatting text, you must **select** the text. Selecting text involves clicking and dragging the I-beam pointer across text to highlight it. You also can click with the pointer in the blank area to the left of text to select lines or paragraphs. Table B-2 describes the many ways to select text. Alice revises the press release by selecting text and replacing it with new text.

 **Steps**

1. **Click before December 9, 2002 and drag the I pointer over the text to select it**
   The date is selected, as shown in Figure B-3.

2. **Type January 13, 2003**
   The text you type replaces the selected text.

3. **Double-click James, type your first name, double-click Callaghan, then type your last name**
   Double-clicking a word selects the entire word.

4. **Place the pointer in the margin to the left of the phone number so that the pointer changes to , click to select the phone number, then type (415) 555-8293**
   Clicking to the left of a line of text with the pointer selects the entire line.

5. **Click the down scroll arrow at the bottom of the vertical scroll bar until the headline Guy Fogg to Speak … is at the top of your document window**
   The scroll arrows or scroll bars allow you to **scroll** through a document. You scroll through a document when you want to display different parts of the document in the document window.

6. **Select SAN FRANCISCO, then type NEW YORK**

7. **In the fourth body paragraph, select the sentence All events will be held at the St. James Hotel., then press [Delete]**
   Selecting text and pressing [Delete] removes the text from the document.

8. **Select and replace text in the second and last paragraphs using the following table:**

select	type
February 12	March 6
St. James Hotel in downtown San Francisco	Waldorf-Astoria Hotel
National Public Radio's Helen DeSaint	New York Times literary editor Isabel Eliot

   The edited press release is shown in Figure B-4.

9. **Click the Save button on the Standard toolbar**
   Your changes to the press release are saved. Always save before and after editing text.

 CLUES TO USE

Replacing text in Overtype mode

Normally you must select text before typing to replace the existing characters, but by turning on Overtype mode you can type over existing characters without selecting them first. To turn Overtype mode on and off on your computer, double-click OVR in the status bar.

On some computers you also can turn Overtype mode on and off by pressing [Insert]. When Overtype mode is on, OVR appears in black in the status bar. When Overtype mode is off, OVR is dimmed.

FIGURE B-3: Date selected in the press release

Selected text

Left document margin

Down scroll arrow

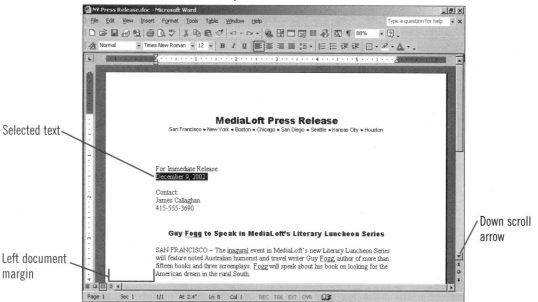

FIGURE B-4: Edited press release

Replacement text

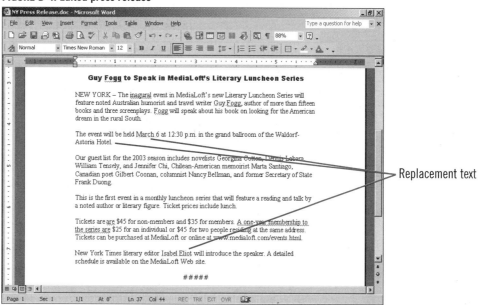

TABLE B-2: Methods for selecting text

to select	use the mouse pointer to
Any amount of text	Drag over the text
A word	Double-click the word
A line of text	Click with the ⤢ pointer to the left of the line
A sentence	Press and hold [Ctrl], then click the sentence
A paragraph	Triple-click the paragraph or double-click with the ⤢ pointer to the left of the paragraph
A large block of text	Click at the beginning of the selection, press and hold [Shift], then click at the end of the selection
Multiple nonconsecutive selections	Select the first selection, then press and hold [Ctrl] as you select each additional selection
An entire document	Triple-click with the ⤢ pointer to the left of any text, click Select All on the Edit menu, or press [Ctrl][A]

Cutting and Pasting Text

Word's editing features allow you to move text from one location to another in a document. The operation of moving text is often called **cut and paste**. When you cut text from a document, you remove it from the document and add it to the **Clipboard**, a temporary storage area for text and graphics that you cut or copy from a document. You cut text by selecting it and using the Cut button or the Cut command on the Edit menu. To insert the text from the Clipboard into the document, you place the insertion point where you want to insert the text, and then use the Paste button or the Paste command on the Edit menu to paste the text at that location. You also can move text by dragging it to a new location using the mouse. Alice reorganizes the information in the press release by moving text using the cut and paste and dragging methods.

1. **Click the Show/Hide ¶ button ¶ on the Standard toolbar**

Formatting marks appear in the document window. **Formatting marks** are special characters that appear on your screen and do not print. Common formatting marks include the paragraph symbol (¶), which shows the end of a paragraph—wherever you press [Enter]; the dot symbol (·), which represents a space—wherever you press [Spacebar]; and the arrow symbol (→), which shows the location of a tab stop—wherever you press [Tab]. Working with formatting marks turned on can help you to select, edit, and format text with precision.

2. **In the third paragraph, select Canadian poet Gilbert Coonan, (including the comma and the space after it), then click the Cut button ✂ on the Standard toolbar**

> **Trouble?**
>
> If the Clipboard task pane opens, close it.

The text is removed from the document and placed on the Clipboard. Word uses two different clipboards: the **system Clipboard** (the Clipboard), which holds just one item, and the **Office Clipboard**, which holds up to 24 items. The last item you cut or copy is always added to both clipboards. You'll learn more about the Office Clipboard in a later lesson.

3. **Place the insertion point before novelists (but after the space) in the first line of the third paragraph, then click the Paste button ▤ on the Standard toolbar**

The text is pasted at the location of the insertion point, as shown in Figure B-5. The Paste Options button ▤ appears below text when you first paste it in a document. You'll learn more about the Paste Options button in the next lesson. For now, you can ignore it.

4. **Press [Ctrl], then click the sentence Ticket prices include lunch. in the fourth paragraph**

The entire sentence is selected.

5. **Press and hold the mouse button over the selected text until the pointer changes to ▧, then drag the pointer's vertical line to the end of the fifth paragraph (between the period and the paragraph mark) as shown in Figure B-6**

> **Trouble?**
>
> If you make a mistake, click the Undo button ↺ on the Standard toolbar, then try again.

The pointer's vertical line indicates the location the text will be inserted when you release the mouse button.

6. **Release the mouse button**

The selected text is moved to the location of the insertion point. It's convenient to move text using the dragging method when the locations of origin and destination are both visible on the screen. Text is not removed to the Clipboard when you move it using the dragging method.

7. **Deselect the text, then click the Save button ▤ on the Standard toolbar**

Your changes to the press release are saved.

FIGURE B-5: Moved text with Paste Options button

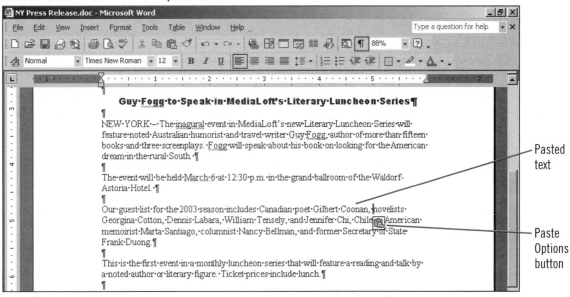

Pasted text

Paste Options button

FIGURE B-6: Text being dragged to a new location

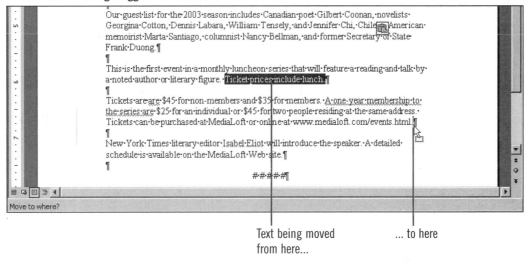

Text being moved from here...

... to here

Using keyboard shortcuts

Instead of using the Cut, Copy, and Paste commands to edit text in Word, you can use the keyboard shortcuts [Ctrl][X] to cut text, [Ctrl][C] to copy text, and [Ctrl][V] to paste text. A shortcut key is a function key, such as [F1], or a combination of keys, such as [Ctrl][S], that you press to perform a command. For example, pressing [Ctrl][S] saves changes to a document just as clicking the Save button or using the Save command on the File menu saves a document. Becoming skilled at using keyboard shortcuts can help you to quickly accomplish many of the tasks you perform frequently in Word. If a keyboard shortcut is available for a menu command, then it is listed next to the command on the menu. To find a more extensive list of shortcut keys, search the Help system using the keyword "shortcuts."

Word 2002

Copying and Pasting Text

Copying and pasting text is similar to cutting and pasting text, except that the text you copy is not removed from the document. Rather, a copy of the text is placed on the Clipboard, leaving the original text in place. You can copy text to the Clipboard by using the Copy command on the Edit menu or the Copy button, or you can copy text by pressing [Ctrl] as you drag the selected text from one location to another. Alice continues to edit the press release by copying text from one location to another.

Trouble?

If the Clipboard task pane opens, close it.

1. In the headline, select **Literary Luncheon**, then click the **Copy button** 📋 on the Standard toolbar

A copy of the text is placed on the Clipboard, leaving the text you copied in place.

2. Place the insertion point before **season** in the third body paragraph, then click the **Paste button** 📋 on the Standard toolbar

"Literary Luncheon" is inserted before "season," as shown in Figure B-7. Notice that the pasted text is formatted differently than the paragraph in which it was inserted.

QuickTip

If you don't like the result of a paste option, try another option or click the Undo button and then paste the text again.

3. Click the **Paste Options button** 📋▾, then click **Match Destination Formatting**

The Paste Options button allows you to change the formatting of pasted text. The formatting of "Literary Luncheon" is changed to match the rest of the paragraph. The options available on the Paste Options menu depend on the format of the text you are pasting and the format of the surrounding text. Table B-3 summarizes the commands used for pasting text.

4. Scroll down if necessary so that the last two paragraphs are visible on your screen

5. In the fifth paragraph, select **www.medialoft.com**, press and hold **[Ctrl]**, then press the mouse button until the pointer changes to 📥

6. Drag the pointer's vertical line to the end of the last paragraph, placing it between **site** and the period, release the mouse button, then release [Ctrl]

The text is copied to the last paragraph. Since the formatting of the text you copied is the same as the formatting of the paragraph in which you inserted it, you can ignore the Paste Options button. Text is not copied to the Clipboard when you copy it using the dragging method.

7. Place the insertion point between **site** and **www.medialoft.com** in the last paragraph, type **at** followed by a space, then click the **Save button** 💾 on the Standard toolbar

Compare your document with Figure B-8.

Using the Undo, Redo, and Repeat commands

Word remembers the editing and formatting changes you make so that you can easily reverse or repeat them. You can reverse the last action you took by clicking the Undo button ↩ on the Standard toolbar, or you can undo a series of actions by clicking the Undo list arrow ↩▾ and selecting the action you want to reverse. When you undo an action using the Undo list arrow, you also undo all the actions above it in the list; that is, all actions that were performed after the action you selected. Similarly, you can keep the changes you just reversed by using the Redo button ↪ and the Redo list arrow ↪▾.

If you want to repeat a change you just made, use the Repeat command on the Edit menu. The name of the Repeat command changes depending on the last action you took. For example, if you just typed "thank you," the name of the command will be Repeat Typing. Clicking the Repeat Typing command will insert "thank you" at the location of the insertion point. You also can repeat the last action you took by pressing [F4].

FIGURE B-7: Text pasted in document

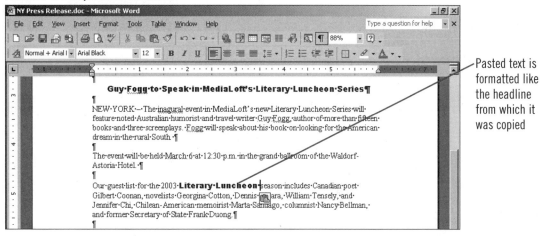

Pasted text is formatted like the headline from which it was copied

FIGURE B-8: Copied text in press release

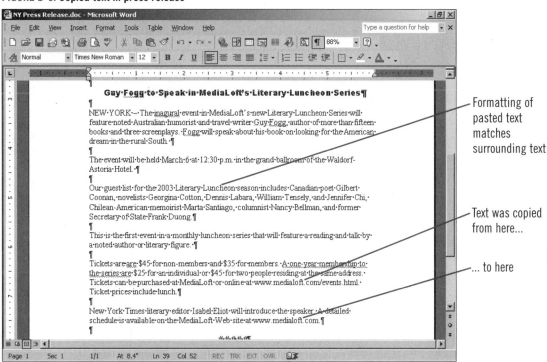

Formatting of pasted text matches surrounding text

Text was copied from here...

... to here

TABLE B-3: Commands used for pasting text

command	use to
Paste command on the Edit menu, Paste button on the Standard toolbar, or [Ctrl][V]	Insert the last item you cut or copied at the location of the insertion point; use the Paste Options button to change the format of the pasted text
Paste Special command on the Edit menu	Insert an item copied or cut from another Office program into a Word document; allows you to embed the object so that you can edit it in its original program; also allows you to create a link to the source file so that changes to the source file are reflected in the Word document
Paste as Hyperlink command on the Edit menu	Paste text so that it is formatted as a hyperlink that jumps to the location from where text was copied; can be used only in conjunction with the Copy command

Using the Office Clipboard

The Office Clipboard allows you to collect text and graphics from files created in any Office Program and insert them into your Word documents. It holds up to 24 items and, unlike the system Clipboard, the items on the Office Clipboard can be viewed. By default, the Office Clipboard opens automatically when you cut or copy two items consecutively. You can also use the Office Clipboard command on the Edit menu to manually display the Office Clipboard if you prefer to work with it open. You add items to the Office Clipboard using the Cut and Copy commands. The last item you collect is always added to both the system Clipboard and the Office Clipboard. ⟡ Alice uses the Office Clipboard to move several sentences in her press release.

Steps

1. In the last paragraph, select the sentence **New York Times literary editor...** (including the space after the period), then click the **Cut button** ✂ on the Standard toolbar
The sentence is cut to the Clipboard.

2. Select the sentence **A detailed schedule is...** (including the ¶ mark), then click ✂
The Office Clipboard opens in the Clipboard task pane, as shown in Figure B-9. It displays the items you cut from the press release. The 📖 icon next to each item indicates the items are from a Word document.

Trouble?

If the Office Clipboard does not open, click Office Clipboard on the Edit menu, click the Undo button on the Standard toolbar two times, click Clear All on the Clipboard task pane, then repeat steps 1 and 2. To restore the default, click Options on the Clipboard task pane, click Show Office Clipboard Automatically to select it, then click outside the menu.

3. Place the insertion point at the end of the second paragraph (before the ¶ mark after Hotel.), then click the **New York Times literary editor...** item on the Office Clipboard
Clicking an item on the Office Clipboard pastes the item in the document at the location of the insertion point. Notice that the item remains on the Office Clipboard even after you pasted it. Items remain on the Office Clipboard until you delete them or close all open Office programs. Also, if you add a 25th item to the Office Clipboard, the first item is deleted.

4. Place the insertion point at the end of the third paragraph (after Duong.), then click the **A detailed schedule is...** item on the Office Clipboard
The sentence is pasted in the document.

QuickTip

To delete an individual item from the Office Clipboard, click the list arrow next to the item, then click Delete.

5. Select the fourth paragraph, which contains the sentence **This is the first event...** (including the ¶ mark), then click ✂
The sentence is cut to the Office Clipboard. Notice that the last item collected displays at the top of the Clipboard task pane. The last item collected is also stored on the system Clipboard.

6. Place the insertion point at the beginning of the third paragraph (before Our...), click the **Paste button** 📋 on the Standard toolbar, then press **[Backspace]**
The "This is the first ..." sentence is pasted at the beginning of the "Our guest list ..." paragraph. You can paste the last item collected using either the Paste command or the Office Clipboard.

7. Place the insertion point at the end of the third paragraph (before the ¶ mark), then press **[Delete]** twice
The ¶ symbols and the blank line between the third and fourth paragraphs are deleted.

QuickTip

Many Word users prefer to work with formatting marks turned on at all times. Experiment for yourself and see which method you prefer.

8. Click the **Show/Hide ¶ button** ¶ on the Standard toolbar
Compare your press release with Figure B-10.

9. Click the **Clear All button** on the Office Clipboard to remove the items from it, close the Clipboard task pane, press **[Ctrl][Home]**, then click the **Save button** 💾
Pressing [Ctrl][Home] moves the insertion point to the top of the document.

FIGURE B-9: Office Clipboard in Clipboard task pane

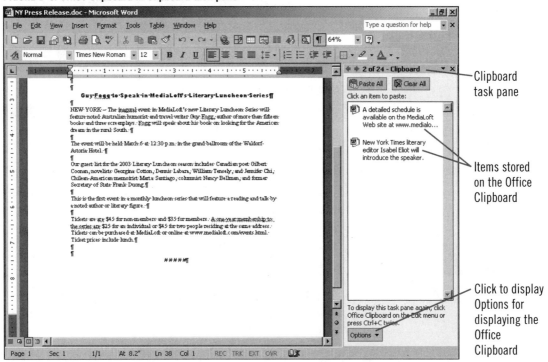

Clipboard task pane

Items stored on the Office Clipboard

Click to display Options for displaying the Office Clipboard

Word 2002

FIGURE B-10: Revised press release

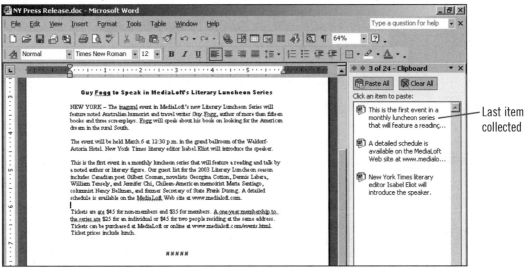

Last item collected

Copying and moving items between documents

The system and Office Clipboards also can be used to copy and move items between Word documents. To copy or cut text from one Word document and paste it into another, first open both documents in the program window. When a document is open in the program window, a Word program button labeled with its filename appears on the taskbar. With multiple documents open, you can copy and move text between documents by copying or cutting the item(s) from one document and then switching to another document and pasting the item(s). To switch between open documents, click the button on the taskbar for the document you want to appear in the document window. The Office Clipboard stores all the items collected from all files, regardless of which document is displayed in the document window. The system Clipboard stores the last item collected from any file.

Word 2002

Using the Spelling and Grammar Checker and the Thesaurus

When you finish typing and revising a document, you can use the Spelling and Grammar command to search the document for misspelled words and grammatical errors. The Spelling and Grammar checker flags possible mistakes, suggests correct spellings, and offers remedies for grammatical errors such as subject-verb agreement, repeated words, and punctuation. Word also includes a Thesaurus, which you can use to look up synonyms for awkward or repetitive words. Alice uses the Spelling and Grammar checker to search her press release for errors. Before beginning the search, she sets the Spelling and Grammar checker to ignore words, such as Fogg, she knows are spelled correctly. She also uses the Thesaurus to find a synonym for "noted."

Trouble?

If Word flags your name or "MediaLoft" as misspelled, right-click those words, then click Ignore All.

QuickTip

To change the language used by Word's proofing tools, click Tools on the menu bar, point to Language, then click Set Language.

Trouble?

You might need to correct other spelling and grammatical errors.

QuickTip

If Word does not offer a valid correction, correct the error yourself.

QuickTip

You also can right-click a word and point to Synonyms on the shortcut menu to see a list of synonyms for a word.

1. **Right-click Fogg in the headline**

   A shortcut menu that includes suggestions for correcting the spelling of "Fogg" opens. You can correct individual spelling and grammar errors by right-clicking text that is underlined with a red or green wavy line and selecting a correction. Although "Fogg" is not in Word's dictionary, it is spelled correctly in the document.

2. **Click Ignore All**

   Clicking Ignore All tells Word not to flag "Fogg" as misspelled.

3. **Press [Ctrl][Home], then click the Spelling and Grammar button 🗹 on the Standard toolbar**

   The Spelling and Grammar: English (U.S.) dialog box opens, as shown in Figure B-11. The dialog box identifies "inagural" as misspelled and suggests possible corrections for the error. The word selected in the Suggestions box is the correct spelling.

4. **Click Change**

   Word replaces the misspelled word with the correctly spelled word. Next, the dialog box indicates "are" is repeated in a sentence.

5. **Click Delete**

   Word deletes the second occurrence of the repeated word. Next, the dialog box flags a subject-verb agreement error and suggests using "is" instead of "are," as shown in Figure B-12. The phrase selected in the Suggestions box is correct.

6. **Click Change**

   The word "is" replaces the word "are" in the sentence and the Spelling and Grammar dialog box closes. Keep in mind that the spelling and grammar feature identifies many common errors, but you cannot rely on it to find and correct all spelling and grammatical errors in your documents. Always proofread your documents carefully.

7. **Click OK to complete the spelling and grammar check, then scroll up until the headline is displayed at the top of your screen**

8. **In the first sentence of the third paragraph, select noted, click Tools on the menu bar, point to Language, then click Thesaurus**

   The Thesaurus: English (U.S.) dialog box opens, as shown in Figure B-13. Possible synonyms for "noted" appear in the dialog box.

9. **Click distinguished in the Replace with Synonym list box, then click Replace**

   The dialog box closes and "distinguished" replaces "noted" in the press release.

10. **Press [Ctrl][Home], then click the Save button 💾 on the Standard toolbar**

FIGURE B-11: Spelling and Grammar: English (U.S.) dialog box

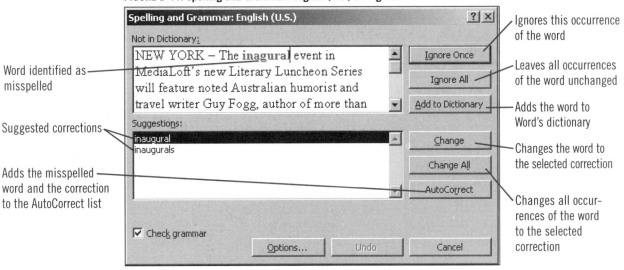

Word identified as misspelled

Suggested corrections

Adds the misspelled word and the correction to the AutoCorrect list

Ignores this occurrence of the word

Leaves all occurrences of the word unchanged

Adds the word to Word's dictionary

Changes the word to the selected correction

Changes all occurrences of the word to the selected correction

FIGURE B-12: Grammar error identified in Spelling and Grammar dialog box

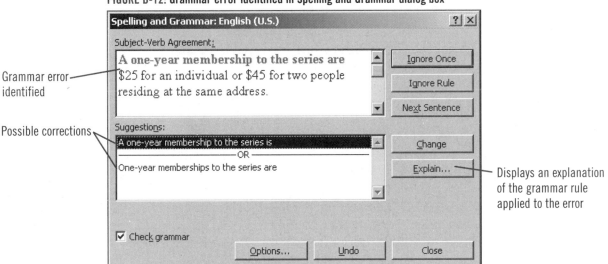

Grammar error identified

Possible corrections

Displays an explanation of the grammar rule applied to the error

FIGURE B-13: Thesaurus: English (U.S.) dialog box

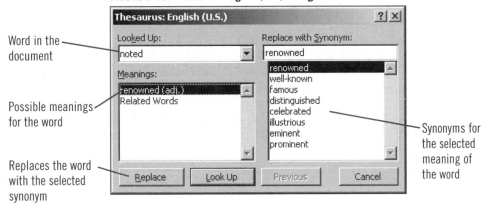

Word in the document

Possible meanings for the word

Replaces the word with the selected synonym

Synonyms for the selected meaning of the word

Finding and Replacing Text

Word's Find and Replace feature allows you to automatically search for and replace all instances of a word or phrase in a document. For example, you might need to substitute "bookstore" for "store," and it would be very time-consuming to manually locate and replace each instance of "store" in a long document. Using the Replace command you can automatically find and replace all occurrences of specific text at once, or you can choose to find and review each occurrence individually. You also can use the Find command to locate and highlight every occurrence of a specific word or phrase in a document. ✐ MediaLoft has decided to change the name of the New York series from "Literary Luncheon Series" to "Literary Limelight Series." Alice uses the Replace command to search the document for all instances of "Luncheon" and replace them with "Limelight."

1. **Click Edit on the menu bar, click Replace, then click More in the Find and Replace dialog box**
   The Find and Replace dialog box opens, as shown in Figure B-14.

2. **Click the Find what text box, then type Luncheon**
   "Luncheon" is the text that will be replaced.

3. **Press [Tab], then type Limelight in the Replace with text box**
   "Limelight" is the text that will replace "Luncheon."

4. **Click the Match case check box in the Search Options section to select it**
   Selecting the Match case check box tells Word to find only exact matches for the uppercase and lowercase characters you entered in the Find what text box. You want to replace all instances of "Luncheon" in the proper name "Literary Luncheon Series." You do not want to replace "luncheon" when it refers to a lunchtime event.

QuickTip

Click Find Next to find, review, and replace each occurrence individually.

5. **Click Replace All**
   Clicking Replace All changes all occurrences of "Luncheon" to "Limelight" in the press release. A message box reports three replacements were made.

6. **Click OK to close the message box, then click Close to close the Find and Replace dialog box**
   Word replaced "Luncheon" with "Limelight" in three locations, but did not replace "luncheon."

7. **Click Edit on the menu bar, then click Find**
   The Find and Replace dialog box opens with the Find tab displayed. The Find command allows you to quickly locate all instances of text in a document. You can use it to verify that Word did not replace "luncheon."

8. **Type luncheon in the Find what text box, click the Highlight all items found in check box to select it, click Find All, then click Close**
   The Find and Replace dialog box closes and "luncheon" is selected in the document.

9. **Deselect the text, click the Save button 🖫 on the Standard toolbar, then click the Print button 🖨 on the Standard toolbar**
   A copy of the finished press release prints. Compare your document to Figure B-15.

10. **Click File on the menu bar, then click Close**

FIGURE B-14: Replace tab in the Find and Replace dialog box

Replace only exact matches of uppercase and lowercase characters

Find only complete words

Use wildcards (*) in a search string

Find words that sound like the Find what text

Find and replace all forms of a word

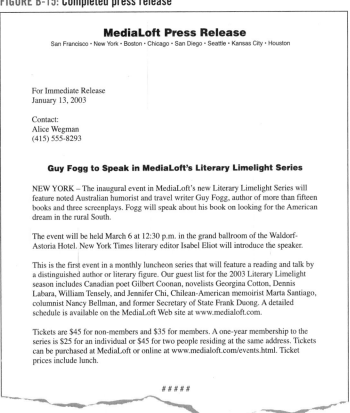

FIGURE B-15: Completed press release

MediaLoft Press Release

San Francisco · New York · Boston · Chicago · San Diego · Seattle · Kansas City · Houston

For Immediate Release
January 13, 2003

Contact:
Alice Wegman
(415) 555-8293

Guy Fogg to Speak in MediaLoft's Literary Limelight Series

NEW YORK – The inaugural event in MediaLoft's new Literary Limelight Series will feature noted Australian humorist and travel writer Guy Fogg, author of more than fifteen books and three screenplays. Fogg will speak about his book on looking for the American dream in the rural South.

The event will be held March 6 at 12:30 p.m. in the grand ballroom of the Waldorf-Astoria Hotel. New York Times literary editor Isabel Eliot will introduce the speaker.

This is the first event in a monthly luncheon series that will feature a reading and talk by a distinguished author or literary figure. Our guest list for the 2003 Literary Limelight season includes Canadian poet Gilbert Coonan, novelists Georgina Cotton, Dennis Labara, William Tensely, and Jennifer Chi, Chilean-American memoirist Marta Santiago, columnist Nancy Bellman, and former Secretary of State Frank Duong. A detailed schedule is available on the MediaLoft Web site at www.medialoft.com.

Tickets are $45 for non-members and $35 for members. A one-year membership to the series is $25 for an individual or $45 for two people residing at the same address. Tickets can be purchased at MediaLoft or online at www.medialoft.com/events.html. Ticket prices include lunch.

\# \# \# \# \#

Inserting text with AutoCorrect

As you type, AutoCorrect automatically corrects many commonly misspelled words. By creating your own AutoCorrect entries, you also can set Word to quickly insert text that you type often, such as your name or contact information, or to correct words you frequently misspell. For example, you could create an AutoCorrect entry so that "Alice Wegman" is automatically inserted whenever you type "aw" followed by a space. To create an AutoCorrect entry, click AutoCorrect Options on the Tools menu. On the AutoCorrect tab in the AutoCorrect dialog box, type the text you want to be automatically corrected in the Replace text box (such as "aw"), type the text you want to be automatically inserted in its place in the With text box (such as "Alice Wegman"), then click Add. The AutoCorrect entry is added to the list. Note that Word inserts an AutoCorrect entry in a document only when you press [Spacebar] after typing the text you want Word to correct. For example, Word will insert "Alice Wegman" when you type "aw" followed by a space, but not when you type "awful."

Using Wizards and Templates

Word includes many templates that you can use to quickly create memos, faxes, letters, reports, brochures, and other professionally designed documents. A **template** is a formatted document that contains placeholder text. To create a document that is based on a template, you replace the placeholder text with your own text and then save the document with a new filename. A **wizard** is an interactive set of dialog boxes that guides you through the process of creating a document. A wizard prompts you to provide information and select formatting options, and then it creates the document for you based on your specifications. You can create a document with a wizard or template using the New command on the File menu. ◢◣ Alice will fax the press release to her list of press contacts, beginning with the *New York Times*. She uses a template to create a fax coversheet for the press release.

1. **Click File on the menu bar, then click New**
   The New Document task pane opens.

2. **Click the General Templates hyperlink in the New Document task pane**
   The Templates dialog box opens. The tabs in the dialog box contain icons for the Word templates and wizards.

3. **Click the Letters & Faxes tab, then click the Professional Fax icon**
   A preview of the Professional Fax template appears in the Templates dialog box, as shown in Figure B-16.

   QuickTip

   Double-clicking an icon in the Templates dialog box also opens a new document based on the template.

4. **Click OK**
   The Professional Fax template opens as a new document in the document window. It contains placeholder text, which you can replace with your own information.

5. **Drag to select Company Name Here, then type MediaLoft**

6. **Click the Click here and type return address and phone and fax numbers placeholder**
   Clicking the placeholder selects it. When a placeholder says Click here… you do not need to drag to select it.

7. **Type MediaLoft San Francisco, press [Enter], then type Tel: (415) 555-8293**
   The text you type replaces the placeholder text.

   QuickTip

   Delete any placeholder text you do not want to replace.

8. **Replace the remaining placeholder text with the text shown in Figure B-17**
   Word automatically inserted the current date in the document. You do not need to replace the current date with the date shown in the figure.

9. **Click File on the menu bar, click Save As, use the Save in list arrow to navigate to the drive or folder where your Project Files are located, type NYT Fax in the File name text box, then click Save**
   The document is saved with the filename NYT Fax.

10. **Click the Print button 🖨 on the Standard toolbar, click File on the menu bar, then click Exit**
    A copy of the fax coversheet prints and the document and Word close.

FIGURE B-16: Letters & Faxes tab in Templates dialog box

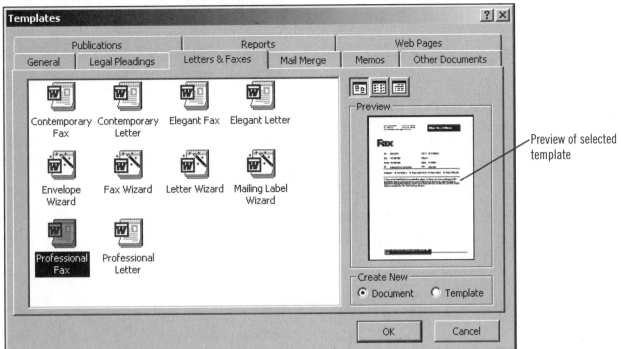

Preview of selected template

FIGURE B-17: Completed fax coversheet document

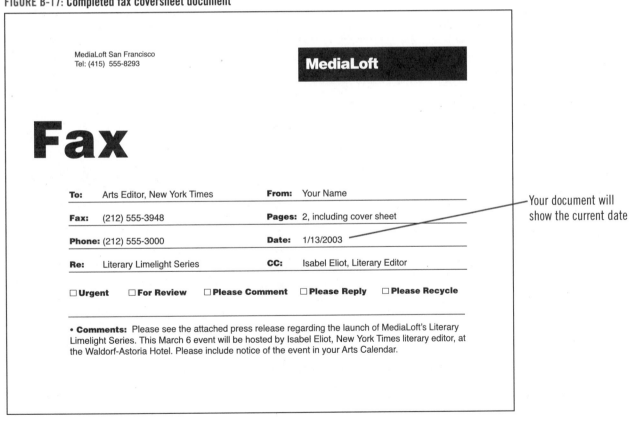

Your document will show the current date

Practice

▶ Concepts Review

Label the elements of the Open dialog box shown in Figure B-18.

FIGURE B-18

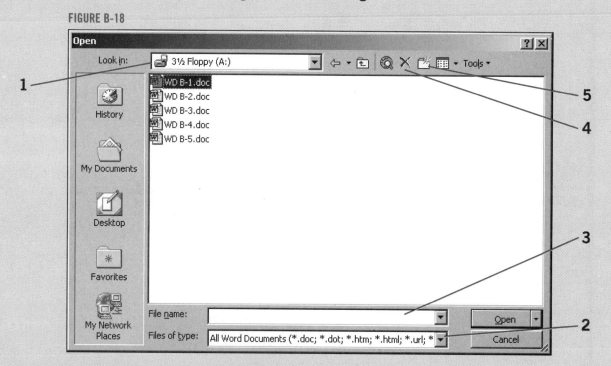

Match each term with the statement that best describes it.

6. System Clipboard
7. Show/Hide
8. Select
9. Thesaurus
10. Undo
11. Template
12. Office Clipboard
13. Paste
14. Replace

a. Feature used to suggest synonyms for words
b. Command used to insert text stored on the Clipboard into a document
c. Command used to reverse the last action you took in a document
d. Temporary storage area for only the last item cut or copied from a document
e. Document that contains placeholder text
f. Temporary storage area for up to 24 items collected from any Office file
g. Command used to locate and replace occurrences of specific text in a document
h. Action that must be taken before text can be cut, copied, or deleted
i. Command used to display formatting marks in a document

Select the best answer from the list of choices.

15. Which of the following is *not* used to open an existing document?
   a. Documents or More documents hyperlink in the New Document task pane
   b. Open command on the Edit menu
   c. Blank document hyperlink in the New Document task pane
   d. Open button on the Standard toolbar

16. To locate and change all instances of a word in a document, which command do you use?
    a. Replace   c. Search
    b. Find   d. Paste

17. Which of the following statements is *not* true?
    a. The last item cut or copied from a document is stored on the system Clipboard.
    b. The Office Clipboard can hold more than one item.
    c. You can view the contents of the Office Clipboard.
    d. When you move text by dragging it, a copy of the text you move is stored on the system Clipboard.

18. Which Word feature corrects errors as you type?
    a. AutoCorrect   c. Spelling and Grammar
    b. Thesaurus   d. Undo and Redo

19. Which command do you use to paste an item created in a different Office program into a Word document so that changes to the source file are reflected in the Word document?
    a. Paste   c. Paste as Hyperlink
    b. Paste Special   d. Office Clipboard

20. What does the symbol ¶ represent when it is displayed in the document window?
    a. Text that is pasted   c. The end of a paragraph
    b. A space   d. A tab stop

 ## Skills Review

1. **Open a document.**
    a. Start Word, click the Open button, then open the file WD B-2 from the drive and folder where your Project Files are located.
    b. Save the document with the filename **CAOS Press Release**.

2. **Select text.**
    a. Select **Today's Date** and replace it with the current date.
    b. Select **Your Name** and **Your Phone Number** and replace them with the relevant information.
    c. Scroll down, then select and replace text in the body of the press release using the following table as a guide:

in paragraph	select	replace with
1	16 and 17	13 and 14
1	fifth	eighth
4	open his renovated Pearl St studio for the first time this year	offer a sneak-preview of his Peace sculpture commissioned by the city of Prague

    d. In the fourth paragraph, delete the sentence **Exhibiting with him will be sculptor Francis Pilo**.
    e. Save your changes to the press release.

3. Cut and paste text.

    a. Display paragraph and other formatting marks in your document if they are not already displayed.

    b. Use the Cut and Paste buttons to switch the order of the two sentences in the fourth paragraph (which begins New group shows…).

    c. Use the drag method to switch the order of the second and third paragraphs.

    d. Adjust the spacing if necessary so that there is one blank line between paragraphs, then save your changes.

4. Copy and paste text.

    a. Use the Copy and Paste buttons to copy **CAOS 2000** from the headline and paste it before the word **map** in the third paragraph.

    b. Change the formatting of the pasted text to match the formatting of the third paragraph, then insert a space between **2000** and **map** if necessary.

    c. Use the drag method to copy **CAOS** from the third paragraph and paste it before the word **group** in the second sentence of the fourth paragraph, then save your changes.

5. Use the Office Clipboard.

    a. Use the Office Clipboard command on the Edit menu to open the Office Clipboard in the task pane.

    b. Scroll so that the first body paragraph is displayed at the top of the document window.

    c. Select the **fifth paragraph** (which begins Studio location maps…) and cut it to the Office Clipboard.

    d. Select the **third paragraph** (which begins Cambridgeport is easily accessible…) and cut it to the Office Clipboard.

    e. Use the Office Clipboard to paste the Studio location maps… item as the new fourth paragraph.

    f. Use the Office Clipboard to paste the Cambridgeport is easily accessible… item as the new fifth paragraph.

    g. Use any method to switch the order of the two sentences in the fourth paragraph (which begins Studio location maps…).

    h. Adjust the spacing if necessary so that there is one blank line between each of the six body paragraphs.

    i. Turn off the display of formatting marks, clear and close the Office Clipboard, then save your changes.

6. Use the Spelling and Grammar checker and the Thesaurus.

    a. Set Word to ignore the spelling of Cambridgeport, if necessary. (*Hint*: Right-click Cambridgeport.)

    b. Move the insertion point to the top of the document, then use the Spelling and Grammar command to search for and correct any spelling and grammatical errors in the press release.

    c. Use the Thesaurus to replace **thriving** in the second paragraph with a different suitable word.

    d. Save your changes to the press release.

7. Find and replace text.

    a. Using the Replace command, replace all instances of **2000** with **2003**.

    b. Replace all instances of the abbreviation **St** with **Street**, taking care to replace whole words only when you perform the replace. (*Hint*: Click More to expand the Find and Replace dialog box.)

    c. Use the Find command to find all instances of **st** in the document, and make sure no errors occurred when you replaced St with Street.

    d. Proofread your press release, correct any errors, save your changes, print a copy, then close the document.

8. Use wizards and templates.

a. Use the New command to open the New Documents task pane.

b. Use the General Templates hyperlink to open the Templates dialog box.

c. Create a new document using the Elegant Fax template.

d. Replace the placeholder text in the document using Figure B-19 as a guide. Delete any placeholders that do not apply to your fax. The date in your fax will be the current date.

e. Scroll to the bottom of the document and replace the placeholder text with your return address.

f. Save the document as **CAOS Fax**, print a copy, close the document, then exit Word.

FIGURE B-19

CAOS 2003

FACSIMILE TRANSMITTAL SHEET

TO:	FROM:
Pat Zabko, Listings Editor	Your Name
COMPANY:	DATE:
Boston Phoenix	9/12/2003
FAX NUMBER:	TOTAL NO. OF PAGES INCLUDING COVER:
(617) 555-2980	2
PHONE NUMBER:	SENDER'S REFERENCE NUMBER:

| RE: | YOUR REFERENCE NUMBER: |
| Cambridgeport Artists Open Studios | |

☐ URGENT   ☐ FOR REVIEW   ☐ PLEASE COMMENT   ☐ PLEASE REPLY   ☐ PLEASE RECYCLE

NOTES/COMMENTS:

A press release regarding the 2003 Cambridgeport Artists Open Studios is included with this fax. Please include this information in the Phoenix Listings.

► Independent Challenge 1

Because of your success in revitalizing a historic theatre in Hobart, Tasmania, you were hired as the director of The Wellington Lyric Theatre in Wellington, New Zealand, to breathe life into its theatre revitalization efforts. After a year on the job, you are launching your first major fund-raising drive. You'll create a fund-raising letter for the Lyric Theatre by modifying a letter you wrote for the theatre in Hobart.

a. Start Word, open the file WD B-3 from the drive and folder where your Project Files are located, then save it as **Lyric Theatre Letter**.

b. Replace the theatre name and address, the date, the inside address, and the salutation with the text shown in Figure B-20.

c. Use the Replace command to replace all instances of **Hobart** with **Wellington**.

d. Use the Replace command to replace all instances of **Tasmanians** with **New Zealanders**.

e. Use the Find command to locate the word **considerable**, then use the Thesaurus to replace the word with a synonym.

f. Create an AutoCorrect entry that inserts **Wellington Lyric Theatre** whenever you type **wlt**.

g. Select each XXXXX and the space that follows it, then type **wlt** followed by a space.

h. Move the fourth body paragraph so that it becomes the second body paragraph.

FIGURE B-20

The Wellington Lyric Theatre
72-74 Hobson Street, Thorndon, Wellington, New Zealand

September 12, 2003

Mr. Colin Fuller
168 Cuba Street
Wellington

Dear Mr. Fuller,

i. Replace Your Name with your name in the signature block.

j. Use the Spelling and Grammar command to check for and correct spelling and grammar errors.

k. Proofread the letter, correct any errors, save your changes, print a copy, close the document, then exit Word.

 # Independent Challenge 2

An advertisement for job openings in Scotland caught your eye and you have decided to apply. The ad, shown in Figure B-21, was printed in last weekend's edition of your local newspaper. You'll use the Letter Wizard to create a cover letter to send with your resume.

a. Read the ad shown in Figure B-21 and decide which position to apply for. Choose the position that most closely matches your qualifications.

b. Start Word and open the Templates dialog box.

c. Double-click Letter Wizard on the Letters & Faxes tab, then select Send one letter in the Office Assistant balloon or Letter Wizard dialog box.

d. In the Letter Wizard—Step 1 of 4 dialog box, choose to include a date on your letter, select Elegant Letter for the page design, select Modified block for the letter style, include a header and footer with the page design, then click Next.

e. In the Letter Wizard—Step 2 of 4 dialog box, enter the recipient's name (Ms. Hillary Price) and the delivery address, referring to the ad for the address information. Also enter the salutation **Dear Ms. Price** using the business style, then click Next.

f. In the Letter Wizard—Step 3 of 4 dialog box, include a reference line in the letter, enter the appropriate position code (see Figure B-21) in the Reference line text box, then click Next.

g. In the Letter Wizard—Step 4 of 4 dialog box, enter your name as the sender, enter your return address (including your country), and select an appropriate complimentary closing. Then, because you will be including your resume with the letter, include one enclosure. Click Finish when you are done.

h. Click Cancel to close the Office Assistant, if necessary. Then save the letter with the filename **Global Dynamics Letter** to the drive and folder where your Project Files are located.

i. Replace the placeholder text in the body of the letter with three paragraphs that address your qualifications for the job:

• In the first paragraph, specify the job you are applying for, indicate where you saw the position advertised, and briefly state your qualifications and interest in the position.

FIGURE B-21

*Global*Dynamics

Career Opportunities in Scotland

Global Dynamics, an established software development firm with offices in North America, Asia, and Europe, is seeking candidates for the following positions in its new Edinburgh facility:

Instructor

Responsible for delivering software training to our expanding European customer base. Duties include delivering hands-on training, keeping up-to-date with product development, and working with the Director of Training to ensure the high quality of course materials. Successful candidate will have excellent presentation skills and be proficient in Microsoft PowerPoint and Microsoft Word. **Position B12C6**

Administrative Assistant

Proficiency with Microsoft Word a must! Administrative office duties include making travel arrangements, scheduling meetings, taking notes and publishing meeting minutes, handling correspondence, and ordering office supplies. Must have superb multi-tasking abilities, excellent communication, organizational, and interpersonal skills, and be comfortable working with e-mail and the Internet. **Position B16F5**

Copywriter

The ideal candidate will have marketing or advertising writing experience in a high tech environment, including collateral, newsletters, and direct mail. Experience writing for the Web, broadcast, and multimedia is a plus. Fluency with Microsoft Word required. **Position C13D4**

Positions offer salary, excellent benefits, moving expenses, and career growth opportunities.

Send resume and cover letter referencing position code to:

**Hillary Price
Director of Recruiting
Global Dynamics
24 Castle Terrace
Edinburgh EH3 9SH
United Kingdom**

Word 2002

- In the second paragraph, describe your work experience and skills. Be sure to relate your experience and qualifications to the position requirements listed in the ad.
- In the third paragraph, politely request an interview for the position and provide your phone number and e-mail address.

j. When you are finished typing the letter, check it for spelling and grammar errors and correct any mistakes.

k. Save your changes to the letter, print a copy, close the document, then exit Word.

▶ Independent Challenge 3

As administrative director of continuing education, you drafted a memo to instructors asking them to help you finalize the course schedule for next semester. Today you'll examine the draft and make revisions before printing it.

a. Start Word and open the file WD B-4 from the drive and folder where your Project Files are located.

b. Open the Save As dialog box, navigate to the drive and folder where your Project Files are located, use the Create New Folder button to create a new folder called **Memos**, then save the document as **Computer Memo** in the Memos folder.

c. Replace Your Name with your name in the From line.

d. Use the Cut and Paste buttons to move the sentence **If you are planning to teach** ... from the first body paragraph to become the first sentence in the last paragraph of the memo.

e. Use the [Delete] key to merge the first two paragraphs into one paragraph.

f. Use the Office Clipboard to reorganize the list of twelve-week courses so that the courses are listed in alphabetical order. (*Hint*: Use the Zoom list arrow to enlarge the document as needed.)

g. Use the dragging method to reorganize the list of one-day seminars so that the seminars are listed in alphabetical order.

h. Use the Spelling and Grammar command to check for and correct spelling and grammar errors.

i. Clear and close the Office Clipboard, save your changes, print a copy, close the document, then exit Word.

℮ Independent Challenge 4

Reference sources—dictionaries, thesauri, style and grammar guides, and guides to business etiquette and procedure—are essential for day-to-day use in the workplace. Much of this reference information is available on the World Wide Web. In this independent challenge, you will locate reference sources on the Web and use some of them to look up definitions, synonyms, and antonyms for words. Your goal is to familiarize yourself with online reference sources so you can use them later in your work.

a. Start Word, open the file WD B-5 from the drive and folder where your Project Files are located, and save it as **Web References**. This document contains the questions you will answer about the Web reference sources you find. You will type your answers to the questions in the document.

b. Replace the placeholder text at the top of the Web References document with your name and the date.

c. Use your favorite search engine to search the Web for grammar and style guides, dictionaries, and thesauri. Use the keywords **grammar**, **usage**, **dictionary**, **glossary**, and **thesaurus** to conduct your search. If your search does not result in links to appropriate reference sources, try the following Web sites: www.bartleby.com, www.dictionary.com, or www.thesaurus.com.

d. Complete the Web References document, then proofread it and correct any mistakes.

e. Save the document, print a copy, close the document, then exit Word.

► **Visual Workshop**

Using the Contemporary Letter template, create the letter shown in Figure B-22. Save the document as **Visa Letter**. Check the letter for spelling and grammar errors, then print a copy.

FIGURE B-22

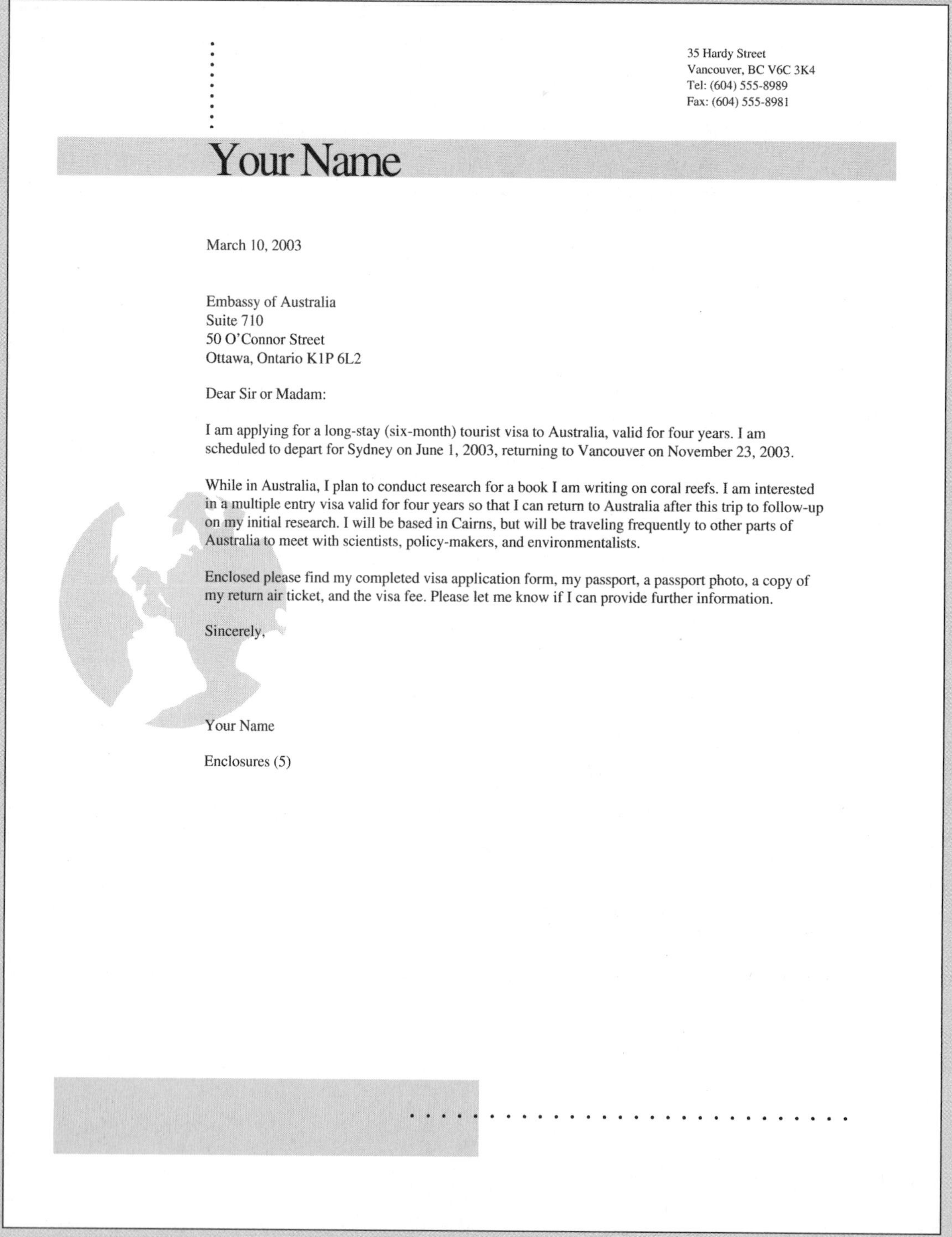

35 Hardy Street
Vancouver, BC V6C 3K4
Tel: (604) 555-8989
Fax: (604) 555-8981

Your Name

March 10, 2003

Embassy of Australia
Suite 710
50 O'Connor Street
Ottawa, Ontario K1P 6L2

Dear Sir or Madam:

I am applying for a long-stay (six-month) tourist visa to Australia, valid for four years. I am scheduled to depart for Sydney on June 1, 2003, returning to Vancouver on November 23, 2003.

While in Australia, I plan to conduct research for a book I am writing on coral reefs. I am interested in a multiple entry visa valid for four years so that I can return to Australia after this trip to follow-up on my initial research. I will be based in Cairns, but will be traveling frequently to other parts of Australia to meet with scientists, policy-makers, and environmentalists.

Enclosed please find my completed visa application form, my passport, a passport photo, a copy of my return air ticket, and the visa fee. Please let me know if I can provide further information.

Sincerely,

Your Name

Enclosures (5)

Formatting

Text and Paragraphs

Objectives

- MOUS ▶ **Format with fonts**
- MOUS ▶ **Change font styles and effects**
- MOUS ▶ **Change line and paragraph spacing**
- MOUS ▶ **Align paragraphs**
- MOUS ▶ **Work with tabs**
- MOUS ▶ **Work with indents**
- MOUS ▶ **Add bullets and numbering**
- MOUS ▶ **Add borders and shading**

Formatting can enhance the appearance of a document, create visual impact, and help illustrate a document's structure. The formatting of a document can also add personality and lend a degree of professionalism to your document. In this unit you learn how to format text using different fonts and font-formatting options. You also learn how to change the alignment, indentation, and spacing of paragraphs, and how to spruce up documents with borders, shading, bullets, and other paragraph-formatting effects. ✐ Isaac Robinson is the marketing director at the MediaLoft Chicago store. Isaac has drafted a quarterly marketing report to send to MediaLoft's headquarters. He now needs to format the report so it is attractive and highlights the significant information. You will work with Isaac as he formats the report.

Formatting with Fonts

Formatting text with different fonts is a quick and powerful way to enhance the appearance of a document. A **font** is a complete set of characters with the same typeface or design. Arial, Times New Roman, Comic Sans, Courier, and Tahoma are some of the more common fonts, but there are hundreds of others, each with a specific design and feel. Another way to alter the impact of text is to increase or decrease its **font size**, which is measured in points. A **point** is ½₂ of an inch. When formatting a document with fonts, it's important to pick fonts that augment the document's purpose. You can apply fonts and font sizes to text by selecting the text and using the Formatting toolbar. ➤ Isaac changes the font and font size of the title and headings in his report, selecting a font that enhances the business tone of the document. By formatting the title and headings in a font different from the body text, he helps to visually structure the report for readers.

Steps

1. Start **Word**, open the file **WD C-1** from the drive and folder where your Project Files are located, then save it as **Chicago Marketing Report**
   The file opens in Print Layout view.

2. Click the **Normal View button** on the horizontal scroll bar, click the **Zoom list arrow** on the Standard toolbar, then click **100%** if necessary
   The document switches to Normal view, a view useful for simple text formatting. The name of the font used in the document, Times New Roman, is displayed in the Font list box on the Formatting toolbar. The font size, 12, appears next to it in the Font Size list box.

3. Select the title **MediaLoft Chicago Quarterly Marketing Report**, then click the **Font list arrow** on the Formatting toolbar
   The Font list showing the fonts available on your computer opens, as shown in Figure C-1. Fonts you have used recently appear above the double line. All the fonts on your computer are listed in alphabetical order below the double line.

4. Click **Arial**
   The font of the report title changes to Arial.

5. Click the **Font Size list arrow** on the Formatting toolbar, then click **20**
   The font size of the title increases to 20 points.

6. Click the **Font Color list arrow** on the Formatting toolbar
   A palette of colors opens.

7. Click **Dark Blue** on the Font Color palette as shown in Figure C-2, then deselect the text
   The color of the report title text changes to dark blue. The active color on the Font Color button also changes to dark blue.

8. Select the heading **Advertising**, click the **Font list arrow**, click **Arial**, click the **Font Size list arrow**, click **14**, click the **Font Color button**, then deselect the text
   The heading is formatted in 14-point Arial with a dark blue color.

9. Scroll down the document and format each of the following headings in 14-point Arial with a dark blue color: **Events**, **Classes & Workshops**, **Publications**, and **Surveys**

10. Press **[Ctrl][Home]**, then click the **Save button** on the Standard toolbar
    Pressing [Ctrl][Home] moves the insertion point to the beginning of the document. Compare your document to Figure C-3.

FIGURE C-1: Font list

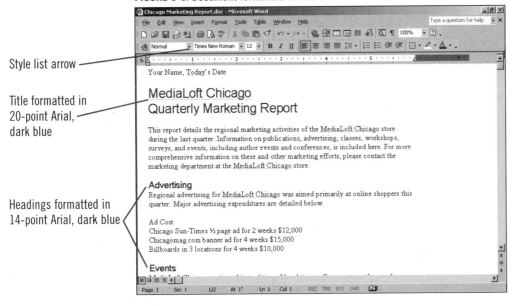

Font list arrow

Font Size list arrow

Font names are formatted in the font itself (your list might differ)

FIGURE C-2: Font Color palette

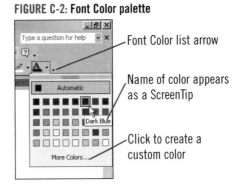

Font Color list arrow

Name of color appears as a ScreenTip

Click to create a custom color

FIGURE C-3: Document formatted with fonts

Style list arrow

Title formatted in 20-point Arial, dark blue

Headings formatted in 14-point Arial, dark blue

Clearing text formatting

If you are unhappy with the way text is formatted, you can use the Clear Formats command to return the text to the default format settings. By default, text is formatted in 12-point Times New Roman and paragraphs are left-aligned and single-spaced. To clear formatting from text, select the text you want to clear, point to Clear on the Edit menu, then click Formats. Alternately, click the Styles list arrow on the Formatting toolbar, then click Clear Formatting. Clearing formatting from text does not delete or change the text itself; it simply formats the text with the default format settings.

Changing Font Styles and Effects

You can dramatically change the appearance of text by applying different font styles, font effects, and character-spacing effects. For example, you can use the buttons on the Formatting toolbar to make text darker by applying **bold**, or to slant text by applying *italic*. You can also use the Font command on the Format menu to apply font effects and character-spacing effects to text. ✎ Isaac spices up the appearance of the text in his document by applying different font styles and effects.

Steps 1234

QuickTip

Click the Underline button U on the Formatting toolbar to underline text.

1. Select **MediaLoft Chicago Quarterly Marketing Report**, then click the **Bold button** B on the Formatting toolbar
   Applying bold makes the characters darker and thicker.

2. Select the **paragraph** under the title, then click the **Italic button** I on the Formatting toolbar
   The paragraph is formatted in italic.

QuickTip

To quickly apply bold to multiple headings, press and hold [Ctrl] as you select each heading, then click B.

3. Scroll down and apply bold to each dark blue heading
   The headings all have a darker, thicker appearance.

4. Scroll up until the subheading Author Events is at the top of your screen, select **Author Events**, click **Format** on the menu bar, then click **Font**
   The Font dialog box opens, as shown in Figure C-4. You can use the Font tab to change the font, font style, size, and color of text, and to add an underline and apply font effects to the selected text.

5. Scroll up the Font list, click **Arial**, click **Bold Italic** in the Font style list box, select the **Small caps check box**, then click **OK**
   The subheading is formatted in Arial, bold, italic, and small caps. When you change text to small caps, the lowercase letters are changed to uppercase letters in a smaller font size.

QuickTip

If you apply formats one by one, then pressing [F4] repeats only the last format you applied.

6. Select **Travel Writers & Photographers Conference**, then press **[F4]**
   Pressing [F4] repeats the last action you took. Because you last applied Arial, bold, italic, and small caps together in one action (using the Font dialog box), the subheading is formatted in Arial, bold, italic, and small caps.

7. Under Author Events, select the book title **Just H20 Please: Tales of True Adventure on the Environmental Frontline**, click I, select **2** in the book title, click **Format** on the menu bar, click **Font**, click the **Subscript check box**, click **OK**, then deselect the text
   As shown in Figure C-5, the book title is formatted in italic and the character 2 is subscript.

QuickTip

To animate the selected text, click the Text Effects tab in the Font dialog box, then select an animation style. The animation appears only when a document is viewed in Word; animation effects do not print.

8. Press **[Ctrl][Home]**, select the **report title**, click **Format** on the menu bar, click **Font**, then click the **Character Spacing tab** in the Font dialog box
   You use the Character Spacing tab to change the scale, or width, of the selected characters, to alter the spacing between characters, or to raise or lower the position of the characters.

9. Click the **Scale list arrow**, click **150%**, click **OK**, deselect the text, then click the **Save button** 🖫 on the Standard toolbar
   Increasing the scale of the characters makes them wider and gives the text a shorter, squat appearance, as shown in Figure C-6.

FIGURE C-4: Font tab in Font dialog box

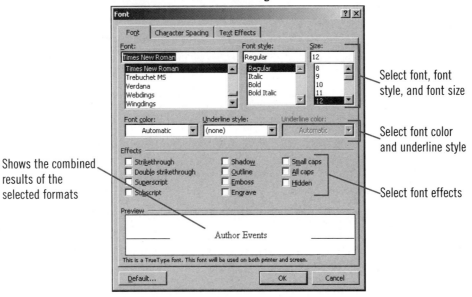

Shows the combined results of the selected formats

Select font, font style, and font size

Select font color and underline style

Select font effects

FIGURE C-5: Font effects applied to text

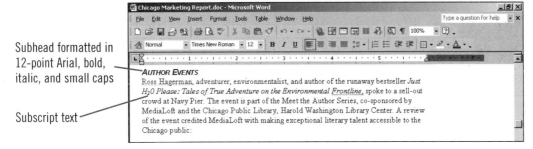

Subhead formatted in 12-point Arial, bold, italic, and small caps

Subscript text

FIGURE C-6: Character-spacing effects applied to text

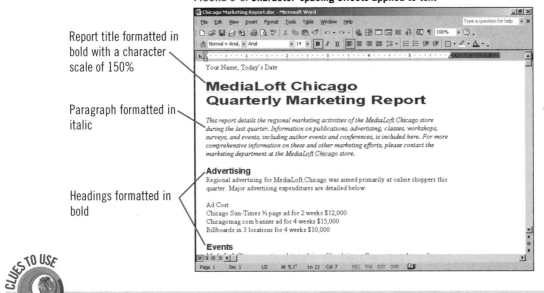

Report title formatted in bold with a character scale of 150%

Paragraph formatted in italic

Headings formatted in bold

Word 2002

Changing the case of letters

The Change Case command on the Format menu allows you to quickly change letters from uppercase to lowercase—and vice versa—saving you the time it takes to retype text you want to change. To change the case of selected text, use the Change Case command to open the Change Case dialog box, then select the case style you want to use. Sentence case capitalizes the first letter of a sentence, title case capitalizes the first letter of each word, and toggle case switches all letters to the opposite case.

Changing Line and Paragraph Spacing

Increasing the amount of space between lines adds more white space to a document and can make it easier to read. Adding space between paragraphs can also open up a document and improve its appearance. You can change line and paragraph spacing using the Paragraph command on the Format menu. You can also use the Line Spacing button to quickly change line spacing. Isaac increases the line spacing of several paragraphs and adds extra space under each heading to give the report a more open feel.

Steps

QuickTip

The checkmark on the Line Spacing list indicates the current line spacing.

1. Place the insertion point in the italicized paragraph under the report title, then click the **Line Spacing list arrow** on the Formatting toolbar
   The Line Spacing list opens. This list includes options for increasing the space between lines.

2. Click **1.5**
   The space between the lines in the paragraph increases to 1.5 lines. Notice that you do not need to select an entire paragraph to change its paragraph formatting; simply place the insertion point in the paragraph you want to format.

QuickTip

Word recognizes any string of text that ends with a paragraph mark as a paragraph, including titles, headings, and single lines in a list.

3. Scroll down until the heading Advertising is at the top of your screen, select the **four-line list** that begins with Ad Cost, click, then click **1.5**
   The line spacing between the selected paragraphs changes to 1.5. To change the paragraph-formatting features of more than one paragraph, you must select the paragraphs.

4. Place the insertion point in the heading **Advertising**, click **Format** on the menu bar, then click **Paragraph**
   The Paragraph dialog box opens, as shown in Figure C-7. You can use the Indents and Spacing tab to change line spacing and the spacing above and below paragraphs. Spacing between paragraphs is measured in points.

QuickTip

Adjusting the space between paragraphs is a more precise way to add white space to a document than inserting blank lines.

5. Click the **After up arrow** in the Spacing section so that 6 pt appears, then click **OK**
   Six points of space are added below the paragraph—the Advertising heading.

6. Select **Advertising**, then click the **Format Painter button** on the Standard toolbar
   The pointer changes to. The **Format Painter** is a powerful Word feature that allows you to copy all the format settings applied to the selected text to other text that you want to format the same way. The Format Painter is especially useful when you want to copy multiple format settings, but you can also use it to copy individual formats.

QuickTip

Using the Format Painter is not the same as using [F4]. Pressing [F4] repeats only the last action you took. You can use the Format Painter at any time to copy multiple format settings.

7. Select **Events** with the pointer, then deselect the text
   Six points of space are added below the Events heading paragraph and the pointer changes back to the I-beam pointer. Compare your document with Figure C-8.

8. Select **Events**, then double-click
   Double-clicking the Format Painter button allows the Format Painter to remain active until you turn it off. By keeping the Format Painter turned on you can apply formatting to multiple items.

9. Scroll down, select the headings **Classes & Workshops**, **Publications**, and **Surveys** with the pointer, then click to turn off the Format Painter
   Six points of space are added below each heading paragraph.

10. Press **[Ctrl][Home]**, then click the **Save button** on the Standard toolbar

FIGURE C-7: Indents and Spacing tab in Paragraph dialog box

Change the spacing above and below paragraphs

Change the line spacing

Spacing After up arrow

Preview of selected settings

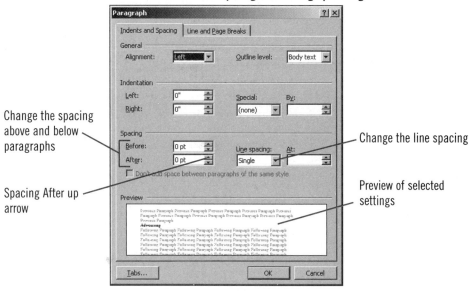

FIGURE C-8: Line and paragraph spacing applied to document

Format Painter button

Line Spacing list arrow

6 points of space added below paragraphs

Line spacing is 1.5

Line spacing is 1

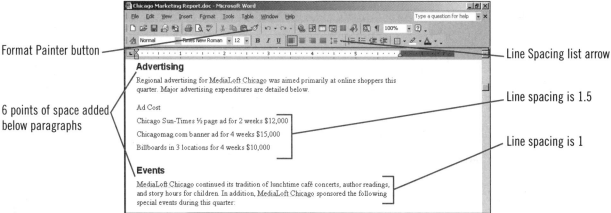

CLUES TO USE

Formatting with styles

You can also apply multiple format settings to text in one step by applying a style. A **style** is a set of formats, such as font, font size, and paragraph alignment, that are named and stored together. To work with styles, click the Styles and Formatting button ![icon] on the Formatting toolbar to open the Styles and Formatting task pane, shown in Figure C-9. The task pane displays the list of available styles and the formats you have created for the current document, if any. To view all the styles available in Word, click the Show list arrow at the bottom of the task pane, then click All Styles.

A **character style**, indicated by a ⓐ character in the list of styles, includes character format settings, such as font and font size. A **paragraph style**, indicated by a ¶ character in the list, is a combination of character and paragraph formats, such as font, font size, paragraph alignment, and paragraph spacing. To apply a style, select the text or paragraph you want to format, then click the style name in the Pick formatting to apply list box.

FIGURE C-9: **Styles and Formatting task pane**

Word 2002

Aligning Paragraphs

Changing paragraph alignment is another way to enhance a document's appearance. Paragraphs are aligned relative to the left and right margins in a document. By default, text is **left-aligned**, which means it is flush with the left margin and has a ragged right edge. Using the alignment buttons on the Formatting toolbar, you can **right-align** a paragraph—make it flush with the right margin—or **center** a paragraph so that it is positioned evenly between the left and right margins. You can also **justify** a paragraph so that both the left and right edges of the paragraph are flush with the left and right margins. Isaac changes the alignment of several paragraphs at the beginning of the report to make it visually more interesting.

Steps

1. Replace **Your Name, Today's Date** with your name, a comma, and the date

2. Select your name and the date, then click the **Align Right button** 📄 on the Formatting toolbar
   The text is aligned with the right margin. In Normal view, the junction of the white and shaded sections of the horizontal ruler indicates the location of the right margin. The left end of the ruler indicates the left margin.

3. Place the insertion point between your name and the comma, press **[Delete]** to delete the comma, then press **[Enter]**
   The new paragraph containing the date is also right-aligned. Pressing [Enter] in the middle of a paragraph creates a new paragraph with the same text and paragraph formatting as the original paragraph.

4. Select the **report title**, then click the **Center button** 📄 on the Formatting toolbar
   The two paragraphs that make up the title are centered between the left and right margins.

QuickTip

Click the Align Left button 📄 on the Formatting toolbar to left-align a paragraph.

5. Place the insertion point in the **Advertising** heading, then click 📄
   The Advertising heading is centered.

6. Place the insertion point in the italicized paragraph under the report title, then click the **Justify button** 📄
   The paragraph is aligned with both the left and right margins, as shown in Figure C-10. When you justify a paragraph, Word adjusts the spacing between words so that each line in the paragraph is flush with the left and the right margins.

7. Place the insertion point in **MediaLoft** in the report title, click **Format** on the menu bar, then click **Reveal Formatting**
   The Reveal Formatting task pane opens in the Word program window, as shown in Figure C-11. The task pane shows the formatting applied to the text and paragraph where the insertion point is located. You can use the Reveal Formatting task pane to check or change the formatting of any character, word, paragraph, or other aspect of a document.

8. Select **Advertising**, then click the **Alignment** hyperlink in the Reveal Formatting task pane
   The Paragraph dialog box opens with the Indents and Spacing tab displayed. It shows the settings for the selected text.

9. Click the **Alignment list arrow**, click **Left**, click **OK**, then deselect the text
   The Advertising heading is left-aligned.

10. Close the Reveal Formatting task pane, then click the **Save button** 📄 on the Standard toolbar

FIGURE C-10: Modified paragraph alignment

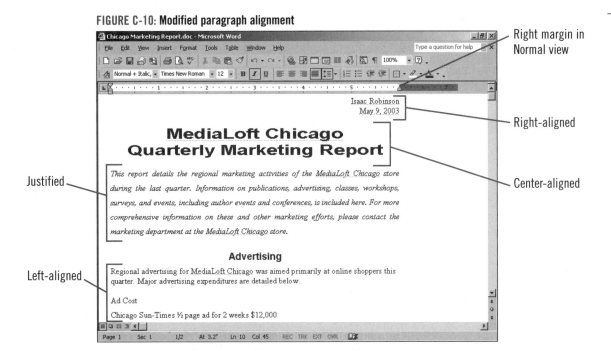

Right margin in Normal view

Right-aligned

Center-aligned

Justified

Left-aligned

FIGURE C-11: Reveal Formatting task pane

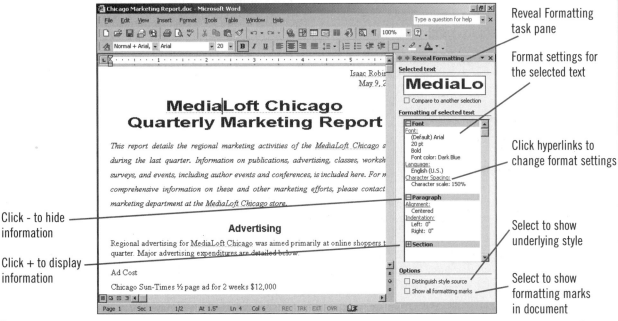

Reveal Formatting task pane

Format settings for the selected text

Click hyperlinks to change format settings

Click - to hide information

Click + to display information

Select to show underlying style

Select to show formatting marks in document

Working with Click and Type

Word's Click and Type feature allows you to automatically apply the paragraph formatting necessary to insert text (or graphics or tables) in a blank area of a document in Print Layout or Web Layout view. As you move the pointer around in a blank area of a document, the pointer changes depending on its location. Double-clicking with a click and type pointer in a blank area of a document automatically applies the appropriate alignment and indentation for that location, so that when you begin typing, the text is already formatted.

The pointer shape indicates which formatting will be applied at each location when you double-click. For example, if you click with the ⫤ pointer, the text you type will be center-aligned. Clicking with I⫶ creates a left tab stop at the location of the insertion point so that the text you type is left-aligned at the tab stop. Clicking with ⫶I right-aligns the text you type. The I≣ pointer creates left-aligned text with a first line indent. The best way to learn how to use Click and Type is to experiment in a blank document.

Unit C

Word 2002

Working with Tabs

Tabs allow you to align text vertically at a specific location in a document. A **tab stop** is a point on the horizontal ruler that indicates the location at which to align text. By default, tab stops are located every ½" from the left margin, but you can also set custom tab stops. Using tabs, you can align text to the left, right, or center of a tab stop, or you can align text at a decimal point or bar character. You set tabs using the horizontal ruler or the Tabs command on the Format menu. ✏ Isaac uses tabs to format the information on advertising expenditures so it is easy to read.

1. Scroll down until the heading Advertising is at the top of your screen, then select the **four-line list** beginning with Ad Cost

   Before you set tab stops for existing text, you must select the paragraphs for which you want to set tabs.

2. Point to the **tab indicator** [L] at the left end of the horizontal ruler

   The icon that appears in the tab indicator indicates the active type of tab; pointing to the tab indicator displays a ScreenTip with the name of the active tab type. By default, left tab is the active tab type. Clicking the tab indicator scrolls through the types of tabs.

3. Click the **tab indicator** to see each of the available tab types, make **left tab** [L] the active tab type, then click the **1" mark** on the horizontal ruler

   A left tab stop is inserted at the 1" mark on the horizontal ruler. Clicking the horizontal ruler inserts a tab stop of the active type for the selected paragraph or paragraphs.

4. Click the **tab indicator** twice so the **Right Tab icon** [▪] is active, then click the **4½" mark** on the horizontal ruler

   A right tab stop is inserted at the 4½" mark on the horizontal ruler, as shown in Figure C-12.

5. Place the insertion point before **Ad** in the first line in the list, press **[Tab]**, place the insertion point before **Cost**, then press **[Tab]**

   Inserting a tab before Ad left-aligns the text at the 1" mark. Inserting a tab before Cost right-aligns Cost at the 4½" mark.

6. Insert a tab at the beginning of each remaining line in the list, then insert a tab before each **$** in the list.

   The paragraphs left-align at the 1" mark. The prices right-align at the 4½" mark.

7. Select the four lines of tabbed text, drag the right tab stop to the **5" mark** on the horizontal ruler, then deselect the text

   Dragging the tab stop moves it to a new location. The prices right-align at the 5" mark.

8. Select the last three lines of tabbed text, click **Format** on the menu bar, then click **Tabs**

   The Tabs dialog box opens, as shown in Figure C-13. You can use the Tabs dialog box to set tab stops, change the position or alignment of existing tab stops, clear tab stops, and apply tab leaders to tabs. **Tab leaders** are lines that appear in front of tabbed text.

9. Click **5"** in the Tab stop position list box, click the **2 option button** in the Leader section, click **OK**, deselect the text, then click the **Save button** [💾] on the Standard toolbar

   A dotted tab leader is added before each 5" tab stop, as shown in Figure C-14.

FIGURE C-12: Left and right tab stops on the horizontal ruler

Right Tab icon in tab indicator

Left tab stop

Right tab stop

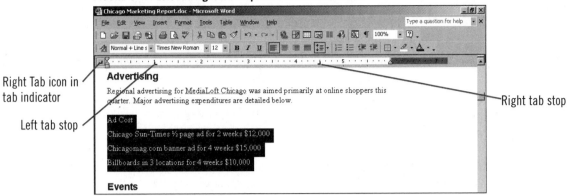

FIGURE C-13: Tabs dialog box

Select the tab stop you want to modify

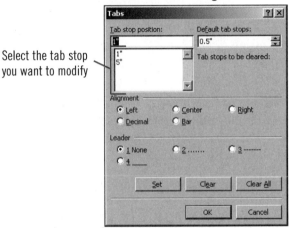

FIGURE C-14: Tab leaders

Tabbed text left-aligned with left tab stop

Tabbed text right-aligned with right tab

Tab leader

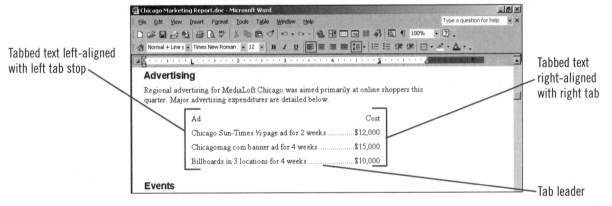

Creating a table

In addition to using tabs to organize text in rows and columns, you can create a table and then enter the text in rows and columns. To create a simple table, place the insertion point where you want to insert the table, click the Insert Table button 🔲 on the Standard toolbar, then, on the grid that appears, drag to select the number of columns and rows you want for the table. When you release the mouse button, an empty table is inserted in the document. To enter or edit text in the table, place the insertion point in a table cell, then type. To move the insertion point from cell to cell, press [Tab] or click in a cell. To format text in a table, select the text, then use the buttons on the Formatting toolbar. The Table menu also includes commands for modifying and formatting tables.

Word 2002

Working with Indents

When you **indent** a paragraph, you move its edge in from the left or right margin. You can indent the entire left or right edge of a paragraph or just the first line. The **indent markers** on the horizontal ruler indicate the indent settings for the paragraph in which the insertion point is located. Dragging the indent markers to a new location on the ruler is one way to change the indentation of a paragraph; using the indent buttons on the Formatting toolbar is another. You can also use the Paragraph command on the Format menu to indent paragraphs. Table C-1 describes different types of indents and the methods for creating each. ⟍ Isaac indents several paragraphs in the report.

1. Press **[Ctrl][Home]**, click the **Print Layout View button** 🔲 on the horizontal scroll bar, click the **Zoom list arrow** on the Standard toolbar, then click **Page Width**
   The document is displayed in Print Layout view, making it easier to see the document margins.

QuickTip

Press [Tab] at the beginning of a paragraph to indent the first line ½". You can also set a custom indent using the Indents and Spacing tab in the Paragraph dialog box.

2. Place the insertion point in the italicized paragraph under the title, then click the **Increase Indent button** 📰 on the Formatting toolbar
   The entire paragraph is indented ½" from the left margin, as shown in Figure C-15. The indent marker ⧗ also moves to the ½" mark on the horizontal ruler. Each time you click the Increase Indent button, the left edge of a paragraph moves another ½" to the right.

3. Click the **Decrease Indent button** 📰 on the Formatting toolbar
   The left edge of the paragraph moves ½" to the left, and the indent marker moves back to the left margin.

Trouble?

Take care to drag only the First Line Indent marker. If you make a mistake, click the Undo button ↺, then try again.

4. Drag the **First Line Indent marker** ▽ to the ¼" mark on the horizontal ruler as shown in Figure C-16
   The first line of the paragraph is indented ¼". Dragging the first line indent marker indents only the first line of a paragraph.

5. Scroll to the bottom of page 1, place the insertion point in the **quote** (the last paragraph), then drag the **Left Indent marker** ⬜ to the ½" mark on the horizontal ruler
   When you drag the Left Indent marker, the First Line and Hanging Indent markers move as well. The left edge of the paragraph is indented ½" from the left margin.

6. Drag the **Right Indent marker** △ to the 5½" mark on the horizontal ruler
   The right edge of the paragraph is indented ½" from the right margin, as shown in Figure C-17.

7. Click the **Save button** 🔲 on the Standard toolbar

TABLE C-1: Types of indents

indent type	description	to create
Left indent	The left edge of a paragraph is moved in from the left margin	Drag the Left Indent marker ⬜ right to the position where you want the left edge of the paragraph to align, or click the Increase Indent button 📰 to indent the paragraph in ½" increments
Right indent	The right edge of a paragraph is moved in from the right margin	Drag the Right Indent marker △ left to the position where you want right edge of the paragraph to end
First-line indent	The first line of a paragraph is indented more than the subsequent lines	Drag the First Line Indent marker ▽ right to the position where you want the first line of the paragraph to start
Hanging indent	The subsequent lines of a paragraph are indented more than the first line	Drag the Hanging Indent marker ⬆ right to the position where you want the hanging indent to start
Negative indent (or Outdent)	The left edge of a paragraph is moved to the left of the left margin	Drag the Left Indent marker ⬜ left to the position where you want the negative indent to start

FIGURE C-15: Indented paragraph

First Line
Indent marker

Hanging Indent
marker

Left Indent
marker

Indented
paragraph

Decrease Indent
button

Increase Indent
button

Right Indent
marker

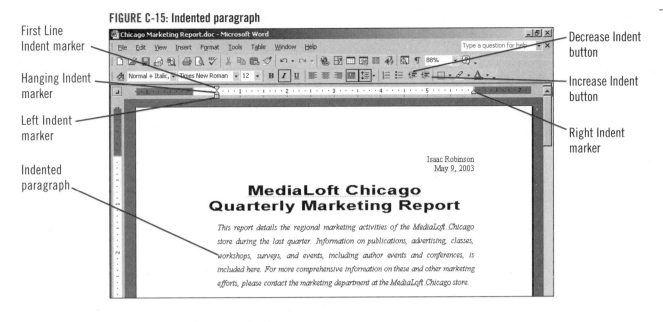

FIGURE C-16: First Line Indent marker being dragged

First Line
Indent marker
being dragged
to the ¼" mark

FIGURE C-17: Paragraph indented from the left and right

Paragraph
indented ½"
from left

Paragraph indented
½" from right

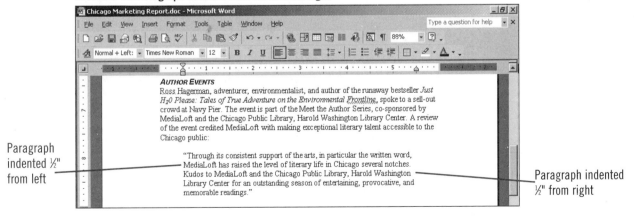

Adding Bullets and Numbering

Formatting a list with bullets or numbering can help to organize the ideas in a document. A **bullet** is a character, often a small circle, that appears before the items in a list to add emphasis. Formatting a list as a numbered list helps illustrate sequences and priorities. You can quickly format a list with bullets or numbering by using the Bullets and Numbering buttons on the Formatting toolbar. You can also use the Bullets and Numbering command on the Format menu to change or customize bullet and numbering styles. 🖋 Isaac formats the lists in his report with numbers and bullets.

1. Scroll down until the first paragraph on the second page (Authors on our...) is at the top of your screen

2. Select the **three-line list of names** under the paragraph, then click the **Numbering button** ▤ on the Formatting toolbar
   The paragraphs are formatted as a numbered list.

> **QuickTip**
>
> To change the numbers to letters, Roman numerals, or another numbering style, right-click the list, click Bullets and Numbering, then select a new numbering style on the Numbered tab.

3. Place the insertion point after **Jack Seneschal**, press **[Enter]**, then type **Polly Flanagan**
   Pressing [Enter] in the middle of the numbered list creates a new numbered paragraph and automatically renumbers the remainder of the list. Similarly, if you delete a paragraph from a numbered list, Word automatically renumbers the remaining paragraphs.

4. Click 1 in the list
   Clicking a number in a list selects all the numbers, as shown in Figure C-18.

5. Click the **Bold button** ▣ on the Formatting toolbar
   The numbers are all formatted in bold. Notice that the formatting of the items in the list does not change when you change the formatting of the numbers. You can also use this technique to change the formatting of bullets in a bulleted list.

> **QuickTip**
>
> To remove a bullet or number, select the paragraph(s), then click ▤ or ▤.

6. Select the **list of classes and workshops** under the Classes & Workshops heading, scrolling down if necessary, then click the **Bullets button** ▤ on the Formatting toolbar
   The five paragraphs are formatted as a bulleted list.

7. With the list still selected, click **Format** on the menu bar, then click **Bullets and Numbering**
   The Bullets and Numbering dialog box opens with the Bulleted tab displayed, as shown in Figure C-19. You use this dialog box to apply bullets and numbering to paragraphs, or to change the style of bullets or numbers.

8. Click the **Square bullets box** or select another style if square bullets are not available to you, click **OK**, then deselect the text
   The bullet character changes to a small square, as shown in Figure C-20.

9. Click the **Save button** ▤ on the Standard toolbar

FIGURE C-18: Numbered list

Numbers selected in numbered list

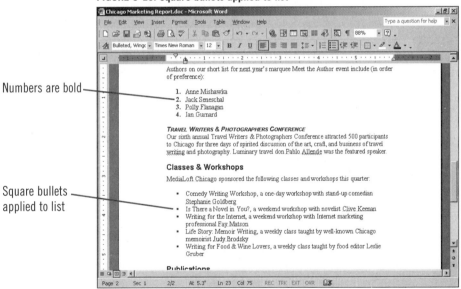

FIGURE C-19: Bulleted tab in the Bullets and Numbering dialog box

Numbered tab contains options for numbered lists

Outline Numbered tab contains options for outlines

Square bullets (your bullet styles might differ)

Click to select different characters and pictures to use as bullets

FIGURE C-20: Square bullets applied to list

Numbers are bold

Square bullets applied to list

Creating outlines

You can create lists with hierarchical structures by applying an outline numbering style to a list. To create an outline, begin by applying an outline numbering style from the Outline Numbered tab in the Bullets and Numbering dialog box, then type your outline, pressing [Enter] after each item. To demote items to a lower level of importance in the outline, place the insertion point in the item, then click the Increase Indent button ⊞ on the Formatting toolbar. Each time you indent a paragraph, the item is demoted to a lower lever in the outline. Similarly, you can use the Decrease Indent button ⊞ to promote an item to a higher level in the outline. You can also create a hierarchical structure in any bulleted or numbered list by using ⊞ and ⊞ to demote and promote items in the list. To change the outline numbering style applied to a list, select a new style from the Outline Numbered tab in the Bullets and Numbering dialog box.

Adding Borders and Shading

Borders and shading can add color and splash to a document. **Borders** are lines you add above, below, to the side, or around words or a paragraph. You can format borders using different line styles, colors, and widths. **Shading** is a color or pattern you apply behind words or paragraphs to make them stand out on a page. You apply borders and shading using the Borders and Shading command on the Format menu. Isaac enhances the advertising expenses table by adding shading to it. He also applies a border under every heading to visually punctuate the sections of the report.

Steps

1. Scroll up until the heading Advertising is at the top of your screen

2. Select the **four paragraphs** of tabbed text under the Advertising heading, click **Format** on the menu bar, click **Borders and Shading**, then click the **Shading tab**
   The Shading tab in the Borders and Shading dialog box is shown in Figure C-21. You use this tab to apply shading to words and paragraphs.

3. Click the **Pale Blue box** in the bottom row of the Fill section, click **OK**, then deselect the text
   Pale blue shading is applied to the four paragraphs. Notice that the shading is applied to the entire width of the paragraphs, despite the tab settings.

4. Select the **four paragraphs**, drag the **Left Indent marker** ▢ to the ¾" mark on the horizontal ruler, drag the **Right Indent marker** △ to the 5¼" mark, then deselect the text
   The paragraphs are indented from the left and right, making the shading look more attractive.

5. Select **Advertising**, click **Format** on the menu bar, click **Borders and Shading**, then click the **Borders tab**
   The Borders tab is shown in Figure C-22. You use this tab to add boxes and lines to words or paragraphs.

QuickTip

When creating custom borders, it's important to select the style, color, and width settings before applying the borders in the Preview section.

6. Click the **Custom box** in the Setting section, click the **Width list arrow**, click ¾ **pt**, click the **Bottom Border button** ▦ in the Preview section, click **OK**, then deselect the text
   A ¾-point black border is added below the Advertising paragraph.

7. Click **Events**, press **[F4]**, then scroll down and use **[F4]** to add a border under each blue heading
   The completed document is shown in Figure C-23.

Trouble?

Adjust the colors in the document if necessary.

8. Click the **Save button** ▦ on the Standard toolbar, click the **Print button** ▦, close the document, then exit Word
   A copy of the report prints. Depending on your printer, colors might appear differently when you print. If you are using a black and white printer, colors will print in shades of gray.

CLUES TO USE

Highlighting text in a document

You can mark important text in a document with highlighting. **Highlighting** is transparent color that is applied to text using the Highlight pointer ⬧ . To highlight text, click the Highlight list arrow ⬧ ▾ on the Formatting toolbar, select a color, then use the I-beam part of the ⬧ pointer to select the text. Click ⬧ to turn off the Highlight pointer. To remove highlighting, select the highlighted text, click ⬧ ▾ , then click None. Highlighting prints, but it is used most effectively when a document is viewed online.

FIGURE C-21: Shading tab in Borders and Shading dialog box

Name of active color appears here

Pale Blue

Click to select a shading pattern

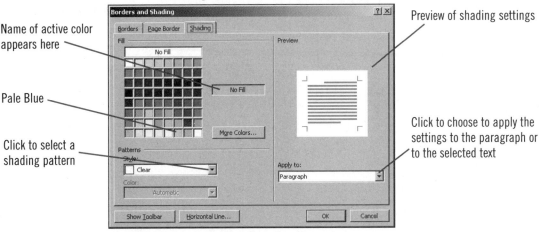

Preview of shading settings

Click to choose to apply the settings to the paragraph or to the selected text

FIGURE C-22: Borders tab in Borders and Shading dialog box

Select border formats before applying them in the Preview section

Select Custom to add a single border

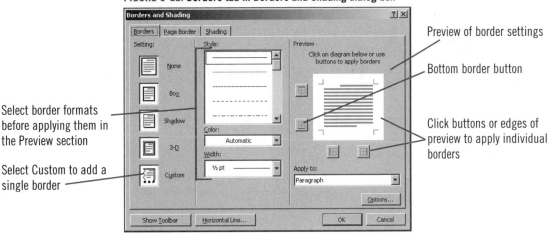

Preview of border settings

Bottom border button

Click buttons or edges of preview to apply individual borders

FIGURE C-23: Borders and shading applied to the document

Border under headings

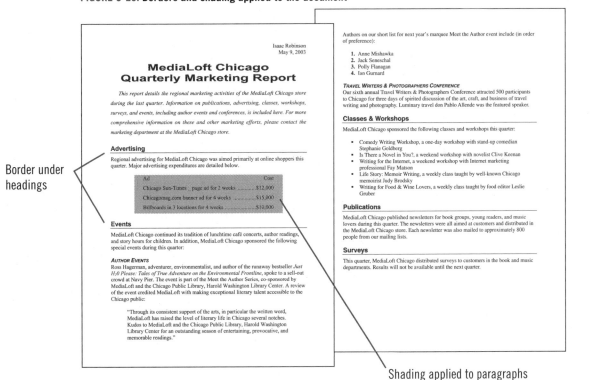

Shading applied to paragraphs

Practice

► Concepts Review

Label each element of the Word program window shown in Figure C-24.

FIGURE C-24

Match each term with the statement that best describes it.

8. **Italic**
9. **Bullet**
10. **Style**
11. **Bold**
12. **Point**
13. **Highlight**
14. **Shading**
15. **Border**

a. A character that appears at the beginning of a paragraph to add emphasis
b. Transparent color that is applied to text to mark it in a document
c. A text style in which characters are slanted
d. Color or a pattern that is applied behind text to make it look attractive
e. A set of format settings
f. A unit of measurement equal to $\frac{1}{72}$ of an inch
g. A line that can be applied above, below, or to the sides of a paragraph
h. A text style in which characters are darker and thicker

Select the best answer from the list of choices.

16. Which button is used to align a paragraph with both the left and right margins?
   a.
   b.
   c.
   d.

17. **What is Times New Roman?**
    a. A character format
    b. A font
    c. A style
    d. A text effect

18. **What is the most precise way to increase the amount of white space between two paragraphs?**
    a. Indent the paragraphs.
    b. Insert an extra blank line between the paragraphs.
    c. Use the Paragraph command to change the spacing below the first paragraph.
    d. Change the line spacing of the paragraphs.

19. **What element of the Word program window can be used to check the font effects applied to text?**
    a. Standard toolbar
    b. Formatting toolbar
    c. Styles and Formatting task pane
    d. Reveal Formatting task pane

20. **Which command would you use to apply color behind a paragraph?**
    a. Borders and Shading
    b. Background
    c. Paragraph
    d. Styles and Formatting

▶ Skills Review

1. **Format with fonts.**
   a. Start Word, open the file WD C-2 from the drive and folder where your Project Files are located, save it as **EDA Report**, then scroll through the document to get a feel for its contents.
   b. Press [Ctrl][Home], format the report title **Concord Springs Economic Development Report Executive Summary** in 22-point Tahoma. Choose a different font if Tahoma is not available to you.
   c. Change the font color of the report title to Blue-Gray.
   d. Format each of the following headings in 14-point Tahoma with the Blue-Gray font color: **Mission Statement, Guiding Principles, Issues, Proposed Actions**.
   e. Press [Ctrl][Home], then save your changes to the report.

2. **Change font styles and effects.**
   a. Apply bold to the report title and to each heading in the report.
   b. Format the paragraph under the Mission Statement heading in italic.
   c. Format the third paragraph under the Issues heading, **Years Population Growth**, in bold small caps, with a Blue-Gray font color.
   d. Change the font color of the two paragraphs under Years Population Growth to Blue-Gray.
   e. Format the paragraph **Source: Office of State Planning** in italic.
   f. Scroll to the top of the report, change the character scale of **Concord Springs Economic Development Report** to 80%, then save your changes.

3. **Change line and paragraph spacing.**
   a. Change the line spacing of the three-line list under the first body paragraph to 1.5 lines.
   b. Add 12 points of space before the Executive Summary paragraph.
   c. Add 12 points of space after each heading in the report.
   d. Add 6 points of space after each paragraph in the list under the Guiding Principles heading.
   e. Add 6 points of space after each paragraph under the Proposed Actions heading.
   f. Press [Ctrl][Home], then save your changes to the report.

4. Align paragraphs.

a. Press [Ctrl][A] to select the entire document, then justify all the paragraphs.

b. Center the two-paragraph report title.

c. Press [Ctrl][End], type your name, press [Enter], type the current date, then right-align your name and the date.

d. Save your changes to the report.

5. Work with tabs.

a. Scroll up and select the four-line list of blue-gray population information.

b. Set left tab stops at the 1¾"-mark and the 3" mark.

c. Insert a tab at the beginning of each paragraph in the list.

d. In the first paragraph, insert a tab before Population. In the second paragraph, insert a tab before 4.5%. In the third paragraph, insert a tab before 53%.

e. Select the first three paragraphs, then drag the second tab stop to the 2¾" mark on the horizontal ruler.

f. Press [Ctrl][Home], then save your changes to the report.

6. Work with indents.

a. Indent the first line of the first body paragraph ½".

b. Indent the paragraph under the Mission Statement heading ½" from the left and ½" from the right.

c. Indent the first line of the paragraph under the Guiding Principles heading ½".

d. Indent the first line of the three body paragraphs under the Issues heading ½".

e. Press [Ctrl][Home], then save your changes to the report.

7. Add bullets and numbering.

a. Apply bullets to the three-line list under the first body paragraph.

b. Change the bullet style to small circles (or choose another bullet style if small circles are not available to you).

c. Change the font color of the bullets to Blue-Gray.

d. Scroll down until the Guiding Principles heading is at the top of your screen.

e. Format the five-paragraph list under Guiding Principles as a numbered list.

f. Format the numbers in 12-point Tahoma bold, then change the font color to Blue-Gray.

g. Scroll down until the Proposed Actions heading is at the top of your screen, then format the paragraphs under the heading as a bulleted list using checkmarks as the bullet style (or choose another bullet style).

h. Change the font color of the bullets to Blue-Gray, press [Ctrl][Home], then save your changes to the report.

8. Add borders and shading.

a. Change the font color of the report title to Light Yellow, then apply Blue-Gray shading.

b. Apply Light Yellow shading to the Mission Statement heading, then add a 1-point Blue-Gray border below the Mission Statement heading.

c. Use the Format Painter to copy the formatting of the Mission Statement heading to the other headings in the report.

d. Under the Issues heading, select the first three lines of tabbed text, which are formatted in Blue-Gray.

e. Apply Light Yellow shading to the paragraphs, then add a 1-point Blue-Gray box border around the paragraphs.

f. Indent the paragraphs 1½" from the left and 1½" from the right.

g. Press [Ctrl][Home], save your changes to the report, view the report in Print Preview, then print a copy. The formatted report is shown in Figure C-25.

h. Close the file and exit Word.

FIGURE C-25

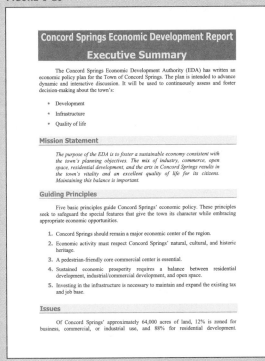

► Independent Challenge 1

You are an estimator for Zakia Construction in the Australian city of Wollongong. You have drafted an estimate for a home renovation job, and need to format it. It's important that your estimate have a clean, striking design, and reflect your company's professionalism.

FIGURE C-26

a. Start Word, open the file WD C-3 from the drive and folder where your Project Files are located, save it as **Zakia Construction**, then read the document to get a feel for its contents. Figure C-26 shows how you will format the letterhead.

b. In the first paragraph, format **ZAKIA** in 24-point Arial Black. (*Hint*: Select a similar font if Arial Black is not available to you.)

c. Format **Construction** in 24-point Arial, then change the character scale to 90%.

d. Format the next four lines in 9-point Arial, right-align them, then add a 1-point border below the last line.

e. In the body of the document, format the title **Proposal of Renovation** in 16-point Arial Black, then center the title.

f. Format the following headings (including the colons) in 12-point Arial Black: **Date, Work to be performed for and at, Scope of work, Payment schedule** and **Agreement**.

g. Format the 14-paragraph list under Scope of work as a numbered list, then apply bold to the numbers.

h. Change the paragraph spacing to add 4 points of space after each paragraph in the list.

i. With the list selected, set a right tab stop at the 5¾" mark, then insert tabs before every price in the list.

j. Apply bold to the two paragraphs—**Total estimated job cost** and **Approximate job time**—below the list.

k. Replace Your Name with your name in the signature block, select the signature block, set a left tab stop at the 3½" mark, then indent the signature block.

l. Examine the document carefully for formatting errors and make any necessary adjustments.

m. Save and print the document, then close the file and exit Word.

Independent Challenge 2

Your employer, The Lange Center for Contemporary Arts in Halifax, Nova Scotia, is launching a membership drive. Your boss has written the text for a flyer advertising Lange membership, and asks you to format it so that it is eye-catching and attractive.

a. Open the file WD C-4 from the drive and folder where your Project Files are located, save it as **Membership Flyer**, then read the document. Figure C-27 shows how you will format the first several paragraphs of the flyer.

FIGURE C-27

MEMBERSHIP DRIVE
2003

What we do for ARTISTS
Since 1982, the artist residency program at the Lange Center for Contemporary Arts has supported the work of more than 1500 artists from all over Canada and from 40 other nations. The residency awards include studio and living space, a monthly stipend to help artists with their expenses, and use of specialized equipment for all types of visual and performance art. Each artist gives a public lecture or performance at the Lange.

b. Select the entire document and format it in 10-point Arial Narrow.

c. Format the first paragraph, **Membership Drive**, in 26-point Arial Narrow, bold, with a white font color. Expand the character spacing by 7 points. Center the paragraph and apply plum shading to the paragraph.

d. Format the second paragraph, **2003**, in 36-point Arial Black, 80% gray font color, with a shadow effect. Expand the character spacing by 25 points and change the character scale to 200%. Center the paragraph.

e. Format each **What we do for…** heading in 12-point Arial, bold, with a plum font color. Add a single line ½-point border under each heading.

f. Format each subheading (**Gallery, Lectures, Library, All members…**, and **Membership Levels**) in 10-point Arial, bold. Add 3 points of spacing before each paragraph.

g. Indent each body paragraph ¼", except for the paragraphs under the What we do for YOU heading.

h. Format the four paragraphs under the All members… subheading as a bulleted list. Use a bullet symbol of your choice and format the bullets in the plum color.

i. Indent the five paragraphs under the Membership Levels heading ¼". For these five paragraphs, set left tab stops at the 1¼" mark and the 2" mark on the horizontal ruler. Insert tabs before the price and before the word **All** in each of the five paragraphs.

j. Format the name of each membership level (**Artistic, Conceptual**, etc.) in 10-point Arial, bold, italic, with a plum font color.

k. Format the **For more information** paragraph in 14-point Arial, bold, with a plum font color. Center the paragraph and add a 6-point dotted black border above the paragraph.

l. Format the last two paragraphs in 11-point Arial Narrow, and center the paragraphs. In the contact information, replace **Your Name** with your name, then apply bold to your name.

m. Examine the document carefully for formatting errors and make any necessary adjustments.

n. Save and print the flyer, then close the file and exit Word.

▶ Independent Challenge 3

One of your responsibilities as program coordinator at Solstice Mountain Sports is to develop a program of winter outdoor learning and adventure workshops. You have written a memo to your boss to update her on your progress. You need to format the memo so it is professional-looking and easy to read.

a. Start Word, open the file WD C-5 from the drive and folder where your Project Files are located, then save it as **Solstice Memo**.

b. Format the heading **Solstice Mountain Sports Memorandum** in 26-point Impact, then center it.

c. In the memo header, replace Today's Date and Your Name with the current date and your name.

d. Select the four-line memo header, set a left tab stop at the ¾" mark, then insert tabs before the date, the recipient's name, your name, and the subject of the memo.

e. Select **Date:**, then apply the character style Strong to it. (*Hint:* Open the Styles and Formatting task pane, click the Show list arrow, click All Styles if necessary, scroll through the alphabetical list of styles to locate the style Strong, then click Strong.)

f. Apply the Strong style to **To:**, **From:**, and **Re:**, then double-space the four lines in the memo header.

g. Apply a 3-point dotted border below the blank line under the memo header. (*Hint:* Turn on formatting marks, select the paragraph symbol below the memo header, then apply a border below it.)

h. Apply the paragraph style Heading 3 to the headings **Overview**, **Workshops**, **Accommodation**, **Fees**, and **Proposed winter programming**.

i. Under the Fees heading, format the words **Workshop fees** and **Accommodation fees** using the Strong style.

j. Add 6 points of space after the Workshop fees paragraph.

k. In the Fees section, apply green highlighting to these sentences: **Workshop fees include materials and equipment.** and **This is a discounted rate.**

l. On the second page of the document, format the list under the Proposed winter programming heading as an outline. Figure C-28 shows the hierarchical structure of the outline. (*Hint:* Format the list as an outline numbered list, then use the Increase Indent and Decrease Indent buttons to change the level of importance of each item.)

m. Change the outline numbering style to the bullet numbering style shown in Figure C-28, if necessary.

n. Save and print the document, then close the file and exit Word.

FIGURE C-28

Proposed winter programming
- ❖ Skiing, Snowboarding, and Snowshoeing
  - ➢ Skiing and Snowboarding
    - ▪ Cross-country skiing
      - • Cross-country skiing for beginners
      - • Intermediate cross-country skiing
      - • Inn-to-inn ski touring
      - • Moonlight cross-country skiing
    - ▪ Telemarking
      - • Basic telemark skiing
      - • Introduction to backcountry skiing
      - • Exploring on skis
    - ▪ Snowboarding
      - • Backcountry snowboarding
  - ➢ Snowshoeing
    - ▪ Beginner
      - • Snowshoeing for beginners
      - • Snowshoeing and winter ecology
    - ▪ Intermediate and Advanced
      - • Intermediate snowshoeing
      - • Guided snowshoe trek
      - • Above tree line snowshoeing
- ❖ Winter Hiking, Camping, and Survival
  - ➢ Hiking
    - ▪ Beginner
      - • Long-distance hiking
      - • Winter summits
      - • Hiking for women
  - ➢ Winter camping and survival
    - ▪ Beginner
      - • Introduction to winter camping
      - • Basic winter mountain skills
      - • Building snow shelters
    - ▪ Intermediate
      - • Basic winter mountain skills II
      - • Ice climbing
      - • Avalanche awareness and rescue

Independent Challenge 4

The fonts you choose for a document can have a major effect on the document's tone. Not all fonts are appropriate for use in a business document, and some fonts, especially those with a definite theme, are appropriate only for specific purposes. The World Wide Web includes hundreds of Web sites devoted to fonts and text design. Some Web sites sell fonts, others allow you to download fonts for free and install them on your computer. In this independent challenge, you will research Web sites related to fonts and find examples of fonts you could use in your work.

a. Start Word, open the file WD C-6 from the drive and folder where your Project Files are located, and save it as **Fonts**. This document contains the questions you will answer about the fonts you find.

b. Use your favorite search engine to search the Web for Web sites related to fonts. Use the keyword **font** to conduct your search. If your search does not result in appropriate links, try looking at the following Web sites: www.1001freefonts.com, www.fontsnthings.com, and www.fontfreak.com.

c. Explore the fonts available for downloading. As you examine the fonts, notice that fonts fall into two general categories: serif fonts, which have a small stroke, called a serif, at the ends of characters, and sans serif fonts, which do not have a serif. Times New Roman is an example of a serif font and Arial is an example of a sans serif font.

d. Type your answers in the Fonts document, save it, print a copy, then close the file and exit Word.

► Visual Workshop

Using the file WD C-7 found in the drive and folder where your Project Files are located, create the menu shown in Figure C-29. (*Hints*: Use Georgia for the font. Change the font size of the heading to 72 points, scale the font to 66%, and expand the spacing by 2 points. For the rest of the text, change the font size to 11 points. Indent all the text ½" from the left and the right. Use paragraph spacing to adjust the spacing between paragraphs so that all the text fits on one page. If the Georgia font is not available to you, choose a different font.) Save the menu as **Rosebud Specials**, then print a copy.

FIGURE C-29

Rosebud Café

· ·

<u>DAILY SPECIALS</u>

MONDAY
Veggie Chili
Hearty veggie chili with melted cheddar in our peasant French bread bowl. Topped with sour cream & scallions.
$5.95

TUESDAY
Greek Salad
Our large garden salad with kalamata olives, feta cheese, and garlic vinaigrette. Served with an assortment of rolls.
$5.95

WEDNESDAY
French Dip
Lean roast beef topped with melted cheddar on our roasted garlic roll. Served with a side of au jus and red bliss mashed potatoes.
$6.95

THURSDAY
Chicken Cajun Bleu
Cajun chicken, chunky blue cheese, cucumbers, leaf lettuce, and tomato on our roasted garlic roll.
$6.50

FRIDAY
Clam Chowder
Classic New England thick, rich, clam chowder in our peasant French bread bowl. Served with a garden salad.
$5.95

SATURDAY
Hot Chicken and Gravy
Delicious chicken and savory gravy served on a thick slice of toasted honest white. Served with red bliss mashed potatoes.
$6.95

SUNDAY
Turkey-Bacon Club
Double-decker roasted turkey, crisp bacon, leaf lettuce, tomato, and sun-dried tomato mayo on toasted triple seed.
$6.50

Your Name
· ·

Unit
D

Formatting

Documents

Objectives

- MOUS ▶ **Set document margins**
- MOUS ▶ **Divide a document into sections**
- MOUS ▶ **Add page breaks**
- MOUS ▶ **Add page numbers**
- MOUS ▶ **Insert headers and footers**
- MOUS ▶ **Edit headers and footers**
- MOUS ▶ **Format columns**
- MOUS ▶ **Insert clip art**

Word's page formatting features allow you to creatively lay out and design the pages of your documents. In this unit, you learn how to change the document margins, determine the page orientation of a document, add page numbers, and insert headers and footers. You also learn how to format text in columns and how to illustrate your documents with clip art. ◢ Alice Wegman has written and formatted the text for a quarterly newsletter for the MediaLoft marketing staff. She is now ready to lay out and design the pages of the newsletter. She plans to organize the articles in columns and to illustrate the newsletter with clip art. You will work with Alice as she formats the newsletter.

Setting Document Margins

Changing a document's margins is one way to change the appearance of a document and control the amount of text that fits on a page. The **margins** of a document are the blank areas between the edge of the text and the edge of the page. When you create a document in Word, the default margins are 1" at the top and bottom of the page, and 1.25" on the left and right sides of the page. You can adjust the size of a document's margins using the Page Setup command on the File menu, or using the rulers. Alice plans the newsletter to be a four-page document when finished. She reduces the size of the document margins so that more text fits on each page.

Steps

1. **Start Word, open the file WD D-1 from the drive and folder where your Project Files are located, then save it as MediaLoft Buzz**
   The newsletter opens in Print Layout view.

2. **Scroll through the newsletter to get a feel for its contents, then press [Ctrl][Home]**
   The newsletter is currently six pages long. Notice the status bar indicates the page where the insertion point is located and the total number of pages in the document.

3. **Click File on the menu bar, click Page Setup, then click the Margins tab in the Page Setup dialog box if necessary**
   The Margins tab in the Page Setup dialog box is shown in Figure D-1. You can use the Margins tab to change the width of the top, bottom, left, or right document margins, to change the orientation of the pages from portrait to landscape, and to alter other page layout settings. **Portrait orientation** means a page is taller than it is wide; **landscape orientation** means a page is wider than it is tall. This newsletter uses portrait orientation.

4. **Click the Top down arrow three times until 0.7" appears, then click the Bottom down arrow until 0.7" appears**
   The top and bottom margins of the newsletter will be .7". Notice that the margins in the Preview section of the dialog box change as you adjust the margin settings.

5. **Press [Tab], type .7 in the Left text box, press [Tab], then type .7 in the Right text box**
   The left and right margins of the newsletter will also be .7". You can change the margin settings by using the arrows or by typing a value in the appropriate text box.

6. **Click OK**
   The document margins change to .7", as shown in Figure D-2. The bar at the intersection of the white and gray areas on the horizontal and vertical rulers indicates the location of the margin. You can also change a document's margins by dragging the bar to a new location. Notice that the status bar indicates the total number of pages in the document is now five.

7. **Click the Zoom list arrow on the Standard toolbar, then click Two Pages**
   The first two pages of the document appear in the document window.

8. **Scroll down to view all five pages of the newsletter, press [Ctrl][Home], click the Zoom list arrow, click Page Width, then click the Save button 🖫 on the Standard toolbar to save the document**

QuickTip

The minimum allowable margin settings depend on your printer and the size of the paper you are using. Word displays a warning message if you set margins that are too narrow for your printer.

QuickTip

Use the Reveal Formatting task pane to quickly check the margin, orientation, paper size, and other page layout settings for a document.

FIGURE D-1: Margins tab in Page Setup dialog box

Default margin settings

Set gutter margin

Select gutter position

Select page orientation

Set mirror margins and other page layout options

Select part of document to apply settings to

Preview of margin settings

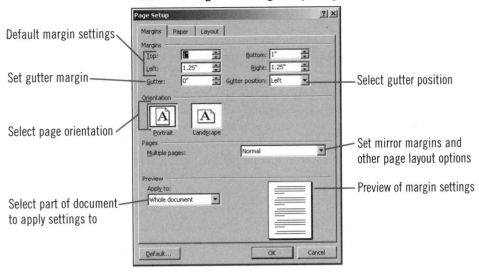

FIGURE D-2: Newsletter with smaller margins

Zoom list arrow

Ruler shows location of left margin

Ruler shows location of right margin

Ruler shows location of top margin

Document margins are narrower

Page 1 is the active page

After adjusting margins, document is five pages long

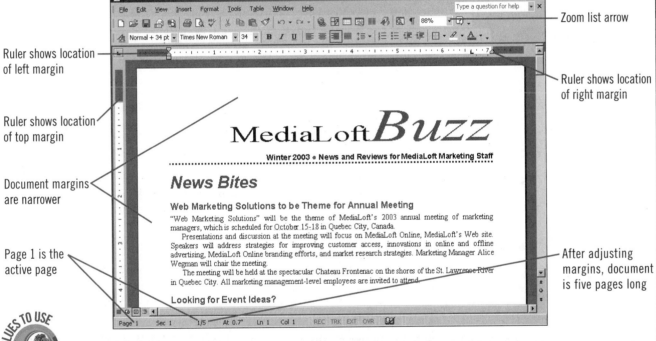

Changing paper size, orientation, and margin settings

By default, the documents you create in Word use an 8½" x 11" paper size in portrait orientation with the default margin settings, but you can adjust these settings in the Page Setup dialog box to create documents of any size, shape, and layout. On the Margins tab, change the orientation of the pages by selecting Portrait or Landscape. To change the layout of multiple pages, use the Multiple pages list arrow to create pages that use mirror margins, include two pages per sheet of paper, or are formatted like a folded booklet. **Mirror margins** are used in documents with facing pages, such as a magazine, where the margins on the left page of the document are a mirror image of the margins on

the right. Documents with mirror margins have inside and outside margins, rather than right and left margins. Another type of margin is a gutter margin, which is used in documents that are bound, such as books. A **gutter** adds extra space to the left or top margin so that the binding does not obscure text. Add a gutter to a document by adjusting the setting in the Gutter text box on the Margins tab. If you want to change the size of the paper used in a document, use the Paper tab in the Page Setup dialog box. Use the Paper size list arrow to select a standard paper size, or enter custom measurements in the Width and Height text boxes.

Word 2002

Dividing a Document into Sections

Dividing a document into sections allows you to format each section of the document with different page layout settings. A **section** is a portion of a document that is separated from the rest of the document by section breaks. **Section breaks** are formatting marks that you insert in a document to show the end of a section. Once you have divided a document into sections, you can format each section with different column, margin, page orientation, header and footer, and other page layout settings. By default, a document is formatted as a single section, but you can divide a document into as many sections as you like. Alice wants to format the body of the newsletter in two columns, but leave the masthead and the headline "News Bites" as a single column. She inserts a section break before the body of the newsletter to divide the document into two sections, then she changes the number of columns in the second section to two.

1. Click the **Show/Hide ¶ button** ¶ on the Standard toolbar to display formatting marks if they are not visible

   Turning on formatting marks allows you to see the section breaks you insert in a document.

QuickTip

When you insert a section break at the beginning of a paragraph, Word inserts the break at the end of the previous paragraph. A section break stores the formatting information for the preceding section.

2. Place the insertion point before the headline **Web Marketing Solutions to be…**, click **Insert** on the menu bar, then click **Break**

   The Break dialog box opens, as shown in Figure D-3. You use this dialog box to insert different types of section breaks. Table D-1 describes the different types of section breaks.

3. Click the **Continuous option button**, then click **OK**

   Word inserts a continuous section break, shown as a dotted double line, above the headline. A continuous section break begins a new section of the document on the same page. The document now has two sections. Notice that the status bar indicates that the insertion point is in section 2.

4. With the insertion point in section 2, click the **Columns button** ▦ on the Standard toolbar

   A grid showing four columns opens below the button. You use the grid to select the number of columns you want to create.

QuickTip

To change the margins or page orientation of a section, place the insertion point in the section, change the margin or page orientation settings on the Margins tab in the Page Setup dialog box, click the Apply to list arrow on the Margins tab, click This section, then click OK.

5. Point to the second column on the grid, then click

   Section 2 is formatted in two columns, as shown in Figure D-4. The text in section 1 remains formatted in a single column. Notice the status bar now indicates the document is four pages long. Formatting text in columns is another way to increase the amount of text that fits on a page. You'll learn more about columns in a later lesson.

6. Click the **Zoom list arrow** on the Standard toolbar, click **Two Pages**, then scroll down to examine all four pages of the document

   The text in section 2—all the text below the continuous section break—is formatted in two columns. Text in columns flows automatically from the bottom of one column to the top of the next.

7. Press **[Ctrl][Home]**, click the **Zoom list arrow**, click **Page Width**, then save the document

TABLE D-1: Types of section breaks

section break	function
Next page	Begins a new a section and moves the text following the break to the top of the next page
Continuous	Begins a new section on the same page
Even page	Begins a new section and moves the text following the break to the top of the next even-numbered page
Odd page	Begins a new section and moves the text following the break to the top of the next odd-numbered page

FIGURE D-3: Break dialog box

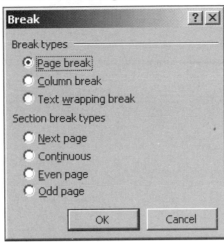

FIGURE D-4: Continuous section break and columns

Text in section 1 is formatted in one column

Insertion point is in section 2

Text in section 2 is formatted in two columns

Section 2 is the active section

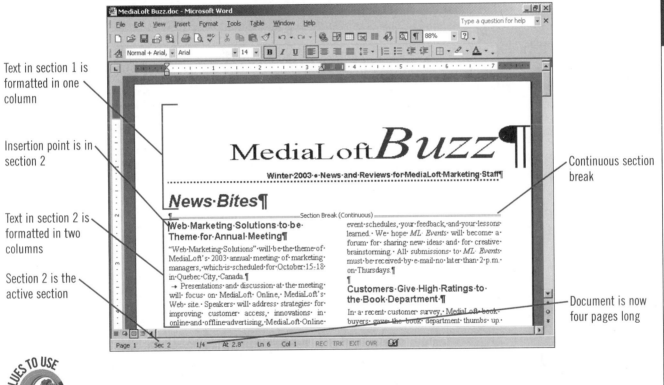

Continuous section break

Document is now four pages long

Changing page layout settings for a section

Dividing a document into sections allows you to vary the layout of a document. In addition to applying different column settings to sections, you can apply different margins, page orientation, paper size, vertical alignment, header and footer, page numbering, and other page layout settings. For example, if you are formatting a report that includes a table with many columns, you might want to change the table's page orientation to landscape so that it is easier to read. To do this, you would insert a section break before and after the table to create a section that contains only the table. Then you would use the Margins tab in the Page Setup dialog box to change the page orientation of the table section to landscape.

To change the page layout settings for an individual section, place the insertion point in the section, open the Page Setup (or Columns) dialog box, select the options you want to change, click the Apply to list arrow, click This section, then click OK. When you select This section in the Apply to list box, the settings are applied to the current section only. If you select Whole document in the Apply to list box, the settings are applied to all the sections in the document.

Adding Page Breaks

As you type text in a document, Word automatically inserts a **soft page break** when you reach the bottom of a page, allowing you to continue typing on the next page. You can also force text onto the next page of a document by using the Break command to insert a **hard page break**. Alice inserts hard page breaks where she knows she wants to begin each new page of the newsletter.

Steps

1. **Scroll down to the bottom of page 1, place the insertion point before the headline Career Corner, click Insert on the menu bar, then click Break**
   The Break dialog box opens. You also use this dialog box to insert page, column, and text-wrapping breaks. Table D-2 describes these types of breaks.

QuickTip

Hard and soft page breaks are always visible in Normal view.

2. **Make sure the Page break option button is selected, then click OK**
   Word inserts a hard page break before "Career Corner" and moves all the text following the page break to the beginning of the next page, as shown in Figure D-5. The page break appears as a dotted line in Print Layout view. Page break marks are visible on the screen but do not print.

3. **Scroll down to the bottom of page 2, place the insertion point before the headline Webcasts Slated for May, press and hold [Ctrl], then press [Enter]**
   Pressing [Ctrl][Enter] is a fast way to insert a hard page break. The headline is forced to the top of the third page.

4. **Scroll down to the bottom of page 3, place the insertion point before the headline Staff News, then press [Ctrl][Enter]**
   The headline is forced to the top of the fourth page.

5. **Press [Ctrl][Home], click the Zoom list arrow on the Standard toolbar, then click Two Pages**
   The first two pages of the document are displayed, as shown in Figure D-6.

6. **Scroll down to view pages 3 and 4, click the Zoom list arrow, click Page Width, then save the document**

CLUES TO USE

Vertically aligning text on a page

By default, text is vertically aligned with the top margin of a page, but you can change the vertical alignment of text so that it is centered between the top and bottom margins, justified between the top and bottom margins, or aligned with the bottom margin of the page. You would vertically align text on a page only when the text does not fill the page; for example, if you are creating a flyer or a title page for a report. To change the vertical alignment of text in a section (or a document), place the insertion point in the section you want to align, open the Page Setup dialog box, use the Vertical alignment list arrow on the Layout tab to select the alignment you want—top, center, justified, or bottom—use the Apply to list arrow to select the part of the document you want to align, then click OK.

FIGURE D-5: Hard page break in document

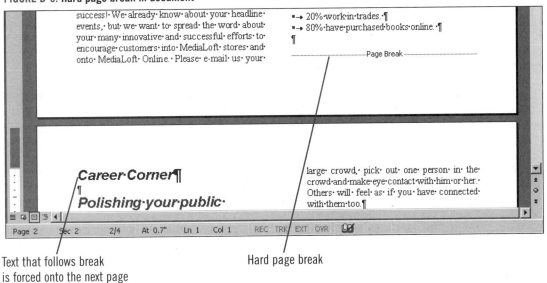

Text that follows break
is forced onto the next page

Hard page break

FIGURE D-6: Pages 1 and 2

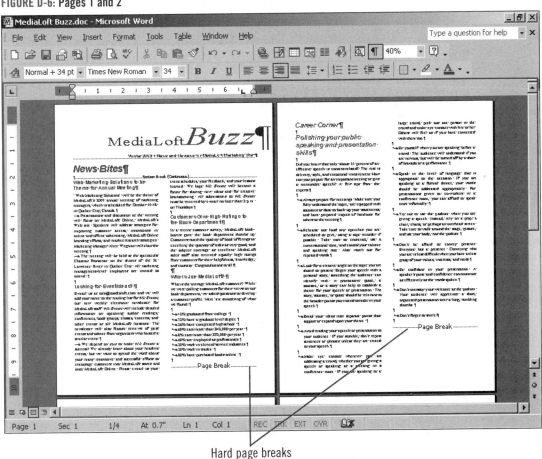

Hard page breaks

TABLE D-2: Types of breaks

break	function
Page break	Forces the text following the break to begin at the top of the next page
Column break	Forces the text following the break to begin at the top of the next column
Text wrapping break	Forces the text following the break to begin at the beginning of the next line

Adding Page Numbers

If you want to number the pages of a multi-page document, you can insert a page number field at the top or bottom of each page. A **field** is a code that serves as a placeholder for data that changes in a document, such as a page number or the current date. When you use the Page Numbers command on the Insert menu to add page numbers to a document, Word automatically numbers the pages for you. ▬▬ Alice adds page numbers to the bottom of each page in the document.

Steps 1234

1. **Click Insert on the menu bar, then click Page Numbers**
   The Page Numbers dialog box opens, as shown in Figure D-7. You use this dialog box to specify the position—top or bottom of the page—and the alignment for the page numbers. Bottom of page (Footer) is the default position.

2. **Click the Alignment list arrow, then click Center**
   The page numbers will be centered between the left and right margins at the bottom of each page.

3. **Click OK, then scroll to the bottom of the first page**
   The page number 1 appears in gray at the bottom of the first page, as shown in Figure D-8. The number is gray, or dimmed, because it is located in the Footer area. When the document is printed, the page numbers appear as normal text. You will learn more about headers and footers in the next lesson.

4. **Click the Print Preview button** 🔍 **on the Standard toolbar, then click the One Page button** ▢ **on the Print Preview toolbar if necessary**
   The first page of the newsletter appears in Print Preview. Notice the page number.

5. **Click the page number with the** 🔍 **pointer to zoom in on the page**
   The page number is centered at the bottom of the page, as shown in Figure D-9.

6. **Scroll down the document to see the page number at the bottom of each page**
   Word automatically numbered the pages of the newsletter.

7. **Click the Multiple Pages button** ▦ **on the Print Preview toolbar, point to the second box in the bottom row on the grid to select 2 x 2 pages, then click**
   All four pages of the newsletter appear in the Print Preview window.

8. **Click Close on the Print Preview toolbar, then save the document**

Inserting date and time fields

Using the Date and Time command on the Insert menu, you can add a field for the current date or the current time into a document. To insert the current date or time at the location of the insertion point, click Date and Time on the Insert menu, then select the date or time format you want to use from the list of available formats in the Date and Time dialog box. To insert the date or time as a field that will be updated automatically each time you open or print the document, select the Update automatically check box, then click OK. If you want to insert the current date or time as static text that does not change each time you open or print the document, deselect the Update automatically check box, then click OK. Word uses the clock on your computer to compute the current date and time.

Once you have inserted a date or time field, you can modify the format by changing the field code: right-click the field, click Edit Field on the shortcut menu, then select a new format in the Field properties list in the Field dialog box. You can edit static text just as you would any other text in Word.

Set location for page number (header or footer)

Set alignment of page number

Clear to hide the page number on the first page

Click to change the numbering format

Preview of page number position

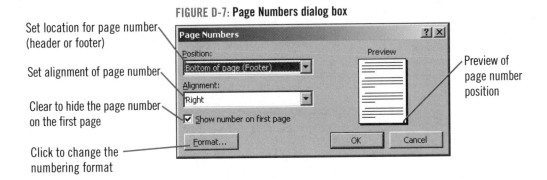

FIGURE D-8: **Page number in document**

Page number is dimmed

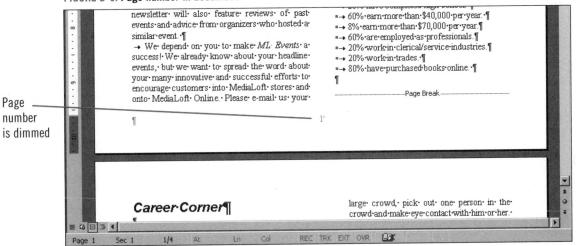

FIGURE D-9: **Page number in Print Preview**

One Page button

Multiple Pages button

Page number in Print Preview

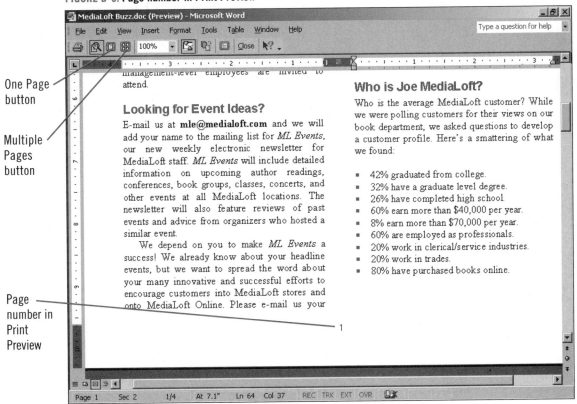

Looking for Event Ideas?

E-mail us at **mle@medialoft.com** and we will add your name to the mailing list for *ML Events*, our new weekly electronic newsletter for MediaLoft staff. *ML Events* will include detailed information on upcoming author readings, conferences, book groups, classes, concerts, and other events at all MediaLoft locations. The newsletter will also feature reviews of past events and advice from organizers who hosted a similar event.

We depend on you to make *ML Events* a success! We already know about your headline events, but we want to spread the word about your many innovative and successful efforts to encourage customers into MediaLoft stores and onto MediaLoft Online. Please e-mail us your

Who is Joe MediaLoft?

Who is the average MediaLoft customer? While we were polling customers for their views on our book department, we asked questions to develop a customer profile. Here's a smattering of what we found:

- 42% graduated from college.
- 32% have a graduate level degree.
- 26% have completed high school.
- 60% earn more than $40,000 per year.
- 8% earn more than $70,000 per year.
- 60% are employed as professionals.
- 20% work in clerical/service industries.
- 20% work in trades.
- 80% have purchased books online.

Word 2002

Inserting Headers and Footers

A **header** is text or graphics that appears at the top of every page of a document. A **footer** is text or graphics that appears at the bottom of every page. In longer documents, headers and footers often contain information such as the title of the publication, the title of the chapter, the name of the author, the date, or a page number. You can add headers and footers to a document by using the Header and Footer command on the View menu to open the Header and Footer areas, and then inserting text and graphics in them. ✒ Alice creates a header that includes the name of the newsletter and the current date.

1. Click **View** on the menu bar, then click **Header and Footer**

The Header and Footer areas open and the document text is dimmed, as shown in Figure D-10. When the document text is dimmed, it cannot be edited. The Header and Footer toolbar also opens. It includes buttons for inserting standard text into headers and footers and for navigating between headers and footers. See Table D-3. The Header and Footer areas of a document are independent of the document itself and must be formatted separately. For example, if you select all the text in a document and then change the font, the header and footer font does not change.

QuickTip

You can change the date format by right-clicking the field, clicking Edit Field on the shortcut menu, and then selecting a new date format in the Field properties list in the Field dialog box.

2. Type **Buzz** in the Header area, press **[Spacebar]** twice, then click the **Insert Date button** 🗓 on the Header and Footer toolbar

Clicking the Insert Date button inserts a date field into the header. The date is inserted using the default date format (usually month/date/year, although your default date format might be different). The word "Buzz" and the current date will appear at the top of every page in the document.

3. Select **Buzz** and the **date**, then click the **Center button** 🖺 on the Formatting toolbar

The text is centered in the Header area. You can also use tabs to center and right-align text in the Header and Footer areas. Notice that the center and right tab stops shown on the ruler do not align with the current margin settings. The tab stops are the default tab stops for the Header and Footer areas, based on the default margin settings. If you change the margins in a document, you need to adjust the tab stops in the Header or Footer area to align with the new margin settings.

QuickTip

Unless you set different headers and footers for different sections, the information you insert in any Header or Footer area will appear on every page in the document.

4. With the text still selected, click the **Font list arrow** on the Formatting toolbar, click **Arial**, click the **Bold button** 🅱, then click in the Header area to deselect the text

The header text is formatted in 12-point Arial bold, as shown in Figure D-11.

5. Click the **Switch Between Header and Footer button** 🖺 on the Header and Footer toolbar

The insertion point moves to the Footer area. A page number field already appears centered in the Footer area.

6. Double-click the **page number** to select the field, click the **Font list arrow**, click **Arial**, click 🅱, then click in the Footer area to deselect the field

The page number is formatted in 12-point Arial bold.

QuickTip

To change the distance between the header and footer and the edge of the page, change the From edge settings on the Layout tab in the Page Setup dialog box.

7. Click **Close** on the Header and Footer toolbar, save the document, then scroll down until the bottom of page 1 and the top of page 2 appear in the document window

The Header and Footer areas close and the header and footer text is dimmed, as shown in Figure D-12. The header text—"Buzz" and the current date—appear at the top of every page in the document, and a page number appears at the bottom of each page.

FIGURE D-10: Header area

Header and Footer toolbar

Header area is open

Document text is dimmed

Insert Date button

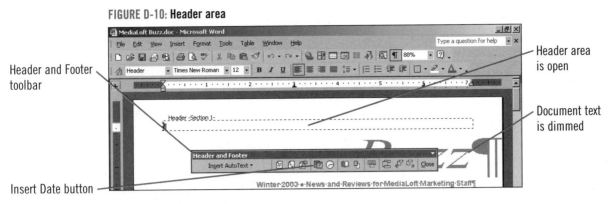

FIGURE D-11: Formatted header text

Information in Header area for section 1 appears on every page

Formatted text is centered in the Header area

Tab stops for the header are set for the default document margins

Switch Between Header and Footer button

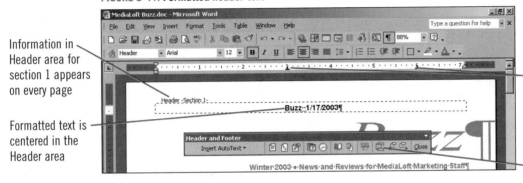

FIGURE D-12: Header and footer in the document

Page number appears in footer on every page

Header text appears in header on every page (your date will differ)

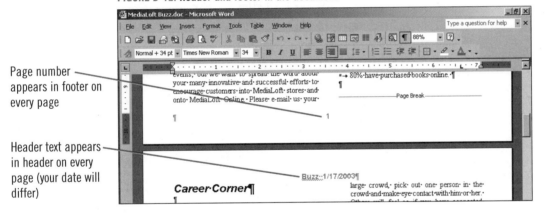

TABLE D-3: Buttons on the Header and Footer toolbar

button	function
Insert AutoText ▾	Inserts an AutoText entry, such as a field for the filename, or the author's name
# Insert Page Number	Inserts a field for the page number so that the pages are numbered automatically
Insert Number of Pages	Inserts a field for the total number of pages in the document
Format Page Number	Opens the Page Number Format dialog box; use to change the numbering format or to begin automatic page numbering with a specific number
Insert Date	Inserts a field for the current date
Insert Time	Inserts a field for the current time
Page Setup	Opens the Page Setup dialog box
Switch Between Header and Footer	Moves the insertion point between the Header and Footer areas

Editing Headers and Footers

To change header and footer text or to alter the formatting of headers and footers you must first open the Header and Footer areas. You can open headers and footers using the Header and Footer command on the View menu, or by double-clicking a header or footer in Print Layout view. ✐ Alice modifies the header by adding a small circle symbol between "Buzz" and the date. She also adds a border under the header text to set it off from the rest of the page. Finally, she removes the header and footer text from the first page of the document.

Steps

1. Place the insertion point at the top of page 2, position the ⬚ pointer over the header text at the top of page 2, then double-click
   The Header and Footer areas open.

2. Place the insertion point between the two spaces after Buzz, click **Insert** on the menu bar, then click **Symbol**
   The Symbol dialog box opens and is similar to Figure D-13. **Symbols** are special characters, such as graphics, shapes, and foreign language characters, that you can insert into a document. The symbols shown in Figure D-13 are the symbols included with the (normal text) font. You can use the Font list arrow on the Symbols tab to view the symbols included with each font on your computer.

3. Scroll the list of symbols if necessary to locate the black circle symbol shown in Figure D-13, select the **black circle symbol**, click **Insert**, then click **Close**
   A circle symbol is added at the location of the insertion point.

4. With the insertion point in the header text, click **Format** on the menu bar, then click **Borders and Shading**
   The Borders and Shading dialog box opens.

5. Click the **Borders tab**, click **Custom** in the Setting section, click the **dotted line** in the Style scroll box (the second line style), click the **Width list arrow**, click **2¼ pt**, click the **Bottom border button** in the Preview section, make sure Paragraph is selected in the Apply to list box, click **OK**, then click **Close** on the Header and Footer toolbar
   A dotted line border is added below the header text, as shown in Figure D-14.

6. Press **[Ctrl][Home]** to move the insertion point to the beginning of the document
   The newsletter already includes the name of the document at the top of the first page, making the header information redundant. You can modify headers and footers so that the header and footer text does not appear on the first page of a document or a section.

7. Click **File** on the menu bar, click **Page Setup** then click the **Layout tab**
   The Layout tab of the Page Setup dialog box includes options for creating a different header and footer for the first page of a document or a section, and for creating different headers and footers for odd- and even-numbered pages in a document or a section. For example, in a document with facing pages, such as a magazine, you might want the publication title to appear in the left-page header and the publication date to appear in the right-page header.

8. Click the **Different first page check box** to select it, click the **Apply to list arrow**, click **Whole document**, then click **OK**
   The header and footer text is removed from the Header and Footer areas on the first page.

9. Scroll to see the header and footer on pages 2, 3, and 4, then save the document

FIGURE D-13: Symbol dialog box

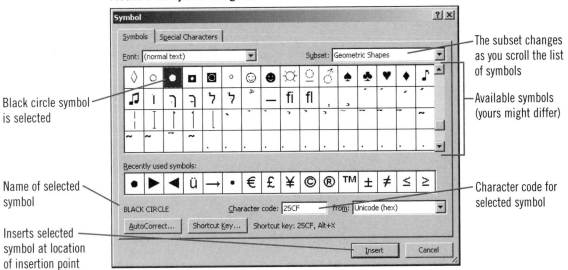

Black circle symbol is selected

The subset changes as you scroll the list of symbols

Available symbols (yours might differ)

Name of selected symbol

Character code for selected symbol

Inserts selected symbol at location of insertion point

FIGURE D-14: Symbol and border added to header

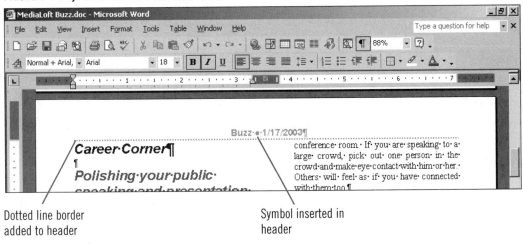

Dotted line border added to header

Symbol inserted in header

CLUES TO USE

Inserting and creating AutoText entries

Word includes a number of built-in AutoText entries, including salutations and closings for letters, as well as information for headers and footers. To insert a built-in AutoText entry at the location of the insertion point, point to AutoText on the Insert menu, point to a category on the AutoText menu, then click the AutoText entry you want to insert. You can also use the Insert AutoText button on the Header and Footer toolbar to insert an AutoText entry from the Header/Footer category into a header or footer.

Word's AutoText feature also allows you to store text and graphics that you use frequently so that you can easily insert them in a document. To create a custom AutoText entry, enter the text or graphic you want to store—such as a company name or logo—in a document, select it, point to AutoText on the Insert menu, and then click New. In the Create AutoText dialog box, type a name for your AutoText entry, then click OK. The text or graphic is saved as a custom AutoText entry. To insert a custom AutoText entry in a document, point to AutoText on the Insert menu, click AutoText, select the entry name on the AutoText tab in the AutoCorrect dialog box, click Insert, then click OK.

Formatting Columns

Formatting text in columns often makes it easier to read. You can apply column formatting to a whole document, to a section, or to selected text. The Columns button on the Standard toolbar allows you to quickly create columns of equal width. In addition, you can use the Columns command on the Format menu to create columns and to customize the width and spacing of columns. To control the way text flows between columns, you can insert a **column break**, which forces the text following the break to move to the top of the next column. You can also balance columns of unequal length by inserting a continuous section break at the end of the last column in a section. ✎ Alice formats the Staff News page in three columns, then she adjusts the flow of text.

1. Scroll to the top of page 4, place the insertion point before **Boston**, click **Insert** on the menu bar, click **Break**, select the **Continuous option button**, then click **OK**

   A continuous section break is inserted before Boston. The newsletter now contains three sections.

QuickTip

To change the width and spacing of existing columns, you can use the Columns dialog box or drag the column markers on the horizontal ruler.

2. Refer to the status bar to confirm that the insertion point is in section 3, click **Format** on the menu bar, then click **Columns**

   The Columns dialog box opens, as shown in Figure D-15.

3. Select **Three** in the Presets section, click the **Spacing down arrow** twice until 0.3" appears, select the **Line between check box**, then click **OK**

   All the text in section 3 is formatted in three columns of equal width with a line between the columns, as shown in Figure D-16.

QuickTip

To create a banner headline that spans the width of a page, select the headline text, click the Columns button, then click 1 Column.

4. Click the **Zoom list arrow** on the Standard toolbar, then click **Whole Page**

   Notice that the third column of text is much shorter than the first two columns. Page 4 would look better if the three columns were balanced—each the same length.

5. Place the insertion point at the end of the third column, click **Insert** on the menu bar, click **Break**, select the **Continuous option button**, then click **OK**

   The columns in section 3 adjust to become roughly the same length.

6. Scroll up to page 3

   The two columns on page 3 are also uneven. The page would look better if the information about the third webcast did not break across the two columns.

QuickTip

If a section contains a column break, you cannot balance the columns by inserting a continuous section break.

7. Click the **Zoom list arrow**, click **Page Width**, scroll to the bottom of page 3, place the insertion point before **Tuesday, June 10**, click **Insert** on the menu bar, click **Break**, click the **Column break option button**, then click **OK**

   The text following the column break is forced to the top of the next column.

8. Click the **Zoom list arrow**, click **Two Pages**, then save the document

   The columns on pages 3 and 4 are displayed, as shown in Figure D-17.

Hyphenating text in a document

Hyphenating a document is another way to control the flow of text in columns. Hyphens are small dashes that break words that fall at the end of a line. Hyphenation diminishes the gaps between words in justified text and reduces ragged right edges in left-aligned text. If a document includes narrow columns, hyphenating the text can help give the pages a cleaner look. To hyphenate a document automatically, point to Language on the Tools menu, click Hyphenation, select the Automatically hyphenate document check box in the Hyphenation dialog box, and then click OK. You can also use the Hyphenation dialog box to change the hyphenation zone—the distance between the margin and the end of the last word in the line. A smaller hyphenation zone results in a greater number of hyphenated words and a cleaner look to columns of text.

FIGURE D-15: Columns dialog box

Select a preset format for columns

Change the number of columns

Select to add a line between columns

Preview of current settings

Set custom widths and spacing for columns

Select part of document to apply format to

Select to create columns of equal width

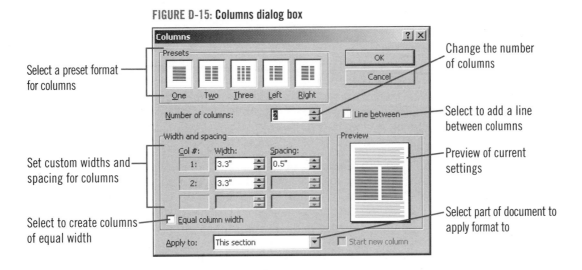

FIGURE D-16: Text formatted in three columns

Column markers show the width and spacing of columns

Text in section 3 is formatted in 3 columns

Section break is at end of section 2

Line added between columns

FIGURE D-17: Completed pages 3 and 4 of newsletter

Text following column break is forced to top of next column

Continuous section break

Column break

Columns in section are balanced

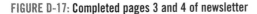

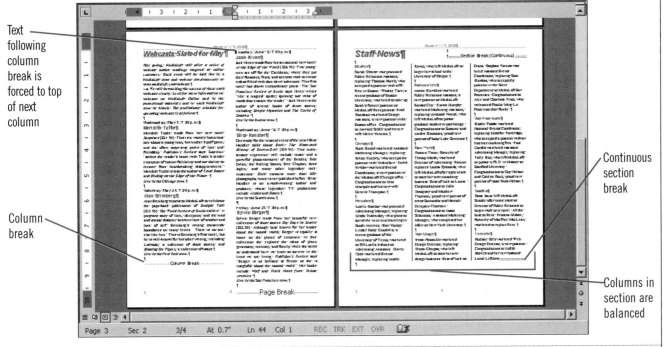

Word 2002

Inserting Clip Art

Illustrating a document with clip art images can give it visual appeal and help to communicate your ideas. **Clip art** is a collection of graphic images that you can insert into a document. Clip art images are stored in the Clip Organizer, a library of the **clips**—media files, including graphics, photographs, sounds, movies, and animations—that come with Word. Clips are organized in collections in the Clip Organizer. You can add a clip to a document using the Clip Art command on the Insert menu. Once you insert a clip art image, you can wrap text around it, resize it, and move it to a different location. ✐ Alice illustrates the second page of the newsletter with a clip art image. After she inserts the image, she wraps text around it, enlarges it, and then moves it so that it is centered between the two columns of text.

1. Click the **Zoom list arrow** on the Standard toolbar, click **Page Width**, scroll to the top of page 2, then place the insertion point before the first body paragraph, which begins **Did you know...**
You will insert the clip art graphic at the location of the insertion point.

2. Click **Insert** on the menu bar, point to **Picture**, then click **Clip Art**
The Insert Clip Art task pane opens, as shown in Figure D-18. You can use this task pane to search for clips related to a keyword.

Trouble?

If the Add Clips to Organizer message box opens, click Later.

3. Select the text in the Search text text box if necessary, type **communication**, then click **Search**
Clips with the keyword "communication" appear in the Insert Clip Art task pane, as shown in Figure D-19. When you point to a clip, a ScreenTip showing the first few keywords applied to the clip, the width and height of the clip in pixels, and the file size and file type for the clip appears.

Trouble?

Select a different clip if the clip shown in Figure D-19 is not available to you.

4. Point to the **clip** shown in Figure D-19, click the **list arrow** that appears next to the clip, click **Insert** on the menu, then close the Insert Clip Art task pane
The clip is inserted at the location of the insertion point. You want to center the graphic on the page. Until you apply text wrapping to a graphic, it is part of the line of text in which it was inserted (an **inline graphic**). To move a graphic independently of text, you must wrap the text around it to make it a **floating graphic**, which can be moved anywhere on a page.

5. Double-click the **clip art image**, click the **Layout tab** in the Format Picture dialog box, click **Tight**, then click **OK**
The text in the first body paragraph wraps around the irregular shape of the clip art image. The white circles that appear on the square edges of the graphic are the **sizing handles**, which appear when a graphic is selected. You can drag a sizing handle to change the size of the image.

QuickTip

To verify the size of a graphic or to set precise measurements, double-click the graphic to open the Format Picture dialog box, then adjust the Height and Width settings on the Size tab.

6. Position the pointer over the **lower-right sizing handle**, when the pointer changes to ↘ drag down and to the right until the graphic is about 2½" wide and 2½" tall
As you drag a sizing handle, the dotted lines show the outline of the graphic. Refer to the dotted lines and the rulers as you resize the graphic. When you release the mouse button, the image is enlarged.

7. With the graphic still selected, position the pointer over the graphic, when the pointer changes to ⊹ drag the graphic down and to the right so it is centered on the page as shown in Figure D-20, release the mouse button, then deselect the graphic
The graphic is now centered between the two columns of text.

Trouble?

If page 3 is a blank page or contains text continued from page 2, reduce the size of the graphic on page 2.

8. Click the **Zoom list arrow**, then click **Two Pages**
The completed pages 1 and 2 are displayed, as shown in Figure D-21.

9. Press **[Ctrl][End]**, press **[Enter]**, type your name, save your changes, print the document, then close the document and exit Word

FIGURE D-18: Insert Clip Art task pane

Type search keyword here

Select collections in which to search for clips

Select type of clips

Click to open the Clip Organizer

Click to search for clips online

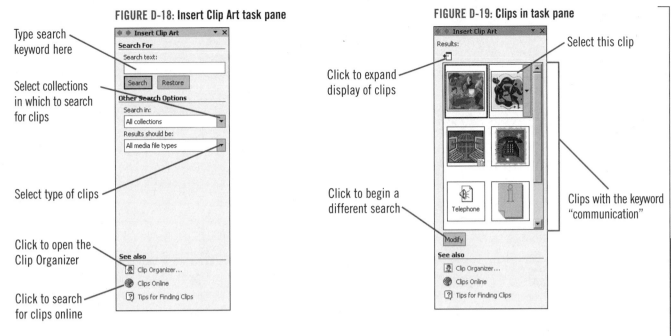

FIGURE D-19: Clips in task pane

Select this clip

Click to expand display of clips

Click to begin a different search

Clips with the keyword "communication"

FIGURE D-20: Graphic being moved to a new location

Sizing handle

Text is wrapped around graphic

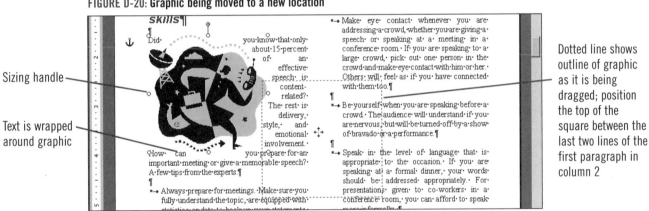

Dotted line shows outline of graphic as it is being dragged; position the top of the square between the last two lines of the first paragraph in column 2

FIGURE D-21: Completed pages 1 and 2 of newsletter

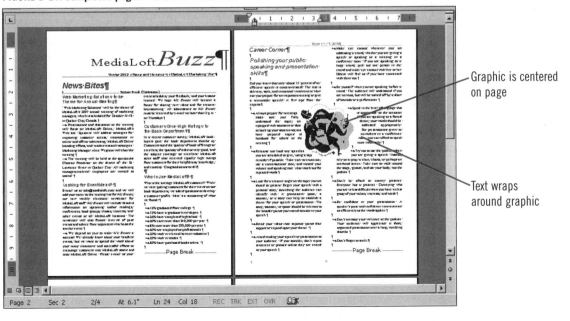

Graphic is centered on page

Text wraps around graphic

Practice

► Concepts Review

Label each element shown in Figure D-22.

FIGURE D-22

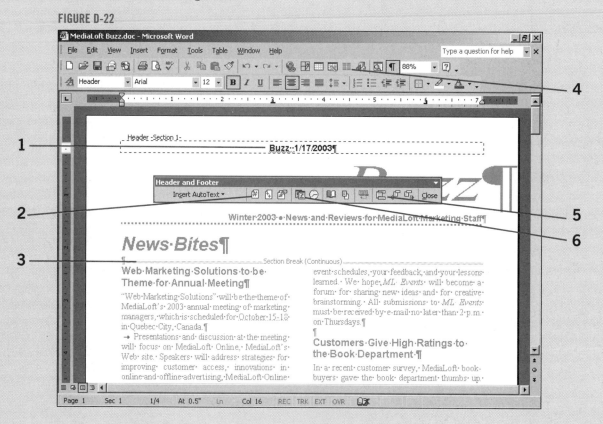

Match each term with the statement that best describes it.

7. **Section break**   a. A formatting mark that forces the text following the mark to begin at the top of the next page

8. **Header**   b. The blank area between the edge of the text and the edge of the page

9. **Footer**   c. A placeholder for information that changes

10. **Field**   d. Text or graphics that appears at the top of every page in a document

11. **Hard page break**   e. An image to which text wrapping has been applied

12. **Margin**   f. A formatting mark that divides a document into parts that can be formatted differently

13. **Inline graphic**   g. An image that is inserted as part of a line of text

14. **Floating graphic**   h. Text or graphics that appears at the bottom of every page in a document

Select the best answer from the list of choices.

15. Which of the following do documents with mirror margins always have?
a. Landscape orientation
b. Inside and outside margins
c. Gutters
d. Different first page headers and footers

16. Which button is used to insert a field into a header or footer?
a. ▨
b. ▣
c. ▨
d. ▨

17. Which type of break do you insert if you want to force text to begin on the next page?
a. Continuous section break
b. Soft page break
c. Hard page break
d. Text wrapping break

18. Which type of break do you insert if you want to balance the columns in a section?
a. Continuous section break
b. Soft page break
c. Column break
d. Text wrapping break

19. What must you do to change an inline graphic to a floating graphic?
a. Resize the graphic
b. Move the graphic
c. Apply text wrapping to the graphic
d. Anchor the graphic

20. Pressing [Ctrl][Enter] does which of the following?
a. Inserts a soft page break
b. Inserts a continuous section break
c. Moves the insertion point to the beginning of the document
d. Inserts a hard page break

▶ Skills Review

1. Set document margins.
a. Start Word, open the file WD D-2 from the drive and folder where your Project Files are located, then save it as **Amherst Fitness**.
b. Change the top and bottom margins to 1.2" and the left and right margins to 1".
c. Save your changes to the document.

2. Divide a document into sections.
a. Scroll down, then insert a continuous section break before the **Facilities** heading.
b. Format the text in Section 2 in two columns, then save your changes to the document.

3. Add page breaks.
a. Insert a hard page break before the heading **Welcome to the Amherst Fitness Center!**, scrolling up if necessary.
b. Scroll down and insert a hard page break before the heading **Services**.
c. Scroll down and insert a hard page break before the heading **Membership**.
d. Press [Ctrl][Home], then save your changes to the document.

4. Add page numbers.
a. Insert page numbers in the document. Center the page numbers at the bottom of the page.
b. View the page numbers on each page in Print Preview, then save your changes to the document.

5. Insert headers and footers.
a. Open the Header and Footer areas, then type your name in the Header area.
b. Press [Tab] twice, then use the Insert Date button on the Header and Footer toolbar to insert the current date.
c. On the horizontal ruler, drag the right tab stop from the 6" mark to the 6½" mark so that the date aligns with the right margin of the document.
d. Move the insertion point to the Footer area.
e. Double-click the page number to select it, then format the page number in bold italic.
f. Close headers and footers, preview the header and footer on each page in Print Preview, close Print Preview, then save your changes to the document.

6. Edit headers and footers.

a. Open headers and footers, then apply italic to the text in the header.

b. Move the insertion point to the Footer area, double-click the page number to select it, then press [Delete].

c. Click the Align Right button on the Formatting toolbar.

d. Use the Symbol command on the Insert menu to open the Symbol dialog box.

e. Insert a black right-pointing triangle symbol, then close the Symbol dialog box.

f. Use the Insert Page Number button on the Header and Footer toolbar to insert a page number.

g. Use the Page Setup button on the Header and Footer toolbar to open the Page Setup dialog box.

h. Use the Layout tab to create a different header and footer for the first page of the document.

i. Scroll to the beginning of the document. If you want your name on the first page of the document, type your name in the First Page Header area, then apply italic to your name.

j. Close headers and footers, preview the header and footer on each page in Print Preview, close Print Preview, then save your changes to the document.

7. Format columns.

a. On page 2, select **Facilities** and the paragraph mark below it, use the Columns button to format the selected text as one column, then center **Facilities** on the page.

b. Balance the columns on page 2 by inserting a continuous section break at the bottom of the second column.

c. On page 3, select **Services** and the paragraph mark below it, format the selected text as one column, then center the text.

d. Balance the columns on page 3.

e. On page 4, select **Membership** and the paragraph mark below it, format the selected text as one column, then center the text.

f. Insert a column break before the **Membership Cards** heading, then save your changes to the document.

8. Insert clip art.

a. On page 1, place the insertion point in the second blank paragraph below **A Rehabilitation and Exercise Facility**. (*Hint*: Place the insertion point to the left of the paragraph mark.)

b. Open the Insert Clip Art task pane. Search for clips related to the keyword **Victories**.

c. Insert the clip shown in Figure D-23. Select a different clip if this one is not available to you.

d. Select the graphic, then drag the lower-right sizing handle up and to the left so that the graphic is about 2" wide and 3" tall. Size the graphic so that all the text and the hard page break fit on page 1. (*Hint*: The sizing handles on inline graphics are black squares.)

e. Scroll to page 3, then place the insertion point before the **Personal Training** heading.

f. In the Insert Clip Art task pane, search for an appropriate clip to illustrate this page. You might try searching using the keywords **sports**, **health**, or **heart**.

g. When you find an appropriate clip, insert it in the document, then close the Insert Clip Art task pane.

h. Double-click the graphic to open the Format Picture dialog box, then click the Layout tab. Apply the Tight text wrapping style to the graphic.

i. Move the graphic so that it is centered below the text at the bottom of the page (below the page break mark). Adjust the size and position of the graphic so that the page looks attractive.

j. Save your changes to the document. Preview the document, print a copy, then close the document and exit Word.

FIGURE D-23

The Amherst Fitness Center

A Rehabilitation and Exercise Facility

Member Services

► Independent Challenge 1

You are the owner of a small catering business in Latona, Ontario called Bon Appetit Catering Services. You have begun work on the text for a brochure advertising your business and are now ready to lay out the pages and prepare the final copy. The brochure will be printed on both sides of an 8½" × 11" sheet of paper, and folded in thirds.

Word 2002

FIGURE D-24

a. Start Word, open the file WD D-3 from the drive and folder where your Project Files are located, then save it as **Bon Appetit**. Read the document to get a feel for its contents.

b. Change the page orientation to landscape, and change all four margins to .6".

c. Format the document in three columns of equal width.

d. Insert a hard page break before the heading **Catering Services**.

e. On page 1, insert column breaks before the headings **Sample Indian Banquet Menu** and **Sample Tuscan Banquet Menu**.

f. On page 1, insert a continuous section break at the end of the third column.

g. Add lines between the columns on the first page, then center the text in the columns.

h. Create a different header and footer for the first page. Type **Call for custom menus designed to your taste and budget** in the First Page Footer area.

i. Center the text in the footer area, format it in 20-point Comic Sans MS, all caps, with a plum font color, then close headers and footers.

j. On page 2, insert a column break before Your Name. Press [Enter] as many times as necessary to move the contact information to the bottom of the second column. Be sure all five lines of the contact information are in column 2 and do not flow to the next column.

k. Replace Your Name with your name, then center the contact information in the column.

l. Insert a column break at the bottom of the second column. Then, type the text shown in Figure D-24 in the third column. Refer to the figure as you follow the instructions for formatting the text in the third column.

m. Format **Bon Appetit Catering Services** in 28-point Comic Sans MS, bold, with a plum font color.

n. Format the remaining text in 12-point Comic Sans MS, with a plum font color. Center the text in the third column.

o. Below Bon Appetit, insert the symbol shown in Figure D-24. (*Hint*: Type the character code 25CA in the Character code text box in the Symbol dialog box to find the symbol.) Change the font color of the symbol to gold.

p. Insert the clip art graphic shown in Figure D-24 or another appropriate clip art graphic. Do not wrap text around the graphic.

q. Add and remove blank paragraphs in the third column of your brochure so that the spacing between elements roughly matches the spacing shown in Figure D-24.

r. Save your changes, preview the brochure in Print Preview, then print a copy. If possible, print the two pages of the brochure back to back so that the brochure can be folded in thirds. Close the document and exit Word.

▶ Independent Challenge 2

You work in the Campus Safety Department at Miller State College. You have written the text for an informational flyer about parking regulations on campus and now you need to format the flyer so it is attractive and readable.

a. Start Word, open the file WD D-4 from the drive and folder where your Project Files are located, then save it as **Parking FAQ**. Read the document to get a feel for its contents.

b. Change all four margins to .7".

c. Insert a continuous section break before **1. May I bring a car to school?** (*Hint*: Place the insertion point before "May.")

d. Scroll down and insert a next page section break before **Sample Parking Permit**.

e. Format the text in section 2 in three columns of equal width with .3" of space between the columns.

f. Hyphenate the document using the automatic hyphenation feature. (*Hint*: If the Hyphenation feature is not installed on your computer, skip this step.)

g. Add a 3-pt dotted line bottom border to the blank paragraph under Miller State College. (*Hint*: Place the insertion point before the paragraph mark under Miller State College, then apply a bottom border to the paragraph.)

h. Add your name to the header. Right-align your name and format it in 10-point Arial.

i. Add the following text to the footer, inserting symbols between words as indicated: **Parking and Shuttle Service Office • 54 Buckley Street • Miller State College • 942-555-2227.**

j. Format the footer text in 10-point Arial Black and center it in the footer. Use a different font if Arial Black is not available to you. If necessary adjust the font and font size so that the entire address fits on one line.

k. Apply a 3-pt dotted line border above the footer text. Make sure to apply the border to the paragraph.

l. Balance the columns in section 2.

m. Add an appropriate clip art image to the upper-right corner of the document, above the border. Make sure the graphic does not obscure the border.

n. Place the insertion point on page 2 (which is section 4). Change the left and right margins in section 4 to 1". Also change the page orientation of section 4 to landscape.

o. Change the vertical alignment of section 4 to Center.

p. Save your changes, preview the flyer in Print Preview, then print a copy. If possible, print the two pages of the flyer back to back. Close the document and exit Word.

▶ Independent Challenge 3

A book publisher would like to publish an article you wrote on stormwater pollution in Australia as a chapter in a forthcoming book called *Environmental Issues for the New Millennium*. The publisher has requested that you format your article like a book chapter before submitting it for publication, and has provided you with a style sheet.

a. Start Word, open the file WD D-5 from the drive and folder where your Project Files are located, then save it as **Stormwater**.

b. Change the font of the entire document to 11-point Book Antiqua. If this font is not available to you, select a different font suitable for the pages of a book. Change the alignment to justified.

c. Change the paper size to 6" × 9".

d. Create mirror margins. (*Hint*: Use the Multiple Pages list arrow.) Change the top and bottom margins to .8", change the inside margin to .4", change the outside margin to .6", and create a .3" gutter to allow room for the book's binding.

e. Change the Zoom level to Two Pages. Create different headers and footers for odd- and even- numbered pages.

f. Change the Zoom level to Page Width. In the odd page header, type **Chapter 7**, insert a symbol of your choice, then type **Stormwater Pollution in the Fairy Creek Catchment**.

g. Format the header text in 9-point Book Antiqua italic, then right-align the text.

h. In the even page header, type your name, insert a symbol of your choice, then insert the current date. (*Hint*: Scroll down or use the Show Next button to move the insertion point to the even page header.)

i. Change the format of the date to include just the month and the year. (*Hint*: Right-click the date field, then click Edit Field.)

j. Format the header text in 9-point Book Antiqua italic. The even page header should be left-aligned.

k. Insert page numbers that are centered in the footer. Format the page number in 10-point Book Antiqua. Make sure to insert a page number field in both the odd and even page footer areas.

l. Format the page numbers so that the first page of Chapter 7 begins on page 53. (*Hint*: Select a page number field, then use the Format Page Number button.)

m. Go to the beginning of the document, press [Enter] 10 times, type **Chapter 7: Stormwater Pollution in the Fairy Creek Catchment**, press [Enter] twice, type your name, then press [Enter] twice.

n. Format the chapter title in 16-point Book Antiqua bold, format your name in 14-point Book Antiqua using small caps, then left-align the text.

o. Save your changes, preview the chapter in Print Preview, print the first three pages of the chapter, then close the document and exit Word.

 # Independent Challenge 4

One of the most common opportunities to use Word's page layout features is when formatting a research paper. The format recommended by the *MLA Handbook for Writers of Research Papers*, a style guide that includes information on preparing, writing, and formatting research papers, is the standard format used by many schools, colleges, and universities. In this independent challenge, you will research the MLA (Modern Language Association) guidelines for formatting a research paper and use the guidelines you find to prepare a sample first page of a research report.

a. Start Word, open the file WD D-6 from the drive and folder where your Project Files are located, then save it as **MLA Style**. This document contains the questions you will answer about MLA style guidelines.

b. Use your favorite search engine to search the Web for information on the MLA guidelines for formatting a research report. Use the keywords **MLA Style** and **research paper format**, to conduct your search. If your search does not result in links to appropriate sources, try the following Web sites: http://webster.commnet.edu/mla.htm or www.mla.org.

c. Look for information on the proper formatting for the following aspects of a research paper: paper size, margins, title page or first page of the report, line spacing, paragraph indentation, page numbers, and works cited.

d. Type your answers to the questions in the MLA Style document, save it, print a copy, then close the document.

e. Using the information you learned, start a new document and create a sample first page of a research report. Use **MLA Format for Research Papers** as the title for your sample report, and make up information about the course and instructor, if necessary. For the body of the report, type several sentences about MLA style. Make sure to format the page exactly as the MLA style dictates.

f. Save the document as **MLA Sample Format** to the drive and folder where your Project Files are located, print a copy, close the document, then exit Word.

► Visual Workshop

Use the file WD D-7, found on the drive and folder where your Project Files are located, to create the article shown in Figure D-25. (*Hint*: Change all four margins to .6". Make the width of the first column 2.2" and the width of the second column 4.8". Format the second column with borders and shading, but take care not to apply shading to the blank paragraph before the Clean Up heading. Select a different clip if the clip shown in the figure is not available to you.) Save the document with the filename **Gardener's Corner**, then print a copy.

FIGURE D-25

GARDENER'S CORNER

Putting a Perennial Garden to Bed

By Your Name

A certain sense of peace descends when a perennial garden is put to bed for the season. The plants are safely tucked in against the elements, and the garden is ready to welcome the first signs of life. When the work is done, you can sit back and anticipate the bright blooms of spring. Many gardeners are uncertain of how to close a perennial garden. This week's column demystifies the process.

Clean up

Debris that is left on top of soil invites garden pests to lay their eggs and spend the winter. Garden clean up can be a gradual process—plants will deteriorate at different rates, allowing you to do a little bit each week.

1. Edge beds and borders and remove stakes and other plant supports.
2. Dig and divide irises, daylilies, and other early bloomers.
3. Cut back plants when foliage starts to deteriorate.
4. Rake all debris out of the garden and pull any weeds that remain.

Plant perennials

Fall is the perfect time to plant perennials! The warm, sunny days and cool nights provide optimal conditions for new root growth.

1. Dig deeply and enhance soil with organic matter.
2. Use a good starter fertilizer to speed up new root growth.
3. Untangle the roots of new plants before planting them.
4. Water deeply after planting as the weather dictates.

Add compost

Organic matter is the key ingredient to healthy soil. If you take care of the soil, your plants will become strong and disease resistant.

1. Use an iron rake to loosen the top few inches of soil.
2. Spread a one to two inch layer of compost over the entire garden.
3. Refrain from stepping on the area and compacting the soil.

To mulch or not to mulch?

Winter protection for perennial beds can only help plants survive the winter. Here's what works and what doesn't:

1. Always apply mulch after the ground is frozen.
2. Never apply generic hay because is contains billions of weed seeds. Also, whole leaves and bark mulch hold too much moisture.
3. Straw and salt marsh hay are excellent choices for mulch.

Getting
Started with Excel 2002

Objectives

► **Define spreadsheet software**
► **Start Excel 2002**
► **View the Excel window**
⌐MOUS⌐ ► **Open and save a workbook**
⌐MOUS⌐ ► **Enter labels and values**
⌐MOUS⌐ ► **Name and move a sheet**
⌐MOUS⌐ ► **Preview and print a worksheet**
► **Get Help**
► **Close a workbook and exit Excel**

In this unit, you will learn how to start Microsoft Excel 2002 and identify elements in the Excel window. You will also learn how to open and save existing files, enter data in a worksheet, manipulate worksheets, and use the extensive Help system. Jim Fernandez is the office manager at MediaLoft, a nationwide chain of bookstore cafés selling books, CDs, DVDs, and videos. MediaLoft cafés sell coffee and pastries. Jim wants you to help him use Excel to analyze a worksheet summarizing budget information for the MediaLoft Café in the New York City store.

Defining Spreadsheet Software

Microsoft Excel is an electronic spreadsheet program that runs on Windows computers. You use an **electronic spreadsheet** to produce professional-looking documents that perform numeric calculations rapidly and accurately. These calculations are updated automatically so that accurate information is always available. See Table A-1 for common ways spreadsheets are used in business. The electronic spreadsheet that you produce when using Excel is also referred to as a **worksheet**. Individual worksheets are stored within a **workbook**, which is a file with the .xls file extension. Each new workbook contains three worksheets. ✏ Jim uses Excel extensively to track MediaLoft finances. Figure A-1 shows a budget worksheet that Jim created using pencil and paper, while Figure A-2 shows the same worksheet Jim created using Excel.

The advantages of using Excel include:

► Enter data quickly and accurately

With Excel, you can enter information faster and more accurately than with pencil and paper. For example, in the MediaLoft NYC Café budget, certain expenses, such as rent, cleaning supplies, and products supplied on a yearly contract (coffee, creamers, sweeteners), remain constant for the year. You can copy the expenses that don't change from quarter to quarter, and then use Excel to calculate Total Expenses and Net Income for each quarter by supplying the data and formulas.

► Recalculate data easily

Fixing typing errors or updating data using Excel is easy, and the results of a changed entry are recalculated automatically. For example, if you receive updated expense figures for Quarter 4, you enter the new numbers and Excel recalculates the worksheet.

► Perform a what-if analysis

The Excel ability to change data and let you quickly view the recalculated results makes it a powerful decision-making tool. For instance, if the salary budget per quarter is increased to $14,500, you can enter the new figure into the worksheet and immediately see the impact on the overall budget. Any time you use a worksheet to ask the question "what if?" you are performing a **what-if analysis**.

► Change the appearance of information

Excel provides powerful features for making information visually appealing and easy to understand. For example, you can use boldface type and colored or shaded text headings or numbers to emphasize important worksheet data and trends.

► Create charts

Excel makes it easy to create charts based on worksheet information. Charts are updated automatically as data changes. The worksheet in Figure A-2 includes a 3-D pie chart that shows the distribution of the budget expenses for the MediaLoft NYC Café.

► Share information with other users

Because everyone at MediaLoft is now using Microsoft Office, it's easy for them to share worksheet data. For example, you can complete the MediaLoft budget that your manager started creating in Excel. Simply access the files you need or want to share through the network or from a disk, or through the use of online collaboration tools (such as intranets and the Internet), and then make any changes or additions.

► Create new worksheets from existing ones quickly

It's easy to take an existing Excel worksheet and quickly modify it to create a new one. When you are ready to create next year's budget, you can open the file for this year's budget, save it with a new filename, and use the existing data as a starting point. An Excel file can also be created using a special format called a **template**, which lets you open a new file based on an existing workbook's design and/or content. Office comes with many prepared templates you can use.

FIGURE A-1: Traditional paper worksheet

MediaLoft NYC Café Budget

	Qtr 1	Qtr 2	Qtr 3	Qtr 4	Total
Net Sales	56,000	84,000	72,000	79,000	291,000
Expenses					
Salary	14,500	14,500	14,500	14,500	58,000
Rent	4,000	4,000	4,000	4,000	16,000
Advertising	3,750	8,000	3,750	3,750	19,250
Cleansers	1,500	1,500	1,500	1,500	6,000
Pastries	2,500	2,500	2,500	2,500	10,000
Milk/Cream	1,000	1,000	1,000	1,000	4,000
Coffee/Tea	4,700	4,750	4,750	4,750	18,950
Sweeteners	300	300	300	300	1,200
Total Expenses	32,250	36,550	32,300	32,300	133,400
Net Income	23,750	47,450	39,700	46,700	157,600

FIGURE A-2: Excel worksheet

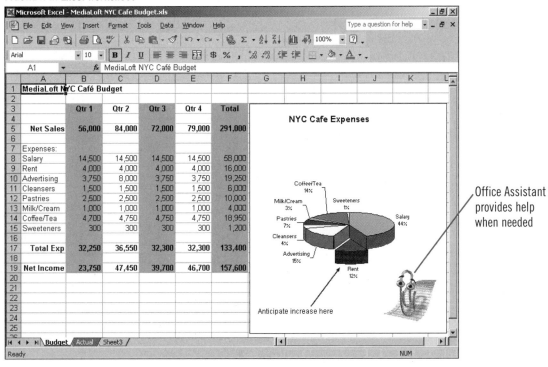

Office Assistant provides help when needed

TABLE A-1: Common business uses for electronic spreadsheets

spreadsheets are used to	by
Maintain values	Calculating numbers
Represent values graphically	Creating charts based on worksheet figures
Create consecutively numbered pages using multiple workbook sheets	Printing reports containing workbook sheets
Organize data	Sorting data in ascending or descending order
Analyze data	Creating data summaries and short-lists using PivotTables or AutoFilters
Create what-if data scenarios	Using variable values to investigate and sample different outcomes

Excel 2002

Starting Excel 2002

To start any Windows program, you use the Start button on the taskbar. A slightly different procedure might be required for computers on a network and those that use Windows-enhancing utilities. If you need assistance, ask your instructor or technical support person. ◄━━━ Jim is ready to begin work on the budget for the MediaLoft Café in New York City. He begins by starting Excel.

Steps 1 2 3 4

1. Point to the **Start button** 🏁 Start on the taskbar
The Start button is on the left side of the taskbar. You use it to start programs on your computer.

2. Click 🏁 Start
Microsoft Excel is located in the Programs folder, which is at the top of the Start menu, as shown in Figure A-3.

3. Point to **Programs**
The Programs menu opens. All the programs on your computer, including Microsoft Excel, are listed on this menu. See Figure A-4. Your program menu might look different, depending on the programs installed on your computer.

Trouble?

If you don't see the Microsoft Excel icon, see your instructor or technical support person.

4. Click the **Microsoft Excel program icon** on the Programs menu
Excel opens and a blank worksheet appears. In the next lesson, you will learn about the elements of the Excel worksheet window.

5. If necessary, click the **Maximize button** 🔲 on the title bar

FIGURE A-3: Start menu

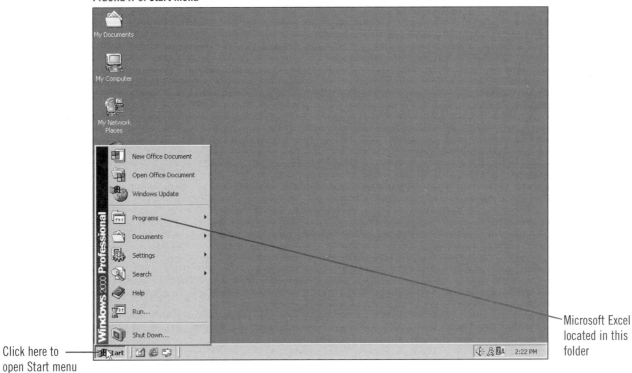

Click here to — open Start menu

Microsoft Excel located in this folder

FIGURE A-4: Programs list

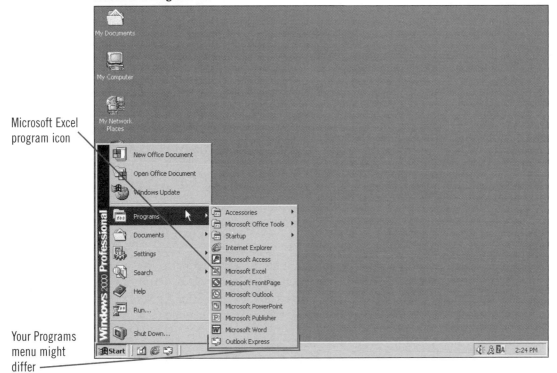

Microsoft Excel program icon

Your Programs menu might differ

Viewing the Excel Window

Excel 2002

When you start Excel, the **worksheet window** appears on your screen. The worksheet window includes the tools that enable you to create and work with worksheets. Jim needs to familiarize himself with the Excel worksheet window and its elements before he starts working with the budget worksheet. Compare the descriptions below to the elements shown in Figure A-5.

Details

▶ The **worksheet window** contains a grid of columns and rows. Columns are labeled alphabetically (A, B, C, etc.) and rows are labeled numerically (1, 2, 3, etc.). The worksheet window displays only a small fraction of the whole worksheet, which has a total of 256 columns and 65,536 rows. The intersection of a column and a row is called a **cell**. Cells can contain text, numbers, formulas, or a combination of all three. Every cell has its own unique location or **cell address**, which is identified by the coordinates of the intersecting column and row. For example, the cell address of the cell in the upper-left corner of a worksheet is A1. The **new workbook pane** appears to the right of the worksheet window and lets you quickly open new or existing workbooks. The **Task pane list arrow** lets you display other panes.

▶ The **cell pointer** is a dark rectangle that outlines the cell you are working in. This cell is called the **active cell**. In Figure A-5, the cell pointer is located at A1, so A1 is the active cell. The column and row headings for the active cell are purple; inactive column and row headings are gray. To activate a different cell, just click any other cell or press the arrow keys on your keyboard to move the cell pointer elsewhere.

> **Trouble?**
>
> If your screen does not display cells in purple and gray as shown in the figure, ask your technical support person to check your Windows color settings.

▶ The **title bar** displays the program name (Microsoft Excel) and the filename of the open worksheet (in this case the default filename, Book1). As shown in Figure A-5, the title bar also contains a control menu box, a Close button, and resizing buttons, which are common to all Windows programs.

▶ The **menu bar** contains menus from which you choose Excel commands. As with all Windows programs, you can choose a menu command by clicking it with the mouse pointer or by pressing [Alt] plus the underlined letter in the menu command name. When you click a menu, only a short list of commonly used commands may appear at first; you can wait or click the double arrows at the bottom of the menu to see expanded menus with more commands.

▶ The **name box** displays the active cell address. In Figure A-5, "A1" appears in the name box, indicating that A1 is the active cell.

▶ The **formula bar** allows you to enter or edit data in the worksheet.

▶ The **toolbars** contain buttons for frequently used Excel commands. The **Standard toolbar** is located just below the menu bar and contains buttons that perform actions within the worksheet. The **Formatting toolbar**—beneath the Standard toolbar—contains buttons that change the worksheet's appearance. Each button contains an image representing its function. For instance, the Print button contains an image of a printer. To choose any button, click it with the left mouse button.

▶ **Sheet tabs** below the worksheet grid let you keep your work in a collection called a **workbook**. Each workbook contains three worksheets by default and can contain a maximum of 255 sheets. Sheet tabs allow you to name your worksheets with meaningful names. **Sheet tab scrolling buttons** help you display hidden worksheets.

▶ The **status bar** is located at the bottom of the Excel window. The left side of the status bar provides a brief description of the active command or task in progress. The right side of the status bar shows the status of important keys such as [Caps Lock] and [Num Lock].

FIGURE A-5: Excel worksheet window elements

Control menu box
Menu bar
Standard toolbar
Formatting toolbar
Name box
Cell pointer highlights active cell
Title bar
Formula bar
Sheet tab scrolling buttons
Sheet tabs
Status bar

Close button
Resizing buttons
Task pane
Task pane list arrow
Pane lets you create new workbooks
Worksheet window
Office Assistant may appear in a different location, or not at all

Working with toolbars and menus in Excel 2002

Although you can configure Excel so that your toolbars and menus modify themselves to conform to your working style, the lessons in this book assume you have turned off personalized menus and toolbars and are working with all menu commands and toolbar buttons displayed. When you use personalized toolbars, the Standard and Formatting toolbars appear on the same row and display only the most frequently used buttons, as shown in Figure A-6. To use a button that is not visible on a toolbar, you click the Toolbar Options button ⬚ at the end of the toolbar, then click the button on the Toolbar Options list. As you work, Excel adds the buttons you use to the visible toolbars and drops the buttons you don't often use to the Toolbar Options list. Similarly, Excel menus adjust to your work habits, so that the commands you use most often appear on shortened menus. You can see all the menu commands by clicking the double arrows at the bottom of a menu. It is often easier to work with full toolbars and menus displayed. To turn off personalized toolbars and menus, click Tools on the menu bar, click Customize, on the Options tab select the Show Standard and Formatting toolbars on two rows and Always show full menus check boxes, and then click Close. The Standard and Formatting toolbars appear on separate rows and display all the buttons, and the menus display the complete list of menu commands. (You can quickly display the toolbars on two rows by clicking a Toolbar Options button and then clicking Show Buttons on Two Rows.)

FIGURE A-6: Toolbars in one row

Toolbar options buttons

Excel 2002

Opening and Saving a Workbook

Sometimes it's more efficient to create a new worksheet by modifying one that already exists. This saves you from having to retype information from previous work. Throughout this book, you will create new workbooks by opening a file from the location where your Project Files are stored, using the Save As command to create a copy of the file with a new name, and then modifying the new file by following the lesson steps. Use the Save command to store changes made to an existing file. It is a good idea to save your work every 10 or 15 minutes and before printing. Saving the files with new names keeps your original Project Files intact, in case you have to start the unit over again or you wish to repeat an exercise. Jim wants you to complete the New York City MediaLoft Café budget that a member of the accounting staff has been working on.

QuickTip

You can also click the Open button 📂 on the Standard toolbar.

1. Click **More Workbooks** in the New Workbook task pane

The Open dialog box opens. See Figure A-7. If no workbooks have been opened on your computer, the command will read "Workbooks."

QuickTip

If you don't see the three-letter extension .xls on the filenames in the Open dialog box, don't worry. Windows can be set up to display or not to display the file extensions.

2. Click the **Look in list arrow**, then click the drive and folder where your Project Files are located

The Look in list arrow lets you navigate to folders and disk drives on your computer. A list of your Project Files appears in the Open dialog box.

3. Click the file **EX A-1**, then click **Open**

The workbook file EX A-1 opens. The new workbook pane no longer appears.

4. Click **File** on the menu bar, then click **Save As**

The Save As dialog box opens, displaying the drive where your Project Files are stored.

QuickTip

You can create a new folder from within the Save As dialog box by clicking 📁 on the dialog box toolbar, typing a name in the Name text box, then clicking OK. To open a file from a folder you create, double-click folders or use the Look in list arrow in the Open dialog box to open the folder, click the filename, then click Open.

5. In the File name text box, select the current filename (if necessary), type **MediaLoft Cafe Budget**, as shown in Figure A-8, then click **Save**

Both the Save As dialog box and the file EX A-1 close, and a duplicate file named MediaLoft Cafe Budget opens, as shown in Figure A-9. The Office Assistant may or may not appear on your screen.

Creating a new workbook

You can create your own worksheets from scratch by opening a new workbook. To create a new workbook, click the New button 🗋 on the Standard toolbar. You can also use the New Workbook pane (located on the right side of the screen) to open a new file. Click the Blank Workbook button 🗋 in the New Workbook pane, and a new workbook will open. Each new workbook automatically contains 3 sheets, although you can insert as many as you need.

FIGURE A-7: Open dialog box

Your folder contents might differ

Your files and folders appear here

Selected filename will appear here

Look in list arrow

My Documents folder opens by default

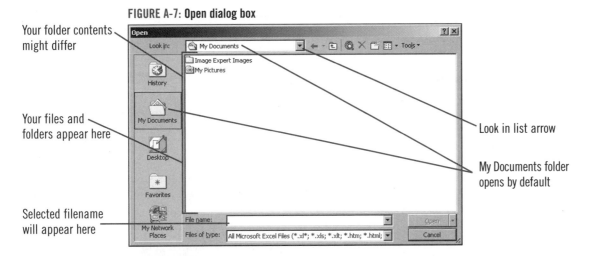

FIGURE A-8: Save As dialog box

Your list of files might differ

Current drive or folder (yours may differ)

Type new filename here

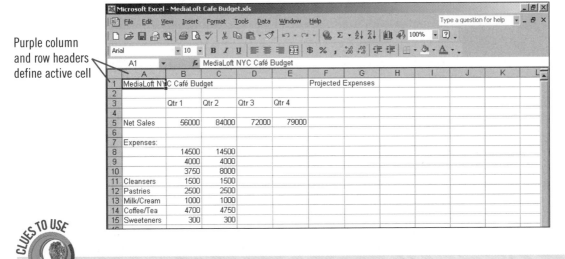

FIGURE A-9: MediaLoft Café Budget workbook

Purple column and row headers define active cell

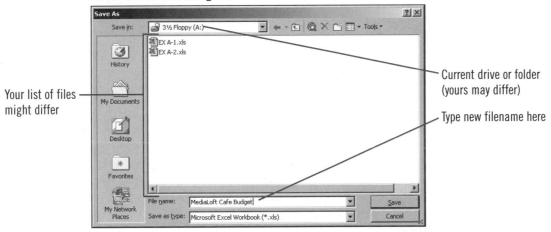

Opening a workbook using a template

You can create a workbook by entering data and formats into a blank workbook, or you can use predesigned workbooks called templates that are included with Excel. Templates let you automatically create workbooks such as balance sheets, expense statements, loan amortizations, sales invoices, or timecards. Templates save you time because they contain labels, values, formulas, and formatting. To open a new document based on a template, click General Templates from the New Workbook task pane, save it under a new name, then add your own information. You may need to have the Office CD available to install the templates.

Entering Labels and Values

Labels help you identify the data in worksheet rows and columns, making your worksheet more readable and understandable. Try to enter all labels in your worksheet before entering the data. Labels can contain text and numerical information not used in calculations, such as dates, times, or addresses. Labels are left-aligned by default. **Values**, which include numbers, formulas, and functions, are used in calculations. Excel recognizes an entry as a value when it is a number or begins with special symbols: +, -, =, @, #, or $. Because Excel treats labels and values differently, you can have a label such as '2003 Sales' without affecting values used in a totals column. All values are right-aligned by default. When a cell contains both text and numbers it is not a valid formula; Excel recognizes the entry as a label. Jim wants you to enter labels identifying the rest of the expense categories, and the values for Qtr 3 and Qtr 4 into the MediaLoft Café Budget worksheet.

1. **Click cell A8 to make it the active cell**

   Notice that the cell address A8 appears in the name box. As you work, the mouse pointer takes on a variety of appearances, depending on where it is and what Excel is doing. Table A-2 lists and identifies some mouse pointers. The labels in cells A8:A15 identify the expenses.

2. **Type Salary, as shown in Figure A-10, then click the Enter button ✓ on the formula bar**

   As you type, the word "Enter" appears in the status bar. Clicking the Enter button indicates that you are finished typing or changing your entry, and the word "Ready" appears in the status bar. Because the cell is still selected, its contents still appear in the formula bar. You can also confirm a cell entry by pressing [Enter], [Tab], or one of the keyboard arrow keys. These three methods also select an adjacent cell. To confirm an entry and leave the same cell selected, you can press [Ctrl][Enter]. If a label does not fit in a cell, Excel displays the remaining characters in the next cell to the right, as long as it is empty. Otherwise, the label is **truncated**, or cut off.

3. **Click cell A9, type Rent, press [Enter] to confirm the entry and move the cell pointer to cell A10, type Advertising in cell A10, then press [Enter]**

   The remaining expense values have to be added to the worksheet.

4. **Click cell D8, press and hold down the left mouse button, drag ✛ to cell E8 then down to cell E15, then release the mouse button**

   You have selected a **range**, which is two or more adjacent cells. The active cell is still cell D8, and the cells in the range are shaded in purple.

5. **Type 14500, press [Enter], type 4000 in cell D9, press [Enter], type 3750 in cell D10, press [Enter], type 1500 in cell D11, press [Enter], type 2500 in cell D12, press [Enter], type 1000 in cell D13, press [Enter], type 4750 in cell D14, press [Enter], type 300 in cell D15, then press [Enter]**

   You will often enter data in multiple columns and rows; selecting a range makes working with data entry easier because pressing [Enter] makes the next cell in the range active. You have entered all the values in the Qtr 3 column, as shown in Figure A-11. The cell pointer is now in cell E8.

6. **Using Figure A-11 as a guide, type the remaining values for cells E8 through E15**

   Before confirming a cell entry, you can click the Cancel button on the formula bar or press [Esc] to cancel or delete the entry. Notice that the AutoCalculate area in the status bar displays "Sum=64550," which is the sum of the figures in the selected range. This sum changes if you change any of the numbers in the selected range.

7. **Click cell D8, type 14550, press [Enter], then select cells D8:E15**

   Notice that the AutoCalculate area in the status bar now says "Sum=64600".

8. **Press [Ctrl][Home] to return to cell A1**

9. **Click the Save button 🖫 on the Standard toolbar**

   You can also press [Ctrl][S] to save a worksheet.

FIGURE A-10: Worksheet with first label entered

Enter button

Name box

Cancel button

Formula bar

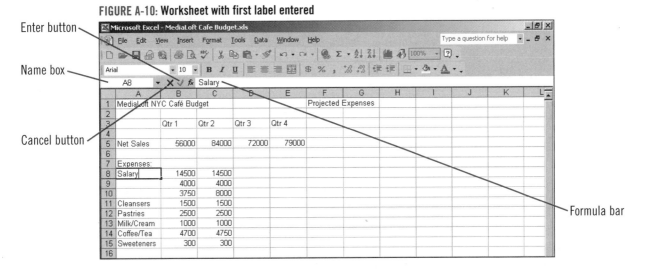

FIGURE A-11: Worksheet with new labels and values

Type these values

Labels entered

Values entered

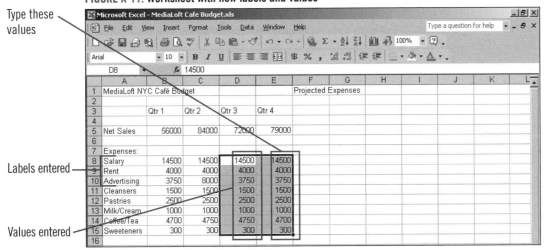

TABLE A-2: Commonly used pointers

name	pointer	use to
Normal	✛	Select a cell or range; indicates Ready mode
Copy	⬉⁺	Create a duplicate of the selected cell(s)
Fill handle	✚	Create an alphanumeric series in a range
I-beam	I	Edit contents of formula bar
Move	⬘	Change the location of the selected cell(s)

Navigating a worksheet

With over a million cells available to you, it is important to know how to move around, or navigate, a worksheet. You can use the arrow keys on the keyboard ([↑] [↓] [←] or [→]) to move a cell or two at a time, or use [Page Up] or [Page Down] to move a screenful at a time. To move a screen to the left press [Alt][Page Up]; to move a screen to the right press [Alt][Page Down]. You can also use the mouse pointer to click the desired cell. If the desired cell is not visible in the worksheet window, use the scroll bars or the Go To command on the Edit menu to move the location into view. To return to the first active cell in a worksheet, click cell A1, or press [Ctrl][Home].

Excel 2002

Excel 2002

Naming and Moving a Sheet

Each workbook initially contains three worksheets, named Sheet1, Sheet2, and Sheet3. When you open a workbook, the first worksheet is the active sheet. To move from sheet to sheet, you can click any sheet tab at the bottom of the worksheet window. The sheet tab scrolling buttons, located to the left of the sheet tabs, allow you to display hidden sheet tabs. To make it easier to identify the sheets in a workbook, you can rename each sheet, add color to the tabs, and then organize them in a logical way. The sheet name appears on the sheet tab. For instance, to better track performance goals, you could name each workbook sheet for an individual salesperson; then you could move the sheets so they appeared in alphabetical order. ◄━━━ Jim wants to be able to easily identify the actual expenses and the projected expenses. He wants you to name two sheets in his workbook, add color to distinguish them, then change their order.

1. Click the **Sheet2 tab**
Sheet2 becomes active; this is the worksheet that contains the actual quarterly expenses. Its tab moves to the front, and Sheet1 moves to the background.

2. Click the **Sheet1 tab**
Sheet1, which contains the projected expenses, becomes active again. Once you have confirmed which sheet is which, you can assign them each a name that you can easily remember.

QuickTip

You can also rename a sheet by right-clicking the tab, clicking Rename, typing the new name, then pressing [Enter].

3. Double-click the **Sheet2 tab**
Sheet 2 becomes the active sheet with the default sheet name ("Sheet2") selected.

4. Type **Actual**, then press **[Enter]**
The new name automatically replaces the default name in the tab. Worksheet names can have up to 31 characters, including spaces and punctuation.

5. Right-click the **Actual tab**, then click **Tab Color**
The Format Tab Color dialog box appears, as shown in Figure A-12.

QuickTip

To delete a worksheet, select the worksheet you want to delete, click Edit on the menu bar, then click Delete sheet. To insert a worksheet, click Insert on the menu bar, then click Worksheet.

6. Click the color **red** (first column, third row), click **OK**, double-click the **Sheet1 tab**, type **Projected**, then press **[Enter]**
Notice that when you renamed Sheet1, the color of the entire Actual tab changed to red. Jim decides to rearrange the order of the sheets, so that Actual comes before Projected.

7. Click the **Actual sheet tab** and hold down the mouse button, then drag it to the left of the **Projected sheet tab**
As you drag, the pointer changes to ▷, the sheet relocation pointer, and a small, black triangle shows its position. See Figure A-13. The first sheet in the workbook is now the Actual sheet. When you have more worksheets than can appear at once, click the leftmost tab scrolling button to display the first sheet tab; click the rightmost navigation button to display the last sheet tab. The left and right buttons move one sheet in their respective directions.

8. Click the **Projected sheet tab**, enter your name in cell **A20**, then press **[Ctrl][Home]**
Your name identifies your worksheet as yours, which is helpful if you are sharing a printer.

9. Click the **Save button** 🖫 on the Standard toolbar

FIGURE A-12: Format Tab Color dialog box

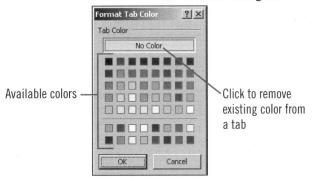

Available colors

Click to remove
existing color from
a tab

FIGURE A-13: Moving Actual sheet before Projected sheet

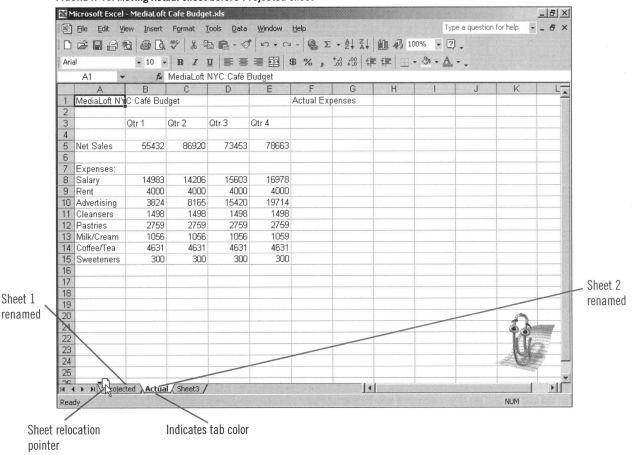

Sheet 1
renamed

Sheet 2
renamed

Sheet relocation
pointer

Indicates tab color

CLUES TO USE

Copying worksheets

There are times when you may want to copy a worksheet. To copy it, press [Ctrl] as you drag the sheet tab and release the mouse button before you release [Ctrl]. You can also move and copy worksheets between workbooks. You must have the workbook that you are copying to, as well as the workbook that you are copying from, open. Select the sheet to copy or move, click Edit on the menu bar, then click Move or Copy sheet. Complete the information in the Move or Copy dialog box. Be sure to click the Create a Copy check box if you are copying rather than moving the worksheet. Carefully check your calculation results whenever you move or copy a worksheet.

Previewing and Printing a Worksheet

After you complete a worksheet, you may want to print it to have a paper copy for reference or to give to others. You can also print a worksheet that is not complete to review your work when you are not at a computer. Before you print a worksheet, you should save any changes. That way, if anything happens to the file as it is being sent to the printer, you will have your latest work saved. Then you should preview it to make sure it will fit on a page the way you want. When you **preview** a worksheet, you see a copy of the worksheet exactly as it will appear on paper. See Table A-3 for a summary of printing tips. ✎ Jim is finished entering the labels and values into the MediaLoft Café budget. He has already saved his changes, so he asks you to preview and print a copy of the worksheet he can review on the way home.

1. Make sure the printer is on and contains paper
If a file is sent to print and the printer is off, an error message appears.

2. Click the **Print Preview button** 🔍 on the Standard toolbar
A miniature version of the worksheet appears on the screen, as shown in Figure A-14. If your worksheet requires more than one page, you could click the Next button or the Previous button to move between pages. Because your worksheet is only one page, the Next and Previous buttons are dimmed.

QuickTip

To print the worksheet using existing settings without previewing it, click 🖨 on the Standard toolbar.

3. Click **Print**
The Print dialog box opens, as shown in Figure A-15.

4. Make sure that the **Active Sheet(s) option button** is selected in the Print what section and that **1** appears in the Number of copies text box in the Copies section
Adjusting the value in the Number of copies text box enables you to print multiple copies. You could also print a selected range by clicking the Selection option button.

QuickTip

After previewing or printing a worksheet, dotted lines appear on the screen indicating individual page breaks in the printout. Page break positions vary with each printer.

5. Click **OK**
A Printing dialog box appears briefly while the file is sent to the printer. Note that the dialog box contains a Cancel button. You can use it to cancel the print job provided you can catch it before the file is sent to the printer.

TABLE A-3: Worksheet printing tips

before you print	recommendation
Save your work	Make sure your work is saved
Check the printer	Make sure that the printer is turned on and is online, that it has paper, and that there are no error messages or warning signals
Preview the worksheet	Check the formatted image for page breaks, page setup (vertical or horizontal), and overall appearance of the worksheet
Check the printer selection	Look in the Print dialog box to verify that the correct printer is selected
Check the Print what options	Verify that you are printing either the active sheet, the entire workbook, or just a selected range

FIGURE A-14: **Print Preview screen**

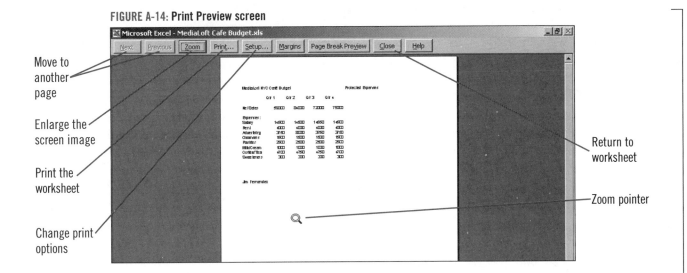

Move to another page

Enlarge the screen image

Print the worksheet

Change print options

Return to worksheet

Zoom pointer

FIGURE A-15: **Print dialog box**

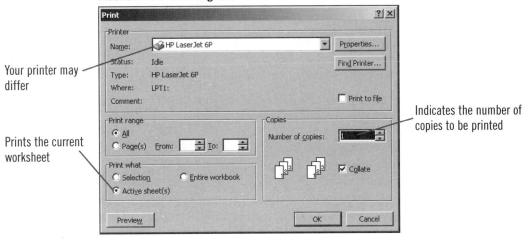

Your printer may differ

Prints the current worksheet

Indicates the number of copies to be printed

Using Zoom in Print Preview

When you are in the Print Preview window, you can enlarge the image by clicking the Zoom button. You can also position the Zoom pointer 🔍 over a specific part of the worksheet page, then click it to view that section of the page. Figure A-16 shows a magnified section of a document. While the image is zoomed in, use the scroll bars to view different sections of the page.

FIGURE A-16: **Enlarging the preview using Zoom**

Getting Help

Excel 2002

Excel features an extensive **Help system** that gives you immediate access to definitions, steps, explanations, and useful tips. The animated Office Assistant provides help in two ways. You can type a **keyword**, a representative word on which Excel can search your area of interest, or you can access a question and answer format to research your Help topic. The Office Assistant provides **Office Assistant Tips** (indicated by a light bulb) on the current action you are performing. You can click the light bulb to display a dialog box containing relevant choices that you can refer to as you work. In addition, you can press [F1] at any time to get immediate help. Alternately, the **Ask a Question list arrow** on the menu bar is always available for asking questions. You can click the text box and type a question at any time to display related help topics. Questions from your current Excel session are stored, and you can access them at any time by clicking the Ask a Question list arrow, then clicking the question of interest. ✎ Jim wants to find out more about ranges so he can work more efficiently with them. He asks you to find more information by using the animated Office Assistant.

Steps

QuickTip

If the Office Assistant is displayed, click it to access Help. If it is not displayed, clicking 🔡 opens the Office Assistant. A previous user may have turned off the Office Assistant. To turn it on, click Help on the menu bar, click Show the Office Assistant, then click the Office Assistant to open the dialog balloon.

1. Click the Microsoft Excel Help button 🔡 **on the Standard toolbar**
An Office Assistant dialog balloon opens, asking what you want to do. You can get information by typing a keyword or question in the white box, known as the **query box**. If the text within the query box is highlighted, your text will automatically replace it. The Office Assistant provides help based on the text in the query box.

2. Type Define a range
See Figure A-18.

3. Click Search
The Office Assistant searches for relevant topics from the Help files in Excel and then displays a list of topics for you to choose from.

QuickTip

Clicking the Print button 🖨 in the Help window prints the information.

4. Click See More, then click Name cells on more than one worksheet
A Help window containing information about ranges opens, as shown in Figure A-19.

5. Read the text, then click the Close button ⊠ **on the Help window title bar**
The Help window closes.

6. Click the Microsoft Excel button on the taskbar to display it, if necessary.
The Office Assistant is no longer visible on the worksheet. Hiding the Office Assistant does not turn it off; it only hides it temporarily.

Changing the Office Assistant

The default Office Assistant character is Clippit, but there are others from which you can choose. To change the appearance of the Office Assistant, right-click the Office Assistant, then click Options. Click the Gallery tab shown in Figure A-17, click the Back and Next buttons until you find an Assistant you want to use, then click OK. (You may need to insert your Microsoft Office CD to perform this task.) Each Office Assistant character makes its own unique sounds. Animate any assistant by right-clicking it, then clicking Animate!

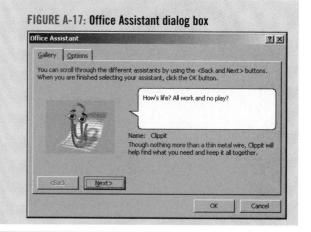

FIGURE A-17: Office Assistant dialog box

FIGURE A-18: Office Assistant

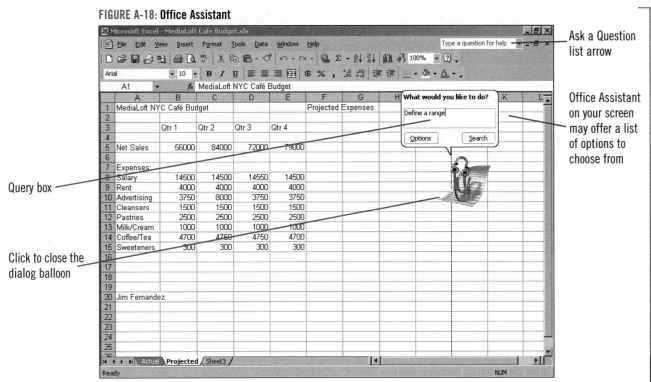

Ask a Question list arrow

Office Assistant on your screen may offer a list of options to choose from

Query box

Click to close the dialog balloon

FIGURE A-19: Help window

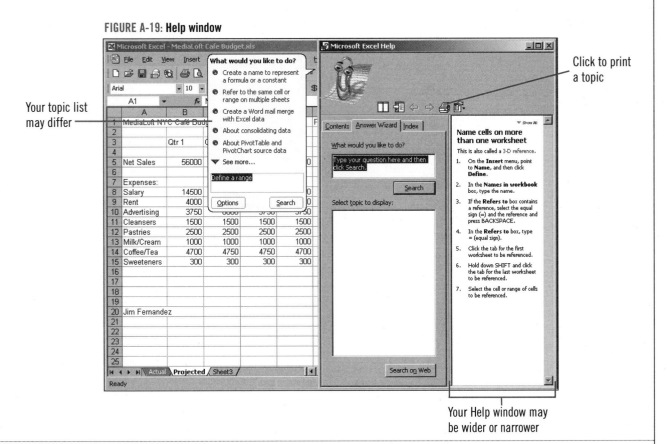

Click to print a topic

Your topic list may differ

Your Help window may be wider or narrower

Excel 2002

Excel 2002

Closing a Workbook and Exiting Excel

When you have finished working, you need to save the workbook file and close it. When you have completed all your work in Excel you need to exit the program. You can exit Excel by clicking Exit on the File menu. ![arrow] Jim has completed his work on the MediaLoft Café budget. He wants you to close the workbook and then exit Excel.

Steps 1 2 3 4

1. Click **File** on the menu bar

The File menu opens. See Figure A-20.

2. Click **Close**

Excel closes the workbook, asking if you want to save your changes; if you have made any changes be sure to save them. You could also click the workbook Close button instead of using the File menu.

QuickTip

To exit Excel and close several files at once, click Exit on the File menu. Excel will prompt you to save changes to each open workbook before exiting.

3. Click **File** on the menu bar, then click **Exit**

You could also click the program Close button to exit the program. Excel closes and you return to the desktop.

FIGURE A-20: Closing a workbook using the File menu

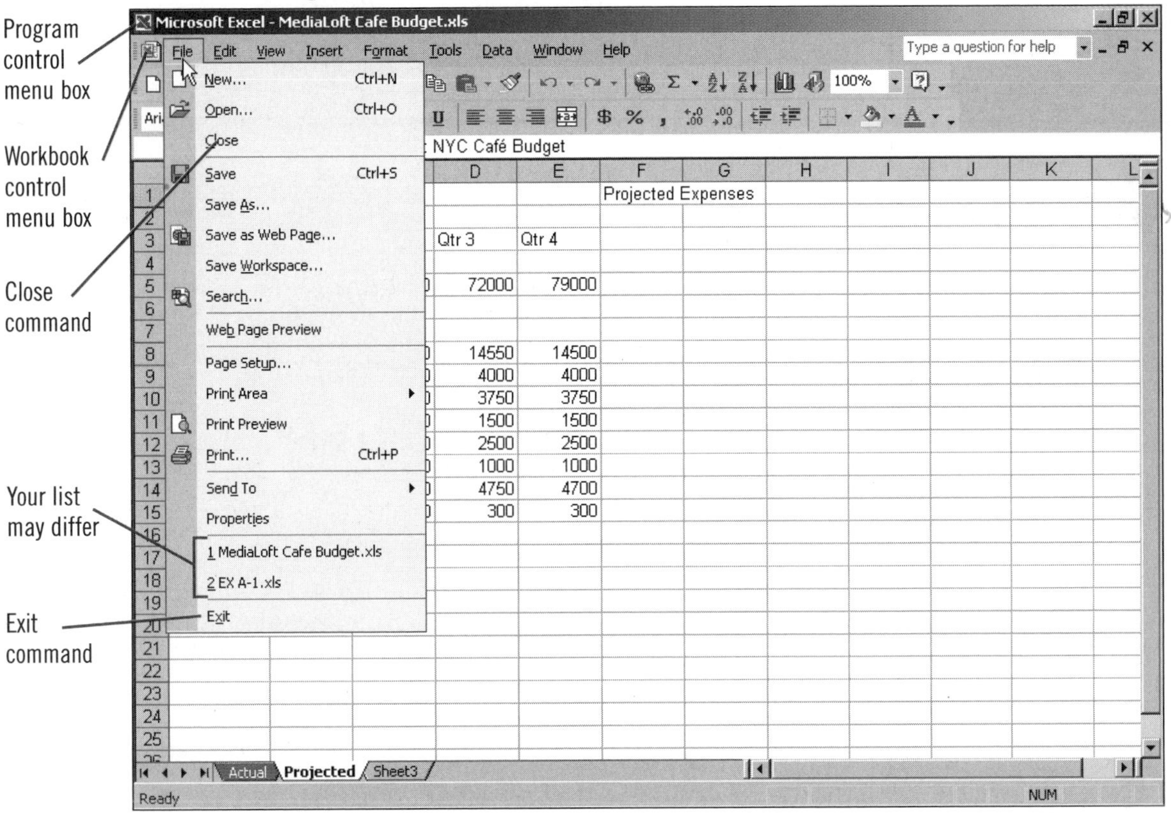

Program control menu box

Workbook control menu box

Close command

Your list may differ

Exit command

	File	Edit	View	Insert	Format	Tools	Data	Window	Help			

New...	Ctrl+N	
Open...	Ctrl+O	
Close		
Save	Ctrl+S	
Save As...		
Save as Web Page...		
Save Workspace...		
Search...		
Web Page Preview		
Page Setup...		
Print Area	▶	
Print Preview		
Print...	Ctrl+P	
Send To	▶	
Properties		
1 MediaLoft Cafe Budget.xls		
2 EX A-1.xls		
Exit		

NYC Café Budget

Projected Expenses

	D	E
Qtr 3		Qtr 4
	72000	79000
	14550	14500
	4000	4000
	3750	3750
	1500	1500
	2500	2500
	1000	1000
	4750	4700
	300	300

Actual **Projected** Sheet3

Ready   NUM

Practice

► Concepts Review

Label the elements of the Excel worksheet window shown in Figure A-21.

FIGURE A-21

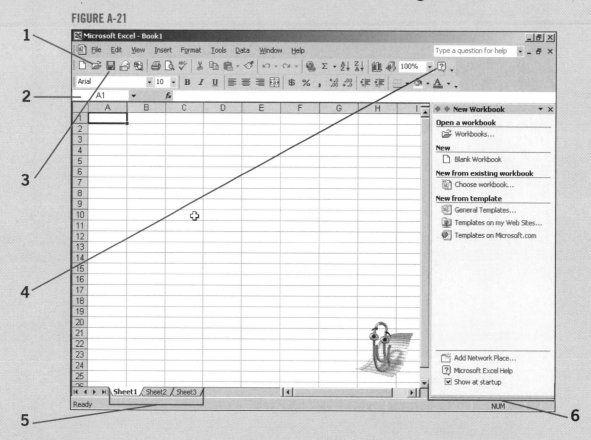

Match each term with the statement that describes it.

7. Cell pointer
8. Formula bar
9. Worksheet window
10. Name box
11. Cell
12. Workbook

a. Area that contains a grid of columns and rows
b. The intersection of a column and row
c. Allows you to enter or edit worksheet data
d. Collection of worksheets
e. Rectangle indicating the active cell
f. Displays the active cell address

Select the best answer from the list of choices.

13. An electronic spreadsheet can perform all of the following tasks, except:
   a. Display information visually.
   b. Calculate data accurately.
   c. Plan worksheet objectives.
   d. Recalculate updated information.

14. Each of the following is true about labels, except:
   a. They are left-aligned by default.
   b. They are not used in calculations.
   c. They are right-aligned by default.
   d. They can include numerical information.

15. Each of the following is true about values, except:
a. They can include labels.
b. They are right-aligned by default.
c. They are used in calculations.
d. They can include formulas.

16. What symbol is typed before a number to make the number a label?
a. "
b. !
c. '
d. ;

17. You can get Excel Help in any of the following ways, except:
a. Clicking Help on the menu bar, then clicking Microsoft Excel Help.
b. Pressing [F1].
c. Clicking 🔲.
d. Minimizing the program window.

18. The following key(s) can be used to confirm cell entries, except:
a. [Enter].
b. [Tab].
c. [Esc].
d. [Ctrl][Enter].

19. Which button is used to preview a worksheet?
a. 🔲
b. 🔲
c. 🔲
d. 🔲

20. Which feature is used to enlarge a Print Preview view?
a. Magnify
b. Enlarge
c. Amplify
d. Zoom

21. Each of the following is true about the Office Assistant, except:
a. It provides tips based on your work habits.
b. It provides help using a question-and-answer format.
c. You can change the appearance of the Office Assistant.
d. It can complete certain tasks for you.

▶ # Skills Review

1. Start Excel 2002.
a. Point to **Programs** in the Start menu.
b. Click the **Microsoft Excel** program icon.
c. In what area of the Start menu are all the programs on your computer located?
d. What appears when Excel opens?

2. Open and save a workbook.
a. Open the workbook EX A-2 from the drive and folder where your Project Files are located.
b. Save the workbook as **MediaLoft Toronto Cafe** using the Save As command on the File menu; use the New Folder button to save it in a new folder called **Toronto** in the drive and folder where your Project Files are located.
c. Close the file.
d. Open it again from the new folder you created.
e. Open a workbook based on the Balance Sheet template: Display the task pane, select General Templates, display the Spreadsheet Solutions tab, then double-click Balance Sheet.
f. Save the workbook as **MediaLoft Balance Sheet** in the drive and folder where your Project Files are stored, then close the workbook.

TABLE-4: MediaLoft Toronto Café

	On-Hand	Cost Each	Sale Price
Water	32	9.57	
Coffee	52	13.71	
Bread	36	15.22	
Muffins	25	16.99	
Sweets	43	11.72	
Sodas	52	9.61	

3. Enter labels and values.

   a. Enter the necessary labels shown in Table A-4.

   b. Enter the values shown in Table A-4.

   c. Clear the contents of cell A9 using the Edit menu, then type **Tea** in cell A9.

   d. Save the workbook using the Save button.

4. Name and move a sheet.

   a. Name the Sheet1 tab **Inventory**, then name the Sheet2 tab **Sales**.

   b. Move the Inventory sheet so it comes after the Sales sheet.

   c. Change the tab color of the Inventory sheet to yellow (third column, fifth row).

   d. Change the tab color of the Sales sheet to aqua (fifth column, fourth row).

   e. Save the workbook.

5. Preview and print a worksheet.

   a. Make the Inventory sheet active.

   b. View it in Print Preview.

   c. Use the Zoom button to get a better look at your worksheet.

   d. Add your name to cell A11, then print one copy of the worksheet.

6. Get Help.

   a. Display the Office Assistant if it is not already displayed.

   b. Ask the Office Assistant for information about creating a formula.

   c. Print the information offered by the Office Assistant, using the Print button in the Help window.

   d. Close the Help window.

7. Close a workbook and exit Excel.

   a. Close the file using the Close command.

   b. If asked if you want to save the worksheet, click **No**.

   c. Exit Excel.

▶ Independent Challenge 1

The Excel Help feature provides definitions, explanations, procedures, and other helpful information. It also provides examples and demonstrations to show you how Excel features work. Topics include elements such as the active cell, status bar, buttons, and dialog boxes, as well as detailed information about Excel commands and options.

   a. Start Excel and open a new workbook using the New Workbook task pane.

   b. Click the **Office Assistant**; display it if necessary using the Show Office Assistant command on the Help menu.

   c. Type a question that will give you information about opening and saving a workbook. (*Hint*: You may have to ask the Office Assistant more than one question.)

   d. Print the information, close the Help window, then exit Excel.

▶ Independent Challenge 2

Spreadsheet software has many uses that can affect the way people work. The beginning of this unit discusses some examples of people using Excel. Use your own personal or business experiences to come up with five examples of how Excel could be used in a business setting.

   a. Start Excel.

   b. Write down five business tasks that you could complete more efficiently by using an Excel worksheet.

   c. Sketch a sample of each worksheet. See Table A-5, a sample payroll worksheet, as a guide.

   d. Open a new workbook and save it as **Sample Payroll** in the drive and folder where your Project Files are stored.

e. Give your worksheet a title in cell A1, then type your name in cell B1.

f. Enter the labels shown in Table A-5. Enter Hours Worked in column C and Hourly Wage in Column E.

g. Enter sample data for Hours Worked and Hourly Wage in the worksheet.

h. Save your work, then preview and print the worksheet.

i. Close the worksheet and exit Excel.

TABLE A-5: **Sample payroll**

Employee Name	Hours Worked	Hourly Wage
Dale Havorford		
Chris Wong		
Sharon Armenta		
Belinda Swanson		
Total		

▶ Independent Challenge 3

You are the office manager for Christine's Car Parts, a small auto parts supplier. Although the company is just three years old, it is expanding rapidly, and you are continually looking for ways to make your job easier. Last year you began using Excel to manage and maintain data on inventory and sales, which has greatly helped you to track information accurately and efficiently. The owner of the company has just approved your request to hire an assistant, who will be starting work in a week. You want to create a short training document that acquaints your new assistant with basic Excel skills.

a. Start Excel.

b. Create a new workbook and save it as **Training Workbook** in the drive and folder where your Project Files are located.

c. Enter a title for the worksheet in cell A1.

d. Make up and enter the values and labels for a sample spreadsheet. Make sure you have labels in column A.

e. Enter your name in cell D1.

f. Change the name of Sheet1 to Sample Data, then change the tab color of the Sample Data to another color.

g. Preview the worksheet, then print it.

h. Open a workbook based on a template from the Spreadsheet Solutions tab in the Templates dialog box. (You may need to insert your Office CD in order to do this.)

i. Save the workbook as **Template Sample**, then close the files and exit Excel.

e Independent Challenge 4

You can use the World Wide Web to help make informed purchasing decisions. Your supervisor has just given you approval for buying a new computer. While cost is not a limiting factor, you do need to provide a list of hardware and software requirements. You can use data found on the World Wide Web and use Excel to create a worksheet that details your purchase decision.

a. Connect to the Internet, then go to the CNET site at computers.com.

b. Use any of the links to locate information about the type of computer you want to purchase.

c. Locate data for the type of system you want using at least two vendors from within this site. When you find systems that meet your needs, print out the information. Be sure to identify each system's key features, such as the processor chip, hard drive capacity, RAM, and monitor size.

d. When you are finished gathering data, disconnect from the Internet.

e. Start Excel, open a new workbook and save it in the drive and folder where your Project Files are stored as **New Computer Data**.

f. Enter the manufacturers' names in columns and computer features (RAM, etc.) in rows. List the systems you found through your research, including the features you want (e.g., CD-ROM drive, etc.) and the cost for each system.

g. List the tax and shipping costs the manufacturer charges.

h. Indicate on the worksheet your final purchase decision by including descriptive text in a prominent cell. Enter your name in one of the cells.

i. Save, preview, and then print your worksheet.

j. Close the file and exit Excel.

► Visual Workshop

Create a worksheet similar to Figure A-22 using the skills you learned in this unit. Save the workbook as **Carrie's Camera and Darkroom** to the drive and folder where your Project Files are stored. Type your name in cell A11, then preview and print the worksheet.

FIGURE A-22

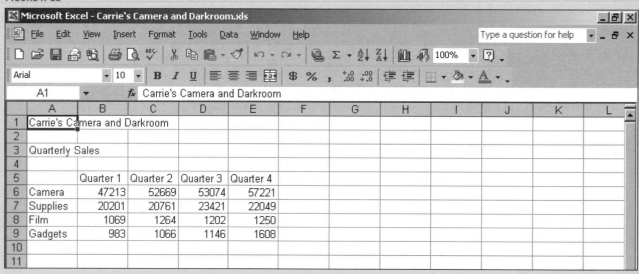

Unit
B

Building
and Editing Worksheets

- ▶ **Plan and design a worksheet**
- `MOUS` ▶ **Edit cell entries**
- `MOUS` ▶ **Enter formulas**
- `MOUS` ▶ **Create complex formulas**
- `MOUS` ▶ **Introduce Excel functions**
- `MOUS` ▶ **Copy and move cell entries**
- `MOUS` ▶ **Understand relative and absolute cell references**
- `MOUS` ▶ **Copy formulas with relative cell references**
- `MOUS` ▶ **Copy formulas with absolute cell references**

Using your understanding of Excel basics, you can now plan and build your own worksheets. When you build a worksheet, you enter labels, values, and formulas into worksheet cells. Once you create a worksheet, you can save it in a workbook file and then print it. ✎ The MediaLoft marketing department has asked Jim Fernandez for an estimate of the average number of author appearances this summer. Marketing hopes that the number of appearances will increase 20% over last year's figures. Jim asks you to create a worksheet that summarizes appearances for last year and forecasts the summer appearances for this year.

Planning and Designing a Worksheet

Before you start entering data into a worksheet, you need to know the purpose and approximate layout of the worksheet. To increase store traffic and sales, MediaLoft encourages authors to come to stores and sign their books. Jim wants to forecast MediaLoft's 2003 summer author appearances. The goal, already identified by the Marketing department, is to increase the year 2002 signings by 20%. Using the planning guidelines below, work with Jim as he plans this worksheet.

In planning and designing a worksheet it is important to:

► **Determine the purpose of the worksheet and give it a meaningful title**

Jim needs to forecast summer appearances for 2003. Jim titles the worksheet "Summer 2003 MediaLoft Author Events Forecast."

► **Determine your worksheet's desired results, or "output"**

Jim needs to begin scheduling author events and will use these forecasts to determine staffing and budget needs if the number of author events increases by 20%. He also wants to calculate the average number of author events because the Marketing department uses this information for corporate promotions.

► **Collect all the information, or "input," that will produce the results you want**

Jim gathers together the number of author events that occurred at four stores during the 2002 summer season, which runs from June through August.

► **Determine the calculations, or formulas, necessary to achieve the desired results**

First, Jim needs to total the number of events at each of the selected stores during each month of the summer of 2002. Then he needs to add these totals together to determine the grand total of summer appearances. Because he needs to determine the goal for the 2003 season, the 2002 monthly totals and grand total are multiplied by 1.2 to calculate the projected 20% increase for the 2003 summer season. He'll use the Average function to determine the average number of author appearances for the Marketing department.

► **Sketch on paper how you want the worksheet to look; identify where to place the labels and values**

Jim decides to put the store locations in rows and the months in columns. He enters the data in his sketch and notes the location of the monthly totals and the grand total. Below the totals, he writes out the formula for determining a 20% increase in 2002 appearances. He also includes a label for the average number of events calculations. Jim's sketch of his worksheet is shown in Figure B-1.

► **Create the worksheet**

Jim enters the labels first, to establish the structure of the worksheet. He then enters the values—the data summarizing the events—into his worksheet. Finally, he enters the formulas necessary to calculate totals, averages, and forecasts. These values and formulas will be used to calculate the necessary output. The worksheet Jim creates is shown in Figure B-2.

FIGURE B-1: Worksheet sketch showing labels, values, and calculations

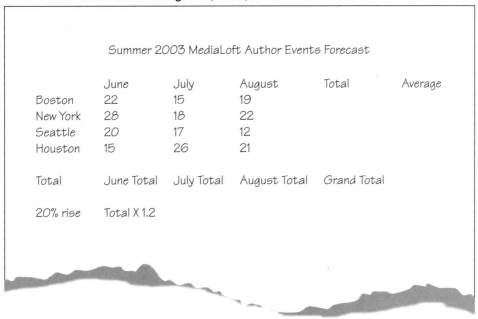

Summer 2003 MediaLoft Author Events Forecast

	June	July	August	Total	Average
Boston	22	15	19		
New York	28	18	22		
Seattle	20	17	12		
Houston	15	26	21		
Total	June Total	July Total	August Total	Grand Total	
20% rise	Total X 1.2				

FIGURE B-2: Jim's forecasting worksheet

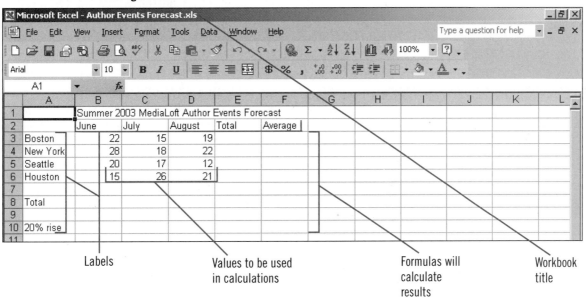

Labels

Values to be used in calculations

Formulas will calculate results

Workbook title

Editing Cell Entries

You can change the contents of a cell at any time. To edit the contents of a cell, you first select the cell you want to edit. Then you have two options: you can click the formula bar or press [F2]. This puts Excel into Edit mode. Alternately, you can double-click any cell and start editing. To make sure you are in Edit mode, look at the **mode indicator** on the far-left side of the status bar. After planning and creating his worksheet, Jim notices that he entered the wrong value for the August Seattle events, and that Houston should replace San Diego. He asks you to edit these entries to correct them.

Steps

QuickTip

In the Open dialog box, you can double-click the file-name to open the workbook in one step.

1. Start Excel, open the workbook **EX B-1** from the drive and folder where your Project Files are stored, then save it as **Author Events Forecast**

2. Click cell **D5**

This cell contains August events for the Seattle store, which you want to change to reflect the correct numbers.

3. Click to the right of **12** in the formula bar

Excel goes into Edit mode, and the mode indicator on the status bar displays "Edit." A blinking vertical line called the **insertion point** appears in the formula bar, and if you move the mouse pointer to the formula bar, the pointer changes to Ⅰ, which is used for editing. See Figure B-3.

4. Press **[Backspace]**, type **8**, then click the **Enter button** ☑ on the formula bar

The value in cell D5 is changed from 12 to 18, and cell D5 remains selected.

5. Click cell **A6**, then press **[F2]**

Excel returns to Edit mode, and the insertion point appears in the cell.

QuickTip

The Undo button ↶ allows you to reverse up to 16 previous actions, one at a time.

6. Press **[Backspace]** nine times, type **Houston**, then press **[Enter]**

The label changes to Houston, and cell A7 becomes the active cell. If you make a mistake, you can click the Cancel button ☒ on the formula bar *before* confirming the cell entry. If you notice the mistake *after* you have confirmed the cell entry, click the Undo button ↶ on the Standard toolbar.

7. Double-click cell **C6**

Double-clicking a cell also puts Excel into Edit mode with the insertion point in the cell.

8. Press **[Delete]** twice, then type **19**

The number of book signings for July in Houston has been corrected. See Figure B-4.

9. Click ☑ to confirm the entry, then click the **Save button** 🖫 on the Standard toolbar

FIGURE B-3: Worksheet in Edit mode

Insertion point in formula bar

Edit mode indicator

Pointer used for editing

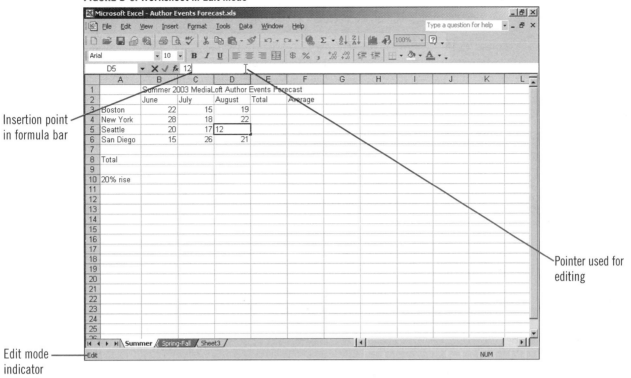

FIGURE B-4: Edited worksheet

Name box

Insertion point in cell

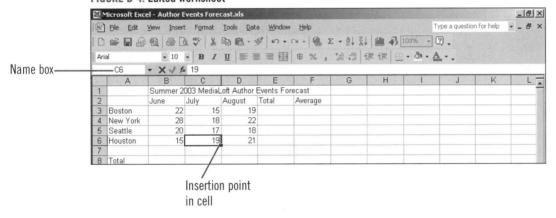

CLUES TO USE

Recovering a lost workbook file

Sometimes while you are using Excel, you may experience a power failure or your computer may "freeze," making it impossible to continue working. If this type of interruption occurs, Excel has a built-in recovery feature that allows you to open and save files that were open at the time of the interruption. When you restart Excel after an interruption, the Document Recovery task pane opens on the left side of your screen displaying both original and recovered versions of the files that were open. If you're not sure which file to open (original or recovered), it's usually better to open the recovered file because it will have retained the latest information. You can, however, open and review all the versions of the file that were recovered and save the best one. Each file listed in the Document Recovery task pane has a list arrow with options that allow you to open the file, save the file, delete the file, or show repairs made to the file.

Excel 2002

Entering Formulas

You use **formulas** to perform numeric calculations such as adding, multiplying, and averaging. Formulas in an Excel worksheet usually start with the equal sign (=), called the **formula prefix**, followed by cell addresses and range names. Arithmetic formulas use one or more **arithmetic operators** to perform calculations; see Table B-1. Using a cell address or range name in a formula is called **cell referencing**. If you change a value in a cell, any formula containing that cell reference will be automatically recalculated using the new value. ⬛︎⬛︎⬛︎ Jim needs to total the values for the monthly author events for June, July, and August. He asks you to create formulas to perform these calculations.

Steps

1. **Click cell B8**
   This is the cell where you want to enter the calculation that totals the number of June events.

2. **Type = (the equal sign)**
   Placing an equal sign at the beginning of an entry tells Excel that a formula is about to be entered, rather than a label or a value. "Enter" appears on the status bar. The total number of June events is equal to the sum of the values in cells B3, B4, B5, and B6.

Trouble?

If you type an incorrect character, press [Backspace].

3. **Type b3+b4+b5+b6**
   Compare your worksheet to Figure B-5. Each cell address in the equation is shown in a matching color in the worksheet. For example, the cell address B3 is written in blue in the equation and is outlined in blue in the worksheet. This makes it easy to identify each cell in a formula.

Trouble?

If the formula instead of the result appears in the cell after you click ☑, make sure you began the formula with = (the equal sign).

4. **Click the Enter button** ☑ **on the formula bar**
   The result, 85, appears in cell B8. Cell B8 remains selected, and the formula appears in the formula bar. Excel is not case-sensitive: it doesn't matter if you type uppercase or lowercase characters when you enter cell addresses. Typing cell addresses is only one way of creating a formula. A more accurate method involves **pointing** at cells using the mouse, then using the keyboard to supply arithmetic operators.

5. **Click cell C8, type =, click cell C3, type +, click cell C4, type +, click cell C5, type +, click cell C6, then click the Enter button** ☑ **on the formula bar**
   When you clicked cell C3, a moving border surrounded the cell. This **moving border** indicates the cell used in the calculation. Moving borders can appear around a single cell or a range of cells. The total number of author appearances for July, 69, appears in cell C8. The pointing method of creating a formula is more accurate than typing, because it is easy to type a cell address incorrectly. Cell D8 also needs a total.

6. **Click cell D8, type =, click cell D3, type +, click cell D4, type +, click cell D5, type +, click cell D6, then click the Enter button** ☑ **on the formula bar**
   The total number of appearances for August, 80, appears in cell D8. Compare your worksheet to Figure B-6.

7. **Click the Save button** ⬛︎ **on the Standard toolbar**

FIGURE B-5: Worksheet showing cells in a formula

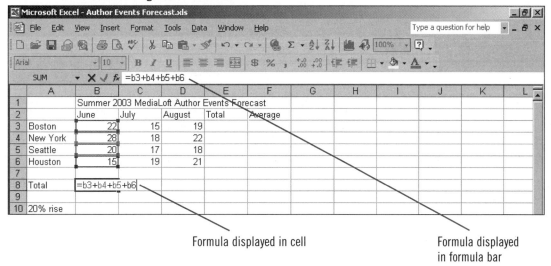

Formula displayed in cell

Formula displayed in formula bar

FIGURE B-6: Completed formulas

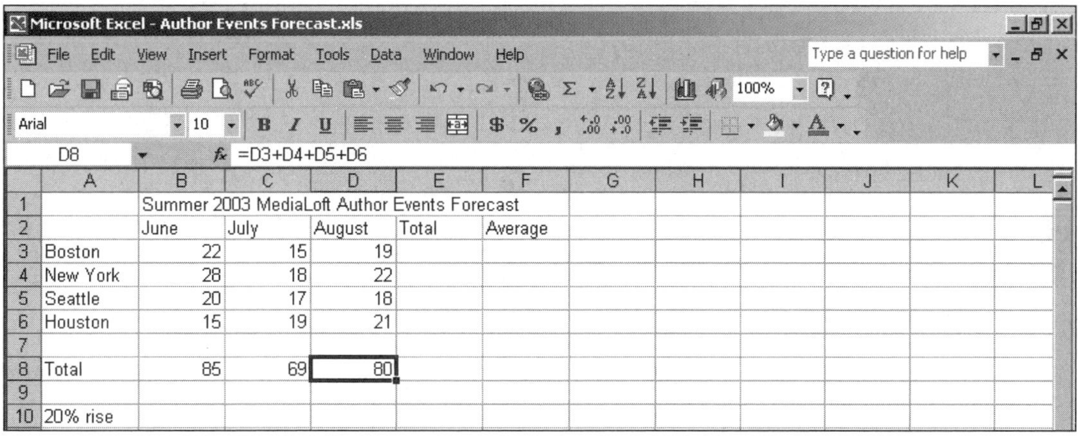

TABLE B-1: Excel arithmetic operators

operator	purpose	example
+	Addition	=A5+A7
–	Subtraction or negation	=A5–10
*	Multiplication	=A5*A7
/	Division	=A5/A7
%	Percent	=35%
^ (caret)	Exponent	=6^2 (same as 6^2)

Creating Complex Formulas

The formula you entered is a simple formula containing one arithmetic operator, the plus sign. You can create a **complex formula**—an equation that uses more than one type of arithmetic operator. For example, you may need to create a formula that uses addition and multiplication. You can use arithmetic operators to separate tasks within a complex equation. In formulas containing more than one arithmetic operator, Excel uses the order of precedence rules to determine which operation to perform first.  Jim wants you to total the values for the monthly author events for June, July, and August, and forecast what the 20% increase in appearances will be. You create a complex formula to perform these calculations.

1. **Click cell B10, type =, click cell B8, then type *.2**
   This part of the formula calculates 20% of the cell contents by multiplying the June total by .2 (or 20%). Because this part of the formula uses multiplication, it will be calculated first according to the rules of precedence.

QuickTip

Press [Esc] to turn off a moving border.

2. **Type +, then click cell B8**
   The second part of the formula adds the 20% increase to the original value of the cell. The mode indicator says Point, indicating you can add more cell references. Compare your worksheet to Figure B-7.

3. **Click ▧ on the formula bar**
   The result, 102, appears in cell B10.

4. **Click cell C10, type =, click cell C8, type *.2, type +, click cell C8, then click ▧**
   The result, 82.8, appears in cell C10.

5. **Click cell D10, type =, click cell D8, type *.2, type +, click D8, then click ▧**
   The result, 96, appears in cell D10. Compare your completed worksheet to Figure B-8.

6. **Click the Save button 🖫 on the Standard toolbar**

Editing formulas

You can edit formulas the same way you edit cell entries: you can click the cell containing the formula then edit it in the formula bar; you can also double-click a cell or press [F2] to enter Edit mode, and then edit the formula in the cell. After you are in Edit mode, use the arrow keys to move the insertion point left or right in the formula. Use [Backspace] or [Delete] to delete characters to the left or right of the insertion point, then type or point to new cell references or operators.

FIGURE B-7: Elements of a complex formula

Microsoft Excel - Author Events Forecast.xls

File Edit View Insert Format Tools Data Window Help

SUM ▼ X ✓ fx =B8*.2+B8

	A	B	C	D	E	F	G
1		Summer 2003 MediaLoft Author Events Forecast					
2		June	July	August	Total	Average	
3	Boston	22	15	19			
4	New York	28	18	22			
5	Seattle	20	17	18			
6	Houston	15	19	21			
7							
8	Total	85	69	80			
9							
10	20% rise	=B8*.2+B8					
11							

FIGURE B-8: Multiple complex formulas

Microsoft Excel - Author Events Forecast.xls

File Edit View Insert Format Tools Data Window Help

D10 ▼ fx =D8*0.2+D8

	A	B	C	D	E	F	G
1		Summer 2003 MediaLoft Author Events Forecast					
2		June	July	August	Total	Average	
3	Boston	22	15	19			
4	New York	28	18	22			
5	Seattle	20	17	18			
6	Houston	15	19	21			
7							
8	Total	85	69	80			
9							
10	20% rise	102	82.8	96			
11							

Formula calculates a 20% increase over the value in cell D8 and displays the result in cell D10

Order of precedence in Excel formulas

A formula can include several mathematical operations. When you work with formulas that have more than one operator, the order of precedence is very important. If a formula contains two or more operators, such as 4+.55/4000*25, the computer performs the calculations in a particular sequence based on these rules: Operations inside parentheses are calculated before any other operations. Exponents are calculated next, then any multiplication and division—from left to right.

Finally, addition and subtraction are calculated from left to right. In the example 4+.55/4000*25, Excel performs the arithmetic operations by first dividing 4000 into .55, then multiplying the result by 25, then adding 4. You can change the order of calculations by using parentheses. For example, in the formula (4+.55)/4000*25, Excel would first add 4 and .55, then divide that amount by 4000, then finally multiply by 25.

Introducing Excel Functions

Functions are predefined worksheet formulas that enable you to perform complex calculations easily. Like formulas, functions always begin with the formula prefix = (the equal sign). You can type functions, or you can use the Insert Function button to select the function you need from a list. The **AutoSum** button on the Standard toolbar enters the most frequently used function, SUM. A function can be used by itself within a cell, or as part of a formula. For example, to calculate monthly sales tax, you could create a formula that adds a range of cells (using the SUM function) and then multiplies the total by a decimal. ⬤➤➤ Jim asks you to use the SUM function to calculate the grand totals in his worksheet and the AVERAGE function to calculate the average number of author events per store.

Steps

1. **Click cell E3**

   This is where you want the total of all Boston author events for June, July, and August.

2. **Click the AutoSum button** Σ **on the Standard toolbar, then click the Enter button** ✓ **on the formula bar**

   The formula =SUM(B3:D3) appears in the formula bar and the result, 56, appears in cell E3. By default, AutoSum adds the values in the cells above the cell pointer. If there are one or fewer values there, AutoSum adds the values to its left—in this case, the values in cells B3, C3, and D3. The information inside the parentheses is the **argument**, or the information Excel uses to calculate the function result. In this case, the argument is the range B3:D3.

3. **Click cell E4, click** Σ, **then click** ✓

   The total for the New York events appears in cell E4.

4. **Click cell E5, then click** Σ

   AutoSum sets up a function to add the two values in the cells above the active cell, but this time the default argument is not correct.

5. **Click cell B5 and hold down the mouse button, drag to cell D5 to select the range B5:D5, then click** ✓

   As you drag, the argument in the SUM function changes to reflect the selected range, and a yellow Argument ToolTip shows the function syntax. You can click any part of the ToolTip to display Help on the function.

6. **Click cell E6, type =SUM(, click cell B6 and drag to cell D6, click** ✓, **click cell E8, type =SUM(, click cell B8 and drag to cell D8, click** ✓, **click cell E10, type =SUM(, click cell B10 and drag to cell D10, then click** ✓

   Compare your screen to Figure B-9. Excel adds the closing parenthesis.

7. **Click cell F3, then click the Insert Function button** *fx* **on the formula bar**

   The Insert Function dialog box and Wizard opens. Here you can select a function from a list. See Table B-2 for frequently used functions. The function you need to calculate averages—named AVERAGE—appears in the Most Recently Used function category.

8. **Click AVERAGE in the Select a function list box, click OK; the Function Arguments dialog box opens; type B3:D3 in the Number 1 text box, as shown in Figure B-10, then click OK**

9. **Click cell F4, click** *fx*, **verify that AVERAGE is selected, click OK, type B4:D4, click OK, click cell F5, click** *fx*, **click AVERAGE, click OK, type B5:D5, click OK, click cell F6, click** *fx*, **click AVERAGE, click OK, type B6:D6, then click OK**

   The result for Boston (cell F3) is 18.66667; the result for New York (cell F4) is 22.66667; the result for Seattle (cell F5) is 18.33333; and the result for Houston (cell F6) is 18.33333, giving you the averages for all four stores.

10. **Enter your name in cell A25, click the Save button** 🖫 **on the Standard toolbar, then click the Print button** 🖨 **on the Standard toolbar**

FIGURE B-9: Worksheet with SUM functions entered

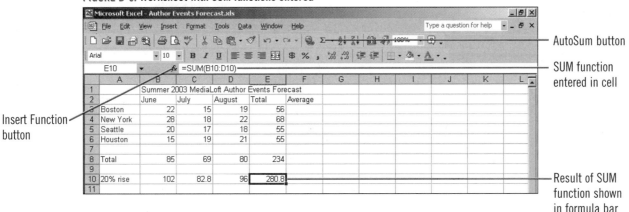

AutoSum button

SUM function entered in cell

Insert Function button

Result of SUM function shown in formula bar

FIGURE B-10: Using Insert Function to create a formula

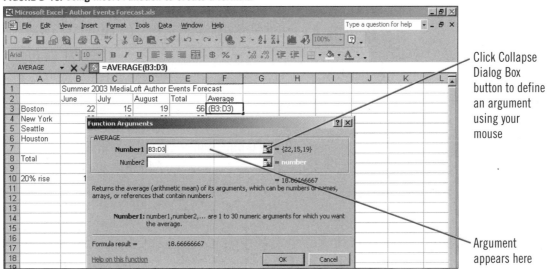

Click Collapse Dialog Box button to define an argument using your mouse

Argument appears here

TABLE B-2: Frequently used functions

function	description
SUM (*argument*)	Calculates the sum of the arguments
AVERAGE (*argument*)	Calculates the average of the arguments
MAX (*argument*)	Displays the largest value among the arguments
MIN (*argument*)	Displays the smallest value among the arguments
COUNT (*argument*)	Calculates the number of values in the arguments

CLUES TO USE

Using the MIN and MAX functions

Other commonly used functions include MIN and MAX. You use the MIN function to calculate the minimum, or smallest, value in a selected range; the MAX function calculates the maximum, or largest, value in a selected range. The MAX function is included in the Most Recently Used function category in the Insert Function dialog box, while both the MIN and MAX function can be found in the Statistical category. These functions are particularly useful in larger worksheets.

Copying and Moving Cell Entries

Using the Cut, Copy, and Paste buttons or the Excel drag-and-drop feature, you can copy or move information from one cell or range in your worksheet to another. When you cut or move information, the original data does not remain in the original location. You can also cut, copy, and paste labels and values from one worksheet to another. ◄▬▬ Jim needs to include the 2003 forecast for spring and fall author events. He's already entered the spring data and will finish entering the labels and data for the fall. He asks you to copy information from the spring report to the fall report.

1. **Click the Spring-Fall sheet tab** of the Author Events Forecast workbook
   The store names in cells A6:A7 are incorrect.

2. **Click the Summer sheet tab**, select the range **A5:A6**, then click the **Copy button** 📋 on the Standard toolbar
   The selected range (A5:A6) is copied to the **Office Clipboard**, a temporary storage area that holds the selected information you copy or cut. A moving border surrounds the selected range until you press [Esc] or copy additional information to the Clipboard. The information you copied remains in the selected range.

Trouble?

If the Clipboard task pane does not open, click Edit on the menu bar, then click Office Clipboard.

3. **Click the Spring-Fall sheet tab**, select the range **A6:A7**, click the **Paste button** 📋 on the Standard toolbar, select the range **A4:A9**, then click 📋
   The Clipboard task pane opens when you copy a selection to the already-occupied Clipboard. You can use the Clipboard task pane to copy, cut, store, and paste up to 24 items. Each item in the pane displays its contents.

QuickTip

After you paste an item, the Paste Options button 📋 appears. If you move the pointer over it, the Paste Options list arrow appears, letting you choose whether to paste the contents or only the formatting.

4. **Click cell A13**, click [Boston New York Seattle Houston Total] in the Clipboard Task Pane to paste the contents in cell A13, then click the **Close button** ❌ in the Task Pane title bar to close it
   The item is copied into the range A13:A18. When pasting an item from the Clipboard into the worksheet, you only need to specify the top-left cell of the range where you want to paste the selection. The Total label in column E is missing from the fall forecast.

5. **Click cell E3**, position the pointer on any edge of the cell until the pointer changes to ↖, then press and hold down **[Ctrl]**
   The pointer changes to the copy pointer ↖⁺.

6. While still pressing **[Ctrl]**, press and hold the **left mouse button**, drag the cell contents to cell **E12**, release the mouse button, then release **[Ctrl]**
   This **drag-and-drop technique** is useful for copying cell contents. As you dragged, an outline of the cell moved with the pointer, as shown in Figure B-11, and a ScreenTip appeared tracking the current position of the item as you moved it. When you released the mouse button, the Total label appeared in cell E12. You can also use drag and drop to move data to a new cell.

Trouble?

When you use drag and drop to move data into occupied cells, Excel asks if you want to replace the existing cells. Click OK to replace the contents with those of the cell you are moving.

7. **Click cell C1**, position the pointer on the edge of the cell until it changes to ↖, then drag the cell contents to **A1**
   You don't use [Ctrl] when moving information with drag and drop. You can easily enter the fall events data into the range B13:D16.

8. Using the information shown in Figure B-12, enter the author events data for the fall into the range **B13:D16**

9. Click the **Save button** 💾 on the Standard toolbar

FIGURE B-11: Using drag-and-drop to copy information

Copy button

Paste button

Copied cell

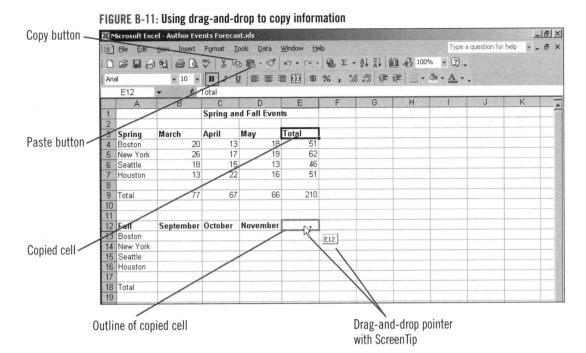

Outline of copied cell

Drag-and-drop pointer
with ScreenTip

FIGURE B-12: Worksheet with fall author event data entered

Sum of selected range appears in status bar

CLUES TO USE

Using the Office Clipboard

The Office Clipboard, shown in the task pane in Figure B-13, lets you copy and paste multiple items such as text, images, tables, or Excel ranges within or between Microsoft Office applications. The Office Clipboard can hold up to 24 items copied or cut from any Office program. The Clipboard task pane displays the items stored on the Office Clipboard. You choose whether to delete the first item from the Clipboard when you copy the 25th item. The collected items remain in the Office Clipboard and are available to you until you close all open Office programs. You can specify when and where to show the Office Clipboard task pane by clicking the options list arrow at the bottom of the Clipboard pane.

FIGURE B-13: Office Clipboard task pane

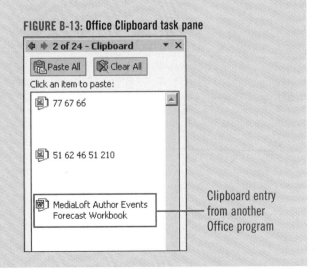

Clipboard entry
from another
Office program

Understanding Relative and Absolute Cell References

As you work in Excel, you will often want to reuse formulas in different parts of the worksheet. This will save you time because you won't have to retype them. For example, you may want to perform a what-if analysis showing one set of sales figures using a lower forecast in one part of the worksheet and another set using a higher forecast in another area. But when you copy formulas, it is important make sure that they refer to the correct cells. To do this, you need to understand relative and absolute cell references. ✎ Jim often reuses formulas in different parts of his worksheets to examine different possible outcomes, so he wants you to understand relative and absolute cell references.

Details

▶ **Use relative references when cell relationships remain unchanged.**

When you create a formula that references other cells, Excel normally does not "record" the exact cell references, but instead the relationship to the cell containing the formula. For example, in Figure B-14, cell E5 contains the formula: =SUM(B5:D5). When Excel retrieves values to calculate the formula in cell E5, it actually looks for "the cell three columns to the left of the formula, which in this case is cell B5", "the cell two columns to the left of the formula" and so on. This way, if you copy the cell to a new location such as cell E6, the results will reflect the new formula location, and will automatically retrieve the values in cells B6, C6, and D6. This is called **relative cell referencing**, because Excel is recording the input cells *in relation to* the formula cell.

In most cases, you will use relative cell references, which is the Excel default. In Figure B-14, the formulas in E5:E9 and in B9:E9 contain relative cell references. They total the "three cells to the left of" or the "four cells above" the formulas.

▶ **Use absolute cell references when one relationship changes.**

There are times when you want Excel to retrieve formula information from a specific cell, and you don't want that cell to change when you copy the formula to a new location. For example, you might have a price in a specific cell that you want to use in all formulas, regardless of their location. If you used relative cell referencing, the formula results would be incorrect, because Excel would use a different cell every time you copied the formula. Therefore you need to use an **absolute cell reference**, a reference that does not change when you copy the formula.

You create an absolute cell reference by placing a $ (dollar sign) before both the column letter and the row number for the cell's address, using the [F4] function key on the keyboard. Figure B-15 displays the formulas used in Figure B-14. The formulas in cells B15 to D18 use absolute cell references to refer to a potential sales increase of 50%, shown in cell B12.

FIGURE B-14: Location of relative references

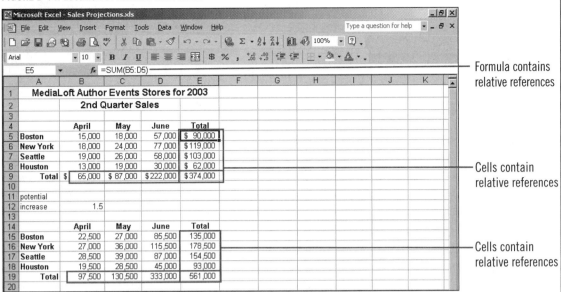

Formula contains relative references

Cells contain relative references

Cells contain relative references

FIGURE B-15: Absolute and relative reference formulas

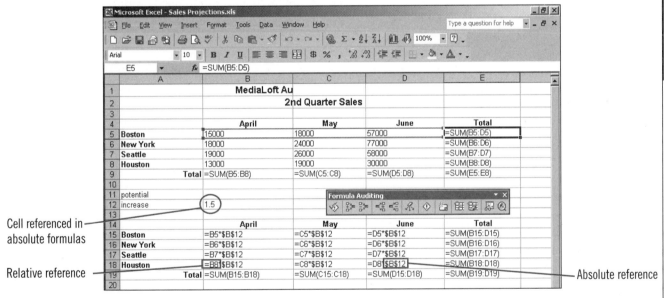

Cell referenced in absolute formulas

Relative reference

Absolute reference

Using a mixed reference

Sometimes when you copy a formula, you'll want to change the row reference but keep the column reference the same. This type of cell referencing combines elements of both absolute and relative referencing and is called a mixed reference. When copied, the mixed reference C$14 changes the column relative to its new location but prevents the row from changing.

In the mixed reference $C14, the column would not change but the row would be updated relative to its location. Like the absolute reference, a mixed reference can be created using the [F4] function key. With each press of the [F4] key, you cycle through all the possible combinations of relative, absolute, and mixed references ($C$14, C$14, $C14, C14).

Excel 2002

Copying Formulas with Relative Cell References

Copying and moving formulas allows you to reuse formulas you've already created. Copying formulas, rather than retyping them, is faster and helps to prevent typing errors. You can use the Copy and Paste commands or the Fill Right method to copy formulas. Jim wants you to copy the formulas that total the appearances by region and by month from the spring to the fall.

Steps

1. **Click cell E4, then click the Copy button** 📋 **on the Standard toolbar**
   The formula for calculating the total number of spring Boston author events is copied to the Clipboard. Notice that the formula =SUM(B4:D4) appears in the formula bar.

QuickTip

To specify components of the copied cell or range prior to pasting, click Edit on the menu bar, then click Paste Special. You can selectively copy formulas, values, comments, validation, and formatting attributes, and specify calculations, as well as transpose cells or paste the contents as a link.

2. **Click cell E13, then click the Paste button** 📋 **on the Standard toolbar**
   The formula from cell E4 is copied into cell E13, where the new result of 59 appears. Notice in the formula bar that the cell references have changed, so that the range B13:D13 appears in the formula. This formula contains **relative cell references**, which tell Excel to copy the formula to a new cell, but to substitute new cell references so that the relationship of the cells to the formula in its new location remains unchanged. In this case, Excel adjusted the formula so that cells D13, C13, and B13—the three cell references immediately to the left of E13—replaced cells D4, C4, and B4, the three cell references to the left of E4. Notice that the bottom-right corner of the active cell contains a small square, called the **fill handle**. You can use the fill handle to copy labels, formulas, and values. This option is called **AutoFill**.

3. **Position the pointer over the fill handle until it changes to ✛, press and hold the left mouse button, then drag the fill handle to select the range E13:E16**
   See Figure B-16.

4. **Release the mouse button**
   A formula similar to the one in cell E13 now appears in the range E14:E16. Again, because the formula uses relative cell references, cells E14 through E16 correctly display the totals for the fall author events. After you release the mouse button, the **AutoFill Options button** appears. If you move the pointer over it and click its list arrow, you can specify what you want to fill and whether or not you want to include formatting.

5. **Click cell B9, click Edit on the menu bar, then click Copy**

Trouble?

If the Clipboard task pane opens, click the Close button. If the Office Assistant appears, right-click it, then click Hide.

6. **Click cell B18, click Edit on the menu bar, then click Paste**
   See Figure B-17. The formula for calculating the September events appears in the formula bar. You also need totals to appear in cells C18, D18, and E18. You could use the fill handle again, but another option is to use a menu command.

7. **Select the range B18:E18**

8. **Click Edit on the menu bar, point to Fill, then click Right**
   The rest of the totals are filled in correctly. Compare your worksheet to Figure B-18.

9. **Click the Save button** 💾 **on the Standard toolbar**

FIGURE B-16: Using the fill handle

12	Fall	September	October	November	Total
13	Boston	22	17	20	59
14	New York	27	16	24	
15	Seattle	19	19	18	
16	Houston	15	25	18	
17					
18	Total				

Formula in cell E13 will be copied to E14:E16

Fill handle

Mouse pointer

FIGURE B-17: Copied formula

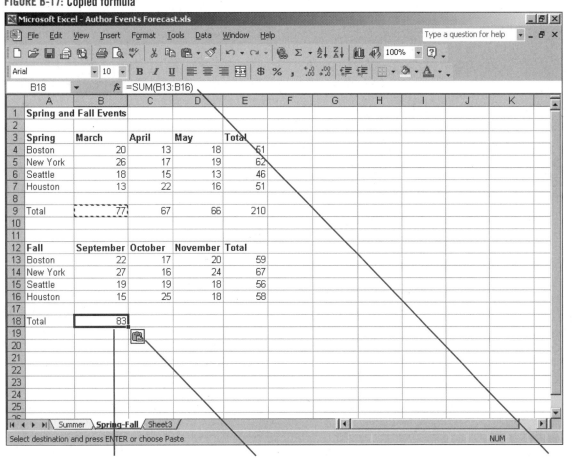

Copied formula result

Paste Options button

Copied formula cell references

FIGURE B-18: Completed worksheet with all formulas copied

12	Fall	September	October	November	Total
13	Boston	22	17	20	59
14	New York	27	16	24	67
15	Seattle	19	19	18	56
16	Houston	15	25	18	58
17					
18	Total	83	77	80	240

Filling cells with sequential text or values

Often, you'll need to fill cells with sequential text: months of the year, days of the week, years, or text plus a number (Quarter 1, Quarter 2, . . .). You can easily fill cells using sequences by dragging the fill handle. As you drag the fill handle, Excel automatically extends the existing sequence. (The contents of the last filled cell appear in the ScreenTip.) Use the Fill Series command on the Edit menu to examine all of the available fill series options.

Copying Formulas with Absolute Cell References

When copying formulas, you might want a cell reference to always refer to a particular cell address. In such an instance, you would use an absolute cell reference. An **absolute cell reference** always refers to a specific cell address when the formula is copied. You create an absolute reference by placing a dollar sign ($) before the row letter and column number of the address (for example $A$1). The staff in the Marketing department hopes the number of author events will increase by 20% over last year's figures. Jim wants you to add a column that calculates a possible increase in the number of spring events in 2003. He asks you to do a what-if analysis and recalculate the spreadsheet several times, changing the percentage by which the number of appearances might increase each time.

1. Click cell **G1**, type **Change**, then press [→]

   You can store the increase factor that will be used in the what-if analysis in cell H1.

2. Type **1.1**, then press **[Enter]**

   The value in cell H1 represents a 10% increase in author events.

3. Click cell **G3**, type **What if?**, then press **[Enter]**

4. Click cell **G4**, type =, click **E4**, type *, click **H1**, then click the **Enter button** on the formula bar

   The result, 56.1, appears in cell G4. This value represents the total spring events for Boston if there is a 10% increase. Jim wants to perform a what-if analysis for all the stores.

5. Drag the fill handle to extend the selection from **G4** to **G7**

   The resulting values in the range G5:G7 are all zeros. When you copy the formula it adjusts so that the formula in cell G5 is =E5*H2. Because there is no value in cell H2, the result is 0, an error. You need to use an absolute reference in the formula to keep the formula from adjusting itself. That way, it will always reference cell H1. You can change the relative cell reference to an absolute cell reference by using [F4].

6. Click cell **G4**, press **[F2]** to change to Edit mode, then press **[F4]**

   When you press [F2], the **range finder** outlines the equation's arguments in blue and green. When you press [F4], dollar signs appear, changing the H1 cell reference to an absolute reference. See Figure B-19.

7. Click ☑ on the formula bar, then drag the fill handle to extend the selection to range **G5:G7**

   The formula correctly contains an absolute cell reference, and the value of G4 remains unchanged at 56.1. The correct values for a 10% increase appear in cells G4:G7. You complete the what-if analysis by changing the value in cell H1 to indicate a 25% increase in events.

8. Click cell **H1**, type **1.25**, then click ☑

   The values in the range G4:G7 change to reflect the 25% increase. Compare your completed worksheets to Figure B-20. Because events only occur in whole numbers, the numbers' appearance can be changed later.

9. Enter your name in cell **A25**, click the **Save button** 🖫 on the Standard toolbar, click the **Print button** 🖨 on the Standard toolbar, close the workbook, then exit Excel

FIGURE B-19: Absolute cell reference in cell G4

Absolute cell references in formula

Incorrect values due to relative references in copied formulas

Microsoft Excel - Author Events Forecast.xls

	A	B	C	D	E	F	G	H	I	J	K
1	Spring and Fall Events						Change	1.1			
2											
3	Spring	March	April	May	Total		What if?				
4	Boston	20	13	18	51		=E4*$H$1				
5	New York	26	17	19	62		0				
6	Seattle	18	15	13	46		0				
7	Houston	13	22	16	51		0				
8											
9	Total	77	67	66	210						

AVERAGE =E4*$H$1

FIGURE B-20: Completed worksheets

Summer 2003 MediaLoft Author Events Forecast

	June	July	August	Total	Average
Boston	22	15	19	56	18.66667
New York	28	18	22	68	22.66667
Seattle	20	17	18	55	18.33333
Houston	15	19	21	55	18.33333
Total	85	69	80	234	
20% rise	102	82.8	96	280.8	

Spring and Fall Events   Change   1.25

Spring	March	April	May	Total	What if?
Boston	20	13	18	51	63.75
New York	26	17	19	62	77.5
Seattle	18	15	13	46	57.5
Houston	13	22	16	51	63.75
Total	77	67	66	210	

Fall	September	October	November	Total	
Boston	22	17	20	59	
New York	27	16	24	67	
Seattle	19	19	18	56	
Houston	15	25	18	58	
Total	83	77	80	240	

CLUES TO USE

Inserting and deleting selected cells

As you add formulas to your workbook, you may need to insert or delete cells, not entire rows or columns. When you do this, Excel automatically adjusts cell references to reflect their new locations. To insert cells, click Insert on the menu bar, then click Cells. The Insert dialog box opens, asking if you want to insert a cell and move the selected cell down or to the right of the new one. To delete one or more selected cells, click Edit on the menu bar, click Delete, and, in the Delete dialog box, indicate which way you want to move the adjacent cells. When using this option, be careful not to disturb row or column alignment that may be necessary to make sense of the worksheet.

Practice

► Concepts Review

Label each element of the Excel worksheet window shown in Figure B-21.

FIGURE B-21

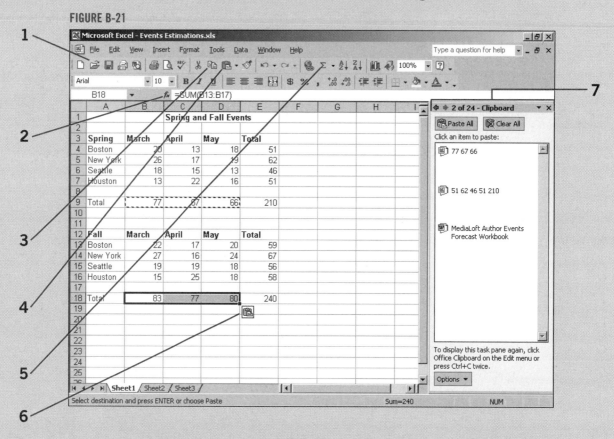

Match the term or button with the statement that describes it.

8. Fill handle

9. Function

10. <image>

11. <image>

12. Formula

a. A predefined formula that provides a shortcut for commonly used calculations

b. A cell entry that performs a calculation in an Excel worksheet

c. Used to copy labels, formulas, and values

d. Adds the selected range to the Office Clipboard.

e. Used to paste cells

Select the best answer from the list of choices.

13. What type of cell reference changes when it is copied?
   - a. Absolute
   - b. Circular
   - c. Looping
   - d. Relative

14. What character is used to make a reference absolute?
   - a. &
   - b. ^
   - c. $
   - d. @

15. Which button is used to enter data in a cell?

a. [↺]   c. [▣]

b. [✕]   d. [✓]

▶ Skills Review

1. Edit cell entries and work with ranges.
 a. Start Excel, open the workbook EX B-2 from the drive and folder where your Project Files are stored then save it as **Office Furnishings**.
 b. Change the quantity of Tables to **27**.
 c. Change the price of Desks to **285**.
 d. Change the quantity of Easels to **18**.
 e. Enter your name in cell A40, then save the workbook.

2. Enter formulas.
 a. In cell B6, use the pointing method to enter the formula **B2+B3+B4+B5**.
 b. In cell D2, use the pointing method to enter the formula **B2*C2**.
 c. Save your work.

3. Create complex formulas.
 a. In cell B8, enter the formula **(B2+B3+B4+B5)/4**.
 b. In cell C8, enter the formula **(C2+C3+C4+C5)/4**.
 c. Save your work.

4. Introduce Excel functions.
 a. Enter the label **Min Price** in cell A9.
 b. In cell C9, enter the function **MIN(C2:C5)**.
 c. Enter the label **Max Price** in cell A10.
 d. Create a formula in cell C10 that determines the maximum price.
 e. Save your work.

5. Copy and move cell entries.
 a. Select the range **A1:C6**, then copy the range to cell A12.
 b. Select the range **D1:E1**, then use drag and drop to copy the range to cell D12.
 c. Move the contents of cell G1 to cell E9, then save your work.

6. Copy formulas with relative cell references.
 a. Copy the formula in D2 into cells D3:D5.
 b. Copy the formula in D2 into cells D13:D16.
 c. Save the worksheet.

7. Copy formulas with absolute cell references.
 a. In cell E10, enter the value **1.375**.
 b. In cell E2, create a formula containing an absolute reference that multiplies D2 and E10.
 c. Use the fill handle to copy the formula in E2 into cells **E3:E5**.
 d. Use the copy and paste buttons to copy the formula in E2 into cells **E13:E16**.
 e. Delete cells A13:E13, shifting the cells up, then edit the formula in cell B16 so the missing reference is removed.
 f. Change the amount in cell E10 to **2.873**.
 g. Select cells A1:E1 and insert cells, shifting cells down.
 h. Enter **Inventory Estimate** in cell A1.
 i. Save, preview, print, and close the workbook, then exit Excel.

▶ Independent Challenge 1

You are the box office manager for the Young Brazilians Jazz Band, a popular new group. Your responsibilities include tracking seasonal ticket sales for the band's concerts and anticipating ticket sales for the next season. The group sells four types of tickets: reserved, general, senior, and student tickets.

The 2003–2004 season includes five scheduled concerts: Spring, Summer, Fall, Winter, and Thaw. You will plan and build a worksheet that tracks the sales of each of the four ticket types for all five concerts.

FIGURE B-22

	A	B	C	D	E	F	G	H
1			2003-2004 Season					
2			Young Brazilians Jazz Band					Increase
3								1.05
4		Reserved	General	Senior	Student			
5	Concerts	Seating	Admission	Citizens	Tickets	Totals		What if?
6	Spring	285	50	30	20	385		404.25
7	Summer	135	25	35	20	215		225.75
8	Fall	130	50	25	20	225		236.25
9	Winter	160	100	30	20	310		325.5
10	Thaw	250	60	35	20	365		383.25
11	Total	960	285	155	100	1500		1575

a. Think about the results you want to see, the information you need to build into these worksheets, and what types of calculations must be performed.

b. Sketch sample worksheets on a piece of paper to indicate how the information should be laid out. What information should go in the columns? In the rows?

c. Start Excel, open a new workbook, then save it as **Young Brazilians** in the drive and folder where your Project Files are stored.

d. Plan and build a worksheet that tracks the sales of each of the four ticket types for all five concerts. Build the worksheets by entering a title, row labels, column headings, and formulas.

e. Enter your own sales data. No concert sold more than 400 tickets, and the Reserved category was the most popular.

f. Calculate the total ticket sales for each concert, the total sales for each of the four ticket types, and the total sales for all tickets.

g. Name the worksheet **Sales Data** and color the tab Red.

h. Copy the Sales Data worksheet to a blank worksheet, name the copied worksheet **5% Increase**, and color the tab aqua.

i. Modify the 5% increase sheet so that a 5% increase in sales of all ticket types is shown in a separate column. See Figure B-22 for a sample worksheet.

j. Enter your name in a worksheet cell.

k. Save your work, preview and print the worksheets, then close the workbook and exit Excel.

▶ Independent Challenge 2

The Beautiful You Salon is a small but growing beauty salon that has hired you to organize its accounting records using Excel. The owners want you to track its expenses using Excel. Before you were hired, one of the bookkeepers entered last year's expenses in a workbook, but the analysis was never completed.

a. Start Excel, open the workbook EX B-3 then save it as **Beautiful You Finances** in the drive and folder where your Project Files are stored. The worksheet includes labels for functions such as the Average, Maximum, and Minimum amounts of each of the expenses in the worksheet.

b. Think about what information would be important for the bookkeeping staff to know.

c. Create your sketch using the existing worksheet as a foundation.

d. Create formulas in the Total column and row using the AutoSum function.

e. Create formulas in the Average, Maximum, and Minimum columns and rows using the appropriate functions, dragging to select the range.

f. Rename Sheet1 **Expenses** and add a color to the tab.

g. Enter your name in a worksheet cell.

h. Save your work, preview and print the worksheet, then close the workbook and exit Excel.

▶ Independent Challenge 3

You have been promoted to computer lab manager at Learn-It-All, a local computer training center. It is your responsibility to make sure there are enough computers for students during scheduled classes. Currently, you have five classrooms: four with IBM PCs and one with Macintoshes. Classes are scheduled Monday, Wednesday, and Friday in two-hour increments from 9 a.m. to 5 p.m. (the lab closes at 7 p.m.), and each room can currently accommodate 30 computers.

You plan and build a worksheet that tracks the number of students who can currently use the available computers per room. You create your enrollment data. Using an additional worksheet, you show the impact of an enrollment increase of 25%.

a. Think about how to construct these worksheets to create the desired output.

b. Sketch sample paper worksheets to indicate how the information should be laid out.

c. Start Excel, open a new workbook, then save it as **Learn-it-All** in the drive and folder where your Project Files are stored.

d. Create a worksheet by entering a title, row labels, column headings, data, and formulas. Name the sheet to easily identify its contents.

e. Create a second sheet by copying the information from the initial sheet.

f. Name the second sheet to easily identify its contents.

g. Add color to each sheet tab.

h. Enter your name in a cell in each sheet.

i. Save your work, preview and print each worksheet, then close the workbook and exit Excel.

Independent Challenge 4

Your company is opening a branch office in Great Britain and your boss is a fanatic about keeping the thermostats at a constant temperature during each season of the year. Because she grew up in the U.S., she is only familiar with Fahrenheit temperatures and doesn't know how to convert them to Celsius. She has asked you to find out the Celsius equivalents for the thermostatic settings she wants to use. She prefers the temperature to be 65 degrees F in the winter, 62 degrees F in the spring, 75 degrees in the summer, and 70 degrees F in the fall. You can use the Web and Excel to determine the new settings.

a. Start Excel, open a new workbook, then save it as **Temperature Conversions** in the drive and folder where your Project Files are stored.

b. Go to the Alta Vista search engine at www.altavista.com and enter search text such as "temperature conversions". You can also use Yahoo!, Excite, Infoseek, or another search engine of your choice. Locate a site that tells you how to convert Fahrenheit temperatures to Celsius. (*Hint:* One possible site you can use to determine these conversions is http://home.clara.net/brianp/, then click on the Temperature link.)

c. Think about how to create an Excel equation that will perform the conversion.

d. Create column and row titles using Table B-3 to get started.

e. In the appropriate cell, create an equation that calculates the conversion of a Fahrenheit temperature to a Celsius temperature.

f. Copy the equation, then paste it in the remaining Celsius cells.

g. Enter your name in a worksheet cell.

h. Save and print your work.

TABLE B-3

Temperature Conversions

Season	Fahrenheit	Celsius
Spring	62	
Winter	68	
Summer	75	
Fall	70	

▶ Visual Workshop

Create a worksheet similar to Figure B-23 using the skills you learned in this unit. Save the workbook as **Annual Budget** in the drive and folder where your Project Files are stored. Enter your name in cell A13, then preview and print the worksheet.

FIGURE B-23

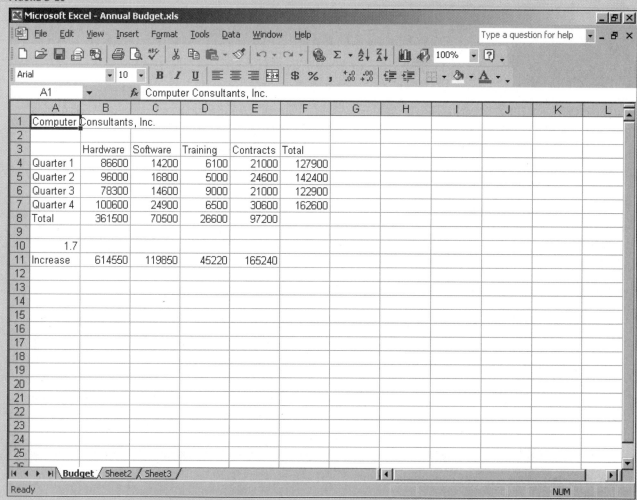

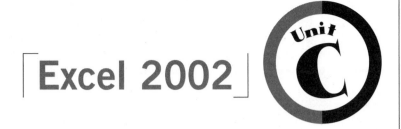
Formatting

a Worksheet

You can use Excel formatting features to make a worksheet more attractive, to make it easier to read, or to emphasize key data. You do this by using different colors and fonts for the cell contents, adjusting column and row widths, and inserting and deleting columns and rows. ✎ The marketing managers at MediaLoft have asked Jim Fernandez to create a workbook that lists advertising expenses for all MediaLoft stores. Jim has prepared a worksheet for the New York City store containing this information, which he can adapt later for use in other stores. He asks you to use formatting to make the worksheet easier to read and to call attention to important data.

Formatting Values

If you enter a value in a cell and you don't like the way the data appears, you can adjust the cell's format. **Formatting** determines how labels and values appear in cells, such as boldface, italic, with or without dollar signs or commas, and the like. Formatting changes only the way a value or label appears; it does not alter cell data in any way. To format a cell, first select it, then apply the formatting. You can format cells and ranges before or after you enter data. ✎ The Marketing department has requested that Jim begin by listing the New York City store's advertising expenses. Jim developed a worksheet that lists advertising invoices. He entered all the information and now wants you to format some of the labels and values. Because some of the changes might also affect column widths, you make all formatting changes before widening the columns.

Steps 1234

QuickTip

Recall that to save a workbook in a different location, you click File on the menu bar, click Save As, click the Save in list arrow and navigate to a new drive or folder, type a new filename if necessary, then click Save.

1. **Start Excel, open the Project File EX C-1 from the drive and folder where your Project Files are stored, then save it as Ad Expenses**

   The store advertising worksheet appears in Figure C-1. You can display numeric data in a variety of ways, such as with decimals or leading dollar signs. Excel provides a special format for currency, which adds two decimal places and a dollar sign.

2. **Select the range E4:E32, then click the Currency Style button 💲 on the Formatting toolbar**

   Excel adds dollar signs and two decimal places to the Cost data. Excel automatically resizes the column to display the new formatting. Another way to format dollar values is to use the comma format, which does not include the $ sign.

QuickTip

Select any range of contiguous cells by clicking the top-left cell, pressing and holding [Shift], then clicking the bottom-right cell. Add a row to the selected range by continuing to hold down [Shift] and pressing [↓], add a column by pressing [→].

3. **Select the range G4:I32, then click the Comma Style button �’ on the Formatting toolbar**

   The values in columns G, H, and I display the comma format. You can also format percentages by using the Formatting toolbar.

4. **Select the range J4:J32, click the Percent Style button % on the Formatting toolbar, then click the Increase Decimal button on the Formatting toolbar to show one decimal place**

   The % of Total column is now formatted with a percent sign (%) and one decimal place. You decide that you prefer the percentages rounded to the nearest whole number.

5. **Click the Decrease Decimal button**

   You can also apply a variety of formats to dates in a worksheet.

6. **Select the range B4:B31, click Format on the menu bar, click Cells, then if necessary click the Number tab**

   The Format Cells dialog box opens with the Number tab in front and the Date category already selected. See Figure C-2.

7. **Select the format 14-Mar-01 in the Type list box, then click OK**

   The dates in column B appear in the format you selected. You decide you don't need the year to appear in the Inv. Due column.

QuickTip

The 3-14-01 format displays a single-digit day (such as 5/9/03) just as 9-May-03 does. The format below it displays the same day as 5/09/03.

8. **Select the range C4:C31, click Format on the menu bar, click Cells, click 14-Mar in the Type list box, then click OK**

   Compare your worksheet to Figure C-3.

9. **Click the Save button 🖫 on the Standard toolbar**

FIGURE C-1: Advertising expense worksheet

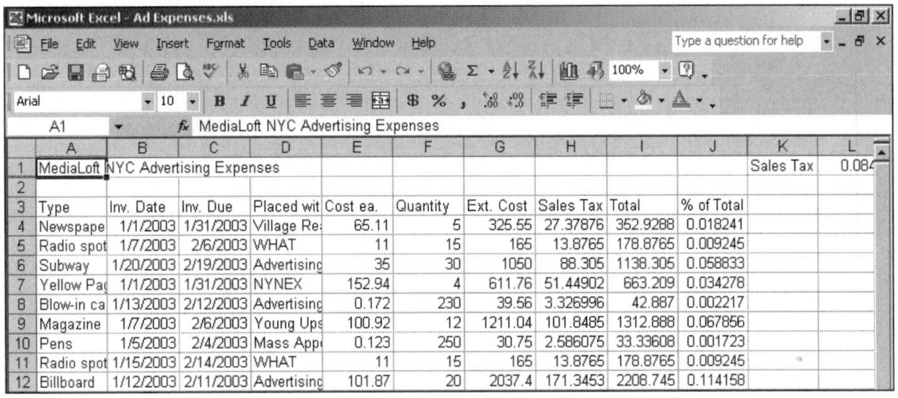

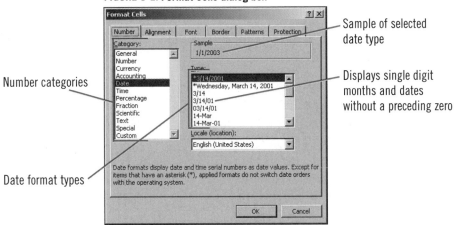

FIGURE C-2: Format Cells dialog box

Sample of selected date type

Number categories

Displays single digit months and dates without a preceding zero

Date format types

FIGURE C-3: Worksheet with formatted values

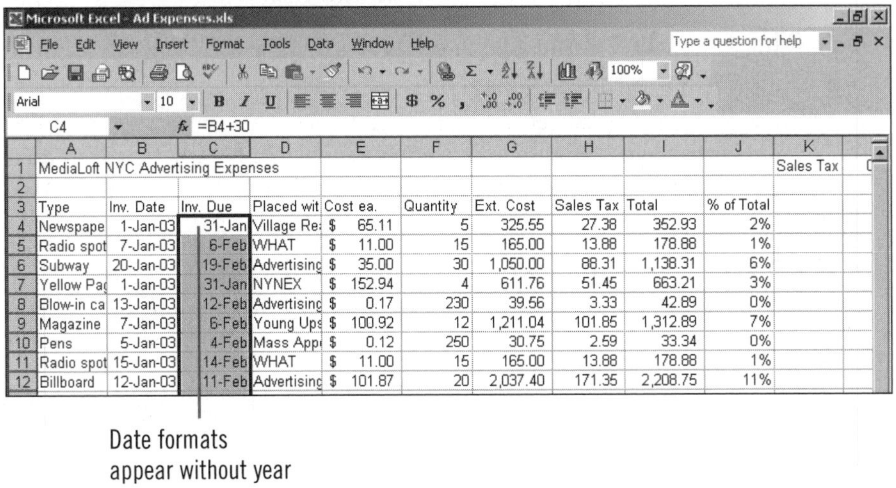

Date formats appear without year

Using the Format Painter

You can "paint" a cell's format into other cells by using the Format Painter button on the Standard toolbar. This is similar to using copy and paste to copy information, but instead of copying cell contents, you copy only the cell format. Select the cell containing the desired format, then click . The pointer changes to . Use this pointer to select the cell or range you want to contain the new format. You can paint a cell's format onto multiple cells by double-clicking , then clicking each cell that you want to paint with .When you are finished painting formats, you can turn off the Format Painter by pressing [Esc] or by clicking again.

Using Fonts and Font Sizes

A **font** is the name for a collection of characters (letters, numerals, symbols, and punctuation marks) with a similar, specific design. The **font size** is the physical size of the text, measured in units called points. A **point** is equal to 1/72 of an inch. The default font in Excel is 10-point Arial. You can change the font, the size, or both of any worksheet entry or section by using the Format command on the menu bar or by using the Formatting toolbar. Table C-1 shows several fonts in different sizes. ✎ Now that the data is formatted, Jim wants you to change the font and size of the labels and the worksheet title so that they stand out more from the data.

Steps

1. Press **[Ctrl][Home]** to select cell A1

QuickTip
You can also open the Format Cells dialog box by right-clicking selected cells, then clicking Format Cells.

2. Click **Format** on the menu bar, click **Cells**, then click the **Font tab** in the Format Cells dialog box
See Figure C-4.

3. Scroll down the **Font list** to see an alphabetical listing of the fonts available on your computer, click **Times New Roman** in the Font list box, click **24** in the Size list box, then click **OK**
The title font appears in 24-point Times New Roman, and the Formatting toolbar displays the new font and size information. You can also change a font and increase the font size by using the Formatting toolbar. The column headings should stand out more from the data.

4. Select the range **A3:J3**, then click the **Font list arrow** [Arial] on the Formatting toolbar
Notice that the fonts on this font list actually look like the font they represent.

5. Click **Times New Roman** in the Font list, click the **Font Size** list arrow [10 ▾], then click **14** in the Font Size list
Compare your worksheet to Figure C-5. Notice that some of the column headings are now too wide to appear fully in the column. Excel does not automatically adjust column widths to accommodate cell formatting; you have to adjust column widths manually. You'll learn to do this in a later lesson.

6. Click the **Save button** 🖫 on the Standard toolbar

TABLE C-1: Types of fonts

font	12 point	24 point	font	12 point	24 point
Arial	Excel	Excel	Playbill	Excel	Excel
Comic Sans MS	Excel	Excel	Times New Roman	Excel	Excel

FIGURE C-4: Font tab in the Format Cells dialog box

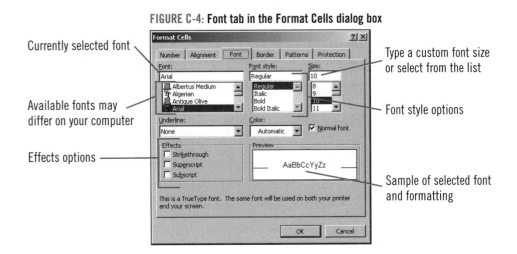

Currently selected font

Available fonts may differ on your computer

Effects options

Type a custom font size or select from the list

Font style options

Sample of selected font and formatting

FIGURE C-5: Worksheet with formatted title and labels

Font and size of active cell or range

Column headings now 14-point Times New Roman

Title after changing to 24-point Times New Roman

Inserting Clip Art

You can add clips to your worksheets to make them look more professional. A **clip** is an individual media file, such as art, sound, animation, or a movie. **Clip art** refers to images such as a corporate logo, a picture, or a photo; Excel comes with many clips that you can use. To add clip art to your worksheet, click Insert on the menu bar, point to Picture, then click Clip Art. The Insert Clip Art task pane appears. Here you can search for clips by typing one or more **keywords** (words related to your subject) in the Search text box, then clicking Search. Clips that relate to your keywords appear in the Clip Art task pane, as shown in Figure C-6. Click the image you want. (If you have a standard Office installation and have a dial-up Internet connection, you will have fewer images available.) You can also add your own images to a worksheet by clicking Insert on the menu bar, pointing to Picture, then clicking From File. Navigate to the file you want, then click Insert. To resize an image, drag its lower right corner. To move an image, drag it to a new location.

FIGURE C-6: Results of search on keyword "magic"

Changing Attributes and Alignment

Attributes are styling formats such as bold, italics, and underlining that you can apply to affect the way text and numbers look in a worksheet. You can also change the **alignment** of labels and values in cells to be left, right, or center. You can apply attributes and alignment options from the Formatting toolbar or from the Alignment tab of the Format Cells dialog box. See Table C-2 for a list and description of the available attribute and alignment toolbar buttons. ◢━━ Now that you have applied new fonts and font sizes to his worksheet labels, Jim wants you to further enhance the worksheet's appearance by adding bold and underline formatting and centering some of the labels.

Steps 1 2 3 4

1. Press **[Ctrl][Home]** to move to cell A1, then click the **Bold button** **B** on the Formatting toolbar
   The title appears in bold.

2. Select the range **A3:J3**, then click the **Underline button** **U** on the Formatting toolbar
   Excel underlines the text in the column headings in the selected range.

   > **QuickTip**
   > Overuse of any attribute can be distracting and make a workbook less readable. Be consistent, adding emphasis the same way throughout.

3. Click cell **A3**, click the **Italics button** **I** on the Formatting toolbar, then click **B**
   The word "Type" appears in boldface italic type. Notice that the Bold, Italics, and Underline buttons are selected.

4. Click **I**
   Excel removes italics from cell A3 but the bold and underline formatting attributes remain.

   > **QuickTip**
   > Use formatting shortcuts on any selected range: [Ctrl][B] to bold, [Ctrl][I] to italicize, and [Ctrl][U] to underline.

5. Select the range **B3:J3**, then click **B**
   Bold formatting is added to the rest of the labels in the column headings. The title would look better if it were centered over the data columns.

6. Select the range **A1:J1**, then click the **Merge and Center button** 🔲 on the Formatting toolbar
   The Merge and Center button creates one cell out of the 10 cells across the row, then centers the text in that newly created large cell. The title "MediaLoft NYC Advertising Expenses" is centered across the 10 columns you selected. You can change the alignment within individual cells using toolbar buttons; you can split merged cells into their original components by selecting the merged cells, then clicking 🔲.

   > **QuickTip**
   > To clear all formatting, click Edit on the menu bar, point to Clear, then click Formats.

7. Select the range **A3:J3**, then click the **Center button** 🔲 on the Formatting toolbar
   Compare your screen to Figure C-7. Although they may be difficult to read, notice that all the headings are centered within their cells.

8. Click the **Save button** 🔲 on the Standard toolbar

Rotating and indenting cell entries

In addition to applying fonts and formatting attributes, you can rotate or indent cell data within a cell to further change its appearance. You can rotate text within a cell by altering its alignment. To change alignment, select the cells you want to modify, click Format on the menu bar, click Cells, then click the Alignment tab. Click a position in the Orientation box, or type a number in the degrees text box to change from the default horizontal alignment, then click OK. You can indent cell contents using the Increase Indent button 📇 on the Formatting toolbar, which moves cell contents to the right one space, or the Decrease Indent button 📇, which moves cell contents to the left one space.

FIGURE C-7: Worksheet with formatting attributes applied

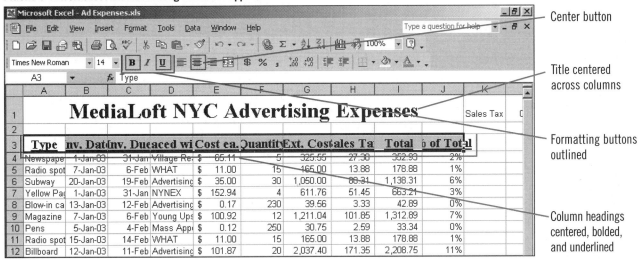

Center button

Title centered across columns

Formatting buttons outlined

Column headings centered, bolded, and underlined

TABLE C-2: Attribute and Alignment buttons on the Formatting toolbar

button	description	button	description
B	Bolds text	▤	Aligns text on the left side of the cell
I	Italicizes text	▤	Centers text horizontally within the cell
U	Underlines text	▤	Aligns text on the right side of the cell
▢▾	Adds lines or borders	▦	Centers text across columns, and combines two or more selected adjacent cells into one cell

Using AutoFormat

Excel has 17 predefined worksheet formats to make formatting easier and to give you the option of consistently styling your worksheets. AutoFormats are designed for worksheets with labels in the left column and top rows, and totals in the bottom row or right column. To use AutoFormat, select the data to be formatted—or place your mouse pointer anywhere within the range to be selected (Excel can automatically detect a range of cells)—click Format on the menu bar, click AutoFormat, select a format from the sample boxes, as shown in Figure C-8, then click OK.

FIGURE C-8: AutoFormat dialog box

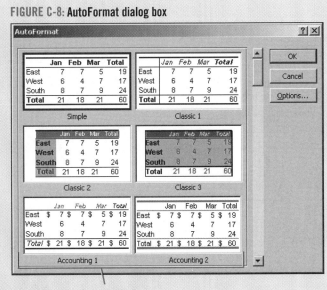

Samples of available formats

Adjusting Column Widths

As you continue formatting a worksheet, you might need to adjust column widths to accommodate a larger font size or style. The default column width is 8.43 characters wide, a little less than one inch. With Excel, you can adjust the column width for one or more columns by using the mouse or the Column command on the Format menu. Table C-3 describes the commands available on the Format Column menu. Jim notices that some of the labels in column A have been truncated and don't fit in the cells. He asks you to adjust the widths of the columns so that the labels appear in their entirety.

Steps 1 2 3 4

1. **Position the pointer on the line between the column A and column B headings**

   The **column heading** is the gray box at the top of each column containing a letter. The pointer changes to ↔, as shown in Figure C-9. You position the pointer on the right edge of the column that you are adjusting. The Yellow Pages entries are the widest in the column.

2. **Click and drag the ↔ pointer to the right until the column displays the Yellow Pages entries fully**

   The **AutoFit** feature lets you use the mouse to resize a column so it automatically accommodates the widest entry in a cell.

QuickTip

To reset columns to the default width, click the column headings to select the columns, click Format on the menu bar, point to Column, click Standard Width, then click OK.

3. **Position the pointer on the column line between columns B and C headings until it changes to ↔, then double-click**

   Column B automatically widens to fit the widest entry, in this case, the column label.

4. **Use AutoFit to resize columns C, D, and J**

   You can also use the Column Width command on the Format menu to adjust several columns to the same width.

5. **Select the range F5:I5**

   Columns can be adjusted by selecting any cell in the column.

6. **Click Format on the menu bar, point to Column, then click Width**

   The Column Width dialog box appears. Move the dialog box, if necessary, by dragging it by its title bar so you can see the selected columns. The column width measurement is based on the number of characters in the Normal font (in this case, Arial).

Trouble?

If "######" appears after you adjust a column of values, the column is too narrow to display the contents. Increase the column width until the values appear.

7. **Type 11 in the Column Width text box, then click OK**

   The column widths change to reflect the new setting. See Figure C-10.

8. **Click the Save button 🖫 on the Standard toolbar**

TABLE C-3: Format Column commands

command	description	command	description
Width	Sets the width to a specific number of characters	Unhide	Unhide(s) column(s)
AutoFit Selection	Fits to the widest entry	Standard Width	Resets width to default widths
Hide	Hide(s) column(s)		

FIGURE C-9: Preparing to change the column width

Resize pointer between columns A and B

Row 2 heading

Column D heading

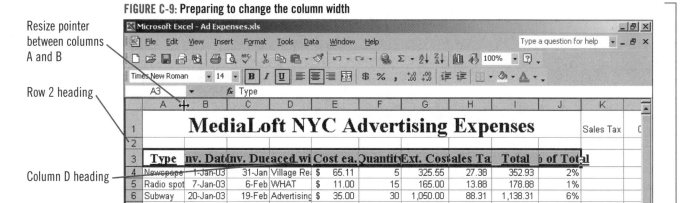

FIGURE C-10: Worksheet with column widths adjusted

Columns widened to display text

Columns widened to same width

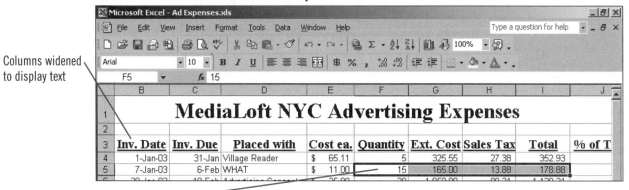

Specifying row height

The Row Height command on the Format menu allows you to customize row height to improve readability. Row height is calculated in points, the same units of measure used for fonts. The row height must exceed the size of the font you are using. Normally, you don't need to adjust row heights manually. If you format something in a row to be a larger point size, Excel will adjust the row to fit the largest point size in the row. You can also adjust row height by placing the ✛ pointer under the row heading and dragging to the desired height.

Excel 2002

Inserting and Deleting Rows and Columns

As you modify a worksheet, you might find it necessary to insert or delete rows and columns to keep your worksheet current. For example, you might need to insert rows to accommodate new inventory products or remove a column of yearly totals that are no longer necessary. Jim has already improved the appearance of his worksheet by formatting the labels and values in the worksheet. Now he decides to improve the overall appearance of the worksheet by inserting a row between the last row of data and the totals. Jim has located a row of inaccurate data and an unnecessary column that he wants you to delete.

1. Right-click cell **A32**, then click **Insert**

The Insert dialog box opens. See Figure C-11. You can choose to insert a column or a row, or you can shift the data in the cells in the active column right or in the active row down. An additional row between the last row of data and the totals will visually separate the totals.

QuickTip

Inserting or deleting rows or columns can cause problems in formulas that contain absolute cell references. After adding rows or columns to a worksheet, be sure to proof your formulas.

2. Click the **Entire row option button**, then click **OK**

A blank row appears between the totals and the Billboard data. Excel inserts rows above the cell pointer and inserts columns to the left of the cell pointer. When you insert a new row, the contents of the worksheet shift down from the newly inserted row. The formula result in cell E33 has not changed. When you insert a new column, the contents of the worksheet shift to the right from the point of the new column. To insert a single row, you can also right-click the row heading immediately below where you want the new row, then click Insert. To insert multiple rows, drag across row headings to select the same number of rows as you want to insert. The Insert Options button appears beside cell A33. When you place ⌖ over ⬚, you can click the list arrow and select from the following options: Format Same As Above, Format same As Below, or Clear Formatting.

3. Click the **row 27 heading**

Hats from Mass Appeal Inc. will no longer be part of the advertising campaign. All of row 27 is selected, as shown in Figure C-12.

QuickTip

Use the Edit menu, or right-click the selected row and click Delete, to remove a selected row. Pressing [Delete] removes the contents of a selected row; the row itself remains.

4. Click **Edit** in the menu bar, then click **Delete**

Excel deletes row 27, and all rows below this shift up one row.

5. Click the **column J heading**

The percentage information is calculated elsewhere and is no longer necessary in this worksheet.

6. Click **Edit** in the menu bar, then click **Delete**

Excel deletes column J. The remaining columns to the right shift left one column.

7. Click the **Save button** 🖫 on the Standard toolbar

FIGURE C-11: Insert dialog box

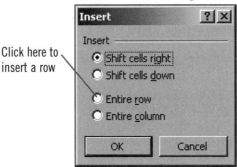

Click here to insert a row

Insert

Insert
- ○ Shift cells right
- ○ Shift cells down
- ○ Entire row
- ○ Entire column

OK   Cancel

FIGURE C-12: Worksheet with row 27 selected

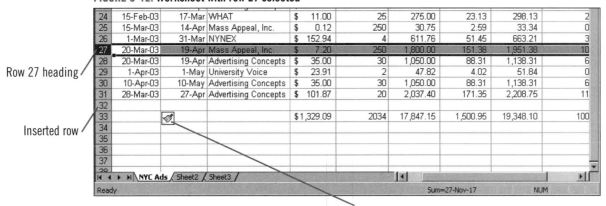

24	15-Feb-03	17-Mar	WHAT	$ 11.00	25	275.00	23.13	298.13	2
25	15-Mar-03	14-Apr	Mass Appeal, Inc.	$ 0.12	250	30.75	2.59	33.34	0
26	1-Mar-03	31-Mar	NYNEX	$ 152.94	4	611.76	51.45	663.21	3
27	20-Mar-03	19-Apr	Mass Appeal, Inc.	$ 7.20	250	1,800.00	151.38	1,951.38	10
28	20-Mar-03	19-Apr	Advertising Concepts	$ 35.00	30	1,050.00	88.31	1,138.31	6
29	1-Apr-03	1-May	University Voice	$ 23.91	2	47.82	4.02	51.84	0
30	10-Apr-03	10-May	Advertising Concepts	$ 35.00	30	1,050.00	88.31	1,138.31	6
31	28-Mar-03	27-Apr	Advertising Concepts	$ 101.87	20	2,037.40	171.35	2,208.75	11
32									
33				$1,329.09	2034	17,847.15	1,500.95	19,348.10	100
34									
35									
36									
37									

Row 27 heading

Inserted row

NYC Ads / Sheet2 / Sheet3 /

Ready   Sum=27-Nov-17   NUM

Insert Options button may appear in a different location, or may not be visible

CLUES TO USE

Adding and editing comments

Much of your Excel work may be in collaboration with teammates with whom you share worksheets. You can share ideas with other worksheet users by adding comments within selected cells. To include a comment in a worksheet, click the cell where you want to place the comment, click Insert on the menu bar, then click Comment. A resizable text box containing the computer's user name opens where you can type your comments. A small, red triangle appears in the upper-right corner of a cell containing a comment. If the comments are not already displayed, workbook users can point to the triangle to display the comment. To see all worksheet comments, as shown in Figure C-13, click View on the menu bar, then click Comments. To edit a comment click the cell containing the comment, click Insert on the menu bar, then click Edit Comment. To delete a comment, right-click the cell containing the comment, then click Delete Comment.

FIGURE C-13: Comments in worksheet

20	Subway	22-Feb-03	24-Mar	Advertising Concepts	$ 35.00
21	Radio spot	1-Feb-03	3-Mar	WHAT	$ 11.00
22	Newspaper	25-Feb-03	27-Mar	Village Reader	$ 65.11
23	Blow-in cards	10-Mar-03	9-Apr		$ 0.17
24	Radio spot	15-Feb-03	17-Mar		$ 11.00
25	Pens	15-Mar-03	14-Apr		$ 0.12
26	Yellow Pages	1-Mar-03	31-Mar		$ 152.94
27	Subway	20-Mar-03	19-Apr	Advertising Concepts	$ 35.00
28	Newspaper	1-Apr-03	1-May		$ 23.91
29	Subway	10-Apr-03	10-May		$ 35.00
30	Billboard	28-Mar-03	27-Apr		$ 101.87
31					
32					$1,321.89
33					
34					

Jim Fernandez: Should we continue with these ads, or expand to other publications?

Jim Fernandez: We need to evaluate whether we should continue these ads.

NYC Ads / Sheet2 / Sheet3 /

Ready

Excel 2002

Applying Colors, Patterns, and Borders

You can use colors, patterns, and borders to enhance the overall appearance of a worksheet and to make it easier to read. You can add these enhancements by using the Patterns or Borders tabs in the Format Cells dialog box or by using the Borders and Color buttons on the Formatting toolbar. You can apply color or patterns to the background of a cell, to a range, or to cell contents. You can also apply borders to all the cells in a worksheet or only to selected cells to call attention to individual or groups of cells. See Table C-4 for a list of border buttons and their functions. Jim asks you to add a pattern, a border, and color to the title of the worksheet to give it a more professional appearance.

Steps

1. Press **[Ctrl][Home]** to select cell **A1**, then click the **Fill Color list arrow** 🖌️▾ on the Formatting toolbar
The color palette appears.

2. Click the **Turquoise** color (fourth row, fifth column)
Cell A1 has a turquoise background, as shown in Figure C-14. Cell A1 spans columns A through I because of the Merge and Center command used for the title.

> **QuickTip**
> Use color sparingly. Too much color can divert the reader's attention from the worksheet data.

3. Click **Format** on the menu bar, then click **Cells**
The Format Cells dialog box opens.

4. Click the **Patterns tab** if it is not already displayed
See Figure C-15. A high contrast between foreground and background increases the readability of cell contents.

5. Click the **Pattern list arrow**, click the **Thin Diagonal Crosshatch pattern** (third row, last column), then click **OK**
A border also enhances a cell's appearance. Unlike underlining, which is a text formatting tool, borders extend the width of the cell.

> **QuickTip**
> You can also draw cell borders using the mouse pointer. Click the Borders list arrow on the Formatting toolbar. Click Draw Borders, then drag to create borders or boxes.

6. Click the **Borders list arrow** ⊞▾ on the Formatting toolbar, then click the **Thick Bottom Border** (second row, second column) on the Borders palette
It can be difficult to view a border in a selected cell.

7. Click cell **A3**
The border is a nice enhancement. Font color can also help distinguish information in a worksheet.

> **QuickTip**
> The default color on the Fill Color and Font Color buttons changes to the last color you selected.

8. Select the range **A3:I3**, click the **Font Color list arrow** 🅰️▾ on the Formatting toolbar, then click **Blue** (second row, third column from the right) on the palette
The text changes color, as shown in Figure C-16.

9. Click the **Print Preview button** 🔍 on the Standard toolbar, preview the first page, click **Next** to preview the second page, click **Close** on the Print Preview toolbar, then click the **Save button** 💾 on the Standard toolbar

FIGURE C-14: Background color added to cell

Cell A1 with turquoise
background

FIGURE C-15: Patterns tab in the Format Cells dialog box

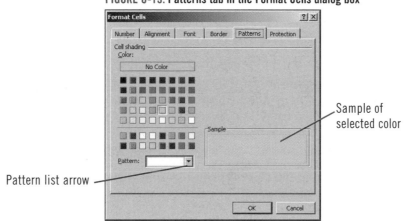

Sample of
selected color

Pattern list arrow

FIGURE C-16: Worksheet with colors, patterns, and border

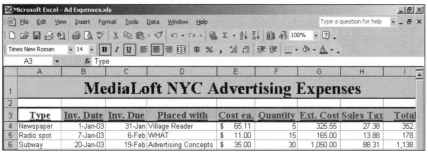

TABLE C-4: Border buttons

button	function	button	function	button	function
	No Border		Bottom Double Border		Top and Thick Bottom Border
	Bottom Border		Thick Bottom Border		All Borders
	Left Border		Top and Bottom Border		Outside Borders
	Right Border		Top and Double Bottom Border		Thick Box Border

Using Conditional Formatting

Formatting makes worksheets look professional and helps distinguish different types of data. You can have Excel automatically apply formatting depending on specific outcomes in cells. You might, for example, want advertising costs above a certain number to appear in red boldface and lower values to appear in blue. Automatically applying formatting attributes based on cell values is called **conditional formatting**. If the data meets your criteria, Excel applies the formats you specify. Jim wants the worksheet to include conditional formatting so that total advertising costs greater than $175 appear in boldface red type. He asks you to create the conditional format in the first cell in the Total cost column.

1. **Click cell G4**
   Use the scroll bars if necessary, to make column G visible.

2. **Click Format on the menu bar, then click Conditional Formatting**
   The Conditional Formatting dialog box opens. Depending on the logical operator you've selected (such as "greater than" or "not equal to"), the Conditional Formatting dialog box displays different input boxes. You can define up to three different conditions that let you determine the outcome, and then assign formatting attributes to each one. You define the condition first. The default setting for the first condition is "Cell Value Is" "between."

3. **To change the current condition, click the Operator list arrow, then click greater than or equal to**
   Because you changed the operator from "between," which required text boxes for two values, only one value text box now appears. The first condition is that the cell value must be greater than or equal to some value. See Table C-5 for a list of options. The value can be a constant, formula, cell reference, or date. That value is set in the third box.

4. **Click the Value text box, then type 175**
   Now that you have assigned the value, you need to specify what formatting you want for cells that meet this condition.

5. **Click Format, click the Color list arrow, click Red (third row, first column), click Bold in the Font style list box, click OK, compare your settings to Figure C-17, then click OK to close the Conditional Formatting dialog box**
   The value in cell G4, 325.55, is formatted in bold red numbers because it is greater than 175, meeting the condition to apply the format. You can copy conditional formats the same way you would copy other formats.

6. **With cell G4 selected, click the Format Painter button on the Standard toolbar, then drag to select the range G5:G30**

7. **Click cell G4**
   Compare your results to Figure C-18. All cells with values greater than or equal to 175 in column G appear in bold red text.

8. **Press [Ctrl][Home] to move to cell A1**

9. **Click the Save button on the Standard toolbar**

FIGURE C-17: Completed Conditional Formatting dialog box

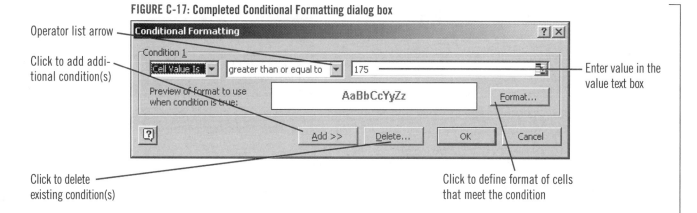

Operator list arrow

Click to add additional condition(s)

Enter value in the value text box

Click to delete existing condition(s)

Click to define format of cells that meet the condition

FIGURE C-18: Worksheet with conditional formatting

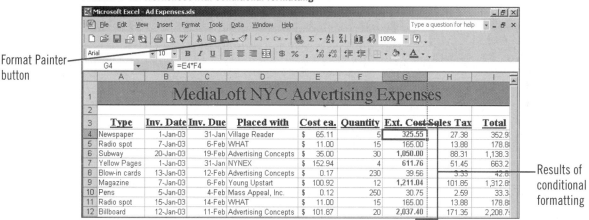

Format Painter button

Results of conditional formatting

TABLE C-5: Conditional formatting options

option	mathematical equivalent	option	mathematical equivalent
Between	$X>Y<Z$	Greater than	$Z>Y$
Not between	$B>C<A$	Less than	$Y<Z$
Equal to	$A=B$	Greater than or equal to	$A \geq B$
Not equal to	$A \neq B$	Less than or equal to	$Z \leq Y$

CLUES TO USE

Deleting conditional formatting

Because it's likely that the conditions you define will change, you can delete any conditional format you define. Select the cell(s) containing conditional formatting, click Format on the menu bar, click Conditional Formatting, then click Delete. The Delete Conditional Format dialog box opens, as shown in Figure C-19. Select the check boxes for any of the conditions you want to delete, click OK, then click OK again. The previously assigned formatting is deleted—leaving the cell's contents intact.

FIGURE C-19: Delete Conditional Format dialog box

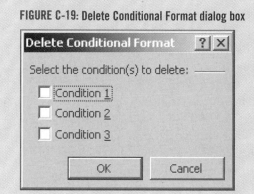

Excel 2002

Checking Spelling

A single misspelled word can cast doubt on the validity and professional value of your entire workbook. Excel includes a spelling checker to help you ensure workbook accuracy. The spelling checker scans your worksheet, displays words it doesn't find in its built-in dictionary, and when possible suggests replacements. To check other sheets in a multiple-sheet workbook, you need to display each sheet and run the spelling checker again. Because the built-in dictionary cannot possibly include all the words that each of us needs, you can add words to the dictionary, such as your company name, an acronym, or an unusual technical term. The spelling checker will no longer consider that word misspelled. Any words you've added to the dictionary using Word, Access, or PowerPoint are also available in Excel. ✎ Because he will distribute this workbook to the marketing managers, Jim asks you to check its spelling.

Steps

Trouble?

If a language other than English is being used, the Spelling English dialog box will list the name of that language.

1. Click the Spelling button ✓ on the Standard toolbar
The Spelling English (U.S.) dialog box opens, as shown in Figure C-21, with MediaLoft selected as the first misspelled word in the worksheet. For any word you have the option to Ignore or Ignore All cases the spell checker flags, or Add the word to the dictionary.

2. Click Ignore All for MediaLoft
The spell checker found the word "cards" misspelled and offers "crabs" as an alternative.

3. Scroll through the Suggestions list, click cards, then click Change
The word "Concepts" is also misspelled and the spell checker suggests the correct spelling.

4. Click Change
When no more incorrect words are found, Excel displays a message indicating that all the words on that worksheet have been checked.

5. Click OK

6. Enter your name in cell A34, then press [Ctrl][Home]

QuickTip

You can set the Excel AutoCorrect feature to correct spelling as you type. Click Tools on the menu bar, then click AutoCorrect Options.

7. Click the Save button 🖫 on the Standard toolbar, then preview the worksheet

8. In the Preview window, click Setup, under Scaling click Fit to option button to print the worksheet on one page, click OK, click Print, then click OK
Compare your printout to Figure C-22.

9. Click File on the menu bar, then click Exit to close the workbook without saving changes and exit Excel

---

CLUES TO USE

Using e-mail to send a workbook

You can use e-mail to send an entire workbook from within Excel. To send a workbook as an e-mail message attachment, open the workbook, click File, point to Send to, then click Mail Recipient (as Attachment). You supply the To and (optional) Cc information, as shown in Figure C-20, then click Send. You can also route a workbook to one or more recipients on a routing list. Click File, point to Send to, then click Routing Recipient. Click Create New Contact and enter contact information, then fill in the Routing slip. Depending on your e-mail program and Web browser, you may have to follow a different procedure.

FIGURE C-20: E-mailing an Excel workbook

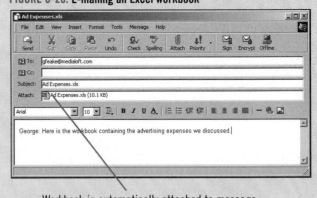

Workbook is automatically attached to message

FIGURE C-21: Spelling English dialog box

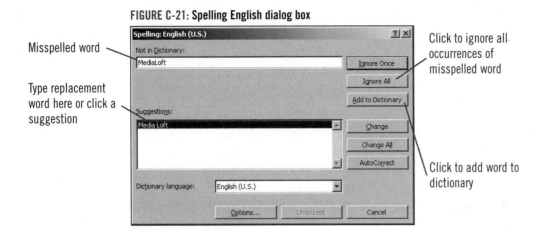

Misspelled word

Click to ignore all occurrences of misspelled word

Type replacement word here or click a suggestion

Click to add word to dictionary

FIGURE C-22: Completed worksheet

MediaLoft NYC Advertising Expenses

Sales Tax   0.0841

Type	Inv. Date	Inv. Due	Placed with	Cost ea.	Quantity	Ext. Cost	Sales Tax	Total
Newspaper	1-Jan-03	31-Jan	Village Reader	$ 65.11	5	325.55	27.38	352.93
Radio spot	7-Jan-03	6-Feb	WHAT	$ 11.00	15	165.00	13.88	178.88
Subway	20-Jan-03	19-Feb	Advertising Concepts	$ 35.00	30	1,050.00	88.31	1,138.31
Yellow Pages	1-Jan-03	31-Jan	NYNEX	$ 152.94	4	611.76	51.45	663.21
Blow-in cards	13-Jan-03	12-Feb	Advertising Concepts	$ 0.17	230	39.56	3.33	42.89
Magazine	7-Jan-03	6-Feb	Young Upstart	$ 100.92	12	1,211.04	101.85	1,312.89
Pens	5-Jan-03	4-Feb	Mass Appeal, Inc.	$ 0.12	250	30.75	2.59	33.34
Radio spot	15-Jan-03	14-Feb	WHAT	$ 11.00	15	165.00	13.88	178.88
Billboard	12-Jan-03	11-Feb	Advertising Concepts	$ 101.87	20	2,037.40	171.35	2,208.75
Newspaper	25-Jan-03	24-Feb	Village Reader	$ 65.11	6	390.66	32.85	423.51
Newspaper	1-Feb-03	3-Mar	University Voice	$ 23.91	2	47.82	4.02	51.84
T-Shirts	3-Feb-03	5-Mar	Mass Appeal, Inc.	$ 5.67	200	1,134.00	95.37	1,229.37
Yellow Pages	1-Feb-03	3-Mar	NYNEX	$ 152.94	4	611.76	51.45	663.21
Newspaper	1-Mar-03	31-Mar	University Voice	$ 23.91	2	47.82	4.02	51.84
Blow-in cards	28-Feb-03	30-Mar	Advertising Concepts	$ 0.17	275	47.30	3.98	51.28
Magazine	27-Feb-03	29-Mar	Young Upstart	$ 100.92	12	1,211.04	101.85	1,312.89
Subway	22-Feb-03	24-Mar	Advertising Concepts	$ 35.00	30	1,050.00	88.31	1,138.31
Radio spot	1-Feb-03	3-Mar	WHAT	$ 11.00	30	330.00	27.75	357.75
Newspaper	25-Feb-03	27-Mar	Village Reader	$ 65.11	6	390.66	32.85	423.51
Blow-in cards	10-Mar-03	9-Apr	Advertising Concepts	$ 0.17	275	47.30	3.98	51.28
Radio spot	15-Feb-03	17-Mar	WHAT	$ 11.00	25	275.00	23.13	298.13
Pens	15-Mar-03	14-Apr	Mass Appeal, Inc.	$ 0.12	250	30.75	2.59	33.34
Yellow Pages	1-Mar-03	31-Mar	NYNEX	$ 152.94	4	611.76	51.45	663.21
Subway	20-Mar-03	19-Apr	Advertising Concepts	$ 35.00	30	1,050.00	88.31	1,138.31
Newspaper	1-Apr-03	1-May	University Voice	$ 23.91	2	47.82	4.02	51.84
Subway	10-Apr-03	10-May	Advertising Concepts	$ 35.00	30	1,050.00	88.31	1,138.31
Billboard	28-Mar-03	27-Apr	Advertising Concepts	$ 101.87	20	2,037.40	171.35	2,208.75
name				$ 1,321.89	1784	16,047.15	1,349.57	17,396.72

Practice

► Concepts Review

Label each element of the Excel worksheet window shown in Figure C-23.

FIGURE C-23

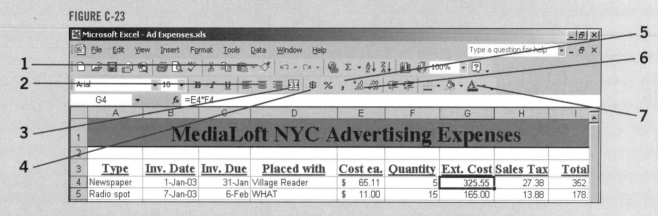

Match each command or button with the statement that describes it.

8. Cells command on the Format menu
9. Delete command on the Edit menu
10. Conditional Formatting
11. 📋
12. $
13. ✓

a. Changes appearance of cell depending on result
b. Erases the contents of a cell
c. Used to check the spelling in a worksheet
d. Used to change the appearance of selected cells
e. Pastes the contents of the Clipboard into the current cell
f. Changes the format to Currency

Select the best answer from the list of choices.

14. Which button increases the number of decimal places in selected cells?
   a.
   b.
   c.
   d.
15. Each of the following operators can be used in conditional formatting, *except*:
   a. Equal to.
   b. Greater than.
   c. Similar to.
   d. Not between.
16. How many conditional formats can be created in any cell?
   a. 1
   b. 2
   c. 3
   d. 4
17. Which button center-aligns the contents of a single cell?
   a.
   b.
   c.
   d.

18. Which of the following is an example of the comma format?
    a. $5,555.55
    b. 5555.55
    c. 55.55%
    d. 5,555.55
19. What is the name of the feature used to resize a column to its widest entry?
    a. AutoResize
    b. AutoFormat
    c. AutoFit
    d. AutoAdjust
20. Which feature applies formatting attributes according to cell contents?
    a. Conditional Formatting
    b. Comments
    c. AutoFormat
    d. Merge and Center

▶ ## Skills Review

1. **Format values.**
   a. Start Excel and open a new workbook.
   b. Enter the information from Table C-6 in your worksheet. Begin in cell A1, and do not leave any blank rows or columns.

TABLE C-6

MediaLoft Great Britain Quarterly Sales Projection			
Department	Average Price	Quantity	Totals
Sports	25	2250	
Computers	40	3175	
History	35	1295	
Personal Growth	25	2065	

   c. Save this workbook as **MediaLoft GB Inventory** in the drive and folder where your Project Files are stored.
   d. Add the bold attribute to the data in the Department column.
   e. Use the Format Painter to paste the format from the data in the Department column to the Department and Totals labels.
   f. Add the italics attribute to the Average Price and Quantity labels.
   g. Apply the Comma format to the Price and Quantity data and reduce the number of decimals in the Quantity column to 0.
   h. Insert formulas in the Totals column (multiply the average price by the Quantity).
   i. Apply the Currency format to the Totals data.
   j. Save your work.
2. **Use fonts and font sizes.**
   a. Select the range of cells containing the column titles.
   b. Change the font of the column titles to Times New Roman.
   c. Increase the font size of the column titles and the title in cell A1 to 14-point.
   d. Resize the columns as necessary.
   e. Select the range of values in the Average Price column.
   f. Format the range using the Currency Style button.
   g. Save your changes.
3. **Change attributes and alignment.**
   a. Select the worksheet title **MediaLoft Great Britain**, then use the Bold button to boldface it.
   b. Use the Merge and Center button to center the title and the Quarterly Sales Projection labels over columns A through D.

   c. Select the label **Quarterly Sales Projection**, then apply underlining to the label.

   d. Select the range of cells containing the column titles, then center them.

   e. Return the underlined, merged and centered Quarterly Sales Projection label to its original alignment.

   f. Move the Quarterly Sales Projection label to cell D2 and change the alignment to Align Right.

   g. Save your changes, then preview and print the workbook.

4. **Adjust column widths.**

   a Use the Format menu to change the size of the Average Price column to **25**.

   b. Use the AutoFit feature to resize the Average Price column.

   c. Use the Format menu to resize the Department column to **18** and the Sold column to **11**.

   d. Change the text in cell C3 to **Sold**, use AutoFit to resize the column, then change the column size to 11.

   e. Save your changes.

5. **Insert and delete rows and columns.**

   a. Insert a new row between rows 4 and 5.

   b. Add MediaLoft Great Britain's newest department—**Children's Corner**—in the newly inserted row. Enter **35** for the average price and **1225** for the number sold.

   c. Add the following comment to cell A5: **New department**.

   d. Add a formula in cell D5 that multiplies the Average Price column by the Sold column.

   e. Add a new column between the Department and Average Price columns with the title **Location**.

   f. Delete the History row.

   g. Edit the comment so it reads "New department. Needs promotion."

   h. Save your changes.

6. **Apply colors, patterns, and borders.**

   a. Add an outside border around the Average Price and Sold data.

   b. Apply a light green background color to the labels in the Department column.

   c. Apply a gold background to the column labels in cells **B3:E3**.

   d. Change the color of the font in the column labels in cells B3:E3 to blue.

   e. Add a 12.5% Gray pattern fill to the title in Row 1. (*Hint*: Use the Patterns tab in the Format Cells dialog box to locate the 12.5% Gray pattern.)

   f. Enter your name in cell A20, then save your work.

   g. Preview and print the worksheet, then close the workbook.

7. **Use conditional formatting.**

   a. Open the Project File EX C-2 from the drive and folder where your Project Files are stored, then save it as **Monthly Operating Expenses**.

   b. Create conditional formatting that changes the monthly data entry to blue if a value is **greater than 2500**, and changes it to red if **less than 700**.

   c. Create a third conditional format that changes the monthly data to green if a value is **between 1000 and 2000**.

   d. Use the Bold button and Center button to format the column headings and row titles.

   e. Make Column A wide enough to accommodate the contents of cells **A4:A9**.

   f. AutoFit the remaining columns.

   g. Use Merge and Center in Row 1 to center the title over columns A–E.

   h. Format the title in cell A1 using 14-point Times New Roman text. Fill the cell with a color and pattern of your choice.

   i. Delete the third conditional format.

   j. Enter your name in cell A20, then apply a green background to it and make the text color yellow.

   k. Use the Edit menu to clear the cell formats from the cell with your name, then save your changes.

8. **Check spelling.**

   a. Check the spelling in the worksheet using the spell checker, correcting any spelling errors.

   b. Save your changes, then preview and print the workbook.

   c. Close the workbook, then exit Excel.

▶ Independent Challenge 1

Beautiful You, a small beauty salon, has been using Excel for several months. Now that the salon's accounting records are in Excel, the manager would like you to work on the inventory. Although more items will be added later, the worksheet has enough items for you to begin your modifications.

a. Start Excel, open the Project File EX C-3 from the drive and folder where your Project Files are stored, then save it as **BY Inventory**.

b. Create a formula that calculates the value of the inventory on hand for each item.

c. Use an absolute reference to calculate the sale price of each item, using the markup percentage shown.

d. Add the bold attribute to the column headings.

e. Make sure all columns are wide enough to display the data and headings.

f. Add a row under #2 Curlers for **Nail Files**, price paid **$0.25**, sold **individually (each)**, with **59** on hand.

g. Verify that all the formulas in the worksheet are correct. Adjust any items as needed, check the spelling, then save your work.

h. Use conditional formatting to call attention to items with a quantity of 25 or fewer on hand. Use boldfaced red text.

i. Add an outside border around the data in the Item column.

j. Delete the row with #3 Curlers.

k. Enter your name in an empty cell, then save the file.

l. Preview and print the worksheet, close the workbook, then exit Excel.

▶ Independent Challenge 2

You volunteer several hours each week with the Community Action Center. You would like to examine the membership list, and decide to use formatting to make the existing data look more professional and easier to read.

a. Start Excel, open the Project File EX C-4 from the drive and folder where your Project Files are stored, then save it as **Community Action**.

b. Remove any blank columns.

c. Format the Annual Revenue figures using the Currency format.

d. Make all columns wide enough to fit their data and headings.

e. Use formatting enhancements, such as fonts, font sizes, and text attributes to make the worksheet more attractive.

f. Center-align the column labels.

g. Use conditional formatting so that Number of Employees data greater than 50 employees appears in a contrasting color.

h. Before printing, preview the file so you know what the worksheet will look like. Adjust any items as necessary, check spelling, enter your name in an empty cell, save your work, then print a copy.

i. Close the workbook then exit Excel.

▶ Independent Challenge 3

Classic Instruments is a Miami-based company that manufactures high-quality pens and markers. As the finance manager, one of your responsibilities is to analyze the monthly reports from your five district sales offices. Your boss, Joanne Bennington, has just asked you to prepare a quarterly sales report for an upcoming meeting. Because several top executives will be attending this meeting, Joanne reminds you that the report must look professional. In particular, she asks you to emphasize the company's surge in profits during the last month and to highlight the fact that the Northeastern district continues to outpace the other districts.

a. Plan a worksheet that shows the company's sales during the first quarter. Assume that all pens are the same price. Make sure you include:
- The number of pens sold (units sold) and the associated revenues (total sales) for each of the five district sales offices. The five sales districts include: Northeastern, Midwestern, Southeastern, Southern, and Western
- Calculations that show month-by-month totals and a three-month cumulative total
- Calculations that show each district's share of sales (percent of Total Sales)
- Formatting enhancements to emphasize the recent month's sales surge and the Northeastern district's sales leadership

b. Ask yourself the following questions about the organization and formatting of the worksheet: How will you calculate the totals? What formulas can you copy to save time and keystrokes? Do any of these formulas need to use an absolute reference? How will you show dollar amounts? What information should be shown in bold? Do you need to use more than one font? Should you use more than one point size?

c. Start Excel, then build the worksheet with your own price and sales data. Enter the titles and labels first, then enter the numbers and formulas. You can use the form in Table C-7 to get started.

d. Save the workbook as **Classic Instruments** in the drive and folder where your Project Files are stored.

e. Adjust the column widths as necessary.

f. Change the height of row 1 to 30 points.

g. Format labels and values, and change the attributes and alignment.

h. Use the AutoFormat feature to add color and formatting to the data.

i. Resize columns and adjust the formatting as necessary.

j. Add a column that calculates a 22% increase in sales dollars. Use an absolute cell reference in this calculation.

k. Create a new column named Increased Sales that adds the projected increase to the Total Sales. (*Hint*: Make sure the current formatting is applied to the new information.)

l. Insert a ClipArt image in an appropriate location, adjusting its size and position as necessary.

m. Enter your name in an empty cell.

n. Check the spelling, then save your work.

o. Preview, then print the file in landscape orientation.

p. Close the file then exit Excel.

TABLE C-7

Classic Instruments

1st Quarter Sales Report

		January		February		March		Total	
Office	Price	Units Sold	Sales	Units Sold	Sales	Units Sold	Sales	Units Sold	Sales
Northeastern									
Midwestern									
Southeastern									
Southern									
Western									

Independent Challenge 4

After saving for many years, you now have enough funds to take that international trip you have always dreamed about. Your well-traveled friends have told you that you should always have the local equivalent of $100 U.S. dollars in cash with you when you enter a country. You decide to use the Web to determine how much money you will need in each country.

a. Start Excel, open a new workbook, then save it as **Currency Conversions** in the drive and folder where your Project Files are stored.

b. Enter column and row labels using the following table to get started.

Currency Equivalents			
$100 in US dollars			
Country	$1 Equivalent	$100 US	Name of Units
Australia			
Canada			
France			
Germany			
Sweden			
United Kingdom			

c. Go to the Alta Vista search engine at www.altavista.com and locate information on currency conversions. (*Hint*: One possible site where you can determine currency equivalents is www.oanda.com/. Use the Quick Converter.)

d. Find out how much cash is equivalent to **$1** in U.S. dollars for the following countries: **Australia**, **Canada**, **France**, **Germany**, **Sweden**, and the **United Kingdom**. Also enter the name of the currency used in each country.

e. Create an equation that calculates the equivalent of **$100** in U.S. dollars for each country in the list, using an absolute value in the formula.

f. Format the entries in columns B and C using the correct currency unit for each country, with two decimal places. (*Hint*: Use the Numbers tab in the Format cells dialog box; choose the appropriate currency format from the Symbol list, using 2 decimal places. For example, use the **F (French) Standard** format for the France row, and so forth.)

g. Create a conditional format that changes the font attributes of the calculated amount in the "$100 US" column to bold and red if the amount is equals or exceeds **500 units** of the local currency.

h. Merge and center the title over the column headings.

i. Add a background color to the title.

j. Apply the AutoFormat of your choice to the conversion table.

k. Enter your name in an empty worksheet cell.

l. Spell check, save, preview, then print the worksheet.

m. If you have access to an e-mail account, e-mail your workbook to your instructor as an attachment.

n. Close the workbook and exit Excel.

► Visual Workshop

Create the worksheet shown in Figure C-24, using skills you learned in this unit. Open the Project File EX C-5 from the drive and folder where your Project Files are stored, then save it as **Projected March Advertising Invoices**. Create a conditional format in the Cost ea. column so that entries greater than 60 appear in red. (*Hint*: The only additional font used in this exercise is Times New Roman. It is 22 points in row 1, and 16 points in row 3.) Spell check the worksheet, then save and print your work.

FIGURE C-24

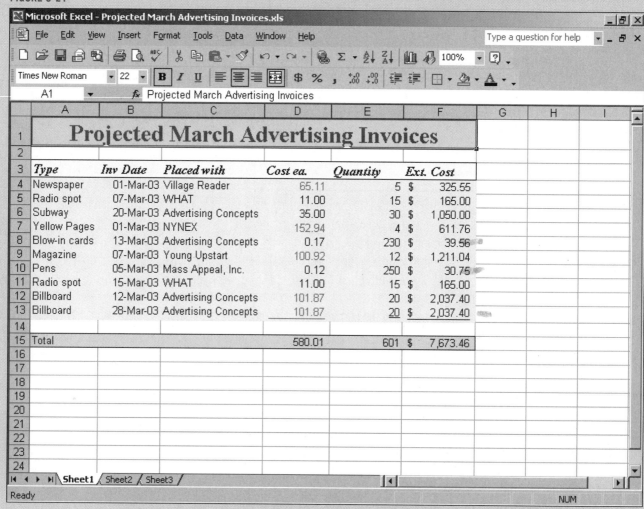

Unit D

Working
with Charts

Objectives

► **Plan and design a chart**
► **Create a chart**
► **Move and resize a chart**
► **Edit a chart**
► **Format a chart**
► **Enhance a chart**
► **Annotate and draw on a chart**
► **Preview and print a chart**

Worksheets provide an effective way to organize information, but they are not always the best format for presenting data to others. Information in a selected range or worksheet can easily be displayed as a chart. Charts, often called graphs, allow you to communicate the relationships in your worksheet data in readily understandable pictures. In this unit, you will learn how to create a chart, how to edit a chart and change the chart type, how to add text annotations and arrows to a chart, and how to preview and print a chart. For the annual meeting Jim Fernandez needs you to create a chart showing the six-month sales history for the MediaLoft stores in the eastern division. He wants to illustrate the growth trend in this division.

Excel 2002

Planning and Designing a Chart

Before creating a chart, you need to plan the information you want your chart to show and how you want it to look.  In early June, the Marketing Department launched a regional advertising campaign for the eastern division. The results of the campaign were increased sales during the fall months. Jim wants his chart for the annual meeting to illustrate the growth trend for sales in MediaLoft's eastern division stores and to highlight this sales increase.

Details

Jim wants you to use the worksheet shown in Figure D-1 and the following guidelines to plan the chart:

▶ **Determine the purpose of the chart and identify the data relationships you want to communicate graphically**

You want to create a chart that shows sales throughout MediaLoft's eastern division from July through December. In particular, you want to highlight the increase in sales that occurred as a result of the advertising campaign.

▶ **Determine the results you want to see, and decide which chart type is most appropriate to use**

Different charts display data in distinctive ways. Some chart types are more appropriate for particular types of data and analyses. How you want your data displayed—and how you want that data interpreted—can help you determine the best chart type to use. Table D-1 describes several different types of charts and indicates when each one is best used. Because you want to compare data (sales in multiple locations) over a time period (the months July through December), you decide to use a column chart.

▶ **Identify the worksheet data you want the chart to illustrate**

You are using data from the worksheet titled "MediaLoft Eastern Division Stores" shown in Figure D-1. This worksheet contains the sales data for the four stores in the eastern division from July through December.

▶ **Sketch the chart, then use your sketch to decide where the chart elements should be placed**

You sketch your chart as shown in Figure D-2. You put the months on the horizontal axis (the **x-axis**) and the monthly sales figures on the vertical axis (the **y-axis**). The x-axis is often called the **category axis** because it often contains the names of data groups, such as months or years. The y-axis is called the **value axis** because it often contains numerical values that help you interpret the size of chart elements. (In a 3-D chart, the y-axis is referred to as the z-axis.) The area inside the horizontal and vertical axes is called the **plot area**. The **tick marks** on the y-axis create a scale of measure for each value. Each value in a cell you select for your chart is a **data point**. In any chart, a **data marker** visually represents each data point, which in this case is a column. A collection of related data points is a **data series**. In this chart, there are four data series (Boston, Chicago, Kansas City, and New York), so you include a **legend** to make it easy to identify them.

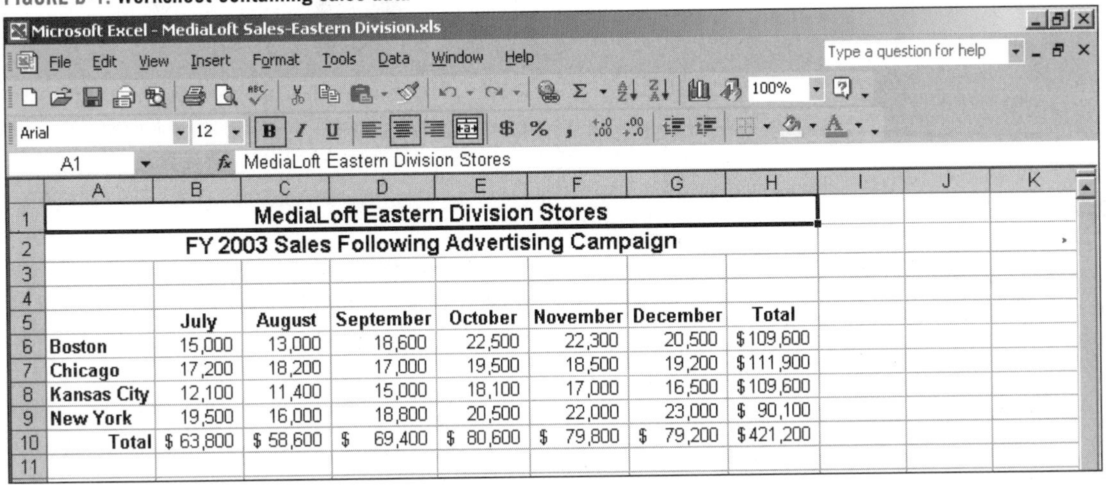

Microsoft Excel - MediaLoft Sales-Eastern Division.xls

File Edit View Insert Format Tools Data Window Help   Type a question for help

Arial   12   B I U

A1   fx MediaLoft Eastern Division Stores

	A	B	C	D	E	F	G	H	I	J	K
1	MediaLoft Eastern Division Stores										
2	FY 2003 Sales Following Advertising Campaign										
3											
4											
5		July	August	September	October	November	December	Total			
6	Boston	15,000	13,000	18,600	22,500	22,300	20,500	$ 109,600			
7	Chicago	17,200	18,200	17,000	19,500	18,500	19,200	$ 111,900			
8	Kansas City	12,100	11,400	15,000	18,100	17,000	16,500	$ 109,600			
9	New York	19,500	16,000	18,800	20,500	22,000	23,000	$ 90,100			
10	Total	$ 63,800	$ 58,600	$ 69,400	$ 80,600	$ 79,800	$ 79,200	$ 421,200			
11											

FIGURE D-2: Column chart sketch

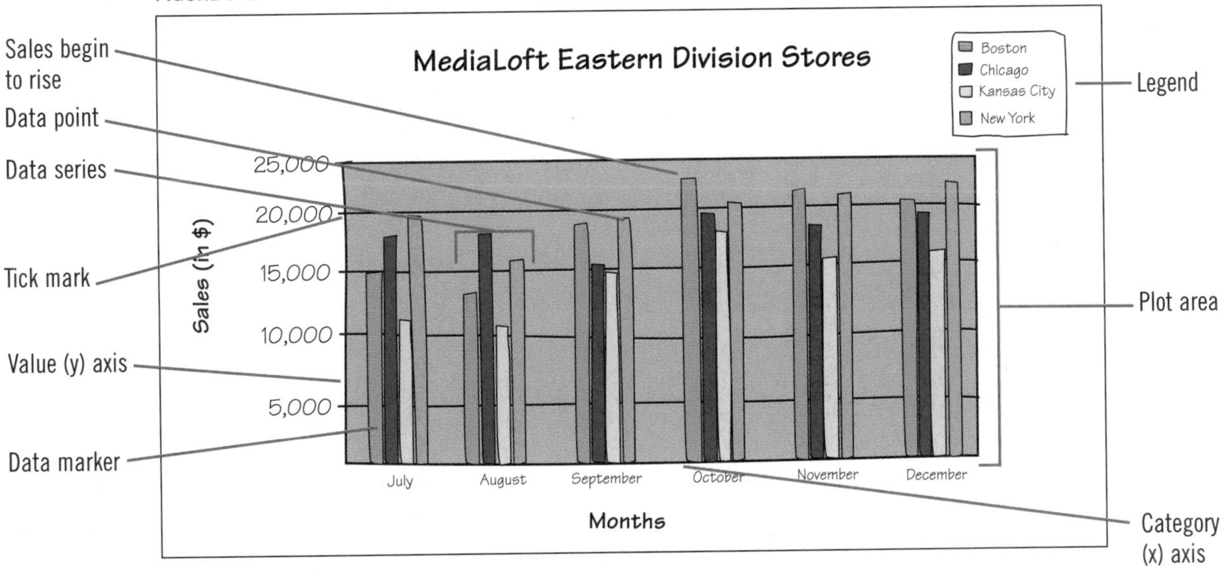

TABLE D-1: Commonly used chart types

type	button	description
Area		Shows how individual volume changes over time in relation to total volume
Bar		Compares distinct object levels over time using a horizontal format; sometimes referred to as a horizontal bar chart in other spreadsheet programs
Column		Compares distinct object levels over time using a vertical format; the Excel default; sometimes referred to as a bar chart in other spreadsheet programs
Line		Compares trends over even time intervals; appears similar to an area chart, but does not emphasize total
Pie		Compares sizes of pieces as part of a whole; used for a single series of numbers
XY (scatter)		Compares trends over uneven time or measurement intervals; used in scientific and engineering disciplines for trend spotting and extrapolation
Combination	none	Combines a column and line chart to compare data requiring different scales of measure

Creating a Chart

To create a chart in Excel, you first select the range containing the data you want to chart. Once you've selected a range, you can use the Excel Chart Wizard to lead you through the process of creating the chart. ➤ Using the worksheet containing the sales data for the eastern division, Jim asks you to create a chart that shows the growth trend that occurred as a result of the advertising campaign.

QuickTip

When charting any data for a given time period, make sure all series are for the same time period, so you don't misrepresent your data.

Trouble?

You can create a chart from non-contiguous cells by pressing the Option key and selecting each range.

1. Start Excel, open the Project File **EX D-1** from the drive and location where your Project Files are stored, then save it as **MediaLoft Sales - Eastern Division**

You want the chart to include the monthly sales figures for each of the eastern division stores, as well as month and store labels. You don't include the Total column and row because the monthly figures make up the totals, and these figures would skew the chart.

2. Select the range **A5:G9**, then click the **Chart Wizard button** 📊 on the Standard toolbar

The selected range contains the data you want to chart. The Chart Wizard opens. The Chart Wizard - Step 1 of 4 - Chart Type dialog box lets you choose the type of chart you want to create. The default chart type is a Clustered Column, as shown in Figure D-3. You can see a preview of the chart using your selected data by clicking, then holding the **Press and Hold to View Sample** button.

3. Click **Next** to accept Clustered Column, the default chart type

The Chart Wizard - Step 2 of 4 - Chart Source Data dialog box lets you choose the data to chart and whether the series appear in rows or columns. You want to chart the effect of sales for each store over the time period. Currently, the rows are accurately selected as the data series, as specified by the Series in option button located under the Data range. Because you selected the data before clicking the Chart Wizard button, Excel converted the range to absolute values and the correct range, =Sheet1!$A$5:$G$9, appears in the Data range text box.

4. Click **Next**

The Chart Wizard - Step 3 of 4 - Chart Options dialog box shows a sample chart using the data you selected. The store locations (the rows in the selected range) are plotted against the months (the columns in the selected range), and Excel added the months as labels for each data series. A legend shows each location and its corresponding color on the chart. The Titles tab lets you add titles to the chart and its axes. Other tabs let you modify the axes, legend, and other chart elements.

5. Click the **Chart title text box**, then type **MediaLoft Sales - Eastern Division**

After a moment, the title appears in the Sample Chart box. See Figure D-4.

6. Click **Next**

In the Chart Wizard - Step 4 of 4 - Chart Location dialog box, you determine the placement of the chart in the workbook. You can display a chart as an object on the current sheet, on any other existing sheet, or on a newly created chart sheet. A **chart sheet** in a workbook contains only a chart, which is linked to the worksheet data. The default selection—displaying the chart as an object in the sheet containing the data—will help Jim emphasize his point at the annual meeting.

QuickTip

If you want to delete a chart, select it, then press [Delete].

7. Click **Finish**

The column chart appears and the Chart toolbar opens, either docked or floating, as shown in Figure D-5. Your chart might be in a different location and look slightly different. You will adjust the chart's location and size in the next lesson. The **selection handles**, the small squares at the corners and sides of the chart's border, indicate that the chart is selected. Anytime a chart is selected, as it is now, a blue border surrounds the worksheet data range, a green border surrounds the row labels, and a purple border surrounds the column labels.

8. Click the **Save button** 💾 on the Standard toolbar

FIGURE D-3: First Chart Wizard dialog box

Selected chart

Chart types

Clustered column chart is the default

Chart subtypes for selected chart

Description of selected chart subtype

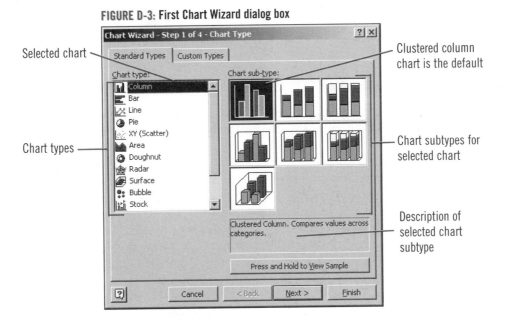

FIGURE D-4: Third Chart Wizard dialog box

Type the chart title here

Sample chart

Title added

Legend

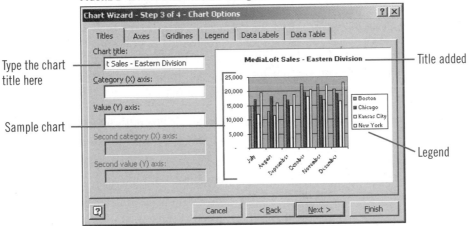

FIGURE D-5: Worksheet with column chart

Column labels

Row labels

Data range

Selected chart object

Chart toolbar title bar

Title

Legend

Selection handles

Month labels on the x-axis

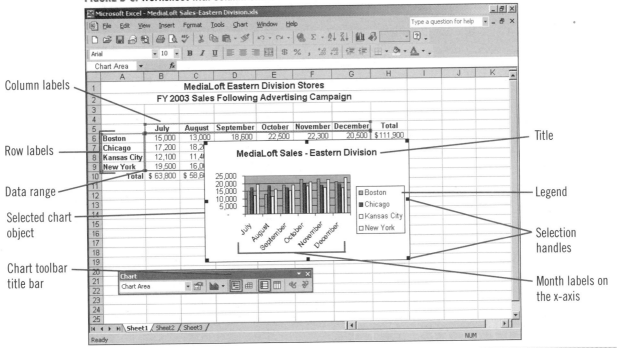

Excel 2002

Moving and Resizing a Chart

Charts are graphics, or drawn objects, and are not located in a specific cell or at a specific range address. An **object** is an independent element on a worksheet. You can select an object by clicking within its borders to surround it with selection handles. You can move a selected chart object anywhere on a worksheet without affecting formulas or data in the worksheet. However, any data changed in the worksheet will automatically be updated in the chart. You can resize a chart to improve its appearance by dragging its selection handles. You can even put a chart on another sheet, and it will still reflect the original data. Chart objects contain other objects, such as a title and legend, which you can move and resize. To move an object, select it, then drag it or cut and copy it to a new location. When you select a chart object, the name of the selected object appears in the Chart Objects list box on the Chart toolbar and in the name box. ✏ Jim wants you to increase the size of the chart, position it below the worksheet data, then change the position of the legend.

QuickTip

The Chart menu only appears on the menu bar when a chart or one of its objects is selected.

1. Make sure the chart is still selected, then position the pointer over the chart
The pointer shape ⩩ indicates that you can move the chart or use a selection handle to resize it. For a table of commonly used chart pointers, refer to Table D-2. On occasion, the Chart toolbar obscures your view. You can dock the toolbar to make it easier to see your work.

2. If the chart toolbar is floating, click the **Chart toolbar's title bar**, drag it to the right edge of the status bar until it docks, then release the mouse button
The toolbar is docked on the bottom of the screen.

QuickTip

Resizing a chart doesn't affect the data in the chart, only the way the chart looks on the sheet.

3. Place ⩩ on a blank area near the edge of the chart, press and hold the left mouse button, using ✛, drag it until the upper-left edge of the chart is at the top of row 13 and the left edge of the chart is at the left border of column A, then release the mouse button
As you drag the chart, you can see a dotted outline representing the chart's perimeter. The chart appears in the new location.

4. Position the pointer on the right-middle selection handle until it changes to ↔ , then drag the right edge of the chart to the right edge of column H
The chart is widened. See Figure D-6.

5. Position the pointer over the top-middle selection handle until it changes to ↕, then drag it to the top of row 12

6. If the labels for the months do not fully appear, position the pointer over the bottom middle selection handle until it changes to ↕, then drag down to display the months
You can move the legend to improve the chart's appearance. You want to align the top of the legend with the top of the plot area.

7. Click the **legend** to select it, then drag the **legend** upward using ⩩ so the top of the legend aligns with the top of the plot area
Selection handles appear around the legend when you click it; "Legend" appears in the Chart Objects list box on the Chart toolbar as well as in the name box, and a dotted outline of the legend perimeter appears as you drag. Changing any label will modify the legend text.

QuickTip

Because the chart is no longer selected, the chart toolbar no longer appears.

8. Click cell **A9**, type **NYC**, then click ☑
See Figure D-7. The legend changes to the text you entered.

9. Click the **Save button** ▣ on the Standard toolbar

FIGURE D-6: Worksheet with resized and repositioned chart

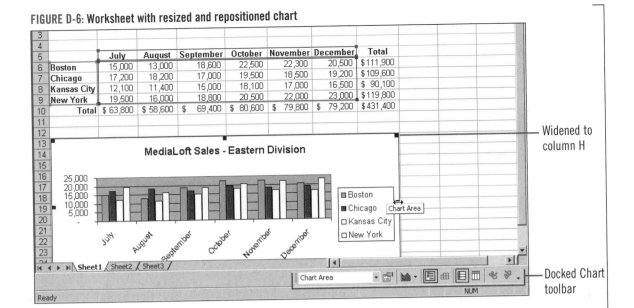

Widened to column H

Docked Chart toolbar

FIGURE D-7: Worksheet with repositioned legend

Repositioned legend

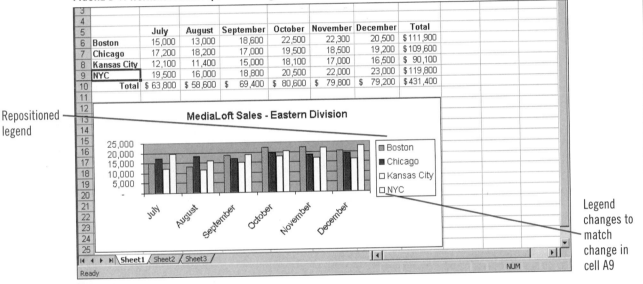

Legend changes to match change in cell A9

TABLE D-2: Commonly used pointers

name	pointer	use	name	pointer	use
Diagonal resizing	↗ or ↘	Change chart shape	I-beam	I	Edit chart text from corners
Draw	+	Create shapes	Move chart	↔↕	Change chart location
Horizontal resizing	↔	Change chart shape from left to right	Vertical resizing	↕	Changes chart shape from top to bottom

Identifying chart objects

There are many objects within a chart, such as bars and axes; Excel makes it easy to identify each of them. Placing the mouse pointer over a chart object displays a ScreenTip identifying it, whether the chart is selected or not. If a chart—or any object in it—is selected, the ScreenTips still appear. In addition, the name of the selected chart object appears in the Chart Object list box on the Chart toolbar and in the name box .

Excel 2002

Editing a Chart

Once you've created a chart, it's easy to modify it. You can change data values in the worksheet, and the chart will automatically be updated to reflect the new data. You can also easily change the type of chart displayed by using the buttons on the Chart toolbar. ✒️ Jim looks over his worksheet and realizes that he entered the wrong data for the Kansas City store in November and December. After you correct this data, he wants to see how the same data looks using different chart types.

Steps 1234

Trouble?

If you cannot see the chart and data together on your monitor, click View on the menu bar, click Zoom, then click 75%.

1. If necessary, scroll the worksheet so that you can see both the chart and row 8, containing the Kansas City sales figures, then place your mouse pointer over the December data point to display **Series "Kansas City" Point "December" Value: 16,500**

2. Click cell **F8**, type **19000** to correct the November sales figure, press [→], type **20500** in cell **G8**, then click ✓
   The Kansas City columns for November and December reflect the increased sales figures. See Figure D-8. The totals in column H and row 10 are also updated.

3. Select the chart by clicking on a blank area within the chart border, then click the **Chart Type list arrow** 📊▾ on the Chart toolbar
   The chart type buttons appear on the Chart Type palette. Table D-3 describes the principal chart types available.

4. Click the **Bar Chart button** 📊 on the palette
   The column chart changes to a bar chart. See Figure D-9. You look at the bar chart, take some notes, then decide to convert it back to a column chart. You now want to see if the large 'increase in sales would be better presented with a three-dimensional column chart.

QuickTip

As you work with charts, experiment with different formats for your charts until you get just the right look.

5. Click the **Chart Type list arrow** 📊▾, then click the **3-D Column Chart button** 📊 on the palette
   A three-dimensional column chart appears. You notice that the three-dimensional column format is more crowded than the two-dimensional format but gives you a sense of volume.

QuickTip

The chart type button displays the last chart type selected.

6. Click the **Chart Type list arrow** 📊▾, then click the **Column Chart button** 📊 on the palette

7. Click the **Save button** 💾 on the Standard toolbar

TABLE D-3: Commonly used chart type buttons

click to display a	click to display a	click to display a	click to display a
📊 area chart	🥧 pie chart	📊 3-D area chart	🥧 3-D pie chart
📊 bar chart	📊 (XY) scatter chart	📊 3-D bar chart	📊 3-D surface chart
📊 column chart	🍩 doughnut chart	📊 3-D column chart	📊 3-D cylinder chart
📈 line chart	📡 radar chart	📈 3-D line chart	🌢 3-D cone chart

FIGURE D-8: Worksheet with new data entered for Kansas City

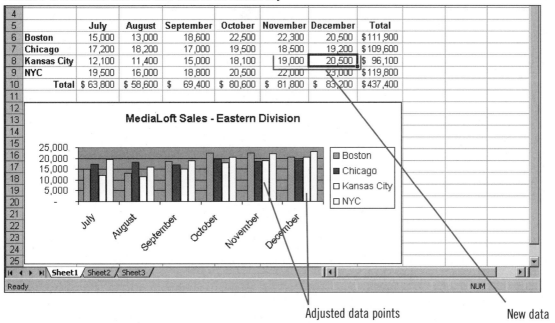

		July	August	September	October	November	December	Total
5		July	August	September	October	November	December	Total
6	Boston	15,000	13,000	18,600	22,500	22,300	20,500	$111,900
7	Chicago	17,200	18,200	17,000	19,500	18,500	19,200	$109,600
8	Kansas City	12,100	11,400	15,000	18,100	19,000	20,500	$ 96,100
9	NYC	19,500	16,000	18,800	20,500	22,000	23,000	$119,800
10	Total	$ 63,800	$ 58,600	$ 69,400	$ 80,600	$ 81,800	$ 83,200	$437,400

Adjusted data points   New data

FIGURE D-9: Bar chart

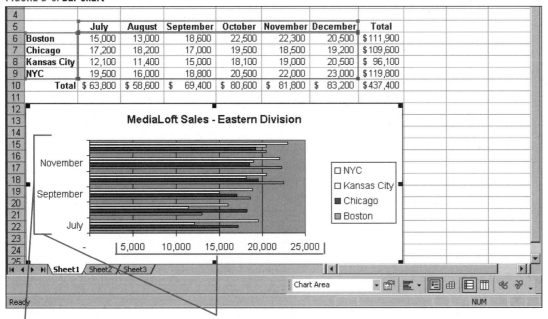

		July	August	September	October	November	December	Total
5		July	August	September	October	November	December	Total
6	Boston	15,000	13,000	18,600	22,500	22,300	20,500	$111,900
7	Chicago	17,200	18,200	17,000	19,500	18,500	19,200	$109,600
8	Kansas City	12,100	11,400	15,000	18,100	19,000	20,500	$ 96,100
9	NYC	19,500	16,000	18,800	20,500	22,000	23,000	$119,800
10	Total	$ 63,800	$ 58,600	$ 69,400	$ 80,600	$ 81,800	$ 83,200	$437,400

Your chart may show more axis labels   Row and column data are reversed

CLUES TO USE

Rotating a 3-D chart

In a three-dimensional chart, other data series in the same chart can sometimes obscure columns or bars. You can rotate the chart to obtain a better view. Click the chart, click the tip of one of its axes (select the Corners object), then drag the handles until a more pleasing view of the data series appears. See Figure D-10.

FIGURE D-10: 3-D chart rotated with improved view of data series

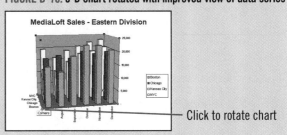

Click to rotate chart

WORKING WITH CHARTS   EXCEL D-9

Excel 2002

Formatting a Chart

After you've created a chart using the Chart Wizard, you can easily modify its appearance. You can use the Chart toolbar and Chart menu to change the colors of data series and to add or eliminate a legend and gridlines. **Gridlines** are the horizontal and vertical lines in the chart that enable the eye to follow the value on an axis. The Chart toolbar buttons are listed in Table D-4. ↗ Jim wants you to make some changes in the appearance of his chart. He wants to see if the chart looks better without gridlines, and he wants to change the color of a data series.

Steps

1. **Make sure the chart is still selected**
   Horizontal gridlines currently extend from the y-axis tick marks across the chart's plot area.

2. **Click Chart on the menu bar, click Chart Options, click the Gridlines tab in the Chart Options dialog box, then click the Major Gridlines check box for the Value (Y) axis to remove the check**
   The gridlines disappear from the sample chart in the dialog box, as shown in Figure D-11.

3. **Click the Major Gridlines check box for the Value (Y) axis to reselect it, then click the Minor Gridlines check box for the Value (Y) axis**
   Both major and minor gridlines appear in the sample. **Minor gridlines** show the values between the tick marks.

4. **Click the Minor Gridlines check box for the Value (Y) axis, then click OK**
   The minor gridlines disappear, leaving only the major gridlines on the Value axis. You can change the color of the columns to better distinguish the data series.

5. **With the chart selected, double-click any light blue column in the NYC data series**
   Handles appear on all the columns in the NYC data series, and the Format Data Series dialog box opens, as shown in Figure D-12.

QuickTip
Add labels, values, and percentages to your chart by using the Data Labels tab in the Chart Options dialog box.

6. **Click the fuchsia box (fourth row, first column) in the Patterns tab, then click OK**
   All the columns for the series become fuchsia, and the legend changes to match the new color. Compare your finished chart to Figure D-13.

7. **Click the Save button 🖫 on the Standard toolbar**

TABLE D-4: Chart enhancement buttons

button	use
🔲	Displays formatting dialog box for the selected object on the chart
📈	Selects chart type (chart type on button changes to last chart type selected)
📋	Adds/deletes legend
⊞	Creates a data table within the chart
📊	Charts data by row
▥	Charts data by column
✎	Angles selected text downward (clockwise)
✎	Angles selected text upward (counter clockwise)

FIGURE D-11: **Chart Options dialog box**

Sample chart appears without gridlines

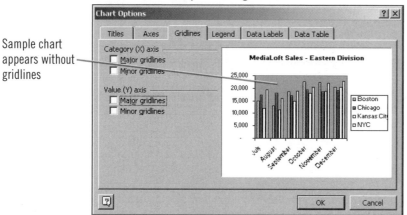

FIGURE D-12: **Format Data Series dialog box**

Sample of selected color

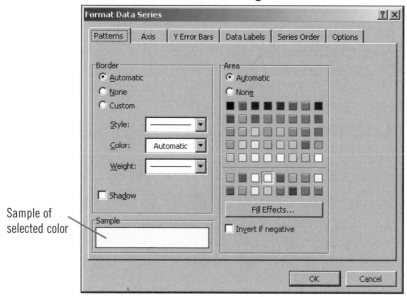

FIGURE D-13: **Chart with formatted data series**

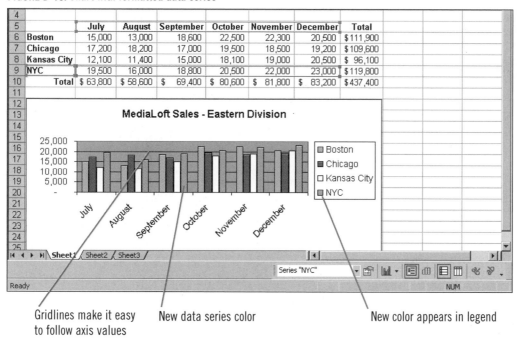

	July	August	September	October	November	December	Total
6 Boston	15,000	13,000	18,600	22,500	22,300	20,500	$111,900
7 Chicago	17,200	18,200	17,000	19,500	18,500	19,200	$109,600
8 Kansas City	12,100	11,400	15,000	18,100	19,000	20,500	$ 96,100
9 NYC	19,500	16,000	18,800	20,500	22,000	23,000	$119,800
10 Total	$ 63,800	$ 58,600	$ 69,400	$ 80,600	$ 81,800	$ 83,200	$437,400

Gridlines make it easy to follow axis values

New data series color

New color appears in legend

Enhancing a Chart

There are many ways to enhance a chart to make it easier to read and understand. You can create titles for the x-axis and y-axis, add graphics, or add background color. You can even format the text you use in a chart. Jim wants you to improve the appearance of his chart by creating titles for the x-axis and y-axis and adding a drop shadow to the title.

Steps

1. Click a blank area of the chart to select it, click **Chart** on the menu bar, click **Chart Options**, click the **Titles tab** in the Chart Options dialog box, then type **Months** in the **Category (X) axis text box**

Descriptive text on the x-axis helps readers understand the chart. The word "Months" appears below the month labels in the sample chart, as shown in Figure D-14.

QuickTip

To edit the text, position the pointer over the selected text box until it changes to I, click, then edit the text.

2. In the **Value (Y) axis text box**, type **Sales (in $)**, then click **OK**

A selected text box containing "Sales (in $)" appears rotated 90 degrees to the left of the y-axis. Once the Chart Options dialog box is closed, you can move the Value or Category axis title to a new position by clicking on an edge of the object then dragging it.

3. Press **[Esc]** to deselect the Value-axis title

Next you decide that a border with a drop shadow will enhance the chart title.

4. Click the chart title, **MediaLoft Sales – Eastern Division**, to select it

QuickTip

The Format button opens a dialog box with the appropriate formatting options for the selected chart element. The ScreenTip for the button changes, depending on the selected object.

5. Click the **Format Chart Title button** on the Chart toolbar to open the Format Chart Title dialog box, make sure the **Patterns tab** is selected, then click the **Shadow check box** to select it

A border with a drop shadow surrounds the title in the Sample area.

6. Click the **Font tab** in the Format Chart Title dialog box, click **Times New Roman** in the Font list, click **Bold Italic** in the Font style list, click **OK**, then press **[Esc]** to deselect the chart title

A border with a drop shadow appears around the chart title, and the chart title text is reformatted.

QuickTip

You can also double-click the Category axis title to open the Format Axis Titles dialog box.

7. Click **Months** (the Category axis title), click , click the **Font tab** if necessary, select **Times New Roman** in the Font list, then click **OK**

The Category axis title appears in the Times New Roman font.

8. Click **Sales (in $)** (the Value axis title), click , click the **Font tab** if necessary, click **Times New Roman** in the Font list, click **OK**, then press **[Esc]** to deselect the title

The Value axis title appears in the Times New Roman font. Compare your chart to Figure D-15.

9. Click the **Save button** on the Standard toolbar

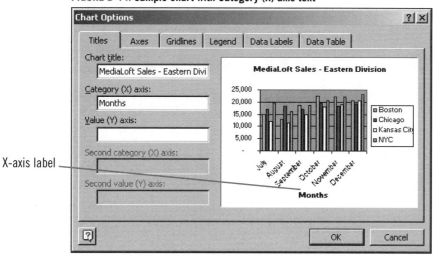

X-axis label

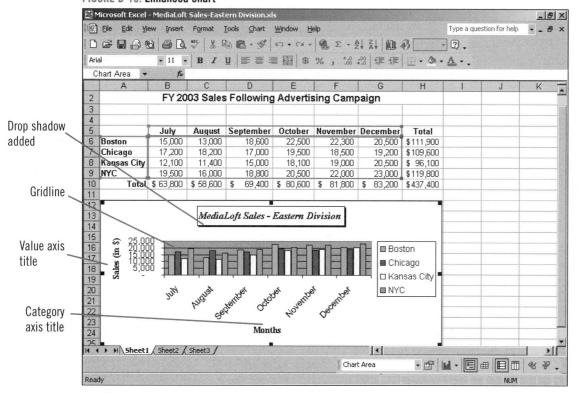

FIGURE D-15: Enhanced chart

Drop shadow
added

Gridline

Value axis
title

Category
axis title

Changing text alignment in charts

You can modify the alignment of axis text to make it fit better within the plot area. With a chart selected, double-click the axis text to be modified. The Format Axis dialog box opens. Click the Alignment tab, then change the alignment by typing the number of degrees in the Degrees text box, or by clicking a marker in the Degrees sample box. When you have made the desired changes, click OK.

Annotating and Drawing on a Chart

You can add arrows and text annotations to point out critical information in your charts. **Text annotations** are labels that you add to a chart to further describe your data. You can draw lines and arrows that point to the exact locations you want to emphasize. ✐ Jim wants you to add a text annotation and an arrow to highlight the October sales increase.

Steps

1. Make sure the chart is selected

To call attention to the Boston October sales increase, you can draw an arrow that points to the top of the Boston October data series with the annotation, "Due to ad campaign." With the chart selected, simply typing text in the formula bar creates annotation text.

2. Type Due to ad campaign, then click the Enter button 🔲

As you type, the text appears in the formula bar. After you confirm the entry, the text appears in a selected text box within the chart window.

Trouble?

If the pointer changes to I or ↔, release the mouse button, click outside the text box area to deselect it, select the text box, then repeat Step 3.

3. Point to an edge of the text box so that the pointer changes to 🔯

4. Drag the text box above the chart, as shown in Figure D-16, then release the mouse button

You can add an arrow to point to a specific area or item in a chart by using the Drawing toolbar.

5. Click the Drawing button 🔲 **on the Standard toolbar**

The Drawing toolbar appears below the worksheet.

QuickTip

To annotate charts, you can also use the Callout shapes on the AutoShapes menu in the Drawing toolbar.

6. Click the Arrow button 🔲 **on the Drawing toolbar, then move the pointer over the chart**

The pointer changes to ┼, and the status bar displays "Click and drag to insert an AutoShape." When you draw an arrow, the point farthest from where you start will have the arrowhead.

QuickTip

You can also insert text and an arrow in the data section of a worksheet by clicking the Text Box button 🔲 on the Drawing toolbar, drawing a text box, typing the text, then adding the arrow.

7. Position ┼ under the t in the word "to" in the text box, press and hold the left mouse button, drag the line to the Boston column in the October sales series, then release the mouse button

An arrow appears, pointing to Boston October sales. The arrow is a selected object in the chart; you can resize, format, or delete it just like any other object. Compare your finished chart to Figure D-17.

8. Click 🔲 **to close the Drawing toolbar**

9. Click the Save button 🔲 **on the Standard toolbar**

FIGURE D-16: Repositioning text annotation

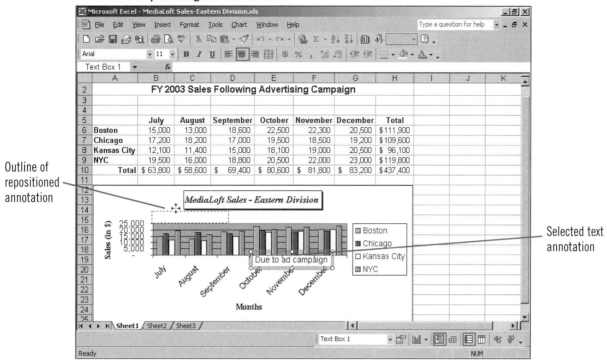

Outline of repositioned annotation

Selected text annotation

FIGURE D-17: Completed chart with text annotation and arrow

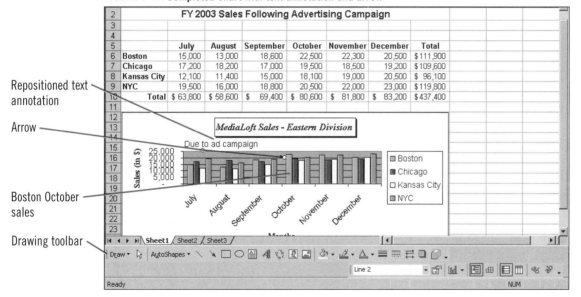

Repositioned text annotation

Arrow

Boston October sales

Drawing toolbar

Exploding a pie slice

Just as an arrow can call attention to a data series, you can emphasize a pie slice by exploding, or pulling it away from, the pie chart. Once the pie chart is selected, click the pie to select it, click the desired slice to select only that slice, then drag the slice away from the pie, as shown in Figure D-18. After you change the chart type, you may need to adjust arrows within the chart.

FIGURE D-18: Exploded pie slice

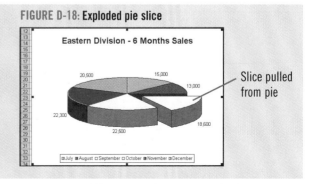

Slice pulled from pie

Previewing and Printing a Chart

After you complete a chart, you will often need to print it. Like previewing a worksheet, previewing a chart lets you see what your chart looks like before you print it. You can print a chart by itself or as part of the worksheet. ✐ Jim wants a printed version of the chart for the annual meeting. He wants you to print the worksheet and the chart together, so that the shareholders can see the actual sales numbers for the eastern division stores.

Steps 1 2 3 4

1. Press **[Esc]** to deselect the arrow and the chart, enter your name in cell **A35**, then press **[Ctrl][Home]**

> **QuickTip**
>
> The preview will show in color if you have a color printer selected.

2. Click the **Print Preview button** 🔍 on the Standard toolbar
The Print Preview window opens. You decide the chart and data would make better use of the page if they were printed in **landscape** orientation—that is, with the text running the long way on the page. You will use Page Setup to change the page orientation.

3. Click **Setup** on the Print Preview toolbar to open the Page Setup dialog box, then click the **Page tab**, if necessary

4. Click the **Landscape option button** in the Orientation section, as shown in Figure D-19, then click **OK**
Because each page has a default left margin of 0.75", the chart and data will print too far over to the left of the page. You can change this setting using the Margins tab.

> **QuickTip**
>
> The printer you have selected may affect the appearance of the preview screen.

5. Click **Setup** on the Print Preview toolbar, click the **Margins tab**, click the **Horizontally check box** (under Center on page), then click **OK**
The data and chart are positioned horizontally on the page. See Figure D-20.

6. Click **Print** to display the Print dialog box, then click **OK**
The data and chart print, and you are returned to the worksheet. If you want, you can choose to preview (and print) only the chart.

7. Select the **chart**, then click the **Print Preview button** 🔍
The chart appears in the Print Preview window. If you wanted to, you could print the chart by clicking the Print button on the Print Preview toolbar.

8. Click **Close** on the Print Preview toolbar

9. Click the **Save button** 💾 on the Standard toolbar, close the workbook, then exit Excel

FIGURE D-19: **Page tab of the Page Setup dialog box**

Landscape option button selected

Depending on your printer, your settings may differ

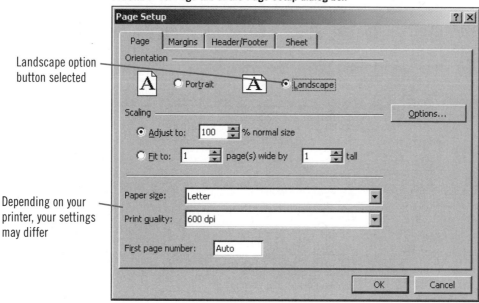

FIGURE D-20: **Chart and data ready to print**

Centered on page

Orientation changed to landscape

Chart and data will print on one page

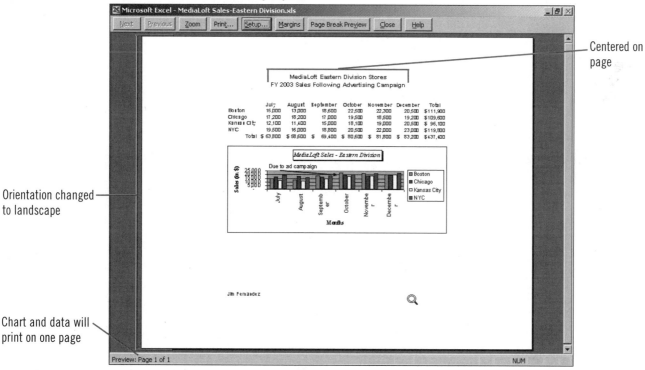

Using the Page Setup dialog box for a chart

When a chart is selected, a different Page Setup dialog box opens than when neither the chart nor data is selected. The Center on Page options are not always available. To accurately position a chart on the page, you can click the Margins button on the Print Preview toolbar. Margin lines appear on the screen and show you exactly how the margins will appear on the page. The exact placement appears in the status bar when you press and hold the mouse button on the margin line. You can drag the lines to the exact settings you want.

Practice

▶ Concepts Review

Label each element of the Excel chart shown in Figure D-21.

FIGURE D-21

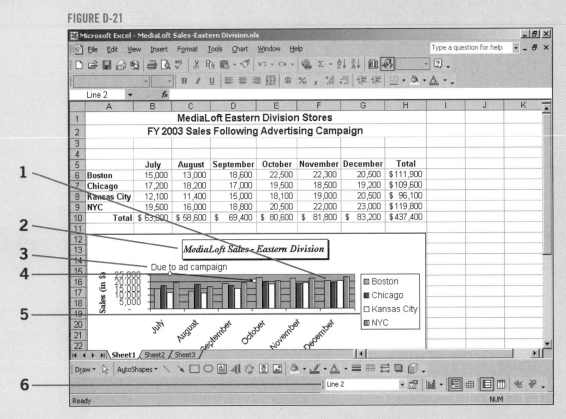

Match each chart type with the statement that describes it.

7. **Column**
8. **Area**
9. **Pie**
10. **Combination**
11. **Line**

a. Shows how volume changes over time
b. Compares data as parts of a whole
c. Displays a column and line chart using different scales of measurement
d. Compares trends over even time intervals
e. Compares data over time—the Excel default

Select the best answer from the list of choices.

12. The object in a chart that identifies patterns used for each data series is a:
   a. Data point.
   b. Plot.
   c. Legend.
   d. Range.

13. What is the term for a row or column on a chart?
a. Range address
b. Axis title
c. Chart orientation
d. Data series

14. The orientation of a page whose dimensions are 11" wide by 8½" tall is:
a. Sideways.
b. Longways.
c. Portrait.
d. Landscape.

15. In a 2-D chart, the Value axis is the:
a. X-axis.
b. Z-axis.
c. D-axis.
d. Y-axis.

16. In a 2-D chart, the Category axis is the:
a. X-axis.
b. Z-axis.
c. D-axis.
d. Y-axis.

17. Which pointer is used to resize a chart object?
a. I
b. ↘
c. ↔↕
d. +

▶ Skills Review

1. Create a chart.
a. Start Excel, open a new workbook, then save it as **MediaLoft Vancouver Software Usage** in the drive and folder where your Project Files are stored.
b. Enter the information from the following table in your worksheet in range A1:F6. Resize columns as necessary.

	Excel	Word	PowerPoint	Access	Publisher
Accounting	27	15	2	7	1
Marketing	13	35	35	15	35
Engineering	25	5	3	1	5
Personnel	15	25	10	10	27
Production	6	5	22	0	25

    c. Save your work.

    d. Select the range containing the data and headings.

    e. Start the Chart Wizard.

    f. In the Chart Wizard, select a clustered column chart, then verify that the series are in rows; add the chart title **Software Usage by Department**, and make the chart an object on the worksheet.

    g. After the chart appears, save your work.

2. Move and resize a chart.

    a. Make sure the chart is still selected.

    b. Move the chart beneath the data.

    c. Resize the chart so it extends to column L.

    d. Move the legend below the charted data. (*Hint*: Change the legend's position by using the Legend tab in the Chart Options dialog box.)

    e. Save your work.

3. Edit a chart.

    a. Change the value in cell B3 to **6**. Notice the change in the chart.

    b. Select the chart.

    c. Resize the chart so the bottom is at row 24.

    d. Use the Chart Type list arrow to change the chart to a 3-D Column Chart.

    e. Rotate the chart to move the data.

    f. Change the chart back to a column chart.

    g. Save your work.

4. Format a chart.

    a. Make sure the chart is still selected.

    b. Use the Chart Options dialog box to turn off the displayed gridlines.

    c. Change the font used in the Category and Value labels to Times New Roman. (*Hint*: Click the axis to select it, then proceed as you would to change an axis title.)

    d. Turn on the major gridlines for the Value axis.

    e. Change the title's font to Times New Roman.

    f. Save your work.

5. Enhance a chart.

    a. Make sure the chart is selected, then select the **Titles tab** in the Chart Options dialog box.

    b. Enter **Software** as the x-axis title.

    c. Enter **Users** as the y-axis title.

    d. Change **Production** in the legend to **Art**. (*Hint*: Change the text entry in the worksheet.)

    e. Add a drop shadow to the title.

    f. Save your work.

6. Annotate and draw on a chart.

a. Make sure the chart is selected, then create the text annotation **Needs More Users**.

b. Position the text annotation beneath the title.

c. Below the text annotation, use the Drawing toolbar to create an arrow similar to the one in Figure D-22 that points to the area containing the Access data.

d. Save your work.

7. Preview and print a chart.

a. In the worksheet, enter your name in cell A30.

b. Preview the chart and data.

c. Change the page orientation to landscape.

d. Center the page contents horizontally and vertically on the page.

e. Print the data and chart from the Print Preview window.

f. Save your work.

g. Preview only the chart, then print it.

h. Close the workbook, then exit Excel.

FIGURE D-22

	Excel	Word	PowerPoint	Access	Publisher
Accounting	27	15	2	7	1
Marketing	6	35	35	15	35
Engineering	25	5	3	1	5
Personnel	15	25	10	10	27
Art	6	5	22	0	25

▶ Independent Challenge 1

You are the operations manager for the Springfield, Oregon Theater Group. Each year the group applies to various state and federal agencies for matching funds. For this year's funding proposal, you need to create charts to document the number of productions in previous years.

a. Sketch a sample worksheet on a piece of paper describing how you will create the charts. Which type of chart is best suited for the information you need to display? What kind of chart enhancements do you want to use? Will a 3-D effect make your chart easier to understand?

b. Start Excel, open the Project File EX D-2, then save it as **Springfield Theater Group** in the drive and folder where your Project Files are stored.

c. Create a column chart for the data, accepting all Chart Wizard defaults.

d. Change at least one of the colors used in a data series.

e. Create at least two additional charts for the same data to show how different chart types display the same data. (*Hint*: Move each chart to a new location, then deselect each chart before using the Wizard to create the next one.)

f. After creating the charts, make the appropriate enhancements. Include chart titles, legends, and value and category axis titles, using the suggestions in the following table:

suggested chart enhancements	
Title	Types and Number of Plays
Legend	Year 1, Year 2, Year 3, Year 4
Value axis title	Number of Plays
Category axis title	Play Types

g. Add data labels.

h. Enter your name in a worksheet cell.

i. Save your work. Before printing, preview the file so you know what the charts will look like. Adjust any items as necessary.

j. Print the worksheet (charts and data).

k. Close the workbook, then exit Excel.

▶ Independent Challenge 2

Beautiful You, a small beauty salon, has been using Excel for several months. One of your responsibilities at the Beautiful You Salon is to re-create the company's records using Excel. Another is to convince the current staff that Excel can help them make daily operating decisions more easily and efficiently. To do this, you've decided to create charts using the previous year's operating expenses, including rent, utilities, and payroll. The manager will use these charts at the next monthly meeting.

a. Decide which data in the worksheet should be charted. Sketch two sample charts. What type of charts are best suited for the information you need to show? What kind of chart enhancements will be necessary?

b. Start Excel, open the Project File EX D-3 from the drive and folder where your Project Files are stored, then save it as **BY Expense Charts**.

c. Create a column chart on the worksheet, containing the expense data for all four quarters.

d. Using the same data, create an area chart and one additional chart using any other appropriate chart type. (*Hint*: move each chart to a new location, then deselect it before using the Wizard to create the next one.)

e. Add annotated text and arrows to the column chart that highlight any important data or trends.

f. In one chart, change the color of a data series, then in another chart, use black-and-white patterns only. (*Hint*: use the Fill Effects button in the Format Data Series dialog box. Then display the Patterns tab. Adjust the Foreground color to black and the Background color to white, then select a pattern.)

g. Enter your name in a worksheet cell.

h. Save your work. Before printing, preview each chart so you know what the charts will look like. Adjust any items as needed.

i. Print the charts.

j. Close the workbook, then exit Excel.

▶ Independent Challenge 3

You are working as an account representative at the Bright Light Ad Agency. You have been examining the expenses charged to clients of the firm. The Board of Directors wants to examine certain advertising expenses and has asked you to prepare charts that can be used in this evaluation.

a. Start Excel, open the Project File EX D-4 from the drive and folder where your Project Files are stored, then save it as **Bright Light**.

b. Decide what types of charts would be best suited for the data in the range A16:B24. Sketch two sample charts. What kind of chart enhancements will be necessary?

c. Use the Chart Wizard to create at least three different types of charts that show the distribution of advertising expenses. (*Hint*: Move each chart to a new location, then deselect it before using the Wizard to create the next one.)

d. Add annotated text and arrows highlighting important data, such as the largest expense.

e. Change the color of at least one data series.

f. Add chart titles and Category and Value axis titles. Format the titles with a font of your choice. Place a drop shadow around the chart title.

g. Enter your name in a worksheet cell.

h. Save your work. Before printing, preview the file so you know what the charts will look like. Adjust any items as needed. Be sure the chart is placed appropriately on the page.

i. Print the charts, close the workbook then exit Excel.

Independent Challenge 4

Your company, Film Distribution, is headquartered in Montreal, and is considering opening a new office in the U.S. They would like you to begin investigating possible locations. You can use the Web to find and compare median pay scales in specific cities to see how relocating will affect the standard of living for those employees who move to the new office.

a. Start Excel, open a new workbook, then save it as **New Location Analysis** in the drive and folder where your Project Files are located.

b. Connect to the Internet, use your browser to go to homeadvisor.msn.com/pickaplace/comparecities.asp. (If this address is no longer current, go to homeadvisor.msn.com or www.homefair.com, and follow links for **Moving and Relocation, Compare Cost of Living**, or similar links to find the information needed for your spreadsheet. You can also use your favorite search engine to locate other sites on cost of living comparisons.)

c. Determine the median incomes for Seattle, San Francisco, Dallas, Salt Lake City, Memphis, and Boston. Record this data on a sheet named Median Income in your workbook. (*Hint*: See the table below for suggested data layout.)

Location	Income
Seattle	
San Francisco	
Dallas	
Salt Lake City	
Memphis	
Boston	

d. Format the data so it looks attractive and professional.

e. Create any type of column chart, with the data series in columns, on the same worksheet as the data. Include a descriptive title.

f. Determine how much an employee would need to earn in Seattle, San Francisco, Dallas, Memphis, and Boston to maintain the same standard of living as if the company chose to relocate to Salt Lake City and pay $75,000. Record this data on a sheet named **Standard of Living** in your workbook.

g. Format the data so it looks attractive and professional.

h. Create any type of chart you feel is appropriate on the same worksheet as the data. Include a descriptive title.

i. Do not display the legends in either chart.

j. Change the color of the data series in the Standard of Living chart to bright green.

k. Remove the major gridlines in the Median Income chart.

l. Format the Value axis in both charts so that the salary income displays a 1000 separator (comma) but no decimal places.

m. Enter your name in a cell in both worksheets.

n. Save the workbook. Preview the chart and change margins as necessary.

o. Print each worksheet, including the data and chart, making setup modifications as necessary.

p. Close the workbook, then exit Excel.

▶ Visual Workshop

Modify a worksheet, using the skills you learned in this unit and using Figure D-23 for reference. Open the Project File EX D-5 from the drive and folder where your Project Files are stored, then save it as **Quarterly Advertising Budget**. Create the chart, then change the chart to reflect Figure D-23. Enter your name in cell A13, save, preview, then print your results.

FIGURE D-23

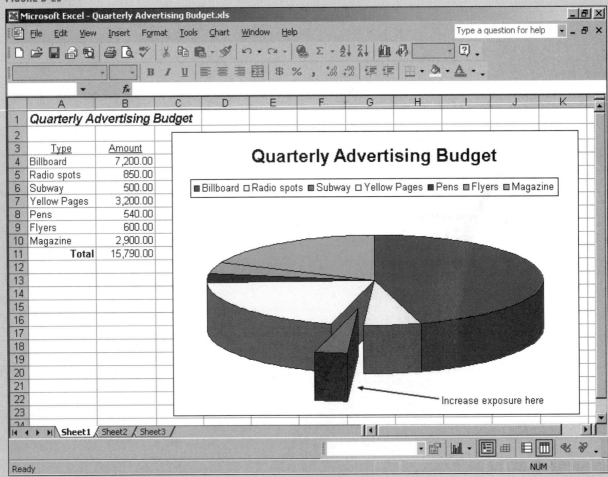

Integrating
Word and Excel

Objectives

► **Understand Integration**
► **Open multiple programs**
► **Copy Word data into Excel**

Now that you have experienced the power of Word and Excel, it is time to learn how to integrate these two programs. When you integrate programs, you combine information from the output of the programs without retyping anything. ▰▰▰ Alice Wegman is a marketing manager for MediaLoft, a nationwide chain of bookstore cafés that sells books, CDs, and videos. Five of the MediaLoft stores noticed that they had an increase in sales soon after they started promoting MediaLoft's participation in a national literacy program. Alice collected the spring quarter sales data for the five stores and compiled this information in a Word document. She decides she wants to communicate this data graphically using Excel charts, so she needs to copy the data to an Excel workbook.

Understanding Integration

Programs in Microsoft Office are designed to work together. The ability to use information across multiple programs, or **integration**, makes it possible to share data among documents and between coworkers. The file from which the information is copied is the **source file**. The file that receives the copied information is the **destination file**. For example, charts created in an Excel worksheet, the source file, can be copied to and edited in a Word document or a PowerPoint presentation, the destination file. Alice decides to review some of the ways that data can be integrated among the Office suite programs and with other programs.

You can use Microsoft Office integration features to:

► Copy and paste data
You can copy information—whether it's text, values, or objects—created in one program into another program using the Copy and Paste commands. You can copy and paste one item at a time using the Windows clipboard, or, if the Office Clipboard task pane is open, you can copy and store up to 24 items. See Figure A-1.

► Drag and drop data
You can also copy selected text, values, or objects into other programs by using the drag-and-drop method. Once the files are opened and the program windows are arranged so that both the source and destination files are visible, you can press and hold [Ctrl] and drag a selection from the source file into the destination file.

► Link and embed objects
If you include data that is subject to change in multiple files, you should link the object you want to copy. A **linked** object maintains a connection to the source file so that the linked objects in both the destination file and the source file are updated when the data is changed in the source file. An **embedded** object maintains a link to the source program, but not to the source file. You can double-click an embedded object to open the source program and edit the object. The source file remains unchanged, however.

► Import and export text and graphics
You can also use files created in programs that are not part of the Office suite by using **filters**, programs built into the Office suite that convert files created in another format.

► Create hyperlinks
You can include hyperlinks in your files to other places in your files, other files, or a location on the Internet. Figure A-2 shows the Insert Hyperlink dialog box, which is used to create a hyperlink. When you click a hyperlink, the file or Web page that the hyperlink is connected to opens.

► Work efficiently using Office eServices
Microsoft maintains a Web site that offers a variety of tools—many of them free—that makes it easy to get the most out of Office, including sharing information. This site, shown in Figure A-3, changes often and offers many exciting features.

► E-mail files
You can share Office files by sending them as attachments to an e-mail message. By clicking the E-mail (as Attachment) button on the Standard toolbar. This opens your e-mail client and attaches the file to the e-mail message. By sending a file and using Office tools such as Tracking and Comments, you can easily incorporate input from your coworkers into your documents.

► Collaborate online
E-mail is one form of online collaboration. You can also use Office program features to share and review documents accessed by multiple users, and you can hold online discussions.

FIGURE A-1: Entries in Office Clipboard

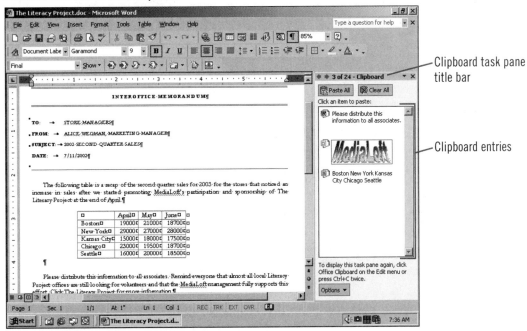

Clipboard task pane title bar

Clipboard entries

FIGURE A-2: Insert Hyperlink dialog box

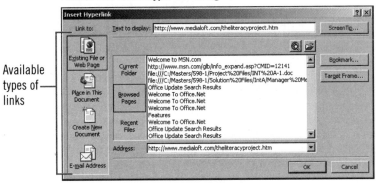

Available types of links

FIGURE A-3: Microsoft eServices on the Web

Opening Multiple Programs

When you are integrating information from one program into another, it is often necessary to have more than one file in more than one program open at the same time. The Windows environment gives you the ability to have more than one program open at a time, and to view them on the same screen simultaneously. This ability is sometimes called **multitasking**. Before integrating the data, Alice starts both Word and Excel. To make integrating the data easier, she aligns each program window side by side on the screen.

Steps

1. Click the **Start button** [Start] on the taskbar, point to **Programs**, then click **Microsoft Word** in the Program list
A blank Word document opens.

2. Click the **Minimize button** in the program window
The Word program window shrinks into a program button on the taskbar. Sometimes the taskbar is hidden.

3. If necessary, move the mouse pointer to the bottom of the screen
The taskbar appears.

4. Click [Start] on the taskbar, point to **Programs**, then click **Microsoft Excel**
A blank Excel workbook opens. The taskbar displays program buttons for Word and Excel, and the button for Excel is a lighter gray, as shown in Figure A-4. The light gray color of the Excel program button indicates that Excel is the active window.

5. Click the **Word program button** on the taskbar
The Word window is maximized and Word becomes the active program. The Excel window is still open, but it is not active. You want to see both windows at the same time.

6. Right-click a blank area on the taskbar
The taskbar shortcut menu appears.

7. Click **Tile Windows Vertically** on the shortcut menu
The two program windows each occupy half the screen. Compare your screen to Figure A-5. The title bars of both windows are gray, and both program buttons on the taskbar are dark gray, indicating that neither program window is active.

FIGURE A-4: Excel workbook active and Word document inactive

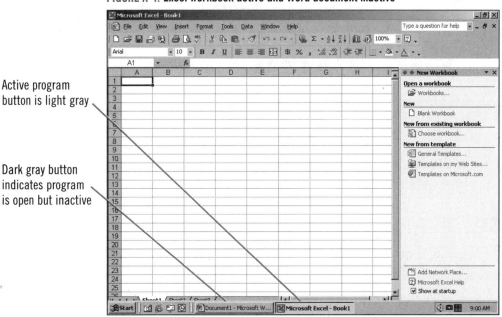

Active program button is light gray

Dark gray button indicates program is open but inactive

FIGURE A-5: Word and Excel windows open

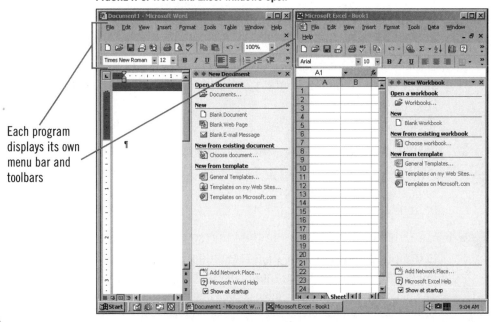

Each program displays its own menu bar and toolbars

CLUES TO USE

Using shortcut keys to switch between open programs

You can switch between open programs by clicking the program buttons on the taskbar or by using the shortcut key combination [Alt][Tab]. Pressing [Alt][Tab] causes the icons and names of open programs (whether or not they are minimized) to appear in the center of the screen, as shown in Figure A-6. To see this on the screen, press and hold [Alt], then press and release [Tab]. If more than one program is open, press and release [Tab] again while still holding down [Alt] to move the selection box to the next icon in the center of the screen. When the program you want to activate is selected, release [Alt].

FIGURE A-6: Using [Alt][Tab] to switch among open programs

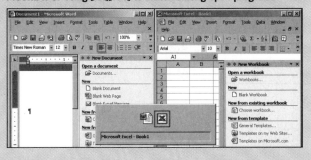

Integration

Copying Word Data into Excel

Moving or copying information from one program to another is just like moving or copying information within a single program. You can use the Cut, Copy, and Paste commands; buttons on the toolbars; or the drag-and-drop method to move or copy information. ◣ Alice typed a memo to the five store managers that includes a Word table containing the spring quarter sales data for all five stores. Alice wants to copy the data from the Word table into an Excel workbook. Later, Alice will be able to create the charts she needs once the data is copied into Excel.

Steps

1. **Click anywhere in the Word program window to make it active**
   Clicking in a window makes the window active.

2. **Open the file INT A-1 from the drive and location where your Project Files are stored, then save it as Manager Memo**
   Once the document is open, it can be saved to the location where your Project Files are stored. Manager Memo appears in the Word program window in Print Layout view.

3. **Replace Alice Wegman's name in the From line with your name**

4. **Scroll down until you can see the table and the body of the memo, then click the right scroll arrow on the horizontal scroll bar so you can see the entire table, as shown in Figure A-7**
   The Word document is the source file, and the blank Excel workbook is the destination file.

5. **Position the pointer in the selection bar next to the top row of the table until the pointer changes to ↗, press and hold the mouse button to select the top row of the table, drag the pointer down until all of the rows are selected, then release the mouse button**

QuickTip

You also can select the Word table, click the Copy button 🗐 on the Word Standard toolbar, click the top, left destination cell in Excel, then click the Paste button 🗐 on the Excel Standard toolbar.

6. **Press and hold [Ctrl], click in the table so the pointer looks like ▓, drag the pointer to the Excel worksheet, position the outline of the table in the range A1:D6 as shown in Figure A-8, then release the mouse button and [Ctrl]**
   The information in the Word table is copied into the Excel worksheet, as shown in Figure A-9. Using drag and drop is the easiest way to copy information from a source file to a target file. You can now work with the data in the Excel workbook.

7. **Click the Save button 🖫 on the Excel Standard toolbar, then save the workbook as Manager Sales in the location where your Project Files are stored**

8. **Close the Manager Sales workbook and exit Excel**

9. **Close the Manager Memo document and exit Word without saving changes**

FIGURE A-7: Manager Memo open

Table in memo

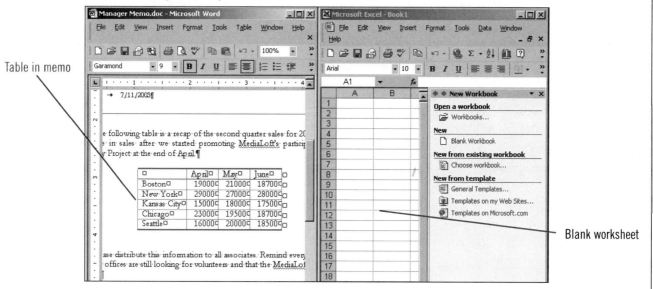

Blank worksheet

FIGURE A-8: Word text dragged and dropped into an Excel worksheet

Drag and drop
copy pointer

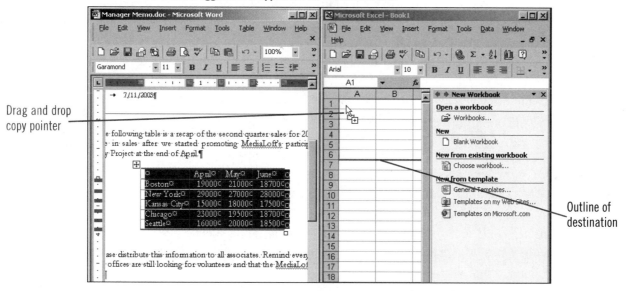

Outline of
destination

FIGURE A-9: Word table data copied into an Excel workbook

Destination
file data

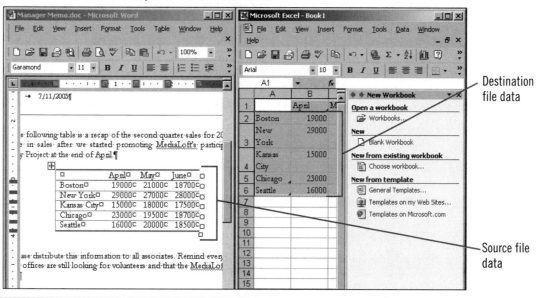

Source file
data

Integration

▶ Independent Challenge 1

The Hispanic Chamber of Commerce realizes that to improve their advertising coverage, they need to hire an outside consultant. A list of promising consultants is being assembled by other Chamber members. Your job is to create a memo that gives them an overview of the Chamber's advertising efforts.

   a. Start Excel, open the Excel file INT A-2 from the location where your Project Files are stored, then save it as **Chamber Statistics**. Start Word, open the Word file INT A-3 from the location where your Project Files are stored, then save it as **Chamber Consultants**.

   b. Examine the Chamber Consultants document and determine what additions you need to make to best inform the prospective consultant.

   c. Examine the chart in the Chamber Statistics workbook. Do you think you can use this chart within the memo, or do you need to create another type of chart to better convey the information? Can you add any enhancements to the chart to make it clearer?

   d. The memo to the board should contain three charts. Create the additional charts you need in Excel; for example, you can create a column chart that shows how much money is spent on each type of advertising, or a bar chart showing the different types of advertisements and the money spent on each one. Add any enhancements, such as text annotations and arrows, that will call attention to the charts in the memo.

   e. Create the document text to accompany each chart, then copy the charts into the document.

   f. Update the date in the Chamber Consultants document to reflect the current date and replace the text after FROM with your name, then preview the document and print a copy.

   g. Save and close the document and the workbook, and exit both programs.

Independent Challenge 2

MediaLoft is considering expanding its stores in the United Kingdom. Before Alice Wegman hires a marketing firm to target this area, she wants to learn about this country's demographics. She has asked you to use the Web to find census data for the United Kingdom, and then prepare a synopsis of the information.

   a. Connect to the Internet and use a search engine to locate Web sites that have information on the United Kingdom census data. If your search does not produce any results, you might try the following sites:
       www.cia.gov/cia/publications/factbook/index.html
       www.felixent.force9.co.uk/europe/uk/07.html

   b. Locate and print data that details age distribution by gender—that is, the percentage of men and women in different age brackets—then disconnect from the Internet.

   c. Start Excel, then create a workbook named **Population Projections**.

   d. Enter data for the information on age distribution by gender, adjusting column widths as necessary.

   e. Format the statistical data using the comma format showing no decimals.

   f. Create a 3-D column chart that graphically describes this data.

   g. Start Word, then create a document named **Population Analysis**.

   h. Create original text that explains the data and the chart you created in Excel.

   i. Copy and paste the Excel data and chart into the Word document.

   j. Include any links that you used to get your data.

   k. Copy and paste the Excel chart into the Word document.

   l. Add your name as the last line in the document, then save and print your work.

   m. Close the document and the workbook, and exit both programs.

Getting
Started with Access 2002

Objectives

- ► **Define database software**
- ► **Learn database terminology**
- ► **Start Access and open a database**
- ⌐MOUS⌐ ► **View the database window**
- ⌐MOUS⌐ ► **Navigate records**
- ⌐MOUS⌐ ► **Enter records**
- ⌐MOUS⌐ ► **Edit records**
- ► **Preview and print a datasheet**
- ► **Get Help and exit Access**

In this unit, you will learn the purpose, advantages, and terminology of Microsoft Access 2002, a database software program. You will learn how to use the different elements of the Access window and how to get help. You'll learn how to navigate through a database, enter and update data, and preview and print data. ✐ Kelsey Lang is a Marketing Manager at MediaLoft, a nationwide chain of bookstore cafés that sells books, music, and videos. Recently, MediaLoft switched to Access for storing and maintaining customer information. Kelsey will use Access to maintain this valuable information for MediaLoft.

Defining Database Software

Microsoft Access 2002 is a database software program that runs on Windows. **Database software** is used to manage data that can be organized into lists of related information, such as customers, products, vendors, employees, projects, or sales. Many small companies record customer, inventory, and sales information in a spreadsheet program such as Microsoft Excel. While this electronic format is more productive than using a paper-based system, Excel still lacks many of the database advantages provided by Access. Refer to Table A-1 for a comparison of the two programs. Kelsey reviews the advantages of database software over manual systems.

The advantages of using Access include:

► Data entry is faster and easier

Before inexpensive microcomputers, small businesses used manual paper systems, as illustrated in Figure A-1, such as index cards, to record each customer, sale, and inventory item. Using an electronic database such as Access, you can create on-screen data entry forms that make managing a database easier, more accurate, and more efficient than manual systems.

► Information retrieval is faster and easier

Retrieving information in a manual system is tedious because the information has to be physically handled, sorted, and stored. Also, one error in filing can cause serious retrieval problems later. With Access you can quickly find, display, and print information about customers, sales, or inventory.

► Information can be viewed and sorted in multiple ways

A manual system allows you to sort information in only one order, unless the information is duplicated for a second arrangement. In such a system, complete customer and product information is recorded for each sale. This can easily compromise data accuracy. Access allows you to view or sort the information from one or more subjects simultaneously. For example, you might want to find all the customers who purchased a particular product, or find all the products purchased by a particular customer. A change made to the data in one view of Access is automatically updated in every other view or report.

► Information is more secure

Paper can be torn, misplaced, and stolen. There is no password required to read a paper document. A flood or fire can destroy the single copy of information in a manual system. If information is stored in an Access database file, you can back up an Access database file on a regular basis and store the file at an offsite location. You can also protect data with a password so only those users with appropriate security clearances can view or manipulate it.

► Information can be shared among several users

An index card system is limited to those users who have physical access to it. If one user keeps a card for an extended period of time, then others cannot use or update that information. Access databases are inherently multiuser. More than one person can be entering, updating, and using the data at the same time.

► Duplicate data entry is minimized

A paper-based system requires that you record the customer and product information for each sale twice—once on the customer index card and once on the inventory index card. With Access, you only need to enter each piece of information once. Figure A-2 shows a possible structure for an Access database that records sales.

FIGURE A-1: Using a manual system to organize sales data

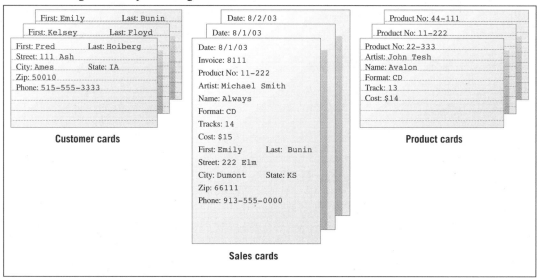

FIGURE A-2: Using Access, an electronic relational database, to organize sales data

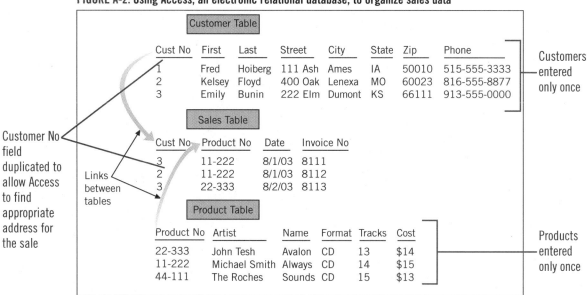

TABLE A-1: Comparing Excel to Access

feature	Excel	Access
Layout	Provides a natural tabular layout for easy data entry	Provides a natural tabular layout as well as customized data entry screens
Storage	Limited to approximately 65,000 records per sheet	Able to store any number of records up to two gigabytes
Linked tables	Manages single lists of information	Allows links between lists of information to reduce data redundancy
Reporting	Limited to the current spreadsheet arrangement of data	Able to create and save multiple report presentations of data
Security	Limited to file and password security options such as marking the file "read-only" or protecting a range of cells	Each user can be given access to only the records and fields they need
Multiuser capabilities	Does not easily allow multiple users to simultaneously enter and update data	Naturally allows multiple users to simultaneously enter and update data
Data entry screens	Provides limited data entry screens	Provides the ability to create extensive data entry screens called forms

Access 2002

Learning Database Terminology

To become familiar with Access, you need to understand basic database terminology. Kelsey reviews the terms and concepts that define a database.

Details

▶ A **database** is a collection of information associated with a topic (for example, sales of products to customers). The smallest piece of information in a database is called a **field**, or category of information, such as the customer's name, city, state, or phone number. A **key field** is a field that contains unique information for each record, such as a social security number for a person or a customer number for a customer. A group of related fields, such as all of the demographic information for one customer, is called a **record**. In Access, a collection of records for a single subject, such as all of the customer records, is called a **table**, as shown in Figure A-3.

▶ An Access database is a **relational database**, in which more than one table, such as the Customer, Sales, and Product tables, can share information. The term "relational database" comes from the fact that two tables are linked, or related, by a common field.

▶ Tables, therefore, are the most important **objects** in an Access database because they contain all of the data within the database. An Access database may also contain six other objects. These other objects serve to increase the usefulness and value of the relational data. The other objects in an Access database besides tables are **queries**, **forms**, **reports**, **pages**, **macros**, and **modules**. They are summarized in Table A-2.

▶ Data can be entered and edited in four of the objects: tables, queries, forms, and pages. The relationship between tables, queries, forms, and reports is shown in Figure A-4. Regardless of how the data is entered, it is physically stored in a table object. Data can be printed from a table, query, form, page, or report object. The macro and module objects provide additional database productivity and automation features. All of the objects (except for the page objects, which create Web pages) are stored in one database file.

TABLE A-2: Access objects and their purpose

object	purpose
Table	Contains all of the raw data within the database in a spreadsheet-like view; tables can be linked with a common field to share information and therefore minimize data redundancy
Query	Provides a spreadsheet-like view of the data similar to tables, but a query can be designed to provide the user with a subset of fields or records from one or more tables; queries are created when a user has a question about the data in the database
Form	Provides an easy-to-use data entry screen, which generally shows only one record at a time
Report	Provides a professional printout of data that may contain enhancements such as headers, footers, and calculations on groups of records
Page	Creates dynamic Web pages which interact with an Access database; also called Data Access Page
Macro	Stores a set of keystrokes or commands, such as the commands to print several reports or to display a toolbar when a form opens
Module	Stores Visual Basic for Applications programming code that extends the functions and automated processes of Access

FIGURE A-3: Tables contain fields and records

Customer Table

Cust No	First	Last	Street	City	State	Zip	Phone
1	Fred	Hoiberg	111 Ash	Ames	IA	50010	515-555-3333
2	Kelsey	Floyd	400 Oak	Lenexa	MO	60023	816-555-8877
3	Emily	Bunin	222 Elm	Dumont	KS	66111	913-555-0000

Fields

Records

Sales Table

Cust No	Product No	Date	Invoice No
3	11-222	8/1/03	8111
2	11-222	8/1/03	8112
3	22-333	8/2/03	8113

Tables

Product Table

Product No	Artist	Name	Format	Tracks	Cost
22-333	John Tesh	Avalon	CD	13	$14
11-222	Michael Smith	Always	CD	14	$15
44-111	The Roches	Sounds	CD	15	$13

FIGURE A-4: The relationship between Access objects

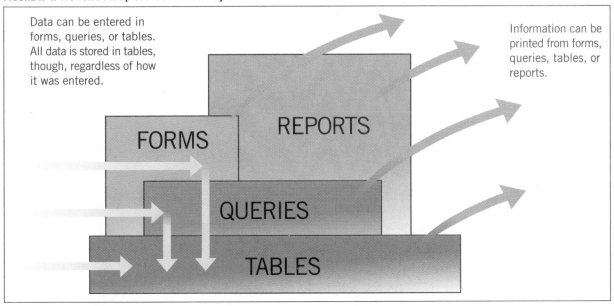

Data can be entered in forms, queries, or tables. All data is stored in tables, though, regardless of how it was entered.

Information can be printed from forms, queries, tables, or reports.

FORMS

REPORTS

QUERIES

TABLES

Starting Access 2002 and Opening a Database

You can start Access by clicking the Access icon on the Windows desktop or on the Microsoft Office shortcut bar. Since not all computers will provide a shortcut icon on the desktop or display the Office shortcut bar, you can always find Access by clicking the Start button on the taskbar, pointing to Programs, and then choosing Access from the Programs menu. You can open a database from within Access or by finding the database file on the desktop, in My Computer, or in Windows Explorer, and then opening it. ✐ Kelsey starts Access and opens the MediaLoft-A database.

1. Click the **Start button** 🎌**Start** on the taskbar

The Start button is the first item on the taskbar, and is usually located in the lower-left corner of your screen. You can use the Start menu to start any program on your computer.

2. Point to **Programs**

Access is generally located on the Programs menu. All the programs stored on your computer can be found on the Programs menu.

Trouble?

If Microsoft Access is not located on the Programs menu, look for it within program group menus such as the Microsoft Office group.

3. Click **Microsoft Access**

Access opens and displays a task pane on the right, from which you can open an existing file or create a new database.

Trouble?

If the task pane does not appear on the right side of your screen, click File on the menu bar, then click New.

4. Click the **Files** or **More files** link in the Open a file section of the task pane

The Open dialog box opens, as shown in Figure A-5. Depending on the databases and folders stored on your computer, your dialog box may look slightly different.

5. Click the **Look in list arrow**, then navigate to the drive and folder where your Project Files are stored

When you have navigated to the correct folder, a list of the Microsoft Access database files in that folder appears in the Open dialog box.

6. Click the **MediaLoft-A** database file, click **Open**, then click the **Maximize button** on the Microsoft Access title bar if the Access window is not already maximized

The MediaLoft-A database opens as shown in Figure A-6.

FIGURE A-5: Open dialog box

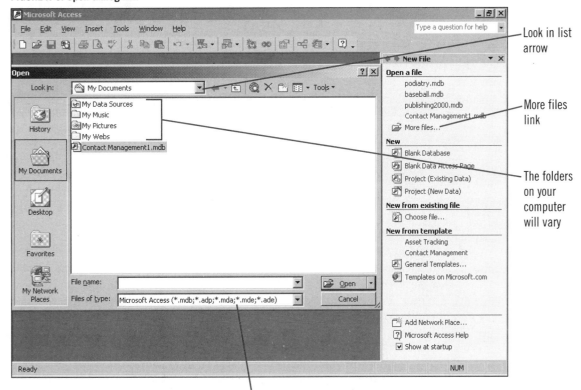

Look in list arrow

More files link

The folders on your computer will vary

Whether or not the file extensions are displayed is determined by a Folder Option setting within Windows Explorer

FIGURE A-6: MediaLoft-A database

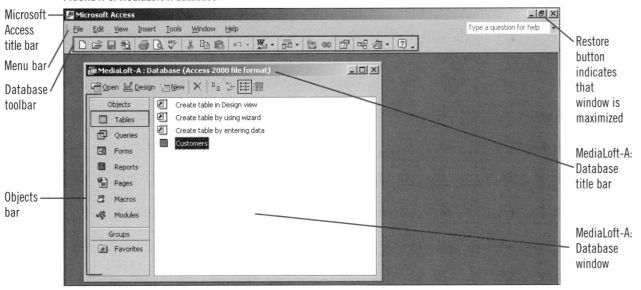

Microsoft Access title bar

Menu bar

Database toolbar

Objects bar

Restore button indicates that window is maximized

MediaLoft-A: Database title bar

MediaLoft-A: Database window

CLUES TO USE

Personalized toolbars and menus in Access 2002

All of the applications within Office 2002 support **personalized toolbars** and **personalized menus** to some extent. "Personalized" means that the toolbars and menus modify themselves to reflect those features that you most commonly use. To view, modify, or reset the toolbar and menu options, click Tools on the menu bar, and then click Customize. On the Options tab you can reset the personalized usage data, eliminate the delay when displaying full menus, and change other toolbar button characteristics.

Viewing the Database Window

When you start Access and open a database, the **database window** displays such common Windows elements as the title bar, menu bar, and toolbar. The **Objects bar** displays the buttons for the seven Access objects as well as the group buttons. The **Groups** area displays other commonly used files and folders, such as the Favorites folder. Clicking the **Objects button** or **Groups button** on the Objects bar alternatively expands and collapses that section. Kelsey explores the MediaLoft-A database.

Steps

1. **Look at each of the Access window elements shown in Figure A-7**
   The Objects bar on the left side of the database window displays the seven object types. The other elements of the database window are summarized in Table A-3. Because the Tables object is selected, the buttons you need to create a new table or to work with the existing table are displayed in the MediaLoft-A Database window.

2. **Click File on the menu bar**
   The File menu contains commands for opening a new or existing database, saving a database in a variety of formats, and printing. The menu commands vary depending on which window or database object is currently in use.

   > **QuickTip**
   > Double-click a menu option to quickly display the full menu.

3. **Point to Edit on the menu bar, point to View, point to Insert, point to Tools, point to Window, point to Help, move the pointer off the menu, then press [Esc] twice**
   All menus close when you press [Esc]. Pressing [Esc] a second time deselects the menu bar.

4. **Point to the New button ☐ on the Database toolbar**
   Pointing to a toolbar button causes a descriptive **ScreenTip** to automatically appear, providing a short description of the button. The buttons on the toolbars represent the most commonly used Access features. Toolbar buttons change just as menu options change depending on which window and database object are currently in use.

5. **Point to the Open button ☞ on the Database toolbar, then point to the Save button ▣ on the Database toolbar**
   Sometimes toolbar buttons or menu options are dimmed, which means they are not currently available. For example, the Paste button ▣ is dimmed because there is nothing on the Clipboard ready to be pasted.

6. **Click Queries on the Objects bar**
   The query object window provides ways to create a new query, and displays the names of previously created queries as shown in Figure A-8. There are three existing query objects displayed within the MediaLoft-A Database window.

7. **Click Forms on the Objects bar, then click Reports on the Objects bar**
   The MediaLoft-A database contains the Customers table, three queries, one form, and three reports.

Viewing objects

You can change the way you view the objects in the database window by clicking the last four buttons on the database window toolbar. You can view the objects as Large Icons ▣▫, Small Icons ▣▫, in a List ▦ (default view), and with Details ▦. The Details view shows a description of the object, as well as the date the object was last modified and the date it was originally created.

FIGURE A-7: MediaLoft-A database screen elements

Access title bar
Menu bar
Database toolbar
Database window toolbar
Click to expand or collapse Objects
Objects buttons
Click to expand or collapse Groups

MediaLoft-A: Database title bar
View buttons

Database window

Status bar

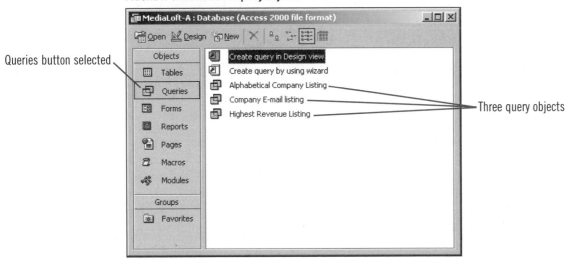

FIGURE A-8: MediaLoft-A query objects

Queries button selected

Three query objects

TABLE A-3: Elements of the database window

element	description
Database toolbar	Contains buttons for commonly performed tasks that affect the entire database (e.g., New, Open, or Relationships) or are common to all database objects (e.g., Print, Copy, or Spelling)
Database window	Allows you to work with the individual objects and groups stored within the database
Menu bar	Contains menus options appropriate for the current view of the database
Objects buttons	Objects buttons on the Objects bar display a list of each type of database object
Database window toolbar	Contains buttons used to open, modify, create, delete, or view objects
Status bar	Displays messages regarding the current database operation
Title bar	Contains the program name or filename of the active database

Navigating Records

Your ability to navigate the fields and records of a database is fundamental to your productivity and success with the database. You can navigate through the information in **Navigation mode** in the table's **datasheet**, a spreadsheet-like grid that displays fields as columns and records as rows. ◄███ Kelsey opens the database and reviews the table containing information about MediaLoft's customers.

QuickTip

You can also double-click an object to open it.

1. Click **Tables** on the Objects bar, click **Customers**, then click the **Open button** 📇 on the MediaLoft-A Database window toolbar

The datasheet for the Customers table opens, as shown in Figure A-9. The datasheet contains 27 customer records with 13 fields of information for each record. **Field names** are listed at the top of each column. The number of the selected record in the datasheet is displayed in the **Specific Record box** (also called the **record number box**) at the bottom of the datasheet window. Depending on the size of your monitor and your screen area settings, you may see a different number of fields. To view more fields, scroll to the right.

2. Press **[Tab]** to move to **Sprint**

Sprint is selected in the first record. The Sprint entry is in the second field, named Company, of the first record.

3. Press **[Enter]**

The focus moves to the Aaron entry in the third column, in the field named First. Pressing either [Tab] or [Enter] moves the focus to the next field. **Focus** refers to which field would be edited if you started typing.

4. Press **[↓]**

The focus moves to the Jacob entry in the field named First of the second record. The **current record symbol** in the **record selector box** also identifies which record you are navigating. The Next Record and Previous Record **navigation buttons** in the lower-left corner of the datasheet can also be used to navigate the datasheet.

Trouble?

If [Ctrl][End] doesn't move the focus to the last field of the last record, you are probably working in Edit mode. Press [Tab] to return to Navigation mode, and then press [Ctrl][End].

5. Press **[Ctrl][End]**

The focus moves to the $6,790.33 entry in the last field, named YTDSales, of the last record. You can also use the Last Record navigation button to move to the last record.

6. Press **[Ctrl][Home]**

The focus moves to the 1 entry in the field named ID of the first record. You can also use the First Record navigation button to move to the first record. A complete listing of navigation keystrokes to move the focus between fields and records is shown in Table A-4.

Changing to Edit mode

If you click a field with the mouse pointer instead of pressing [Tab] or [Enter] to navigate through the datasheet, you change from **Navigation** mode to Edit mode. In **Edit mode**, Access assumes that you are trying to make changes to that particular field value, so key strokes such as [Ctrl][End], [Ctrl][Home], [→] and [←] move the insertion point *within* the field. To return to Navigation mode, press [Tab] or [Enter] (thus moving the focus to the next field), or press [↑] or [↓] (thus moving the focus to a different record).

FIGURE A-9: Customers datasheet

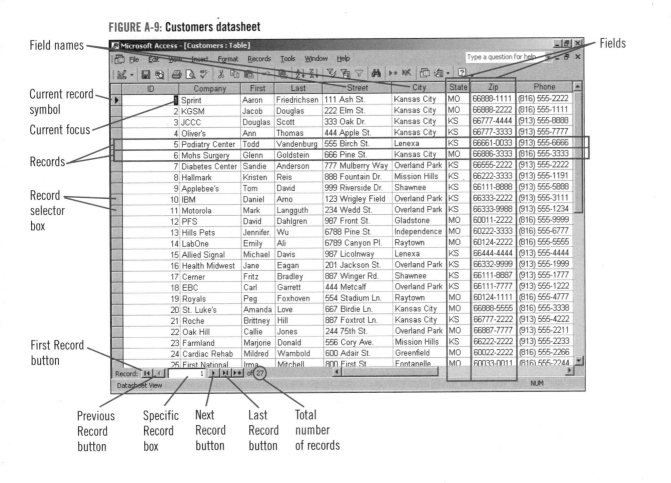

TABLE A-4: Navigation mode keyboard shortcuts

shortcut key	to move to the
[Tab], [Enter] or [→]	Next field of the current record
[Shift][Tab] or [←]	Previous field of the current record
[Home]	First field of the current record
[End]	Last field of the current record
[Ctrl][Home]	First field of the first record
[Ctrl][End]	Last field of the last record
[↑]	Current field of the previous record
[↓]	Current field of the next record
[Ctrl][↑]	Current field of the first record
[Ctrl][↓]	Current field of the last record
[F5]	Specific record entered in the Specific Record box

Entering Records

The ability to add records into a database is a critical task that is usually performed on a daily basis. You can add a new record by clicking the **New Record button** ▶∗ on the Table Datasheet toolbar or by clicking the New Record navigation button. A new record is always added at the end of the datasheet. You can rearrange the order of the records in a datasheet by sorting them, which you will learn later. ◀▬▬▬ Kelsey is ready to add two new records in the Customers table. First, she maximizes the datasheet window.

Steps 1234

1. Click the **Maximize button** ▣ in the window title bar of the Customers Table datasheet

   Maximizing both the Access and datasheet windows displays the most information possible on the screen, and allows you to see more fields and records.

2. Click the **New Record button** ▶∗ on the Table Datasheet toolbar, then press **[Tab]** to move through the ID field and into the Company field

   The ID field is an **AutoNumber** field. Each time you add a record, Access automatically displays the next available integer in the AutoNumber field when you start entering data in that record. You cannot type into an AutoNumber field. The AutoNumber field logs how many records have been added to the datasheet since the creation of the table. It does not tell you how many records are currently in the table because Access will not reuse an AutoNumber value that was assigned to a record that has been deleted.

3. Type **CIO**, press **[Tab]**, type **Taylor**, press **[Tab]**, type **McKinsey**, press **[Tab]**, type **420 Locust St.**, press **[Tab]**, type **Lenexa**, press **[Tab]**, type **KS**, press **[Tab]**, type **66111-8899**, press **[Tab]**, type **9135551189**, press **[Tab]**, type **9135551889**, press **[Tab]**, type **9/6/69**, press **[Tab]**, type **taylor@cio.com**, press **[Tab]**, type **5433.22**, then press **[Enter]**

   The value of 28 was automatically entered in the ID field for this record. Notice that the Navigation buttons indicate that you are now working on record 29 of 29.

4. Enter the new record for Cooper Michaels shown below

in field:	type:	in field:	type:
ID	[Tab]	Zip	65555-4444
Company	Four Winds	Phone	913-555-2289
First	Cooper	Fax	913-555-2889
Last	Michaels	Birthdate	8/20/68
Street	500 Sunset Blvd.	Email	coop@4winds.com
City	Manhattan	YTDSales	5998.33
State	KS		

5. Press **[Tab]**, then compare your updated datasheet with Figure A-10

   You should have 29 records. You can confirm that you have 29 records by using the navigation buttons.

FIGURE A-10: Customers table with two new records

Table datasheet toolbar

Both windows are maximized

New Record button

Two new records

ID	Company	First	Last	Street	City	State	Zip	Phone
7	Diabetes Center	Sandie	Anderson	777 Mulberry Way	Overland Park	KS	66555-2222	(913) 555-2222
8	Hallmark	Kristen	Reis	888 Fountain Dr.	Mission Hills	KS	66222-3333	(913) 555-1191
9	Applebee's	Tom	David	999 Riverside Dr.	Shawnee	KS	66111-8888	(913) 555-5888
10	IBM	Daniel	Arno	123 Wrigley Field	Overland Park	KS	66333-2222	(913) 555-3111
11	Motorola	Mark	Langguth	234 Wedd St.	Overland Park	KS	66333-9988	(913) 555-1234
12	PFS	David	Dahlgren	987 Front St.	Gladstone	MO	60011-2222	(816) 555-9999
13	Hills Pets	Jennifer	Wu	6788 Pine St.	Independence	MO	60222-3333	(816) 555-6777
14	LabOne	Emily	Ali	6789 Canyon Pl.	Raytown	MO	60124-2222	(816) 555-5555
15	Allied Signal	Michael	Davis	987 Licolnway	Lenexa	KS	66444-4444	(913) 555-4444
16	Health Midwest	Jane	Eagan	201 Jackson St.	Overland Park	KS	66332-9999	(913) 555-1999
17	Cerner	Fritz	Bradley	887 Winger Rd.	Shawnee	KS	66111-8887	(913) 555-1777
18	EBC	Carl	Garrett	444 Metcalf	Overland Park	KS	66111-7777	(913) 555-1222
19	Royals	Peg	Foxhoven	554 Stadium Ln.	Raytown	MO	60124-1111	(816) 555-4777
20	St. Luke's	Amanda	Love	667 Birdie Ln.	Kansas City	MO	66888-5555	(816) 555-3338
21	Roche	Brittney	Hill	887 Foxtrot Ln.	Kansas City	KS	66777-2222	(913) 555-4222
22	Oak Hill	Callie	Jones	244 75th St.	Overland Park	MO	66887-7777	(913) 555-2211
23	Farmland	Marjorie	Donald	556 Cory Ave.	Mission Hills	KS	66222-2222	(913) 555-2233
24	Cardiac Rehab	Mildred	Wambold	600 Adair St.	Greenfield	MO	60022-2222	(816) 555-2266
25	First National	Irma	Mitchell	800 First St.	Fontanelle	MO	60033-0011	(816) 555-2244
26	IKON	Ralph	Gregory	500 Maple St.	Adair	MO	60044-0022	(816) 555-2288
27	St. Thomas	Frances	Gustaphson	400 Russel Ln.	Casey	MO	60055-0055	(816) 555-5556
28	CIO	Taylor	McKinsey	420 Locust St.	Lenexa	KS	66111-8899	(913) 555-1189
29	Four Winds	Cooper	Michaels	500 Sunset Blvd.	Manhattan	KS	65555-4444	(913) 555-2289
(AutoNumber)								

Record: 30 of 30

Datasheet View   NUM

New Record button

Moving datasheet columns

You can reorganize the fields in a datasheet by dragging the field name left or right. Figure A-11 shows how the mouse pointer changes to as the Email field is moved to the left. The black vertical line between the Fax and Birthdate fields represents the new location for the field you are moving. Release the mouse button when you have appropriately positioned the field.

FIGURE A-11: Moving a field

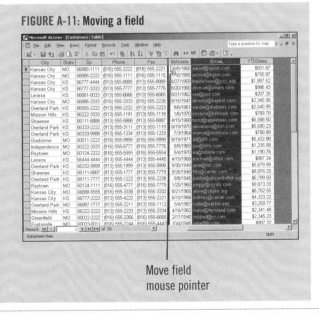

Move field mouse pointer

Access 2002

Editing Records

Updating existing information is another important daily task. To change the contents of an existing record, click the field you want to change, then type the new information. You can delete unwanted data by clicking the field and using the [Backspace] or [Delete] keys to delete text to the left or right of the insertion point. Other data entry keystrokes are summarized in Table A-5. Kelsey needs to make some corrections to the datasheet of the Customers table. She starts by correcting an error in the Street field of the first record.

1. **Press [Ctrl][Home] to move to the first record, click to the right of 111 Ash St. in the Street field, press [Backspace] three times to delete St., then type Dr.**
   When you are editing a record, the **edit record symbol**, which looks like a small pencil, appears in the record selector box to the left of the current record, as shown in Figure A-12.

2. **Click to the right of Hallmark in the Company field in record 8, press [Spacebar], type Cards, then press [↓] to move to the next record**
   You do not need to explicitly save new records or changes to existing records because Access saves the new data as soon as you move to another record or close the datasheet.

3. **Click Shawnee in the City field for record 17, then press [Ctrl]['']**
   The entry changes from "Shawnee" to "Overland Park." Pressing [Ctrl]['] inserts the data from the same field in the previous record.

4. **Click to the left of EBC in the Company field for record 18, press [Delete] to remove the E, press [Tab] to move to the next field, then type Doug**
   "EBC" becomes "BC" in the Company field, and "Doug" replaces "Carl" in the First field. Notice the edit record symbol in the record selector box to the left of record 18. Since you are still editing this record, you can undo the changes using the [Esc] key.

5. **Press [Esc]**
   The Doug entry changes back to Carl. Pressing [Esc] once removes the current field's editing changes.

6. **Press [Esc] again**
   Pressing [Esc] a second time removes all changes made to the record you are currently editing. The Company entry is restored to EBC. The ability to use [Esc] in Edit mode to remove data entry changes is dependent on whether or not you are still editing the record (as evidenced by the edit record symbol to the left of the record). Once you move to another record, the changes are saved, and you return to Navigation mode. In Navigation mode you can no longer use [Esc] to remove editing changes, but you can click the **Undo button** on the Table Database toolbar to undo the last change you made.

7. **Press [↓] to move to Peg in the First field of record 19, type Peggy, then press [↓] to move to record 20**
   Since you are no longer editing record 19, [Esc] has no effect on the last change.

QuickTip

The ScreenTip for the Undo button displays the action you can undo.

8. **Click the Undo button on the Table Datasheet toolbar**
   You undo the last edit and Peggy is changed back to Peg. Some areas of Access allow you to undo multiple actions, but a datasheet allows you to undo only your last action.

9. **Click anywhere in the Allied Signal (ID 15) record, click the Delete Record button on the Table Datasheet toolbar, then click Yes**
   The message warns that you cannot undo a record deletion operation. Notice that the Undo button is dimmed, indicating that it cannot be used at this time.

FIGURE A-12: Editing records

Print Preview button

Edit symbol

ID	Company	First	Last	Street	City	State	Zip	Phone
1	Sprint	Aaron	Friedrichsen	111 Ash Dr.	Kansas City	MO	66888-1111	(816) 555-2222
2	KGSM	Jacob	Douglas	222 Elm St.	Kansas City	MO	66888-2222	(816) 555-1111
3	JCCC	Douglas	Scott	333 Oak Dr.	Kansas City	KS	66777-4444	(913) 555-8888
4	Oliver's	Ann	Thomas	444 Apple St.	Kansas City	KS	66777-3333	(913) 555-7777
5	Podiatry Center	Todd	Vandenburg	555 Birch St.	Lenexa	KS	66661-0033	(913) 555-6666
6	Mohs Surgery	Glenn	Goldstein	666 Pine St.	Kansas City	MO	66886-3333	(816) 555-3333
7	Diabetes Center	Sandie	Anderson	777 Mulberry Way	Overland Park	KS	66555-2222	(913) 555-2222
8	Hallmark	Kristen	Reis	888 Fountain Dr.	Mission Hills	KS	66222-3333	(913) 555-1191
9	Applebee's	Tom	David	999 Riverside Dr.	Shawnee	KS	66111-8888	(913) 555-5888
10	IBM	Daniel	Arno	123 Wrigley Field	Overland Park	KS	66333-2222	(913) 555-3111
11	Motorola	Mark	Langguth	234 Wedd St.	Overland Park	KS	66333-9988	(913) 555-1234
12	PFS	David	Dahlgren	987 Front St.	Gladstone	MO	60011-2222	(816) 555-9999
13	Hills Pets	Jennifer	Wu	6788 Pine St.	Independence	MO	60222-3333	(816) 555-6777
14	LabOne	Emily	Ali	6789 Canyon Pl.	Raytown	MO	60124-2222	(816) 555-5555
15	Allied Signal	Michael	Davis	987 Licolnway	Lenexa	KS	66444-4444	(913) 555-4444
16	Health Midwest	Jane	Eagan	201 Jackson St.	Overland Park	KS	66332-9999	(913) 555-1999
17	Cerner	Fritz	Bradley	887 Winger Rd.	Shawnee	KS	66111-8887	(913) 555-1777
18	EBC	Carl	Garrett	444 Metcalf	Overland Park	KS	66111-7777	(913) 555-1222
19	Royals	Peg	Foxhoven	554 Stadium Ln.	Raytown	MO	60124-1111	(816) 555-4777
20	St. Luke's	Amanda	Love	667 Birdie Ln.	Kansas City	MO	66888-5555	(816) 555-3338
21	Roche	Brittney	Hill	887 Foxtrot Ln.	Kansas City	KS	66777-2222	(913) 555-4222
22	Oak Hill	Callie	Jones	244 75th St.	Overland Park	MO	66887-7777	(913) 555-2211
23	Farmland	Marjorie	Donald	556 Cory Ave.	Mission Hills	KS	66222-2222	(913) 555-2233
24	Cardiac Rehab	Mildred	Wambold	600 Adair St.	Greenfield	MO	60022-2222	(816) 555-2266
25	First National	Irma	Mitchell	800 First St.	Fontanelle	MO	60033-0011	(816) 555-2244

Record: 1 of 29

Datasheet View NUM

Insertion point

TABLE A-5: Edit mode keyboard shortcuts

editing keystroke	action
[Backspace]	Deletes one character to the left of the insertion point
[Delete]	Deletes one character to the right of the insertion point
[F2]	Switches between Edit and Navigation mode
[Esc]	Undoes the change to the current field
[Esc][Esc]	Undoes all changes to the current record
[F7]	Starts the spell check feature
[Ctrl][']	Inserts the value from the same field in the previous record into the current field
[Ctrl][;]	Inserts the current date in a Date field

CLUES TO USE

Resizing datasheet columns

You can resize the width of a field in a datasheet by dragging the thin black line that separates the field names to the left or right. The mouse pointer changes to ⟷ as you make the field wider or narrower.

Release the mouse button when you have resized the field. To adjust the column width to accommodate the widest entry in the field, double-click the thin black line that separates the field names.

Previewing and Printing a Datasheet

After entering and editing the records in a table, you can print the datasheet to obtain a hard copy of it. Before printing the datasheet, you should preview it to see how it will look when printed. Often you will want to make adjustments to margins and page orientation. ✎ Kelsey is ready to preview and print the datasheet.

QuickTip

If you want your name to appear on the printout, enter it as a new record in the datasheet before printing.

1. **Click the Print Preview button 🔍 on the Table Database toolbar**
   The datasheet appears as a miniature page in the Print Preview window, as shown in Figure A-14. The Print Preview toolbar provides options for printing, viewing more than one page, and sending the information to Word or Excel.

2. **Click the 🔍 pointer on the top of the datasheet**
   By magnifying this view of the datasheet, you can see Customers, the name of the table, in the center of the header. Today's date is positioned in the right section of the header.

3. **Scroll down to view the bottom of the page**
   The word "Page" and the current page number are positioned in the center of the footer.

4. **Click the Two Pages button 🔲 on the Print Preview toolbar**
   The navigation buttons in the lower-left corner are dimmed, indicating that the entire print-out fits on two pages. To make further changes, use the Page Setup dialog box.

5. **Click File on the menu bar, then click Page Setup**
   The Page Setup dialog box opens, as shown in Figure A-15. This dialog box provides options for changing margins, removing the headings (the header and footer), and changing page orientation from portrait (default) to landscape by using the Page tab.

6. **Double-click 1 in the Top text box, type 2, then click OK**
   The modified datasheet appears in the Print Preview window.

7. **Click the Print button 🖨 on the Print Preview toolbar, then click the Close button ⃞Close**
   The datasheet appears on the screen.

CLUES TO USE

Hiding fields

Sometimes you may not want all the fields of a datasheet to appear on the printout. To temporarily hide a field, click anywhere in the field, click Format on the menu bar, and then click Hide Columns. To redisplay the column, click Format, then click Unhide Columns. The Unhide Columns dialog box, shown in Figure A-13, opens. The unchecked boxes indicate which columns are currently hidden.

These fields are currently hidden

FIGURE A-13: Unhide Columns dialog box

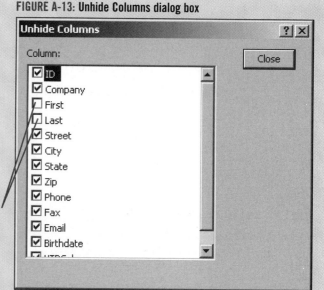

FIGURE A-14: Datasheet in print preview (portrait orientation)

Print Preview toolbar

Print button

Two pages button

Close button

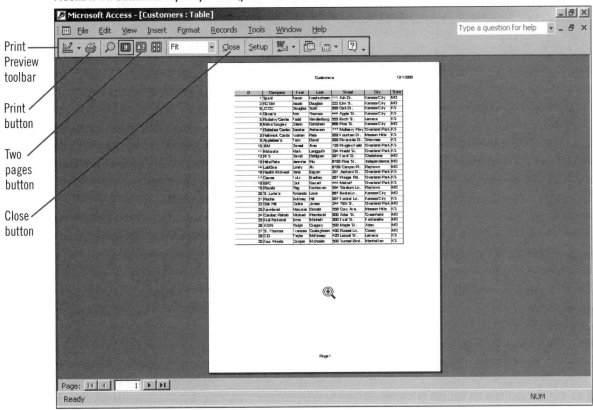

FIGURE A-15: Page Setup dialog box

Top margin measurement

Click the Page tab for page orientation options (portrait vs. landscape)

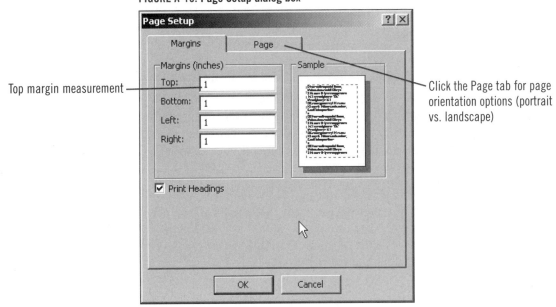

Access 2002

Getting Help and Exiting Access

When you have finished working in your database, you need to close the object you were working in, such as a table datasheet, and then close the database. To close a table, click File on the menu bar and then click Close, or click the object's Close button ⊠ located in the upper-right corner of the menu bar. Once you have closed all open objects, you can exit the program. As with most programs, if you try to exit Access and have not yet saved changes to open objects, Access will prompt you to save your changes. You can use the Help system to learn more about the program. ◄━━━ Kelsey has finished working with Access for now, so she closes the Customers table and MediaLoft-A database. Before exiting, she learns more about the Help system, and then exits Access.

1. **Click the Close button ⊠ for the Customers datasheet**
   If you make any structural changes to the datasheet such as moving, resizing, or hiding columns, you are prompted to save those changes. The MediaLoft-A database window is now active.

2. **Click the Close button ⊠ for the MediaLoft-A Database, as shown in Figure A-16**
   The MediaLoft-A database is closed, but Access is still running, so you could open another database or explore the Help system to learn more about Access.

3. **Click the Ask a question box, type naming fields, then press [Enter]**
   A list of potential Help topics that relate to your entry appears. Using the Help text box is similar to initiating keyword searches via the Office Assistant or using the Answer Wizard. Help menu options and terminology are further explained in Table A-6.

4. **Click About renaming a field in a table**
   The Help manual opens to the specific page that explains how to rename an existing field in a table. **Glossary terms** are shown as blue hyperlinks. Clicking a blue hyperlink displays a definition for that word in green text.

Trouble?

If you do not see the Contents, Answer Wizard, and Index tabs to the left of the Help window, click the Show Help button 🔲 on the Help toolbar.

5. **Click the Show All link in the upper-right corner of the Microsoft Access Help window**
   An expanded view of the Help page with all subcategories and definitions appears as shown in Figure A-17. The Show All link now becomes the Hide All link.

6. **Click the Contents tab, double-click Microsoft Access Help, double-click Working with Data, double-click Adding, Editing, or Deleting Data, click Delete a record, then click the Show All link in the upper-right corner of the Microsoft Access Help window**
   Searching for information by using the Contents tab is similar to locating information by starting with a broad Table of Contents, then continuing to narrow the subject matter into smaller areas.

7. **Click the Close button ⊠ for the Microsoft Access Help window**
   Whether you prefer to browse the Help manual by typing key words into the Ask a question box, drilling down through the Contents, interacting with the Office Assistant, or through some other method, it is important to realize that you're using the same Help system, but accessing it in different ways.

QuickTip

If your Project Files are stored on a floppy disk, do not remove your floppy disk from drive A until you have completely exited Access.

8. **Click File on the menu bar, then click Exit**

FIGURE A-16: Closing a database

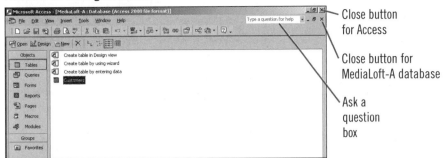

Close button for Access

Close button for MediaLoft-A database

Ask a question box

FIGURE A-17: Microsoft Access Help window

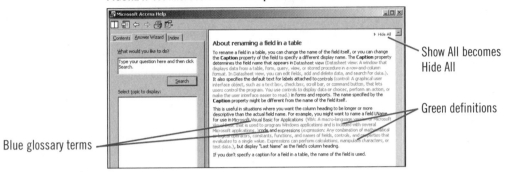

Show All becomes Hide All

Green definitions

Blue glossary terms

TABLE A-6: Help menu options

Help menu option	description
Microsoft Access Help	Opens the Office Assistant which prompts you for a keyword search of the Help manual
Show the Office Assistant	Presents the **Office Assistant**, an automated character that provides tips and interactive prompts while you are working
Hide the Office Assistant	Temporarily closes the Office Assistant for the working session
What's This	Changes the mouse pointer to ⬚?. Click an area, icon, or menu option using this special mouse pointer to get a short description of that item.
Office on the Web	If you are connected to the Web, provides additional Microsoft information and support articles stored at the Microsoft Web site
Sample Databases	Provides easy access to the sample databases installed with Access 2002
Detect and Repair	Analyzes a database for possible data corruption and attempts to repair problems
About Microsoft Access	Provides the version and product ID of Access

Compact on Close

The Compact on Close option found on the General tab of the Options dialog box compacts and repairs your database each time you close it. To open the Options dialog box, click Tools on the menu bar, and then click Options. While the Compact on Close feature works extremely well if your database is stored on your hard drive or on another large storage device, it can cause problems if your Project File is stored on a floppy disk. The Compact on Close process creates a temporary file that is just as large as the original database file. This temporary file is used during the compaction process, and is deleted after the procedure successfully finishes. Therefore, if your database file grows larger than half of the available storage space on your floppy disk, the Compact on Close process will not be able to create the necessary temporary file or successfully compact the database. Such an error might result in a harmless error message or, in the worst case, a corrupt database.

Practice

► Concepts Review

Label each element of the Access window shown in Figure A-18.

FIGURE A-18

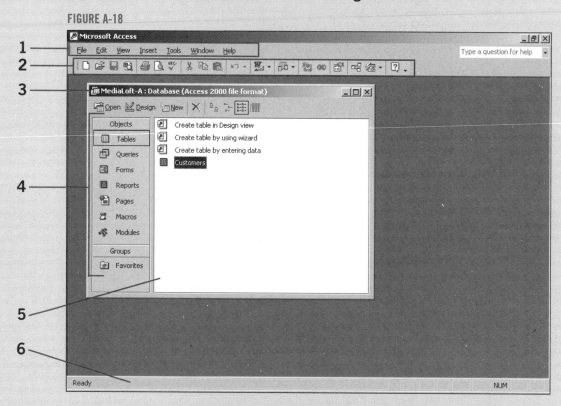

Match each term with the statement that describes it.

7. **Objects**
8. **Table**
9. **Record**
10. **Field**
11. **Datasheet**

a. A group of related fields, such as all of the demographic information for one customer
b. A collection of records for a single subject, such as all the customer records
c. A category of information in a table, such as a customer's name, city, or state
d. A spreadsheet-like grid that displays fields as columns and records as rows
e. Seven types of these are contained in an Access database and are used to enter, enhance, and use the data within the database

Select the best answer from the list of choices.

12. **Which of the following is NOT a typical benefit of relational databases?**
   a. Easier data entry
   b. Faster information retrieval
   c. Minimized duplicate data entry
   d. Automatic trend analysis

13. **Which of the following is NOT an advantage of managing data with a relational database versus a spreadsheet?**
   a. Doesn't require planning before data is entered
   b. Allows links between lists of information
   c. Provides greater security
   d. Allows multiple users to enter data simultaneously

14. The object that holds all of the data within an Access database is the:
   a. Query.
   b. Table.
   c. Form.
   d. Report.

15. The object that provides an easy-to-use data entry screen is the:
   a. Table.
   b. Query.
   c. Form.
   d. Report.

16. What displays messages regarding the current database operation?
   a. Status bar
   b. Title bar
   c. Database toolbar
   d. Object tabs

► Skills Review

1. Define database software.
   a. Identify five disadvantages of using a noncomputerized system to organize database information.
   b. Identify five advantages of managing database information in Access versus using a spreadsheet.

2. Learn database terminology.
   a. Explain the relationship between a field, a record, a table, and a database.
   b. Identify the seven objects of an Access database, and explain the main purpose of each.
   c. Which object of an Access database is most important? Why?

3. Start Access and open a database.
   a. Click the Start button, point to Programs, then click Microsoft Access.
   b. Open the **Recycle-A** database from the drive and location where your Project Files are stored.
   c. Identify the following items. (*Hint*: To create a printout of any screen, press [Print Screen] to capture an image of the screen to the Windows clipboard, start any word-processing program, then click the Paste button. Print the document that now contains a picture of the opening database window, and identify the elements on the printout.)
   • Database toolbar
   • Recycle-A database window
   • Menu bar
   • Object buttons
   • Objects bar
   • Status bar

4. View the database window.
   a. Maximize both the Access window and the Recycle-A database window.
   b. Click each of the Object buttons, then write down the object names of each type that exist in the Recycle-A database.

5. Navigate records.
   a. Open the Clubs table.
   b. Press [Tab] or [Enter] to move through the fields of the first record.
   c. Press [Shift][Tab] to move backward through the fields of the first record.
   d. Press [Ctrl][End] to move to the last field of the last record.
   e. Press [Ctrl][Home] to move to the first field of the first record.
   f. Click the Last Record navigation button to quickly move to the Oak Hill Patriots record.

6. Enter records.

a. In the Clubs table, click the New Record button, then add the following two records:

Name	Street	City	State	Zip	Phone	FName	LName	Club Number
EBC Angels	10100 Metcalf	Overland Park	KS	66001	555-7711	Steve	Grigsby	8
Friends of the Zoo	111 Holmes	Kansas City	MO	65001	555-8811	Jim	Wheeler	9

b. Move the Club Number field from the last column of the datasheet to the first column.

7. Edit records.

a. In the Clubs table, change the Name field in the first record from Jaycees to **JC Club**.

b. Change the Name field in the second record from Boy Scouts #1 to **Oxford Cub Scouts**.

c. Change the LName field in the fifth record from Perry to **Griffiths**.

d. Enter your name and unique information as a new record using **99** as the Club Number.

e. Delete the record for Club Number 8.

8. Preview and print a datasheet.

a. Preview the Clubs table datasheet.

b. Use the Page Setup option on the File menu to change the page orientation from portrait to landscape.

c. Print the Clubs table datasheet.

9. Get Help and exit Access.

a. Close the Clubs table object, saving the changes.

b. Close the Recycle-A database, but leave Access running.

c. Search for the Help topics by entering the keyword **subdatasheet** into the Ask a question box. Click the link for the About subdatasheets option.

d. Click the Show All link to display all of the glossary terms, then click the Print button on the Help window toolbar to print that page.

e. Close the Microsoft Access Help window.

f. Exit Access.

► Independent Challenge 1

Ten examples of database tables are given below. For each example, write a brief answer for the following.

a. What field names would you expect to find in each table?

b. Provide an example of two possible records for each table.

- Telephone directory
- College course offerings
- Restaurant menu
- Cookbook
- Movie listing
- Encyclopedia
- Shopping catalog
- Corporate inventory
- Party guest list
- Members of the House of Representatives

Independent Challenge 2

You are working with several civic groups to coordinate a community-wide cleanup effort. You have started a database called Recycle-A that tracks the clubs, their trash deposits, and the trash centers that are participating.

a. Start Access.

b. Open the **Recycle-A** database from the location where your Project Files are stored, then write down the number of records and fields in each of the tables.

c. Open the datasheet for the Centers table. An expand button appears as a small plus sign to the left of the Name field for each record. Click the expand button to the left of each of the records in the Centers datasheet. A subdatasheet for each Center will appear. Count the records in each subdatasheet. How many records are in the subdatasheets, and what does this tell you about the relationship between the Centers and Deposits tables?

d. Close the Centers table, and then open the datasheet for the Clubs table. Click the expand button to the left of each of the Club records and count the records in each subdatasheet. How many records are in the subdatasheets, and what does this tell you about the relationship between the Clubs and Deposits tables?

e. Close the Clubs table, then exit Access.

▶ Independent Challenge 3

You are working with several civic groups to coordinate a community-wide cleanup effort. You have started a database called Recycle-A that tracks the clubs, their trash deposits, and the trash centers that are participating.

a. Start Access and open the **Recycle-A** database from the location where your Project Files are stored.

b. Add the following records to the Clubs table:

Club Number	Name	Street	City	State	Zip	Phone	FName	LName
10	Take Pride	222 Lincoln Way	Olathe	KS	66001	555-2211	David	Reis
11	Cub Scouts #321	333 Ward Pkwy.	Kansas City	MO	65002	555-8800	Jacob	Langguth

c. Edit the following records in the Clubs table. The Street field has changed for Club Number 6 and the Phone and FName fields have changed for Club Number 7.

Club Number	Name	Street	City	State	Zip	Phone	FName	LName
6	Girl Scouts #1	55 Oak Terrace	Shawnee	KS	68777	555-4444	Jonathan	Bacon
7	Oak Hill Patriots	888 Switzer	Overland Park	KS	66444	555-9988	Cynthia	Ralston

d. If you haven't entered a record containing your own information, enter this record using **99** as the Club Number.

e. Print the datasheet.

f. Close the Clubs table, close the Recycle-A database, then exit Access.

Independent Challenge 4

The World Wide Web can be used to research information about almost any topic. In this exercise, you'll go to Microsoft's Web site for Access, and explore what's new about Access 2002.

a. Connect to the Internet, and use your browser to go to the www.microsoft.com/access Web page.

b. Web sites change often, but there will probably be a link that provides a tour of Access 2002, or an introduction to Access 2002. Click that link and follow the tour or introduction. Based on what you learned, describe two new things that you discovered about Access 2002.

c. Go back to the www.microsoft.com/access or www.microsoft.com/office Web page, then click the appropriate hyperlinks to find out how Office XP suites are organized. You might find this information within a pricing or ordering link. Find the Web page that describes what is included in the various Office XP suites and print it. On the printout, identify which suites include Access.

 Visual Workshop

Open the **Recycle-A** database from the drive and folder where your Project Files are stored, then open the Centers table datasheet. Modify the records in the existing Centers table to reflect the changes shown in Figure A-19. The Street field for the first record has changed, the ContactLast field for the first three records have changed, and two new records have been added. Also, enter a new record using your name as the contact with **99** as the Center Number. Print the datasheet, close the Centers table, close the Recycle-A database, then exit Access.

FIGURE A-19

	Center Nu	Name	Street	City	State	Zip	Phone	ContactFirst	ContactLast	Hazardous
+	1	Trash 'R Us	989 Main St.	Lenexa	KS	61111	555-7777	Ben	Garrett	☑
+	2	You Deliver	12345 College	Overland Park	KS	63444	555-2222	Jerry	Welch	☑
+	3	County Landfill	12444 Pflumm	Lenexa	KS	64222	555-4422	Jerry	Anderson	☐
+	4	Cans and Stuff	543 Holmes	Kansas City	MO	60011	555-2347	Gretchen	Pratt	☐
+	5	We Love Trash	589 Oak St.	Kansas City	KS	60022	555-3456	Mitchell	Arno	☑
*										▒

Record: I◄ ◄ 1 ► ►I ►* of 5

Using
Tables and Queries

Now that you are familiar with some of the basic Access terminology and features, you are ready to plan and build your own database. Your first task is to create the tables that store the data. Once the tables are created and the data is entered, you can use several techniques for finding specific information in the database, including sorting, filtering, and building queries. ◢▬▬ Kelsey Lang, a marketing manager at MediaLoft, wants to build and maintain a database containing information about MediaLoft's products. The information in the database will be useful when Kelsey provides information for future sales promotions.

Access 2002

Planning a Database

The most important object in a database is the table object. Tables store the **raw data**, the individual pieces of information stored in the fields in the database. When you design a table, you identify the fields of information the table will contain and the type of data to be stored in each field. Some databases contain multiple tables linked together. Kelsey plans her database containing information about MediaLoft's products.

Details

In planning a database it is important to:

▶ **Determine the purpose of the database and give it a meaningful name**
The database will store information about MediaLoft's music products. You decide to name the database MediaLoft, and name the first table Music Inventory.

▶ **Determine what reports you want the database to produce**
You want to be able to print inventory reports that list the products by artist, type of product (CD, cassette, minidisk), quantity in stock, and price. These pieces of information will become the fields in the Music Inventory table.

▶ **Collect the raw data that will be stored in the database**
The raw data for MediaLoft's products might be stored on index cards, in paper reports, and in other electronic formats, such as word processing documents, spreadsheets, or accounting system files. You can use Access to import data from many other electronic sources, which greatly increases the efficiency of your data entry.

▶ **Sketch the structure of each table, including field names and data types**
Using the data you collected, identify the field name and data type for each field in each table as shown in Figure B-1. The **data type** determines what type of information you can enter in a field. For example, a field with a Currency data type does *not* accept text. Properly defining the data type for each field helps you maintain data consistency and accuracy. Table B-1 lists the data types available within Access.

CLUES TO USE

Choosing between the Text and Number data type

When assigning data types, avoid choosing the Number data type for a telephone or zip code field. Although these fields generally contain numbers, they should still be Text data types. Consider the following: You may want to enter 1-800-BUY-BOOK in a telephone number field. This would not be possible if the field is designated as a Number data type. Also, when you sort the fields, you want them to sort alphabetically, like Text fields. For example, with the zip codes 60011 and 50011-8888, if the zip code field is designated as a Number data type, the zip codes would be interpreted incorrectly as the values 60,011 and 500,118,888, and sorted in that order, too.

FIGURE B-1: Music Inventory fields and data types

Field Name	Data Type
RecordingID	AutoNumber
RecordingTitle	Text
RecordingArtist	Text
MusicCategory	Text
RecordingLabel	Text
Format	Text
NumberofTracks	Number
PurchasePrice	Currency
RetailPrice	Currency
Notes	Memo

TABLE B-1: Data types

data type	description of data	size
Text	Text information or combinations of text and numbers, such as a street address, name, or phone number	Up to 255 characters
Memo	Lengthy text such as comments or notes	Up to 65,536 characters
Number	Numeric information used in calculations, such as quantities	Several sizes available to store numbers with varying degrees of precision
Date/Time	Dates and times	Size controlled by Access to accommodate dates and times across thousands of years (for example, 1/1/1850 and 1/1/2150 are valid dates)
Currency	Monetary values	Size controlled by Access; accommodates up to 15 digits to the left of the decimal point and four digits to the right
AutoNumber	Integers assigned by Access to sequentially order each record added to a table	Size controlled by Access
Yes/No	Only one of two values stored (Yes/No, On/Off, True/False)	Size controlled by Access
OLE Object	Objects and files linked or embedded (OLE) that are created in other programs, such as pictures, sound clips, documents or spreadsheets	Up to one gigabyte
Hyperlink	Web addresses	Size controlled by Access
Lookup Wizard	Invokes a wizard that helps link the current table to another table or list through the current field.	Size controlled through the choices made in the Lookup Wizard

Access 2002

Creating a Table

After you plan the structure of the table, your next step is to create the actual database file. This file will eventually contain the table and all of the other objects within the database file such as queries, forms, and reports. When you create a database, you start by naming it, and then you can build the first table object and enter data. Access offers several methods for creating the database and the first table. For example, you can import a table from another data source such as a spreadsheet, or use the Access **Table Wizard** to create a table from scratch. The Table Wizard provides interactive help to create the field names and data types for each field. ✎ Kelsey is ready to create the MediaLoft database. She uses the Table Wizard to create the Music Inventory table.

Trouble?

If the task pane does not appear in the Access window, click File on the menu bar, then click New.

1. Start Access, click the **Blank Database link** in the New section of the task pane as shown in Figure B-2
   The File New Database dialog box opens.

2. Type **MediaLoft** in the File name text box, click the **Save in list arrow**, navigate to the drive and folder where your Project Files are stored, then click **Create**
   The MediaLoft database file is created and saved where your Project Files are stored. There are many ways to create the first table in the database, but the Table Wizard offers an efficient and easy way to get started.

Trouble?

If the Create table by using wizard option does not appear in the database window, click Tools on the menu bar, then click Options. On the View tab, make sure that the New object shortcuts check box is selected, then click OK.

3. Double-click **Create table by using wizard** in the MediaLoft Database window
   The Table Wizard dialog box opens, as shown in Figure B-3. The Table Wizard offers 25 business and 20 personal sample tables from which you can select sample fields. The Recordings sample table in the Personal database category most closely matches the fields you want to include in the Music Inventory table.

4. Click the **Personal option button**, scroll down and click **Recordings** in the Sample Tables list box, then click the **Select All Fields button** >>
   At this point, you can change the suggested field names to better match your needs.

5. Click **RecordingArtistID** in the Fields in my new table list box, click **Rename Field**, type **RecordingArtist** in the Rename field text box, then click **OK**

6. Click **Next**
   The second Table Wizard dialog box allows you to name the table and determine if Access should set the **primary key**, a special field that contains unique information for each record in a table.

Trouble?

If you are viewing an empty datasheet, click the Design View button 🔲 on the Table Datasheet toolbar.

7. Type **Music Inventory**, make sure the **Yes, set a primary key for me option button** is selected, click **Next**, click the **Modify the table design option button**, then click **Finish**
   The table opens in Design View, shown in Figure B-4, which allows you to add, delete, or modify the fields in the table. The **key symbol** indicates that the RecordingID field has been designated as the primary key field.

FIGURE B-2: New File task pane

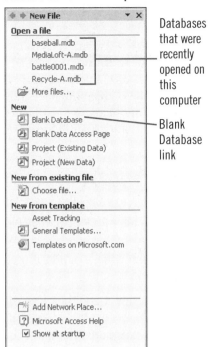

Databases that were recently opened on this computer

Blank Database link

FIGURE B-3: Table Wizard

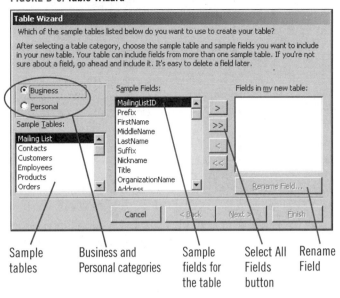

Sample tables

Business and Personal categories

Sample fields for the table

Select All Fields button

Rename Field

FIGURE B-4: Music Inventory table in Design view

Music Inventory table

Key field symbol

Field names

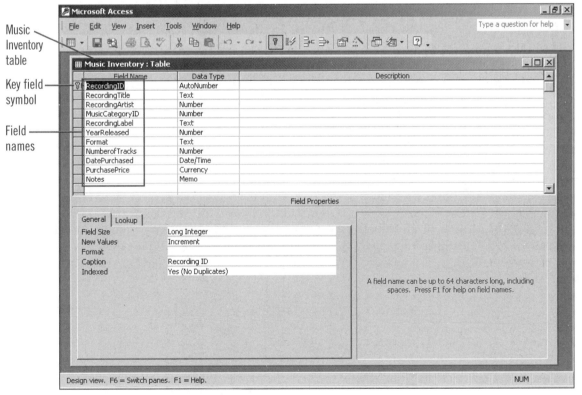

Modifying a Table

Each database object has a **Design View** in which you can modify its structure. The Design View of a table allows you to add or delete fields, add **field descriptions**, or change other field properties. Field **properties** are additional characteristics of a field such as its size or default value. Using the Table Wizard, Kelsey was able to create a Music Inventory table very quickly. Now in Design View she further modifies the fields to meet her specific needs. MediaLoft doesn't track purchase dates or release dates, but it does need to store retail price information in the database.

QuickTip

Deleting a field from a table deletes any data stored in that field for all records in the table!

1. In Design View of the Music Inventory table, click **DatePurchased** in the Field Name column, click the **Delete Rows button** on the Table Design toolbar, click **YearReleased** in the Field Name column, click to delete the field, click the **Notes** field, then click the **Insert Rows button**

   The Year Released and Date Purchased fields are deleted from the table. A new row appears above the Notes field in which you can enter a new field name.

QuickTip

You can also choose a data type by pressing its first letter such as C for Currency.

2. Type **RetailPrice**, press **[Tab]**, click the **Data Type list arrow**, then click **Currency**

   The new field is added to the Music Inventory table, as shown in Figure B-5. Both the RecordingArtist and MusicCategoryID fields have a Number data type, but it should be Text.

3. Click the **Number** Data Type for the RecordingArtist field, click the **Data Type list arrow**, click **Text**, click the **Number** Data Type for the MusicCategoryID field, click the **Data Type list arrow**, then click **Text**

   Now, descriptive words can be entered in these fields rather than just numbers. You must work in the Design View of a table to make structural changes to fields such as changing the data type.

4. Click to the right of **MusicCategoryID**, press **[Backspace]** twice to delete ID, then click the **Save button** on the Table Design toolbar

   Field names can include any combination of letters, numbers and spaces, up to 64 characters long. The only special characters that are not allowed include the period (.), exclamation point (!), accent grave (`), and square brackets [ ]. Field descriptions are optional, but help to further describe the field.

QuickTip

The Field Description entry appears in the status bar when that field has the focus in Datasheet View.

5. Click the **MusicCategory Description cell**, then type **classical, country, folk, gospel, jazz, new age, rap, or rock**

   The **Field Size** property limits the number of characters allowed for each field.

6. Make sure the **MusicCategory** field is still selected, double-click **50** in the Field Size cell, then type **9**

   The longest entry in the MusicCategory field, classical, is only nine characters. The finished Music Inventory table Design View should look like Figure B-6.

QuickTip

The Datasheet View button becomes the Design View button when working in Datasheet View.

7. Click the **Datasheet View button** on the Table Design toolbar, click **Yes** to save the table, then type the following record into the new datasheet:

in field:	type:	in field:	type:
Recording ID	[Tab]	Format	CD
Recording Title	No Words	Number of Tracks	12
RecordingArtist	Brickman, Jim	Purchase Price	10
Music Category ID	New Age	RetailPrice	13
Recording Label	Windham Hill	Notes	[Tab]

8. Close the Music Inventory table, then close the MediaLoft database

   Data is saved automatically, so you were not prompted to save the record when you closed the datasheet.

FIGURE B-5: Music Inventory table with new RetailPrice field

Save button

Datasheet View button

DatePurchased and YearReleased fields are deleted

RetailPrice field is selected

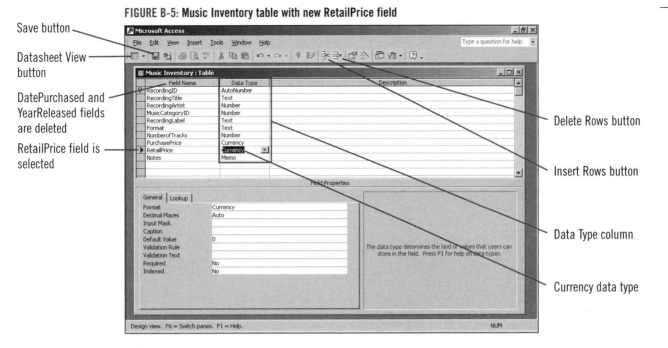

Delete Rows button

Insert Rows button

Data Type column

Currency data type

FIGURE B-6: Modifying field properties

MusicCategory field name changed

MusicCategory field is selected

Field Size entry changed from 50 to 9

Field Properties pane

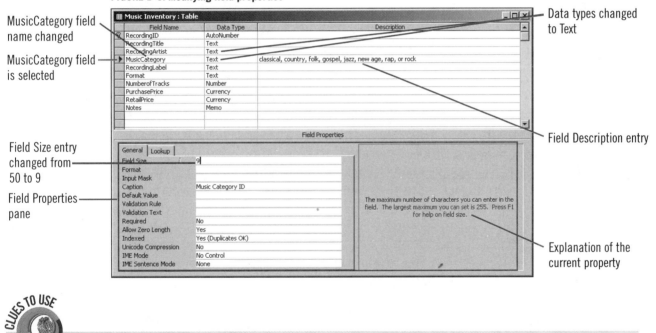

Data types changed to Text

Field Description entry

Explanation of the current property

CLUES TO USE

Learning about field properties

Properties are the characteristics that define the field. Two properties are required for every field: Field Name and Data Type. Many other properties, such as Field Size, Format, Caption, and Default Value are defined in the Field Properties pane found in the Design View of the table. As you add more property entries, you are generally restricting the amount or type of data that can be entered in the field, which in turn increases data entry accuracy. For example, you might change the Field Size property for a State field to 2 in order to eliminate an incorrect entry such as FLL. The Field Properties change depending on the data type of the selected field. For example, there would be no Field Size property for a Birth Date field, because Access controls the size of fields with a Date/Time data type. The Caption property is used to override the field name with an easy-to-read caption on datasheets, forms, and reports. Database designers often insist on field names without spaces because they are easier to reference in other Access objects. Yet database *users* would rather view field names with spaces when entering data. That's why the tables created by the wizards have field names without spaces, but display more readable captions on the datasheet.

Formatting a Datasheet

Although you primarily use the report object to create professional printouts from an Access database, you can print a datasheet too. Although you cannot create custom headings or insert graphic images on a datasheet as you can with a report, you can change the fonts, colors, and gridlines to dramatically change the appearance of the datasheet. Kelsey has entered some information about MediaLoft's music products into the Music Inventory table of the MediaLoft-B database. Now she will print the Music Inventory datasheet after formatting it with a new font and gridline color.

1. Click the **Open button** on the Database toolbar, select the **MediaLoft-B** database from the drive and folder where your Project Files are stored, then click **Open**

2. Click the **Music Inventory** table in the MediaLoft-B database window, then click the **Open button** on the database window toolbar

   The Music Inventory table on the Database window toolbar contains 58 records, as shown in Figure B-7. Formatting options for a datasheet are found on the Format menu or on the Formatting (Datasheet) toolbar. When you format a datasheet, every record in the datasheet is formatted the same way.

3. Click **Format** on the menu bar, click **Font**, scroll and click **Comic Sans MS** in the Font list, then click **OK**

   Comic Sans MS is an informal font that simulates handwritten text, but is still very readable. By default, the Formatting (Datasheet) toolbar does not appear in Datasheet View, but toolbars are easily turned on and off using the View menu.

4. Click **View** on the menu bar, point to **Toolbars**, then click **Formatting (Datasheet)**.

   The Formatting (Datasheet) toolbar contains the most common formatting options for changing the font, colors, and gridlines of the datasheet.

5. Click the **Line/Border Color button list arrow**, click the **red** box, click the **Gridlines button list arrow**, then click the **Gridlines: Horizontal** box

   In addition to formatting changes, you may wish to change the page setup options before you print a datasheet.

6. Select **Cook, Jesse** in the Artist field of the first record, type your last name, your first name, click **File** on the menu bar, click **Page Setup**, click the **Page tab**, click the **Landscape option button**, then click **OK**

   Your name is in the Artist field of the first record to uniquely identify your printout.

7. Click the **Print Preview button** on the Table Datasheet toolbar, click the **Next Page button** in the Print Preview Navigation buttons to view page 2, then click the **Print button**

   The First Page and Previous Page buttons will be dimmed if you are viewing the first page of the datasheet. The Next Page and Last Page buttons will be dimmed if you are viewing the last page of the datasheet. By default, the table name and current date print in the datasheet header, and the page number prints in the datasheet footer as shown in Figure B-8.

8. Click the **Close button** for the preview window, click **No** when asked to save the changes to the layout of the table, double-click the **Music Inventory** table to reopen the datasheet, then study the first record

   The font and gridline formatting changes were *not* saved when you answered No to the question about saving changes to the layout. Your name entry in the Artist field of the first record *was* automatically saved by Access. Remember, all data entries and data edits are automatically saved as you move between records or close a datasheet.

FIGURE B-7: Music Inventory table datasheet

	RecordingID	Title	Artist	Category	Label	Format	Tracks	V
▶	1	Gravity	Cook, Jesse	New Age	Columbia	CD	15	
	2	Come Walk With Me	Adams, Oleta	Gospel	CBS Records	CD	10	
	3	Greatest Hits	Winans, BeBe & CeCe	Gospel	Benson	Vinyl	9	
	4	Tribute	Yanni	New Age	MCA	CD	10	
	5	World Café	Tree Frogs	Rap	New Stuff	CD	12	
	6	Relationships	Winans, BeBe & CeCe	Gospel	Capitol	CD	14	
	7	No Words	Brickman, Jim	New Age	Windham Hill	CD	10	
	8	God's Property	Nu Nation	Rap	B-Rite Music	Cassette	13	
	9	Message	4 Him	Gospel	Benson	CD	13	
	10	Sacred Road	Lantz, David	New Age	Narada	Cassette	12	
	11	Mariah Carey	Carey, Mariah	Rock	Columbia	CD	11	
	12	Ironman Triathlon	Tesh, John	New Age	GTS Records	Cassette	9	
	13	Daydream	Carey, Mariah	Rock	Columbia	CD	12	
	14	Heartsounds	Lantz, David	New Age	Narada	CD	14	
	15	The Roches	Roches, The	Folk	Warner Bros. Records	Cassette	10	
	16	Can We Go Home Now	Roches, The	Folk	Ryko	CD	11	
	17	Live at the Red Rocks	Tesh, John	New Age	GTS Records	CD	16	
	18	I'll Lead You Home	Smith, Michael	Gospel	Reunion	CD	14	
	19	Winter Song	Tesh, John	New Age	GTS Records	CD	12	
	20	December	Winston, George	New Age	Windham	CD	12	
	21	Time, Love & Tenderness	Bolton, Michael	Rock	Sony Music	CD	10	

Record: ⏮ ◀ 1 ▶ ⏭ ▶* of ⟨58⟩

58 total records

FIGURE B-8: Previewing the formatted datasheet

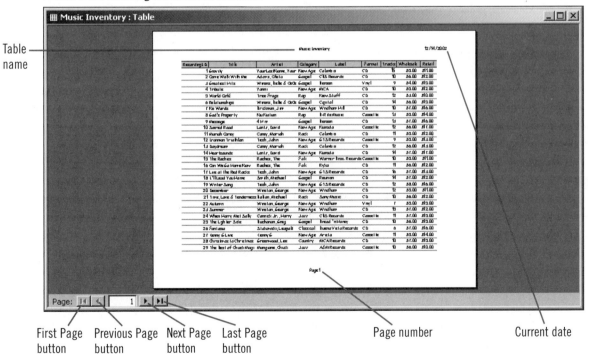

Table name

First Page button   Previous Page button   Next Page button   Last Page button   Page number   Current date

Understanding Sorting, Filtering, and Finding

The records of a datasheet are automatically sorted according to the data in the primary key field. Often, however, you may want to view or print records in an entirely different sort order, or you may want to display a subset of the records, such as those within the same music category or those below a certain retail price. Access makes it easy to sort, find data, and filter a datasheet by using buttons on the Table Datasheet toolbar, summarized in Table B-2.  Kelsey studies the sort, find, and filter features to better learn how to find and retrieve information.

► **Sorting** refers to reorganizing the records in either ascending or descending order based on the contents of a field. In ascending order, Text fields sort from A to Z, Number and Currency fields from the lowest to the highest value, and Date/Time fields from the oldest date to the date furthest into the future. In Figure B-9 the Music Inventory table has been sorted in ascending order on the Artist field. Notice that in a Text field, numbers sort before letters.

► **Filtering** means temporarily isolating a subset of records, as shown in Figure B-10. For example, by using a filter, you can produce a listing of all music with the value "Rock" in the Category field. To redisplay all of the records in the datasheet, click the Remove Filter button. The filtered subset can be formatted and printed just like the entire datasheet.

► **Finding** refers to locating a specific piece of data, such as "Amy." The Find and Replace dialog box is shown in Figure B-11. The options in this dialog box are summarized below.

- **Find What:** Provides a text box for your search criteria. The search criteria might be Amy, Beatles, or Capitol Records.

- **Look In:** Determines whether Access looks for the search criteria in the current field or in the entire datasheet.

- **Match:** Determines whether the search criteria must exactly match the contents of the whole field, any part of the field, or the start of the field.

- **Search:** Allows you to search the entire datasheet (All) or just those records before (Up) or after (Down) the current record.

- **Match Case:** Determines whether the search criteria is case sensitive (e.g., NH vs. Nh vs. nh).

- **Search Fields As Formatted:** Determines whether the search criteria is compared to the actual value of the field or the formatted appearance of the value (e.g., 10 vs. $10.00).

- **Replace tab:** Provides a Replace With text box for you to specify replacement text. For example, you can find every occurrence of CD and replace it with Compact Disc.

Using wildcards

Wildcards are symbols you use as substitutes for characters to locate data that matches your Find criteria. Access uses these wildcards: the **asterisk (*)** represents any group of characters, the **question mark (?)** stands for any single character, and the **pound sign (#)** stands for a single number digit. For example, to find any word beginning with S, type s* in the Find What text box.

FIGURE B-9: Music Inventory datasheet sorted by Artist

Records are sorted in ascending order by Artist

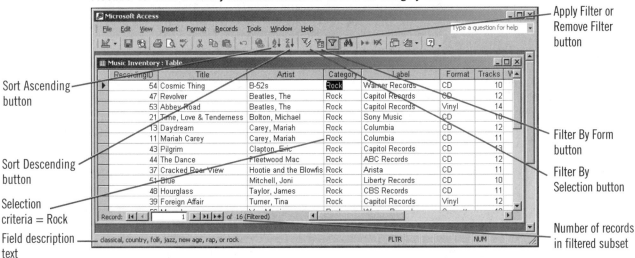

FIGURE B-10: Music Inventory datasheet filtered for Rock in the Category field

Apply Filter or Remove Filter button

Sort Ascending button

Sort Descending button

Selection criteria = Rock

Field description text

Filter By Form button

Filter By Selection button

Number of records in filtered subset

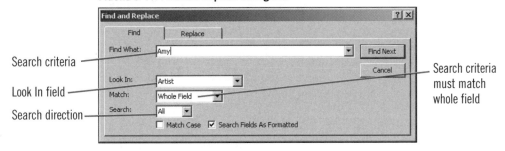

FIGURE B-11: Find and Replace dialog box

Search criteria

Look In field

Search direction

Search criteria must match whole field

TABLE B-2: Sort, Filter, and Find buttons

name	button	purpose
Sort Ascending	⏬	Sorts records based on the selected field in ascending order (0 to 9, A to Z)
Sort Descending	⏫	Sorts records based on the selected field in descending order (Z to A, 9 to 0)
Filter By Selection	⏣	Filters records based on selected data and hides records that do not match
Filter By Form	⏲	Filters records based on more than one selection criteria by using the Filter By Form window
Apply Filter or Remove Filter	▽	Applies or removes the filter
Find	🔍	Searches for a string of characters in the current field or all fields

Sorting Records and Finding Data

The sort and find features are powerful tools that help you work more efficiently whether you are working with data in a datasheet or viewing it through a form. ✒ Kelsey needs to create several different printouts of the Music Inventory datasheet to satisfy various departments. The marketing department wants the records sorted by Title and by Artist. The accounting department wants the records sorted from the highest retail price to the lowest.

Steps 1234

1. **In the Music Inventory datasheet, click any value in the Title field, then click the Sort Ascending button [⬇] on the Table Datasheet toolbar**
   The records are sorted in ascending order by the values in the Title field, as shown in Figure B-12.

2. **Click any cell in the Artist field, then click [⬇]**
   The records are sorted in ascending order by the values in the Artist field.

3. **Scroll to the right to view the Retail field, click any value in the Retail field, then click the Sort Descending button [⬆] on the Table Datasheet toolbar**
   The products that sell for the highest retail price are listed first. Access also lets you find all records based on search criteria.

4. **Click any value in the Title field, then click the Find button [🔍] on the Table Datasheet toolbar**
   The Find and Replace dialog box opens with Title selected as the Look In field. You have been asked to find the titles that may be hot sellers during the Christmas season.

5. **Type Christmas in the Find What text box, click the Match list arrow, then click Any Part of Field, as shown in Figure B-13**
   "Christmas" is the search criteria. Access will find all occurrences of the word Christmas in the Title field, whether it is the first, middle, or last part of the title.

6. **Click Find Next, then drag the title bar of the Find and Replace dialog box up and to the right to better view the datasheet**
   If you started the search at the top of the datasheet, A Family Christmas is the first title found.

7. **Click Find Next to find the next occurrence of the word Christmas, then click Find Next as many times as it takes to move through all the records**
   When no more occurrences of the search criteria Christmas are found, Access provides a dialog box that tells you that no more matching records can be found.

8. **Click OK when prompted that Access has finished searching the records, then click Cancel to close the Find and Replace dialog box**

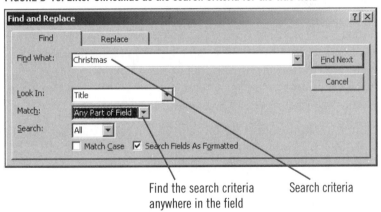

RecordingID	Title	Artist	Category	Label	Format	Tracks	V
55	A Christmas Album	Grant, Amy	Folk	Reunion Records	CD	11	
46	A Family Christmas	Tesh, John	New Age	GTS Records	CD	14	
32	A Winter's Solstice	Windham Hill Artists	New Age	Windham	CD	10	
53	Abbey Road	Beatles, The	Rock	Capitol Records	Vinyl	14	
22	Autumn	Winston, George	New Age	Windham	Vinyl	7	
51	Blue	Mitchell, Joni	Rock	Liberty Records	CD	10	
16	Can We Go Home Now	Roches, The	Folk	Ryko	CD	11	
35	Christmas	Mannheim Steamroller	New Age	Sony Music	CD	11	
28	Christmas to Christmas	Greenwood, Lee	Country	MCA Records	CD	10	
31	Closeup	Sandborn, David	Jazz	MCA Records	Cassette	10	
2	Come Walk With Me	Adams, Oleta	Gospel	CBS Records	CD	10	
54	Cosmic Thing	B-52s	Rock	Warner Records	CD	10	
37	Cracked Rear View	Hootie and the Blowfis	Rock	Arista	CD	11	
13	Daydream	Carey, Mariah	Rock	Columbia	CD	12	
52	Decade	Young, Neil	Rock	A&M Records	CD	10	
20	December	Winston, George	New Age	Windham	CD	12	
26	Fantasia	Stokowski, Leopold	Classical	Buena Vista Records	CD	6	
40	Favorite Overtures	Bernstein, Leonard	Classical	CBS Records	Vinyl	5	
39	Foreign Affair	Turner, Tina	Rock	Capitol Records	Vinyl	12	
42	Garth Brooks Live	Brooks, Garth	Country	Liberty Records	CD	10	
8	God's Property	Nu Nation	Rap	B-Rite Music	Cassette	13	

Record: 1 of 58

Records are sorted ascending by Title

FIGURE B-13: Enter Christmas as the search criteria for the Title field

Find and Replace

Find / Replace

Find What: Christmas

Look In: Title

Match: Any Part of Field

Search: All

☐ Match Case ☑ Search Fields As Formatted

Find Next
Cancel

Find the search criteria anywhere in the field

Search criteria

CLUES TO USE

Using more than one sort field

The telephone book sorts records by last name (**primary sort field**) and when ties occur on the last name (for example, two Smiths), the telephone book further sorts the records by first name (**secondary sort field**). Access allows you to sort by more than one field using the query object, which you will learn more about later in this unit. Queries allow you to use more than one sort field by specifying sort criteria in Query Design View.

Filtering Records

Filtering the datasheet temporarily displays only those records that match criteria. **Criteria** are rules or limiting conditions you set. For example, you may want to show only those records where the Category field is equal to Rap, or where the PurchasePrice field is less than $10. Once you have filtered a datasheet or form to display a subset of records, you can still sort the records and find data just as if you were working with all of the records. ◄▬▬▬ The accounting department asked Kelsey for a listing of cassettes with a retail price of $15 or more. Kelsey uses the datasheet filter buttons to fulfill this request.

Steps

1. In the Music Inventory datasheet, click the **RecordingID** field, click the **Sort Ascending button** on the Table Datasheet toolbar, click any occurrence of **Cassette** in the Format field, then click the **Filter By Selection button** on the Table Datasheet toolbar

Twelve records are selected, as shown in Figure B-14. Filter By Selection is a fast and easy way to filter the records for an exact match (in this case, where the Format field value is *equal to* Cassette). To filter for comparative data and to specify more complex criteria including **comparison operators** (for example, where PurchasePrice is *equal to or greater than* $15), you must use the Filter By Form feature. See Table B-3 for more information on comparison operators.

> **QuickTip**
> If criteria become lengthy, you can widen a column to display the entire criteria entry just as you can widen columns in a datasheet. If you need to clear previous criteria, click the Clear Grid button ☒.

2. Click the **Filter By Form button** on the Table Datasheet toolbar, scroll to the right to click the **Retail** criteria cell, then type **>=15**

The Filter By Form window is shown in Figure B-15. The previous Filter By Selection criteria, Cassette in the Format field, is still in the grid. Access distinguishes between text and numeric entries by placing quotation marks around text entries. Filter By Form is more powerful than Filter By Selection because it allows you to enter criteria for more than one field at a time so that *both* criteria must be true in order for the record to be shown in the resulting datasheet.

3. Click the **Apply Filter button** on the Filter/Sort toolbar, then scroll to the right to display the Retail field

Only two records are true for both criteria, as shown in Figure B-16. The Record Navigation buttons in the lower-left corner of the datasheet display how many records were chosen for the filtered subset. The Apply Filter button becomes the Remove Filter button after a filter is applied.

> **QuickTip**
> Be sure to remove existing filters before you apply a new filter or you will end up filtering a subset of records versus the entire datasheet.

4. Click the **Remove Filter button** on the Table Datasheet toolbar

The datasheet redisplays all 58 records.

5. Click any value in the Label field, click ☒, click **A&M Records** in the Label field if it is not already selected, then click ☒

Using sort and filter skills, you quickly found the five records that met the A&M Records criteria.

6. Close the datasheet, then click **Yes** if prompted to save the changes to the Music Inventory table

Saving a table layout saves the last sort order, but filters are always removed when you close a datasheet, regardless of whether you save the changes to the layout.

FIGURE B-14: Music Inventory datasheet filtered for Cassette in the Format field

Records are
sorted in
ascending order
by RecordingID

12 records
are selected

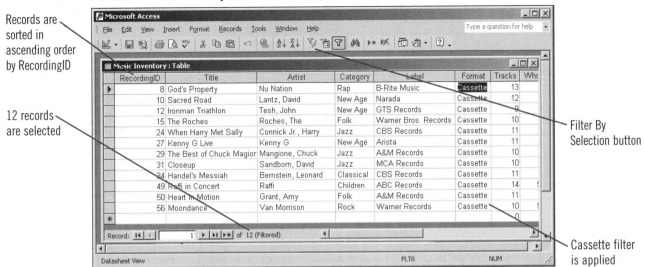

Filter By
Selection button

Cassette filter
is applied

FIGURE B-15: Filter By Form grid

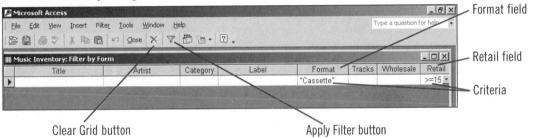

Format field

Retail field

Criteria

Clear Grid button

Apply Filter button

FIGURE B-16: Two records matched Filter By Form criteria

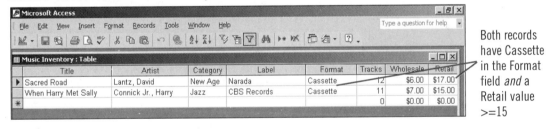

Both records
have Cassette
in the Format
field *and* a
Retail value
>=15

TABLE B-3: Comparison operators

operator	description	expression	meaning
>	Greater than	>500	Numbers greater than 500
>=	Greater than or equal to	>=500	Numbers greater than or equal to 500
<	Less than	<"Braveheart"	Names from A to Braveheart, but not Braveheart
<=	Less than or equal to	<="Bridgewater"	Names from A through, and including, Bridgewater
<>	Not equal to	<>"Cyclone"	Any name except for Cyclone

CLUES TO USE

Searching for blank fields

Is Null and Is Not Null are two other types of common criteria. Is Null criteria will find all records where no entry has been made in the field. Is Not Null will find all records where there is any entry in the field, even if the entry is 0. Primary key fields cannot have a null entry.

Access 2002

Creating a Query

A **query** is a database object that creates a datasheet of specified fields and records from one or more tables. It displays the answer to a question about the data in your database. You can edit, navigate, sort, find, and filter a query's datasheet just like a table's datasheet. A query is similar to a filter, but much more powerful. For example, a query is a saved object within the database whereas a **filter** is a temporary view of the data whose criteria is discarded when you close the datasheet or form that is being filtered. Table B-4 compares the two. Kelsey uses the Simple Query Wizard to build a query.

Steps

1. Click Queries on the Objects bar, then double-click Create query by using wizard
The Simple Query Wizard dialog box opens, allowing you to choose the table or query which contains the fields you want to display in the query. You select the fields in the order that you want them to appear on the final query datasheet.

QuickTip
You can double-click a field to move it from the Available Fields list to the Selected Fields list.

2. Click Category in the Available Fields list, click the Select Single Field button ▸, click Title, click ▸, click Artist, click ▸, click Tracks, then click ▸
The Simple Query Wizard dialog box should look like Figure B-17. The fields shown in the Available Fields list are determined by what table or query is selected in the Tables/Queries list.

3. Click Next, click Next to accept the Detail option, then click Finish to accept the suggested query title and to view the data
The Music Inventory Query's datasheet opens with all 58 records, but with only the four fields that you requested in the query wizard, as shown in Figure B-18. You can use a query datasheet to edit or add information.

4. Double-click 10 in the Tracks cell for record 7, No Words, then type 11
The Specific Record box indicates what record you are currently editing. Editing data through a query datasheet changes the data in the underlying table just as if you were working directly in the table's datasheet. A query does *not* produce a duplicate set of data, but rather, displays the original table data in a new arrangement. A query is sometimes called a **logical view** of the data. Any data additions, deletions, or editions you make through a query datasheet are actually made to the original data stored in the table object.

5. Click the Design View button ▨ on the Query Datasheet toolbar
The **Query Design View** opens, showing you a **field list** for the Music Inventory table in the upper portion of the window, and the fields you have requested for this query in the **query design grid** in the lower portion of the window.

QuickTip
Criteria is not case sensitive so country and Country produce the same results.

6. Click the Criteria cell for the Category field, then type country as shown in Figure B-19
Query Design View is used to add, delete, or change the order of fields, sort the records, or add criteria to limit the number of records shown in the resulting datasheet. Any change made in Query Design View is saved with the query object.

7. Click the Datasheet View button ▦ on the Query Design toolbar
The resulting datasheet has four records that match the country criteria in the Category field. To save this query with a more descriptive name than the one currently displayed in the query title bar, use the Save As command on the File menu.

8. Click File on the menu bar, click Save As, type Country Music in the Save Query 'Music Inventory Query' To text box, click OK, then close the query datasheet
Both the original Music Inventory Query and the modified Country Music queries are saved in this database. You can double-click a query to reopen the datasheet in the same way as you can open the datasheet of a table.

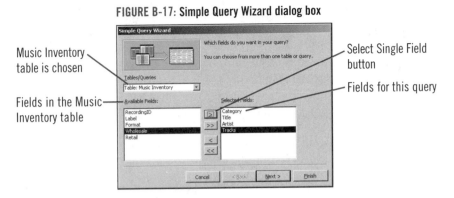

FIGURE B-17: Simple Query Wizard dialog box

Music Inventory table is chosen

Fields in the Music Inventory table

Select Single Field button

Fields for this query

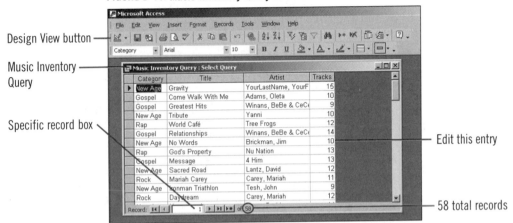

FIGURE B-18: Music Inventory Query datasheet

Design View button

Music Inventory Query

Specific record box

Edit this entry

58 total records

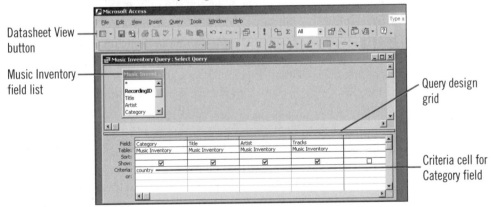

FIGURE B-19: Query Design View

Datasheet View button

Music Inventory field list

Query design grid

Criteria cell for Category field

TABLE B-4: Queries vs. filters

Characteristics	filters	queries
Are saved as an object in the database	No	Yes
Can be used to select a subset of records in a datasheet	Yes	Yes
Can be used to select a subset of fields in a datasheet	No	Yes
Its resulting datasheet can be used to enter and edit data	Yes	Yes
Its resulting datasheet can be used to sort, filter, and find records	Yes	Yes
Is commonly used as the source of data for a form or report	No	Yes
Can calculate sums, averages, counts, and other types of summary statistics across records	No	Yes
Can be used to create calculated fields	No	Yes

Modifying a Query

Whether an existing query is created through the use of a wizard or built from scratch in Query Design View, to modify the query you work in Query Design View in the same way you modify existing tables by working in Table Design View. Query Design View is where you employ powerful query features such as defining complex criteria, defining multiple sort orders, and building calculated fields. ✏️ Kelsey wants to modify the Country Music query in a variety of ways. She uses Query Design View to make the changes and then she prints the resulting datasheet.

Steps ₁₂₄₃

QuickTip

Right-click an object and click Design View from the shortcut menu to open it in this view.

1. Click the **Country Music query** in the MediaLoft-B Database window, then click the **Design button** 🔲 on the database window toolbar
   Query Design View opens, displaying the current fields and criteria for the Country Music query. To add fields to the query, you drag the fields from the field list to the position in the query design grid where you want them to appear on the datasheet.

Trouble?

If the field list in the upper portion of Query Design View is not visible, use the Query Design scroll bars to move to the top and left part of the window.

2. Scroll in the Music Inventory field list, then drag the **Retail field** to the **Tracks Field cell** in the query design grid as shown in Figure B-20
   The Retail field is added to the query design grid between the Artist and Tracks fields. You can also delete fields in the existing query grid.

3. Click the **field selector** for the Category field, then press the **Delete** key
   Deleting a field from Query Design View does not have any affect on the data stored in the underlying table. Deleting a field from a query means that this field will not be displayed on the datasheet for this query.

4. Click the **Sort cell** for the Title field, click the **Sort list arrow**, click **Ascending**, click the **Sort cell** for the Artist field, click the **Sort list arrow**, click **Ascending**, then click the **Datasheet View button** 🔲 on the Query Design toolbar to view the resulting datasheet
   Since sort orders are evaluated in a left-to-right order and there are no duplicate values in the primary sort order (Title), the secondary sort order (Artist) is never used to further determine the order of the records. To change the primary and secondary sort orders for a query, use Query Design View.

Trouble?

Click the field selector for a field to select it, release the mouse button, then drag the field selector for the chosen field. A thin, black, vertical bar will indicate where the field will be positioned as you drag it.

5. Click 🔲 on the Query Datasheet toolbar, click the **field selector** for the Artist field to select it, then drag the **field selector** for the Artist field to the first column position in the query design grid as shown in Figure B-21
   The primary sort order will now be determined by the Artist field, and the secondary sort order by the Title field.

6. Click 🔲 to view the resulting datasheet
   Study records 4 and 5, which contain the same Artist value, "Beatles, The." Note that the records are further sorted by the values in the Title field. You can specify as many sort orders as you desire in Query Design View, but they are always evaluated in a left-to-right order. You can also add multiple criteria values in Query Design View.

7. Click 🔲, click the first **Criteria cell** for the Retail field, type **>=15**, click the first **Criteria cell** for the Tracks field, type **>=12**, then click 🔲 to view the resulting datasheet as shown in Figure B-22
   Twelve records are selected that matched both criteria. The query design grid row into which query criteria is entered is extremely important. Criteria entered on the same row must *both* be true for the record to be selected. Criteria entered on different rows are evaluated separately, and a record need only be true for *one* row of criteria in order to be selected for the resulting datasheet.

8. Click the **Print button** 🖨 on the Query Datasheet toolbar, close the datasheet without saving changes, close the MediaLoft-B database, then exit Access

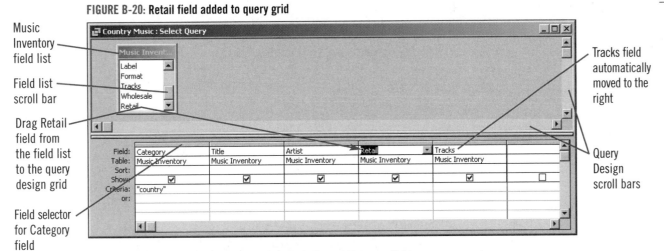

FIGURE B-20: Retail field added to query grid

Music Inventory field list

Field list scroll bar

Drag Retail field from the field list to the query design grid

Field selector for Category field

Tracks field automatically moved to the right

Query Design scroll bars

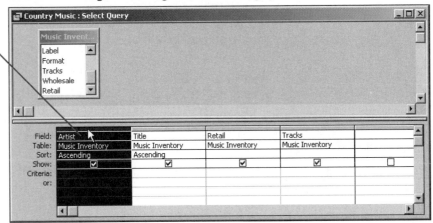

FIGURE B-21: Sorting records using the Artist and Category fields

Artist field has been moved by dragging the field selector

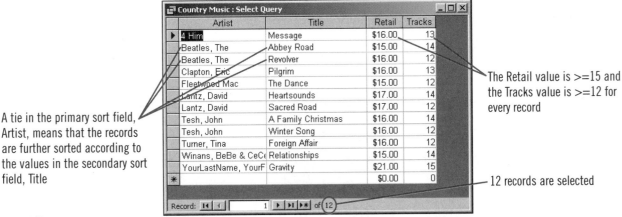

FIGURE B-22: The final datasheet

A tie in the primary sort field, Artist, means that the records are further sorted according to the values in the secondary sort field, Title

The Retail value is >=15 and the Tracks value is >=12 for every record

12 records are selected

Understanding And and Or criteria

Criteria placed on different rows of the query design grid are Or criteria. In other words, a record may be true for *either* row of criteria in order for it to be displayed on the resulting datasheet. Placing additional criteria in the *same* row, however, creates And criteria. Records must meet the criteria for *all* of the criteria on one row in order to be chosen for that datasheet. As

you add additional rows of criteria (Or criteria) to the query design grid, you increase the number of records displayed on the resulting datasheet because the record needs to be true for the criteria in only *one* of the rows in order to be displayed on the datasheet for that query.

Practice

► Concepts Review

Label each element of the Select Query window shown in Figure B-23.

FIGURE B-23

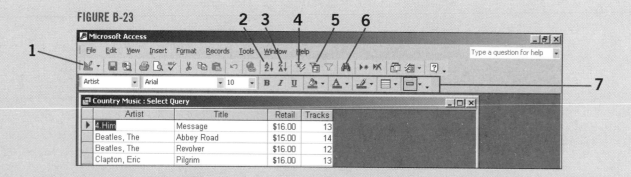

Match each term with the statement that describes it.

8. **Primary key**   a. Determines what type of data can be stored in each field
9. **Table Wizard**   b. Provides interactive help to create the field names and data types for each field in a new table
10. **Filter**   c. A database object that creates a datasheet of specified fields and records from one or more tables
11. **Data type**   d. A field that contains unique information for each record
12. **Query**   e. Creates a temporary subset of records

Select the best answer from the list of choices.

13. Which data type would be best for a field that was going to store birth dates?
    a. Text
    b. Number
    c. AutoNumber
    d. Date/Time
14. Which data type would be best for a field that was going to store Web addresses?
    a. Text
    b. Memo
    c. OLE
    d. Hyperlink
15. Which data type would be best for a field that was going to store telephone numbers?
    a. Text
    b. Number
    c. OLE
    d. Hyperlink
16. Each of the following is true about a filter, *except*:
    a. It creates a temporary datasheet of records that match criteria.
    b. The resulting datasheet can be sorted.
    c. The resulting datasheet includes all fields in the table.
    d. A filter is automatically saved as an object in the database.
17. Sorting refers to:
    a. Reorganizing the records in either ascending or descending order.
    b. Selecting a subset of fields and/or records to view as a datasheet from one or more tables.
    c. Displaying only those records that meet certain criteria.
    d. Using Or and And criteria in the query design grid.

▶ Skills Review

1. Plan a database.

a. Plan a database that will contain the names and addresses of physicians. You might use a telephone book to gather information.

b. On paper, sketch the Table Design view of a table that will hold this information. Write the field names in one column and the data types for each field in the second column.

2. Create a table.

a. Start Access and use the Blank Access database option to create a database. Save the file as **Doctors** in the drive and folder where your Project Files are stored.

b. Use the Table Wizard to create a new table. Use the Contacts sample table found in the Business database category.

c. Choose each of the sample fields in the following order: ContactID, FirstName, LastName, Address, City, StateOrProvince, PostalCode, Title.

d. Rename the StateOrProvince field as **State**.

e. Name the table **Addresses**, and allow Access to set the primary key field.

f. Click the Modify the table design option button in the last Table Wizard dialog box, then click Finish.

3. Modify a table.

a. In the first available blank row (after the Title field), add a new field called **PhoneNumber** with a Text data type.

b. Change the Field Size property of the State field from 20 to **2**.

c. Insert a field named **Suite** with a Text data type between the Address and City fields.

d. Add the description **M.D. or D.O.** to the Title field.

e. Save the Addresses table, display the Addresses datasheet, and enter one record using your own information in the name fields. Remember that the ContactID field is specified with an AutoNumber data type that automatically increments the value in that field when you start making an entry in any other field.

f. Use the Page Setup dialog box to change the Page Orientation to Landscape. Preview the datasheet. If it doesn't fit on one page, return to the datasheet and resize the columns until the record previews on a single page, and then print that page.

g. Close the Doctors database.

4. Format a datasheet.

a. Open the **Doctors-B** database from the drive and folder where your Project Files are stored. Open the Doctor Addresses table datasheet.

b. Change the font of the datasheet to Arial Narrow, and the font size to 9.

c. Change the gridline color to black, and remove the vertical gridlines.

d. Change the Page Orientation to Landscape and all of the margins to 0.5". Preview the datasheet (it should fit on one page), then print and close it without saving the formatting changes.

5. Understand sorting, filtering, and finding.

a. On a sheet of paper, identify three ways that you might want to sort an address list, such as the Doctor Addresses datasheet. Be sure to specify both the field you would sort on and the sort order (ascending or descending).

b. On a sheet of paper, identify three ways that you might want to filter an address list, such as the Doctor Addresses datasheet. Be sure to specify both the field you would filter on and the criteria that you would use.

6. Sort records and find data.

a. Open the Doctor Addresses datasheet, sort the records in ascending order on the Last field, then list the first two last names on paper.

b. Sort the Doctor Addresses records in descending order on the Zip field, then list the first two doctors on paper.

c. Find the records in which the Address1 field contains Baltimore in any part of the field. How many records did you find?

d. Find the records where the Zip field contains **64012**. How many records did you find?

Access 2002

7. Filter records.

a. In the Doctor Addresses datasheet, filter the records for all physicians with the Title **D.O.** Print this datasheet with narrow margins and in landscape orientation so that it fits on one page.

b. In the Doctor Addresses datasheet, filter the records for all physicians with **M.D.** in the Title field and **64012** in the Zip field, then print this datasheet with narrow margins and in landscape orientation so that it fits on one page.

c. Close the Doctor Addresses datasheet, and save the layout changes.

8. Create a query.

a. Use the Query Wizard to create a new query based on the Doctor Addresses table with the following fields: First, Last, City, State, Zip.

b. Name the query **Doctors in Missouri**, then view the datasheet.

c. In Query Design View, add the criteria **MO** to the State field, then view the datasheet.

d. Change Mark Garver's last name to **Garvey**.

e. Change Samuel Harley's first and last name to your first and last name, then save the query.

9. Modify a query.

a. Modify the Doctors in Missouri query to include only those doctors in Kansas City, Missouri. Be sure that the criteria is in the same row so that both criteria must be true for the record to be displayed.

b. Save the query with the name **Doctors in Kansas City Missouri**. Print the query results, then close the query datasheet.

c. Modify the Doctors in Kansas City Missouri query so that the records are sorted in ascending order on the last name, then add the DoctorNumber field as the first field in the datasheet.

d. Print and save the sorted datasheet for that query, then close the datasheet.

e. Close the Doctors-B database then exit Access.

▶ Independent Challenge 1

You want to start a database to track your personal video collection.

a. Start Access and create a new database called **Movies** in the drive and folder where your Project Files are located.

b. Using the Table Wizard, create a table based on the Video Collection sample table in the Personal category with the following fields: MovieTitle, YearReleased, Rating, Length, DateAcquired, PurchasePrice.

c. Rename the YearReleased field as **Year** and the PurchasePrice field as **Purchase**.

d. Accept the default name **Video Collection** for the table and allow Access to set a primary key field.

e. Modify the Video Collection table in Design View with the following changes:
  - Delete the Rating Field.
  - Change the Length field to a Number data type.
  - Change the DateAcquired field name to **DatePurchased**.
  - Add a field between Year and Length called **PersonalRating** with a Number data type.
  - In the Description of the PersonalRating field, enter: **My personal rating on a scale from 1 (bad) to 10 (great)**.
  - Add a field between PersonalRating and Length fields called **Rated** with a Text data type.
  - In the Description of the Rated field, enter: **G, PG, PG-13, R**.
  - Change the Field Size property of the Rated field to **5**.

f. Save the Video Collection table, and then open it in Datasheet View.

g. Enter five records with sample data from videos you own or movies you've seen, print the datasheet, close the Video Collection table, close the Movies database, then exit Access.

▶ Independent Challenge 2

You work for a marketing company that sells medical supplies to doctors' offices.

a. Start Access and open the **Doctors-B** database from the drive and folder where your Project Files are located, then open the Doctors Addresses table datasheet.

b. Filter the records to find all those physicians who live in **Grandview**, modify column widths so that all data is visible, edit William Baker's last name to your last name, change the paper orientation to landscape, preview, then print the datasheet.

c. Sort the filtered records by last name, change the cell color to silver (use the Fill/Back Color button on the Formatting toolbar or the Background Color list found in the Datasheet Formatting dialog box), change the font style to bold, then print the datasheet.

d. Close the Doctors Addresses datasheet without saving the changes.

e. Using the Query Wizard, create a query with the following fields: First, Last, Phone.

f. Name the query **Telephone Query**. Sort the records in ascending order by last name, then print the datasheet. Close the query without saving the changes.

g. In Query Design View of the Telephone Query, delete the First field, then add the Title field between the existing Last and Phone fields. Add an ascending sort order to the Phone field. Save, view, and print the datasheet.

h. In Query Design View of the Telephone Query, add the State field to the fourth column. Add criteria so that only those records where there is no entry in the State field are displayed on the resulting datasheet. (*Hint*: Use **Is Null** criteria for the State cell.)

i. View the datasheet, and then change Sanderson's last name to your last name. Print and close the Telephone Query without saving the changes. Close the Doctors-B database, then exit Access.

▶ Independent Challenge 3

You want to create a database to keep track of your personal contacts.

a. Start Access and create a new database called **People** in the drive and folder where your Project Files are located.

b. Using the Table Wizard, create a table based on the Addresses sample table in the Personal category with the following fields: FirstName, LastName, SpouseName, Address, City, StateOrProvince, PostalCode, EmailAddress, HomePhone, Birthdate.

c. Name the table **Contact Info**, allow Access to set the primary key field, and choose the Enter data directly into the table option in the last Table Wizard dialog box.

d. Enter at least five records into the table, making sure that two people have the same last name. Use your name for one of the records. Note that the Contact InfoID field has an AutoNumber data type.

e. Sort the records in ascending order by last name, then save and close the Contact Info datasheet.

f. Using the Query Wizard, create a query with the following fields from the Contact Info table in this order: LastName, FirstName, Birthdate. Name the query **Birthday List**.

g. In Query Design View, sort the records in ascending order by LastName and then by FirstName.

h. Save the query as **Sorted Birthday List**, then view the query. Change the Birthdate value to **1/6/71** for your record.

i. Modify the datasheet by making font and color changes, print it, then close it without saving it.

j. Open the datasheet for the Contact Info table and observe the Birthdate value for your record. On a piece of paper, explain why the 1/6/71 value appears in the datasheet for the table when you made the edit in the Sorted Birthday List query.

k. Explain why the 1/6/71 value was saved even though you closed the query without saving the layout changes.

l. Close the Contact Info table, close the People database, then exit Access.

Independent Challenge 4

You are on the staff of an economic development team whose goal is to encourage tourism in the Baltic Sea region. You have created an Access database called Baltic-B to track important fields of information on the countries in that region, and will use the Internet to find information about the area.

a. Start Access and open the **Baltic-B** database from the drive and folder where your Project Files are located.

b. Open the Countries table datasheet, then click the expand button to the left of Norway as well as to the left of Oslo using Figure B-24 as a guide.

c. This arrangement of data shows you how events are tracked by city, and how cities are tracked by country in the Baltic-B database.

d. Connect to the Internet, and then go to www.yahoo.com, www.ask.com, or any general search engine to conduct some research for your database. Your goal is to enter at least one city record (the country's capital city) for each country. Be sure to enter the Population data for that particular city, rather than for the entire country. You can enter the data by expanding the country record subdatasheets as shown for Norway in Figure B-24, or by entering the records directly into the Cities datasheet.

e. Return to the search engine, and research upcoming tourist events for Oslo, Norway. Enter three more events for Oslo into the database. You can enter the data into the Event subdatasheet shown in Figure B-24, or enter the records directly into the Events datasheet by opening the Events table datasheet. If you enter the records into the Events datasheet, remember that the CityID field value for Oslo is 1.

f. Open the Countries datasheet, expand all records so that all of the cities for each country as well as all of the events for Oslo appear. Print the expanded datasheet.

g. Close the Countries datasheet, close the Baltic-B database, then exit Access.

FIGURE B-24

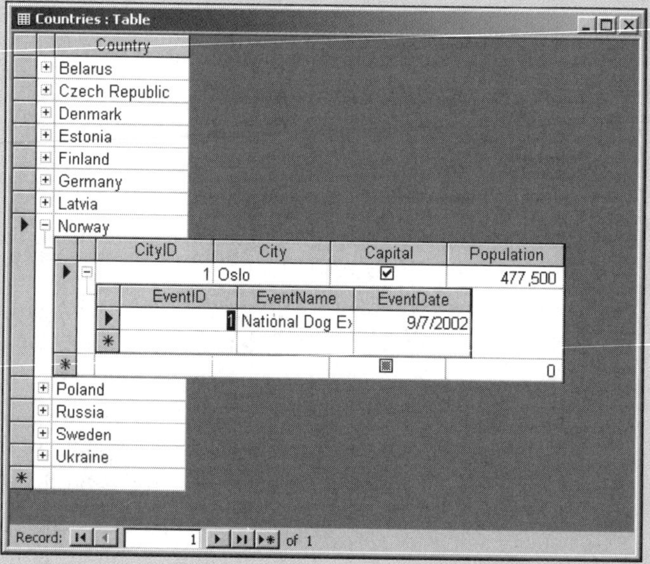

Countries : Table
Country
+ Belarus
+ Czech Republic
+ Denmark
+ Estonia
+ Finland
+ Germany
+ Latvia
− Norway

CityID	City	Capital	Population
1	Oslo	☑	477,500

EventID	EventName	EventDate
1	National Dog Ex	9/7/2002
*		

			0
+ Poland			
+ Russia			
+ Sweden			
+ Ukraine			
*			

Record: ◄◄ ◄ 1 ► ►► ►* of 1

► Visual Workshop

Open the **MediaLoft-B** database from the drive and folder where your Project Files are located. Create a query based on the Music Inventory table that displays the datasheet shown in Figure B-25. Notice that only the Jazz category is displayed and that the records are sorted in a descending order on the Retail field. Change the Title of the first record to include your last name, then print the datasheet. Save the query as **Jazz Selections** in the MediaLoft-B database.

FIGURE B-25

	Category	Retail	Artist	Title	Tracks
►	Jazz	$15.00	Connick Jr., Harry	When Harry Met Sally	11
	Jazz	$13.00	Sandborn, David	Closeup	10
	Jazz	$10.00	Mangione, Chuck	The Best of Chuck Mangione	10
*		$0.00			0

Record: ◄◄ ◄ 1 ► ►► ►* of 3

Using

Forms

Objectives

- ► **Plan a form**
- _{MOUS} ► **Create a form**
- _{MOUS} ► **Move and resize controls**
- _{MOUS} ► **Modify labels**
- _{MOUS} ► **Modify text boxes**
- _{MOUS} ► **Modify tab order**
- _{MOUS} ► **Enter and edit records**
- _{MOUS} ► **Insert an image**

A **form** is an Access database object that allows you to present information in a format that makes the task of entering and editing data quick and easy. Forms are the primary object used to find, enter, and edit data. Although the datasheet view of a table or query can be used to navigate, enter, and edit data, all of the fields for one record are sometimes not visible unless you scroll left or right. A form solves that problem by allowing you to design the layout of fields on the screen, and typically displays the data for only one record at a time. A form also supports graphical elements such as pictures, buttons, and tabs, which make the form's arrangement of data easy to understand and use. ✐ Fellow employees are excited about the MediaLoft music inventory database. They have asked Kelsey Lang to create a form to make it easier to access, enter, and update inventory data.

Planning a Form

Properly organized and well-designed forms make a tremendous difference in the productivity of the end user. Since forms are the primary object used to enter and edit data, time spent planning a form is time well spent. Forms are often built to match a **source document** (for example, an employment application or a medical history form) to facilitate fast and accurate data entry. Now, however, it is becoming more common to type data directly into the database rather than first recording it on paper. Therefore, form design considerations, such as clearly labeled fields and appropriate formatting, are extremely important. Other form design considerations include how the user tabs from field to field, and what type of **control** is used to display the data. See Table C-1 for more information on form controls.  Kelsey considers the following form design considerations when planning her Music Inventory form.

► **Determine the overall purpose of the form**
Interview the users to determine how the form will be used. Name your form with its specific purpose such as "Music Inventory Entry Form" rather than a generic name such as "Music."

► **Determine the underlying record source**
The **record source** is defined by either a table or query object. The record source determines the data that the form will display.

► **Gather the source documents used to design your form**
It's a good idea to sketch the form by hand, making sure that you list every element, including fields, text, and graphics that you want the form to display.

► **Determine the best type of control to use for each item on the form**
Figures C-1 and C-2 show examples of several controls. **Bound controls** display data from the underlying record source and are also used to edit and enter data. **Unbound controls** do not change from record to record and exist only to clarify and enhance the appearance of the form.

TABLE C-1: Form Controls

name	used to:	bound or unbound
Label	Provide consistent descriptive text as you navigate from record to record; the label is the most common type of unbound control	Unbound
Text box	Display, edit, or enter data for each record from an underlying record source; the text box is the most common type of bound control	Bound
List box	Display a list of possible data entries	Bound
Combo box	Display a list of possible data entries for a field, and also provide a text box for an entry from the keyboard; a combination of the list box and text box controls	Bound
Tab control	Create a three-dimensional aspect to a form	Unbound
Check box	Display "yes" or "no" answers for a field; if the box is checked, it means "yes"	Bound
Toggle button	Display "yes" or "no" answers for a field; if the button is pressed, it means "yes"	Bound
Option button	Display a choice for a field	Bound
Option group	Display and organize choices (usually presented as option buttons) for a field	Bound
Bound object frame	Display OLE (Object Linking and Embedding) data, such as a picture	Bound
Unbound object frame	Display a picture or clip art image that doesn't change from record to record	Unbound
Line and Rectangle	Draw lines and rectangles on the form	Unbound
Command button	Provide an easy way to initiate a command or run a macro	Unbound

FIGURE C-1: Form controls

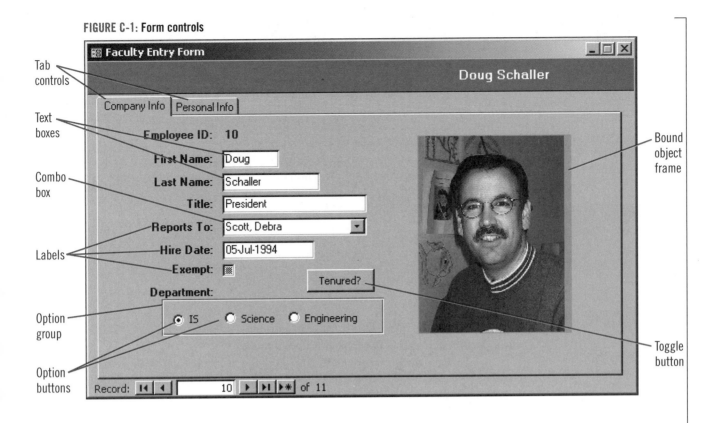

Tab controls

Text boxes

Combo box

Labels

Option group

Option buttons

Bound object frame

Toggle button

FIGURE C-2: Form controls

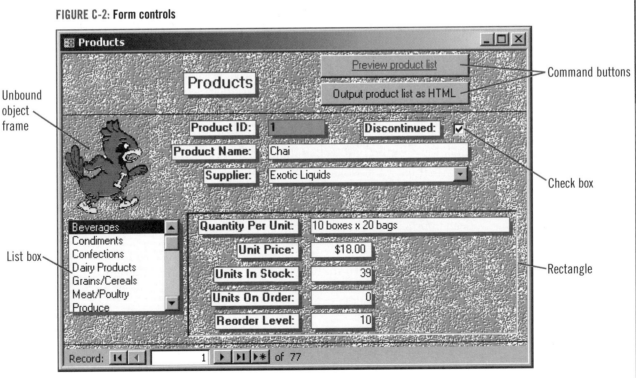

Unbound object frame

List box

Command buttons

Check box

Rectangle

Creating a Form

There are many ways to create a form. You can create a form from scratch using **Form Design View**, or you can use the **Form Wizard** to provide guided steps for the form development process. The Form Wizard prompts you to select the record source for the form, choose an overall layout, choose a style, and title the form. The Form Wizard is an easy way to create an initial version of a form. Table C-2 summarizes the ways to create a form. No matter what technique is used to create a form, you use Form Design View to modify an existing form object. ✎▬ Kelsey made some notes on how she'd like the final Music Inventory form arranged. Now she uses the Form Wizard to get started.

Steps 1 2 3 4

1. Start Access, click the **More files** link in the New File task pane, then open the **MediaLoft-C** database from the drive and folder where your New File Project Files are located

QuickTip

You can also double-click the Create form by using wizard option in the database window to start the Form Wizard.

2. Click **Forms** on the Objects bar in the MediaLoft-C Database window, then click the **New button** 🔲 on the database window toolbar
   The New Form dialog box opens, presenting the various techniques used to create a new form.

3. Click **Form Wizard** in the New Form dialog box, click the **Choose the table or query where the object's data comes from list arrow**, click **Music Inventory**, then click **OK**
   The Music Inventory table will serve as the record source for this form. If this database contained multiple tables or queries, these additional objects would have been presented as well as the Music Inventory table.

4. Click the **Select All Fields button** ▶▶, click **Next**, click the **Columnar layout option button**, click **Next**, click the **Standard** style, click **Next**, then click **Finish** to accept the title and to open the form to view or enter information
   The Music Inventory form opens in **Form View**, as shown in Figure C-3. Descriptive labels appear in the first column, and text boxes that display data from the underlying record source appear in the second column. A check box control displays the Yes/No data in the PeoplesChoice field. You can enter, edit, find, sort, and filter records using a form.

5. Click the **Title text box**, click the **Sort Ascending button** ⬆ on the Form View toolbar, then click the **Next Record button** ▶ in the Record Navigation buttons four times to move to the fifth record
   Abbey Road is the fifth record when the records are sorted in ascending order by the Title field. Information about the current record number and total number of records appears in the Record Navigation buttons area.

6. Click the **Last Record button** ▶❙ in the Record Navigation buttons
   World Café by the Tree Frogs is the last record when the records are sorted in ascending order by the Title field.

7. Click **Rap** in the Category text box, then click the **Filter By Selection button** 🖼 on the Form View toolbar
   Six records have the value of Rap in the Category field. The sort, filter, and find buttons work the same way in a form as they do in a datasheet.

8. Close the Music Inventory form
   The last sort order is automatically saved when you close a form. Filters are automatically removed when you close a form just as they are for a datasheet.

FIGURE C-3: **Music Inventory form**

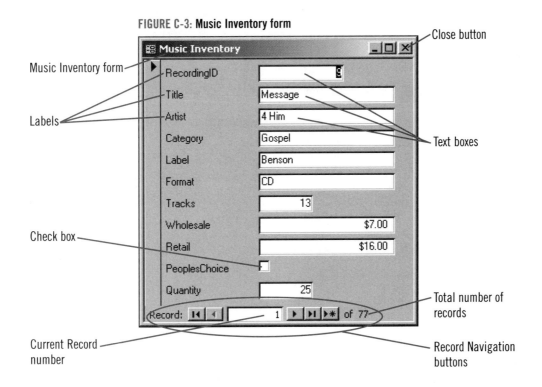

Music Inventory form → Music Inventory

Close button

Labels

Text boxes

- RecordingID: 8
- Title: Message
- Artist: 4 Him
- Category: Gospel
- Label: Benson
- Format: CD
- Tracks: 13
- Wholesale: $7.00
- Retail: $16.00
- PeoplesChoice: ☐
- Quantity: 25

Check box

Record: 1 of 77

Total number of records

Current Record number

Record Navigation buttons

TABLE C-2: **Form creation techniques**

technique	description
Design View	Provides a layout screen in which the form developer has complete control over the data, layout, and formatting choices that will be displayed by the form. Since Form Design View is the most powerful and flexible technique used to create a form, it is also the most complex. Form Design View is also used to modify all existing forms, regardless of how they were created.
Form Wizard	Provides a guided series of steps to create a form. Prompts for record source, layout, style, and title.
AutoForm	Instantly creates a form that displays all the fields in the chosen record source. There are five different AutoForm options (Columnar, Tabular, Datasheet, PivotTable, and PivotChart) that correspond to five different form layouts in the New Form dialog box.
Chart Wizard	Provides a guided series of steps to create a graphical arrangement of data in the form of a business chart such as a bar, column, line, or pie chart that is placed on a form.
PivotTable Wizard	Provides a guided series of steps to create a summarized arrangement of data in a PivotTable View of a form. Fields used for the column and row headings determine how the data is grouped and summarized.

CLUES TO USE

Using the AutoForm button

You can quickly create a form by clicking a table or query object in the Database window, then clicking the New Object: AutoForm button 🔳 on the Database toolbar. The New Object: AutoForm button offers no prompts or dialog boxes; it instantly creates a columnar form that displays all the fields in the selected table or query.

Moving and Resizing Controls

After you create a form, you can work in Form Design View to modify the size, location, and appearance of existing controls. Form Design View also allows you to add or delete controls. Kelsey moves and resizes the controls on the form to improve the layout.

Trouble?

Be sure you open the Design View of the Music Inventory form and not the Music Inventory table.

1. **Click the Music Inventory form, click the Design button** ▨ **on the database window toolbar, then click the Maximize button** ▣ **for the form**
   Maximizing the form makes it easier to modify the form. In Form Design View, several elements that help you design the form may automatically appear. The **Toolbox toolbar** contains buttons that allow you to add controls to the form. The **field list** contains the fields in the record source. The vertical and horizontal rulers help you position controls on the form. These items are shown in Figure C-4. You work with the Toolbox and field list when you add or change existing controls. If you are not working with the Toolbox or the field list you can toggle them off to unclutter your screen.

QuickTip

Press [F8] to open the field list.

2. **If the Toolbox toolbar is visible, click the Toolbox button** ⚒ **on the Form Design toolbar to toggle it off, and if the field list is visible, click the Field List button** ▤ **on the Form Design toolbar to toggle it off**
   Before moving, resizing, deleting, or changing a control in any way, you must select it.

3. **Click the PeoplesChoice check box**
   Sizing handles appear in the corners and on the edges of selected controls. When you work with controls, the mouse pointer shape is very important. Pointer shapes are summarized in Table C-3.

QuickTip

If you make a mistake, click the Undo button ↺ and try again. In Form Design View, you can undo up to 20 actions.

4. **Point to the selected PeoplesChoice check box so that the pointer changes to** ✋, **then drag the control so that it is positioned to the right of the RecordingID text box and the right edge of the check box is at the 4.5 inch mark on the horizontal ruler**
   The form will automatically widen to accommodate the new position for the check box. Also, when you move a bound control, such as a text box or check box, the accompanying unbound label moves with it. The field name for the selected control appears in the **Object list box**.

QuickTip

If you undo too many actions, click Edit on the menu bar, then click Redo.

5. **Select and move the Quantity and Tracks text boxes using the** ✋ **pointer to match their final locations as shown in Figure C-5**
   Moving a text box automatically moves its associated label. If you want to move only the text box or only the label, you would use the ☝ mouse pointer. Resizing controls also improves the design of the form.

QuickTip

You can move controls one **pixel** (picture element) at a time by pressing [Ctrl] and an arrow key. You can resize controls one pixel at a time by pressing [Shift] and an arrow key.

6. **Click the Retail text box, use the** ↔ **pointer to drag the middle-right edge sizing handle left to the 2 inch mark on the horizontal ruler, click the Wholesale text box, then use the** ↔ **pointer to drag the middle-right edge sizing handle left to the 2 inch mark**
   Moving and resizing controls requires great concentration and mouse control. Don't worry if your screen doesn't *precisely* match the figure, but *do* make sure that you understand how to use the move and resize mouse pointers used in Form Design View. Precision and accuracy naturally develop with practice, but even experienced form designers regularly rely on the Undo button.

7. **Click the Form View button** ▤ **on the Form Design toolbar to view the final form as shown in Figure C-6**

FIGURE C-4: Design View of the Music Inventory form

Field List button

Label

Field list

Vertical ruler

Text box

Toolbox button

Horizontal ruler

Toolbox toolbar

PeoplesChoice
check box

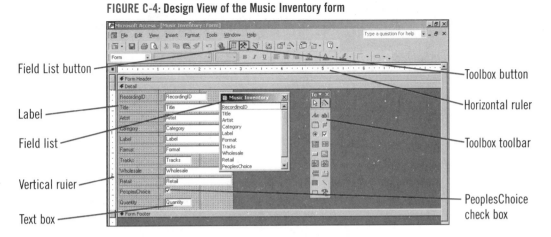

FIGURE C-5: Controls have been moved

Form View button

Object list box

PeoplesChoice label and check
box have been moved

Text boxes have been moved

Sizing handles indicate which
control is selected

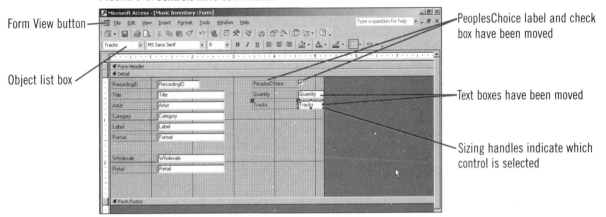

FIGURE C-6: Reorganized Music Inventory form

Labels

Text boxes have
been resized

Text boxes

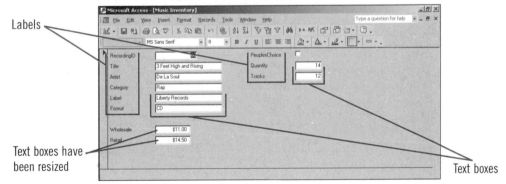

TABLE C-3: Form Design View mouse pointer shapes

shape	when does this shape appear?	action
⟋	When you point to any unselected control on the form (the default mouse pointer)	Single-clicking with this mouse pointer *selects* a control
✋	When you point to the edge of a selected control (but not when you are pointing to a sizing handle)	Dragging this mouse pointer moves all selected controls
👆	When you point to the larger sizing handle in the upper-left corner of a selected control	Dragging this mouse pointer *moves only the single control* where the pointer is currently positioned, not other controls that may also be selected
↔ ↕ ⤡ ⤢	When you point to any sizing handle (except the larger one in the upper-left corner)	Dragging this mouse pointer *resizes* the control

Modifying Labels

When you create a form with the Form Wizard, it places a label to the left of each text box that displays the name of the field. Often, you'll want to modify those labels to be more descriptive or user-friendly. You can modify a label control by directly editing it in Form Design View, or you can make the change in the property sheet of the label. The **property sheet** is a comprehensive listing of all **properties** (characteristics) that have been specified for that control. Kelsey modifies the labels of the Music Inventory form to be more descriptive.

1. Click the **Design View button** on the Form View toolbar, click the **RecordingID label** to select it, click between the **g** and **I** in the RecordingID label, then press **[Spacebar]** to insert a space

   Directly editing labels in Form Design View is tricky because you must single-click the label to select it, then precisely click where you want to edit it. If you double-click the label, you will open its property sheet.

2. Click the **Title label**, click the **Properties button** on the Form Design toolbar, then click the **Format tab**, as shown in Figure C-7

   The **Caption** property controls the text displayed by the label control. The property can be found on either the Format or the All tabs. The All tab presents a complete list of all the properties for a control.

3. Click to the left of **Title** in the Caption property, type **Recording**, press **[Spacebar]**, then click to toggle the property sheet off

   Don't be overwhelmed by the number of properties available for each control on the form. Over time, you may want to learn about most of these properties, but in the beginning you'll be able to make the vast majority of the property changes through menu and toolbar options rather than by accessing the property sheet itself. For example, you may wish to right-align the labels in the first column so that they are closer to their respective text boxes. You could directly modify the Text Align property in the property sheet for each label, or make the same property changes using the Formatting (Form/Report) toolbar.

4. Click the **Recording ID label**, then click the **Align Right button** on the Formatting (Form/Report) toolbar

   The Recording ID label caption is now much closer to its associated text box. See Table C-4 for a list of techniques to quickly select several controls so that you can apply alignment and formatting changes to more than one control simultaneously.

5. Click the **0.5 inch** mark on the horizontal ruler to select the first column of controls as shown in Figure C-8, then click

   All the labels in the first column are right-aligned.

6. Click the **Save button** on the Form Design toolbar, then click the **Form View button** on the Form Design toolbar to view the changes in Form View

FIGURE C-7: Examining the property sheet for a label

Recording ID label has been changed

Title label is selected

Format tab

Caption property

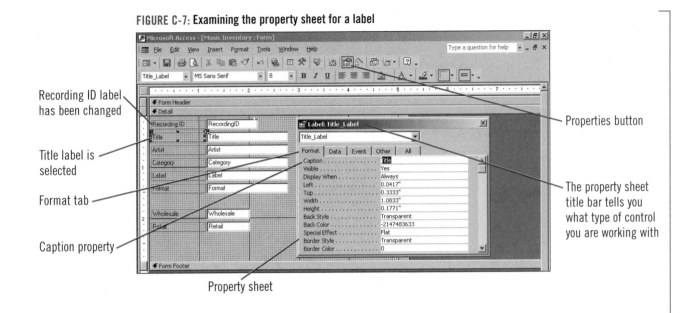

Properties button

The property sheet title bar tells you what type of control you are working with

Property sheet

FIGURE C-8: Selecting several labels at the same time

Clicking in the 0.5" mark in the horizontal ruler

All labels in the first column are selected

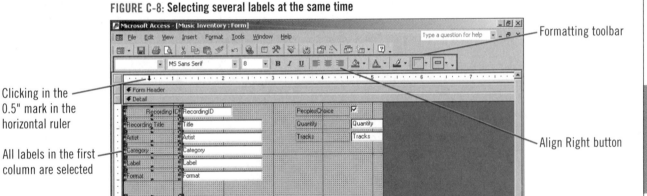

Formatting toolbar

Align Right button

TABLE C-4: Selecting more than one control

technique	description
Click, [Shift]+click	Click a control, then press and hold [Shift] while clicking other controls; each one is selected
Drag a selection box	Drag a selection box (an outline box you create by dragging the pointer in Form Design View); every control that is in or is touched by the edges of the box is selected
Click in the ruler	Click in either the horizontal or vertical ruler to select all controls that intersect the selection line
Drag in the ruler	Drag through either the horizontal or vertical ruler to select all controls that intersect the selection line as it is dragged through the ruler

Modifying Text Boxes

Text boxes are generally used to display data from underlying fields and are therefore *bound* to that field. A text box control may also serve as a **calculated control** when it stores an **expression**, a combination of symbols that calculates a result. Sample expressions include calculating the current page number, determining the current date, calculating a grade point average, or manipulating text values. ◀▬▬ Kelsey wants the Music Inventory form to calculate the profit for each record. She creates a calculated control by entering an expression within a text box to find the difference between the values in the Retail and Wholesale fields.

Steps

1. Click the **Design View button** 🖎 on the Form View toolbar, click the **Toolbox button** 🛠 on the Form View toolbar, then click the **Text Box button** 🔤 on the Toolbox toolbar
   The mouse pointer changes to ⁺🔤.

2. Click just below the **Retail text box** on the form, then use ✋ to move the new text box and label control into the position shown in Figure C-9
   Adding a new text box automatically added a new label with the default caption Text22:. The number in the default caption depends on how many controls you have previously added to the form. You can create the calculated control by typing the expression directly in the text box.

3. Click **Unbound** in the new text box, type **=[Retail]-[Wholesale]**, then press **[Enter]**
   All expressions start with an equal sign (=). When referencing a field name within an expression, square brackets surround the field name. You must type the field name exactly as it appears in the Table Design View, but you do not need to worry about capitalization.

4. Click the **Text22: label** to select it, click the **Text22: label** again to edit it, double-click **Text22**, type **Profit** as the new caption, press **[Enter]**, then click the **Form View button** 📧 to view the changes as shown in Figure C-10
   The Profit for the first record is calculated as $3.50 and displays as 3.5. Property changes such as applying a Currency format can be made in Form View.

5. Click **3.5** in the Profit text box, click **View** on the menu bar, then click **Properties**
   Monetary values such as the calculated Profit field should be right-aligned and display with a dollar sign and two digits to the right of the decimal point.

6. Click the **Format tab** in the Text Box property sheet if not already selected, click the **Format property list arrow**, click **Currency**, scroll through the property sheet to display the **Text Align property**, click the **Text Align property list arrow**, then click **Right**
   A short description of the selected property appears in the status bar. Some changes to a form, such as moving, deleting, or adding controls, can only be accomplished in Form Design View.

7. Click 🖎, click 🗐 to toggle off the property sheet, use ✋ to switch the position of the **Retail and Wholesale text boxes**, move and align the **Profit label** under the Wholesale label, resize the **Profit text box** to be the same size as the Wholesale text box, then click 📧
   The final form is shown in Figure C-11.

FIGURE C-9: Adding a text box

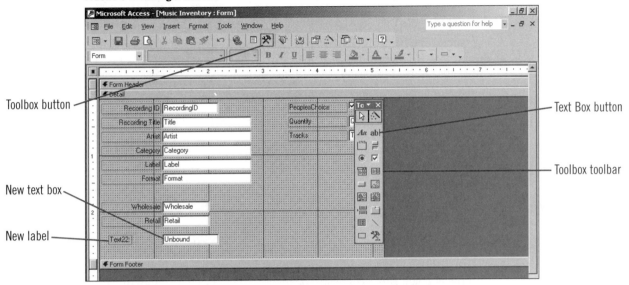

Toolbox button

New text box

New label

Text Box button

Toolbox toolbar

FIGURE C-10: Displaying a calculation

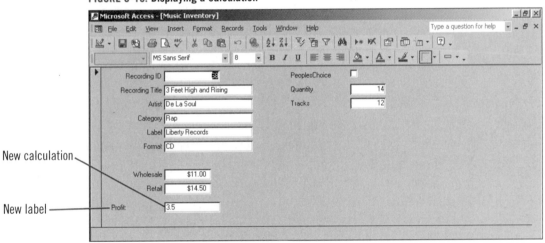

New calculation

New label

FIGURE C-11: Updated Music Inventory form

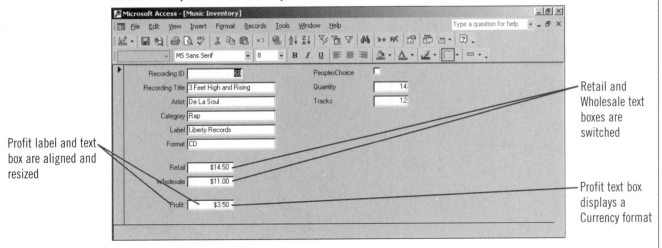

Profit label and text box are aligned and resized

Retail and Wholesale text boxes are switched

Profit text box displays a Currency format

Access 2002

Modifying Tab Order

Once all of the controls have been added, moved, and resized on the form, you'll want to check the tab order. The **tab order** is the order in which the **focus** (the active control) moves as you press [Tab] in Form View. Because the form is the primary object by which users will view, edit, and enter data, careful attention to tab order is essential to maintain the user's productivity and satisfaction with the form. ✦▬▬ Kelsey checks the tab order of the Music Inventory form, then changes the tab order as necessary in Form Design View.

QuickTip

You can also press [Enter] to move the focus from field to field in a form.

1. **Press [Tab] 11 times watching the focus move through the bound controls of the form**
Currently, focus moves back and forth between the left and right columns of controls. For efficient data entry, you want the focus to move down through the first column of text boxes before moving to the second column.

2. **Click the Design View button** ⧉ **on the Form View toolbar, click View on the menu bar, then click Tab Order**
The Tab Order dialog box allows you to change the tab order of controls in three sections: Form Header, Detail, and Form Footer. You can expand these sections in Form Design View by dragging the bottom edge of a section down to open it. Right now, all of the controls are positioned in the form's Detail section. See Table C-5 for more information on form sections. To change tab sequence, drag the **row selector**, positioned to the left of the field name, up or down. A black line will show you the new placement of the field in the list.

QuickTip

Click the Auto Order button in the Tab Order dialog box to automatically set a left-to-right, top-to-bottom tab order for the current arrangement of controls on the form.

3. **Click the Retail row selector in the Custom Order list, drag it up and position it just below Format, click the Wholesale row selector, drag it under Retail, click the Tracks row selector, drag it under Quantity, click the Text22 row selector, then drag it under Wholesale, as shown in Figure C-12**
Text22 represents the name of the text box that contains the profit calculation. If you wanted to give it a more descriptive name, you could have changed its Name property. The **Name property** for a text box is analogous to the Caption property for a label.

QuickTip

In Form Design View, press [Ctrl][.] to switch to Form view. In Form View, press [Ctrl][,] to switch to Form Design View.

4. **Click OK in the Tab Order dialog box, click the Save button** ⧉ **, then click the Form View button** ⧉ **on the Form Design toolbar**
Although nothing visibly changes on the form, the tab order is different.

5. **Press [Enter] 11 times to move through the fields of the form with the new tab order**
The focus now moves through all of the text boxes of the first column, and then moves through the second column.

6. **Continue pressing [Enter] until you reach the Retail value of the second record (which should be $15.00), type 16, then press [Enter]**
Changing the value in either the Retail or the Wholesale fields will automatically recalculate the value in the Profit field. Recording ID 55 now shows a profit of $6.00.

7. **Press [Enter] to move the focus to the Profit field, attempt to type 77, and observe the message in the status bar**
Even though the calculated control can receive the focus, its value cannot be directly edited in Form view. As the message indicates, its value is bound to the expression [Retail]-[Wholesale].

FIGURE C-12: Tab Order dialog box

Form Header section is closed

Detail section

Form Footer section is closed

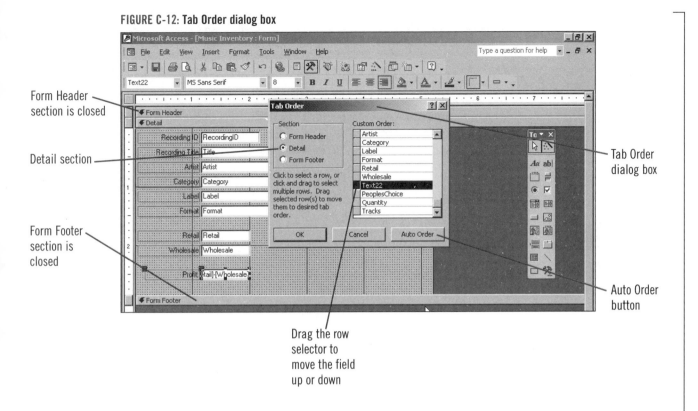

Tab Order dialog box

Auto Order button

Drag the row selector to move the field up or down

TABLE C-5: Form sections

section	description
Form Header	Controls placed in the Form Header section print only once at the top of the printout; by default, this section is closed in Form Design View
Detail	Controls placed in the Detail section display in Form View and print once for every record in the underlying table or query object; all controls created by the Form Wizard are placed in this section
Form Footer	Controls placed in the Form Footer section print only once at the end of the printout; by default, this section is closed in Form Design View

Entering and Editing Records

The most important reasons for using a form are to find, enter, or edit records in the underlying record source. You can also print a form, but printing all records in a form layout often produces a very long printout because of the vertical orientation of the fields. ✐ Kelsey uses the Music Inventory form to add a new record to the Music Inventory table. Then she prints only the new record.

1. Click the **New Record button** ▶✱ on the Form View toolbar

A new, blank record is displayed. The Recording ID field is an AutoNumber field that will automatically increment when you begin to enter data. The Specific Record box indicates the current record number.

QuickTip

A New Record button is also located on the Navigation buttons.

QuickTip

To enter a check in a check box press [Spacebar].

2. Press [Tab] to move the focus to the **Recording Title text box**, type **Your Name Dancers** to insert your name in the record, then enter the rest of the information shown in Figure C-13

The Profit text box shows the calculated result of $6.00. The new record is stored as record 78 in the Music Inventory table.

Trouble?

Don't click the Print button on the Form View toolbar unless you want *all* of the records to print.

3. Click **File** on the menu bar, click **Print** to open the Print dialog box, click the **Selected Record(s) option button** in the Print Range section, then click **OK**

Forms are also often used to find, edit, or delete existing records in the database.

4. Click the **Recording Title text box**, click the **Find button** 🔍 on the Form View toolbar to open the Find and Replace dialog box, type **Mermaid Avenue** in the Find What text box, then click **Find Next**

Record 46 appears behind the Find and Replace dialog box, as shown in Figure C-14.

QuickTip

As the confirmation message indicates, you cannot undo the deletion of a record.

5. Click **Cancel** in the Find and Replace dialog box, click the **Delete Record button** ▶✕ on the Form View toolbar, then click **Yes** to confirm the deletion

Forms are also a great way to filter the records to a specific subset of information.

6. Click **Gospel** in the Category text box, click the **Filter By Form button** 🗐 on the Form View toolbar, click the **Category list arrow**, click **Gospel**, click the **Or tab** in the lower-left corner of the Filter By Form window, click the **Category list arrow**, click **Children**, then click the **Apply Filter button** 🔽 on the Filter/Sort toolbar

Eight records were found that matched the Gospel or Children criteria in the Category field.

7. Click the **Print Preview button** 🔍 on the Form View toolbar, then click the **Last Page button** ▶❙ in the Navigation buttons

Previewing the records helps to determine how many pages the printout would be. Since about three records print on a page, your printout is three pages long.

8. Click the **Close button** 𝖢𝗅𝗈𝗌𝖾 on the Print Preview toolbar, then click the **Remove Filter button** 🔽 on the Form View toolbar so that all 77 records in the Music Inventory table are redisplayed

FIGURE C-13: Entering a new record into a form

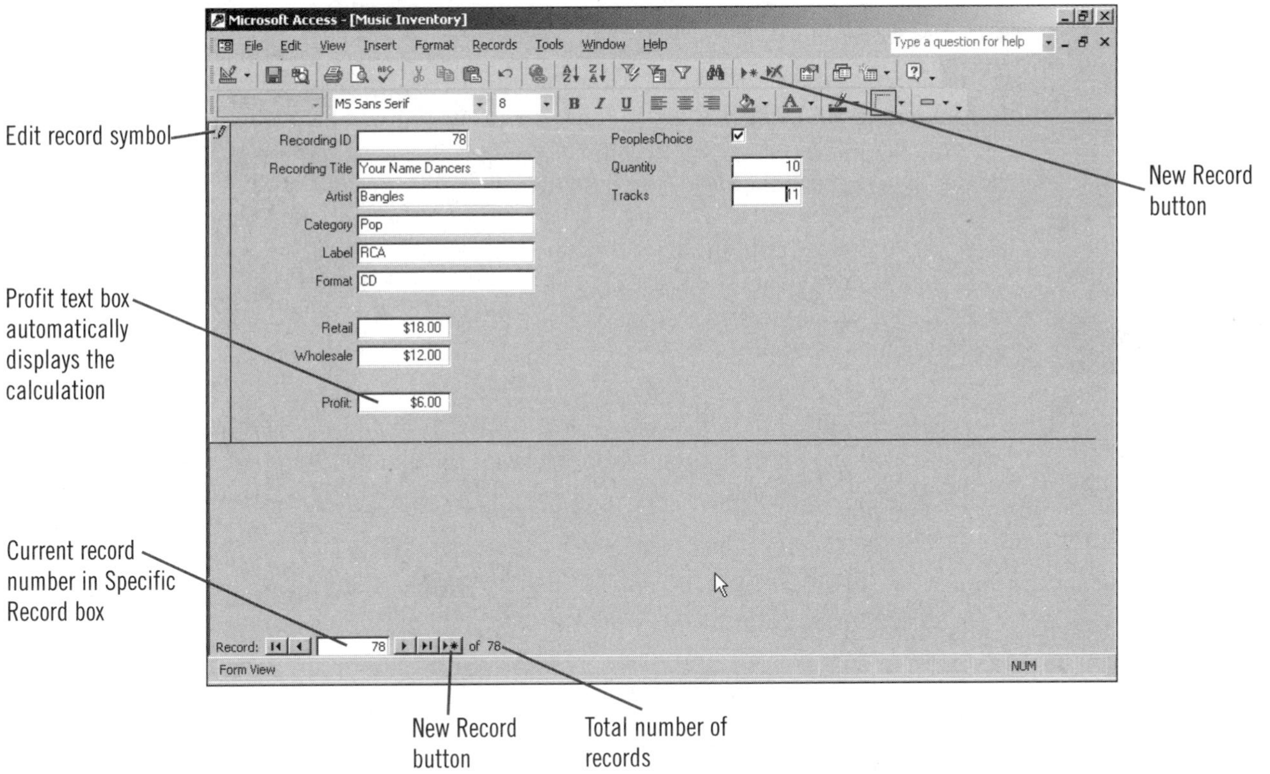

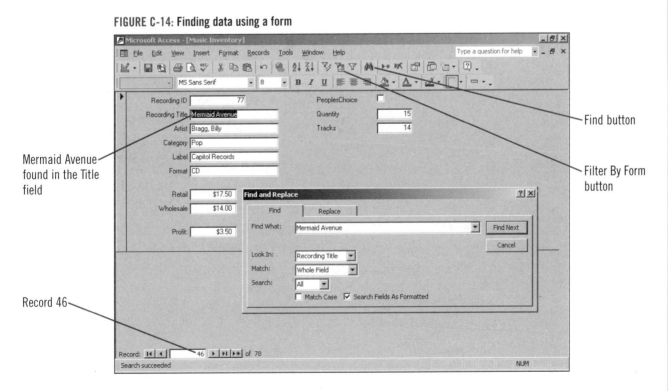

Edit record symbol

Profit text box automatically displays the calculation

New Record button

Current record number in Specific Record box

New Record button

Total number of records

FIGURE C-14: Finding data using a form

Mermaid Avenue found in the Title field

Find button

Filter By Form button

Record 46

Inserting an Image

Graphic images, such as pictures, a logo, or clip art, can add style and professionalism to a form. Images are added to a form as either bound or unbound controls. The form section in which they are placed is also significant. For example, if you add an **unbound image** such as a company logo to the Form Header section, the image will appear at the top of the form in Form View as well as at the top of a printout. If you add the same unbound image to the Detail section, it would appear multiple times because the Detail section is reproduced once for every record. **Bound images** are tied to a field defined with an OLE Object data type and store multimedia data such as pictures or sound clips. Kelsey adds the MediaLoft logo and a descriptive title to the Form Header section using an unbound image control.

1. Click the **Design View button** on the Form View toolbar, place the pointer on the bottom edge of the **Form Header section** so that the pointer changes to ⊥, then drag the bottom of the Form Header section to the **1 inch** mark on the vertical ruler
   The Form Header section is open.

2. Click the **Image button** on the Toolbox toolbar, then click the pointer in the **Form Header section** at the **1 inch** mark on the horizontal ruler
   The Insert Picture dialog box opens.

3. Click the **Look in list arrow**, navigate to the drive and folder where your Project Files are located, click **Smallmedia**, then click **OK**
   The MediaLoft logo is inserted into the Form Header, as shown in Figure C-15. Placing a title in the Form Header section adds a finishing touch to the form.

4. Click the **Label button** on the Toolbox toolbar, click the ⁺A pointer to the right of the **MediaLoft logo** in the Form Header section, type **MediaLoft Music**, then press **[Enter]**
   Labels can be formatted to enhance the appearance on the form.

5. Click the **Font Size list arrow**, click **24**, double-click a **sizing handle** so that the label **MediaLoft Music** is completely displayed, click the **Font/Fore Color list arrow**, click the dark blue box (second from the right on the top row), click the **Save button**, then click the **Form View button** to observe the changes, as shown in Figure C-16
   You can spell check the records to correct any errors. The Spelling dialog box has options to ignore all values in a particular field, ignore a single occurrence of a word, ignore all occurrences of a word, plus other options.

QuickTip

[F7] is the quick keystroke to open the Spelling dialog box.

6. Click the **Spelling button** on the Form View toolbar, click **Ignore 'Artist' Field** in the Spelling dialog box as shown in Figure C-17, click **Ignore All** in the Spelling dialog box to skip all occurrences of Ryko, click **Ignore 'Title' Field** to ignore Closeup and all other entries in the Title field, click **Ignore All** to skip all occurrences of Arista, click **Ignore All** to skip all occurrences of Narada, click **Ignore All** to skip all occurrences of Gramaphone, click **Change** to change Recrds to Records, then click **OK**
   To add an entry such as Ryko to the custom dictionary, you would click the Add button in the Spelling dialog box.

7. Find and print the record for RecordingID 78, which displays Your Name Dancers in the Recording Title

8. Close the Music Inventory form, close the MediaLoft-C database, then exit Access

FIGURE C-15: Adding an image to the Form Header section

1" mark on the horizontal ruler

1" mark on the vertical ruler

MediaLoft logo

Label button

Image button

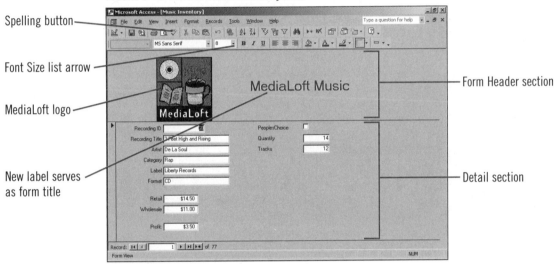

FIGURE C-16: The final Music Inventory form

Spelling button

Font Size list arrow

MediaLoft logo

New label serves as form title

Form Header section

Detail section

FIGURE-C-17: Spelling dialog box

Ignore single occurrence of a word

Change word to selected suggestion

Ignore all entries in the Artist field

Ignore all occurrences of a word

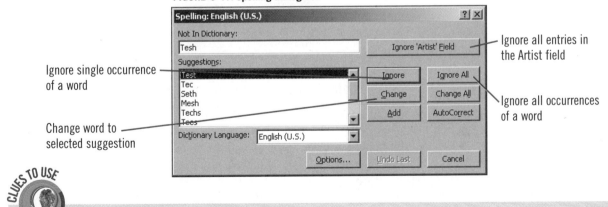

CLUES TO USE

Using the Custom Dictionary

The **custom dictionary** is a supplemental dictionary to which you add words that are spelled correctly, such as proper names, but which are not already stored in the default Access dictionary. Since the custom dictionary file is used across all Office applications on a particular computer, do not add words to it unless you are the only user of that computer.

Practice

► Concepts Review

Label each element of Form View shown in Figure C-18.

FIGURE C-18

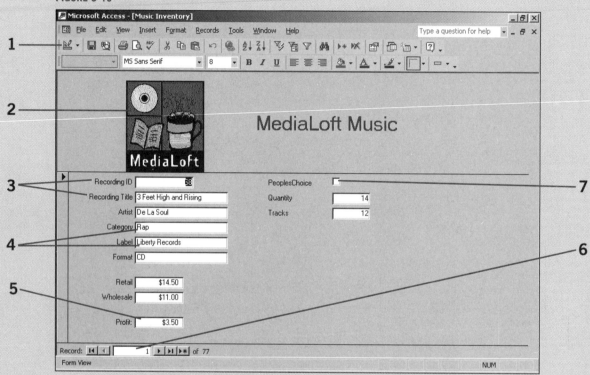

Match each term with the statement that describes it.

8. Sizing handles

9. Detail section

10. Bound control

11. Tab order

12. Form

13. Calculated control

a. An Access database object that allows you to arrange the fields of a record in any layout and is used to enter, edit, and delete records

b. Used on a form to display data from a field

c. Squares that appear in the corners and edges of the selected control

d. The way in which the focus moves from one bound control to the next

e. Uses a text box and an expression to display an answer

f. Controls placed here print once for every record in the underlying table or query object

Select the best answer from the list of choices.

14. Every element on a form is called a:
    a. Property.
    b. Control.
    c. Piece.
    d. Handle.

15. The mouse pointer that is used to resize a control is:
    a. ⟷
    b. ↔
    c. ✋
    d. 👆

16. The most common bound control is the:
    a. Label.
    b. Text box.
    c. Combo box.
    d. Check box.

17. The most common unbound control is the:
    a. Label.
    b. Text box.
    c. Combo box.
    d. Image.

18. The _____ View is used to move or resize form controls.
    a. Form
    b. Datasheet
    c. Print Preview
    d. Design

19. The _____ control is commonly used to display data on a form from a field with a Yes/No data type.
    a. Text box
    b. Label
    c. Check box
    d. Combo box

20. The _____ dictionary is a supplemental dictionary to which you add words that are spelled correctly, such as proper names.
    a. Custom
    b. Caption
    c. Name
    d. User

▶ Skills Review

1. **Plan a form.**
    a. Plan a form to use for entering business contacts by looking at several business cards.
    b. Write down the organization of the fields on the form.
    c. Determine what type of control you will use for each bound field.
    d. Identify the labels you would like to display on the form.

2. **Create a form.**
    a. Start Access and open the **Membership-C** database from the drive and folder where your Project Files are located.
    b. Click the Forms button in the Membership-C Database window, then double-click the Create form by using wizard option.
    c. Base the form on the CONTACTS table, and include all of the fields.
    d. Use a Columnar layout, a Standard style, and title the form **Contact Entry Form**.
    e. Display the form in Form View.

3. **Move and resize controls.**
    a. Open and maximize the Design View window for the Contact Entry Form.
    b. Move the LNAME text box and corresponding label to the right of the FNAME text box.
    c. Move the DUESOWED and DUESPAID text boxes and corresponding labels to the right of the address controls.
    d. Resize the PHONE and ZIP text boxes to be the same size as the CITY text box.
    e. Move the PHONE text box and corresponding label between the FNAME and COMPANY controls. The resulting form should look similar to Figure C-19.

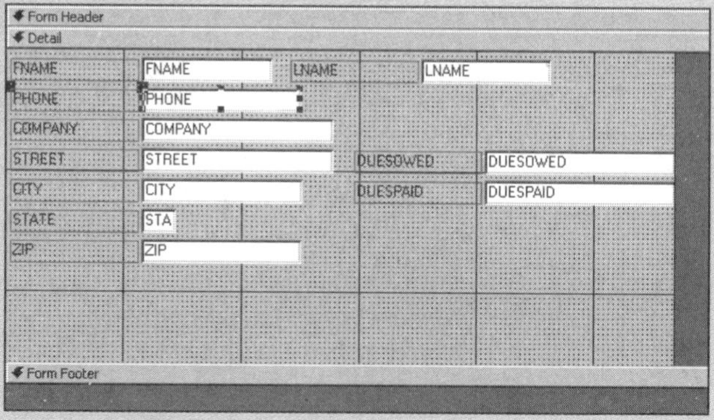

4. **Modify labels.**
    a. Right-align all of the labels. Be careful to right-align the labels, and not the text boxes.
    b. Edit the caption of the FNAME label to **FIRST NAME**, the LNAME label to **LAST NAME**, the DUESOWED label to **DUES OWED**, and the DUESPAID label to **DUES PAID**.

5. **Modify text boxes.**
    a. Add a new text box below the DUESPAID text box.
    b. Type the expression =**[DUESOWED]-[DUESPAID]** in the new unbound text box. (*Hint:* Remember that you must use the *exact field names* as defined in Table Design View in a calculated expression.)
    c. In the property sheet for the new calculated control, change the Format property to Currency.
    d. Right-align the new calculated control.
    e. Change the accompanying label from Text20: to **BALANCE**.
    f. Move and resize the new calculated control and label so that it is aligned beneath the DUESOWED and DUES-PAID controls.

6. **Modify tab order.**
    a. Change the Tab order so that pressing [Tab] moves the focus through the text boxes in the following order: FNAME, LNAME, PHONE, COMPANY, STREET, CITY, STATE, ZIP, DUESOWED, DUESPAID, Text20 (the calculated control).
    b. Save your changes, open the form in Form View, then test the new tab order.

FIGURE C-19

7. Enter and edit records.

a. Use the Contact Entry Form to enter the following new records:

	FIRST NAME	LAST NAME	PHONE	COMPANY	STREET
Record 1	Jane	Eagan	555-1166	Cummins Construction	1515 Maple St.
Record 2	Connie	Sinclaire	555-2277	Motorola	1010 Green St.

	CITY	STATE	ZIP	DUES OWED	DUES PAID
1 con't.	Fontanelle	KS	50033	$50.00	$25.00
2 con't.	Bridgewater	KS	50022	$50.00	$50.00

b. Find the Connie Sinclaire record, enter your last name in the COMPANY text box, then print that record.

c. Find the Lois Goode record, enter **IBM** in the COMPANY text box, change Barnes in the STREET field to **your last name**, then print that record.

d. Filter for all records with a ZIP entry of 64145. How many records did you find? Write the answer on the back of the previous printout.

e. Sort the filtered 64145 zip code records in ascending order by LAST NAME, change the street name for this record to **your last name**, then print this record.

8. Insert an image.

a. In Form Design View, expand the Form Header section to the 1" mark on the vertical ruler.

b. Use the Image control to insert the **Hand.bmp** file in the left side of the Form Header. (*Note:* The Hand.bmp file is on the drive and folder where your Project Files are located.)

c. Centered and below the graphic file, add the label **MEMBERSHIP INFORMATION** in a 24-point font. Be sure to resize the label so that all of the text is visible.

d. Below the MEMBERSHIP INFORMATION label, add your name as a label.

e. View the form in Form View, then spell check the records.

f. Sort the records in descending order based on the COMPANY values. Print only the first record.

g. Save and close the form, close the database, then exit Access.

▶ Independent Challenge 1

As the office manager of a cardiology clinic, you need to create a data entry form for new patients.

a. Start Access, open the **Clinic-C** database from the drive and folder where your Project Files are located.

b. Using the Form Wizard, create a form that includes all the fields in the Demographics table, using the Columnar layout and Standard style. Title the form **Patient Entry Form**.

c. In Form Design View, move the DOB, Gender, Ins Code, and Entry Date controls to a second column to the right of the existing column. DOB should be next to Last Name.

d. Switch the positions of the State and ZIP controls.

FIGURE C-20

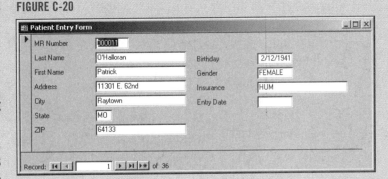

e. Modify the Medical Record Number label to **MR Number**, the Address 1 label to **Address**, the DOB label to **Birthday**, and the Ins Code label to **Insurance**. Be sure to modify the labels, not the text boxes. The final organization of the form is shown in Figure C-20.

f. Change the tab order so that State is before Zip.

g. Use the newly created form to add a record using your own personal information. Enter **2002** for the MR Number, **BCBS** for the Insurance, and **2/1/02** for the Entry Date.

h. Print only the new record that you just added.

i. Save and close the Patient Entry Form, close the Clinic-C database, then exit Access.

► Independent Challenge 2

As office manager of a cardiology clinic, you want to build a form that quickly calculates a height-to-weight ratio value based on information in the Outcomes Data table.

a. Start Access, then open the **Clinic-C** database from the drive and folder where your Project Files are located.

b. Using the Form Wizard, create a form based on the Outcomes Data table with only the following fields: MR#, Height, and Weight.

c. Use the Columnar layout and Standard style, and name the form **Height to Weight Ratio Form**.

d. In Design View, use the Text Box button to add a text box and accompanying label below the Weight text box.

e. Enter the expression **=[Height]/[Weight]** in the unbound text box.

f. Modify the calculated expression's label from Text6: to **Ratio**.

g. Resize the Ratio label so that it is closer to the calculated expression control, then right-align all of the labels.

h. Change the format property of the calculated control to Fixed.

i. Open the Form Header section about 0.5", then add a label to that section with your name as the caption.

j. Save and view the form, then print the form for the record with the MR Number of 006494.

k. Sort the records in descending order by Height, change the value in the Weight field to **200**, then print this record.

l. Close the Height to Weight Ratio Form, close the Clinic-C database, then exit Access.

► Independent Challenge 3

As office manager of a cardiology clinic, you want to build a form to enter new insurance information.

a. Open the **Clinic-C** database from the drive and folder where your Project Files are located.

b. Using the Form Wizard, create a form based on the Insurance Company Information table, and include all of the fields.

c. Use the Columnar layout, Standard style, and accept **Insurance Company Information** as the title.

d. Edit the Caption of the Insurance Company Name label to **Insurance Company**. Be sure to modify the Insurance Company Name label, not the text box.

e. Resize the State text box so that it is the same size as the City text box.

f. Expand the Form Header section, then add the graphic image **Medical.bmp** to the left side of the Form Header section. The Medical.bmp file is in the drive and folder where your Project Files are located.

g. Add a label **Insurance Entry Form** and another for **your name** to the right of the medical clip art in the Form Header section.

h. Increase the size of the Insurance Entry Form label to 18 points. Resize the label to display the entire caption.

i. Switch to Form View, then find the record for the Cigna Insurance Company. Change Sherman in the City field to your last name, then print this record.

j. Filter for all records with a State entry of KS. How many records did you find? Write the answer on the back of the previous printout.

k. Save and close the Insurance Company Information Form, close the Clinic-C database, then exit Access.

Independent Challenge 4

You are on the staff of an economic development team whose goal is to encourage tourism in the Baltic Sea region. You have created an Access database called Baltic-C to track important fields of information for the countries in that region, and will use the Internet to find information about the area and enter it into existing forms.

a. Start Access and open the **Baltic-C** database from the drive and folder where your Project Files are located.

b. Connect to the Internet, then go to www.about.com, www.alltheweb.com, or any general search engine to conduct research for your database. Your goal is to find information for at least one new city record for each country.

c. Open the Countries form. You can enter the data you found on the Internet for each city by using the City fields shown in Figure C-21. This arrangement of data organizes cities within countries using a main form/subform arrangement. The main form contains a single text box tied to the Country field. The subform presents a datasheet of four City fields. Be sure to enter the Population data for that particular city, rather than for the entire country. CityID is an AutoNumber field, so it will automatically increment as you enter the City, Capital, and Population data.

FIGURE C-21

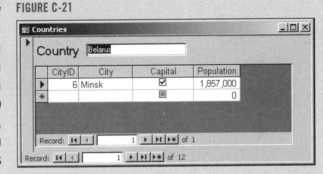

d. Close the Countries form, then open the Countries table datasheet. Click all of the expand buttons to the left of each of the Country records to show the city records that you just entered through the Countries form, then print the expanded datasheet. Close the Countries table.

e. Open the Cities form and find the Olso, Norway record shown in Figure C-22. This form shows another main form/subform arrangement. The main form contains fields that describe the city, whereas the subform contains a datasheet with fields that describe the events for that city.

f. Return to the search engine, and research upcoming tourist events for Copenhagen, Denmark.

g. In the Cities form, find the Copenhagen record, then enter three events for Copenhagen. EventID is an AutoNumber field, so it will automatically increment as you enter the EventName and EventDate information.

h. Print the Copenhagen record, close the Cities form, close the Baltic-C database, then exit Access.

FIGURE C-22

▶ Visual Workshop

Open the **Clinic-C** database, then use the Form Wizard to create the form based on the Demographics table, as shown in Figure C-23. Notice that the label **Patient Form** is 24 points and has been placed in the Form Header section. The clip art, Medstaff.bmp, can be found in the drive and folder where your Project Files are located. The image has been placed on the right side of the Detail section, and many controls were moved and resized. Also notice that the labels are right-aligned. To change the background color of the Detail section to white, double-click the Detail section bar in Form Design View, then modify the Back Color property on the Format tab of the property sheet to **16777215**, the value that corresponds to white. Enter your own name and gender for the first record, then print it.

FIGURE C-23

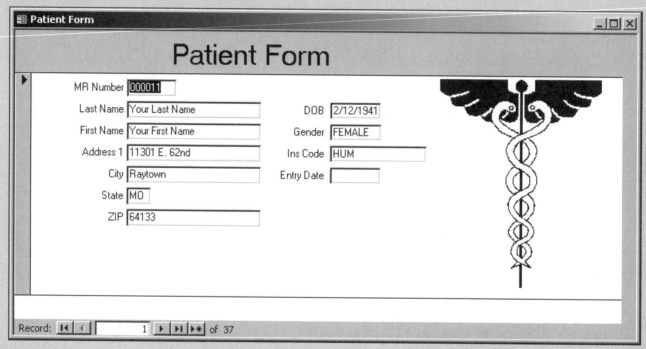

Using

Reports

Objectives

- ► **Plan a report**
- MOUS ► **Create a report**
- MOUS ► **Group records**
- MOUS ► **Change the sort order**
- MOUS ► **Add a calculation**
- MOUS ► **Align controls**
- MOUS ► **Format controls**
- ► **Create mailing labels**

A **report** is an Access object used to create professional printouts. The record source for an Access report is either a table or a query object. A report is created using commands and tools similar to those used to create a form. Although you can print a datasheet or form, reports are the primary object used to create professional printouts because reports provide many more printing options. For example, a report may include formatting embellishments such as multiple fonts and colors, extra graphical elements such as clip art and lines, and multiple headers and footers. Reports are also very powerful analysis tools. A report can calculate subtotals, averages, counts, or other statistics for groups of records. You cannot enter or edit data through a report. ▰▰▰ Kelsey Lang, a marketing manager at MediaLoft, wants to produce some reports to distribute to MediaLoft employees.

Planning a Report

Hard copy reports are often the primary tool used to communicate database information at meetings, with clients or customers, or with top executives. Time spent planning your report not only increases your productivity but also ensures that the report meets its intended objectives. Creating a report is similar to creating a form, and you work with bound, unbound, and calculated controls in Report Design View just as you do in Form Design View. Reports, however, have more sections than forms. The report **section** determines how often and where controls placed within that section print in the final report. See Table D-1 for more information on report sections. 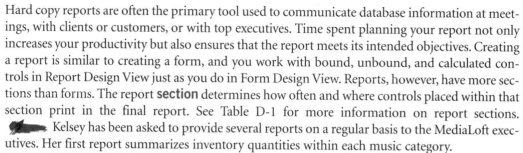 Kelsey has been asked to provide several reports on a regular basis to the MediaLoft executives. Her first report summarizes inventory quantities within each music category.

Kelsey uses the following guidelines to plan her report:

▶ **Identify a meaningful title for the report**

The title should clearly identify the purpose of the report and be meaningful to those who will be reading the report. The title is created with a label control placed in the Report Header section.

▶ **Determine the information (the fields and records) that the report will show**

You can base a report on a table, but usually you create a query to gather the specific fields from the one or more tables upon which the report is based. If you base the report on a query, you are also able to set criteria within the query to limit the number of records displayed by the report.

▶ **Determine how the fields should be organized on the report**

Most reports display fields in a horizontal layout across the page, but you can arrange them any way you want. Just as in forms, bound text box controls are used on a report to display the data stored in the underlying fields. These text boxes are generally placed in the report **Detail** section. The Detail section of a report is always visible in Report Design View.

▶ **Determine how the records should be sorted and/or grouped within the report**

In an Access report, **grouping** means to sort records in a particular order *plus* provide a section before the group of records called the Group Header section and a section after the group of records called the Group Footer section. The **Group Header** section contains controls that introduce the upcoming group of records. The **Group Footer** section holds controls that calculate statistics such as subtotals for the preceding group of records.

The ability to group records is extremely powerful. For example, you might group the records of an address report by the State field. Since State is the grouping field, you would be able to add the State Header and State Footer sections to the report. In the State Header section you might add a text box bound to the State field that displays the name of the state before listing the Detail records for that state. In the State Footer section you might add a text box that contains an expression to count the number of records within each state. You might want to further sort the records by the City field, so that the Detail records printed for each state would be listed in ascending order based on the value of the City field.

Group Header and Footer sections are opened by specifying a Yes value to these field properties in the Sorting and Grouping dialog box, opened by clicking the Sorting and Grouping button ▤ on the Report Design toolbar.

▶ **Identify any other descriptive information that should be placed at the beginning or end of the report, or at the top or bottom of each page**

You will use the **Report Header**, **Report Footer**, **Page Header**, and **Page Footer** sections to add information that you wish to print on every page, or at the beginning or end of the report. For example, you might add a text box that contains an expression to display the current date in the Page Header section, or you might add a text box that contains an expression to display the current page number in the Page Footer section. The Report Header and Report Footer sections of a report can be opened using the Report Header/Footer option on the View menu in Report Design View.

Kelsey sketched her first report as shown in Figure D-1.

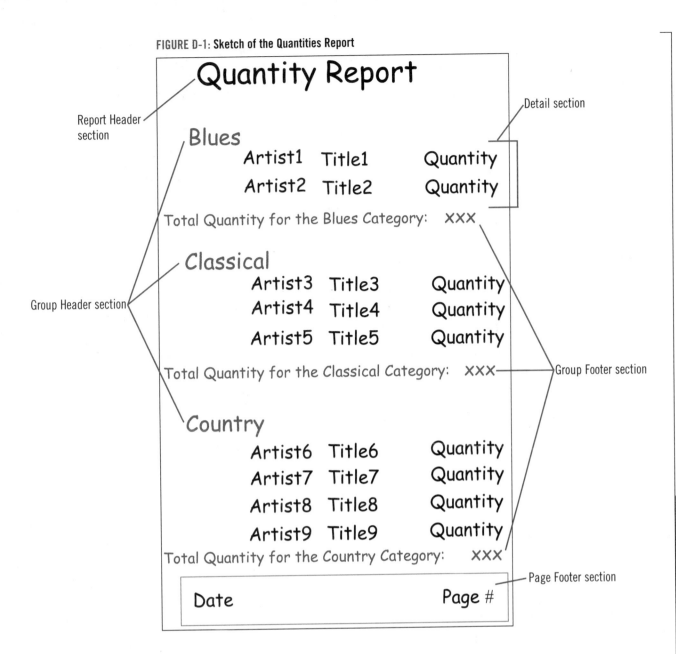

Quantity Report

Report Header section

Detail section

Blues

Artist1 Title1   Quantity
Artist2 Title2   Quantity

Total Quantity for the Blues Category: xxx

Classical

Artist3 Title3   Quantity
Artist4 Title4   Quantity
Artist5 Title5   Quantity

Group Header section

Total Quantity for the Classical Category: xxx

Group Footer section

Country

Artist6 Title6   Quantity
Artist7 Title7   Quantity
Artist8 Title8   Quantity
Artist9 Title9   Quantity

Total Quantity for the Country Category: xxx

Page Footer section

Date   Page #

TABLE D-1: Report sections

section	where does this section print?	which controls are most commonly placed in this section?
Report Header	At the top of the first page of the report	Label controls containing the report title; can also include clip art, a logo image, or a line separating the title from the rest of the report
Page Header	At the top of every page (but below the Report Header on page one)	Text box controls containing a page number or date expression
Group Header	Before every group of records	Text box control for the field by which the records are grouped
Detail	Once for every record	Text box controls for the rest of the fields in the recordset (the table or query upon which the report is built)
Group Footer	After every group of records	Text box controls containing calculated expressions, such as subtotals or counts, for the records in that group
Page Footer	At the bottom of every page	Text box controls containing a page number or date expression
Report Footer	At the end of the entire report	Text box controls containing expressions such as grand totals or counts that calculate a value for all of the records in the report

Creating a Report

You can create reports in Access in Report Design View, or you can use the Report Wizard to help you get started. The **Report Wizard** asks questions that guide you through the initial development of the report, similar to the Form Wizard. Your responses to the Report Wizard questions specify the fields you want to view in the report, the style and layout of the report, and how you want the records to be sorted, grouped, and analyzed. Another way to quickly create a report is by selecting a table or query, clicking the New Object list arrow ▣▾ on the Database toolbar, and then clicking AutoReport. AutoReport, however, does not give you a chance to review the options provided by the Report Wizard. Kelsey uses the Report Wizard to create the Quantities Report she planned on paper.

Steps

1. Start Access, click the **More files link** in the Open a file section of the New File task pane, then open the **MediaLoft-D** database from the drive and folder where your Project Files are located

   This database contains a Music Inventory table and a query object from which you will base your reports.

2. Click **Reports** on the Objects bar in the MediaLoft-D database window, then double-click **Create report by using wizard**

   The Report Wizard dialog box opens. The Selection Quantities query has the fields you need for this report.

3. Click the **Tables/Queries list arrow**, click **Query: Selection Quantities**, click **Category** in the Available Fields list, then click the **Select Single Field button** ⊳

   The Category field moves from the Available Fields list to the Selected Fields list.

Trouble?

If you did not select the fields in the correct order, click the Remove Single Field button ◁ to move fields from the Selected Fields list back to the Available Fields list.

4. Double-click **Title**, double-click **Artist**, then double-click **Quantity**

   The four fields are selected and the first dialog box of the Report Wizard should look like Figure D-2. The Report Wizard also asks grouping and sorting questions that determine the order and amount of detail provided on the report.

5. Click **Next**, click **Next** to move past the grouping levels question, click the **first sort order list arrow** in the Report Wizard dialog box, then click **Category**

   You can use the Report Wizard to specify up to four sort fields in either an ascending or descending sort order for each field.

Trouble?

Click Back to review previous dialog boxes within a wizard.

6. Click **Next**, click **Next** to accept the **Tabular** layout and **Portrait** orientation, click **Corporate** for the style, click **Next**, type **Quantities Report** for the report title, verify that the **Preview the report option button** is selected, then click **Finish**

   The Quantities Report opens in Print Preview, as shown in Figure D-3. It is very similar to the sketch created earlier. Notice that the records are sorted by the Category field.

FIGURE D-2: Report Wizard dialog box

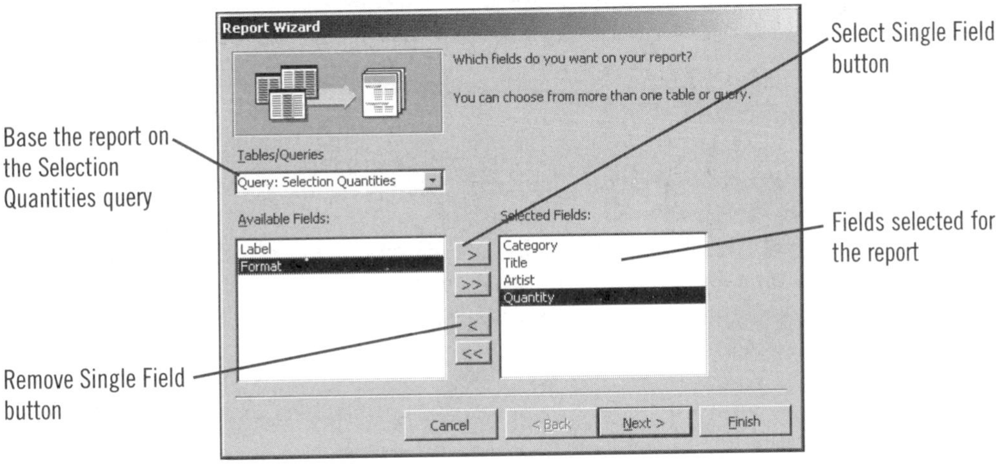

Base the report on the Selection Quantities query

Remove Single Field button

Select Single Field button

Fields selected for the report

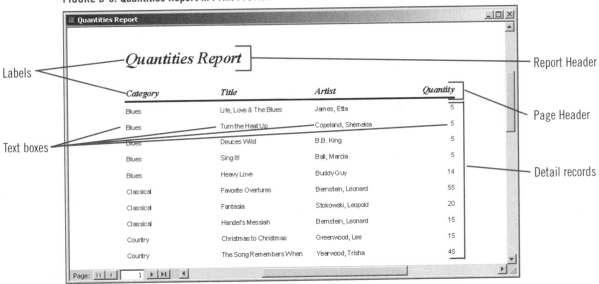

FIGURE D-3: Quantities Report in Print Preview

Labels

Text boxes

Report Header

Page Header

Detail records

Why reports should be based on queries

Although you can use the first dialog box of the Report Wizard to select fields from different tables without first creating a query to collect those fields into one object, it is not recommended. If you later decide that you want to add more fields to the report or limit the number of records in the table, you will find it very easy to add fields or criteria to an underlying query object to meet these new needs. To accomplish this same task without using an intermediary query object requires that you change the Record Source property of the report itself, which most users find more difficult than working with a query.

Grouping Records

Grouping refers to sorting records on a report *in addition to* providing an area above and below the group of records in which additional controls can be placed. These two special sections of the report are called the Group Header and Group Footer. You can create groups on a report through the Report Wizard, or you can change an existing report's grouping and sorting fields in Report Design View. Just as with forms, you make all structural changes to a report in the object's Design View. Kelsey wants to group the Quantities Report by the Category field instead of simply sorting it by Category. In addition, she wants to add controls to the Group Header and Group Footer to clarify and summarize information within the report.

Steps

1. Click the **Design View button** on the Print Preview toolbar to switch to Report Design View

   Report Design View shows you the sections of the report as well as the controls within each section. It is difficult to visually distinguish labels and text boxes in Report Design View, but you can always open the property sheet and view its title bar to determine the type of control you're working with. Report Design View is where you change grouping and sorting fields.

2. Click the **Sorting and Grouping button** on the Report Design toolbar, click the **Group Header text box**, click the **Group Header list arrow**, click **Yes**, click the **Group Footer text box**, click the **Group Footer list arrow**, then click **Yes**

   Specifying Yes for the Group Header and Group Footer properties opens those sections of the report in Report Design View. The dialog box is shown in Figure D-4.

3. Click to close the Sorting and Grouping dialog box, click the **Category text box** in the Detail section, then drag the **text box** with the 🖐 pointer straight up into the Category Header section

   Trouble?
   Be careful to drag the Category text box in the Detail section rather than the Category label in the Page Header section.

   By placing the Category text box in the Category Header, it will print once for each new category value rather than once for each record. You can add a calculated control to subtotal each category of records by placing a text box in the Category Footer section, and entering an expression into the text box.

4. If the Toolbox toolbar is not visible, click the **Toolbox button** on the Report Design toolbar, click the **Text Box button** on the Toolbox toolbar, then click in the **Category Footer section** directly below the Quantity text box

   Your screen should look like Figure D-5. You can modify the label and text box controls in the Category Footer section to describe and define the Quantity field subtotal.

5. Click the **Text13: label** in the Category Footer section to select it, double-click **Text13**, type **Subtotal**, then press **[Enter]**

   Trouble?
   If you double-click the label itself (versus Text13), you will open the control's property sheet.

6. Click the **unbound text box control** in the Category Footer section to select it, click **Unbound** within the text box control to edit it, type **=sum([Quantity])**, then press **Enter**

   The expression that calculates the sum of the Quantity field is now in the text box control. Calculated expressions start with an equal sign. When entering an expression, the field name is not case sensitive, but it must be surrounded by square brackets and match the field name as defined in Table Design View.

7. Click the **Print Preview button** on the Report Design toolbar

   Since the Category text box was moved to the Category Header section, it prints only once per group of records as shown in Figure D-6. Each group of records is followed by a Group Footer that includes the Subtotal label as well as a calculated field that subtotals the Quantity field for that group of records.

8. Click the **Close button** on the Print Preview toolbar, click to toggle off the Toolbox, click the **Save button**, then close the Quantities Report

FIGURE D-4: Sorting and Grouping dialog box

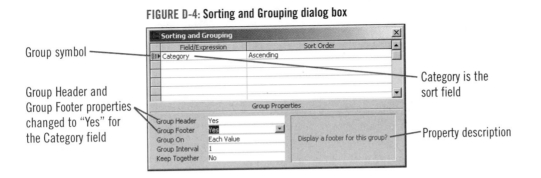

Group symbol

Group Header and Group Footer properties changed to "Yes" for the Category field

Category is the sort field

Property description

FIGURE D-5: Quantities Report in Report Design View

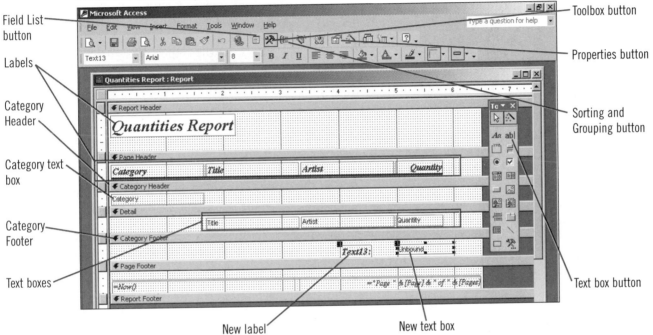

Field List button

Labels

Category Header

Category text box

Category Footer

Text boxes

Toolbox button

Properties button

Sorting and Grouping button

Text box button

New label

New text box

FIGURE D-6: The Quantities Report grouped by the Category field

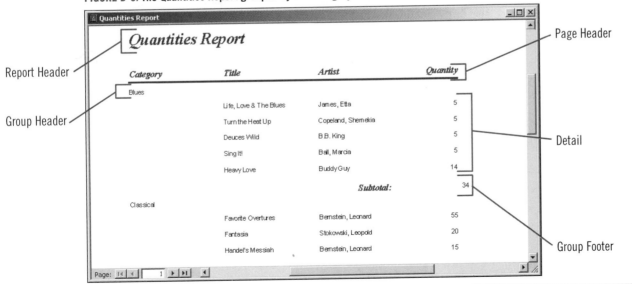

Report Header

Group Header

Page Header

Detail

Group Footer

Changing the Sort Order

The grouping field acts as a primary sort field. You can define additional sort fields too. When you sort records within a group, you order the Detail records according to a particular field. The Report Wizard prompts you for group and sort information at the time you create the report, but you can also group and sort an existing report by using the Sorting and Grouping dialog box in Report Design View. ✎ Kelsey wants to modify the Quantities Report so that the Detail records are sorted by the Artist field within the Category group.

Steps 1234

1. **Right-click the Quantities Report, then click Design View**
   The Quantities Report opens in Design View.

2. **Click the Sorting and Grouping button [≣] on the Report Design toolbar, click the Field/Expression text box in the second row, click the Field/Expression list arrow, then click Artist as shown in Figure D-7**
   Both the Group Header and Group Footer Group property values are set to No, which indicates that the Artist field is providing a sort order only.

3. **Click [≣] to toggle the Sorting and Grouping dialog box off, then click the Print Preview button [▣] on the Report Design toolbar**
   Part of the report is shown in Print Preview, as shown in Figure D-8. You can use the buttons on the Print Preview toolbar to view more of the report.

> **QuickTip**
> The grid will expand to 4 × 5 pages if you keep dragging to expand it.

4. **Click the One Page button [▣] on the Print Preview toolbar to view one miniature page, click the Two Pages button [▣] to view two pages, click the Multiple Pages button [▣], then drag to the right in the grid to show 1 × 4 Pages as shown in Figure D-9**
   The Print Preview window displays the four pages of the report. You can click the Zoom pointers [🔍] and [🔍] to change the zoom magnification.

> **QuickTip**
> You can also type a number into the Fit text box to zoom at a specific percent.

5. **Point to the last subtotal on the last page of the report with the [🔍] pointer, click to read the number 92 in the last subtotal of the report, then click again to view all four pages of the report in the Preview window**
   To zoom the preview to a specific percentage, click the Fit button list arrow [Fit ▾] on the Print Preview toolbar, then click a percentage. The Fit option automatically adjusts the preview to display all pages in the report.

6. **Click the Close button [Close] on the Print Preview toolbar, then click the Save button [▣] on the Report Design toolbar**

Adding a field to a report

To add a field from the underlying table or query object to the report, click the Field List button [▣] on the Report Design toolbar, then drag the field from the field list to the appropriate position on the report.

This action creates both a label control that displays the field name and a bound text box control that displays the value of the field on the resulting report.

FIGURE D-7: Specifying a sort order

Group symbol
Artist field is selected
Grouping sections are turned off for the Artist field

Ascending sort order
Field/Expression list arrow

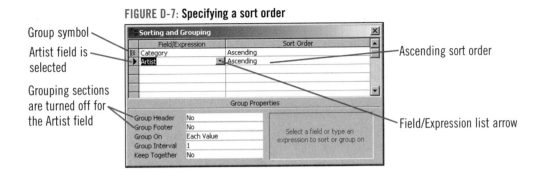

FIGURE D-8: The Quantities Report sorted by Artist

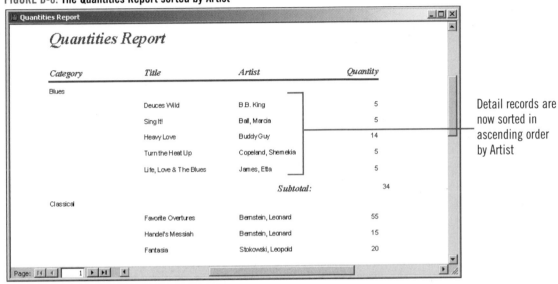

Detail records are now sorted in ascending order by Artist

FIGURE D-9: Print Preview

Fit button list arrow
Drag to 1 × 4 Pages
One Page button
Two Pages button
Multiple Pages button

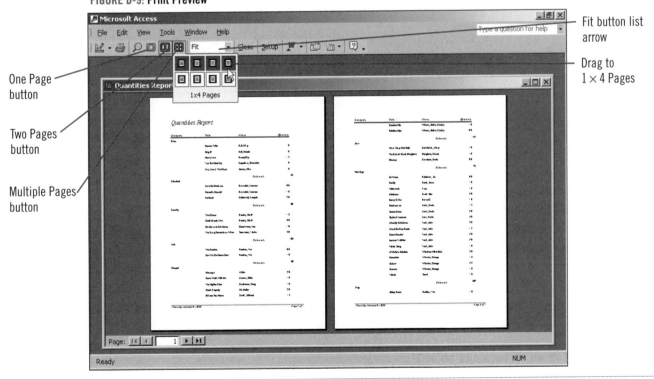

Adding a Calculation

In a report, you create a **calculation** by entering an expression into an unbound text box. When a report is previewed or printed, the expression is evaluated and the resulting calculation is placed on the report. An **expression** is a combination of fields, operators (such as +, −, / and *), and functions that result in a single value. Many times, expressions include functions such as SUM or COUNT. A **function** is a built-in formula provided by Access that helps you quickly create a calculation. See Table D-2 for examples of common expressions that use Access functions. Notice that every calculated expression starts with an equal sign, and when it uses a function, the arguments for the function are placed in parentheses. **Arguments** are the pieces of information that the function needs to create the final answer. Kelsey adds another calculation to the Quantities Report that counts the number of records within each music category.

Steps

1. Make sure the Quantities Report is in Report Design View, right-click the **=Sum([Quantity])** **text box** in the Category Footer section, click **Copy** on the shortcut menu, right-click in a **blank area** in the left part of the Category Footer section, then click **Paste** on the shortcut menu as shown in Figure D-10

   Modifying a copy of the existing calculated expression control saves time and reduces errors.

2. Click the new **Subtotal label** in the Category Footer section to select it, double-click **Subtotal** to select the text, type **count**, then press **[Enter]**

   The label is only descriptive text. The text box to the right of the Count label will contain the expression that calculates the count. Right now, however, it still calculates a sum of the Quantity values instead of a count of Quantity values.

3. Click the new **=Sum([Quantity]) text box** in the Category Footer section to select it, double-click the **Sum** function within the expression to select it, type **count**, then press **[Enter]**

   The expression now counts the number of records in each group.

4. Click the **Save button** 🖫 on the Report Design toolbar

   When you save a report object, you are saving the report definition, not the data displayed by the report. The data that the report displays was automatically saved as it was previously entered into the database. Once a report object is saved, it will always show the most up-to-date data when you preview or print the report.

5. Click the **Print Preview button** 🔍 on the Report Design toolbar, click the **Zoom list arrow** ⬜, click **100%,** then scroll the Preview window as shown in Figure D-11

TABLE D-2: Common Access expressions

category	sample expression	description
Arithmetic	=[Price]*1.05	Multiplies the Price field by 1.05 (adds 5% to the Price field)
Arithmetic	=[Subtotal]+[Shipping]	Adds the value of the Subtotal field to the value of the Shipping field
Page Number	="Page "&[Page]	Displays the word Page, a space, and the current page number
Text	=[FirstName]& " "&[LastName]	Displays the value of the FirstName and LastName fields in one control separated by a space
Text	=Left([ProductNumber],2)	Uses the **Left** function to display the first two characters in the ProductNumber field
Aggregate	=Avg([Freight])	Uses the **Avg** function to display an average of the values in the Freight field
Date	=Date()	Uses the **Date** function to display the current date in the form of mm-dd-yy

FIGURE D-10: Copying and pasting a calculated control

Copy button

Paste button

New label control

New text box control

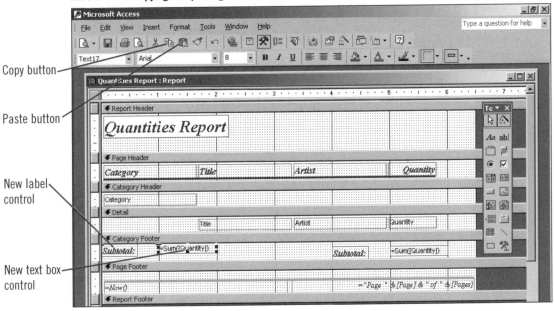

FIGURE D-11: Previewing the Count calculated control

New label control

New text box control

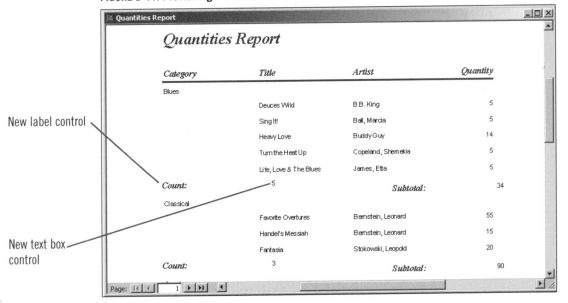

Access 2002

Using the Office Clipboard

The Office Clipboard lets you copy and paste multiple items within or between the Microsoft Office applications. To view the Clipboard task pane, click Edit on the menu bar, then click Clipboard. The Clipboard can collect up to 24 items, and you can

paste any of these items at any time. Click the Options button within the Office Clipboard task pane to set Clipboard characteristics such as when it will automatically appear.

Aligning Controls

Once the information that you want to present has been added to the appropriate section of a report, you may also want to rearrange the data on the report. Aligning controls in columns and rows makes the information easier to read. There are several **alignment** commands. You can left-, right-, or center-align a control *within its own border* using the Alignment buttons on the Formatting (Form/Report) toolbar, or you can align the edges of controls *with respect to one another* using the Align command on the Format menu. ◄▬▬▬ Kelsey aligns several controls on the Quantities Report to improve the readability of the report, and give it a more professional look.

1. Click the **Design View button** 📐 on the Print Preview toolbar, then click in the **vertical ruler** to the left of the Count label in the Category Footer section
   All four controls in the Category Footer section are selected. Text boxes that display numeric fields are right-aligned by default. The label and text box that you added in the Category Footer section that display calculated expressions are left-aligned by default.

2. Click the **Align Right button** 📑 on the Formatting (Form/Report) toolbar
   Your screen should look like Figure D-12. Now the information displayed by these controls is right-aligned within the border of that control.

3. With the four controls still selected, click **Format** on the menu bar, point to **Align**, then click **Bottom**
   The bottom edges of the four controls are now aligned with respect to one another. You can also align the right or left edges of controls in different sections.

4. Click the **Quantity label** in the Page Header section, press and hold [**Shift**], click the **Quantity text box** in the Detail section, click the **=Sum([Quantity])** text box in the Category Footer section, release [**Shift**], click **Format** on the menu bar, point to **Align**, then click **Right**
   The right edges of the Quantity label, Quantity text box, and Quantity calculated controls are aligned. With the edges at the same position and the information right-aligned within the controls, the controls form a perfect column on the final report.

5. Click the **blue line** below the labels between the Artist and and Quantity Fields in the Page Header section, press and hold [**Ctrl**], press the **Down Arrow key [↓]** twice to move the line down two pixels, then release [**Ctrl**]
   You can also move and resize controls using the mouse, but precise movements are often easier to accomplish using quick keystrokes. Pressing the arrow keys while holding [Ctrl] moves the selected control one pixel (picture element) at a time in the direction of the arrow. Pressing the arrow keys while holding [Shift] resizes the selected control.

6. With the blue line still selected, press and hold [**Shift**], then press the **Right Arrow key [→]** as many times as necessary to extend the line to the right edge of the Quantity label
   The extended line better defines the sections on the page.

7. Click the **Save button** 💾, click the **Print Preview button** 🔍, then scroll and zoom so that your report looks similar to Figure D-13

Click here to
select all the
controls in the
Category
Footer section

Four controls
are right-
aligned

Formatting
(Form/Report)
toolbar

Align Right
button

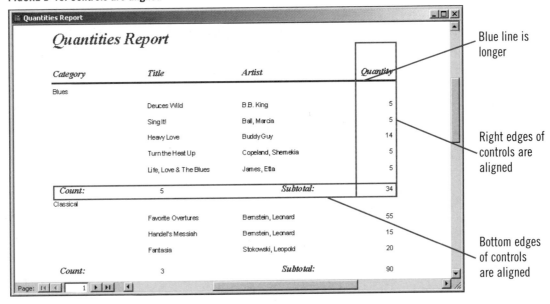

FIGURE D-13: **Controls are aligned**

Blue line is
longer

Right edges of
controls are
aligned

Bottom edges
of controls
are aligned

Access 2002

Formatting Controls

Formatting refers to enhancing the appearance of the information. Table D-3 lists several of the most popular formatting commands found on the Formatting (Form/Report) toolbar. Although the Report Wizard automatically applies many formatting embellishments to a report, you often want to improve upon the appearance of the report to fit your particular needs. ✐ Kelsey doesn't feel that the music category information is prominent on the report, so she wants to format that control to change its appearance.

Steps

1. **Click the Design View button** 📝 **on the Print Preview toolbar, then click the Category text box in the Category Header section**
   Before you can format any control, it must be selected.

2. **Click the Font Size list arrow** `8 ▾` **on the Formatting (Form/Report) toolbar, click 11, then click the Bold button** `B` **on the Formatting (Form/Report) toolbar**
   Increasing the font size and applying bold are common ways to make information more visible on a report. You can also change the colors of the control.

> **QuickTip**
>
> When the color on the Fill/Back Color 🖌, Font/Fore Color ▲, or Line/Border ✎ button displays the color you want, you simply click the button to apply that color.

3. **With the Category text box still selected, click the Font/Fore Color list arrow** `▲▾`, **then click the red box (third row, first column on the left) as shown in Figure D-14**
   Many buttons on the Formatting (Form/Report) toolbar include a list arrow that you can click to reveal a list of formatting choices. When you click the color list arrow, a palette of available colors is displayed.

4. **With the Category text box still selected, click the Fill/Back Color list arrow** `🖌▾`, **then click the light gray box (fourth row, last column on the right)**
   Be careful about relying too heavily on color formatting. Background shades often become solid black boxes when printed on a black-and-white printer or fax machine. Fortunately, Access allows you to undo up to your 20 most recent actions in Report Design View.

> **QuickTip**
>
> The quick keystroke for Undo is [CTRL][Z]. The quick keystroke for Redo is [CTRL][Y].

5. **With the Category text box still selected, click the Undo button** ↺ **on the Report Design toolbar to remove the background color, click** ↺ **to remove the font color, click Edit on the menu bar, then click Redo Property Setting to redo the font color**
   If you undo more actions than desired, use the Redo command on the Edit menu to redo the last undone action. The Redo menu command changes depending on the last undone action, and it can be used to redo up to 20 undone actions.

> **QuickTip**
>
> If you want your name on the printout, switch to Report Design view and add your name as a label to the Page Header section.

6. **Click the Line/Border Color list arrow** `✎▾`, **click the blue box (second row, sixth column), then click the Print Preview button** 🔍
   The screen should look like Figure D-15.

7. **Click File on the menu bar, click Print, type 1 in the From text box, type 1 in the To text box, click OK, then click the Close button** `Close` **on the Print Preview toolbar**

8. **Click the Save button** 💾, **then close the Quantities Report**

FIGURE D-14: Working with color formats

Font size

Bold button

Fill/Back Color
button

Font/Fore Color
button

Category text box
is selected

Line/Border
Color button

Blue

Light gray

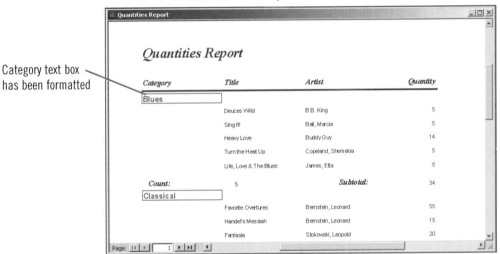

FIGURE D-15: Formatted Quantities Report

Category text box
has been formatted

TABLE D-3: Useful formatting commands

button	button name	description
B	Bold	Toggles bold on or off for the selected control(s)
I	Italic	Toggles italics on or off for the selected control(s)
U	Underline	Toggles underline on or off for the selected control(s)
≡	Align Left	Left-aligns the selected control(s) within its own border
≡	Center	Center-aligns the selected control(s) within its own border
≡	Align Right	Right-aligns the selected control(s) within its own border
⬥	Fill/Back Color	Changes the background color of the selected control(s)
A	Font/Fore Color	Changes the text color of the selected control(s)
✎	Line/Border Color	Changes the border color of the selected control(s)
▢	Line/Border Width	Changes the style of the border of the selected control(s)
▭	Special Effect	Changes the special visual effect of the selected control(s)

Creating Mailing Labels

Mailing Labels are used for many business purposes such as identifying folders in a filing cabinet, labeling products for sale, or providing addresses for mass mailings. Once you enter data into your Access database, you can easily create mailing labels from this data using the **Label Wizard** that creates a report object. ✎ Kelsey has been asked to create labels for the display cases in the MediaLoft stores with the Artist and Title fields only. The labels are to be printed in alphabetical order by Artist and then by Title. Kelsey uses the Label Wizard to get started.

Steps 1 2 3 4

1. Click **Reports** on the Objects bar in the MediaLoft-D database window (if not already selected), click the **New button** 🔲, click **Label Wizard** in the New Report dialog box, click the **Choose the table or query where the object's data comes from list arrow**, click **Music Inventory**, then click **OK**

   The Label Wizard dialog box opens as shown in Figure D-16. Avery is the default manufacturer, and produces a wide variety of labels measured in both millimeters and inches, but many other international label manufacturers can also be chosen. Avery 5160 labels are one of the most popular sizes in the United States, and are measured in inches.

2. Click the **English** option button (if not already selected), scroll and click **5160** in the Product number list, then click **Next**

   The next wizard dialog box allows you to change the font, font size, and other text attributes.

3. Click the **Font size list arrow**, click **11**, click the **Font name list arrow**, scroll and click **Comic Sans MS**, then click **Next**

   The next wizard dialog box asks you to set up the **prototype label**, a sample format upon which the final mailing labels will be created. Any text, spaces, or punctuation that you want on the prototype label must be entered from the keyboard.

   > **Trouble?**
   >
   > If your fields are on the same line, you did not press [Enter] after each line. Select and delete the fields, then redo Step 4.

4. Double-click **Artist**, press **[Enter]**, then double-click **Title**

   Your screen should look like Figure D-17.

5. Click **Next**, double-click **Artist** for the primary sort field, then double-click **Title** for the secondary sort field

   Artist is specified as the primary sort field and Title as the secondary sort field so that the labels will be printed in ascending order based on the value in the Artist field, with records from the same artist further sorted in ascending order by the value in the Title field.

6. Click **Next**, type **Artist-Title Labels** to name the report, click **Finish**, click **OK** if prompted about the size of the columns, then click the **Zoom pointer** 🔍 to see a full page of labels

   The labels should look like Figure D-18.

7. Click the **Close button** on the Print Preview toolbar, then click the **Save button** 🔲

8. Click **File** on the menu bar, then click **Exit** to exit Access

FIGURE D-16: Label Wizard

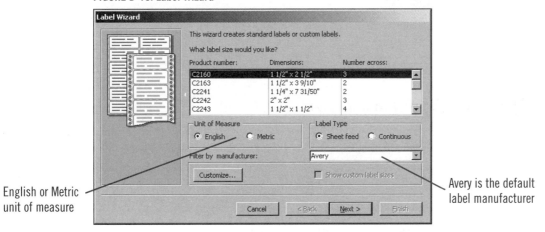

English or Metric
unit of measure

Avery is the default
label manufacturer

FIGURE D-17: The prototype label

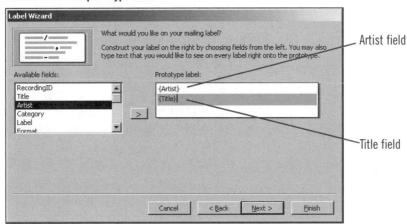

Artist field

Title field

FIGURE D-18: The Artist-Title Labels report

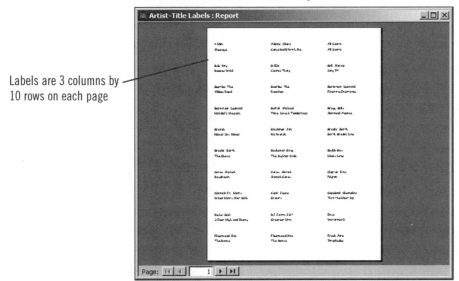

Labels are 3 columns by
10 rows on each page

Practice

► Concepts Review

Label each element of the Report Design View window shown in Figure D-19.

FIGURE D-19

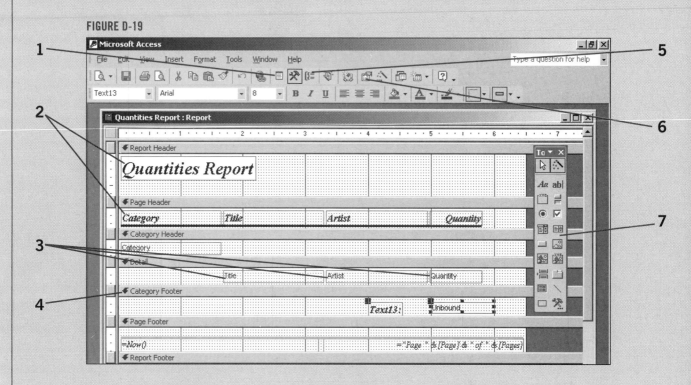

Match each term with the statement that describes it.

8. Function
9. Section
10. Detail section
11. Report
12. Formatting
13. Grouping

a. Determines where a control will display on the report
b. Sorting records *plus* providing a section before and after the group of records
c. Access object used to create paper printouts
d. Enhancing the appearance of the way information displays in the report
e. A built-in formula provided by Access that helps you quickly create a calculated expression
f. Prints once for every record

Select the best answer from the list of choices.

14. **Press and hold which key to select more than one control in Report Design View?**
    a. [Ctrl]
    b. [Alt]
    c. [Shift]
    d. [Tab]
15. **Which type of control is most commonly placed in the Detail section?**
    a. Label
    b. Text box
    c. Combo box
    d. List box
16. **Which type of control is most commonly placed in the Page Header section?**
    a. Label
    b. Combo box
    c. Command button
    d. Bound image
17. **A calculated expression is most often placed in which report section?**
    a. Report Header
    b. Detail
    c. Formulas
    d. Group Footer
18. **Which of the following would be the appropriate expression to count the number of records using the FirstName field?**
    a. =Count(FirstName)
    b. =Count[FirstName]
    c. =Count{FirstName}
    d. =Count([FirstName])
19. **To align the edges of several controls with respect to one another, you use the alignment commands on the:**
    a. Formatting toolbar.
    b. Standard toolbar.
    c. Print Preview toolbar.
    d. Format menu.
20. **To display the Clipboard task pane, you would choose the Office Clipboard from which menu?**
    a. Format
    b. Edit
    c. View
    d. Tools

▶ Skills Review

1. Plan a report.

   a. Plan a report to use for tracking job opportunities as if you were looking for a new job. To gather the raw data for your report, find a newspaper or Web site with job listings in your area of interest.

   b. Identify the Report Header, Group Header, and Detail sections of the report by using sample data based on the following information:

     • The title of the report should be **Job Opportunity Report**.

     • The records should be grouped by the Job Title field. For example, if you are interested in working with computers, job titles might be Database Specialist or Computer Analyst. Include at least two job title groupings in your sample report.

     • The Detail section should include information on the company, contact person, and telephone number for each job opportunity.

2. Create a report.

   a. Start Access and open the **Club-D** database from the drive and folder where your Project Files are located.

   b. Use the Report Wizard to create a report based on the CONTACTS table.

   c. Include the following fields in the following order for the report: STATUS, FNAME, LNAME, DUESOWED, DUESPAID

   d. Do not add any grouping or sorting fields.

   e. Use the Tabular layout and Portrait orientation.

   f. Use a Bold style and title the report **Contact Status Report**.

   g. Preview the first page of the new report.

3. Group records.

   a. In Report Design View, open the Sorting and Grouping dialog box, and group the report by the STATUS field in ascending order. Open both the Group Header and Group Footer sections for the STATUS field, then close the Sorting and Grouping dialog box.

   b. Move the STATUS text box in the Detail section up to the left edge of the STATUS Header section.

   c. Preview the first page of the new report.

4. Change the sort order.

   a. In Report Design View, open the Sorting and Grouping dialog box, then add LNAME as a sort field in ascending order immediately below the STATUS field.

   b. Close the Sorting and Grouping dialog box, then preview the first page of the new report.

5. Add a calculation.

   a. In Report Design View, add a text box control in the STATUS Footer section directly below the DUESOWED text box that is in the Detail section.

   b. Delete the accompanying label to the left of the unbound text box.

   c. Add another text box control in the STATUS Footer section directly below the DUESPAID text box in the Detail section.

   d. Delete the accompanying label to the left of the new unbound text box.

   e. Modify the unbound text boxes added to the STATUS Footer section so that they subtotal the DUESOWED and DUESPAID fields, respectively. The calculated expressions will be =Sum([DUESOWED]) and =Sum([DUESPAID]).

   f. Add your name as a label to the Report Header section.

   g. Preview both pages of the report, then print both pages of the report.

6. Align controls.

   a. In Report Design View, right-align the new calculated controls in the STATUS Footer section.

   b. Select the DUESOWED text box in the Detail section, and the =Sum([DUESOWED]) calculated expression in the STATUS Footer section, then right-align the controls with respect to one another.

c. Select the DUESPAID text box in the Detail section, and the =Sum([DUESPAID]) calculated expression in the STATUS Footer section, then right-align the controls with respect to one another.

d. Select the two calculated controls in the STATUS Footer section, then align the bottoms of the controls with respect to one another.

7. **Format controls.**

a. Select the two calculated controls in the STATUS Footer section, click the Properties button, then change the Format property on the Format tab to Currency. Close the property sheet.

b. Select the STATUS text box in the STATUS Header section, change the font size to 12 points, bold and italicize the control, then change the Fill/Back color to bright yellow. The Report Design View should look like Figure D-20.

FIGURE D-20

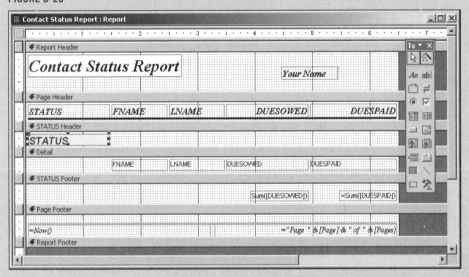

c. Save, preview, print, then close the report.

8. **Create mailing labels.**

a. Use the Label Wizard and the CONTACTS table to create mailing labels using Avery metric labels.

b. The text should be formatted with an Arial 10 point font, Light (font weight), black (text color), with the product number L7668, and with no italic or underline attributes.

c. Organize the prototype label as follows:
FNAME LNAME
COMPANY
STREET
CITY, STATE ZIP
You have to enter spaces between the FNAME and LNAME fields as well as between the CITY, STATE, and ZIP fields. Also, you have to type a comma after the CITY field.

d. Sort the labels by the ZIP field.

e. Save and name the report **Mailing Labels**, then view the report.

f. Close the Club-D database then exit Access.

Access 2002

▶ Independent Challenge 1

You have been hired to create a report for a physical therapy clinic.

- **a.** Start Access then open the **Therapy-D** database from the drive and folder where your Project Files are located.
- **b.** Use the Report Wizard to create a report using all of the fields from the Location Financial Query.
- **c.** View your data by Survey, group by Street, sort by PatientLast, click the Summary Options button, then sum both the AmountSent and AmountRecorded fields.
- **d.** Use the Stepped layout, Portrait orientation, and Soft Gray style.
- **e.** Name the report **Location Financial Report**.
- **f.** Modify the AmountSent and AmountRecorded labels in the Page Header section to **Sent** and **Recorded**, respectively.
- **g.** Change the font/fore color of the labels in the Page Header section to bright blue.
- **h.** Widen the Street text box in the Street Header section to twice its current size, and change the border color to bright blue.
- **i.** Add your name as a label to the Report Header section.
- **j.** Save, then print the report.
- **k.** Close the Therapy-D database then exit Access.

▶ Independent Challenge 2

You have been hired to create a report for a physical therapy clinic.

- **a.** Start Access and open the **Therapy-D** database from the drive and folder where your Project Files are located.
- **b.** Use the Report Wizard to create a report using all of the fields from the Therapist Satisfaction Query except for the Initials and First fields.
- **c.** View the data by Survey. Do not add any grouping levels and do not add any sorting levels.
- **d.** Use the Tabular layout, Portrait orientation, and Casual style.
- **e.** Title the report **Therapist Satisfaction Report**, then view the report.
- **f.** In Report Design View, add your name as a label in the Report Header section, then print the report.
- **g.** Group the report by Last, and open both the Group Header and Group Footer sections for the Last field.
- **h.** Use the Sorting and Grouping dialog box to further sort the records by PatientLast. Close the Sorting and Grouping dialog box.
- **i.** Move the Last text box from the Detail section up into the Last Header section.
- **j.** Remove bold from all of the labels in the Page Header section, then widen the title label in the Report Header section to make sure all of the text appears when previewed.
- **k.** Using the Text Box button on the Toolbar, add two text boxes in the Last Footer section. Place them directly below the Courtesy and Knowledge text boxes that are in the Detail section. Delete the labels that accompany the new text boxes.
- **l.** Insert an expression into the new unbound text boxes to create the calculated controls =Avg([Courtesy]) and =Avg([Knowledge]), respectively.
- **m.** Resize the new calculated controls so that they are the same size as the Courtesy and Knowledge text boxes in the Detail section.
- **n.** Use the property sheet for the two new calculated controls to change the Format property on the Format tab to Fixed.
- **o.** Right-align the two new calculated controls within their own borders. Also, align the right edge of the =Avg([Courtesy]) and the Courtesy text boxes with respect to each other. Right-align the edges of the =Avg([Knowledge]) and Knowledge text boxes with respect to each other.
- **p.** Align the top edges of the new calculated controls with respect to each other.

q. If the report is wider than 6.5" wide, drag the right edge of the report to the left so that the final report is no wider than 6.5".

r. Save, then preview the report. The report should look like Figure D-21.

s. Print the report, close the Therapy-D database, then exit Access.

FIGURE D-21

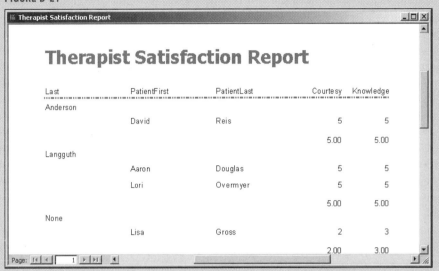

▶ Independent Challenge 3

Use the knowledge and skills that you have acquired about Access to create an attractive report that includes information about colleges and universities that offer programs in computer science. Create a database containing this information, and then design a report that displays the data. Gather information from libraries, friends, and the Web to enter into the database.

a. Start Access then create a new database called **Colleges** in the drive and folder where your Project Files are located. Include any fields you feel are important, but make sure you include the institution's name, state, and whether it is a four- or two-year school.

b. Find information on schools that offer programs in computer science. If you are using the Web, use any available search engines.

c. Compile a list of at least five institutions, and enter the five records into a table named **Computer Science Schools**.

d. Create a report that includes all the fields in the table **Computer Science Schools**, and group by the field that contains the information on whether the college is a four- or two-year school.

e. Sort the records by the state, then by the institution's name.

f. Use an appropriate style and title for your report. Insert your initials at the end of the report title.

g. Save, preview, then print the report.

h. Close the Colleges database, then exit Access.

Independent Challenge 4

You are on the staff of an economic development team whose goal is to encourage tourism in the Baltic Sea region. You have created an Access database called Baltic-D to track important fields of information for the countries in that region. You have been using the Internet to find information about events and demographics in the area and entering that information into the database using existing forms. You need to create and then print reports to present to the team.

  a. Start Access and open the **Baltic-D** database from the drive and folder where your Project Files are located.

  b. Connect to the Internet, then go to www.google.com, www.lycos.com, or another search engine to conduct research for your database. Your goal is to find three upcoming events for Helsinki, Finland, and to print the Web pages.

  c. Open the Cities form, find the Helsinki record, and enter three events for Helsinki into the Events fields. EventID is an AutoNumber field, so it will automatically increment as you enter the EventName and EventDate information.

  d. Use the Report Wizard to create a report based on the Baltic Area Festivals query. Use all of the fields. View the data by Cities, do not add any more grouping levels, and sort the records in ascending order by EventDate.

  e. Use a Stepped layout, a Portrait orientation, and a Corporate style.

  f. Title the report **Baltic Area Events**.

  g. Switch to Report Design View to apply additional formatting embellishments as desired.

  h. Add your name as a label to the Report Header section.

  i. Save, print, then close the report. Exit Access.

 Visual Workshop

Open the **Club-D** database from the drive and folder where your Project Files are located to create the report based on the CONTACTS table. The report is shown in Figure D-22. The Report Wizard, Stepped Layout, and the Corporate style were used to create this report. Note that the records are grouped by the CITY field and sorted within each group by the LNAME field. A calculated control that counts the number of records is displayed in the City Footer. Add a label with your name to the Report Header section, then save and print the report.

FIGURE D-22

Membership by City			*Your Name*
CITY	**LNAME**	**FNAME**	**PHONE**
Belton			
	Duman	Mary Jane	555-8844
	Hubert	Holly	555-6004
	Mayberry	Mitch	555-0401
Count: 3			
Kansas City			
	Alman	Jill	555-6931
	Bouchart	Bob	555-3081
	Collins	Christine	555-3602
	Diverman	Barbara	555-0401

Integrating

Word, Excel, and Access

► **Merge data between Access and Word**
► **Use Mail Merge to create a form letter**
► **Export an Access table to Excel**

You have learned how to use Word, Excel, and Access individually to accomplish specific tasks more efficiently. Now you will learn how to integrate files created with these programs so that you can use the best features of each one. ✏ Maria Abbott, the general sales manager for MediaLoft, wants to establish a profile of MediaLoft's corporate customers so that she can incorporate this information into the annual report. To do this, she creates a survey and mails it to these customers. She also wants to export the Access database of corporate customer names and addresses to an Excel worksheet so that she can create an Excel chart showing corporate sales by state and include this chart in the report.

Unit B
Integration

Merging Data Between Access and Word

Companies often keep a database of customer names and addresses, which they use to send form letters to their customers. With Office, you can combine, or **merge**, data from an existing Access table with a Word document to automatically create personalized form letters. Maria wants to survey MediaLoft's corporate customers. She has written a form letter using Word, and she wants to merge her form letter with the customer names and addresses that already exist in an Access table.

Steps

QuickTip

If you plan to do the steps in this unit again, be sure to make and use a copy of the Access file MediaLoft-IB.

Trouble?

If the Access window remains on top as the active window, click the Word program button on the taskbar.

1. Start Access, open the file **MediaLoft-IB.mdb** from the location where your Project Files are stored, click the **Tables button** on the Objects bar if necessary, make sure **Customers** is selected, then click the **Open button** on the Database window toolbar
The datasheet for the Customers table opens. The Customers table is the **data source** for the mail merge.

2. Click **Tools** on the menu bar, point to **Office Links**, then click **Merge It with Microsoft Word**
The Microsoft Word Mail Merge Wizard dialog box opens, as shown in Figure B-1. The Mail Merge Wizard links your data to a Microsoft Word document. The customer survey form letter already exists as a Word document, so the default option, Link your data to an existing Microsoft Word document, is correct.

3. Click **OK**
The Select Microsoft Word Document dialog box opens.

4. Select the file **INT B-1.doc** from the location where your Project Files are stored, then click **Open**
Word opens and the document INT B-1 appears in the document window.

5. If the Word program window does not fill the screen, click the Word program window **Maximize button**, then if necessary, click the **Show/Hide ¶ button** on the Standard toolbar to display formatting marks
Compare your screen to Figure B-2. The Mail Merge task pane is open. The Mail Merge task pane contains hyperlinks to commands that you use to perform a mail merge. The Mail Merge task pane is organized like a wizard, so there are actually six different Mail Merge task panes. This one is Step 3 of 6. The Mail Merge toolbar appears below the Formatting toolbar. The buttons on the Mail Merge toolbar are used to perform many of the same commands as the hyperlinks in the Mail Merge task pane. The document you just opened is the **main document** for the mail merge.

6. Replace Maria Abbott's name with **Your Name**

7. Save the document as **Survey Form Letter** to the drive and location where your Project Files are stored

FIGURE B-1: Microsoft Word Mail Merge Wizard dialog box

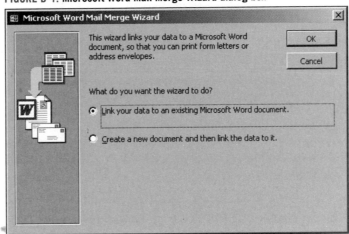

FIGURE B-2: Main document

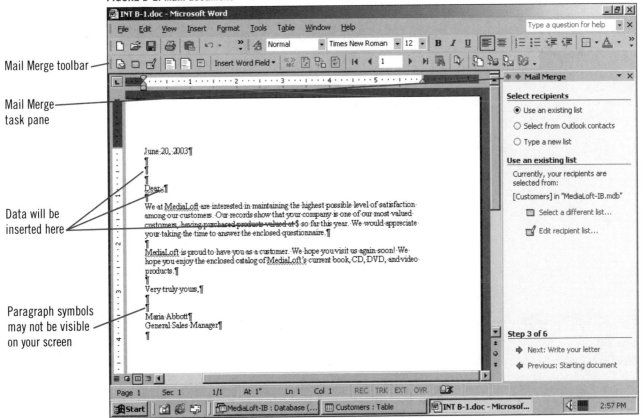

Mail Merge toolbar

Mail Merge task pane

Data will be inserted here

Paragraph symbols may not be visible on your screen

TABLE B-1: Mail Merge buttons

name	button	name	button	name	button
	Insert Address Block		Highlight Merge Fields		Find Entry
	Insert Greeting Line		Match Fields		Check for Errors
	Insert Merge Fields		First Record		Merge to New Document
	View Merged Data		Last Record		Merge to Printer

Using Mail Merge to Create a Form Letter

Once you have opened and linked the form letter and the Access table, you are ready to insert **merge fields**, placeholders for the merged data, into the letter. When you perform the mail merge, Access looks for the merge fields in the main document and replaces them with the appropriate fields from the data source. ✎ After opening the data source and selecting the main document, Maria needs to insert merge fields into the main document.

Steps 1234

1. Click the **Next: Write your letter hyperlink** in the task pane, click to the **left of the colon** in the greeting, then click the 📄 **More items hyperlink** in the Mail Merge task pane
   The Insert Merge Field dialog box opens. This dialog box contains a list of fields in the Access database. You need to insert the field representing each customer's first name.

QuickTip

Click the Highlight Merge Fields button 📄 on the Mail Merge toolbar to highlight the merge fields.

2. Click **First**, click **Insert**, click **Close**, position the pointer to the right of the $ (dollar sign) in the first paragraph, click the 📄 **More items hyperlink** in the Mail Merge task pane, click **YTDSales**, click **Insert**, then click **Close**
   The First and the YTDSales fields are inserted between angled brackets in the form letter.

3. Position the insertion pointer in the **second empty paragraph** below the date, then click the 📄 **Address block hyperlink** in the Mail Merge task pane
   The Insert Address Block dialog box opens. You use this dialog box to determine the appearance of information in the address block.

4. Click **Joshua Randall Jr.** in the recipient's name format list, then click **Match Fields**
   The Match Fields dialog box opens, similar to Figure B-3. If the field names in the data source you are using approximately match the field names in the Match Fields list on the left, the corresponding field name from your data source will be listed in the drop-down lists on the right side of the dialog box. The Mail Merge field name "Address 1" wasn't matched with anything in the MediaLoft-IB database.

5. Click the **Address 1 list arrow**, click **Street**, compare your settings to Figure B-3, click **OK**, then click **OK** to close the Insert Address Block dialog box
   The Address Block field appears in the document, as shown in Figure B-4.

6. Click the **Next: Preview your letters hyperlink** in the Mail Merge task pane
   The data from the first record (David Friedrichsen at Sprint) appears correctly in the main document.

QuickTip

Click the 📄 Edit recipient list hyperlink to open Access and edit the database. Click Exclude this recipient to exclude the current record from the final mail merge.

7. Click the **Next Record button ⏭** in the task pane
   The data from the second record (Liz Douglas at KGSM) appears in the document. Maria decides to merge the letters into one file so she can examine the final product before printing.

QuickTip

To merge the files directly to the printer, click the Print hyperlink in the task pane.

8. Click the **Next: Complete the merge hyperlink** in the task pane, click the 📄 **Edit individual letters hyperlink** in the task pane, then click **OK** in the Merge to New Document dialog box

9. Click the **Save button 💾** on the Standard toolbar, save the document as **Survey Letters** to the location where your Project Files are stored, click **File** on the menu bar, click **Print**, click the **Current page option button** to print only the first form letter, then click **OK**
   The first form letter prints.

10. Click **File** on the menu bar, click **Exit**, then click **No** to save changes to Survey Form Letter
    Word closes and returns you to Access.

FIGURE B-3: Match Fields dialog box

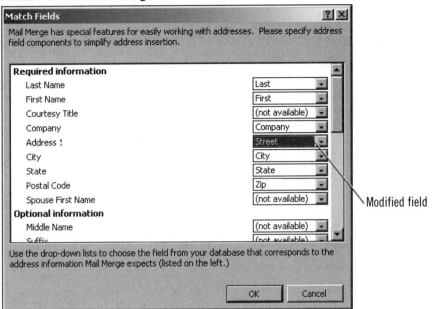

Modified field

FIGURE B-4: Main document with merge fields inserted

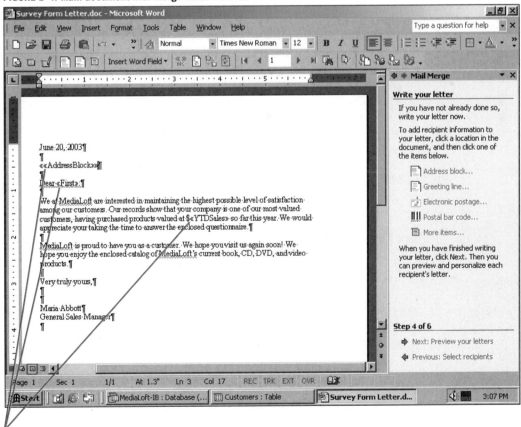

Inserted merge
fields

Unit B
Integration

Exporting an Access Table to Excel

You can export data in an Access table to Excel and several other Office programs. When you export a table, a copy of the data is created in a format acceptable to the other program, and the original data remains intact. Maria wants to export the Customers table in the MediaLoft-IB database into Excel so that she can analyze the data. At some point, she will create a chart that shows the distribution of MediaLoft's corporate customer sales.

Steps

1. **Make sure that the Customers table datasheet is still open, click Tools on the menu bar, point to Office Links, then click Analyze It with Microsoft Excel**

   The exported data appears in an Excel workbook named Customers that contains only one worksheet, also named Customers. When you import data into Excel, only one worksheet is supplied, although you can add more.

2. **If necessary, click the Excel program window Maximize button** ▣

   Maria does not need the Phone, Fax, Birthdate, or E-mail columns.

QuickTip

The green triangle in the upper-left corner of the cells in column H is an error indicator. In this case, it appears because the Zip code appears to be a number, but it is formatted as text. You can ignore it.

3. **Scroll to the right, select the I through L column selector buttons, click Edit on the menu bar, click Delete, then press [Ctrl][Home] to return to cell A1**

   All the remaining columns are now visible on the screen.

4. **Click Data on the menu bar, then click Sort**

   The Sort dialog box opens, similar to Figure B-5. Notice that the Header row option button at the bottom of the dialog box is selected. This means that the first row in the worksheet will not be sorted.

5. **Click the Sort by list arrow, scroll down and click State, click the first Then by list arrow, scroll down and click YTDSales**

   Compare your dialog box to Figure B-5.

6. **Click OK**

   The data is now sorted in ascending order by state, and within each state, by year-to-date sales. Compare your screen to Figure B-6.

7. **Click File on the menu bar, click Page Setup, click the Page tab if necessary, click the Landscape option button, click Print, then click OK**

   The worksheet prints on one page.

8. **Scroll down and enter Your Name in cell A30, press [Ctrl][Home], click File on the menu bar, click Save As, switch to the drive and folder where you are saving your Project Files, then click Save**

   Your changes are saved to the file Customers in the location where your Project Files are stored.

9. **Click File on the menu bar, click Exit to exit Excel, in the Access program window, click File on the menu bar, then click Exit to exit Access**

FIGURE B-5: Sort dialog box

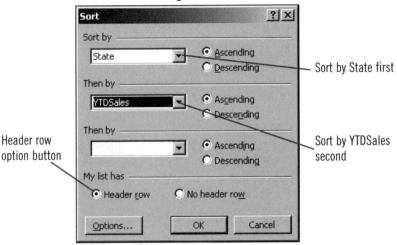

FIGURE B-6: Excel worksheet with sorted data

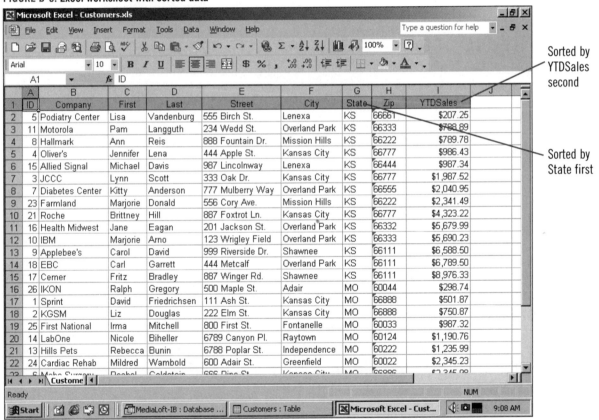

Integration

Exporting an Access table to Word

You can export an Access table to Microsoft Word by using the Publish It with MS Word feature. To export a table, open the Access database with the table you want to export, select the table name or open the table datasheet, click Tools on the menu bar, point to Office Links, then click Publish It with Microsoft Word. The table is exported to a Word table in a new Word document, and the document file is automatically saved in rich text format with the same name as the Access table.

▶ Independent Challenge 1

As the administrator for Monroe High School, you want to keep track of student records and generate reports for the principal and school district. You need to create a database containing information about the students currently enrolled in the high school. Once the database table is complete, export the table information to Excel and Word to create reports.

a. Start Access and create a new database called **Student Records**.

b. Create a table called **Student Info**. Decide what fields should be included in the database, but make sure you include fields for each student's first name, last name, address, phone number, gender, birth date, grade level, and cumulative grade point average (GPA).

c. Create a form to facilitate the entry of your student records, then print one record to show a sample of the form.

d. Add 20 records to your table, then sort the students by last name and then by first name.

e. Export the Student Info table to an Excel worksheet, then resize the columns to fit the table.

f. Scroll down to row C23 and enter **Your Name** in cell 23.

g. Print out your results, then save your worksheet as **Student Info** to the location where your Project Files are stored. Close the worksheet and exit Excel.

h. In Access, use the Publish It with MSWord command to export the Student Info table to a Word table, resize columns to fit the table, then format the table to make the document more attractive.

i. Change the page orientation to Landscape, sort the table by grade level and then by last name, then format the table to make the document more attractive.

j. Press [Enter] twice at the bottom of the document, then type your name.

k. Save the **Student Info** document in the location where your Project Files are stored, print it, close the document, then exit Word.

l. Close the Student Records database and exit Access.

Independent Challenge 2

MediaLoft sponsors the Pleasantown Players, a regional theater group that is supported by ticket revenues and private donations. You have been asked to help the theater group by writing a fundraising letter and merging it with a database of selected MediaLoft corporate customers. To maximize your results, you decide to send out the initial mailing to customers who have spent more than $2,000 at MediaLoft so far this year. You need to modify the current Customers table and create a query to find the appropriate customers. Then you need to create a form letter, which you will merge with the data stored in the query.

a. Open the Project File MediaLoft-IB.mdb from the location where your Project Files are stored, create a query called **Highest Revenue Listing** to find corporate customers who have spent more than $2,000 at MediaLoft so far this year. You are going to merge this query with a form letter, so make sure you include all the fields you will merge into the letter in the query.

b. Create a main document (form letter) in Word called **Funding Letter** in the location where your Project Files are stored. Use all the fields you feel are necessary. In the letter, you want to tell customers how important it is to support local, nonprofessional theater. For the letter content, tell the customers about the Pleasantown Players. Invent any information that adds informative, persuasive facts to your funding request.

c. Type your name in the signature block in the letter.

d. Merge the document Funding Letter and the query you created into a new document named **Pleasantown Letters**.

e. Print the current page of the Pleasantown Letters file.

f. Save your changes to the document, close the document, exit Word, then close the databse and exit Access.

Getting
Started with PowerPoint 2002

Objectives

► **Define presentation software**
► **Start PowerPoint 2002**
► **View the PowerPoint window**
[MOUS] ► **Use the AutoContent Wizard**
[MOUS] ► **View a presentation**
[MOUS] ► **Save a presentation**
► **Get Help**
[MOUS] ► **Print and close the file, and exit PowerPoint**

Microsoft PowerPoint 2002 is a presentation program that transforms your ideas into professional, compelling presentations. With PowerPoint, you can create individual slides and display them as an electronic slide show on your computer, video projector, or even via the Internet. ✦ Maria Abbott is the general sales manager at MediaLoft, a nationwide chain of bookstore cafés that sells books, CDs, and videos. Maria needs to familiarize herself with the basics of PowerPoint and learn how to use PowerPoint to create professional presentations.

Defining Presentation Software

Presentation software is a computer program you can use to organize and present information. Whether you are giving a sales pitch or explaining your company's goals and accomplishments, presentation software can help make your presentation effective and professional. You can use PowerPoint to create presentations, as well as notes for the presenter and handouts for the audience. Table A-1 explains the items you can create using PowerPoint. 🖉 Maria wants to create a presentation that explains a new advertising campaign that MediaLoft is developing. She is not familiar with PowerPoint, so she gets right to work exploring its capabilities. Figure A-1 shows a handout she created using a word processor for a recent presentation. Figure A-2 shows how the same handout might look in PowerPoint.

Maria can easily complete the following tasks using PowerPoint:

► Present information in a variety of ways

With PowerPoint, you can present information using a variety of methods. For example, you can print handout pages or an outline of your presentation for your audience, or you can display your presentation as an electronic slide show on your computer, using either a projection machine or the Internet.

► Enter and edit data easily

Using PowerPoint, you can enter and edit data quickly and efficiently. When you need to change a part of your presentation, you can use the advanced word-processing and outlining capabilities of PowerPoint to edit your content rather than re-create it.

► Change the appearance of information

PowerPoint has many features that can transform the way text, graphics, and slides look. By exploring these capabilities, you will discover how easy it is to change the appearance of your presentation.

► Organize and arrange information

Once you start using PowerPoint, you won't have to spend much time making sure your information is correct and in the right order because, with PowerPoint you can quickly and easily rearrange and modify any piece of information in your presentation.

► Incorporate information from other sources

Often, when you create presentations, you use information from other sources. With PowerPoint, you can import information from spreadsheet, database, and word-processing files prepared in programs such as Microsoft Excel, Microsoft Access, Microsoft Word, and Corel WordPerfect, as well as graphics from a variety of sources.

► Show a presentation on any computer running Windows 2000 or Windows 98

PowerPoint has a powerful feature called the PowerPoint Viewer, which you can use to show your presentation on computers running Windows 2000 or Windows 98 that do not have PowerPoint installed. The PowerPoint Viewer displays a presentation as an on-screen slide show.

FIGURE A-1: Traditional handout

- Marketing 2003
  - Maria Abbott

- Marketing Summary
  - Market: past, present, and future
    - Review changes in market share
    - Leadership
    - Market Shifts
    - Costs
    - Pricing and competition

- Product Definition
  - Personal ad space in e-commerce market

- Competition
  - The competitive landscape
    - The players
    - Strengths and weaknesses
    - Product ratings

FIGURE A-2: PowerPoint handout

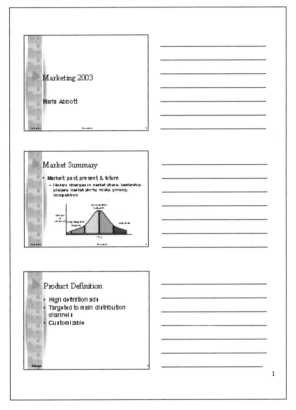

TABLE A-1: Ways to present information using PowerPoint

item	use
On-screen presentations	Run a slide show directly from your computer
Web presentations	Broadcast a presentation on the Web or on an intranet that others can view, complete with video and audio
Online meetings	View or work on a presentation with your colleagues in real time
Color overheads	Print PowerPoint slides directly to transparencies on your color printer
Black-and-white overheads	Print PowerPoint slides directly to transparencies on your black-and-white printer
Notes	Print notes that help you remember points about each slide when you speak to a group
Audience handouts	Print handouts with two, three, or six slides on a page
Outline pages	Print the outline of your presentation to show the main points

Starting PowerPoint 2002

To start PowerPoint, you must first start Windows, and then click the Start button on the taskbar and point to the Programs folder, which usually contains the Microsoft PowerPoint program icon. If the Microsoft PowerPoint icon is not in the Programs folder, it might be in a different location on your computer. If you are using a computer on a network, you might need to use a different starting procedure. ◄━━━ Maria starts PowerPoint to familiarize herself with the program.

Steps 1 2 3 4

1. **Make sure your computer is on and the Windows desktop is visible**

   If any program windows are open, close or minimize them.

2. **Click the Start button on the taskbar, then point to Programs**

   The Programs menu opens, showing a list of icons and names for all your programs, as shown in Figure A-3. Your screen might look different, depending on which programs are installed on your computer.

Trouble? ▶

If you have trouble finding Microsoft PowerPoint on the Programs menu, check with your instructor or technical support person.

3. **Click Microsoft PowerPoint on the Programs menu**

   PowerPoint starts, and the PowerPoint window opens, as shown in Figure A-4.

CLUES TO USE

Creating a PowerPoint shortcut icon on the desktop

You can make it easier to start PowerPoint by placing a shortcut on the desktop. To create the shortcut, click the Start button, then point to Programs. On the Programs menu, point to Microsoft PowerPoint, then right-click Microsoft PowerPoint. In the shortcut menu that appears, point to Send To, then click Desktop (create shortcut). Windows places a shortcut icon named Microsoft PowerPoint on your desktop. In the future, you can start PowerPoint by simply double-clicking this icon, instead of using the Start menu. You can edit or change the name of the shortcut by right-clicking the shortcut icon, clicking Rename on the shortcut menu, and then editing as you would any item name in Windows. If you are working in a computer lab, you may not be allowed to place shortcuts on the desktop. Check with your instructor or network administrator before attempting to add a shortcut.

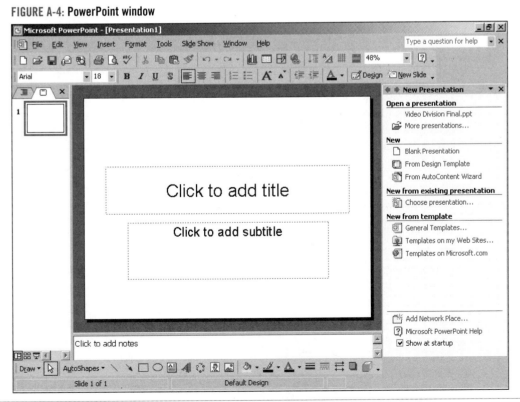

Microsoft
PowerPoint
program

Start button

Your list of
programs may
be different

FIGURE A-4: PowerPoint window

PowerPoint 2002

Viewing the PowerPoint Window

When you first open PowerPoint, a blank slide appears in the PowerPoint window. PowerPoint has different **views** that allow you to see your presentation in different forms. By default, the PowerPoint window opens in **Normal view**, which is the primary view that you use to write, edit, and design your presentation. Normal view is divided into three areas called **panes**: the pane on the left containing the Outline and Slide tabs, the slide pane, and the notes pane. You move around in each pane by using its scroll bars. The PowerPoint window and the specific parts of Normal view are described below. ⟶ Maria examines the elements of the PowerPoint window. Find and compare the elements described below, using Figure A-5 as a guide.

Details

► The **title bar** contains the program name, the title of the presentation, a program Control Menu button, resizing buttons, and the program Close button.

► The **menu bar** contains the names of the menus you use to choose PowerPoint commands, as well as the Ask a Question box and the Close Window button.

► The **Standard toolbar** contains buttons for commonly used commands, such as copying and pasting. The **Formatting toolbar** contains buttons for the most frequently used formatting commands, such as changing font type and size. The toolbars on your screen may be displayed on one line instead if two. See the Clues to Use for more information on how toolbars are displayed.

► The **Outline tab** displays your presentation text in the form of an outline, without graphics. In this tab, it is easy to move text on or among slides by dragging text to reorder the information.

► The **Slides tab** displays the slides of your presentation as small images, called **thumbnails**. You can quickly navigate through the slides in your presentation using this tab. You can also add, delete, or rearrange slides on this tab.

► The **slide pane** contains the current slide in your presentation, including all text and graphics.

► The **notes pane** is used to type notes that reference a slide's content. You can print these notes and refer to them when you make a presentation or print them as handouts and give them to your audience. The notes pane is not visible to the audience when you give a slide presentation.

► The **task pane** contains sets of hyperlinks for commonly used commands. The commands are grouped into 10 different task panes. The commands include creating new presentations, opening existing ones, searching for documents, and using the Office clipboard. You can also perform basic formatting tasks from the task pane such as changing the slide layout, slide design, color scheme, or slide template of a presentation.

► The **Drawing toolbar**, located at the bottom of the PowerPoint window, contains buttons and menus that let you create lines, shapes, and special effects.

► The **view buttons**, at the bottom of the Outline tab and Slides tab area, allow you to quickly switch between PowerPoint views.

► The **status bar**, located at the bottom of the PowerPoint window, shows messages about what you are doing and seeing in PowerPoint, including which slide you are viewing.

FIGURE A-5: Presentation window in Normal view

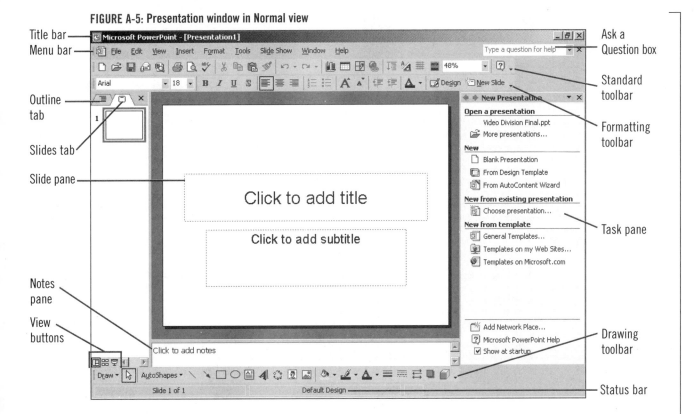

Title bar

Menu bar

Outline tab

Slides tab

Slide pane

Notes pane

View buttons

Ask a Question box

Standard toolbar

Formatting toolbar

Task pane

Drawing toolbar

Status bar

Toolbars in PowerPoint 2002

PowerPoint 2002 offers personalized toolbars and menus, which modify themselves to your working style. When you use personalized toolbars and menus, the Standard and Formatting toolbars appear on the same row and display only the most frequently used buttons. To use a button that is not visible on a toolbar, click the Toolbar Options button [»] at the end of the toolbar, and then click the button that you wish to appear on the Toolbar Options list. As you work, PowerPoint adds the buttons you use to the visible toolbars and drops the buttons you haven't used in a while to the Toolbar Options list. Similarly, PowerPoint menus adjust to your work habits, so that the commands you use most often appear on shortened menus. To view additional menu commands, click the double arrows at the bottom of a menu.

The lessons in this book assume you have turned off personalized menus and toolbars and are working with all menu commands and toolbar buttons displayed. To turn off personalized toolbars and menus so that you can easily find the commands that are referenced in this book, click Tools on the menu bar, click Customize, select the Show Standard and Formatting toolbars on two rows and Always show full menus checkboxes on the Options tab, and then click Close. The Standard and Formatting toolbars will then appear on separate rows and display all the buttons, and the menus will display the complete list of menu commands. (You can also quickly display the toolbars on two rows by clicking either Toolbar Options button and then clicking Show Buttons on Two Rows.)

PowerPoint 2002

Using the AutoContent Wizard

The quickest way to create a presentation is with the AutoContent Wizard. A **wizard** is a series of steps that guides you through a task (in this case, creating a presentation). Using the AutoContent Wizard, you choose a presentation type from the wizard's list of sample presentations. Then you indicate what type of output you want. Next, you type the information for the title slide and the footer. The AutoContent Wizard then creates a presentation with sample text you can use as a guide to help formulate the major points of your presentation. ➤ Maria decides to start her presentation by opening the AutoContent Wizard.

Steps 123 4

1. **In the New Presentation task pane, point to the From AutoContent Wizard hyperlink under New**
   The mouse pointer changes to 🖑. The pointer changes to this shape any time it is positioned over a hyperlink.

Trouble?

If the Office Assistant appears and asks if you would like help, click No.

2. **Click the From AutoContent Wizard hyperlink**
   The AutoContent Wizard dialog box opens, as shown in Figure A-6. The left section of the dialog box outlines the contents of the AutoContent Wizard, and the text in the right section explains the current wizard screen.

3. **Click Next**
   The Presentation type screen appears. This screen contains category buttons and types of presentations. Each presentation type contains suggested text for a particular use. By default, the presentation types in the General category are listed.

4. **Click the category Projects, click Reporting Progress or Status in the list on the right, then click Next**
   The Presentation style screen appears, asking you to choose an output type.

5. **If necessary, click the On-screen presentation option button to select it, then click Next**
   The Presentation options screen requests information that will appear on the title slide of the presentation and in the footer at the bottom of each slide.

6. **Click in the Presentation title text box, then type New Ad Campaign**

7. **Press [Tab], then type your name in the Footer text box**

8. **Make sure the Date last updated and Slide number check boxes are selected**

9. **Click Next, then click Finish**
   The AutoContent Wizard opens the presentation based on the Reporting Progress or Status presentation type you chose. Sample text for each slide is listed on the left in the Outline tab, and the title slide appears on the right side of the screen. A text box with information appears next to Slide 1. Notice that the task pane is no longer visible. The task pane can be easily opened the next time you need it. Compare your screen to Figure A-7.

FIGURE A-6: AutoContent Wizard opening screen

Green box identifies current screen name

Step 3

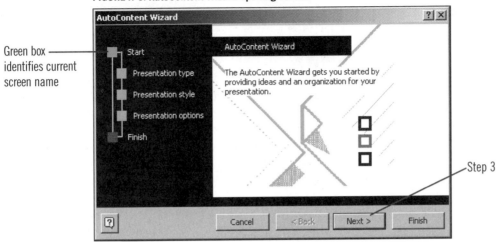

FIGURE A-7: Presentation created with AutoContent Wizard

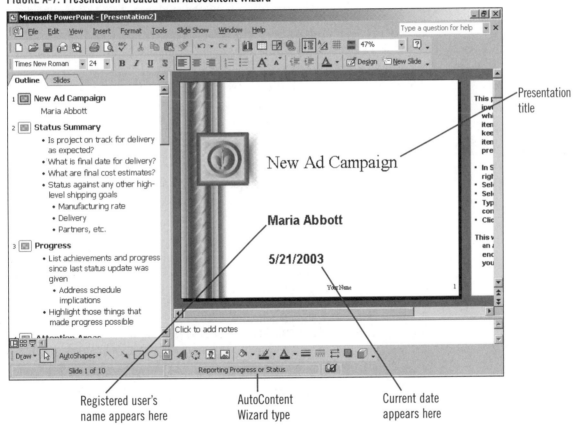

Presentation title

Registered user's name appears here

AutoContent Wizard type

Current date appears here

About Wizards and the PowerPoint installation

As you use PowerPoint, you may find that not all AutoContent Wizards are available to you. The wizards available depend on your PowerPoint installation. A typical installation gives you a minimal set of wizards, templates, and other features. Some may be installed so that the program requests the Office CD "on first use"; in other words, the first time you request that feature. If you find that a feature you want is not installed, insert the Office CD as directed. If you are working on a networked computer or in a lab, see your technical support person for assistance.

Viewing a Presentation

This lesson introduces you to the four PowerPoint views: Normal view, Slide Sorter view, Slide Show view, and Notes Page view. Each PowerPoint view shows your presentation in a different way and allows you to manipulate your presentation differently. To move easily among most of the PowerPoint views, use the view buttons located at the bottom of the pane containing the Outline and Slides tabs. Table A-3 provides a brief description of the PowerPoint views. ◀━━ Maria examines each PowerPoint view, starting with Normal view.

Steps 1234

1. In the Outline tab, click the small **slide icon** 🔲 next to Slide 3

The text for Slide 3 is selected in the Outline tab and Slide 3 appears in the slide pane as shown in Figure A-8. Notice that the status bar also indicates the number of the slide you are viewing.

2. Click the **Previous Slide button** ⯅ at the bottom of the vertical scroll bar twice so that Slide 1 (the title slide) appears

The scroll box in the vertical scroll bar moves back up the scroll bar. The gray slide icon on the Outline tab indicates which slide is displayed in the slide pane. As you scroll through the presentation, notice the sample text on each slide created by the AutoContent Wizard.

> **QuickTip**
>
> Click the right horizontal scroll arrow in the slide pane to view all of the text to the right of the slide.

3. Click the **Slides tab**

Thumbnails of all the slides in your presentation appear on the Slide tab and the slide pane enlarges. A text box to the right of Slide 1 in the slide pane describes a tip for working with this presentation. Tips like this appear when you create some presentations using the AutoContent Wizard.

4. Click the **Slide Sorter View button** 🔡

A thumbnail of each slide in the presentation appears as shown in Figure A-9. You can examine the flow of your slides and easily move them to change their order.

5. Double-click the first slide in Slide Sorter view

The slide that you clicked appears in Normal view.

6. Click the **Slide Show (from current slide) button** 🖥

The first slide fills the entire screen. In this view, you can practice running through your slides as they would appear in an electronic slide show.

7. Click the **left mouse button**, press **[Enter]**, or press **[Spacebar]** to advance through the slides one at a time until you see a black slide, then click once more to return to Normal view

After you view the last slide in Slide Show view, a black slide, indicating that the slide show is finished, appears. When you click the black slide (or press [Spacebar] or [Enter]), you automatically return to the view you were in before you ran the slide show, in this case, Normal view.

> **Trouble?**
>
> If you don't see a menu command, click the double arrow at the bottom of the menu.

8. Click **View** on the menu bar, then click **Notes Page**

Notes Page view appears, showing a reduced image of the current slide above a large text box. You can enter text in this box and then print the notes page for your own use to help you remember important points about your presentation. To switch to Notes Page view, you must choose Notes Page from the View menu; there is no Notes Page View button.

FIGURE A-8: Normal view with the Outline tab displayed

Slides tab

Slide icon

Slide Show (from current slide) button

Slide Sorter View button

Normal View button

Current slide number

Previous Slide button

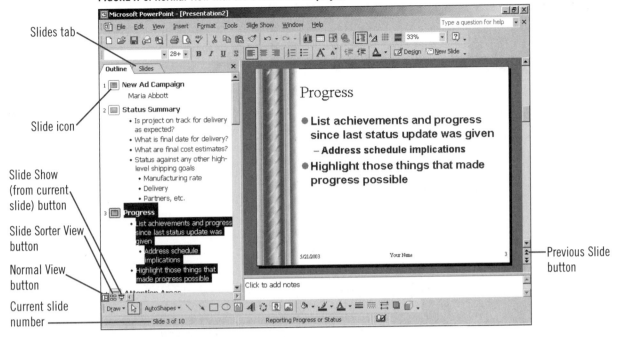

FIGURE A-9: Slide Sorter view

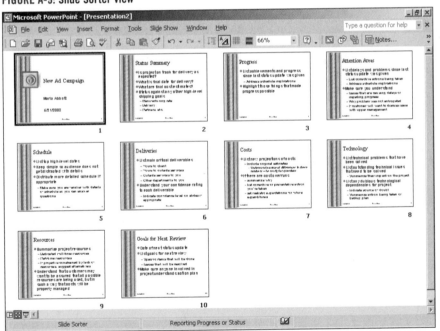

TABLE A-3: PowerPoint views

view name	button	button name	description
Normal	⊞	Normal View	Displays the pane that contains the Outline tab and Slide tab, slide pane, and notes panes at the same time; use this view to work on your presentation's content, layout, and notes concurrently
Slide Sorter	🔡	Slide Sorter View	Displays a thumbnail of all slides in the order in which they appear in your presentation; use this view to rearrange and add special effects to your slides
Slide Show	🖵	Slide Show (from current slide)	Displays your presentation as an electronic slide show
Notes Page			Displays a reduced image of the current slide above a large text box where you can enter notes

Saving a Presentation

To store your presentation permanently, you must save it as a file on a disk. As a general rule, you should save your work about every 10 or 15 minutes and before printing. You use either the Save command or the Save As command on the File menu to save your presentation for the first time. When you want to make a copy of an existing presentation under a different name, use the Save As command; otherwise, use the Save command to save your changes to a presentation file. ✐▬▬▬ Maria saves her presentation as New Ad Campaign.

Steps

1. **Click File on the menu bar, then click Save As**
   The Save As dialog box opens, similar to Figure A-10.

2. **Click the Save in list arrow, then navigate to the drive and folder where your Project Files are located**
   A default filename, which PowerPoint takes from the presentation title you entered, appears in the File name text box. If your drive or folder contains any PowerPoint files, their filenames appear in the white area in the center of the dialog box.

Trouble?

Don't worry if you see the extension .ppt after the filename in the list of filenames, even though you didn't type it. Windows can be set up to show or hide the file extensions.

3. **If necessary, drag to select the default presentation name in the File name text box, type New Ad Campaign, then click Save**
   Filenames can be up to 255 characters long; you may use lower- or uppercase letters, symbols, numbers, and spaces. The Save As dialog box closes, and the new filename appears in the title bar at the top of the Presentation window. You decide you want to save the presentation in Normal view instead of in Notes Page view.

4. **Click the Normal View button** 🔲
   The presentation view changes from Notes Page view to Normal view.

QuickTip

To save a file quickly, you can press the shortcut key combination [Ctrl][S].

5. **Click the Save button** 🔲 **on the Standard toolbar**
   The Save command saves any changes you made to the file to the same location you specified when you used the Save As command. Save your file frequently while working with it to protect the presentation.

FIGURE A-10: Save As dialog box

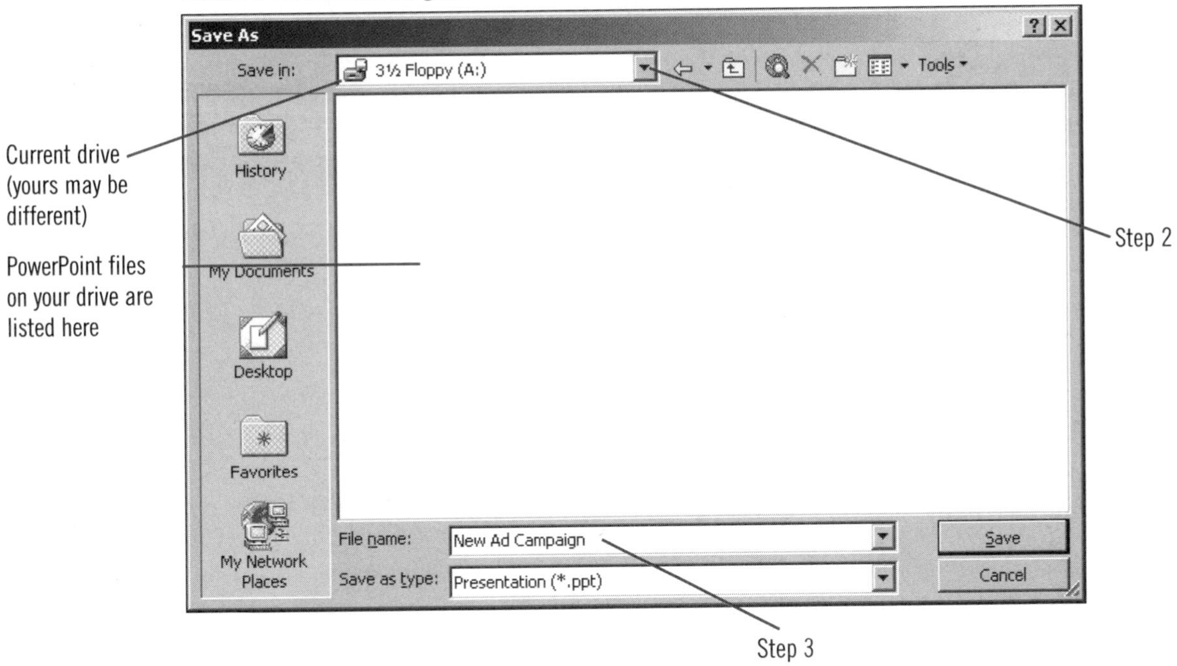

Current drive
(yours may be
different)

PowerPoint files
on your drive are
listed here

Step 2

Step 3

PowerPoint 2002

Saving fonts with your presentation

When you create a presentation, it uses the fonts that are installed on your computer. If you need to open the presentation on another computer, the fonts might look different if that computer has a different set of fonts. To preserve the look of your presentation on any computer, you can save, or embed, the fonts in your presentation. Click File on the menu bar, then click Save As. The Save As dialog box opens. Click Tools, click Save Options, then click the Embed

TrueType fonts check box in the Save Options dialog box. Click OK to close the Save Options dialog box, then click Save. Now the presentation will look the same on any computer that opens it. Using this option, however, significantly increases the size of your presentation on disk, so only use it when necessary. You can freely embed any TrueType font that comes with Windows. You can embed other TrueType fonts only if they have no license restrictions.

Getting Help

PowerPoint 2002

PowerPoint has an extensive Help system that gives you immediate access to definitions, reference information, and feature explanations. Help information appears in a separate window that you can move and resize. ◆▬▬ Maria is finished working with her presentation for now, so she decides to learn about PowerPoint's printing capabilities.

Steps

QuickTip

Clicking the Ask a Question box list arrow displays a list of recently searched for Help topics.

1. **Click in the Ask a Question box** on the menu bar, type **printing**, then press **[Enter]**

   A list appears below the Ask a Question box displaying hyperlinks to Help topics related to printing. See Figure A-11.

2. **Click the About printing hyperlink**

   The Microsoft PowerPoint Help window opens and displays information in the right pane about printing in PowerPoint. See Figure A-12. The Help window on your screen might be a different size than the one shown in the figure. Three hyperlinks to subtopics, identified by small blue arrows, are listed below the Help information in the right pane. To see any of these topics, simply click the topic. The left pane of the Help window shows three tabs that you can use to continue searching for other Help topics. The Contents tab contains Help topics organized in outline form. To open a Help window about a topic, double-click it. On the Answer Wizard tab, you search for a key word in all the Help topics, similar to the Ask a Question box. The Index tab contains an alphabetical list of Help topics. Type the word you want help on in text box 1, and the list in box 2 scrolls to that word. Click Search to view related topics in text box 3, then click the topic you want to read about.

QuickTip

If the Office Assistant is visible, you can click it to open the dialog balloon and search PowerPoint Help to display the same topics as shown in Figure A-11. To quickly open the Office Assistant dialog balloon, click the animated character, click the Microsoft PowerPoint Help button [?] on the Standard toolbar, or press [F1].

3. **Click each of the sub topics in the right pane, then read the information in the window**

   You will need to scroll down to read all the information. After reading a particular Help topic, you can search for another topic using one of the tabs on the Help window.

4. **Click the Answer Wizard tab**, if necessary, select all of the text in the What would you like to do text box, if necessary, type **print slides**, then click **Search**

   Topics related to printing slides in PowerPoint appear in the Select topic to display list box.

5. **Click the Print slides topic**

   Read the information in the right pane on how to print slides.

6. **Click the Close button** ☒ in the Microsoft PowerPoint Help window title bar

   The Help window closes, and you return to your presentation. The rest of the figures in this text do not show the Office Assistant.

QuickTip

To turn off the Office Assistant completely, right-click the Assistant, click Options, deselect the Use the Office Assistant check box, then click OK.

7. If the Office Assistant is visible, click **Help** on the menu bar, then click **Hide the Office Assistant**

   If you have hidden the Office Assistant several times, a dialog balloon may open asking if you want to turn it off permanently.

8. If a dialog balloon opens asking if you want to turn off the Office Assistant permanently, click the option you prefer in the Office Assistant dialog balloon, then click **OK**

   Selecting Hide the Office Assistant only hides it temporarily; it will reappear later to give you tips.

FIGURE A-11: Ask a Question list for the topic "printing"

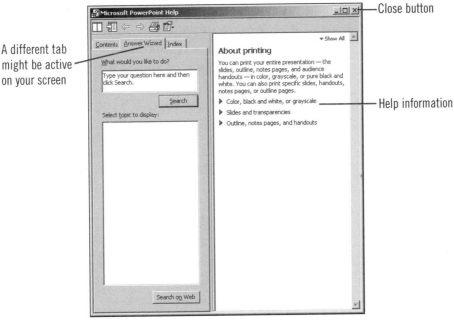

Type term to search for here

Topics related to search term

FIGURE A-12: Help window

A different tab might be active on your screen

Close button

Help information

Recovering lost presentation files

Sometimes while you are working on a presentation, PowerPoint may freeze, making it impossible to continue working on your presentation, or you may experience a power failure that causes your computer to shut down. If this type of interruption occurs, PowerPoint has a built-in recovery feature that allows you to open and save files that were open during the interruption. When you start PowerPoint again after an interruption, the Document Recovery task pane opens on the left side of your screen, displaying both original and recovered versions of the PowerPoint files that were open. If you're not sure which file to open (original or recovered), it's usually better to open the recovered file because it will have retained the latest information. You can, however, open and review all the versions of the file that was recovered and select the best one to save. Each file listed in the Document Recovery task pane has a list arrow with options that allow you to open the file, save the file, delete the file, or show repairs made to the file.

Printing and Closing the File, and Exiting PowerPoint

You print your presentation when you have completed it or when you want to review your work. Reviewing hard copies of your presentation at different stages of production gives you an overall perspective of its content and look. When you are finished working on your presentation, close the file containing your presentation and exit PowerPoint. Maria is done working on her presentation for now, so after saving her presentation, she prints the slides and notes pages of the presentation so she can review them later; then she closes the file and exits PowerPoint.

1. Click **File** on the menu bar, then click **Print**

The Print dialog box opens, similar to Figure A-13. In this dialog box, you can specify which slide format you want to print (slides, handouts, notes pages, etc.) as well as the number of pages to print and other print options. The default options, Slides and Grayscale, are already selected in the Print what area at the bottom of the dialog box.

2. In the Print range section in the middle of the dialog box, click the **Slides option button** to select it, type **3** to print only the third slide, then click **OK**

The third slide prints. If you have a black-and-white printer, the slide prints in shades of gray. To save paper, it's often a good idea to print in handout format, which lets you print up to nine slides per page.

3. Click **File** on the menu bar, then click **Print**

The Print dialog box opens again. The options you choose in the Print dialog box remain there until you close the presentation.

4. Click the **All option button** in the Print range section, click the **Print what list arrow**, click **Handouts**, click the **Slides per page list arrow** in the Handouts section, then click **6**, if necessary

5. Click the **Color/grayscale list arrow**, click **Pure Black and White**, then click **OK**

The presentation prints as audience handouts on two pages. The presentation prints without any gray tones.

6. Click **File** on the menu bar, then click **Print**

The Print dialog box opens again.

7. Click the **Print what list arrow**, click **Outline View**, then click **OK**

The presentation outline prints.

8. Click **File** on the menu bar, then click **Close**

If you have made changes to your presentation, a Microsoft PowerPoint alert box opens asking you if you want to save changes you have made to the New Ad Campaign file, as shown in Figure A-14.

9. If necessary, click **Yes** to close the alert box

10. Click **File** on the menu bar, then click **Exit**

The presentation and the PowerPoint program close, and you return to the Windows desktop.

FIGURE A-13: Print dialog box

Your printer name may be different

Step 2

Click to select item to print

Step 5

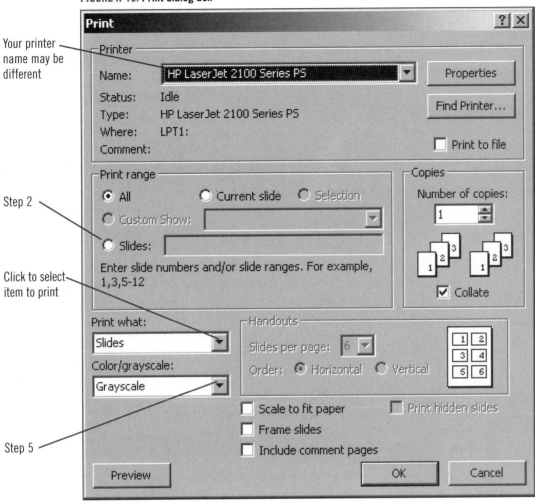

FIGURE A-14: Save changes message box

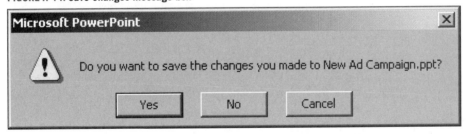

Viewing your presentation in grayscale or black and white

Viewing your presentation in pure black and white or in grayscale (using shades of gray) is very useful when you will be printing a presentation on a black-and-white printer and you want to make sure your text is readable. To see how your color presentation looks in grayscale or black and white, click the Color/Grayscale button ▦ on the Standard toolbar, then select either the Grayscale command or the Pure Black and White command. The Grayscale View toolbar appears. You can use the Grayscale View toolbar to select different settings to view your presentation. If you don't like the way an object looks in black and white or grayscale view, you can change its color. Right-click the object, point to Black and White Setting or Grayscale Setting (depending on which view you are in), and choose from the options on the submenu.

Practice

► Concepts Review

Label the elements of the PowerPoint window shown in Figure A-15.

FIGURE A-15

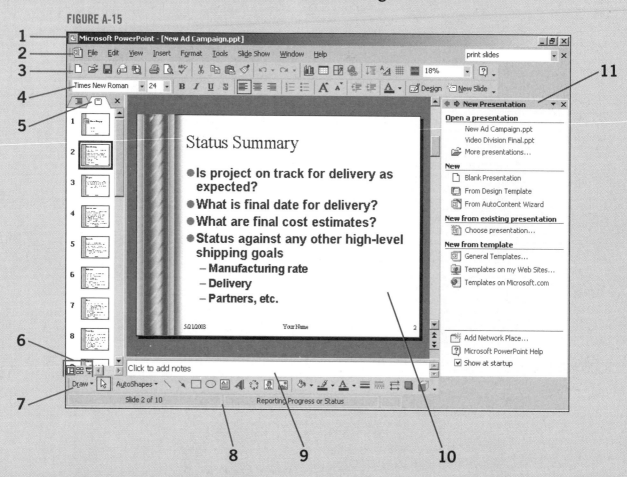

Match each term with the statement that describes it.

12. **AutoContent Wizard**
13. **Task pane**
14. **Slide Sorter view**
15. **Normal view**
16. **Outline tab**

a. Displays hyperlinks of common commands
b. Displays the text of your presentation in an outline form
c. Series of dialog boxes that guides you through creating a presentation and produces a presentation with suggestions for content
d. Displays the Outline and Slide tabs, as well as the slide and notes panes
e. Shows all your slides as thumbnails

Select the best answer from the list of choices.

17. **PowerPoint can help you create all of the following, *except*:**
    a. Notes pages.
    b. Outline pages.
    c. An on-screen presentation.
    d. A movie.

18. **The buttons you use to switch between the PowerPoint views are called:**
    a. Screen buttons.
    b. PowerPoint buttons.
    c. View buttons.
    d. Toolbar buttons.

19. **All of the following are PowerPoint views, *except*:**
    a. Slide Sorter view.
    b. Notes Page view.
    c. Current Page view.
    d. Normal view.

20. **The view that allows you to view your electronic slide show with each slide filling the entire screen is called:**
    a. Presentation view.
    b. Slide Sorter view.
    c. Slide Show view.
    d. Electronic view.

21. **Which wizard helps you create and outline your presentation?**
    a. Presentation Wizard
    b. OrgContent Wizard
    c. AutoContent Wizard
    d. Pick a Look Wizard

22. **How do you switch to Notes Page view?**
    a. Press [Shift] and click in the notes pane
    b. Click the Notes Page View button
    c. Click View on the menu bar, then click Notes Page
    d. All of the above

23. **How do you save changes to your presentation after you have saved it for the first time?**
    a. Click Save As on the File menu, select a filename from the list, then assign it a new name
    b. Click the Save button on the Standard toolbar
    c. Click Save As on the File menu, then click Save
    d. Click Save As on the File menu, specify a new location and filename, then click Save

PowerPoint 2002

► Skills Review

1. Start PowerPoint and view the PowerPoint window.
a. Identify as many elements of the PowerPoint window as you can without referring to the unit material.
b. For any elements you cannot identify, refer to the unit.

2. Use the AutoContent Wizard.
a. Start the AutoContent Wizard, then select a presentation category and type. (*Hint*: If you see a message saying you need to install the feature, insert your Office CD in the appropriate drive and click OK. If you are working in a networked computer lab, see your technical support person for assistance. If you are unable to load additional templates, click No as many times as necessary, then select another presentation type.)
b. Select the output options of your choice.
c. Enter appropriate information for the opening slide, enter your name as the footer text, and complete the wizard to show the first slide of the presentation.

3. View a presentation and run a slide show.
a. View each slide in the presentation to become familiar with its content.
b. When you are finished, return to Slide 1.
c. Click the Outline tab and review the presentation contents.
d. Change to Notes Page view and see if the notes pages in the presentation contain text, then return to Normal view.
e. Examine the presentation contents in Slide Sorter view.
f. View all the slides of the presentation in Slide Show view, and end the slide show to return to Slide Sorter view.

4. Save a presentation.
a. Change to Notes Page view.
b. Open the Save As dialog box.
c. Navigate to the drive and folder where your Project Files are located.
d. Name your presentation **Practice**.
e. Click Tools, then click Save Options.
f. Choose the option to embed the fonts in your presentation, as shown in Figure A-16, then click OK.
g. Save your file.
h. Go to a different view than the one you saved your presentation in.
i. Save the changed presentation.

FIGURE A-16

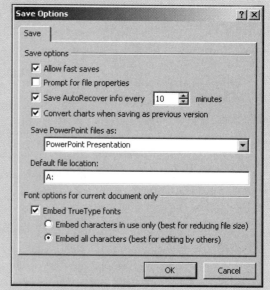

5. **Get Help.**

   a. Type **creating presentations** in the Ask a Question box, then press [Enter].

   b. Click the About creating presentations hyperlink.

   c. Scroll down, and read the information.

   d. Click the Index tab, then type a word you want help with in text box 1.

   e. Click a word in the list in list box 2 if it did not jump to the correct word, then click Search.

   f. Click a topic in the list in box 3 and read about it.

   g. Explore a number of topics that interest you.

   h. When you have finished exploring the Index tab, switch to the Contents tab.

   i. On the Contents tab, double-click any book icon to view the Help subjects (identified by page icons), then click the page icons to review the Help information. Explore a number of topics that interest you.

   j. When you have finished exploring the Contents tab, close the Help window and hide the Office Assistant, if necessary.

6. **Print and close the file, and exit PowerPoint.**

   a. Print slides 2 and 3 as slides in grayscale. (*Hint*: In the Slides text box, type 2-3.)

   b. Print all the slides as handouts, 9 slides per page, in pure black and white.

   c. Print the presentation outline.

   d. Close the file, saving your changes.

   e. Exit PowerPoint.

▶ Independent Challenge 1

You have just gotten a job as a marketing assistant at Events, Inc, a catering firm specializing in clambakes and barbecues for large company events. John Hudspeth, the marketing manager, has some familiarity with PowerPoint. He has printed his presentation as grayscale, but he cannot see all of his text, and he wants to know how to solve this problem.

a. If PowerPoint is not already running, start it.

b. Use PowerPoint Help to find the answer to John's question.

c. Write down which Help feature you used (Ask a Question box, Index, etc.) and the steps you followed.

d. Print the Help window that shows the information you found. (*Hint*: Click the Print button at the top of the Help window.)

e. Exit PowerPoint.

PowerPoint 2002

▶ Independent Challenge 2

You are in charge of marketing for ArtWorks, Inc., a medium-size company that produces all types of art for corporations to enhance their work environment. The company has a regional sales area that includes areas throughout western Europe. The president of ArtWorks has asked you to plan and create the outline of the PowerPoint presentation he will use to convey his marketing plan to the sales department.

   a. If necessary, start PowerPoint.
   b. Start the AutoContent Wizard. (*Hint*: If the task pane is not visible, click View on the menu bar, then click Task Pane.)
   c. On the Presentation type screen, choose the Sales/Marketing category, then choose Marketing Plan from the list.
   d. Assign the presentation an appropriate title, and include your name as the footer text.
   e. Scroll through the outline that the AutoContent Wizard produces. Does it contain the type of information you thought it would?
   f. Plan and take notes on how you would change and add to the sample text created by the wizard. What information do you need to promote ArtWorks to companies?
   g. Switch views. Run through the slide show at least once.
   h. Save your presentation with the name **ArtWorks** to the drive and folder where your Project Files are located.
   i. Print your presentation as handouts (6 slides per page).
   j. Close the presentation and exit PowerPoint.

▶ Independent Challenge 3

You have recently been promoted to sales manager at Alison Industries. Part of your job is to train sales representatives to go to potential customers and give presentations describing your company's products. Your boss wants you to find an appropriate PowerPoint presentation template that you can use for your next training presentation to recommend strategies to the sales representatives for closing sales. She wants a printout so she can evaluate it.

   a. If necessary, start PowerPoint.
   b. Start the AutoContent Wizard. (*Hint*: If the task pane is not visible, click View on the menu bar, then click Task Pane.)
   c. Examine the available AutoContent Wizards and select one that you could adapt for your presentation. (*Hint*: If you see a message saying you need to install additional templates, insert your Office CD in the appropriate drive and click OK. If you are working in a networked computer lab, see your technical support person for assistance. If you are unable to load additional templates, click No as many times as necessary, then select another presentation type.)
   d. Enter an appropriate slide title and include your name as the footer text.
   e. Print the presentation as an outline, then print the first slide in pure black and white.
   f. Write a brief memo to your boss describing which wizard you think will be most helpful, referring to specific slides in the outline to support your recommendation.
   g. Save the presentation as **Sales Training** to the drive and folder where your project files are located.
   h. Close the presentation and exit PowerPoint.

Independent Challenge 4

In this unit, you've learned about PowerPoint basics such as how to start PowerPoint, view the PowerPoint window, use the AutoContent Wizard, and run a slide show. There are many Web sites that provide information about how to use PowerPoint more effectively.

Use the Web to access information about one of the following topics:

- Information on how to use PowerPoint effectively
- Tips on how to increase your productivity using PowerPoint

a. Connect to the Internet, then go to Microsoft's Web site at www.microsoft.com. Your screen should look similar to Figure A-17.

b. Click the Office hyperlink, then locate the Using Microsoft PowerPoint page.

c. Research and gather information on using PowerPoint.

d. Start a word processing program and create and save a new blank document as **PowerPoint Productivity Tips** to the drive and folder where your Project Files are located.

e. Type your name at the top of the document.

FIGURE A-17

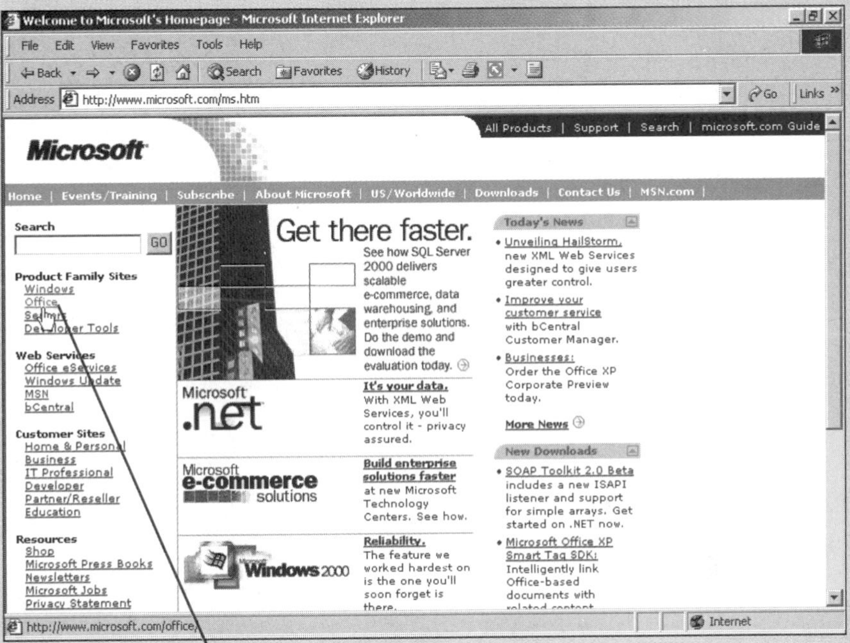

Click the Office link to locate information on PowerPoint

f. Write a brief summary report of the information you compile. Your report should include at least five tips or instructions on how to use PowerPoint more effectively or how to increase your productivity using PowerPoint. For each tip or instruction, include the exact URL where you found the tip. (*Hint*: Click in the Address or Location box in your browser window to select the current URL, click Edit on the menu bar, click Copy, then use the Paste command in the word processor to paste the exact URL in your document.)

g. Save your final document, print it, then close the document and exit the word processor.

▶ Visual Workshop

Create the presentation shown in Figure A-18 using the Project Overview AutoContent Wizard in the Projects category. Make sure you include your name as the footer. Save the presentation as Phase 3A to the drive and folder where your Project Files are located. Print the slides as handouts, six slides per page, in pure black and white.

FIGURE A-18

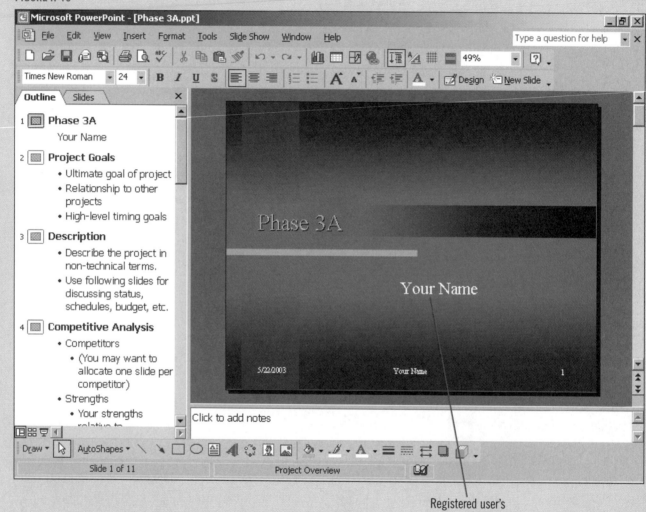

Registered user's name appears here

Creating
a Presentation

► **Plan an effective presentation**

MOUS ► **Enter slide text**

MOUS ► **Create a new slide**

MOUS ► **Enter text in the Outline tab**

MOUS ► **Add slide headers and footers**

MOUS ► **Choose a look for a presentation**

MOUS ► **Check spelling in a presentation**

MOUS ► **Evaluate a presentation**

Now that you are familiar with PowerPoint basics, you are ready to plan and create your own presentation. To do this, you first enter and edit the presentation text, and then you can focus on the design and look of your presentation. PowerPoint helps you accomplish these tasks with the AutoContent Wizard and with a collection of professionally prepared slide designs, called **design templates**, which can enhance the look of your presentation. In this unit, you create a presentation using a PowerPoint design template. Maria Abbott, general sales manager at MediaLoft, needs to prepare a marketing presentation on a new service that MediaLoft is planning to introduce later in the year. She begins by planning her presentation.

Planning an Effective Presentation

Before you create a presentation using PowerPoint, you need to plan and outline the message you want to communicate and consider how you want the presentation to look. When preparing the outline, you need to consider where you are giving the presentation and who your audience will be. It is also important to know what resources you might need, such as a computer or projection equipment. ✐ Using Figure B-1 and the planning guidelines below, follow Maria as she outlines the presentation message.

In planning a presentation, it is important to:

▶ **Determine the purpose of the presentation**
When you have a well-defined purpose, developing an outline for your presentation is much easier. Maria needs to present a marketing plan for a new Internet service that MediaLoft is planning to launch later in the year.

▶ **Determine the message you want to communicate, then give the presentation a meaningful title and outline your message**
If possible, take time to adequately develop an outline of your presentation content before creating the slides. Maria starts her presentation by defining the new service, describing the competition, and stating the product positioning. See Figure B-1.

▶ **Determine the audience and the delivery location**
The presentation audience and delivery location can greatly affect the type of presentation you create. For example, if you had to deliver a presentation to your staff in a small, dimly lit conference room, you may create a very simple presentation; however, if you had to deliver a sales presentation to a client in a formal conference room with many windows, you may need to create a very professional-looking presentation. Maria will deliver her presentation in a large conference room to MediaLoft's marketing management team.

▶ **Determine the type of output—black-and-white or color overhead transparencies, on-screen slide show, or an online broadcast—that best conveys your message, given time constraints and computer hardware availability**
Because Maria is speaking in a large conference room to a large group and has access to a computer and projection equipment, she decides that an on-screen slide show is the best output choice for her presentation.

▶ **Determine a look for your presentation which will help communicate your message**
You can choose one of the professionally designed templates that come with PowerPoint, modify one of these templates, or create one of your own. Maria wants a simple and artistic template to convey the marketing plan.

▶ **Determine what additional materials will be useful in the presentation**
You need to prepare not only the slides themselves but also supplementary materials, including speaker notes and handouts for the audience. Maria uses speaker notes to help remember a few key details, and she will pass out handouts for the audience to use as a reference.

FIGURE B-1: Outline of the presentation content

1. iMedia
   -Proposed Marketing Plan
   -Maria Abbott
   -May 26, 2003
   -General Sales Manager
2. Product Definition
   -Internet media service provider
      -Music and video
      -Articles and trade papers
      -Historical papers archive
   -Publishing service
      -Papers, articles, books, games, and more...
3. Competition
   -Bookstores
   -Internet stores
   -Media services
   -Ratings
4. Product Positioning
   -Only licensed media download service provider
   -Only interactive service provider
   -Only publishing service provider

CLUES TO USE

Using templates from the Web

When you create a presentation, you have the option of using one of the design templates supplied with PowerPoint, or you can use a template from another source, such as a Web server or Microsoft's Office Template Gallery Web site. To create a presentation using a template from a Web server, start PowerPoint, open the New Presentation task pane, then click the Templates on my Web Sites hyperlink. The New from Templates on my Web Sites dialog box opens. Locate and open the template you want to use, then save it with a new name. To use a template from Microsoft's Office Template Gallery, open the New Presentation task pane, then click the Templates on Microsoft.com hyperlink. Your Web browser opens to the Microsoft Office Template Gallery Web site. Locate the PowerPoint template you want to use, then click the Edit in Microsoft PowerPoint hyperlink to open and save the template in PowerPoint. The first time you use the Template Gallery, you must install Microsoft Office Template Gallery and accept the license agreement.

Entering Slide Text

Each time you start PowerPoint, a new presentation with a blank title slide appears in Normal view. The title slide has two **text placeholders** that are boxes with dashed-line borders where you enter text. The top text placeholder on the title slide is the **title placeholder**, labeled "Click to add title." The bottom text placeholder on the title slide is the **main text placeholder**, labeled "Click to add subtitle." To enter text in a placeholder, simply click the placeholder and then type your text. After you enter text in a placeholder, the placeholder becomes a text object. An **object** is any item on a slide that can be manipulated. Objects are the building blocks that make up a presentation slide. ✐ Maria begins working on her presentation by starting PowerPoint and entering text on the title slide.

Steps 1 2 3 4

1. **Start PowerPoint**

   A new presentation appears displaying a blank slide.

2. **Move the pointer over the title placeholder labeled "Click to add title" in the slide pane**

   The pointer changes to I when you move the pointer over the placeholder. In PowerPoint, the pointer often changes shape, depending on the task you are trying to accomplish.

3. **Click the title placeholder**

   The **insertion point**, a blinking vertical line, indicates where your text will appear in the title placeholder. A **selection box**, the slanted line border, appears around the title placeholder, indicating that it is selected and ready to accept text. See Figure B-2.

Trouble?

If you press a wrong key, press [Backspace] to erase the character, then continue to type.

4. **Type iMedia**

   PowerPoint center-aligns the title text within the title placeholder, which is now a text object. Notice that text appears on the slide thumbnail on the Slides tab.

5. **Click the main text placeholder in the slide pane**

   A wavy, red line may appear under the word "iMedia" in the title object indicating that the automatic spellchecking feature in PowerPoint is active. Don't worry if it doesn't appear on your screen.

6. **Type Proposed Marketing Plan, then press [Enter]**

   The insertion point moves to the next line in the text placeholder.

7. **Type Maria Abbott, press [Enter], type May 26, 2003, press [Enter], then type General Sales Manager**

   Notice that the AutoFit Options button ⊞ appears near the text object. The AutoFit Options button on your screen tells you that PowerPoint has automatically decreased the size of all the text in the text object to fit in the text object.

8. **Click the Autofit Options button ⊞, then click Stop Fitting Text to This Placeholder on the shortcut menu**

   The text in the main text box changes back to its original size as shown in Figure B-3. The text object looks a little crowded.

Trouble?

If the insertion point is blinking in a blank line after completing this step, press [Backspace] one more time.

9. **Position I to the right of 2003, drag to select the entire line of text, press [Backspace], then click outside the main text object in a blank area of the slide**

   The text and the line it occupied are deleted and the Autofit Options button closes. Clicking a blank area of the slide deselects all selected objects on the slide.

10. **Click the Save button 🖫 on the Standard toolbar, then save your presentation as iMedia 1 to the drive and folder where your Project Files are stored**

FIGURE B-2: Slide with selected title placeholder

Selection box

Title placeholder

Insertion point

Main text placeholder

Mouse pointer

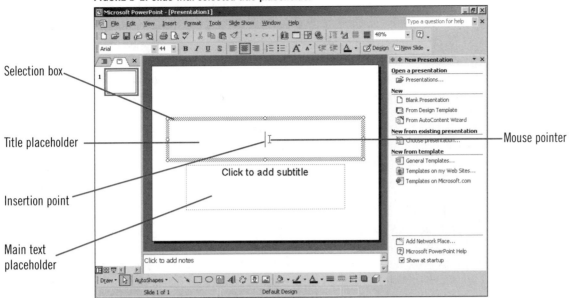

FIGURE B-3: Title slide with text

Red, wavy line indicates automatic spellchecking is on

iMedia

Proposed Marketing Plan
Maria Abbott
General Sales Manager

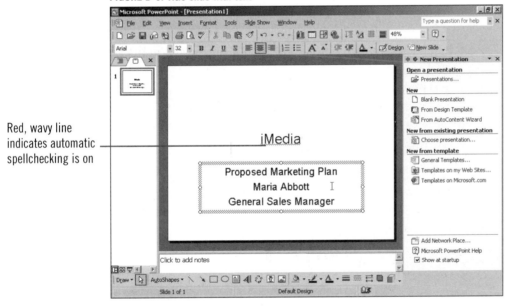

Using Speech Recognition

Speech recognition technology lets you enter text and issue commands by talking into a standard microphone connected to your computer. It is an Office-wide program that you must install and set up before you can use it. To start using Speech Recognition, start Word, click Tools on the menu bar, then click Speech. You might be prompted to install the Speech Recognition files using the Office CD. Once you have installed the Speech Recognition files, the Speech Recognition component will be available in all Office programs. The Training Wizard is a series of paragraphs that you read into your computer's microphone. These training sessions teach the Speech module to recognize your voice. They also teach you the speed and level of clarity with which you need to speak so that the program can understand you. Training sessions improve the performance of the Speech Recognition module. If you don't use the training sessions, the Speech Recognition module may be inaccurate.

Creating a New Slide

To help you create a new slide easily, PowerPoint offers 27 predesigned slide layouts. A **slide layout** determines how all of the elements on a slide are arranged. Slide layouts include a variety of placeholder arrangements for different objects, including titles, text, clip art, tables, charts, diagrams, and media clips, and are organized by layout type in the following categories: text layouts, content layouts, text and content layouts, and other layouts. You have already used the title slide layout in the previous lesson. Table B-1 describes some of the placeholders you'll find in the slide layouts. To continue developing the presentation, Maria needs to create a slide that defines the new service MediaLoft is developing.

1. Click the **New Slide button** 🖾 on the Formatting toolbar

A new blank slide appears after the current slide in your presentation and the Slide Layout task pane opens, as shown in Figure B-4. The new slide in the slide pane contains a title placeholder and a **body text** placeholder for a bulleted list. Notice that the status bar indicates Slide 2 of 2 and that the Slides tab now contains two slide thumbnails. The Slide Layout task pane identifies the different PowerPoint slide layouts that you can use in your presentation. A selection box appears around the Title and Text slide layout identifying it as the currently applied layout for the slide. You can easily change the current slide's layout by clicking a slide layout icon in the Slide Layout task pane.

2. Point to the **Title and 2-Column Text layout** (last layout in the Text Layouts section) in the Slide Layout task pane

When you place your pointer over a slide layout icon, a selection list arrow appears. You can click the list arrow to choose options for applying the layout. After a brief moment, a ScreenTip also appears that identifies the slide layout by name.

3. Click the **Title and 2-Column Text layout**

A slide layout with two text placeholders replaces the Title and Text slide layout.

4. Type **Product Definition**, then click the **left body text placeholder** in the slide pane

The text you type appears in the title placeholder, and the insertion point appears next to a bullet in the left body text placeholder.

5. Type **Internet media provider**, then press **[Enter]**

A new first-level bullet automatically appears when you press [Enter].

6. Press **[Tab]**

The new first-level bullet indents and becomes a second-level bullet.

7. Type **Music and video**, press **[Enter]**, type **Articles and trade papers**, press **[Enter]**, then type **Historical papers archive**

The left text object has four bullet points.

8. Press **[Ctrl][Enter]**, then type **Publishing service**

Pressing [Ctrl][Enter] moves the insertion point to the next text placeholder. Because this is a two-column layout, the insertion point moves to the other body text placeholder on the slide.

9. Press **[Enter]**, press **[Tab]**, type **Papers**, press **[Enter]**, type **Articles**, press **[Enter]**, type **Books**, press **[Enter]**, type **Games and more...**, click in a blank area of the slide, then click the **Save button** 🖫 on the Standard toolbar

Your changes to the file are saved. Compare your screen with Figure B-5.

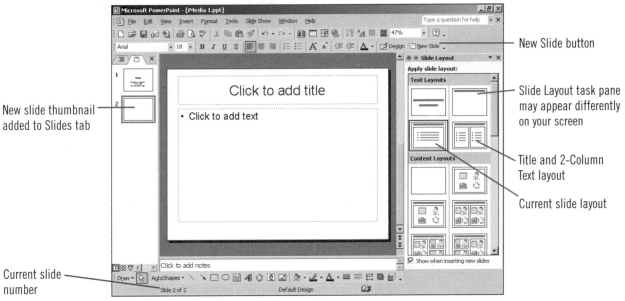

New Slide button

New slide thumbnail added to Slides tab

Slide Layout task pane may appear differently on your screen

Title and 2-Column Text layout

Current slide layout

Current slide number

FIGURE B-5: New slide with Title and 2-Column Text slide layout

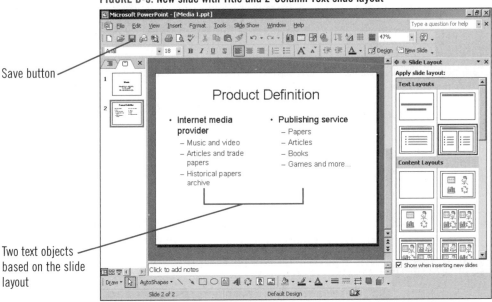

Save button

Two text objects based on the slide layout

TABLE B-1: Slide Layout placeholders

placeholder	symbol	description
Bulleted List		Inserts a short list of related points
Clip Art		Inserts a picture from the Clip Gallery
Chart		Inserts a chart created with Microsoft Graph
Diagram or Organization Chart		Inserts a diagram or organizational chart
Table		Inserts a table
Media Clip		Inserts a music, sound, or video clip
Content		Inserts objects such as a table, a chart, clip art, a picture, a diagram or organizational chart, or a media clip

PowerPoint 2002

Entering Text in the Outline Tab

You can enter presentation text on the slide, as you've learned already, or, if you'd rather focus on the presentation text without worrying about how it's arranged, you can enter it in the Outline tab. As in a regular outline, the headings, or titles, appear first; beneath the titles, the subpoints, or body text, appear. Body text appears as one or more lines of bulleted text indented under a title. Maria switches to the Outline tab to enter body text for two more slides.

Steps 1 2 3 4

1. **Click the Outline tab to the left of the slide pane**
   The Outline tab enlarges to display the text of your slides. The slide icon for Slide 2 is highlighted, indicating that it's selected. Notice the numbers 1 and 2 that appear to the left of the first-level bullets for Slide 2, indicating that there are two body text objects on the slide.

2. **Point to the Title and Text layout (second row, first column) in the Slide Layout task pane, click the list arrow, then click Insert New Slide**
   A new slide, Slide 3, with the Title and Text layout appears as the current slide below Slide 2. A selected slide icon ▦ appears next to the slide number when you add a new slide to the outline. See Figure B-6. Text that you enter next to a slide icon becomes the title for that slide.

3. **Click next to the Slide 3 slide icon in the Outline tab, type Competition, press [Enter], then press [Tab]**
   A new slide was inserted when you pressed [Enter], but because you want to enter body text for the slide you just created, you indented this line to make it part of Slide 3.

4. **Type Bookstoes, press [Enter], type E-sites, press [Enter], type Media services, press [Enter], type Ratings, then press [Enter]**
   Make sure you typed "Bookstoes" without the "r" as shown.

5. **Press [Shift][Tab]**
   The bullet that was created when you pressed [Enter] changes to a new slide icon.

6. **Type Product Positioning, press [Ctrl][Enter], type Licensed media download provider, press [Enter], type Publishing service provider, press [Enter], type Interactive service provider, then press [Ctrl][Enter]**
   Pressing [Ctrl][Enter] while the cursor is in the body text object creates a new slide with the same layout as the previous slide. Two of the bulleted points you just typed for Slide 4 are out of order, and you don't need the new Slide 5 you just created.

7. **Click the Undo button ↺ on the Standard toolbar**
   Clicking the Undo button undoes the previous action. Slide 5 is deleted and the insertion point moves back up to the last bullet in Slide 4.

8. **Position the pointer to the left of the last bullet in Slide 4 in the Outline tab**
   The pointer changes to ⬌↕.

9. **Drag the mouse pointer up until the pointer changes to ↕ and a vertical indicator line appears above the second bullet point in Slide 4, then release the mouse button**
   The third bullet point moves up one line in the outline and trades places with the second bullet point, as shown in Figure B-7.

10. **Click the Slides tab, click the Slide 2 icon in the Slides tab, then save your work**
    Slide 2 of 4 should appear in the status bar.

FIGURE B-6: Normal view with Outline tab open

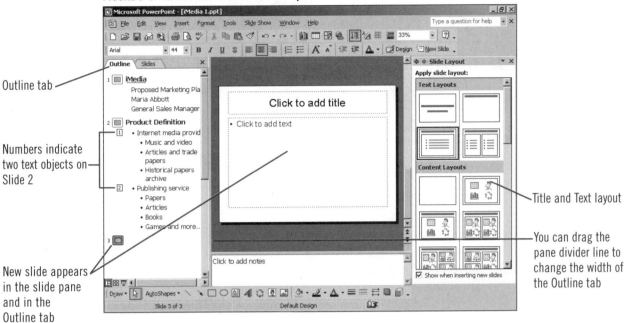

Outline tab

Numbers indicate two text objects on Slide 2

New slide appears in the slide pane and in the Outline tab

Title and Text layout

You can drag the pane divider line to change the width of the Outline tab

FIGURE B-7: Bulleted item moved up on the Outline tab

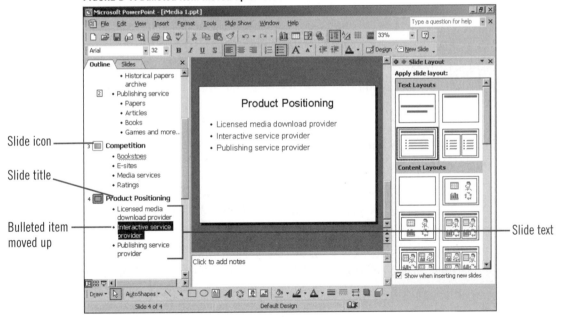

Slide icon

Slide title

Bulleted item moved up

Slide text

What do I do if I see a lightbulb on a slide?

If you have the Office Assistant showing, you may see a yellow lightbulb in your presentation window. The lightbulb is part of the PowerPoint Help system and it can mean several things. First, the Office Assistant might have a suggestion for an appropriate piece of clip art for that slide. Second, the Office Assistant might have a helpful tip based on the task you are performing. This is known as a context-sensitive tip.

Third, the Office Assistant might have detected a style, such as a word in the slide title that should be capitalized, which is inconsistent with preset style guidelines. When you see a lightbulb, you can click it, read the dialog balloon, and click the option you prefer, or you can ignore it. If the Office Assistant is hidden or turned off, the lightbulb will not appear.

Adding Slide Headers and Footers

Header and footer text, such as your company or product name, the slide number, and the date, can give your presentation a professional look and make it easier for your audience to follow. On slides, you can add text only to the footer; however, notes or handouts can include both header and footer text. Footer information that you apply to the slides of your presentation is visible in the PowerPoint views and when you print the slides. Notes and handouts header and footer text is visible when you print notes pages, handouts, and the outline. ◣ Maria wants to add footer text to the slides of her presentation.

1. **Click View on the menu bar, then click Header and Footer**
   The Header and Footer dialog box opens, as shown in Figure B-8. The Header and Footer dialog box has two tabs: one for slides and one for notes and handouts. The rectangles at the bottom of the Preview box identify the default position of the three types of footer text on the slides. Two of the Footer check boxes are selected by default, so two of the rectangles at the bottom of the Preview box are darkened.

2. **Click the Date and time check box to deselect it**
   The first dark rectangle at the bottom of the Preview box lightens. The middle dark rectangle identifies where the Footer text—the only check box still selected—will appear on the slide. The rectangle on the right, therefore, shows where the slide number will appear if that check box is selected.

   QuickTip

   If you want the original date that you opened or created the presentation to appear, select the Fixed date option and type the date in the Fixed text box.

3. **Click the Date and time check box, then click the Update automatically option button**
   Now every time you view the slide show or print the slides of the presentation, the current date will appear in the footer.

4. **Click the Update automatically list arrow, then click the fourth option in the list**
   The date format changes.

5. **Click the Slide number check box, click in the Footer text box, then type your name**
   The Preview box changes to show that all three footer placeholders are selected.

6. **Click the Don't show on title slide check box**
   Selecting this check box prevents the footer information you entered in the Header and Footer dialog box from appearing on the title slide. Compare your screen to Figure B-9.

7. **Click Apply to All**
   The dialog box closes and the footer information is applied to all of the slides in your presentation except the title slide. You can apply footer information to just one slide in the presentation if you want.

8. **Click the Slide 1 icon in the Slides tab, click View on the menu bar, then click Header and Footer**
   The Header and Footer dialog box opens displaying all of the options that you selected earlier in this lesson. You want to show your name in all the footer on the title slide.

   Trouble?

   If you click Apply to All in Step 10, click the Undo button on the Standard toolbar and repeat Steps 9 and 10.

9. **Click the Date and time check box, the Slide number check box, and the Don't show on title slide check box to deselect them**
   Only the text in the Footer text box will appear on the title slide.

10. **Click Apply, then save your work**
    Clicking Apply applies the footer information to just the current slide.

FIGURE B-8: Header and Footer dialog box

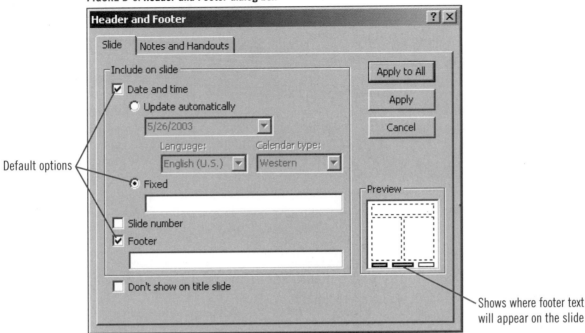

Default options

Shows where footer text will appear on the slide

FIGURE B-9: Completed Header and Footer dialog box

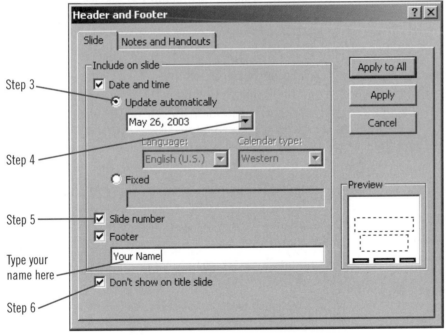

Step 3

Step 4

Step 5

Type your name here

Step 6

PowerPoint 2002

Entering and printing notes

You can add notes to your slides when there are certain facts you want to remember during a presentation or when there is information you want to hand out to your audience. Notes do not appear on the slides themselves when you run a slide show. Use the Notes pane in Normal view or Notes Page view to enter notes about your slides. To enter notes on a slide, click in the Notes pane, then type. If you want to insert graphics on the notes pages, you must use Notes Page view instead of the Notes pane. To open Notes Page view, click View on the menu, then click Notes Page. You can print your notes using the Notes Pages option in the Print dialog box. The notes page can also be a good handout to give your audience for their use. Don't enter any notes, and print the notes pages; the slides will print as thumbnails with space to the right for notes.

Choosing a Look for a Presentation

To help you design your presentation, PowerPoint provides a number of design templates so you don't have to spend time creating the right presentation look. A **design template** has borders, colors, text attributes, and other elements arranged in a specific format that you can apply to one or all the slides in your presentation. In most cases, you would apply one template to an entire presentation; you can, however, apply multiple templates to the same presentation. You can use a design template as is, or you can modify any element to suit your needs. Unless you know something about graphic design, it is often easier and faster to use or modify one of the templates supplied with PowerPoint. No matter how you create your presentation, you can save it as a template for future use. Maria decides to use an existing PowerPoint template.

Steps

1. Click the **Other Task Panes list arrow** ▾ in the task pane title bar, then click **Slide Design – Design Templates**

   The Slide Design task pane appears, similar to the one shown in Figure B-10. This task pane is split into sections: the three hyperlinks that open sub-task panes at the top of the pane; the Used in This Presentation section, which identifies the templates currently applied to the presentation (in this case, the Default Design template); the Recently Used section, which identifies up to five templates you have applied recently (this section will not appear on your screen if no one has used any other templates); and the Available For Use section, which lists all of the standard PowerPoint design templates that you can apply to a presentation.

2. Scroll down to the **Available For Use section** of the Slide Design task pane, then place your pointer over the **Balance template** (first row, second column)

   A selection list arrow appears next to the Balance template icon. The list arrow provides options for you to choose from when applying design templates. To really determine how a design template will look on your presentation, you need to apply it. You can apply as many templates as you want until you find one that you like.

3. Click the **Balance template list arrow**, then click **Apply to All Slides**

   The Balance template is applied to all the slides. Notice the new slide background color, the new graphic elements, and the new slide text color. The scales in the background of this template don't fit with the presentation content.

4. Click the **Fireworks template list arrow** (sixth row, first column), then click **Apply to Selected Slides**

   The Fireworks template is applied to the title slide of the presentation. This design template doesn't fit with the presentation content either.

5. Click the **Blends template list arrow** (second row, first column), then click **Apply to All Slides**

   This simple and colorful design template looks good with the presentation content and fits the MediaLoft company image.

6. Click the **Next Slide button** ▾ three times

   Preview all the slides in the presentation to see how they look.

7. Click the **Previous Slide button** ▴ three times to return to Slide 1

   Compare your screen to Figure B-11.

8. Save your changes

FIGURE B-10: Normal view with Slide Design task pane open

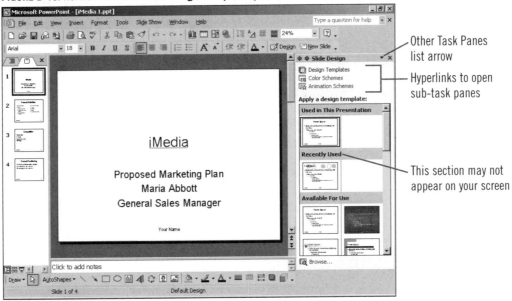

Other Task Panes list arrow

Hyperlinks to open sub-task panes

This section may not appear on your screen

FIGURE B-11: Blends template design applied

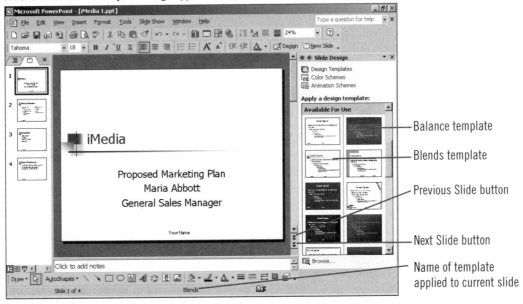

Balance template

Blends template

Previous Slide button

Next Slide button

Name of template applied to current slide

CLUES TO USE

Using design templates

You are not limited to using the templates PowerPoint provides; you can either modify a PowerPoint template or create your own. For example, you might want to use your company's color as a slide background or incorporate your company's logo on every slide. If you modify an existing template, you can keep, change, or delete any color, graphic, or font. To create a new template, click Blank Presentation on the New Presentation task pane. Add the design elements you want, then open the Save As dialog box. Click the Save as type list arrow, and choose Design Template, then name your template, and click Save. PowerPoint will automatically add the file extension .pot to the filename, save the template to the Office Templates folder, and add it to the Slide Design task pane. You can then use your customized template as a basis for future presentations. To apply a template that you created to an existing presentation, open the presentation, then choose the template in the Slide Design task pane. The design template will be applied to your current presentation.

Checking Spelling in the Presentation

PowerPoint 2002

As your work nears completion, you need to review and proofread your presentation thoroughly for errors. You can use the spellchecking feature in PowerPoint to check for and correct spelling errors. This feature compares the spelling of all the words in your presentation against the words contained in its electronic dictionary. You still must proofread your presentation for punctuation, grammar, and word-usage errors because the spellchecker recognizes only misspelled words, not misused words. For example, the spellchecker would not identify "The Test" as an error, even if you had intended to type "The Best."  Maria has finished adding and changing text in the presentation, so she checks her work.

Steps

> **Trouble?**
>
> If your spellchecker doesn't find the word "iMedia," then a previous user may have accidentally added it to the custom dictionary. Skip Steps 1 and 2 and continue with the lesson.

1. **Make sure that Slide 1 is selected in the Slide tab, then click the Spelling button** **on the Standard toolbar**

   PowerPoint begins to check the spelling in your entire presentation. When PowerPoint finds a misspelled word or a word it doesn't recognize, the Spelling dialog box opens, as shown in Figure B-12. For an explanation of the commands available in the Spelling dialog box, see Table B-2. In this case, PowerPoint does not recognize "iMedia" on Slide 1. It suggests that you replace it with the word "Media." You want the word to remain as you typed it.

2. **Click Ignore All**

   Clicking Ignore All tells the spellchecker to ignore all instances of this word in this presentation. The next word the spellchecker identifies as an error is the word "Bookstoes" in the text body for Slide 3. In the Suggestions list box, the spellchecker suggests "Bookstores."

> **QuickTip**
>
> The spellchecker does not check the text in inserted pictures or objects. You'll need to spell check text in inserted objects, such as charts, using their original application.

3. **Click Bookstores in the Suggestions list box, then click Change**

   If PowerPoint finds any other words it does not recognize, either change them or ignore them. When the spellchecker finishes checking your presentation, the Spelling dialog box closes, and a PowerPoint alert box opens with a message saying the spelling check is complete.

4. **Click OK**

   The alert box closes. Maria is satisfied with her presentation so far and decides to print it.

> **QuickTip**
>
> Click Preview in the Print dialog box or click the Print Preview button on the Standard toolbar to see what your presentation printout will look like.

5. **Click File on the menu bar, then click Print**

6. **Make sure Slides is selected in the Print what list box, click the Color/grayscale list arrow, then click Pure Black and White**

7. **Click the Frame slides check box to select it, as shown in Figure B-13**

   The slides of your presentation print with a frame around each page.

8. **Click OK, return to Slide 1 in Normal view, then save your presentation**

Checking spelling as you type

PowerPoint checks your spelling as you type. If you type a word that is not in the electronic dictionary, a wavy, red line appears under it. To correct the error, right-click the misspelled word. A pop-up menu appears with one or more suggestions. You can select a suggestion, add the word you typed to your custom dictionary, or ignore it. To turn off automatic spellchecking, click Tools on the menu bar, then click Options to open the Options dialog box. Click the Spelling and Style tab, and in the Spelling section, click the Check spelling as you type check box to deselect it. To temporarily hide the wavy, red lines, click the Hide all spelling errors check box to select it.

FIGURE B-12: Spelling dialog box

Unrecognized word
Selected word from Suggestions list
Alternate spellings

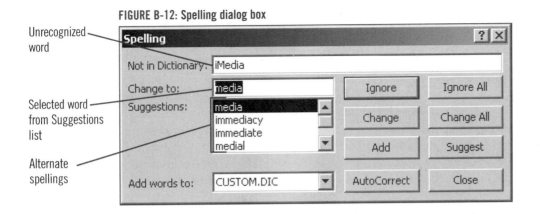

FIGURE B-13: Print dialog box

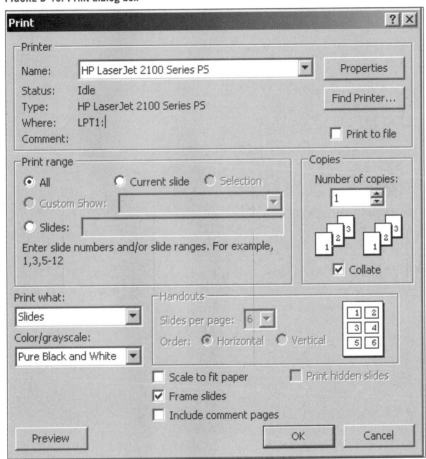

TABLE B-2: Spelling dialog box commands

command	description
Ignore/Ignore All	Continues spellchecking without making any changes to the identified word (or all occurrences of the identified word)
Change/Change All	Changes the identified word (or all occurrences) to the suggested word
Add	Adds the identified word to your custom dictionary; spellchecker will not flag it again
Suggest	Suggests an alternative spelling for the identified word
AutoCorrect	Adds the suggested word as an AutoCorrect entry for the highlighted word
Add words to	Lets you choose a custom dictionary where you store words you often use but that are not part of the PowerPoint dictionary

Evaluating a Presentation

As you create a presentation, keep in mind that good design involves preparation. An effective presentation is both focused and visually appealing—easy for the speaker to present and easy for the audience to understand. The visual elements (colors, graphics, and text) can strongly influence the audience's attention and interest and can determine the success of your presentation. See Table B-3 for general information on the impact a visual presentation has on an audience. Maria evaluates her presentation's effectiveness.

1. Click the **Slide Show button**, then press **[Enter]** to move through the slide show

2. When you are finished viewing the slide show, click the **Slide Sorter View button**
   Maria decides that Slide 4 should come before Slide 3.

3. Drag **Slide 4** between Slides 2 and 3, then release the mouse button
   The thin, black line that moved with the pointer indicates the slide's new position. The final presentation is shown in Slide Sorter view. Compare your screen to Figure B-14. For contrast, Figure B-15 shows a poorly designed slide.

4. When you are finished evaluating your presentation according to the following guidelines, save your changes, then close the presentation and exit PowerPoint

In evaluating a presentation, it is important to:

► **Keep your message focused**
Don't put everything you plan to say on your presentation slides. Keep the audience anticipating further explanations to the key points shown.

► **Keep your text concise**
Limit each slide to six words per line and six lines per slide. Use lists and symbols to help prioritize your points visually. Your presentation text provides only the highlights; use notes to give more detailed information. Maria's presentation focuses attention on the key issues. She will supplement the information with further explanation and details during her presentation.

► **Keep the design simple, easy to read, and appropriate for the content**
A design template makes the presentation consistent. If you design your own layout, keep it simple and use design elements sparingly. Use similar design elements consistently throughout the presentation; otherwise, your audience will get confused. Maria used a simple design template; the colored box cluster and horizontal line give the presentation an interesting, somewhat artistic, look, which is appropriate for a casual professional presentation.

► **Choose attractive colors that make the slide easy to read**
Use contrasting colors for slide background and text to make the text readable. If you are giving an on-screen presentation, you can use almost any combination of colors that look good together.

► **Choose fonts and styles that are easy to read and emphasize important text**
As a general rule, use no more than two fonts in a presentation and vary the font size, using nothing smaller than 24 points. Use bold and italic attributes selectively.

► **Use visuals to help communicate the message of your presentation**
Commonly used visuals include clip art, photographs, charts, worksheets, tables, and movies. Whenever possible, replace text with a visual, but be careful not to overcrowd your slides. White space on your slides is OK!

FIGURE B-14: The final presentation in Slide Sorter view

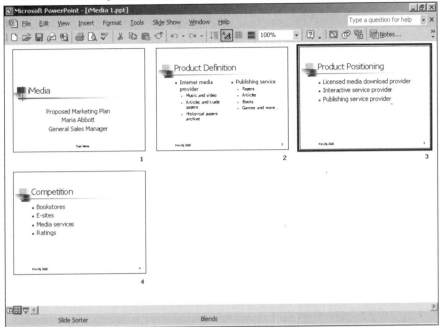

FIGURE B-15: A poorly designed slide in Normal view

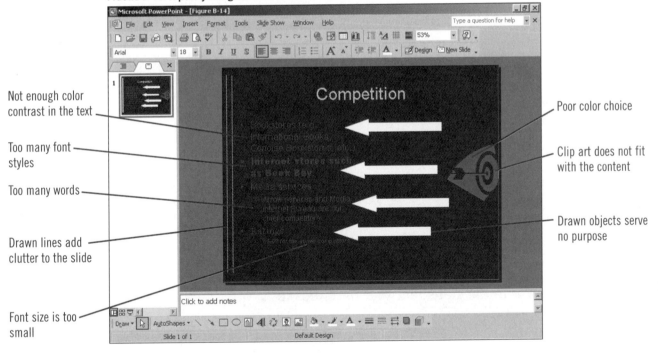

Not enough color contrast in the text

Too many font styles

Too many words

Drawn lines add clutter to the slide

Font size is too small

Poor color choice

Clip art does not fit with the content

Drawn objects serve no purpose

TABLE B-3: Audience impact from a visual presentation

impact	description
Visual reception	Most people receive up to 75% of all environmental stimuli through the human sense of sight
Learning	Up to 90% of what an audience learns comes from visual and audio messages
Retention	Combining visual messages with verbal messages can increase memory retention by as much as 30%
Presentation goals	You are twice as likely to achieve your communication objectives using a visual presentation
Meeting length	You are likely to decrease the average meeting length by 25% when you use visual presentation

Source: Presenters Online, www.presentersonline.com

Practice

▶ Concepts Review

Label each element of the PowerPoint window shown in Figure B-16.

FIGURE B-16

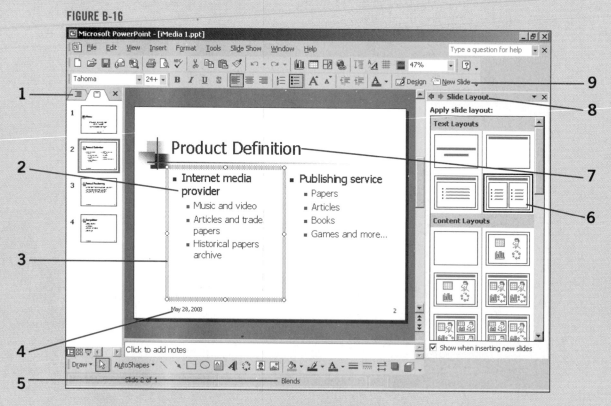

Match each term with the statement that describes it.

10. Selection box
11. Insertion point
12. Slide icon
13. Design template
14. Text placeholder
15. Slide layout

a. A specific design, format, and color scheme that is applied to all the slides in a presentation
b. A blinking vertical line that indicates where your text will appear in a text object
c. Determines how all of the elements on a slide are arranged
d. The slanted line border that appears around a text placeholder, indicating that it is ready to select text
e. A box with a dashed border in which you can enter text
f. In Outline view, the symbol that represents a slide

Select the best answer from the list of choices.

16. What is the definition of a slide layout?
- **a.** A slide layout automatically applies all the objects you can use on a slide.
- **b.** A slide layout determines how all the elements on a slide are arranged.
- **c.** A slide layout applies a different template to the presentation.
- **d.** A slide layout puts all your slides in order.

17. When you type text in a text placeholder, it becomes:
- **a.** A label.
- **b.** A text label.
- **c.** A selection box.
- **d.** A text object.

18. When the spellchecker identifies a word as misspelled, which of the following is not a choice?
- **a.** To ignore this occurrence of the error
- **b.** To change the misspelled word to the correct spelling
- **c.** To have the spellchecker automatically correct all the errors it finds
- **d.** To ignore all occurrences of the error in the presentation

19. When you evaluate your presentation, you should make sure it follows which of the following criteria?
- **a.** The slides should include every piece of information to be presented so the audience can read it.
- **b.** The slides should use as many colors as possible to hold the audience's attention.
- **c.** Many different typefaces will make the slides more interesting.
- **d.** The message should be clearly outlined without a lot of extra words.

20. According to the unit, which of the following is *not* a guideline for planning a presentation?
- **a.** Determine the purpose of the presentation
- **b.** Determine what you want to produce when the presentation is finished
- **c.** Determine which type of output you will need to best convey your message
- **d.** Determine who else can give the final presentation

21. Which of the following statements is *not* true?
- **a.** You can customize any PowerPoint template.
- **b.** The spellchecker will identify "there" as misspelled if the correct word for the context is "their."
- **c.** Speaker notes do not appear during the slide show.
- **d.** PowerPoint has many colorful templates from which to choose.

22. Where else can you enter slide text?
- **a.** Outline tab
- **b.** Outline view
- **c.** Notes Page view
- **d.** Slides tab

Skills Review

1. Enter slide text.

a. Start PowerPoint if necessary.

b. In the slide pane in Normal view, enter the text **Product Marketing** in the title placeholder.

c. In the main text placeholder, enter **Ian Kuvick**.

d. On the next line of the placeholder, enter **Manager**.

e. On the next line of the placeholder, enter **Oct. 11, 2003**.

f. Deselect the text object.

g. Save the presentation as **RouterJet Testing** to the drive and folder where your Project Files are located.

2. Create new slides.

a. Create a new slide.

b. Review the text in Table B-4, then select the appropriate slide layout.

c. Enter the text from Table B-4 into the new slide.

d. Create a new bulleted list slide using the Slide Layout task pane.

e. Enter the text from Table B-5 into the new slide.

f. Save your changes.

3. Enter text on the Outline tab.

a. Open the Outline tab.

b. Create a new bulleted list slide after the last one.

c. Enter the text from Table B-6 into the new slide.

d. Move the third bullet point in the text object to the second position.

e. Switch back to the Slides tab.

f. Save your changes.

4. Add slide headers and footers.

a. Open the Header and Footer dialog box.

b. Type today's date into the Fixed text box.

c. Add the slide number to the footer.

d. Type your name in the Footer text box.

e. Apply the footer to all of the slides.

f. Open the Header and Footer dialog box again, then click the Notes and Handouts tab.

g. Enter today's date in the Fixed text box.

h. Type the name of your class in the Header text box.

i. Type your name in the Footer text box.

j. Apply the header and footer information to all the notes and handouts.

k. Save your changes.

TABLE B-4

Text Object	Text to Insert
Slide title	RouterJet Project Tests - Ian
First indent level	Focus: Component System
Second indent level	User access components Security components Network components System components
First indent level	Data Files and Report
Second indent level	Compile component data files Define component interface parameters Write function data report

TABLE B-5

Text Object	Text to Insert
Slide title	RouterJet Project Tests - Elaine
First indent level	Focus: Network Integration
Second indent level	Server codes and routes File transfer Data conversion Platform functionality ratings

TABLE B-6

Text Object	Text to Insert
Slide title	RouterJet Project Tests - Rajesh
First indent level	Focus: Software QA
Second indent level	User access testing Software compatibility testing Platform testing

5. **Choose a look for a presentation.**
   a. Open the Slide Design task pane.
   b. Locate the Network template, then apply it to all the slides. (*Hint*: The template designs are sorted in alphabetical order.)
   c. Move to Slide 1.
   d. Locate the Crayons template, then apply it to Slide 1.
   e. Save your changes.

6. **Check spelling in a presentation.**
   a. Perform a spelling check on the document and change any misspelled words. Ignore any words that are correctly spelled but that the spellchecker doesn't recognize.
   b. Save your changes.

7. **Evaluate a presentation.**
   a. View Slide 1 in Slide Show view, then move through the slide show.
   b. Evaluate the presentation using the points described in the lesson as criteria.
   c. Preview your presentation.
   d. Print the outline of the presentation.
   e. Print the slides of your presentation in grayscale with a frame around each slide.
   f. Save your changes, close the presentation, and exit PowerPoint.

► Independent Challenge 1

You are an independent distributor of natural foods in Tucson, Arizona. Your business, Harvest Natural Foods, has grown progressively since its inception eight years ago, but sales and profits have leveled off over the last nine months. In an effort to stimulate growth, you decide to acquire two major natural food dealers, which would allow Harvest Natural Foods to expand its territory into surrounding states. Use PowerPoint to develop a presentation that you can use to gain a financial backer for the acquisition.

a. Start PowerPoint. Choose the Maple design template. Enter **Growth Plan** as the main title on the title slide, and **Harvest Natural Foods** as the subtitle.
b. Save the presentation as **Harvest Proposal** to the drive and folder where your Project Files are located.
c. Add five more slides with the following titles: Slide 2–Background; Slide 3–Current Situation; Slide 4–Acquisition Goals; Slide 5–Our Management Team; Slide 6–Funding Required.
d. Enter text into the text placeholders of the slides. Use both the slide pane and the Outline tab to enter text.
e. Create a new slide at the end of the presentation. Enter concluding text on the slide, summarizing the main points of the presentation.
f. Check the spelling in the presentation.
g. View the presentation as a slide show, then view the slides in Slide Sorter view. Evaluate your presentation and make any changes you feel are necessary.
h. Add your name as a footer on the notes and handouts, print handouts (6 slides per page), and then print the presentation outline.
i. Save your changes, close your presentation, then exit PowerPoint.

Independent Challenge 2

You have been asked to give a one-day course at a local adult education center. The course is called "Personal Computing for the Slightly Anxious Beginner" and is intended for adults who have never used a computer. One of your responsibilities is to create presentation slides that outline the course materials.

Plan and create presentation slides that outline the course material for the students. Create slides for the course introduction, course description, course text, grading policies, and a detailed syllabus. Create your own course material, but assume the following: the school has a computer lab with IBM-compatible computers and Microsoft Windows software; each student has a computer; the prospective students are intimidated by computers but want to learn; and the course is on a Saturday from 9 to 5, with a one-hour lunch break.

a. Think about the results you want to see, the information you need, and the type of message you want to communicate.

b. Write an outline of your presentation. What content should go on the slides? Remember that your audience has never used computers before and will need computer terms defined.

c. Start PowerPoint and create the presentation by entering the title slide text.

d. Create the required slides as well as an ending slide that summarizes your presentation.

e. Add a design template. Choose one that is appropriate to your presentation message and your intended audience.

f. Check the spelling in the presentation.

g. Save the presentation as **Class 1** to the drive and folder where your Project Files are located.

h. View the slide show.

i. View the slides in Slide Sorter view, and evaluate your presentation. Adjust it as necessary so that it is focused, clear, concise, and readable. Make sure none of the slides is too cluttered.

j. Add your name as a footer on the notes and handouts, print handouts (6 slides per page), and then print the presentation outline.

k. Save your changes, close your presentation, then exit PowerPoint.

 # Independent Challenge 3

You are the training director for Events, Ltd, a German company in Berlin that coordinates special events, including corporate functions, weddings, and private parties. You regularly train groups of temporary employees that you can call on as coordinators, kitchen and wait staff, and coat checkers for specific events. The company trains 10 to 15 new workers each month for the peak season between May and September. One of your responsibilities is to orient new temporary employees at the next training session.

Plan and create presentation slides that outline your employee orientation. Create slides for the introduction, agenda, company history, dress requirements, principles for interacting successfully with guests, and safety requirements. Create your own presentation and company material, but assume the following: Events Ltd is owned by Jan Negd-Sorenson; the new employee training class lasts four hours, and your orientation lasts 15 minutes; the training director's presentation lasts 15 minutes; and the dress code requires uniforms, supplied by Events, Ltd (white for daytime events, black and white for evening events).

a. Think about the results you want to see, the information you need, and the message you want to communicate.

b. Write a presentation outline. What content should go on the slides?

c. Start PowerPoint and create the presentation by entering the slide text for all your slides.

d. Create a slide that summarizes your presentation.

e. Create an ending slide with the following information:

Events, Ltd

Gubener Strase 49, 10243 Berlin

(Berlin-Friedrichshain)

TEL.: 293755, FAX: 29375799

f. Check the spelling in the presentation.

g. Save the presentation as **Training Class** to the drive and folder where your Project Files are located.

h. View the slide show, then view the slides in Slide Sorter view. Evaluate your presentation, make any changes necessary so that the final version is focused, clear, concise, and readable.

i. Add your name as a footer on the notes and handouts, print the presentation as handouts (2 slides per page), then print the presentation outline.

j. Save your changes, close your presentation, then exit PowerPoint.

 # Independent Challenge 4

One of the best things about PowerPoint is the flexibility you have in creating your presentations, but that same flexibility can result in slides that may appear cluttered, unorganized, and hard to read. Unit B introduced you to some concepts that you can use to help create good presentations using PowerPoint. Use the Web to research more guidelines and tips on creating effective presentations.

Plan and create a presentation that explains these tips to an audience of beginning PowerPoint users. The information you find on the Web should include the following topics:

- Message organization
- Text arrangement and amount
- Slide layout and design
- Presentation development
- Room layout and delivery
- Equipment

a. Connect to the Internet, then use a search engine to locate Web sites that have information on presentations. Use the keywords **presentation tips** to conduct your search. If your search does not produce any results, you might try the following sites:

www.presentersonline.com

www.boxlight.com

www.ljlseminars.com

b. Review at least two Web sites that contain information about presentation tips and guidelines.

c. Start PowerPoint. Title the presentation **Presentation Tips**.

d. Create a presentation with at least five slides. Each slide should contain one main tip with supporting information about that tip.

e. Add a final slide titled **Presentation Tip URLs**. List the URLs from which you obtained the information you used in your presentation.

f. Apply an appropriate design template.

g. Save the presentation as **Presentation Tips** to the drive and folder where your Project Files are located.

h. Add your name as a footer to the slides and notes and handouts, check the spelling in the presentation, then view the final presentation as a slide show.

i. View your presentation in Slide Sorter view and evaluate it. Make any changes necessary so that the final version is focused, clear, concise, and readable.

j. Save your final presentation, print the slides as handouts, 2 per page, then close the presentation and exit PowerPoint.

PowerPoint 2002

▶ Visual Workshop

Create the marketing presentation shown in Figures B-17 and B-18. Add today's date as the date on the title slide. Save the presentation as **Sales Project** to the drive and folder where your Project Files are located. Review your slides in Slide Show view, add your name as a footer to the slides and the notes and handouts. Print the first slide of your presentation as a slide, and print the outline. Save your changes, close the presentation, and exit PowerPoint.

FIGURE B-17

FIGURE B-18

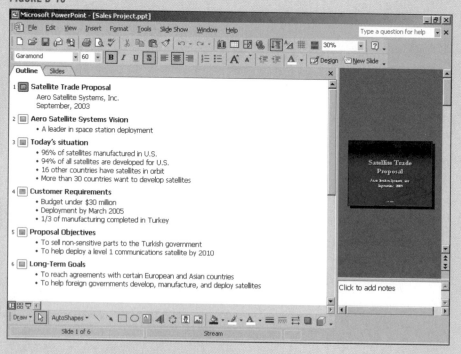

Modifying
a Presentation

Objectives

- ► **Open an existing presentation**
- MOUS ► **Draw and modify an object**
- MOUS ► **Edit drawing objects**
- ► **Align and group objects**
- MOUS ► **Add and arrange text**
- MOUS ► **Format text**
- MOUS ► **Import text from Microsoft Word**
- MOUS ► **Customize the color scheme and background**

After you create the basic outline of your presentation and enter text, you need to add visuals to your slides to communicate your message in the most effective way possible. In this unit, you open an existing presentation; draw and modify objects; add, arrange, and format text; change a presentation color scheme; and revise a presentation. Maria Abbott continues to work on the iMedia marketing presentation by drawing and modifying objects. Maria uses the PowerPoint drawing and text-editing features to bring the presentation closer to a finished look.

PowerPoint 2002

Opening an Existing Presentation

Sometimes the easiest way to create a new presentation is by changing an existing one. Revising a presentation saves you from typing duplicate information. You simply open the file you want to change, then use the Save As command to save a copy of the file with a new name. Whenever you open an existing presentation in this book, you will save a copy of it with a new name—this keeps the original file intact. Saving a copy does not affect the original file. ➤ Maria wants to add visuals to her presentation, so she opens the presentation she has been working on.

Steps 1234

1. Start PowerPoint

Trouble?

If the dialog box on your screen does not show a preview box, click the Views button list arrow ▦▾ in the dialog box toolbar, then select Preview.

2. Click the **Choose presentation hyperlink** in the New Presentation task pane under New from existing presentation
The New from Existing Presentation dialog box opens. See Figure C-1.

3. Click the **Look in list arrow**, then locate the drive and folder where your Project Files are stored
A list of your Project Files appears in the dialog box.

QuickTip

To open the file without opening a copy, click the More presentations hyperlink under Open a presentation in the task pane, or click the Open button 📂 on the Standard toolbar.

4. Click **PPT C-1**
The first slide of the selected presentation appears in the preview box on the right side of the dialog box.

5. Click **Create New**
A copy of the file named PPT C-1 opens in Normal view. The title bar displays the temporary filename "Presentation2."

6. Click **File** on the menu bar, then click **Save As**
The Save As dialog box opens. See Figure C-2.

7. Make sure the Save in list box shows the location of your Project Files and that the current filename in the File name text box is selected, then type **iMedia 2**
Compare your screen to the Save As dialog box in Figure C-2.

8. Click **Save** to close the Save As dialog box and save the file
The file is saved with the name iMedia 2.

Trouble?

If you have another PowerPoint presentation open and it appears next to this presentation, close it, then repeat Step 9.

9. Click the **Slide Design button** 🖋 on the Formatting toolbar, click **Window** on the menu bar, then click **Arrange All**
You can work with the task pane opened or closed. Many of the figures in this book show only the window that contains the slide and notes panes and the Slide and Outline tabs.

FIGURE C-1: Open dialog box

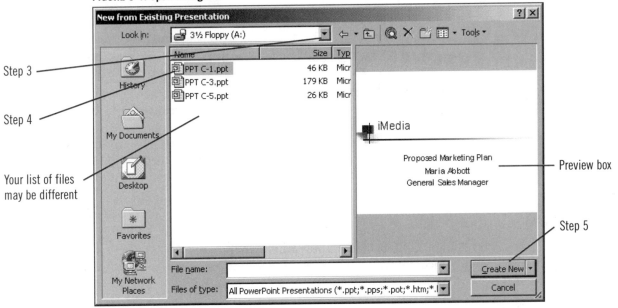

Step 3

Step 4

Your list of files may be different

Preview box

Step 5

FIGURE C-2: Save As dialog box

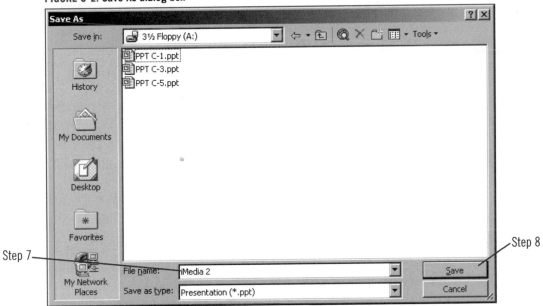

Step 7

Step 8

Searching for a Presentation

You click the Search button 🔍 on the Standard toolbar to open the Search task pane, where you can search for specific text in files located on your computer's hard drive, your local network, your Microsoft Outlook mailbox, and your network places. When you conduct a search from the Search task pane, all the files that contain the search text you specify are displayed. For example, a search for the text "book club" will yield a list of all the files in the locations you specified that contain the text "book club" in the filename, contents, or properties. Once you have found the file you want, you can open and edit the file in its application, create a new document based on the file, create a link from the file to the Office clipboard, or view the file's properties.

PowerPoint 2002

Drawing and Modifying an Object

Using the drawing commands in PowerPoint, you can draw and modify lines, shapes, and pictures to enhance your presentation. Lines and shapes that you create with the PowerPoint drawing tools are objects that you can modify and move at any time. These drawn objects have graphic attributes that you can change, such as fill color, line color, line style, shadow, and 3-D effects. To add drawing objects to your slides, use the buttons on the Drawing toolbar at the bottom of the screen above the status bar. Maria decides to draw an object on Slide 3 of her marketing presentation to add impact to her message.

Steps

1. In the Slides tab, click the **Slide 3 thumbnail**
   Slide 3, titled "Competition," appears in the slide pane.

2. Press and hold **[Shift]**, then click the **body text object**
   A dotted selection box with small circles called **sizing handles** appears around the text object. If you click a text object without pressing [Shift], a selection box composed of slanted lines appears, indicating that the object is active and ready to accept text, but it is not selected. When an object is selected, you can change its size, shape, or attributes by dragging one of the sizing handles.

Trouble?

If you are not satisfied with the size of the text object, resize it again.

3. Position the pointer over the right, middle sizing handle, then drag the sizing handle to the left until the text object is about half its original size as shown in Figure C-3
   When you position the pointer over a sizing handle, it changes to ←→. It points in different directions depending on which sizing handle it is positioned over. When you drag a sizing handle, the pointer changes to +, and a dotted outline representing the size of the text object appears.

QuickTip

Position the pointer on top of a button to see its name.

4. Click the **AutoShapes button** AutoShapes ▾ on the Drawing toolbar, point to **Block Arrows**, then click the **Right Arrow button** ⇨ (first row, first item)
   After you select a shape from the AutoShapes menu and move the pointer over the slide, the pointer changes to +.

QuickTip

If your arrow object is not approximately the same size as the one shown in Figure C-4, press [Shift] and drag one of the corner sizing handles to resize the object.

5. Position + in the blank area of the slide to the right of the text object, press **[Shift]**, drag down and to the right to create an arrow object, as shown in Figure C-4, then release the mouse button and **[Shift]**
   When you release the mouse button, an arrow object appears on the slide, filled with the default color and outlined with the default line style, as shown in Figure C-4. Pressing [Shift] while you create the object maintains the object's proportions as you change its size.

6. Click the **Line Color list arrow** ✏️▾ on the Drawing toolbar, then point to the **red square** (second square from the right)
   A ScreenTip appears identifying this color as the Follow Accent and Hyperlink Scheme Color.

7. Click the **red square**
   PowerPoint applies the red color to the selected object's outline.

8. Click the **Fill Color list arrow** 🎨▾ on the Drawing toolbar, then click the **yellow square** (third square from the right, called Follow Accent Scheme Color)
   PowerPoint fills the selected object with yellow.

9. Click the **Save button** 💾 on the Standard toolbar to save your changes

FIGURE C-3: Resizing a text object

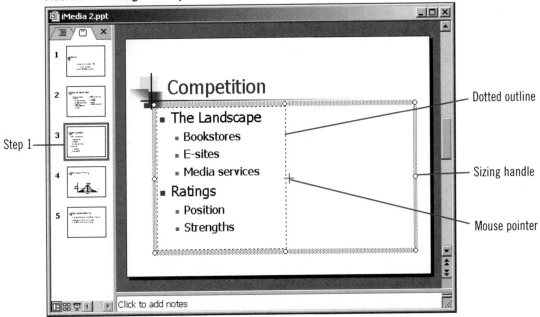

Step 1 ──

Dotted outline

Sizing handle

Mouse pointer

FIGURE C-4: Arrow object on slide

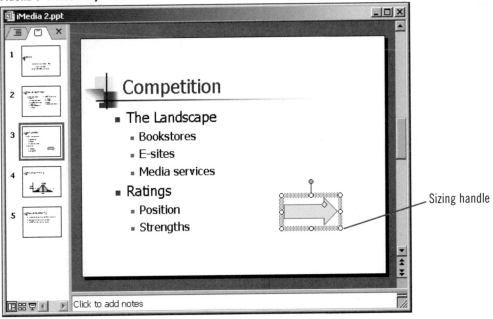

Sizing handle

Understanding PowerPoint Objects

In PowerPoint, you often work with multiple objects on the same slide. These may be text objects or graphic objects, such as drawn objects, clip art, or charts. To help you organize objects on a slide, you can align, group, and stack the objects using the Align or Distribute, Group, and Order commands on the Draw menu on the Drawing toolbar. When you align objects, you place their edges (or their centers) on the same plane. For example, you might want to align two squares vertically (one above the other) so that their left edges are in a straight vertical line. When you group objects, you combine two or more objects into one object. It's often helpful to group objects into one when you have finished positioning them on the slide. When you stack objects, you determine their order, that is, which ones are in front and which are in back. You can use the stacking order of objects to overlap them to create different effects.

PowerPoint 2002

PowerPoint 2002

Editing Drawing Objects

PowerPoint allows you to manipulate the size and shape of objects on your slide. You can alter the appearance of any object by changing its shape or by adjusting its dimensions. You can add text to most PowerPoint objects. You also can move or copy objects. ━━━━ Maria wants three arrows on her slide, and she wants them all to be the same shape and size. She changes the shape of the arrow object, and then makes two copies of it. She then rotates one arrow to complete her graphic.

Steps

1. Click the **arrow object** to select it, if necessary
   In addition to sizing handles, two other handles appear on the selected object. You use the **adjustment handle**—a small yellow diamond—to change the appearance of an object, usually its most prominent feature, like the size of the head of an arrow. You use the **rotate handle**—a small green circle—to rotate the object.

2. Press **[Shift]**, then drag the right, middle sizing handle to the right approximately 1"

Trouble?

PowerPoint uses a hidden grid to align objects; it forces objects to "snap" to the grid lines. If you have trouble aligning the object with the text, press and hold down [Alt] while dragging the object to turn off the grid.

3. Position the pointer over the middle of the selected arrow object so that it changes to ⁺↖, then drag the **arrow** so that the bottom of the arrow aligns with the bottom of the word "Position" in the text box
   A dotted outline appears as you move the arrow object to help you position it. Compare your screen to Figure C-5 and make any necessary adjustments.

4. Position ⁺↖ over the arrow object, then press and hold **[Ctrl]**
   The pointer changes to ↖, indicating that PowerPoint will make a copy of the arrow object when you drag the mouse.

QuickTip

You can use PowerPoint rulers to help you align objects. To display the rulers, position the pointer in a blank area of the slide, right-click, then click Ruler on the shortcut menu.

5. While holding down **[Ctrl]**, drag the **arrow object** up until the dotted lines indicate that the copy aligns with the bottom of the words "Media services" in the text box, then release the mouse button
   A copy of the first arrow object appears.

6. Position ⁺↖ over the second arrow object, press and hold **[Ctrl]**, then drag a **copy** of the arrow object up the slide until it aligns with the bottom of the first bullet point in the text box
   You now have three identical objects on your slide.

7. Type **Adopters**
   The text appears in the center of the active object, in this case, the top arrow. The text is now part of the object, so if you move or rotate the object, the text will move with it.

QuickTip

You can also use the Rotate or Flip commands on the Draw menu button on the Drawing toolbar to rotate or flip objects 90 or 180 degrees.

8. Position the pointer over the rotate handle of the selected arrow object so that it changes to ↻, then drag the **rotate handle** to the left until the arrow head is pointing straight up
   If you need to make any adjustments to the arrow object, drag the rotate handle again. Compare your screen with Figure C-6.

9. Click the **middle arrow object**, type **Price**, click the **bottom arrow object**, type **Performance**, then click in a blank area of the slide

10. Click the **Save button** 🖫 on the Standard toolbar to save your changes

FIGURE C-5: Slide showing resized arrow object

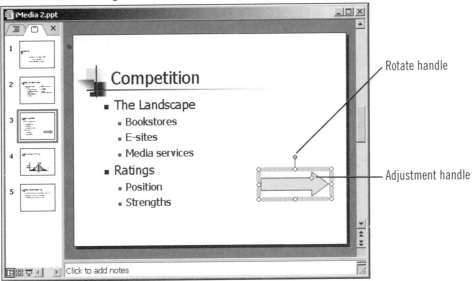

Rotate handle

Adjustment handle

FIGURE C-6: Slide showing duplicated arrow object

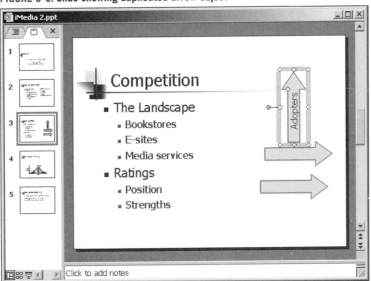

More Ways to Change Objects

You can layer objects over one another by changing their stacking order, or you can change the appearance of an object by making it three-dimensional or by applying a shadow effect. To change the stacking order of an object, select the object, click the Draw button on the Drawing toolbar, point to Order, then click one of the menu commands shown in Figure C-7. To make an object three-dimensional, select it, click the 3-D Style button on the Drawing toolbar, then click one of the buttons on the pop-up menu shown in Figure C-8. To add a shadow to an object, select it, click the Shadow Style button on the Drawing toolbar, then click one of the buttons on the pop-up menu shown in Figure C-9.

FIGURE C-7: Order menu

FIGURE C-8: 3-D menu

FIGURE C-9: Shadow menu

Aligning and Grouping Objects

After you create objects, modify their appearance, and edit their size and shape, you can position them on the slide, align them, and then group them. The Align command aligns objects relative to each other by snapping the selected objects to a grid of evenly spaced vertical and horizontal lines. The Group command groups objects into one object to make editing and moving them much easier. ✎ Maria positions, aligns, and groups the arrow objects on the slide.

Steps

1. Position ✛ over the **Adopters arrow object**, then drag it down the slide until it is in the same position as in Figure C-10

2. Click the **Price arrow object**, press and hold [Shift], then click the **Performance arrow object**
   The two objects are now selected.

3. Click the **Draw button** `Draw ▼` on the Drawing toolbar, then point to **Align or Distribute**
   A menu of alignment and distribution options appears. The top three options align objects vertically; the next three options align objects horizontally.

4. Click **Align Center**
   The arrow objects align vertically on their centers.

5. Press and hold [Shift], click the **Adopters arrow object**, click `Draw ▼`, then click **Group**
   The arrow objects group to form one object without losing their individual attributes. Notice the sizing handles now appear around the outer edge of the grouped object, not around each individual object.

6. Right-click a blank area of the slide, then click **Grid and Guides** on the shortcut menu
   The Grid and Guides dialog box opens.

7. Click the **Display drawing guides on screen check box**, then click **OK**
   The PowerPoint guides appear as dotted lines on the slide. (The dotted lines may be very faint on your screen.) The guides intersect at the center of the slide. They will help you position the arrow object.

8. Position ▷ over the **horizontal guide** in a blank area of the slide, press and hold the mouse button until the pointer changes to a guide measurement, then drag the guide down until the guide measurement box reads approximately **0.50**

9. Press [Shift], drag the **grouped arrow object** over the horizontal guide until the center sizing handles are approximately centered over the guide
   Pressing [Shift] while you drag an object constrains its movement to vertical or horizontal. Compare your screen with Figure C-11.

10. Right-click a blank area of the slide, click **Grid and Guides** on the shortcut menu, click the **Display drawing guides on screen check box**, click **OK**, then click the **Save button** 🖫 on the Standard toolbar to save your changes
    The guides are no longer displayed on the slide.

FIGURE C-10: Repositioned arrow object

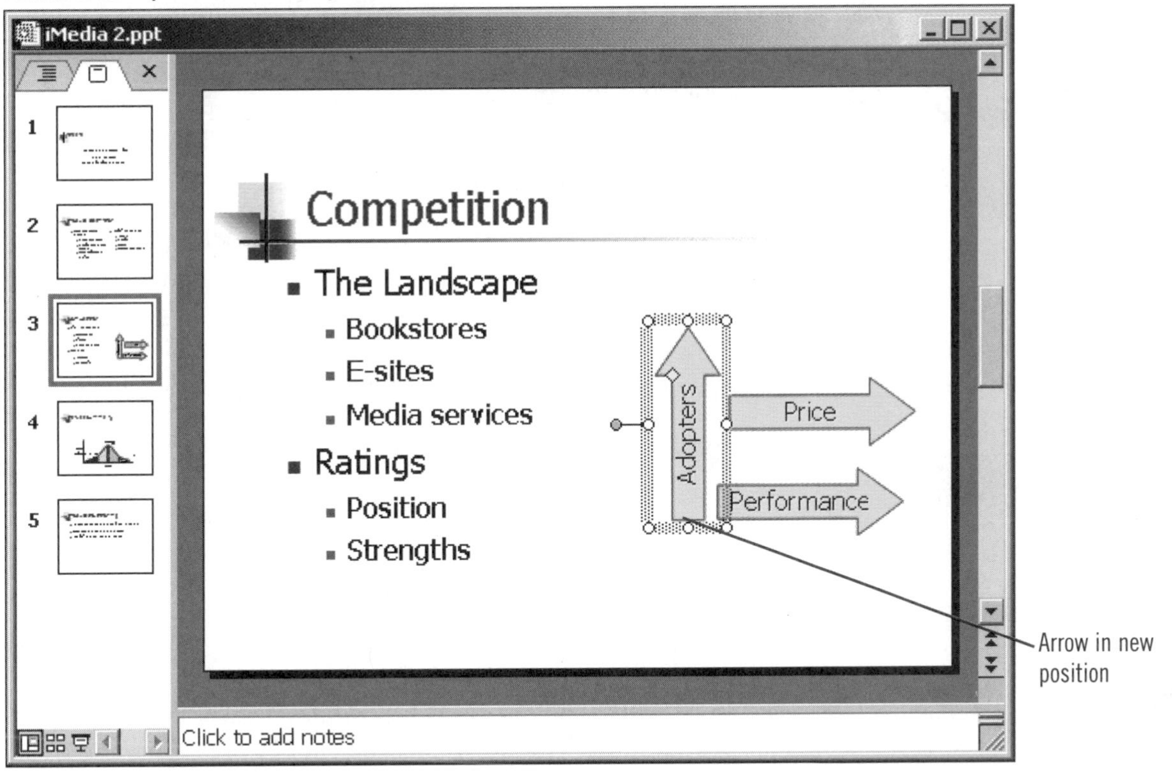

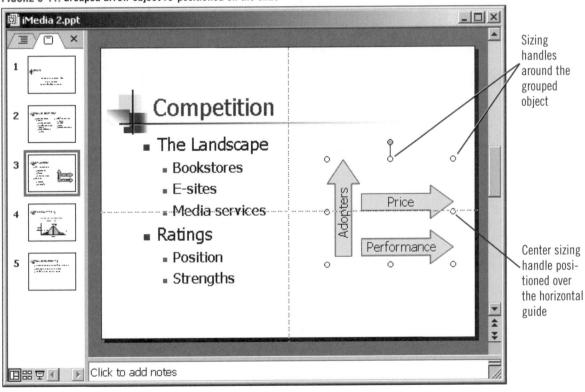

Arrow in new position

FIGURE C-11: Grouped arrow object re-positioned on the slide

Sizing handles around the grouped object

Center sizing handle positioned over the horizontal guide

Adding and Arranging Text

Using the advanced text-editing capabilities of PowerPoint, you can easily add, insert, or rearrange text. The PowerPoint slide layouts allow you to enter text in prearranged text placeholders. If these text placeholders don't provide the flexibility you need, you can use the Text Box button on the Drawing toolbar to create your own text objects. With the Text Box button, you can create two types of text objects: a text label, used for a small phrase where text doesn't automatically wrap to the next line inside the box; and a word-processing box, used for a sentence or paragraph where the text wraps inside the boundaries of the box. ➤ Maria has a slide that contains information on the typical cycle of a product. Now, she uses the Text Box button to create a word-processing box to enter a label for the information on the slide.

Steps 1 2 3 4

1. In the Slides tab, click the **Slide 4 thumbnail**

2. Click the **Text Box button** 🔳 on the Drawing toolbar
   The pointer changes to ↓.

3. Position ↓ about 1" from the left side of the slide, above the top of the chart on the slide, then drag toward the right side of the slide to create a word-processing box
   Your screen should look similar to Figure C-12. When you begin dragging, an outline of the box appears, indicating how wide a text object you are drawing. After you release the mouse button, an insertion point appears inside the text object, ready to accept text.

4. Type **Market, players, shifts and competition**
   Notice that the word-processing box increases in size as your text wraps inside the object. There is a mistake in the text. It should read "Market shifts."

5. Double-click the word **shifts** to select it

6. Position the pointer on top of the selected word and press and hold the mouse button
   The pointer changes to ▨.

7. Drag the word **shifts** to the right of the word **Market** in the text box, then release the mouse button
   A dotted insertion line appears as you drag, indicating where PowerPoint will place the word when you release the mouse button. The word "shifts" moves next to the word "Market."

8. Position ▨ over the text box border, then drag it to the center of the slide
   Your screen should look similar to Figure C-13.

9. Click a blank area of the slide outside the text object, then click the **Save button** 💾 on the Standard toolbar to save your changes

FIGURE C-12: Word-processing box ready to accept text

Slanted lines indicate the word-processing box is ready to accept text

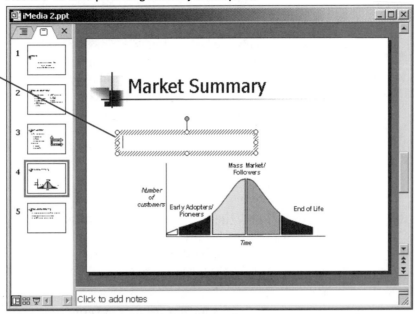

FIGURE C-13: Text added to the word-processing box

Your text might wrap differently depending on the size of your word-processing box

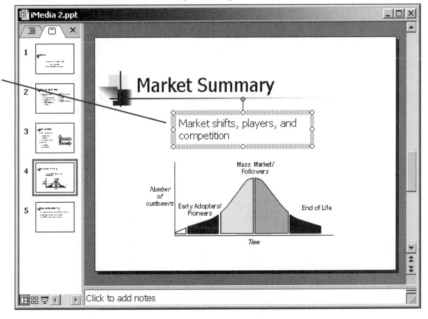

Revising a Presentation

You can send a copy of a presentation over the Internet to others for them to review, edit, and add comments. To send your presentation out for review, you can use Microsoft Outlook, which automatically tracks changes made by reviewers, or you can use any other compatible e-mail program. To send a presentation to reviewers using Outlook, click File on the menu bar, point to Send To, then click Mail Recipient (for Review). Outlook opens and a "Review Request" e-mail with the PowerPoint presentation attached to it is automatically created for you to send to reviewers. Reviewers can use any version of PowerPoint to review, edit, and comment on their copy of your presentation. Once a reviewer is finished with the presentation and sends it back to you, you can combine their changes and comments with your original presentation using PowerPoint's Compare and Merge Presentations feature. When you do this, the Revisions task pane opens with commands that allow you to accept or reject reviewers' changes.

Formatting Text

Once you have entered and arranged the text in your presentation, you can change and modify the way the text looks to emphasize your message. Important text needs to be highlighted in some way to distinguish it from other text or objects on the slide. Less important information needs to be de-emphasized. For example, if you have two text objects on the same slide, you could draw attention to one text object by changing its color or size. To change the way text looks, you need to select it, then choose a Formatting command. ✐━━ Maria uses some of the commands on the Formatting and Drawing toolbars to change the way the new text box looks on Slide 4.

Steps

1. On Slide 4, press **[Shift]**, then click the **word-processing text box**
If a text box is already active because you have been entering text in it, you can select the entire text box by clicking on its border with ⌖. The entire text box is selected. Any changes you make will affect all the text in the selected text box. Changing the text's size and appearance will help emphasize it.

> **QuickTip**
> You can also click the Font Size list arrow `12 ▾`, then click the font size you want from the list.

2. Click the **Increase Font Size button** Ⓐ on the Formatting toolbar
The text increases in size to 28 points.

3. Click the **Italic button** *I* on the Formatting toolbar
The text changes from normal to italic text. The Italic button, like the Bold button, is a toggle button, which you click to turn the attribute on or off.

> **QuickTip**
> The Font Color button can also be found on the Drawing toolbar.

4. Click the **Font Color list arrow** Ⓐ▾ on the Formatting toolbar
The Font Color menu appears, showing the eight colors used in the current presentation and the More Colors command, which lets you choose additional colors.

5. Click **More Colors**, then click the **green cell** in the middle row of the color hexagon, second from the left, as shown in Figure C-14
The Current color and the New color appear in the box in the lower-right corner of the dialog box.

6. Click **OK**
The text in the word-processing box changes to green, and the green is added as the ninth color in the set of colors used in the presentation.

7. Click the **Font list arrow** on the Formatting toolbar
A list of available fonts opens with the font used in the text box selected in the list.

8. Click the down scroll arrow, then click **Times New Roman**
The Times New Roman font replaces the original font in the text object.

> **QuickTip**
> If you want to align a word or a sentence in a text box without aligning all of the text in the text box, select the text, then click one of the alignment buttons on the Formatting toolbar.

9. Click the **Center button** ▤ on the Formatting toolbar
All the text in the text box is aligned to the center of the text box.

10. Drag the text box so it is centered over the chart, resize the text box so the text wraps as shown in Figure C-15, click a blank area of the slide outside the text object to deselect it, then click the **Save button** 🖫 on the Standard toolbar
Compare your screen to Figure C-15.

FIGURE C-14: Colors dialog box

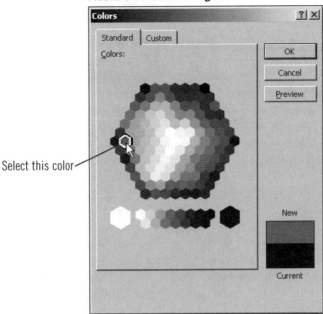

Select this color ──►

FIGURE C-15: Slide showing formatted text box

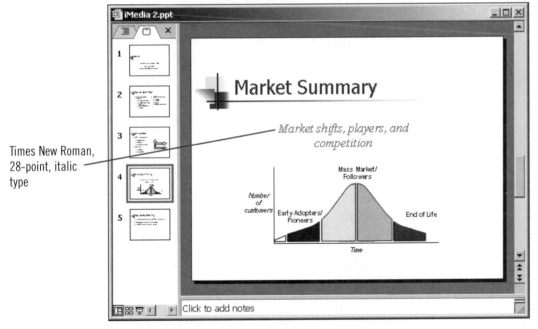

Times New Roman, 28-point, italic type

Replacing Text and Attributes

As you review your presentation, you may decide to replace certain words throughout the entire presentation. You can automatically modify words, sentences, text case, and periods. To replace specific words or sentences, use the Replace command on the Edit menu. To automatically add or remove periods from title or body text and to automatically change the case of title or body text, click Options on the Tools menu, click the Spelling and Style tab, then click Style Options to open the Style Options dialog box. Click the Case and End Punctuation tab, if necessary. The options on the Visual Clarity tab in the Style Options dialog box control the legibility of bulleted text items on the slides.

Importing Text from Microsoft Word

PowerPoint makes it easy to insert information from other sources, such as Microsoft Word, into a presentation. If you have an existing Word document or outline, you can import it into PowerPoint to create a new presentation or additional slides in an existing presentation. Documents saved in Microsoft Word format (.doc), Rich Text Format (.rtf), plain text format (.txt), and HTML format (.htm) can be inserted into a presentation. When you import a Microsoft Word or a Rich Text Format document into a presentation, PowerPoint creates an outline structure based on the styles in the document. For example, a Heading 1 style in the Word document becomes a slide title in PowerPoint and a Heading 2 style becomes the first level of text in a bulleted list. If you insert a plain text format document into a presentation, PowerPoint creates an outline based on the tabs at the beginning of the document's paragraphs. Paragraphs with no tab become slide titles; paragraphs with one tab indent become first-level text in bulleted lists; paragraphs with two tabs become second-level text in bulleted lists; and so on. ◄ One of Maria's colleagues from the Product Fulfillment department sent her a Word document containing a description of the new product. Maria inserts this document into her presentation.

Steps

1. **Click the Outline tab, then click the Slide 5 icon** 🖵
Slide 5 appears in the slide pane. Each time you click a slide icon in the Outline tab, the slide title and text are highlighted indicating the slide is selected. Before you insert information into a presentation, you must first designate where you want the information to be placed. The document will be inserted after the selected slide.

2. **Click Insert on the menu bar, then click Slides from Outline**
The Insert Outline dialog box opens.

3. **Locate the Word document PPT C-2 in the drive and folder where your Project Files are stored, then click Insert**
Three new slides (6, 7, and 8) are added to the presentation as shown in Figure C-16. Slide 6 is highlighted showing you where the information from the Word document begins.

4. **Read the text for the new Slide 6 in the slide pane, click the Slide 7** 🖵 **icon in the Outline tab, then review the text on that slide**
Slide 7 is selected.

5. **Click the Slides tab, then click the Slide 8 thumbnail**
After reviewing the text on this slide, Maria realizes that someone else will cover this information in another presentation.

6. **Right-click the Slide 8 thumbnail, then click Delete Slide on the shortcut menu**
Slide 8 is deleted from the presentation and Slide 7 appears in the slide pane again. Compare your screen to Figure C-17.

7. **Click the Save button** 🖫 **on the Standard toolbar to save your changes**

> **Trouble?**
>
> If a message dialog box opens telling you that you need to install a converter, click Yes, and insert the Office CD when prompted. Check with your instructor or technical support person if you have trouble.

FIGURE C-16: Outline tab showing imported text

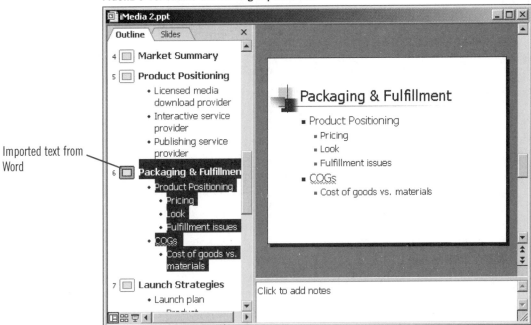

Imported text from Word

FIGURE C-17: Presentation after deleting slide

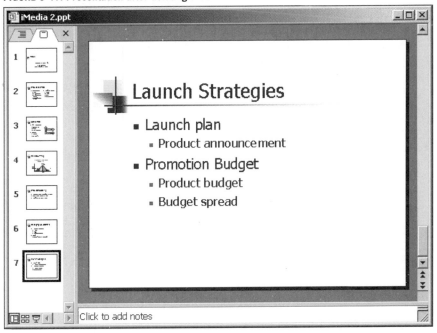

Inserting Slides from Other Presentations

To insert slides into the current presentation, click Insert on the menu bar, then click Slides from Files. Click Browse in the Slide Finder dialog box, then locate the presentation from which you want to copy slides. In the Select slides section, select the slide(s) you want to insert, click Insert, then click Close. The new slides automatically take on the design of the current presentation. If both presentations are open, you can copy the slides from one presentation to another. Change the view of each presentation to Slide Sorter view, select the desired slides, then copy and paste them (or use drag and drop) into the desired presentation. You can then rearrange the slides in Slide Sorter view if necessary.

Customizing the Color Scheme and Background

Every PowerPoint presentation has a **color scheme**, a set of eight coordinated colors, that determines the colors for the slide elements in your presentation: slide background, text and lines, shadows, title text, fills, accents, and hyperlinks. The design template that is applied to a presentation determines its color scheme. See Table C-1 for a description of the slide color scheme elements. The **background** is the area behind the text and graphics. Every design template in PowerPoint—even the blank presentation template—has a color scheme that you can use or modify. You can change the background color and appearance independent of changing the color scheme. Maria changes the color scheme and modifies the background of the presentation.

1. **Click the Color Schemes hyperlink in the Slide Design task pane**
   The current, or default, color scheme is selected with a black border as shown in Figure C-18. Additional color schemes designed specifically for the applied design template (in this case, the Blends template) are also shown.

2. **Click the color scheme icon in the third row, first column in the Slide Design task pane**
   The new color scheme is applied to all the slides in the presentation. In this case, the new color scheme changes the color of the slide graphics and title text, but the bulleted text and background remain the same.

3. **Click Format on the menu bar, then click Background**
   The Background dialog box opens.

4. **In the Background fill section, click the list arrow below the preview of the slide, click Fill Effects, then click the Gradient tab, if necessary**

5. **Click the One color option button in the Colors section, click the Color 1 list arrow, click the purple square (called Follow Accent and Hyperlink Scheme Color)**
   The purple color fills the Color 1 list arrow and the four variant previews in the Variants section, showing that the background will be shaded with purple.

6. **Drag the Brightness scroll box all the way to the right (towards Light) in the Colors section**
   The four variant previews change color.

7. **Click the From corner option button in the Shading Styles section, then click the lower-right variant**
   Compare your screen to Figure C-19.

8. **Click OK, then click Apply to All**
   The slide background is now shaded from purple (lower-right) to white (upper-left).

9. **Click the Slide Sorter View button** 📇**, click the Zoom list arrow on the Standard toolbar, then click 50%**
   The final presentation appears in Slide Sorter view. Compare your screen to Figure C-20.

10. **Add your name as a footer on the notes and handouts, print the slides as handouts (4 slides per page), click the Save button** 💾 **on the Standard toolbar to save your changes, close the presentation, then exit PowerPoint**

FIGURE C-18: Slide Design task pane

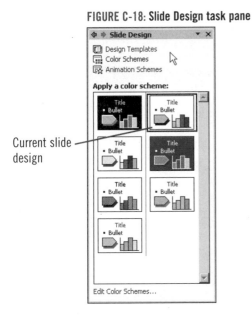

Current slide design

FIGURE C-19: Completed Fill Effects dialog box

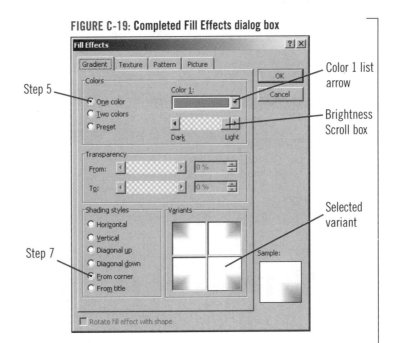

Color 1 list arrow

Brightness Scroll box

Selected variant

Step 5

Step 7

FIGURE C-20: Final presentation in Slide Sorter view

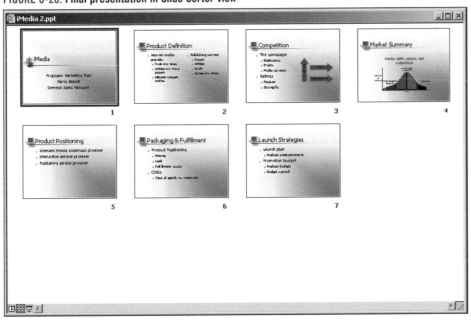

TABLE C-1: Color scheme elements

scheme element	description
Background color	Color of the slide's canvas, or background
Text and lines color	Used for text and drawn lines; contrasts with the background color
Shadows color	Color of the shadow of the text or other object; generally a darker shade of the background color
Title text color	Used for slide title; like the text and line colors, contrasts with the background color
Fills color	Contrasts with both the background and the text and line colors
Accent colors	Colors used for other objects on slides, such as bullets
Accent and hyperlink colors	Colors used for accent objects and for hyperlinks you insert
Accent and followed hyperlink color	Color used for accent objects and for hyperlinks after they have been clicked

PowerPoint 2002

Practice

► Concepts Review

Label the elements of the PowerPoint window shown in Figure C-21.

FIGURE C-21

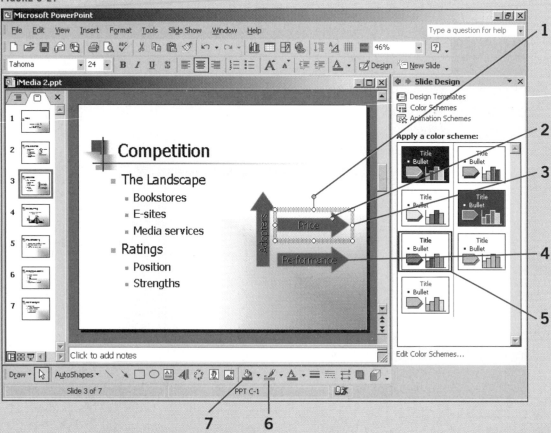

Match each term or button with the statement that describes it.

8. Word-processing box
9. Text label
10.
11. Rotate handle
12. Adjustment handle

a. Used to turn an object
b. Creates a text object on a slide
c. Used to change the shape of an object
d. A text object that does not word wrap
e. A text object made by dragging to create a box after clicking the Text Box button

Select the best answer from the list of choices.

13. How do you change the size of a PowerPoint object?
   a. Drag a sizing handle
   b. Click the Resize button
   c. Drag the adjustment handle
   d. You can't change the size of a PowerPoint object

14. What would you use to position objects at a specific place on a slide?
   a. PowerPoint placeholders
   b. PowerPoint guides and rulers
   c. PowerPoint lines
   d. PowerPoint anchor lines

15. PowerPoint objects can be:
   a. Grouped and aligned.
   b. Resized and modified.
   c. Converted to pictures.
   d. Both A and B.

16. What does the adjustment handle do?
   a. Adjusts the size of an object
   b. Adjusts the position of an object
   c. Changes the appearance of an object
   d. Changes the angle adjustment of an object

17. What is the easiest way to line objects along their centers on a slide?
   a. Group the objects together
   b. Use the Align Center command
   c. Place the objects on the edge of the slide
   d. Use PowerPoint anchor lines

18. What does *not* happen when you group objects?
   a. Objects lose their individual characteristics.
   b. Objects are grouped together as a single object.
   c. Sizing handles appear around the grouped object.
   d. The grouped objects have a rotate handle.

19. What is *not* true about guides?
   a. Slides can have only one vertical and one horizontal guide.
   b. You can press [Ctrl] and drag a guide to create a new one.
   c. You can drag a guide off the slide to delete it.
   d. A PowerPoint guide is a dotted line.

20. What is a slide background?
   a. The pasteboard off the slide
   b. A picture
   c. The area behind text and graphics
   d. The slide grid

21. What is *not* true about a presentation color scheme?
   a. Every presentation has a color scheme.
   b. The color scheme determines the colors of a slide.
   c. You can't change the background color without changing the color scheme.
   d. There are eight colors to every color scheme.

▶ Skills Review

1. Open an existing presentation.
   a. Start PowerPoint.
   b. Open the file PPT C-3 from the drive and folder where your Project Files are stored.
   c. Save it as **Cafe Report** to the location where your Project Files are stored.

2. Draw and modify an object.

a. On Slide 3, add the Lightning Bolt AutoShape from the Basic Shapes category on the AutoShapes menu. Make it as large as possible on the right side of the slide.

b. On the Line Color menu, click No Line.

c. Change the fill color to light green (named Follow Accent Scheme Color).

d. Click the 3-D Style button on the Drawing toolbar, then click the 3-D Style 5 button.

e. Rotate the bolt so it points from the upper-right to the lower-left.

f. Move the object on the slide so it looks similar to Figure C-22.

g. Deselect the object and save your changes.

3. Edit drawing objects.

FIGURE C-22

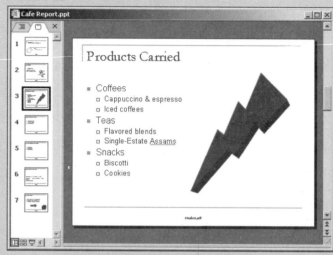

a. On Slide 7, resize the arrow object so it is about ½" shorter. (*Hint*: You might want to resize the bulleted list text object so it does not interfere with your work.)

b. Drag the arrow next to the left side of the box.

c. Use the adjustment handle to lengthen the arrow's head about ¼", then insert the text **Satisfaction**. Enlarge the arrow object so that all the text fits inside it, if necessary.

d. Make two copies of the arrow and arrange them to the left of the first one so that they are pointing in succession to the box.

e. Replace the word **Satisfaction** on the middle arrow with the word **Growth**.

f. Replace the word **Satisfaction** on the left arrow object with the word **Products**.

g. Insert the word **Success** in the cube object.

h. Change all the objects' text font to Arial italic. Enlarge the cube as necessary so the word **Success** fits in it.

i. Save your changes.

4. Align and group objects.

FIGURE C-23

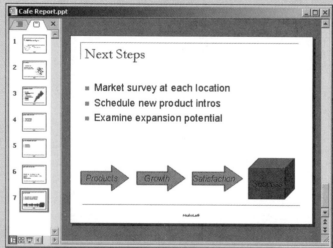

a. Align the middles of the four objects.

b. Group the arrow objects and the cube together.

c. Display the guides, then move the vertical guide left to about 4.58 and the horizontal guide down to about 2.75.

d. Align the grouped object so its bottom-left resize handle snaps to where the guides intersect. (*Hint*: If your object does not snap to the guides, open the Grid and Guides dialog box, and make sure the Snap objects to grid check box is checked.)

e. Hide the guides, then save your changes. Compare your screen with Figure C-23.

5. Add and arrange text.

a. Add a fourth item to the body text box on Slide 2 that reads **Next steps**.

b. Near the bottom of the slide, below the graphic, create a word-processing box about 3" wide, and in it enter the text: **A relaxing café is a reading haven.** (If the AutoCorrect feature is active, the accent will be added to the *e* in *café* automatically when you press [Spacebar].)

c. Drag the word **relaxing** in front of the word **reading**.

d. Save your changes.

6. Format text.

a. On Slide 2, select the word-processing text box that you added, so that formatting commands will apply to all the text in the box.

b. Change the font color to the dark green color (named Follow Title Text Scheme Color), increase its font size to 28 points, then, if necessary, resize the word-processing box so the text fits on one line.

c. Select the body text box to the left of the picture, then align the words to the center.

d. Go to Slide 6, then align the words **Business Day, August 2003** to the right.

e. Change the font color of the text box to the brown color (named Follow Accent and Hyperlink Scheme Color).

f. Go to Slide 7, select the text in the cube, then change the font color to a light fluorescent green. (*Hint*: Use the Colors dialog box.)

g. Go to Slide 1 and change the title text font to Arial Black, 48 points.

h. Deselect the text object, then save your changes.

7. Import text from Microsoft Word.

a. Click Slide 6 in the Slides tab.

b. Import the Word file PPT C-4. Check the formatting of each new slide.

c. In the Slides tab, drag Slide 9 below Slide 10.

d. In the Slides tab, delete Slide 7, Market Surveys.

e. Save your changes.

8. Customize the color scheme and background.

a. Open the Slide Design task pane and click the Color Schemes hyperlink.

b. Apply the bottom color scheme in the right column in the list to all the slides.

c. Open the Background dialog box, then the Fill Effects dialog box.

d. On the Gradient tab, select the Two colors option.

e. Select the Diagonal up shading style and the upper-right variant.

f. Apply this background to all slides.

g. Add your name as a footer to the notes and handouts.

h. Save your changes, then print the slides as handouts (4 slides per page). Your presentation in Slide Sorter view should look similar to Figure C-24.

i. Close the file and exit PowerPoint.

FIGURE C-24

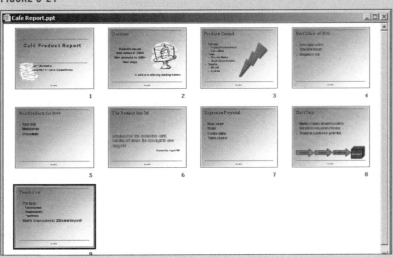

► Independent Challenge 1

In this unit, you learned that when you work with multiple objects on a PowerPoint slide, there are ways to arrange them so your information appears neat and well-organized. Using a word-processing program, write a summary explaining how to perform each of these tasks in PowerPoint. Make sure you explain what happens to the objects when you perform these tasks. Also explain *why* you would perform these tasks.

a. Start the word processor, open a new document, then save the file as **Arranging Objects** to the drive and folder where your Project Files are stored.
b. Explain the six different ways to align objects.
c. Explain the concept of grouping objects.
d. Add your name as the first line in the document, save your changes, print the document, close the document, then exit the word processor.

► Independent Challenge 2

You work for Chicago Language Systems, a major producer of language-teaching CD-ROMs with accompanying instructional books. Twice a year, the company holds title meetings to determine the new title list for the following production term and to decide which current CD titles need to be revised. As the director of acquisitions, you chair the September Title Meeting and present the basic material for discussion.

a. Start PowerPoint, open the file PPT C-5 from the drive and folder where your Project Files are stored, and save it as **Title Meeting 9-26-03**.
b. Add an appropriate design template to the presentation.
c. Insert the Word outline PPT C-6 after Slide 6.
d. Examine all of the slides in the presentation and apply italic formatting to all product and book titles.
e. Format the text so that the most important information is the most prominent.
f. Add appropriate shapes that emphasize the most important parts of the slide content. Format the objects using color and shading. Use the Align and Group commands to organize your shapes.
g. Evaluate the color scheme and the background colors. Delete any slides you feel are unnecessary, and make any changes you feel will enhance the presentation.
h. Spell check, view the final slide show, and evaluate your presentation. Make any necessary changes.
i. Add your name as footer text on the notes and handouts, save the presentation, print the slides as handouts, close the file, and exit PowerPoint.

► Independent Challenge 3

The Software Learning Company is dedicated to the design and development of instructional software that helps college students learn software applications. You need to design five new logos for the company that incorporate the new company slogan: "Software is a snap!" The marketing group will decide which of the five designs looks best. Create your own presentation slides, but assume that the company colors are blue and green.

a. Sketch your logos and slogan designs on a piece of paper. What text and graphics do you need for the slides?
b. Start PowerPoint, create a new blank presentation, and save it as **Software Learning** to the drive and folder where your Project Files are stored.

c. Create five different company logos, each one on a separate slide. Use the shapes on the AutoShapes menu, and enter the company slogan using the Text tool. (*Hint:* Use the Title only layout.) The logo and the marketing slogan should match each other in tone, size, and color; and the logo objects should be grouped together to make it easier for other employees to copy and paste. Use shadings and shadows appropriately.

d. Add a background color if it is appropriate for your logo design.

e. Spell check, view the final slide show, and evaluate your presentation. Delete any slides you feel are unnecessary, and make any necessary changes.

f. Add your name as footer text, save the presentation, print the slides and notes pages (if any), close the file, and exit PowerPoint.

 # Independent Challenge 4

Your company is planning to offer 401(k) retirement plans to all its employees. The Human Resources Department has asked you to construct and deliver a brief presentation about 401(k) plans to the employees. To find the necessary information for the presentation, you decide to use the Web. The information you find on the Web should answer the following questions:

- What is a 401(k) plan?
- How does a 401(k) plan work?
- How much can I contribute to my 401(k) plan at work?
- When do I have to start taking money from my 401(k) account?
- Is there a penalty for early withdrawal?

a. Connect to the Internet, then use a search engine to locate Web sites that have information on 401(k) plans. If your search does not produce any results, you might try the following sites:
   www.401k.com
   www.quicken.com

b. Review at least two Web sites that contain information about 401(k) plans. Print the Home pages of the Web sites you use to gather data for your presentation.

c. Start PowerPoint. On the title slide, title the presentation **401(k) Plans: What Employees Need to Know**. The presentation should contain at least five slides, including the title slide. Refer to the bulleted list as you create your content.

d. Save the presentation as **401(k) Plans** to the drive and folder where your Project Files are stored.

e. Apply a template to the presentation, customize the slide background, create a new color scheme, and save the color scheme as a standard scheme.

f. Use text formatting as necessary to make text visible and help emphasize important points.

g. At least one slide should contain an object from the AutoShapes menu. Customize the object's size and color.

h. Add your name as a footer to the slides, spell check the presentation, and view the final presentation.

i. Save the final version of the presentation, print the slides, then close the file, and exit PowerPoint.

► Visual Workshop

Create a one-slide presentation that looks like the one shown in Figure C-24. Use a text box for each bullet. Group the objects in the bottom logo. (Hint: The top rectangle object uses the 3-D menu.) If you don't have the exact fonts, use something similar. Add your name as a footer on the slide, save the presentation as **SASLtd** to the drive and folder where your Project Files are stored, then print the slide.

FIGURE C-25

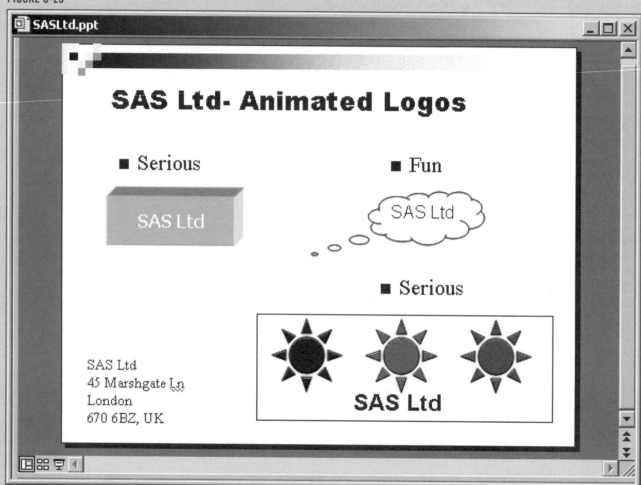

Enhancing

a Presentation

Objectives

- MOUS ► **Insert clip art**
- MOUS ► **Insert, crop, and scale a picture**
- MOUS ► **Embed a chart**
- ► **Enter and edit data in the datasheet**
- ► **Format a chart**
- MOUS ► **Create tables in PowerPoint**
- MOUS ► **Use slide show commands**
- MOUS ► **Set slide show timings and transitions**
- MOUS ► **Set slide animation effects**

After completing the content of your presentation, you can supplement your slide text with clip art or graphics, charts, and other visuals that help communicate your content and keep your slide show visually interesting. In this unit, you learn how to insert three of the most common visual enhancements: a clip art image, a picture, and a chart. These objects are created in other programs. After you add the visuals, you rehearse the slide show and add special effects. ✐ Maria Abbott has changed her presentation based on feedback from her colleagues. Now she wants to revise the marketing presentation to make it easier to understand and more interesting to watch.

Inserting Clip Art

PowerPoint includes many professionally designed images, called **clip art**, that you can place in your presentation. Using clip art is the easiest and fastest way to enhance your presentations. In Microsoft Office, clip art and other media files, including photographs, movies, and sounds, are stored in a file index system called the Microsoft Clip Organizer. The Clip Organizer sorts the clip art into groups, including My Collections, Office Collections, and Web Collections. The Office Collections group holds all the media files that come with Microsoft Office. You can customize the Clip Organizer by adding clips to a collection, moving clips from one collection to another, or creating a new collection. As with drawing objects, you can modify clip art images by changing their shape, size, fill, or shading. Clip art is available from many sources outside of the Clip Organizer, including Microsoft Design Gallery Live on Microsoft's Web site and collections on CD-ROMs. ✐ Maria wants to add a picture from the Media Gallery to one of the slides and then adjust its size and placement.

Steps

1. Start PowerPoint, open the presentation **PPT D-1** from the location where your Project Files are stored, save it as **iMedia 3**, click **View** on the menu bar, click **Task Pane**, click **Window** on the menu bar, then click **Arrange All**

Trouble?

If the Add Clips to Organizer dialog box opens asking if you want to catalog all media files, click Later.

2. Go to **Slide 7**, titled "Launch Strategies," then click the **Insert Clip Art button** 🖾 on the Drawing toolbar
   The Insert Clip Art task pane opens. Each piece of clip art in the Clip Organizer is identified by keywords that describe the clip art. At the top of the task pane in the Search For section, you can enter a keyword and search for specific types of clip art. If you want to search for specific clips, such as clip art, photographs, movies, or sounds, in certain collections, select options under Other Search Options in the task pane. At the bottom of the task pane, you can click one of the hyperlinks to locate other pieces of clip art or to read tips on how to find clip art.

3. Select any text in the **Search text box**, type **plans**, then click **Search**
   PowerPoint searches for clips identified by the keyword "plans."

QuickTip

You can change the slide layout prior to inserting a piece of clip art. Apply any of the "content" slide layouts except the Blank layout, then click the Insert Clip Art button in the Content placeholder to insert a piece of clip art.

4. Scroll down in the Insert Clip Art task pane, then click the **clip art thumbnail** shown in Figure D-1
   The clip art object appears on the slide and the Picture toolbar opens. PowerPoint automatically changes the slide layout to the Title, Text, and Content layout, which decreases the size of the body text box and positions the clip art object on the right side of the slide. The Automatic Layout Options button 🖼 appears below the clip art, which tells you that the slide layout has been changed. You can click the Automatic Layout Options button to select commands that control the automatic changes to the slide layout. If you don't have the clip art picture shown in Figure D-1 in your Clip Organizer, select a similar picture.

5. Place the pointer over the **lower-left sizing handle** and drag the **handle** up to the right about ½"
   The clip art object proportionally decreases in size.

6. Place the pointer over the **Rotate handle** and drag the **handle** to the left so the clip art object is slightly tilted

QuickTip

You can also use the keyboard arrow keys or the Nudge command on the Draw menu button to reposition any selected object by small increments.

7. Drag the **clip art object** up to the right of the text object so it matches Fig D-2
   Compare your screen to Figure D-2 and make any necessary adjustments.

8. Click a blank area of the slide, then save your changes

FIGURE D-1: Screen showing Insert Clip Art task pane

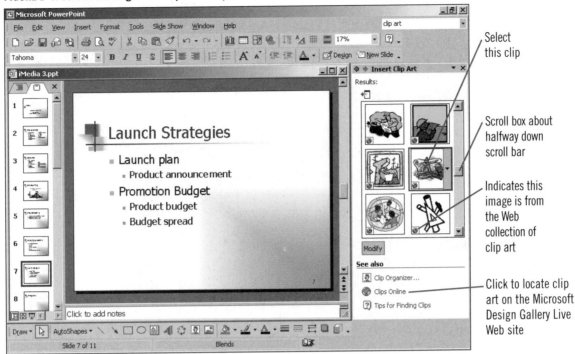

Select this clip

Scroll box about halfway down scroll bar

Indicates this image is from the Web collection of clip art

Click to locate clip art on the Microsoft Design Gallery Live Web site

FIGURE D-2: Slide with clip art object resized and repositioned

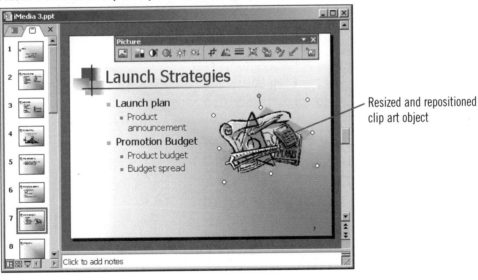

Resized and repositioned clip art object

Find more clips online

If you can't find the clips you need in the Clip Organizer, you can easily use clips from the Microsoft Design Gallery Live Web site. To get clips from the Design Gallery Live Web site, click the Clips Online hyperlink at the bottom of the Insert Clip Art task pane. This will launch your Web browser and automatically connect you to the site. Read the License Agreement carefully; it specifies how you are permitted to use clips from this site. Click Accept to agree to the terms of the License Agreement and continue using the site. The Design Gallery Live window opens. You can search the site by keyword or browse by category. Each clip you download is automatically inserted into the Clip Organizer Web Collections folder.

Inserting, Cropping, and Scaling a Picture

A picture in PowerPoint is a scanned photograph, a piece of line art, clip art, or other artwork that is created in another program and inserted into a PowerPoint presentation. You can insert 18 types of pictures. As with other PowerPoint objects, you can move or resize an inserted picture. You can also crop pictures. **Cropping** a picture means to hide a portion of the picture. Although you can easily change a picture's size by dragging a corner resize handle, you can also **scale** it to change its size by a specific percentage. Maria inserts a picture that has previously been saved to a file, crops and scales it, then adjusts its background.

Steps

1. Go to **Slide 9**, titled "Distribution," then click the **Insert Picture button** on the Drawing toolbar
   The Insert Picture dialog box opens.

2. Select the file **PPT D-2** from the location where your Project Files are stored, then click **Insert**
   The picture appears on the slide, and the Picture toolbar opens. The slide layout changes to the Title, Text, and Content layout. The slide might look better using the original slide layout.

3. Click the **Automatic Layout Options button**, then click **Undo Automatic Layout**
   The slide layout changes back to the original Title and Text layout and the picture moves to the center of the slide. The body text box is too large in this layout.

4. Click, then click **Redo Automatic Layout**
   The picture would fit better on the slide if it didn't show the boxes on the left side of the picture.

5. Click the **Crop button** on the Picture toolbar, then place the pointer over the left, middle sizing handle of the picture
   When the Crop button is active, the sizing handles appear as straight black lines. The pointer changes to ⊣.

6. Press and hold **[Alt]**, then drag the left edge of the picture to the right until the dotted line indicating the left edge of the picture has cut out the boxes, as shown in Figure D-3, then click
   Pressing [Alt] while dragging or drawing an object in PowerPoint overrides the automatic snap-to-grid setting. Now the picture needs to be enlarged and positioned into place.

7. Click the **Format Picture button** on the Picture toolbar, click the **Size tab**, make sure the **Lock aspect ratio check box** is selected, click and hold the **Height up arrow** until the Height and Width percentages reach **200%**, then click **OK**
   When you are scaling a picture and Lock aspect ratio is selected, the ratio of height to width remains the same. The white background is distracting.

8. With the picture still selected, click the **Set Transparent Color button** on the Picture toolbar, then click the **white background** in the picture with the pointer
   The white background is no longer visible, and the picture contrasts well with the background.

9. Drag the **picture** to center it in the blank area on the right side of the slide, deselect it, then save your changes
   See Figure D-4.

FIGURE D-3: Using the cropping pointer to crop the picture

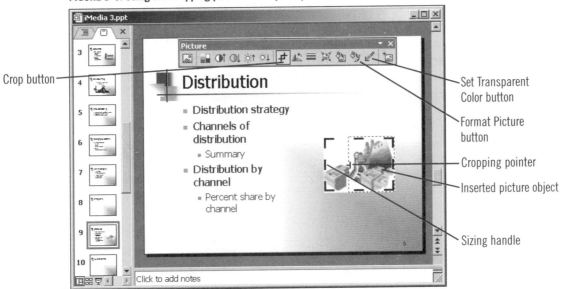

Crop button

Set Transparent
Color button

Format Picture
button

Cropping pointer

Inserted picture object

Sizing handle

FIGURE D-4: Completed slide with the cropped and resized graphic

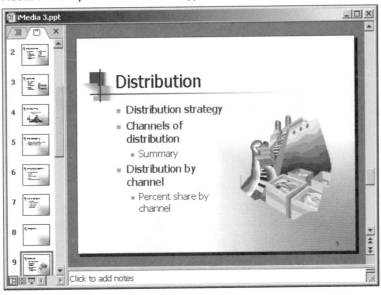

PowerPoint 2002

CLUES TO USE

Ways to use graphics with PowerPoint

You can insert pictures with a variety of graphics file **formats**, or file types, in PowerPoint. Most of the clip art that comes with PowerPoint is in Windows metafile format and has the .wmf file extension. You can change the colors in a .wmf graphic object by selecting it, then clicking the Recolor Picture button on the Picture toolbar. You can then replace each color in the graphic with another color. A graphic in .wmf format can be ungrouped into its separate PowerPoint objects, then edited with any of the PowerPoint drawing tools. You cannot recolor or ungroup pictures (files with the .bmp or .tif

extension). The clip art you inserted in the last lesson is in .wmf format, and the picture you inserted in this lesson is in .tif format.

You can also save PowerPoint slides as graphics and later use them in other presentations, in graphics programs, and on Web pages. Display the slide you want to save, then click Save As from the File menu. In the Save As dialog box, click the Save as type list arrow, and scroll to the desired graphics format. Name the file, click OK, then click the desired option when the alert box appears asking if you want to save all the slides or only the current slide.

Embedding a Chart

Often, the best way to communicate information is with a visual aid such as a chart. PowerPoint comes with a program called **Microsoft Graph** that you can use to create charts for your slides. A **chart** is the graphical representation of numerical data. Every chart has a corresponding **datasheet** that contains the numerical data displayed by the chart. Table D-1 lists the chart types available in Microsoft Graph. When you insert a chart object into PowerPoint, you are actually embedding it. **Embedding** an object means that the object becomes part of the PowerPoint file, but you can double-click on the embedded object to display the tools of the program in which the object was created. If you modify the embedded object, the original object file does not change. Maria wants to embed a chart object into one of her slides.

Steps

1. Go to **Slide 10**, titled "Success Metrics," click the **Other Task Panes list arrow** on the task pane title bar, then click **Slide Layout**
The Slide Layout task pane opens with the Title and Text layout selected.

2. Click the **Title and Content layout** in the Slide Layout task pane under Content Layouts
Remember to use the ScreenTips to help locate the correct layout. A content placeholder appears on the slide displaying six buttons in the middle of the placeholder. Each of these buttons represents a different object, such as a table, picture, or chart, that you can apply to your slide.

3. Click the **Insert Chart button** in the content placeholder
Microsoft Graph opens and embeds a default datasheet and chart into the slide, as shown in Figure D-5. The datasheet consists of rows and columns. The intersection of a row and a column is called a **cell**. Cells are referred to by their row and column location; for example, the cell at the intersection of column A and row 1 is called cell A1. Cells along the left column and top row of the datasheet typically contain **data labels** that identify the data in a column or row; for example, "East" and "1st Qtr" are data labels. Cells below and to the right of the data labels contain the data values that are represented in the chart. Each column and row of data in the datasheet is called a **data series**. Each data series has corresponding **data series markers** in the chart, which are graphical representations such as bars, columns, or pie wedges. The gray boxes along the left side of the datasheet are called **row headings** and the gray boxes along the top of the datasheet are called **column headings**. Notice that the PowerPoint Standard and Formatting toolbars have been replaced with the Microsoft Graph Standard and Formatting toolbars, and the menu bar has changed to include Microsoft Graph commands.

4. Move the pointer over the datasheet
The pointer changes to ✛. Cell A1 is the **active cell**, which means that it is selected. The active cell has a heavy black border around it.

5. Click cell **B3**, which contains the value 46.9
Cell B3 is now the active cell.

6. Click a blank area of the slide to exit Graph then click again to deselect the chart object
Graph closes and the PowerPoint menu bar and toolbars appear.

7. Save your changes

FIGURE D-5: Datasheet and chart in the PowerPoint window

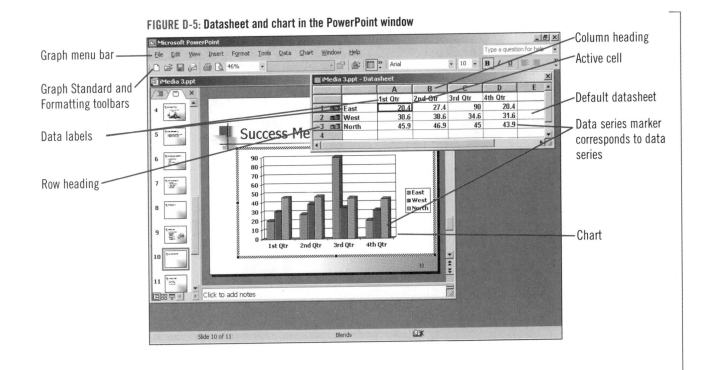

Graph menu bar

Graph Standard and Formatting toolbars

Data labels

Row heading

Column heading

Active cell

Default datasheet

Data series marker corresponds to data series

Chart

TABLE D-1: Microsoft Graph chart types

chart type	looks like	use to
Column		Track values over time or across categories
Bar		Compare values in categories or over time
Line		Track values over time
Pie		Compare individual values to the whole
XY (Scatter)		Compare pairs of values
Area		Show contribution of each data series to the total over time
Doughnut		Compare individual values to the whole with multiple series
Radar		Show changes in values in relation to a center point
Surface		Show value trends across two dimensions
Bubble		Indicate relative size of data points
Stock		Show stock market information or scientific data
Cylinder, cone, pyramid		Track values over time or across categories

Entering and Editing Data in the Datasheet

After you embed the default chart into your presentation, you need to replace the data labels and cell data in the sample datasheet with the correct information. If you have data in a spreadsheet or other source, you can import it into Microsoft Graph; otherwise you can type your own information into the datasheet. As you enter data or make changes to the datasheet, the chart automatically changes to reflect your alterations. ◄▬▬ Maria enters the projected revenue figures for the first year of iMedia operation.

Steps 1234

1. **Double-click the chart on Slide 10**

   The chart is selected and the datasheet opens. The labels representing the quarters across the top are correct, but the row labels need adjusting, and the data needs to be replaced with iMedia's projected quarterly sales figures for each product type.

QuickTip

Double-click the column divider lines between the column headings to automatically resize the column width to accommodate the widest entry.

2. **Click the East row label, type Media, then press [Enter]**

   After you press [Enter], the data label in row 2 becomes selected. Pressing [Enter] in the datasheet moves the active cell down one cell; pressing [Tab] in the datasheet moves the active cell to the right one cell.

3. **Type Publish, then press [Tab]**

   Cell A2 becomes active. Notice in the chart, below the datasheet, that the data labels you typed are now in the legend to the right of the chart. The information in row 3 of the datasheet is not needed.

4. **Click the row heading for row 3, then press [Delete]**

   Clicking the row heading for row 3 selects the entire row. The default information in row 3 of the datasheet is deleted and the columns in the chart adjust accordingly.

Trouble?

If you can't see a column or a row, resize the datasheet window or use the scroll bars to move another part of the datasheet into view.

5. **Click cell A1, type 36,000, press [Enter], type 47,000, press [Tab], then press [↑] to move to cell B1**

   Notice that the height of each column in the chart changes to reflect the numbers you typed.

6. **Enter the rest of the numbers shown in Figure D-6 to complete the datasheet**

   The chart currently shows the columns grouped by quarter, and the legend represents the rows in the datasheet. The icons in the row headings indicate that the row labels appear in the legend. It would be more effective if the columns were grouped by iMedia product with the legend representing the columns in the datasheet.

Trouble?

If you don't see the By Column button on the Standard toolbar, click a Toolbar Options button ≫ on a toolbar to locate buttons that are not visible on your toolbar.

7. **Click the By Column button 🖼 on the Standard toolbar**

   The division labels are now on the horizontal axis of the chart, and the quarters are listed in the legend. The groups of data markers (the columns) now represent the projected revenue for each product by quarter. Notice that the small column chart graphics that used to be in the row headings in the datasheet have now moved to the column headings, indicating that the series are now in columns.

8. **Click the slide outside the chart area, compare your chart to Figure D-7, then save the presentation**

   The datasheet closes, allowing you to see your entire chart. This chart layout clearly shows iMedia's projected revenue for the first year it's in operation.

FIGURE D-6: Datasheet showing iMedia's projected revenue

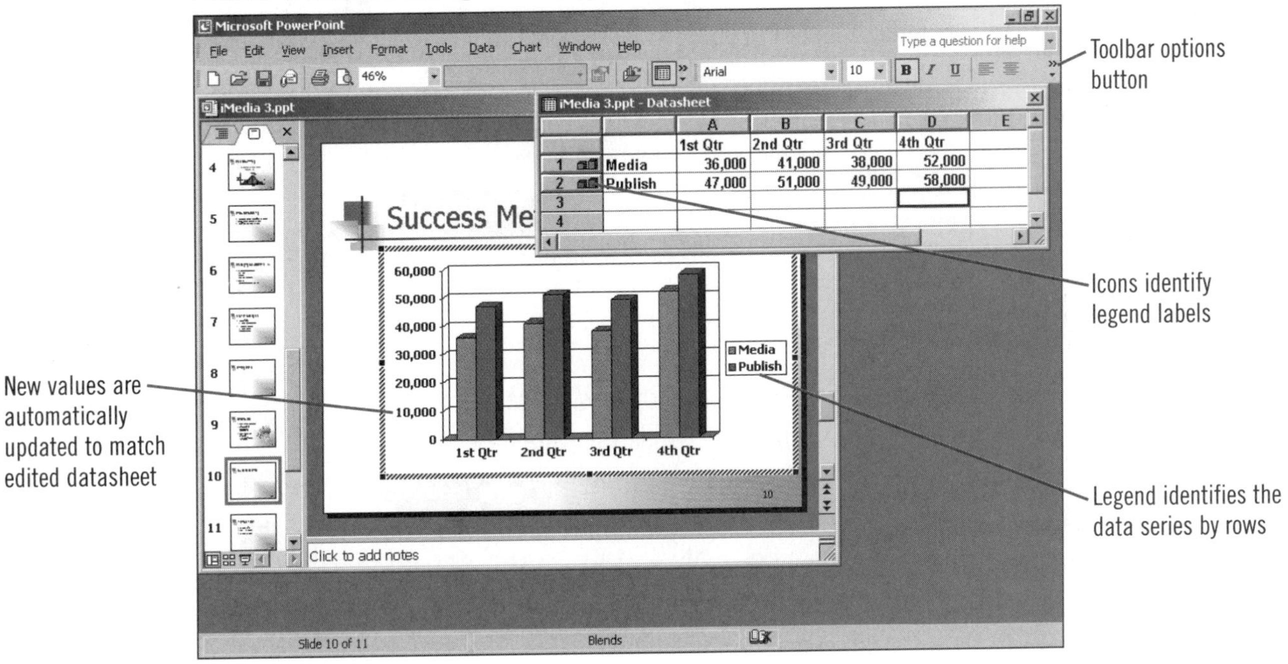

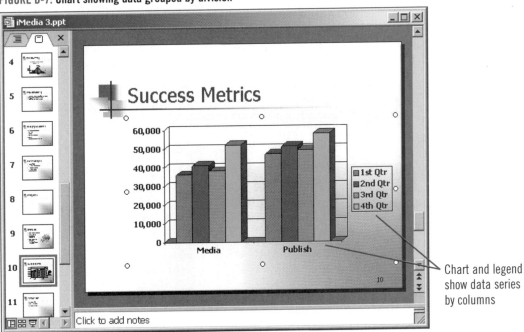

Toolbar options button

Icons identify legend labels

New values are automatically updated to match edited datasheet

Legend identifies the data series by rows

FIGURE D-7: Chart showing data grouped by division

Chart and legend show data series by columns

Series in Rows vs. Series in Columns

If you have difficulty visualizing the difference between the Series in Rows and the Series in Columns commands on the Data menu, think about the legend. **Series in Rows** means that the information in the rows will become the legend in the chart, and the column labels will be on the horizontal axis.

Series in Columns means that the information in the columns will become the legend in the chart, and the row labels will be on the horizontal axis. Microsoft Graph places a small graphic representing the chart type on the axis items that are currently represented by the chart series items (bars, etc.).

Formatting a Chart

Microsoft Graph lets you change the appearance of the chart to emphasize certain aspects of the information you are presenting. You can change the chart type (for example pie, column, bar, or line), create titles, format the chart labels, move the legend, add arrows, or format the data series markers. Like other objects in PowerPoint, you can change the fill color, pattern, line style and color, and style of most elements in a chart. ✐━━ Maria wants to improve the appearance of her chart by formatting the vertical and horizontal axes and by inserting a title.

Steps 1 2 3 4

1. Double-click the **chart** to reopen Microsoft Graph, then click the **Close button** ☒ in the Datasheet window to close the datasheet
The Microsoft Graph menu and toolbar remain at the top of the window.

QuickTip
If you don't see the Currency Style button on the Formatting toolbar, click a Toolbar Options button ⯈ on a toolbar to locate buttons that are not visible on your toolbar.

2. Click one of the **revenue numbers** on the vertical axis to select the axis, then click the **Currency Style button** 🅢 on the Formatting toolbar
Before you can format any object on the chart, you need to select it. The numbers on the vertical axis appear with dollar signs and two decimal places. You don't need to show the two decimal places, because all the values are whole numbers.

3. Click the **Decrease Decimal button** 🔢 on the Formatting toolbar twice
The numbers on the vertical axis now have dollar signs and show only whole numbers. See Figure D-8. The division names on the horizontal axis would be easier to see if they were larger.

4. Click one of the **division names** on the horizontal axis, click the **Font Size list arrow** 18 ▾ on the Formatting toolbar, then click **20**
The font size changes from 18 points to 20 points for both labels on the horizontal axis. The chart would be easier to read if it had a title and axis labels.

5. Click **Chart** on the menu bar, click **Chart Options**, then click the **Titles tab**, if necessary
The Chart Options dialog box opens. Here, you can change the chart title, axes, gridlines, legend, data labels, and the data table.

6. Click in the **Chart title text box**, then type **iMedia Projected Revenue**
The preview box changes to show you the chart with the title.

7. Press **[Tab]** twice to move the insertion point to the Value (Z) axis text box, then type **Revenue**
In a 3-D chart, the vertical axis is called the Z-axis, and the depth axis, which you don't usually work with, is the Y-axis. You decide to move the legend to the bottom of the chart.

8. Click the **Legend tab**, click the **Bottom option button**, then click **OK**
The legend moves to the bottom of the chart, and a new chart title and axis title appear on the chart. The axis title would look better and take up less space if it were rotated 90 degrees.

9. Right-click the **"Revenue" label** on the vertical axis, click **Format Axis Title**, click the **Alignment tab**, drag the **red diamond** in the Orientation section up to a vertical position so the spin box reads 90 degrees, click **OK**, then click a blank area of the slide
Graph closes and the PowerPoint toolbars and menu bar appear.

10. Drag the **chart** to the center of the slide, click a blank area of the slide, then save your changes
Compare your screen to Figure D-9.

FIGURE D-8: Chart showing applied Currency style

Currency style applied to chart numbers

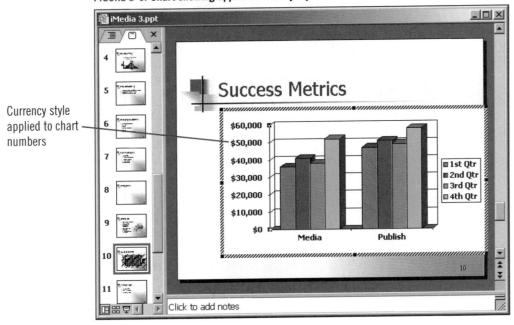

FIGURE D-9: Slide showing formatted chart

Chart title

Value (Z) axis title

Legend

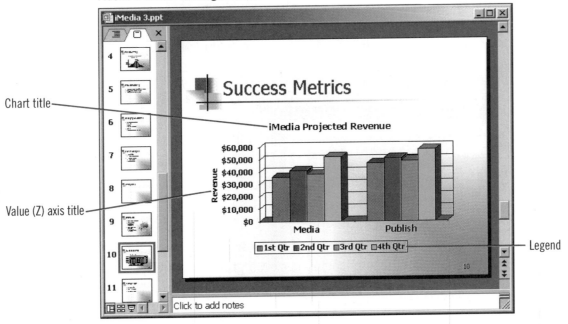

Customizing charts

You can easily customize the look of any chart in Microsoft Graph. Click the chart to select it, then double-click any data series element (a column, for example) to open the Format Data Series dialog box. Use the tabs to change the element's fill color, border, shape, or data label. You can even use the same fill effects you apply to a presentation background. In 3-D charts, you can change the chart depth as well as the distances between series.

PowerPoint 2002

Creating Tables in PowerPoint

As you create your PowerPoint presentation, you may need to insert information in a row and column format. A table you create in PowerPoint is ideal for this type of information layout. There are three ways to create a table in PowerPoint: the Insert Table button on the Standard toolbar, the Table command on the Insert menu and any of the content slide layouts. Once you have created a table, you can use the buttons on the Tables and Borders toolbar or on the Formatting toolbar to format it. ✏ Maria creates a table describing iMedia's different pricing plans.

Steps 1 2 3 4

1. Go to **Slide 8**, then click the **Insert Table button** 🔲 on the Standard toolbar
   A cell grid appears that allows you to specify the number of columns and rows you want in your table.

Trouble?

If the Tables and Borders toolbar does not open, click View on the menu bar, point to Toolbars, then click Tables and Borders. If the toolbar obscures part of the table, drag it out of the way.

2. Move your pointer over the grid to select a **3 × 3 cell area** ("3 × 3 Table" appears at the bottom of the cell grid), then click your mouse button
   A table with three columns and three rows appears on the slide, and the Tables and Borders toolbar opens. The first cell in the table is selected and ready to accept text.

3. Type **Plan 1**, press **[Tab]**, type **Plan 2**, press **[Tab]**, type **Plan 3**, then press **[Tab]**
   Don't worry if the table borders seem to disappear. The text you typed appears in the top three cells of the table. Pressing [Enter] moves the insertion point to the next line in the cell.

4. Enter the rest of the table information shown in Figure D-10, pressing **[Tab]** after each entry except the last one
   The table would look better if it were formatted.

5. Drag to select the column headings in the top row of the table
   The text in the first row becomes highlighted.

QuickTip

You can change the height or width of any table cell by dragging its top or side borders.

6. Click the **Center Vertically button** 🔲 on the Tables and Borders toolbar, then click the **Center button** 🔲 on the Formatting toolbar
   The text is centered horizontally and vertically.

7. With the text in the first row still selected, click the **Fill Color list arrow** 🔲 on the Tables and Borders toolbar, click the **green color** in the second row, then click a blank area of the slide
   The top row is filled with the color green.

8. Select the text in the other two rows, vertically center the text, then fill these three rows with the **white color** in the first row of the Fill Color list
   The table would look better if the last two rows were a little farther away from the cell edges.

QuickTip

You can use the Format Table dialog box to apply a diagonal line through any table cell. Click the Borders tab, then click the diagonal line button.

9. With the bottom two rows still selected, click **Format** on the menu bar, click **Table**, click the **Text Box tab**, click the **Left up scroll arrow** until it reads **.25**, click **OK**, click a blank area of the slide, then save the presentation
   The Tables and Borders toolbar closes and the table is no longer selected. Compare your screen with Figure D-11.

FIGURE D-10: The new table before formatting

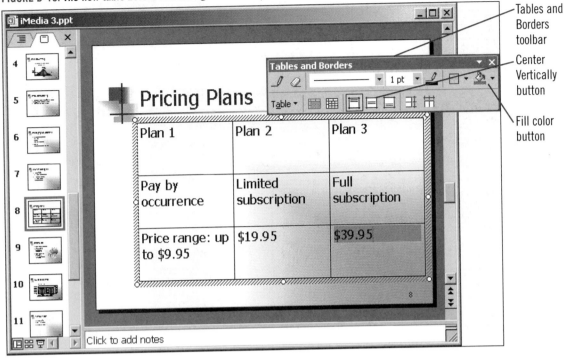

Tables and Borders toolbar

Center Vertically button

Fill color button

FIGURE D-11: Formatted table

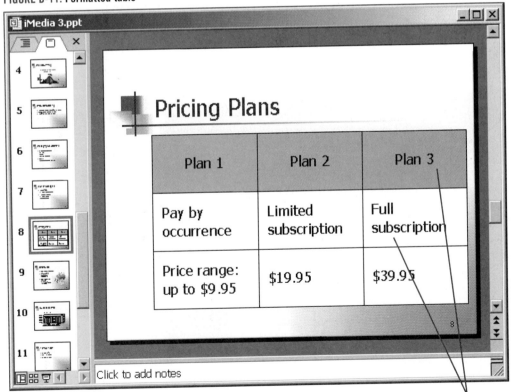

Text vertically centered in the cells

Using Slide Show Commands

With PowerPoint, you can show a presentation on any compatible computer using Slide Show view. As you've seen, Slide Show view fills your computer screen with the slides of your presentation, showing them one at a time, similar to how a slide projector shows slides. Once your presentation is in Slide Show view, you can use a number of slide show options to tailor the show. For example, you can draw on, or **annotate**, slides or jump to a specific slide. ✎ Maria runs a slide show of her presentation and practices using some of the custom slide show options to make her presentation more effective.

Steps

1. Go to **Slide 1**, then click the **Slide Show button** 🖵
The first slide of the presentation fills the screen.

2. Press **[Spacebar]**
Slide 2 appears on the screen. Pressing [Spacebar] or clicking the left mouse button is the easiest way to move through a slide show. Another way is to use the keys listed in Table D-2. You can also use the Slide Show shortcut menu for on-screen navigation during a slide show.

> **QuickTip**
> You can also access the Slide Show shortcut menu by moving the mouse pointer, then clicking the Slide Show menu icon that appears in the lower-left corner of the screen.

3. Right-click anywhere on the screen, point to **Go** on the shortcut menu, then click **Slide Navigator**
The Slide Navigator dialog box opens and displays a list of the presentation slides.

4. Click **9. Distribution** in the Slide titles list box, then click **Go To**
The slide show jumps to Slide 9. You can emphasize major points in your presentation by annotating the slide during a slide show using the Pen tool.

5. Right-click the slide, point to **Pointer Options** on the shortcut menu, then click **Pen**
The pointer changes to ✎.

6. Press and hold **[Shift]** and drag ✎ to draw a line under each of the bulleted points on the slide
Holding down [Shift] constrains the Pen tool to straight horizontal or vertical lines. Compare your screen to Figure D-12. While the annotation pen is visible, mouse clicks do not advance the slide show; however, you can still move to the next slide by pressing [Spacebar] or [Enter].

7. Right-click the slide, point to **Screen** on the shortcut menu, click **Erase Pen**, then press **[Ctrl][A]**
The annotations on Slide 9 are erased and the pointer returns to ⌕.

> **QuickTip**
> If you know the slide number of a slide you want to jump to during a slide show, type the number, then press [Enter].

8. Right-click the slide, point to **Go**, point to **By Title**, then click **3 Competition** on the shortcut menu
Slide 3 appears.

9. Press **[Home]**, then click the left mouse button, press **[Spacebar]**, or press **[Enter]** to advance through the slide show
After the black slide that indicates the end of the slide show appears, the next click ends the slide show and returns you to Normal view.

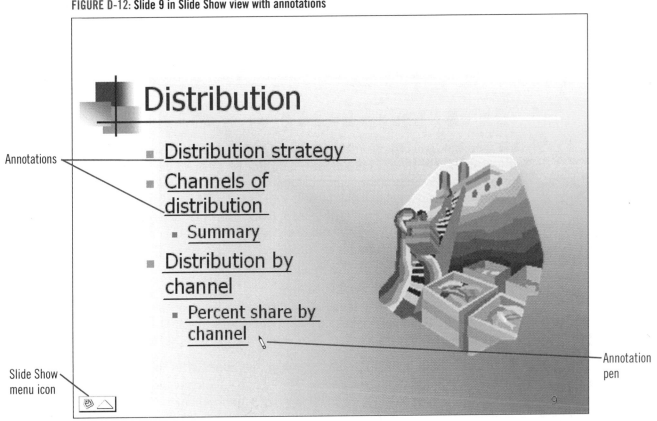

Annotations

Slide Show menu icon

Annotation pen

TABLE D-2: Slide Show keyboard controls

control	description
[Enter], [Spacebar], [PgDn], [N], [↓], or [→]	Advances to the next slide
[E]	Erases the annotation drawing
[Home], [End]	Moves to the first or last slide in the slide show
[H]	Displays a hidden slide
[↑] or [PgUp]	Returns to the previous slide
[W]	Changes the screen to white; press again to return
[S]	Pauses the slide show; press again to continue
[B]	Changes the screen to black; press again to return
[Ctrl][P]	Changes pointer to ✎
[Ctrl][A]	Changes pointer to ⬚
[Esc]	Stops the slide show

Setting Slide Show Timings and Transitions

In a slide show, you can preset when and how each slide appears on the screen. You can set the **slide timing**, which is the amount of time a slide is visible on the screen. Each slide can have different timings. Setting the right slide timing is important because it determines how long you have to discuss the material on each slide. You can also set **slide transitions**, which are the special visual and audio effects you apply to a slide that determine how it moves in and out of view during the slide show. Maria decides to set her slide timings for 10 seconds per slide and to set transitions for all her slides.

Steps

1. Click the **Slide Sorter View button** 🔡

   Slide Sorter view shows a thumbnail of the slides in your presentation. The number of slides you see on your screen depends on the current zoom setting in the Zoom box on the Standard toolbar. Notice that the Slide Sorter toolbar appears next to the Standard toolbar.

2. Click the **Slide Transition button** 🖼 on the Slide Sorter toolbar

   The Slide Transition task pane opens. The list box at the top of the task pane contains the slide transitions that you can apply to the slides of your presentation. You can change the speed of slide transitions or add a sound to a slide that plays during a slide show in the Modify transition section. Determine how slides progress during a slide show—either manually or with a slide timing—in the Advance slide section.

3. Make sure the **On mouse click check box** is selected in the Advance slide section, click the **Automatically after check box** to select it, select the number in the Automatically after text box, type **10**, then click **Apply to All Slides**

   The timing between slides is 10 seconds. The timing appears under each slide. When you run the slide show, each slide will remain on the screen for 10 seconds. You can override a slide's timing and speed up the slide show by pressing [Spacebar], [Enter], or clicking the left mouse button.

4. Scroll down the list of transitions at the top of the task pane, click **Wheel Clockwise, 4 Spokes**, then click **Apply to All Slides**

   You can apply a transition to one slide or to all of the slides in your presentation. The selected slide, Slide 1, displays the slide transition immediately after you apply the transition to all the slides. All of the slides now have the Wheel Clockwise transition applied to them as indicated by the transition icon under each slide. See Figure D-13. The slide transition would have more impact if it were slowed down.

5. Click the **Speed list arrow** under Modify Transition in the task pane, click **Medium**, then click **Apply to All Slides**

6. Scroll down the slide pane and click **Slide 11**, click the **Sound list arrow** under Modify transition in the task pane, scroll down the list, then click **Chime**

   The sound plays when you apply the sound to the slide. The sound will now play when Slide 11 appears during the slide show.

7. Press [Home], click **Slide Show** at the bottom of the task pane, and watch the slide show advance automatically

8. When you see the black slide at the end of the slide show, press [Spacebar]

   The slide show ends and returns to Slide Sorter view with Slide 1 selected.

QuickTip

If you don't see the Slide Transition button on the Slide Sorter toolbar, click a Toolbar Options button 》 on a toolbar to locate buttons that are not visible on your toolbar.

QuickTip

Click the transition icon under any slide to see its transition play.

QuickTip

To end a slide show, press [Esc] or click End Show in the Slide Show shortcut menu.

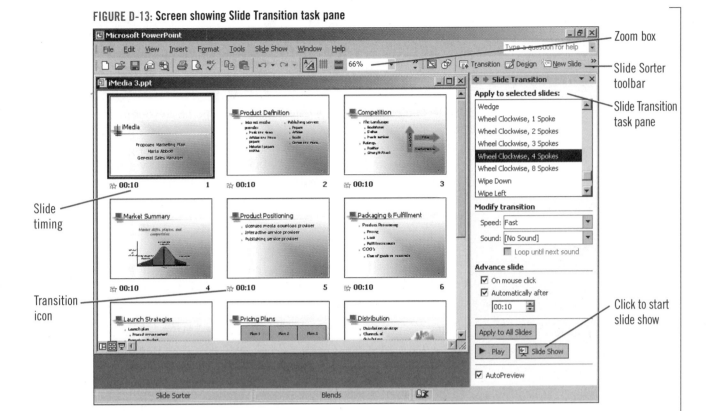

Zoom box

Slide Sorter toolbar

Slide Transition task pane

Slide timing

Transition icon

Click to start slide show

Rehearsing slide show timing

You can set different slide timings for each slide. For example, you can have the title slide appear for 20 seconds, the second slide for 3 minutes, and so on. You can set timings by clicking the Rehearse Timings button 🕲 on the Slide Sorter toolbar or by choosing the Rehearse Timings command on the Slide Show menu. The Rehearsal dialog box shown in Figure D-14 opens. It contains buttons to pause between slides and to advance to the next slide. After opening the Rehearsal dialog box, practice giving your presentation. PowerPoint keeps track of how long each slide appears and sets the timing accordingly. You can view your rehearsed timings in Slide Sorter view. The next time you run the slide show, you can use the timings you rehearsed.

FIGURE D-14: Rehearsal dialog box

Rehearsal ▼ ✕

0:00:04   0:00:04

Click to pause

Time elapsed while viewing current slide

Click to reset the clock to zero for the current slide

Total elapsed time for all slides

PowerPoint 2002

Setting Slide Animation Effects

Animation effects let you control how the graphics and main points in your presentation appear on the screen during a slide show. You can animate text, images, or even individual chart elements, or you can add sound effects. You can set custom animation effects or use one of PowerPoint's animation schemes. An **animation scheme** is a set of predefined visual effects for the slide transition, title text, and bullet text of a slide. ✏️ Maria wants to animate the text and graphics of several slides in her presentation using PowerPoint's animation schemes.

Steps 1234

1. Click **Slide 2**, press and hold down **[Ctrl]**, then click **Slides 3, 5, 6, 7**, and **9**
   All of the selected slides have bulleted lists on them. The bullets can be animated to appear one at a time during a slide show.

2. Click the **Other Task Panes list arrow** 🔽, click **Slide Design – Animation Schemes**, scroll down the Apply to selected slides list to the **Exciting section**, then click **Neutron**
   Each of the selected slides previews the Neutron animation scheme.

3. Click **Slide 1**, then click **Slide Show** at the bottom of the task pane
   The Neutron animation scheme is displayed on the selected slides. You can also animate objects on a slide by setting custom animations. To set custom animation effects, the target slide must be in Slide view.

4. Double-click **Slide 3** in Slide Sorter view, click **Slide Show** on the menu bar, then click **Custom Animation**
   The Custom Animation task pane opens, similar to Figure D-15. Objects that are already animated appear in the Custom Animation task pane list in the order in which they will be animated. **Animation tags** on the slide label the order in which elements are animated during a slide show.

5. Click the grouped **arrow object** to select it, then click **Add Effect** in the Custom Animation task pane
   A menu of animation effects appears.

6. Point to **Entrance**, then click **More Effects**
   The Add Entrance Effect dialog box opens. All of the effects in this dialog box allow an object to enter the slide using a special effect.

7. Scroll down to the **Exciting section**, click **Pinwheel**, then click **OK**
   The arrow object now has the pinwheel effect applied to it as shown in Figure D-15.

8. Run the Slide Show again from Slide 1
   The special effects make the presentation more interesting to view.

9. Click the **Slide Sorter View button** ⊞, click the **Zoom list arrow** on the Standard toolbar, then click **50**
   Figure D-16 shows the completed presentation in Slide Sorter view at 50% zoom.

10. Add your name as a footer on the notes and handouts, save your presentation, print it as handouts, six slides per page, then close the presentation and exit PowerPoint

QuickTip

Keep in mind that the animation effects you choose give a certain "flavor" to your presentation. They can be serious and businesslike or humorous. Choose appropriate effects for your presentation content and audience.

QuickTip

If you want the parts of a grouped object to fly in individually, then you must ungroup them first.

QuickTip

If you want to change the order in which objects are animated on the slide, select the object you want to change in the Custom Animation list in the task pane, then click the appropriate Re-Order arrow below the list.

FIGURE D-15: Screen with Custom Animation task pane open

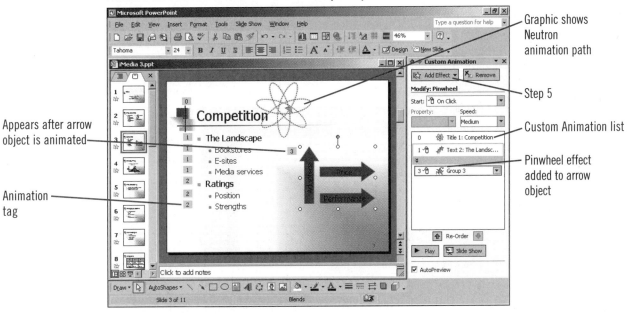

Graphic shows Neutron animation path

Step 5

Custom Animation list

Pinwheel effect added to arrow object

Appears after arrow object is animated

Animation tag

FIGURE D-16: Completed presentation in Slide Sorter view

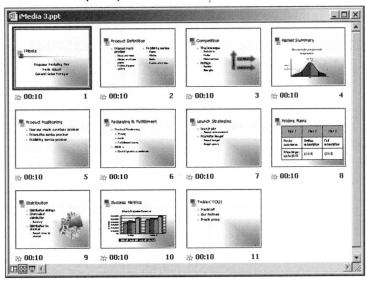

Presentation Checklist

You should always rehearse your slide show. If possible, rehearse your presentation in the room and with the computer that you will use. Use the following checklist to prepare for the slide show:

✓ Is **PowerPoint** or **PowerPoint Viewer** installed on the computer?

✓ Is your **presentation file** on the hard drive of the computer you will be using? Try putting a shortcut for the file on the desktop. Do you have a backup copy of your presentation file on a floppy disk?

✓ Is the **projection device** working correctly? Can the slides be seen from the back of the room?

✓ Do you know how to control **room lighting** so that the audience can see both your slides and their handouts and notes? You may want to designate someone to control the lights if the controls are not close to you.

✓ Will the **computer** be situated so you can advance and annotate the slides yourself? If not, designate someone to advance them for you.

✓ Do you have enough copies of your **handouts**? Bring extras. Decide when to hand them out, or whether you prefer to have them waiting at the audience members' places when they enter.

Practice

▶ Concepts Review

Label each element of the PowerPoint window shown in Figure D-17.

FIGURE D-17

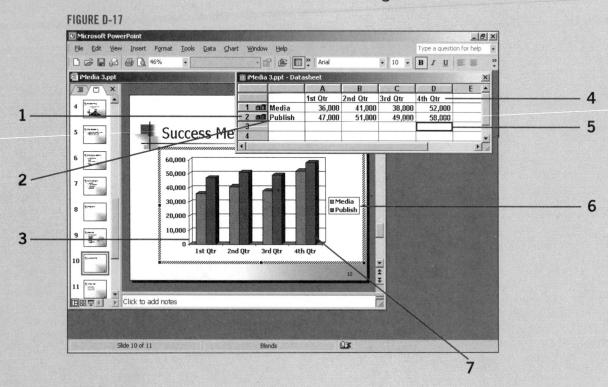

Match each term with the statement that describes it.

8. Chart
9. Embedded object
10. Animation effect
11. Data series markers
12. Clip Organizer
13. Scaling

a. Resizing an object by a specific percentage
b. A graphic representation of a datasheet
c. Graphic representations of data series
d. The special way text and objects appear on a slide
e. An object on a slide from which you can access another program's tools
f. A file index system that organizes images

Select the best answer from the list of choices.

14. PowerPoint animation effects let you control:
   a. The order in which text and objects are animated.
   b. The direction from which animated objects appear.
   c. Which text and images are animated.
   d. All of the above.

15. Which of the following is *not* true of a Microsoft Graph chart?
   a. A graph is made up of a datasheet and chart.
   b. You can double-click a chart to view its corresponding datasheet.
   c. An active cell has a black selection rectangle around it.
   d. You cannot import data from other programs into a datasheet.

▶ Skills Review

1. Insert clip art.

a. Open the presentation PPT D-3 from the drive and folder where your Project Files are stored, then save it as **CD Product Report**.

b. Go to Slide 2, search for CD clip art, then insert a piece of clip art.

c. On the Picture tab of the Format Picture dialog box, click the Color list arrow, then click Grayscale.

d. Drag the graphic so the top of the graphic aligns with the body text box and it is centered in the blank area on the right of the slide, then save your changes.

2. Insert, crop, and scale a picture.

a. Go to Slide 6 and insert the picture file PPT D-4.

b. Crop about ¾" off the left side of the picture.

c. Drag the graphic so its top is aligned with the top line of text.

d. Scale the graphic 25% larger than its original size.

e. Reposition the graphic, then make the white background transparent.

f. Save your changes.

3. Embed a chart.

a. Go to Slide 3, **2003 CD Sales by Quarter**, and apply the Title and Content layout.

b. Start Microsoft Graph.

c. Deselect the chart object and save your changes.

4. Enter and edit data in the datasheet.

a. Open Graph again.

b. Enter the information shown in Table D-4 into the datasheet.

c. Delete any unused rows of default data.

d. Place the data series in columns.

e. Save your changes.

TABLE D-4

	1st Qtr	2nd Qtr	3rd Qtr	4th Qtr
East Div.	12.5	10.6	11.9	15.2
West Div.	14.7	16.4	12.8	19.0

5. Format a chart.

a. Close the datasheet but leave Graph running.

b. Change the region names font on the X-axis to 20-point and regular font style (no bold).

c. Apply the Currency Style with no decimals to the values on the vertical axis.

d. Insert the chart title **Division Sales**.

e. Add the title **In Millions** to the Z-axis, then change the alignment of this label to vertical.

f. Change the legend text font to 16-point Arial font and regular font style (no bold).

g. Exit Graph and save your changes.

6. Create a table.

a. Insert a new slide after Slide 2 using the Title and Content slide layout.

b. Add the slide title **CD Sales by Type**.

c. Click the Insert Table button in the placeholder, then insert a table with two columns and five rows.

d. Enter **Type** in the first cell and **Sales** in the second cell in the first row.

e. In the left column, enter the following: **Rock, Pop, Classical**, and **Jazz/Blues**.

f. In the right column, add sales figures between 20,000 and 80,000 for each CD type.

g. Format the table using fills, horizontal and vertical alignment, and other features.

h. Save your changes.

7. Use slide show commands.

a. Begin the slide show at Slide 1, then proceed through the slide show to Slide 3.

b. On Slide 3, use the Pen to draw straight-line annotations under the labels on the horizontal axis.

c. Erase the pen annotations, then change the pointer back to an arrow.

d. Go to Slide 2 using the Go command on the Slide Show shortcut menu.

e. Press [End] to move to the last slide.

f. Return to Normal view.

8. Set slide show timings and transitions.

a. Switch to Slide Sorter view, then open the Slide Transition task pane.

b. Specify that all slides should advance after eight seconds.

c. Apply the Newsflash transition effect to all slides.

d. View the slide show to verify the transitions are correct, then save your changes.

9. Set slide animation effects.

a. Switch to Normal view, then open the Custom Animation task pane.

b. Switch to Slide 7, apply the (Entrance) Fly In animation effect to the Shuttle image, and the (Entrance) Ascend animation effect to the bulleted list. (*Hint*: Look in the Moderate section after clicking More effects.)

c. Go to Slide 2, apply the (Emphasis) Flicker animation effect to the text object. (*Hint*: Look in the Moderate section after clicking More effects.)

d. Apply the (Exit) Faded Zoom animation effect to the CD graphic. (*Hint*: Look in the Subtle section after clicking More effects.)

e. Run the slide show from the beginning to check the animation effects.

f. Add your name as a footer to the notes and handouts, then print the presentation as handouts (4 slides per page).

g. Save your changes, close the presentation, and exit PowerPoint.

▶ Independent Challenge 1

You are a financial management consultant for Pacific Coast Investments, located in San José, California. One of your primary responsibilities is to give financial seminars on different financial investments and how to determine which funds to invest in. In this challenge, you enhance the look of the slides by adding and formatting objects and adding animation effects and transitions.

a. Open the file PPT D-5 from the location where your Project Files are stored, and save it as **Fund Seminar**.

b. Add your name as the footer on all slides and handouts.

c. Apply the Title and Chart layout to Slide 6, and enter the data in Table D-5 into the datasheet.

d. Format the chart. Add titles as necessary.

e. Add an appropriate clip art item to Slide 2.

f. On Slide 4, use the Align and Group commands to organize the shapes.

TABLE D-5

	1 year	3 year	5 year	10 year
Bonds	4.2%	5.2%	7.9%	9.4%
Stocks	7.5%	8.3%	10.8%	12.6%
Mutual Funds	6.1%	6.3%	6.4%	6.1%

g. Spell check the presentation, then save it.

h. View the slide show, evaluate your presentation, and add a template of your choice. Make changes if necessary.

i. Set animation effects, slide transitions, and slide timings, keeping in mind that your audience includes potential investors who need the information you are presenting to make decisions about where to put their hard-earned money. View the slide show again.

j. Print the slides as handouts (6 slides per page), then close the presentation, and exit PowerPoint.

▶ Independent Challenge 2

You are the manager of the Maryland University Student Employment Office. The office is staffed by work-study students; new students start every semester. Create a presentation that you can use to train them.

a. Plan and create the slide presentation. As you plan your outline, make sure you include slides that will help explain to the work-study staff the main features of the office, including its employment database, library of company directories, seminars on employment search strategies, interviewing techniques, and resume development, as well as its student consulting and resume bulk-mailing services. Add more slides with more content if you wish.

b. Use an appropriate design template.

c. Add clip art and photographs available in the Clip Organizer to help create visual interest.

d. Save the presentation as **Student Employment** to the location where your Project Files are stored. View the slide show and evaluate the contents of your presentation. Make any necessary adjustments.

e. Add transitions, special effects, and timings to the presentation. Remember that your audience is university students who need to assimilate a lot of information in order to perform well in their new jobs. View the slide show again to evaluate the effects you added.

f. Add your name as a footer to slides and handouts. Spell check, save, and print the presentation as handouts (4 slides per page), then close the presentation and exit PowerPoint.

▶ Independent Challenge 3

You are the managing development engineer at JM Design, Inc, an international sports design company located in Ottawa, Ontario, Canada. JM Design designs and manufactures items such as bike helmets, bike racks, and kayak paddles, and markets these items primarily to countries in North America and Western Europe. You need to create a quarterly presentation that outlines the progress of the company's newest technologies, and present it.

a. Plan and create a slide show presentation that includes two new technologies.

b. Use an appropriate design template.

c. Add one chart and one table in the presentation that shows details (such as performance results, testing criteria, etc.) about the new technologies.

d. Include at least two slides that explain how the new technologies will appeal specifically to individual countries in the European and North American markets.

e. Use slide transitions, animation effects, and slide timings. View the slide show to evaluate the effects you added.

f. Add your name as a footer to the handouts. Save the presentation as **JM Design** to the location where your Project Files are stored. Print it as handouts (4 slides per page), then close the presentation and exit PowerPoint.

Independent Challenge 4

You work for Asset Advisors, a small investment firm. You have been asked to complete a basic investing presentation started by your boss. Most of the information has already been entered into the PowerPoint presentation; you just need to add a template and a table to complete the presentation. To find the data for the table, you need to use the Web to locate certain information.

You'll need to find the following information on the Web:
- Data for a table that compares the traditional IRA with the Roth IRA.
- Data for a table that compares at least two other retirement plans.

a. Open the file PPT D-6 from the location where your Project Files are stored, and save it as **Retirement Presentation**.
b. Connect to the Internet, then use a search engine to locate Web sites that have information on retirement plans. If your search does not produce any results, you might try the following sites:

www.vanguard.com
www.investorguide.com
www.quicken.com

c. Review at least two Web sites that contain information about retirement plans. Print the Home pages of the Web sites you use to gather data for your presentation.
d. Apply the Title and Table layout to Slide 7, then enter the data you found that compares the IRA retirement plans.
e. Apply the Title and Table layout to Slide 8, then enter the data you found that compares the other retirement plans.
f. Apply a template to the presentation, then customize the slide background and the color scheme.
g. Format the Autoshape objects on Slides 4 and 5.
h. Use text formatting to help emphasize important points, then add your name as a footer to the handouts.
i. Spell check the presentation, view the final presentation, save the final version, then print the handouts.

▶ Visual Workshop

Create a slide that looks like the example in Figure D-18. Add your name as a footer on the slide. Save the presentation as **Costs** to the location where your Project Files are stored.

FIGURE D-18

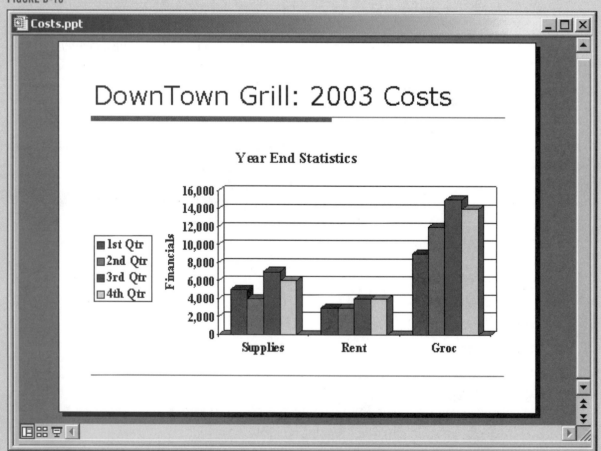

Integrating

Word, Excel, Access, and PowerPoint

Objectives

- ► Understand embedding and linking
- ► Insert a Word outline into a PowerPoint presentation
- ► Embed an Excel chart into a PowerPoint slide
- ► Link an Excel worksheet to a PowerPoint slide
- ► Update a linked Excel worksheet in PowerPoint
- ► Export a PowerPoint presentation to Word

PowerPoint can be easily integrated with the other Office programs. For example, to help you develop a PowerPoint presentation, you can insert a document from Word, or objects, such as an Excel worksheet, directly into the slides of your presentation. In this unit Maria Abbott, MediaLoft's general sales manager, creates a company status presentation that will be used at this year's executive meeting. To complete the presentation, Maria gathers some data herself and collects more from other employees at MediaLoft. Because everyone at MediaLoft uses Microsoft Office, Maria knows that all the files are compatible.

Understanding Embedding and Linking

Sometimes the easiest way to add information to a PowerPoint presentation is to insert information or an object created in another Office program. For example, you might have an existing Excel chart that you can insert to complete a presentation. There are two ways to add objects to the slides of your presentation; you can embed them or you can link them. The **source file** is the original file that contains the data or object that you want to paste, such as a chart in an Excel workbook or a table in a Word document. The **source program** is the program used to create the source file. The **destination file** is the file that the data or object is pasted into, and the **destination program** is the program used to create the destination file. ✎ Maria wants to learn more about embedding and linking.

► **Embedding objects**

When you **embed** an object, you are actually copying an object from its source file and pasting it into a destination file. Once embedded, an object becomes a part of the destination file, and the object is stored in the destination file. You can open the source program and manipulate an embedded object as long as you have access to the source program (either installed on your computer or over a network). Because an embedded object's data is stored in the destination file, the destination file's size increases relative to the file size of the embedded object. To embed an object in most Office programs, you use the Object command on the Insert menu, or you can use the Copy command in the source file and the Paste or Paste Special command in the destination file.

► **Linking objects**

When you **link** an object to a PowerPoint slide, a representation, or picture, of the object is placed on the slide instead of the actual object; this representation of the object is connected, or linked, to the original file. The object is still stored in the source file, unlike an embedded object that is stored directly in a slide. Any changes you make to a linked object's source file are reflected in the linked object. You can open the source file and make changes to the linked object as long as you have access to the source program (either installed on your computer or over a network), and to the source file. To link an object to most Office programs, you use the Object command on the Insert menu, and then click the Link check box in the Insert Object dialog box. You can also copy the object in its source program, click the Paste Special command on the Edit menu in the destination file, and then click the Paste Link option button. The differences between embedding and linking are summarized in Table C-1.

► **Editing embedded and linked objects**

To edit an embedded object, double-click the object. The source program starts, and the menu and toolbars of the source program appear. Changes made to an embedded object in its source program are reflected in the destination file, but these modifications do not affect the original object in the source file because embedded objects have no link to their source files. See Figure C-1.

To edit a linked object, double-click the object to open its source file in its source program, and then make your changes. Close the linked object's source program window when you are finished making changes. The changes made to a linked file are reflected in both the source file and in the linked object in the destination file. See Figure C-2.

FIGURE C-1: Embedding an object

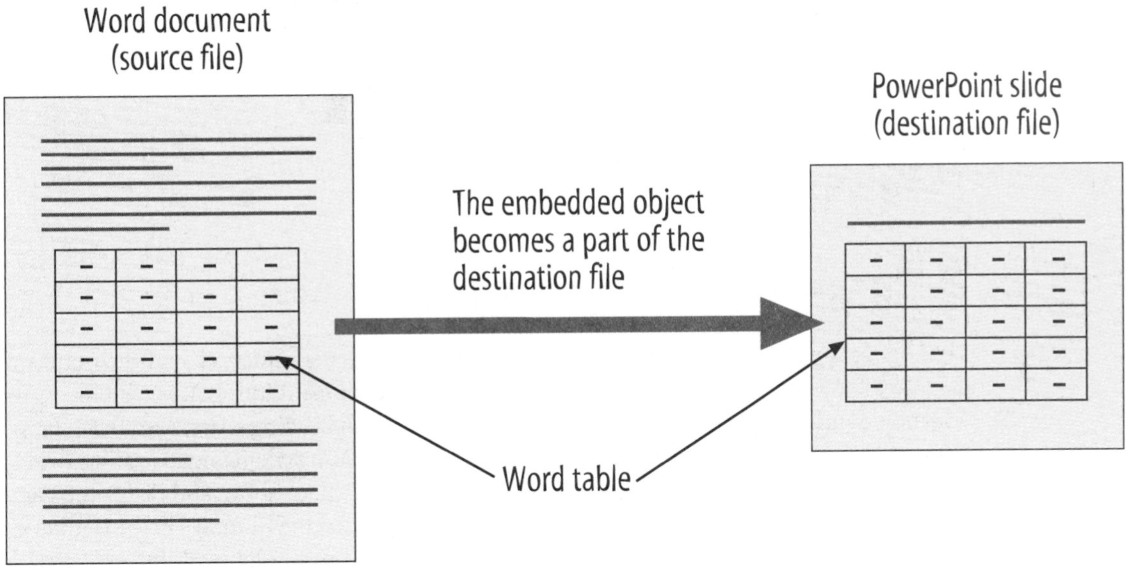

Word document
(source file)

PowerPoint slide
(destination file)

The embedded object
becomes a part of the
destination file

Word table

FIGURE C-2: Linking an object

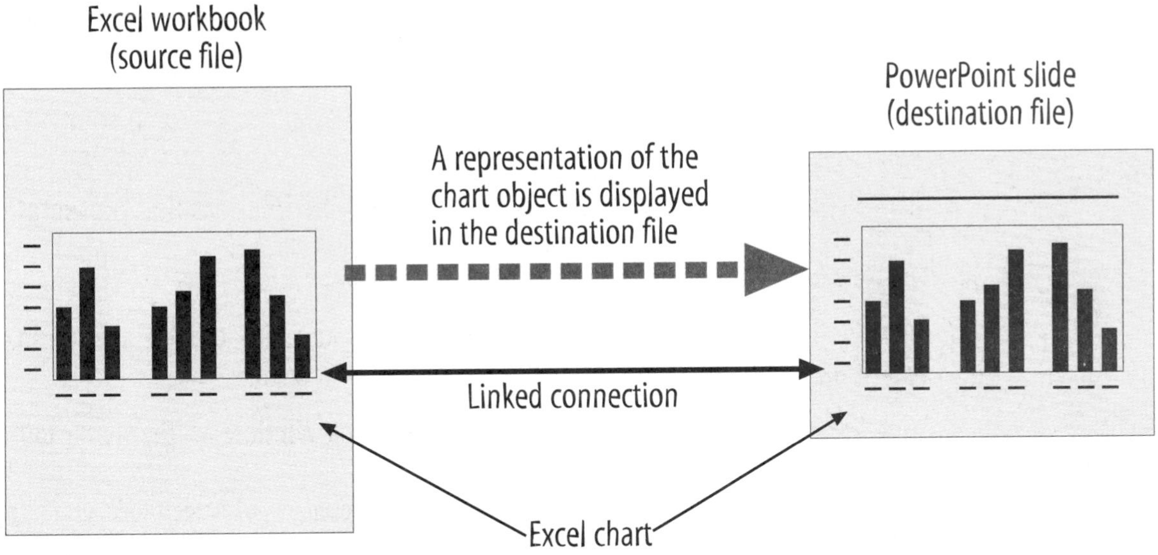

Excel workbook
(source file)

PowerPoint slide
(destination file)

A representation of the
chart object is displayed
in the destination file

Linked connection

Excel chart

TABLE C-1: Embedding vs. Linking

action	situation
Embed	You are the only user of an object, and you want the object to be a part of your presentation.
Embed	You want to access the object in its source program, even if the source file is not available.
Embed	You want to update the object manually while working in PowerPoint.
Link	You always want your object to have the latest information.
Link	The object's source file is shared on a network or where other users have access to the file and can change it.
Link	You want to keep your presentation file size small.

Inserting a Word Outline into a PowerPoint Presentation

Although it is very easy to create an outline in PowerPoint, it is unnecessary if the outline already exists in a Word document. You can easily insert a Word document into PowerPoint to create a presentation outline. The Word document can be formatted with heading styles. A **style** is a named collection of font attributes and paragraph formats; for example, a style named Heading 1 might be a paragraph formatted as 16-point, bold Arial font with extra space above and below the paragraph. When you insert a Word outline formatted with heading styles, the headings in the outline are converted to text levels in PowerPoint. For example, every Word paragraph with the style Heading 1 is converted to a new slide, and every Word paragraph with the style Heading 2 is converted to a subpoint under a slide title. If the Word outline you are inserting doesn't use styles, the outline is converted into slides based on the structure of the document; that is, each new paragraph indicates a new slide, and each new paragraph followed by a tab indicates a subpoint. Maria inserts a Word outline created by Alice Wegman, MediaLoft's marketing manager, into her presentation.

Steps

1. Start PowerPoint

A new blank presentation opens.

2. Click the **Choose presentation hyperlink** under New from existing presentation in the task pane

The New from Existing Presentation dialog box opens.

3. Open the file **INT C-1.ppt** from the location where your Project Files are stored, then save it as **Company Status**

> **Trouble?**
>
> Close any other open presentations, then repeat Step 5.

4. Click **View** on the menu bar, click **Task Pane**, click **Window** on the menu bar, then click **Arrange All**

Now your screen matches the figures in this unit. Compare your screen to Figure C-3. The presentation currently contains two slides.

5. Click anywhere in the text of **Slide 2** in the Outline tab

When you insert the Word document, it begins with a new slide after the current slide.

6. Click **Insert** on the menu bar, then click **Slides from Outline**

The Insert Outline dialog box opens.

> **Trouble?**
>
> If you see a message saying that PowerPoint needs to install this feature, insert your Office CD in the appropriate drive and click Yes. Ask your instructor or technical support person for assistance.

7. Select the file **INT C-2.doc** from the location where your Project Files are stored, click **Insert**, then scroll in the Outline tab to see the new slides

The Word document is inserted as five new slides. See Figure C-4. You can insert a Word document in the Slide or Outline tab in Normal view. Once an outline is inserted into a presentation, you can edit it as if it had been created in PowerPoint.

8. Make sure **Slide 3** is selected in the Outline tab, click the **Slides tab**, then click the thumbnails for **Slides 4-7** to view each new slide

FIGURE C-3: Maria's slide presentation

Presentation contains two slides

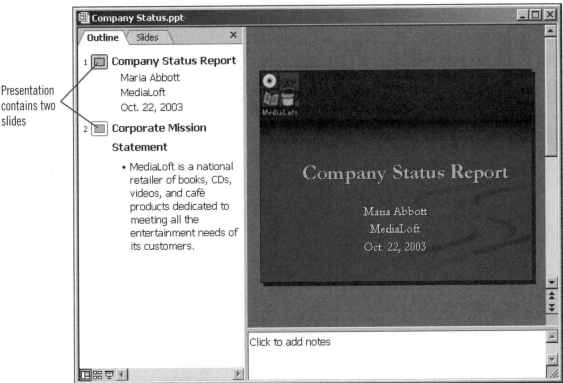

FIGURE C-4: New slides inserted in the Outline tab

Slides inserted from Word outline

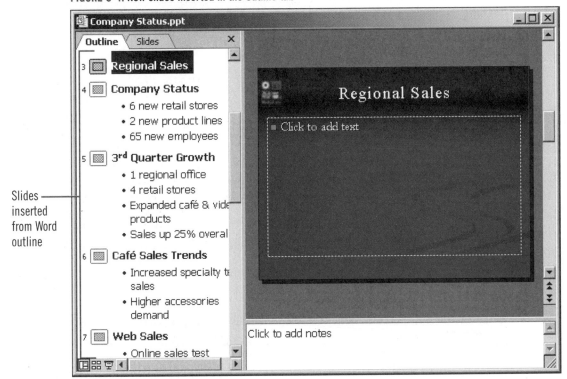

Embedding an Excel Chart into a PowerPoint Slide

You can easily embed an Excel chart into a PowerPoint presentation. Because it is embedded, you can double-click a chart to edit it using Excel tools. The original Excel chart object remains unchanged. Maria decides to include in her presentation an Excel chart that she received from the Accounting Department. She wants to format the chart after she adds it to her presentation, so she embeds it.

Steps

1. Click the **Slide 3 thumbnail** on the Slides tab, click the **Other Task Panes list arrow** on the task pane title bar, click **Slide Layout**, then click the **Title Only layout** under Text Layouts

2. Click **Insert** on the menu bar, then click **Object**
   The Insert Object dialog box opens.

QuickTip

You can reposition the chart on the slide by dragging it.

3. Click the **Create from file option button**, click **Browse**, select the file **INT C-3.xls** from the location where your Project Files are stored, click **OK**, then click **OK** in the Insert Object dialog box
   The Excel chart appears on the slide. Compare your screen to Figure C-5.

4. Click the **Fill Color list arrow** on the Drawing toolbar, then click the **light purple square (labeled Follow Title Text Scheme Color)**
   The chart text would be more readable if it were larger.

Trouble?

If the Chart toolbar does not appear, click View on the menu bar, point to Toolbars, then click Chart.

5. Double-click the **chart object**
   The PowerPoint menu bar and toolbars are replaced with the Excel menu bar and toolbars, and the Excel Chart toolbar appears.

6. Click the **Chart Objects list arrow** [Chart Area] on the Chart toolbar, click **Chart Title**, click the **Format Chart Title button** on the Chart toolbar, click the **Font tab**, click **28** in the Size list, then click **OK**
   The change in the Excel chart is reflected in the embedded object in PowerPoint. Because this is an embedded object, editing the object does not alter the original Excel file.

7. Double-click the **vertical axis** to open the Format Axis dialog box, click the **Font tab**, click **16** in the Size list, click **OK**, then repeat this for the **horizontal axis**

8. Repeat Step 7 to make the **legend** larger, then resize the legend to display all the text, if necessary

9. Drag the corner selection handles and reposition the worksheet object until it is approximately the same size and in the same position as in Figure C-6

10. Click outside the chart object to exit Excel, then click outside the chart object again to deselect it
    Compare your slide to Figure C-6.

FIGURE C-5: Embedded chart object

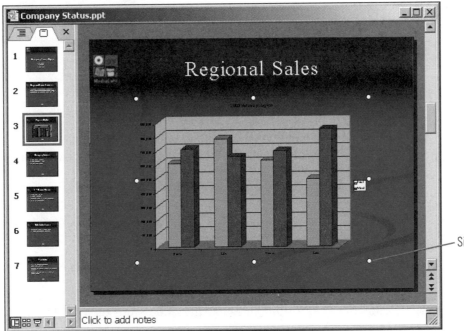

Sizing handle

FIGURE C-6: Formatted Excel chart embedded in a slide

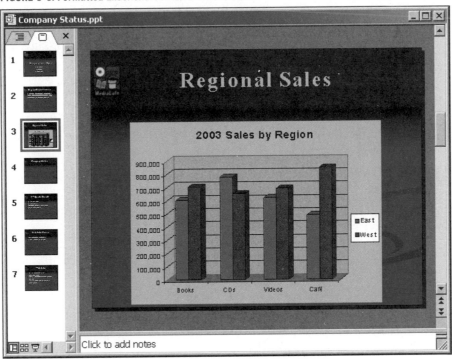

CLUES TO USE

Embedding objects using Paste Special

You can also embed an object or selected information from another Office program into PowerPoint by copying and pasting the information. For example, assume that you want to embed a worksheet from an Excel file. Open the Excel file that contains the worksheet, select the worksheet, and copy it to the Clipboard. Open your PowerPoint presentation, click Edit on the menu bar, click Paste Special, then click OK in the Paste Special dialog box.

Linking an Excel Worksheet to a PowerPoint Slide

You can connect objects to your presentation by establishing a link between the file that created the object and the PowerPoint presentation that contains the object. When you modify a linked object, either in its source file or in the destination file, the object changes in both files when you update the link. Maria needs to insert an Excel worksheet from Jeff Shimada, the director of café operations, into her presentation. Jeff saved the worksheet to MediaLoft's company network of computers. Maria decides to link the worksheet because she knows Jeff will have to update the worksheet before the presentation.

Steps

QuickTip

If you plan to do the steps in this unit again, be sure to make a copy of the Excel file Cafe Profit before you proceed.

1. Click the **Slide 6 thumbnail** on the Slides tab, then change the layout to **Title and Text over Content** under Text and Content layouts in the task pane

2. Click **Insert** on the menu bar, then click **Object**
   The Insert Object dialog box opens. You want to create a linked object from an existing file.

3. Click the **Create from file option button**, click **Browse**, select the file **Cafe Profit.xls** from the location where your Project Files are stored, then click **OK**

4. Click the **Link check box** in the Insert Object dialog box to select it
   Compare your screen to Figure C-7.

5. Click **OK**
   The Excel worksheet is linked to the PowerPoint slide. The worksheet would be easier to read if it were larger.

Trouble?

If Excel opens while you are trying to resize or move the worksheet, click the Close button in the Excel program window.

6. Drag the corner selection handles and reposition the worksheet object until it is approximately the same size and in the same position as in Figure C-8
   The chart text is difficult to read against the dark background.

7. Click the **Fill Color list arrow** on the Drawing toolbar, click the **white color cell** (second from left), then click a blank area of the slide to deselect the object
   Compare your screen to Figure C-8.

8. Save your work

FIGURE C-7: **Insert Object dialog box**

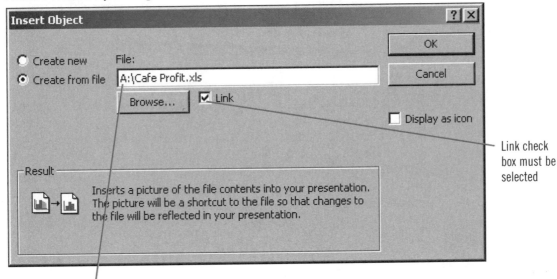

Link check box must be selected

Excel worksheet filename appears here

FIGURE C-8: **Formatted Excel worksheet linked to a slide**

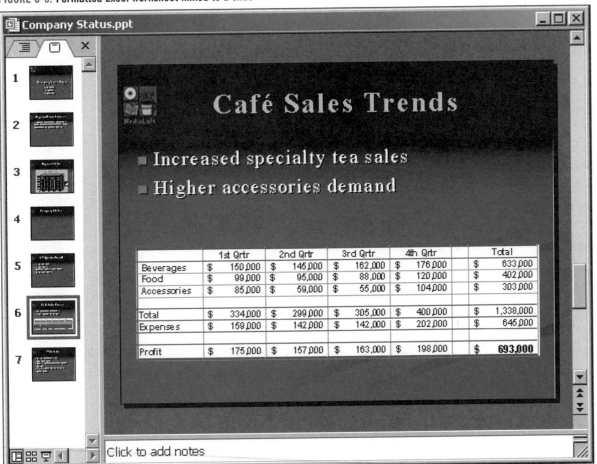

Updating a Linked Excel Worksheet in PowerPoint

To edit or change the information in a linked object, you must open the object's source file. You can open the object's source file and the program it was created in by double-clicking the linked object in the destination file. If you modify a linked object's source file in the source file program, PowerPoint asks you if you want to automatically update the file in the linked presentation the next time you open the PowerPoint file. ✒️ Maria needs to update the linked worksheet because the wrong number was reported for accessory sales for the third quarter.

Steps

Trouble?

To edit or open a linked object in your presentation, the object's source program and source file must be available on your computer or network.

1. Double-click the **worksheet object** on slide 6
   Excel opens in a small window, showing the linked worksheet, and the Excel program button appears on the taskbar.

2. Click the **Maximize button** ▢ in the Excel program window if necessary

3. Click cell **D4**, type **74,000**, then press **[Enter]**
   The number you typed appears in cell D4. Notice that the numbers in cells D6, D9, G4, and G9 all change to reflect the new number in cell D4.

4. Click the **Close button** ☒ in the Excel program window, then click **Yes** to save the changes
   Microsoft Excel closes, and the linked Excel worksheet shows the change you made in Excel. If you opened the file named Cafe Profit.xls in Excel, you would see this same change in the worksheet. Compare your screen to Figure C-9.

5. Click the **Spelling button** ✓ on the Standard toolbar and correct any spelling errors in the presentation

6. Click the **Save button** 🖫 on the Standard toolbar to save the changes you made

7. Click the **Slide Sorter View button** ⊞ below the Slide tab, click in the **Zoom box** on the Standard toolbar, type **50**, then press **[Enter]**
   Compare your screen to Figure C-10. You changed the zoom percentage so you can see all of the slides in the window.

8. Double-click **Slide 1**, then click the **Slide Show button** 🖵 and view the final presentation

9. Add your name as a footer to all slides and handouts

10. Click **File** on the menu bar, click **Print**, select **Pure Black and White** in the Color/grayscale list, select **Handouts** in the Print what list, select **3 Slides per page**, then click **OK** to print the slides

FIGURE C-9: Data change reflected in linked worksheet

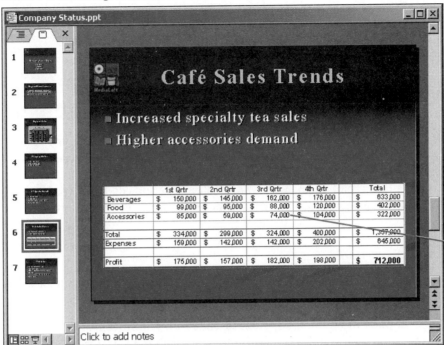

Modified data in Excel worksheet

FIGURE C-10: The final presentation in Slide Sorter view

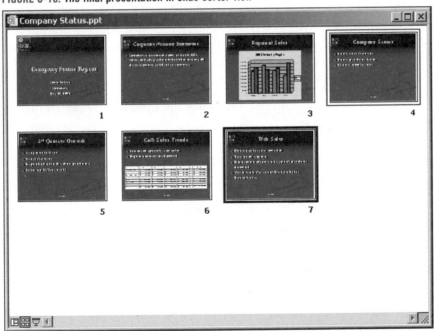

Updating links

If the PowerPoint file is closed when you change the source file, the linked object will still be able to reflect the changes you made in the source file. When you open the file containing the linked object, a dialog box opens reminding you that the file contains links and asking if you want to update the links now. Click OK to update the links, or click Cancel to leave the linked object unchanged. If you choose Cancel, you can still update the link later. Click Edit on the menu bar, then click Links to open the Links dialog box. Click the filename of the link you want to update, then click Update Now.

Exporting a PowerPoint Presentation to Word

You can export a PowerPoint presentation to Word. When you choose the Send To Microsoft Word command on the File menu, Word starts and the outline of the current PowerPoint presentation is exported to a Word document. You can choose one of five layouts for the Word document. Once the PowerPoint outline is in Word, you can save and edit the document. ✎⃝▬▬ Maria wants to create handouts with blank lines so the audience can take notes during the presentation.

1. Click File on the menu bar, point to Send To, then click Microsoft Word

The Send to Microsoft Word dialog box opens, similar to Figure C-11.

> **QuickTip**
>
> To print speaker notes with your slides, choose either the Notes next to slides option or the Notes below slides option. To print fewer pages, choose the Notes next to slides option or the Blank lines next to slide option; the slides will print three per page.

2. Click the Blank lines next to slides option button

You want your handouts to automatically reflect any changes you make to the presentation.

3. Click the Paste link option button at the bottom of the dialog box

4. Click OK

Microsoft Word opens, and the slides appear in a table in a new document. This process may take a little while to complete. See Figure C-12. The slide numbers are in the first column, the slides are in the second column, and blank lines appear next to the slides in the third column. There are three slides per page.

5. Select the first column, then click the Bold button B on the Formatting toolbar

6. Press [Ctrl][End], then type your name

7. Save the Word file as Handouts for Status Meeting to the drive and location where your Project Files are stored

8. Click the Print button 🖶 on the Standard toolbar

The handouts print.

9. Click the Close button on the Word program window, then click the Close button on the PowerPoint program window, saving changes if prompted

The programs close.

FIGURE C-11: **Send to Microsoft Word dialog box**

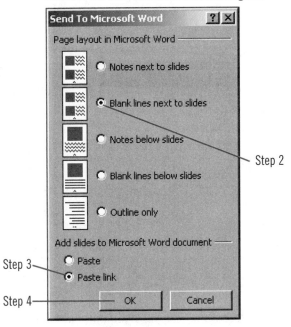

Step 2

Step 3

Step 4

FIGURE C-12: **Exported PowerPoint presentation in Word**

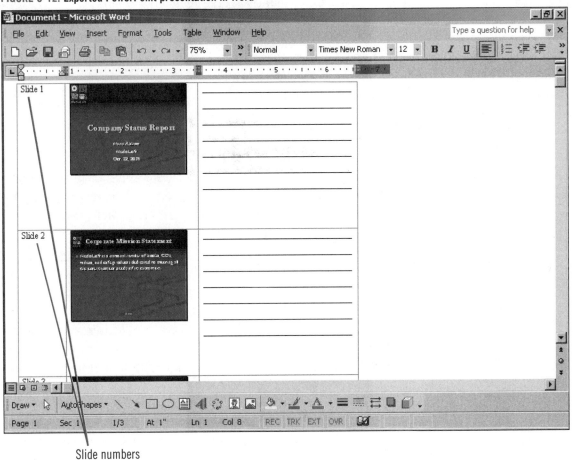

Slide numbers

Independent Challenge 1

You are responsible for recommending which software packages your company should purchase. You have decided to recommend Microsoft Office. Create a PowerPoint presentation illustrating the advantages of each program in the Microsoft Office suite. Your presentation should also contain slides that show how first-time computer users feel about computers and why Microsoft Office is a good choice for them. Information about first-time computer users is provided in the Word file INT C-4.doc in the location where your Project Files are stored. Think about what you want the presentation to say and what graphics you want to use.

a. Plan your presentation, determining its purpose and the look that will help communicate your message.

b. Start PowerPoint, create a presentation, insert your name as the footer on all slides and handouts, then save the presentation as **Office Review** to the location where your Project Files are stored.

c. Insert the Word document INT C-4.doc into your presentation outline. This file contains information about how first-time computer users feel about computers.

d. Add slides explaining why Office is a good choice for your company and explaining the advantages of each of the Office suite programs. Your final presentation should contain at least 10 slides.

e. Create the title slide for your presentation, then save your work.

f. Add an appropriate design template, graphics, and slide show special effects to the presentation. Check each of the slides created from the outline and make sure they convey the information clearly.

g. Check the spelling in your presentation.

h. Run the slide show and evaluate your presentation. Is your message clear? Are the slides visually appealing? Make any changes necessary and save the presentation.

i. Print the slides and outline of your presentation, then close all open files and programs.

 ## Independent Challenge 2

To augment the Census Bureau's data on marriage and birthrate statistics, you have been asked to prepare a PowerPoint presentation that will run continuously in the lobby at the local census office. Charts on the data need to be linked to PowerPoint slides because data is occasionally updated. Use the data found in the two worksheets in the Excel file INT C-5.xls in the location where your Project Files are stored. Create a presentation that explains this data.

a. Start Excel, open the file INT C-5.xls from the location where your Project Files are stored, then save it as **Statistics**.

b. Create at least four charts using the data in the Marriages worksheet, and create one chart using the data in the Birthrates worksheet.

c. Examine the data and the charts you created, then create a new Word document containing an outline for your presentation. Summarize the data and explain what the charts show.

d. Type your name at the top of the document, save it as **Stat Outline** to the location where your Project Files are stored, then print this outline.

e. Start PowerPoint and open a new presentation. Apply a template of your choice. Insert your name as a footer on all slides and handouts, then save it as **Bureau** to the location where your Project Files are stored.

f. Create a title slide for the presentation, then insert the file Stat Outline.doc into the presentation.

g. Link the four charts in the Marriages worksheet to slides in the presentation. Update one of the numbers in the worksheet from within PowerPoint and verify that the number in the presentation is also updated.

h. Add the chart in the Birthrates worksheet to a slide in the presentation.

i. Create handouts in Word so the audience can take notes. Link the presentation in case you make changes. Type your name as the last line in the file, then save this file as **Bureau Handouts** to the location where your Project Files are stored.

j. Switch back to the presentation, then add slide show special effects, such as transitions and animation effects, to the slides.

k. Check the spelling in your presentation, then run the final slide show and evaluate your presentation.

l. Save and print the slides of your presentation.

m. Switch back to the Bureau Handouts file in Word, update the link, then save and print the document. (*Hint*: To update the link, use the Links command on the Edit menu.)

n. Close all open files and programs, saving any changes.

▶ Independent Challenge 3

You have been hired as an associate in the Marketing department at Nomad Ltd, an outdoor sporting gear and adventure travel company. Nomad recently completed a big marketing campaign promoting its bicycle tour packages. Nomad now needs to focus in its other tour packages. Sales of some tour packages, such as bungee jumping, have decreased lately. Concerned about the falling sales, the Nomad board of directors has suggested adding rock climbing and jeep tours to the Nomad tour line to broaden Nomad's customer base. Your job is to develop a marketing presentation that addresses these concerns.

You decide to send a questionnaire to customers who have taken tour packages to ask how they can be improved. You need several charts to show tour trends and the potential sales for the new tours.

a. Start Word and open the file INT C-6.doc from the drive and location where your Project Files are stored. Add your name to the bottom of the letter, then save it as **Cover Letter**. This is the cover letter for the questionnaire.

b. Use the Insert Picture command to add the Nomad logo to the top of the letter. The logo, named Nomad.tif, is in the location where your Project Files are stored. Save your changes, then close the document.

c. Start Access and open the file Customer Data from the location where your Project Files are stored. Create a query that lists all of the information about customers who have taken the bungee tour. Save the query as **Bungee Customers**.

d. Use Mail Merge to merge the cover letter and the Access query you have created. Insert the date and appropriate merge fields in the cover letter. Save the merged file, print the first letter, then close the merged file.

e. Start Excel and open the INT C-7.xls file from the location where your Project Files are stored. Save it as **Tour Type**. This worksheet contains data for road bike, mountain bike, and bungee tour sales. Create two charts on this worksheet: one that compares the sales numbers of the tours and the other that shows the tours as a percentage of all tours. Use drawing tools and color, if appropriate, to point out weak sales. Name this worksheet **Current**.

f. Copy the data from the Current worksheet to a new worksheet. In the new worksheet, add a formula that calculates an increase in the bungee tour sales numbers by 20%, then show this increase in your charts. Use drawing tools and color, if appropriate, to indicate which figures are speculative. Name this worksheet **Bungee Increase**.

g. Copy the increased bungee tour sales data to another new worksheet, then add two more rows for the rock climbing and jeep tours. Assume that their sales equal the sales of the increased bungee tour sales. Create two more charts to show the new tours. Name this worksheet **New Tours**.

h. Add titles to all three charts to identify them. Use drop shadows and other formatting effects to make them more attractive.

i. Start PowerPoint and create a new presentation. Save it as **Tour Evaluation** to the location where your Project Files are stored. This presentation illustrates your marketing ideas to increase sales.

j. Create a title slide, then insert the Word outline INT C-8.doc from the location where your Project Files are stored. Add to the outline your own ideas on how to strengthen bungee tour sales and generate new sales for the new tours. You can suggest additional tours, too.

k. Include any relevant Excel charts on your slides by using the method you feel is best: linking or embedding. Use drawing tools and color, if appropriate, to point out the new tours.

l. Use templates, clip art, animation effects, and any other PowerPoint features you want to create an effective and professional-looking presentation.

m. Insert your name as a footer on all sides and handouts, then print the presentation as handouts (six slides per page).

n. Save and close all files, then close all open programs.

Independent Challenge 4

You work for Royal Canadian Tours, a travel agency in Calgary, Alberta, Canada. Your agency specializes in railroad tour packages throughout Canada. To prepare for a large convention you need to develop a PowerPoint presentation that illustrates the primary rail tours your company offers. You need to develop a 10-slide presentation that briefly describes your company and at least two rail tour packages your company offers. To find data for your presentation, you need to use the Web to locate certain information.

You'll need to find the following information on the Web:

- General data for a table that compares at least two rail tour packages
- Schedule and destination locations
- Information about services provided on the train, as well as information about attractions along the route

a. Connect to the Internet, then use a search engine to locate Web sites that have information on Canadian rail tours. If your search does not produce any results, you might try the following sites:

www.cprtours.com

www.rkymtnrail.com

www.viarail.ca

Review at least two Web sites that contain information about rail tour packages. Print the Home pages of the Web sites you use to gather data for your presentation.

b. Start Word, add your name to the bottom of the document, then save it as **Rail Tours** to the location where your Project Files are stored. This is the outline for your presentation.

c. Create an outline with the information you've gathered on the Internet. Remember to include enough information for at least 10 slides.

d. Insert the outline into a new PowerPoint presentation and save it as **Royal Tours** to the location where your Project Files are stored.

e. Two slides should include information on schedules and destination cities.

f. Create a new slide, title it **Royal Tours Comparison**, then create a table that compares the features of at least two tour packages.

g. Create a new Excel worksheet and save it as **Royal Tours Data** to the drive and folder where your Project Files are stored. Create a worksheet that identifies the number of people that have toured using the Royal Canadian Tours rail packages over the last three years. Name this worksheet **RCT Tours**. Create your own data, but assume that the number of people have ranged between 10,000 and 50,000, depending on the cost of the tour package. Give a total number of people at the bottom of the worksheet for each year. Link this worksheet to a slide in the presentation.

h. Use templates, clip art, transitions, and any other PowerPoint features you want to create an effective and professional-looking presentation.

i. Insert your name as a footer on all slides and handouts in the presentation, then save and print the presentation as handouts, two slides per page.

j. Save and close all files, then close all open programs.

Integrating

Office Applications with Internet Explorer

Objectives

► **Plan a Web publication**
► **Create a Web page**
► **Format a Web page**
► **Create a Web page from a Word document**
► **Create a Web page from an Access table**
► **Create a Web page from an Excel workbook**
► **Create Web pages from a PowerPoint presentation**
► **Add hyperlinks**

The Web page features of Office XP give you the tools to easily create professional Web pages from scratch or to convert existing Office documents into Web pages. A **Web page** is a file that can be stored on a special computer called a **Web server** so it can be viewed on the World Wide Web or an intranet using a browser. Web pages use **Hypertext Markup Language (HTML)** formatting. HTML is the programming language used to describe how each element of a Web page should appear when viewed with a browser. ━━━ Karen Rosen is the director of human resources at MediaLoft. Karen wants to create a set of Web pages that she will eventually post, or **publish**, on the MediaLoft intranet to help new employees learn more about employee benefits and programs. Karen uses Office XP to create the Web pages.

Planning a Web Publication

A **Web publication** is a group of associated Web pages focused on a particular theme or topic. It is important to plan your Web pages carefully before creating them. Planning a Web publication involves thinking about the content to include, determining the design to use, sketching the organization of the Web pages, and including the links between them.  Karen plans the content and organization of her Web pages and outlines the steps involved in creating the Web publication and posting it to the MediaLoft intranet.

Details

In planning her Web pages, Karen is careful to:

► **Sketch each Web page**

Draw a sketch of how you want each page to look and diagram the links between pages. Karen identifies the content that will be useful to employees. She then determines the documents she wants to include on the intranet, sketches the layout, and adds notes, as shown in Figure D-1.

► **Create each Web page**

You can save an existing Office file as a Web page, or you can start with a blank document and create a new Web page. Word includes Web page templates that make it easy to create many standard types of Web pages from scratch. If you want to create a Web page from an existing file, you can use the features in each Office program to convert the file to HTML. Karen will create a new Web page in Word and then convert several existing Office files to HTML files.

► **Format each Web page**

You can use Word to edit most Web page documents—even those not created in Word—and to add images and apply visual themes and backgrounds to Web pages. Karen will use the tools available in Word to enhance the appearance of the Web pages in her Web publication. She will apply a common visual theme to each Web page and insert the MediaLoft company logo on the Welcome page.

► **View each Web page using a browser**

Before finalizing the content and design of each Web page, view the Web page in your browser to make sure it is readable and formatted properly. If necessary, you can use Word to make editing and formatting corrections. Karen will view the Web pages in Internet Explorer to make sure they look as expected.

► **Format hyperlinks**

Once you have finalized the text and graphics of your Web pages, you can add hyperlinks to connect them. Before publishing your Web publication, view it again in your browser to test each hyperlink and make sure it works as you intended. Karen's sketch indicates that she will create links between the home page, which is the Welcome page, and each Web page in the publication. Also, she will eventually create links to the MediaLoft Training page and to the MediaLoft Human Resources page after publishing the Web publication on the MediaLoft intranet.

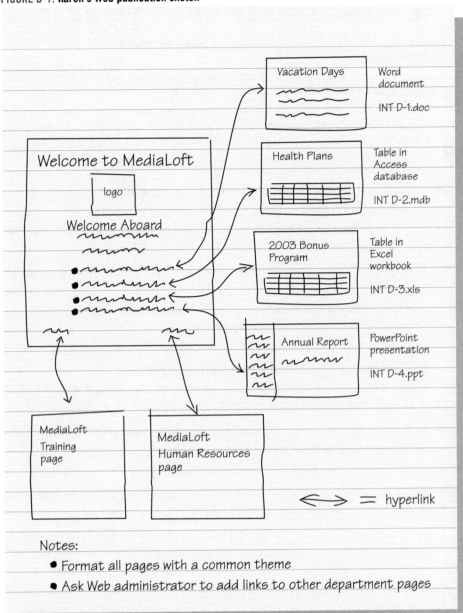

Naming Web Pages

Determining the filenaming conventions and the folder structure you will use for your Web pages is an important aspect of planning a Web publication. Different operating systems place different restrictions on filenames, so it's important to find out what operating system your Web server uses and name your files accordingly. It's safest to name Web pages using the standard eight-dot-three naming convention, which specifies that a filename have a maximum of eight letters followed by a period and three-letter file extension – mypage.htm or chap_1.htm, for example. Therefore, if you intend to publish to the Web, filenames should use all lowercase letters and include no special characters or blank spaces. Valid characters include letters, numbers, and the underscore character. It's also advisable to create a system for naming the Web pages in a large Web publication so that you can easily locate and organize the files.

Unit D

Integration

Creating a Web Page

To create a Web page, you must create a document that uses HTML formatting. HTML places codes, called **tags**, around the elements of a Web page to describe how each element should appear when viewed using a browser. When you create an HTML document in Word, Word automatically inserts the HTML tags for you. A quick way to create a Web page in Word is to start with a Web page template. Word includes templates for many standard types of Web pages, such as a table of contents page or a frequently asked questions (FAQ) page. ➤ Karen uses a Web page template in Word to create the basic structure of the home page, the MediaLoft Welcome page. When completed, the Welcome page will include links to the other Web pages.

Steps

Trouble?

If the New Document task pane is not open, click File on the menu bar, then click New.

1. **Start Word, click the General Templates hyperlink in the New Document task pane, then click the Web Pages tab in the Templates dialog box**
   The Web Pages tab of the Templates dialog box, shown in Figure D-2, includes templates for creating different types and styles of Web pages. It also includes the Web Page Wizard.

2. **Click the Simple Layout icon, verify that the Create New Document option button is selected, then click OK**
   A new Web page document based on the Simple Layout template opens in the document window in Web Layout view. Web Layout view displays a document as it would look when viewed in a Web browser. The text is placeholder text that you will replace with your own information.

3. **Click Format on the menu bar, then click Theme**
   The Theme dialog box opens and displays a list of themes. A **theme** is a predesigned set of formats that you can apply to Web pages to give them a consistent look.

Trouble?

Choose a different theme if Willow is not available to you.

4. **Scroll to the bottom of the Choose a Theme list box, click Willow, examine the preview that appears in the Sample of theme Willow box, then click OK**
   The Willow theme is applied to the Web page.

QuickTip

If you want your name on the printed solution, add it to the page title when you save the Web pages.

5. **Click the Save button 🖫 on the Standard toolbar, click Change Title in the Save As dialog box, type Welcome to MediaLoft in the Set Page Title dialog box, then click OK**
   The page title appears in the title bar when the Web page is viewed with a browser, so it's important to assign a page title that not only describes the Web page but that you would want visitors to see.

Trouble?

The file extension might not appear in your title bar; Windows can be set to display or not display file extensions.

6. **Drag to select Simple Web Page.htm in the File name text box, type Welcome, make sure the drive and folder where your Project Files are stored is displayed in the Save in list box, then click Save**
   The document file is saved as a Web page in HTML format. The filename Welcome.htm appears in the title bar when the document is viewed in Word. Word automatically created a folder named Welcome_files in the same location as the HTML file to contain all the files used in the Web page, such as the files for the graphics, background, bullets, and other Web page elements.

7. **Select Main Heading Goes Here, type Welcome to MediaLoft, select Section 1 Heading Goes Here, type Welcome Aboard, replace the next paragraph with the paragraph shown in Figure D-3, press [Enter] twice, then type the four-line list shown in Figure D-3**
   Later you will format each item in the list as a hyperlink to another Web page.

8. **Press [Enter] twice, type MediaLoft Training page, press [Enter], then type MediaLoft Human Resources page**
   Later you will format these items to create hyperlinks to the Training page and to the Human Resources page.

9. **Use the pointer to select the remaining placeholder text, press [Delete], then click** 🖫

FIGURE D-2: Web Pages tab in Templates dialog box

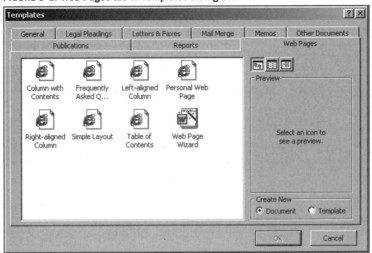

FIGURE D-3: Text entered for the Welcome page

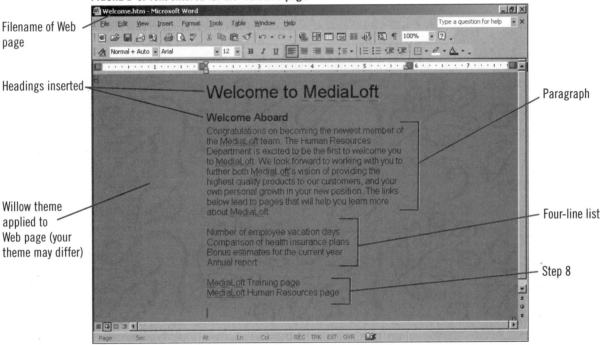

Filename of Web page

Headings inserted

Willow theme applied to Web page (your theme may differ)

Paragraph

Four-line list

Step 8

Choosing Web page content and style

Examining the style, layout, and content of other Web pages can inspire new ideas about how to present information in your own Web publications. A well-designed Web page is not only readable and eye-catching, but communicates a visual message that complements the purpose of the Web publication. By viewing a wide variety of Web pages, you will develop a sense of what kinds of styles, formats, and elements help to communicate messages effectively. When creating a Web publication, keep in mind that the design and tone of your Web pages express your personality or the character of your company to the world.

Unit
D

Integration

Formatting a Web Page

When you format an HTML document in Word, you use the same tools you use to format print documents. For example, when you apply bold to text by using the Bold button on the Formatting toolbar, Word automatically inserts the HTML tags necessary for the Web browser to interpret and then display the text as bold. ✎ Karen uses Word's formatting tools to enhance the appearance of her Web page. She also inserts the MediaLoft logo in the Web page.

Steps

1. Select the heading **Welcome to MediaLoft**, click the **Bold button** **B** on the Formatting toolbar, then click the **Center button** on the Formatting toolbar
   The heading text becomes darker and thicker and is centered between the left and right margins of the page. Although you cannot see the HTML tags for bolding and centering the text, Word added them automatically to the file.

QuickTip

The styles shown on the Style list are the HTML-compatible styles included in the theme.

2. Select the heading **Welcome Aboard**, click the **Style list arrow** on the Formatting toolbar, then click **Heading 2**
   The heading is formatted in the Heading 2 style. A **style** is a set of formats, such as font, font size, and paragraph alignment, that are named and stored together. Each theme includes styles that you can apply to text to format it quickly and easily.

3. Select the four-line list that begins with Number of employee, click the **Bullets button** on the Formatting toolbar, then deselect the text
   The four lines change to a bulleted list using the bullet style included in the theme. See Figure D-4.

4. Place the insertion point at the beginning of the heading **Welcome Aboard,** press **[Enter],** then place the insertion point in the blank line between the headings
   The new blank line will be the location for the MediaLoft logo.

5. Click **Insert** on the menu bar, point to **Picture**, then click **From File**
   The Insert Picture dialog box opens.

6. Navigate to the location where your Project Files are stored, select **MLoft.jpg**, then click **Insert**
   The MediaLoft logo is inserted between the two headings.

Trouble?

If the Picture toolbar opens when you select the graphic, close the toolbar.

7. Select the logo, click , then deselect the logo
   The logo is centered. Web Layout view displays a document as it will look when viewed in a browser, but you can confirm the appearance of a Web page by opening it in Internet Explorer.

8. Click **File** on the menu bar, click **Web Page Preview**, then maximize the Internet Explorer window if necessary
   The Welcome to MediaLoft Web page opens in the Internet Explorer window, as shown in Figure D-5.

9. Close Internet Explorer, save the changes to the document, then close the document

FIGURE D-4: Headings and list formatted

Heading is bold
and centered

Heading 2 style
applied to text

Bullet characters
are included with
the theme

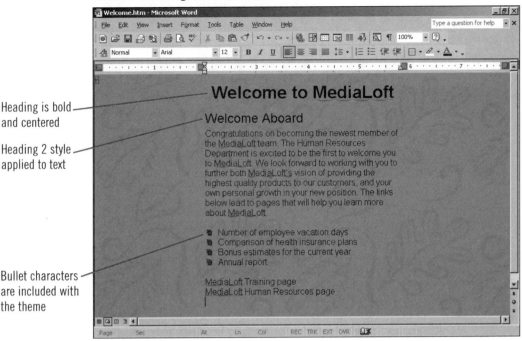

FIGURE D-5: Completed Welcome page in Internet Explorer

Page Title appears
in title bar

Logo is centered

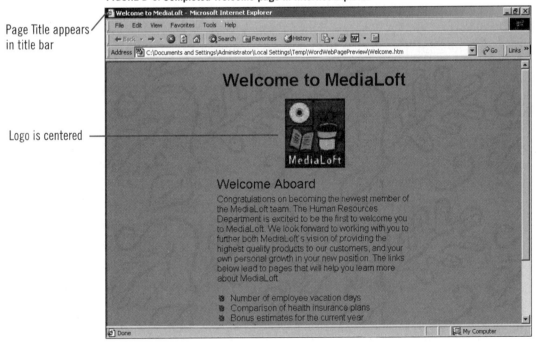

Creating a Web Page from a Word Document

By saving a file in HTML format, you can easily create Web pages from existing Office files. Saving a file as HTML converts the file from the Office format to HTML to make it available on the Web or an intranet. After you convert an Office file to HTML, you can format it using Word. As noted in her original sketch, Karen plans to create Web pages using several existing Office documents. She starts by creating a Web page about company vacation days from a Word document file.

Steps

Trouble?

If the file INT D-1.doc does not appear your list of Project Files in the Open dialog box, change the Files of type list box to display "All Files" or "All Word Documents".

1. In Word, open **INT D-1.doc** from the drive and folder where your Project Files are stored
   The document, which contains a description of MediaLoft's policy on vacation days for employees, opens in Normal view.

2. Click **File** on the menu bar, then click **Save as Web Page**
   The Save As dialog box opens. Notice that the Save as type is Web page (*.htm;*.html). In order to save a file as a Web page, you need to specify a page title and filename.

3. Click **Change Title**, type **Vacation Days** in the Set Page Title dialog box, click **OK**, type **Vacation** in the File name text box, make sure the drive or folder where your Project Files are located is displayed in the Save in list box, then click **Save**
   Word saves a copy of the document in HTML format and switches to Web Layout view. The filename in the titlebar is Vacation.htm.

4. Select the heading **Vacation Days**, click the **Style list arrow** on the Formatting toolbar, click **Heading 1**, then click the **Center button** on the Formatting toolbar

5. Press **[Ctrl][End]** to move the insertion point to the end of the document, press **[Enter]**, then type **Return to Welcome page**
   You will later format "Return to Welcome page" as a hyperlink.

6. Select the five-line list that begins with After completing, click the **Bullets button** on the Formatting toolbar, then deselect the text
   The list is formatted as a bulleted list. Your Vacation Days Web page should match Figure D-6.

7. Click **Format** on the menu bar, click **Theme**, click **Willow** (or the theme you selected in the previous lesson) in the Choose a Theme list box, then click **OK**
   The Willow theme is applied to the Web page, as shown in Figure D-7. The completed Vacation Days Web page now matches the appearance of the Welcome page you created.

8. Save the changes to the document, click **File** on the menu bar, click **Web Page Preview**, then examine the Web page in Internet Explorer

9. Close Internet Explorer, then close the document

FIGURE D-6: Vacation Days Web page

Heading formatted in Heading 1 style and centered

Bulleted list; your bullet style might differ

Text for hyperlink

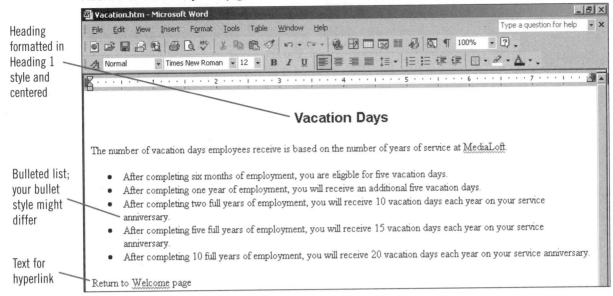

FIGURE D-7: Completed Vacation Days Web page

Theme applied to Web page elements

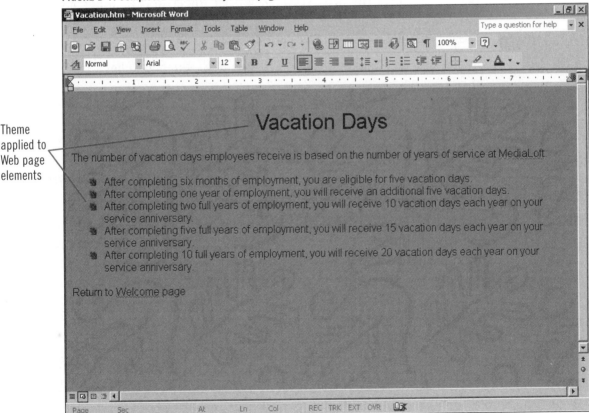

Creating a Web Page from an Access Table

Like Word, Access allows you to save data as Web pages. You can create static HTML documents from table, form, and query datasheets, as well as from reports. When you save data as a static HTML document, the resulting Web page reflects the data at the time the document was saved; subsequent updates to the data are not reflected in the HTML document. Once you save data in HTML format, you can format the file using Word. ▰▰▰▰▰ Karen wants to create a Web page that contains a table comparing the health insurance plans available to MediaLoft employees. This information is stored in an Access database table. She exports the table to HTML and then formats it using Word.

Steps

1. Start Access, click the **More files** link in the New File task pane, open **INT D-2.mdb** from the drive and folder where your Project Files are stored, click **Tables** on the Objects bar in the INT D-2 database window, click the **Open button** 🔳 on the Database Window toolbar, review the datasheet, then close the datasheet

   The Health Plans table is selected automatically in the INT D-2 database window.

2. Click **File** on the menu bar, then click **Export**

   The Export Table 'Health Plans' To dialog box opens, as shown in Figure D-8. You have the option of exporting the data only, or you can export the data and the table format to HTML.

3. Click the **Save as type list arrow**, click **HTML Documents (*.html;*.htm)**, click the **Save formatted check box**, then click **Export**

   The HTML Output Options dialog box opens.

4. Remove the check mark from the **Select a HTML Template check box** if necessary, then click **OK**

   After a few moments, although there are no apparent changes on the screen, the table is exported.

Trouble?

If a message box opens asking if you want to make Word your default Web page editor, click No.

5. Exit Access, then open the file **Health Plans.html** in Word

   The table opens in Word in Web Layout view.

6. Click **Format** on the menu bar, click **Theme**, click **Willow** (or the theme you selected in the previous lessons) in the Choose a Theme list box, then click **OK**

   The theme is applied to the Health Plans Web page.

7. Press **[Ctrl][End]** to move the insertion point to the bottom of the table, press **[Enter]**, then type **Return to Welcome page**

   Later you will format this text as a hyperlink.

8. Select the table heading **Health Plans**, click the **Style list arrow** on the Formatting toolbar, scroll down, click **Table Theme**, click the **Style list arrow**, click **Heading 1**, click the **Center button** 🔳 on the Formatting toolbar, then deselect the text

   The table is formatted with the table format settings included with the theme. Also, the table heading is formatted in the Heading 1 style and centered in the table. The Web page appears as shown in Figure D-9.

9. Save your changes to the document, click **File** on the menu bar, then click **Web Page Preview**

   The Web page opens in Internet Explorer, as shown in Figure D-10.

10. Close Internet Explorer, then close the document

FIGURE D-8: Export Table 'Health Plans' to dialog box

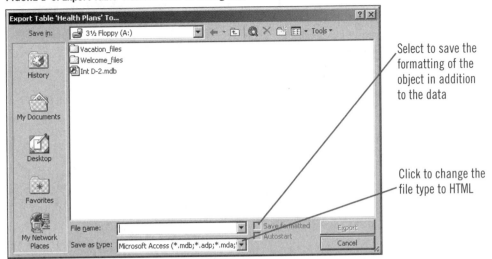

Select to save the formatting of the object in addition to the data

Click to change the file type to HTML

FIGURE D-9: Completed Health Plans Web page in Word

Table from Access database formatted in the Willow theme

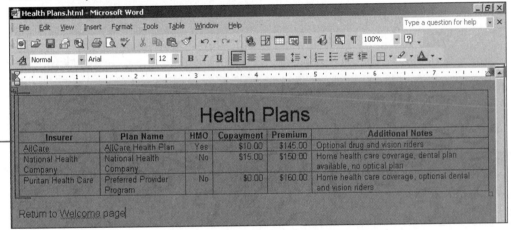

FIGURE D-10: Health Plans Web page in Internet Explorer

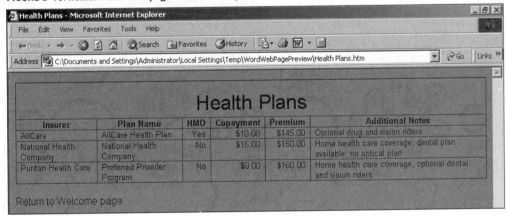

Using Access to create static and dynamic Web pages

You can convert Access objects to static or dynamic Web pages. A static HTML page contains only the information contained in the database at the time you converted the object to a Web page. A Data Access page, on the other hand, is dynamically linked to the database file so that changes to the data are reflected in the Web page and changes made to the data through the Web page are reflected in the underlying table.

Creating a Web Page from an Excel Workbook

Like Word and Access, you can create Web pages using existing Excel files. Excel lets you specify worksheet ranges to use as sources for Web pages, instead of having to include all of the worksheets or cells in a workbook. ✎ Karen wants to add another Web page to the Welcome publication. Titled "2003 Bonus Program", this page will highlight MediaLoft's bonus program and show the estimated bonus percentages for employees by quarter and by department. Karen creates this page from an existing Excel workbook.

Steps

QuickTip

If you want users to be able to enter and calculate data on the Web page, you can click the Add Interactivity check box.

1. **Start Excel, open the Project File INT D-3.xls, click and drag to select the range A1:G7, click File on the menu bar, then click Save as Web Page**
   The Save As dialog box opens. You use this dialog box in Excel to specify the page title and filename for the Web page.

2. **Select the Selection: $A$1:$G$7 option button, click Change Title, type 2003 Bonus Program Estimates in the Set Page Title dialog box, then click OK**
   The title will appear as the page title in the browser title bar and as a heading centered over the table in the Web page.

3. **Type Bonus in the File name text box, click Save, then exit Excel without saving changes to the file INT D-3.xls**

Trouble?

If you do not see the Bonus.htm file in the folder with your Project Files, click the Files of type list arrow, then click All Files. If the file opens in Excel, exit Excel, then repeat Step 4. Make sure you use the Open in Microsoft Word option to open the file correctly.

4. **In Word, click the Open button ☞ on the Standard toolbar, click Bonus.htm in the Open dialog box, click the Open button list arrow, then click Open in Microsoft Word**
   The 2003 Bonus Program Web page opens in Word, as shown in Figure D-11. The page title you created is added as a heading centered above the table.

5. **Press [Ctrl][End], press [Enter], type Return to Welcome page, click Format on the menu bar, click Theme, click Willow (or the theme you chose in the previous lessons) in the Choose a Theme list box, then click OK**
   The theme is applied to the document.

6. **Place the insertion point in the first row of the table, which contains the heading 2003 Bonus Program, click Table on the menu bar, point to Delete, then click Rows**
   The first row of the table is deleted.

7. **Place the insertion point in the table, click Table on the menu bar, point to AutoFit, then click AutoFit to Window**
   The width of the table columns is adjusted so that the table fills the document window.

8. **Select the heading 2003 Bonus Program Estimates, click the Style list arrow on the Formatting toolbar, click Heading 1, click the Center button ▤ on the Formatting toolbar, then deselect the text**
   Now the table and the Web page are formatted with the same theme and font styles as the other Web pages you are creating for the MediaLoft intranet, as shown in Figure D-12.

9. **Save your changes to the document, click Yes to overwrite the file, click File on the menu bar, then click Web Page Preview**
   The Web page opens in Internet Explorer, as shown in Figure D-13.

10. **Close Internet Explorer, then close the document**

FIGURE D-11: 2003 Bonus Program Estimates Web page in Word

Page title is
added as a
heading

Table from
Excel work-
book

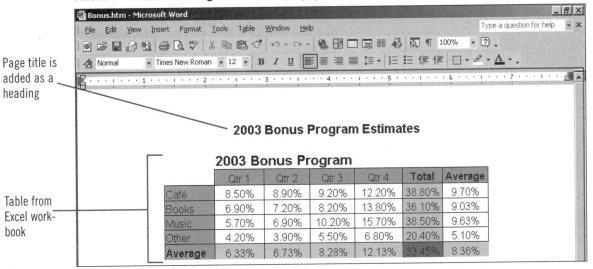

FIGURE D-12: Completed 2003 Bonus Program Estimates Web page

Theme
applied

Table
formatted
to fit the
window

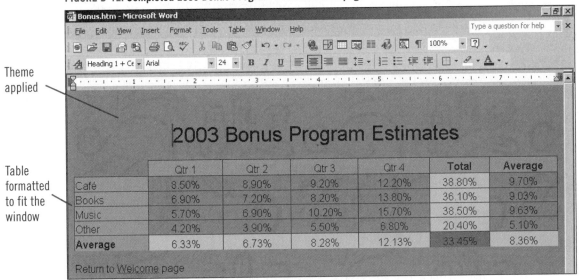

FIGURE D-13: 2003 Bonus Programs Web page in Internet Explorer

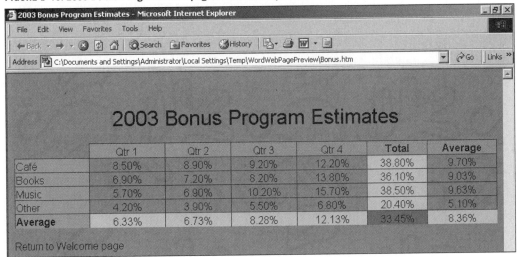

Integration

Creating Web Pages from a PowerPoint Presentation

PowerPoint presentations contain multiple screens of information, called slides. When you convert a PowerPoint presentation to HTML format, PowerPoint creates a separate Web page for each slide and groups the pages in a folder. This differs from the other Office files where only one HTML file is created for each file or Access object converted. When viewing your presentation with a browser, the audience can navigate through the Web pages much as they would navigate through the slides in PowerPoint. Karen converts a PowerPoint presentation from the company's annual report to HTML format. She then formats a hyperlink back to the home page.

Trouble?

Click or press any key to view the next slide.

QuickTip

If you want your name on the printed solution, add it to the page title.

1. Start PowerPoint, open the Project File **INT D-4.ppt**, click **Slide Show** on the menu bar, click **View Show**, then view the entire presentation
   The presentation's six slides outline the company's accomplishments and goals.

2. Click **File** on the menu bar, click **Save as Web Page**, click **Change Title** in the Save As dialog box, type **Annual Report** in the Set Page Title dialog box, click **OK**, type **AR Presentation** in the File name text box, then click **Save**
   PowerPoint exports the presentation to HTML format. It may take several minutes to save the file. Because PowerPoint creates a group of associated Web pages when you save a presentation as HTML, you could consider the Web pages based on this presentation as a publication within your publication.

3. Click **File** on the menu bar, then click **Web Page Preview**
   The presentation opens in Internet Explorer, as shown in Figure D-14. The title of each slide in the presentation appears in the left frame of the browser window. When you point to a title, the pointer changes to the hyperlink pointer and the title is highlighted. You can click a title in the left frame to open that Web page, or you can click the Previous Slide and Next Slide buttons at the bottom of the browser window to view the slides.

4. Click the **PowerPoint program button** on the taskbar to switch to PowerPoint, display **slide 1**, place the insertion point after **2002** on the title slide, press **[Enter]** twice, click the **Decrease Font Size button** on the Formatting toolbar three times, then type **Return to Welcome page**
   You want this text to be a hyperlink to the Welcome page. Because the PowerPoint Web publication is a group of pages instead of a single page, you must use PowerPoint to create the actual link, whereas in other Office files you can create all your links in Word.

5. Select **Return to Welcome page**, then click the **Insert Hyperlink button** on the Standard toolbar
   The Insert Hyperlink dialog box opens. You use the Insert Hyperlink dialog box to select the Web page, document, or e-mail address to which you want to link the selected text.

6. Select the **Welcome.htm** file, then click **OK**
   The hyperlink to the Welcome file is created. You will test the link in the next lesson.

7. Save your changes to the presentation, click **File** on the menu bar, then click **Web Page Preview**
   Internet Explorer displays the first slide from the presentation, as shown in Figure D-15.

8. View the entire presentation in Internet Explorer, close Internet Explorer, then exit PowerPoint

FIGURE D-14: Annual Report presentation in Internet Explorer

Title of current slide

Slide titles

Left frame

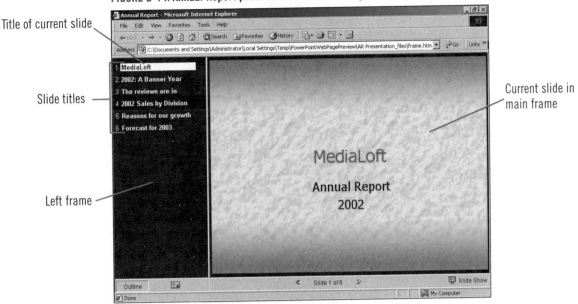

Current slide in
main frame

FIGURE D-15: Title slide with hyperlink added

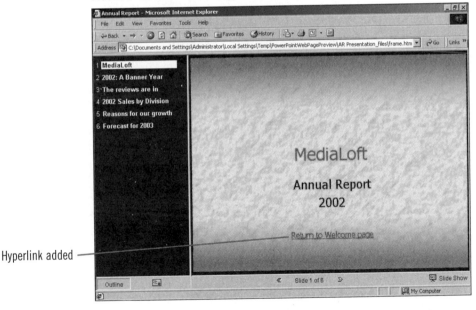

Hyperlink added

Using frames

Frames help users to navigate a group of associated Web pages. It is most useful to organize a Web page using frames when you want common navigation elements for all the Web pages in a publication. Although frames are convenient, you have to consider that some older Web browsers may not support them. A popular way to address this problem is to create two versions of a publication—one with frames and one without—and to offer a choice between the two on the publication's home page. If time or resources limit you to one version, then base your decision on your audience's capabilities. For example, if you create a page for a company intranet and know that every computer has the latest version of a browser installed, adding frames to your publication makes sense. However, if you create a page for a Web publication and want the largest possible audience, using frames excludes some users from viewing your publication.

Adding Hyperlinks

After you create the Web pages for your publication, you need to add hyperlinks both between pages of the publication and from the publication to other Web pages so that your audience can easily navigate the Web site. Karen's sketch shows links from the Welcome page to each of the other Web pages in the publication. It also shows a link back to the Welcome page from each associated page. She begins by adding hyperlinks to the Welcome page.

Steps 1 2 3 4

1. In Word, open the Project File **Welcome.htm**, then scroll down until the bulleted list is visible in the document window

2. Select **Number of employee vacation days**, but not the bullet character, then click the **Insert Hyperlink button** on the Standard toolbar
   The Insert Hyperlink dialog box opens, as shown in Figure D-16.

3. Select **Vacation.htm**, then click **OK**
   The text for the first bullet is formatted as a hyperlink—underlined and formatted in the hyperlink font style used by the theme. The hyperlink you created is a **relative link**, or a link that gives another page's address in relation to the current page. Creating relative links allows you to publish the pages to the Web or an intranet in their current directory structure and have the links remain accurate.

4. Move the mouse pointer over the **Number of employee vacation days** hyperlink
   A ScreenTip appears above the hyperlink, as shown in Figure D-17. By default the ScreenTip shows the path and filename of the linked page, but you can customize the ScreenTip text by clicking the ScreenTip button in the Insert Hyperlink dialog box or in the Edit Hyperlink dialog box.

5. Repeat Steps 2 through 4 to create and verify the relative links for the three remaining lines of bulleted text—link the second bullet to the **Health Plans.html** file, link the third bullet to the **Bonus.htm** file, link the fourth bullet to the **AR Presentation.htm** file—then save the **Welcome.htm** file

6. Press **[Ctrl]**, then click the **Number of employee vacation days** hyperlink
   You can follow a hyperlink in Word by pressing [Ctrl] and clicking the hyperlink. The Vacation Days Web page opens in Internet Explorer.

7. Click the **Edit with Microsoft Word button** on the Internet Explorer toolbar, select **Return to Welcome page** in the Vacation.htm document that opens in Word, click , select **Welcome.htm** in the Insert Hyperlink dialog box, click **OK**, save, then close the document
   The text is formatted as a hyperlink to the Welcome page.

8. Repeat Steps 6 through 7 to add a hyperlink back to the Welcome page on the Health Plans and Bonus Web pages, then close all open files except for the Welcome file in Word
   You already created the hyperlink to the Welcome page in the Annual Report presentation.

9. Save the **Welcome** file in Word, click **File** on the menu bar, click **Web Page Preview**, then use the hyperlinks in the Web publication to view each Web page in Internet Explorer and return to the Welcome page

10. Click the **Print button** in Internet Explorer to print each Web page, exit Internet Explorer, then exit Word
    You have successfully created and tested the links between the files in your Web publication. Eventually, Karen will add links on the Welcome page to take users to the Training page and the Human Resources page on the MediaLoft intranet site.

QuickTip

Use **absolute links**, which contain a fixed address, when you don't want the addresses of your links to change at all.

QuickTip

To edit a hyperlink, right-click it, then click Edit Hyperlink on the shortcut menu. To remove a hyperlink, right-click it, then click Remove Hyperlink.

QuickTip

If you want your name on the printed solution, add it to the bottom of the Web page below the hyperlink.

FIGURE D-16: Insert Hyperlink dialog box

Hyperlink text that appears on the Web page

Current drive or folder

Name of linked file appears here

Files and folders in current drive or folder

Click to change ScreenTip text

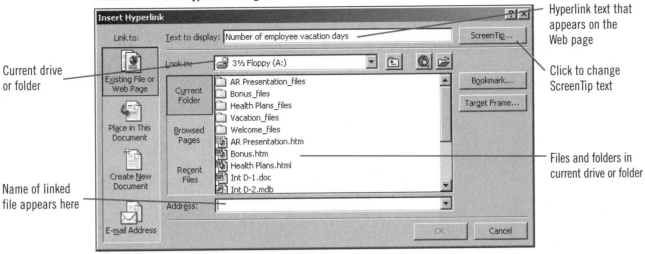

FIGURE D-17: Welcome page with hyperlink added

ScreenTip appears when you point to a hyperlink

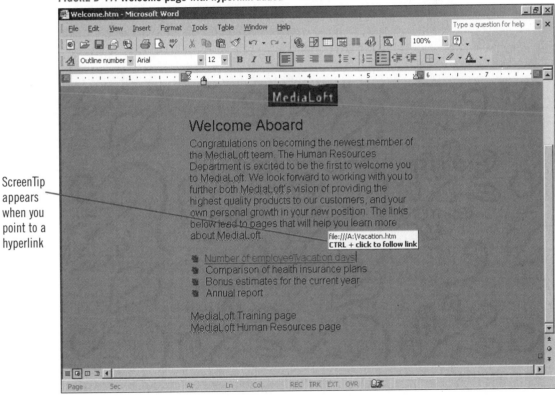

Publishing your Web pages

Your Web publication is not available to anyone outside your local computer network or workgroup until you publish it by placing a copy either on the Web or an on intranet server. Remember, the links you create on your home page are one-way: they help users viewing your page to find other interesting pages, but do not help others locate your page in the first place. Try the following to advertise your Web publication: ask friends and colleagues to create links to your home page on their pages; ask the administrator of your server to add your home page to the index of the site's Web pages; or e-mail information about your publication to groups, organizations, or people with Web sites. To publish effectively on an intranet, send a memo to employees who you think might be interested in your page or ask the network administrator and the owners of other relevant pages to add links to your publication on their pages.

▶ Skills Review

1. Plan a Web publication.

a. Using a pencil and a sheet of paper, sketch an outline of a Web publication for the MediaLoft Sales department, including a Sales News home page, a report on the results of a recent customer survey, a table of contact information for sales representatives, a table of recent sales figures, and a presentation from the eastern division. The Web publication will be posted to the MediaLoft intranet site.

b. Draw arrows on your sketch to indicate the hyperlinks between the pages in the publication.

2. Create a Web page.

a. Start Word, then create a new document using the Table of Contents Web page template.

b. Save the document as a Web page to the drive and folder where your Project Files are stored. Use the filename **TOC** and the Web page title **Sales News home page**.

c. Apply the Blends theme to the Web page. If Blends is not available to you, select a different theme.

d. Replace the template text with the text shown in Figure D-18, then delete the remaining placeholder text.

e. Save the changes.

FIGURE D-18

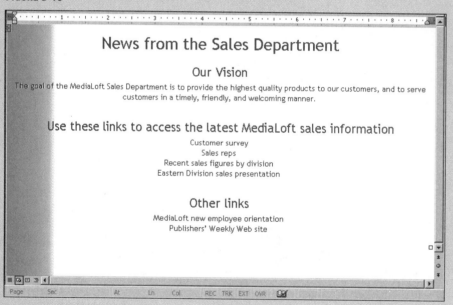

3. Format a Web page.

a. Apply the Heading 3 style to the Our Vision, Use these links…, and Other links headings.

b. Apply the Normal style to the vision statement.

c. Apply the Normal style to the links listed under the Use these links…, and Other links headings.

d. Format the links as a bulleted list.

e. Insert a blank line above the Our Vision heading.

f. Insert the Project File MLoft.jpg on the blank line you created. The file is a graphic file of the MediaLoft logo.

g. Center the logo.

h. Save the changes, preview the Web page in Internet Explorer, close Internet Explorer, then close the TOC file.

4. **Create a Web page from a Word document.**

   a. Open the Project File INT D-5.doc in Word.

   b. Save the file as a Web page with the page title **Customer Survey** and the filename **Survey**.

   c. Apply the Blends theme to the page.

   d. Apply the Heading 1 style to the heading **MediaLoft 2003 Customer Survey**, then center the heading.

   e. Apply the Heading 3 style to the heading **Customer Profile**.

   f. Format the five-line list that begins with percentages under the Customer Profile paragraph as a bulleted list.

   g. Apply the Heading 3 style to the headings Purchasing Habits, Preferred Genres, and Customer Satisfaction.

   h. Select the chart and center it.

   i. Press [Ctrl][End], press [Enter] twice, then type **Return to Sales News home page** at the bottom of the Web page.

   j. Save the changes, preview the Web page in Internet Explorer, close Internet Explorer, then close the Survey file.

5. **Create a Web page from an Access table.**

   a. Start Access, then open the Project File INT D-6.mdb in Access.

   b. Open the Sales Reps Table datasheet, review the records, then close the datasheet.

   c. Export the Sales Rep table as a formatted HTML document. Use the filename **Sales Reps**.

   d. Exit Access, then open the Sales Reps file in Word.

   e. Apply the Blends theme to the page.

   f. Use the Style list arrow to apply the Table Theme style to the table.

   g. AutoFit the table to fit the window. (*Hint*: Click in the table, click Table on the menu bar, point to AutoFit, then click AutoFit to Window.)

   h. Apply the Heading 1 style to the table heading Sales Reps, then center the heading.

   i. Press [Ctrl][End], press [Enter], then type **Return to Sales News home page** at the bottom of the Web page.

   j. Save the changes, preview the Web page in Internet Explorer, close Internet Explorer, then close the Survey file.

6. **Create a Web page from an Excel workbook.**

   a. Start Excel, then open the Project File INT D-7.xls in Excel.

   b. Select the range A1:H6, then save the selected range as a Web page with the filename **Division Sales** and the title **MediaLoft 2003 Monthly Sales by Division**.

   c. Exit Excel without saving changes, then open the Division Sales file in Word.

   d. Delete the first two rows of the table. (*Hint*: Select the rows, right-click, then click Delete Rows.)

   e. Press [Ctrl][End, press [Enter], then type **Return to Sales News home page** at the bottom of the Web page.

   f. Apply the Blends theme to the page.

   g. Apply the Heading 1 style to the heading MediaLoft 2003…, then center the heading.

   h. Save the changes, click Yes to overwrite the file, then preview the Web page in Internet Explorer.

   i. Close Internet Explorer, then close the Division Sales file.

7. **Create Web pages from a PowerPoint presentation.**

   a. Start PowerPoint, open the Project File INT D-8.ppt, then view the presentation.

   b. Place the insertion point after 2003 Fiscal Year on the title slide, press [Enter] twice, use the Decrease Font Size button to reduce the font size to 18 points, then type **Return to Sales News home page**.

   c. Format the text as a hyperlink to the file TOC.htm.

   d. Save the presentation as a Web page with the page title **Eastern Division Report** and the filename **Eastern Presentation**.

   e. Preview the entire presentation in Internet Explorer.

   f. Close Internet Explorer, close the file, then exit PowerPoint.

8. Add hyperlinks.

a. In Word, open the file TOC.htm, then scroll to the bottom of the Web page.

b. Format each item in the bulleted list of links under the Use these links… heading as a hyperlink to the appropriate Web page. Use the Web pages you created in the previous steps. (*Hint*: If you make a mistake and link the wrong file to a hyperlink, right-click the hyperlink, click Remove Hyperlink, then create the hyperlink again.)

c. Format the text MediaLoft new employee orientation as a hyperlink to the Project File Employee.htm.

d. Format the text Publishers' Weekly Web site as a hyperlink. To do this, type the URL **www.publishersweekly.com** in the Address text box in the Insert Hyperlink dialog box.

e. If you want your name on the printed solution, press [Enter] twice at the bottom of the Web page, then type your name.

f. Save the changes to the TOC.htm file.

g. In Word, open each additional Web page you created and format the text Return to Sales News home page as a hyperlink to the file TOC.htm. If you want your name on the printed solution, add it to the bottom of each Web page below the hyperlink. Save your changes, then close each file when you finish.

h. Return to the TOC.htm file in Word, then preview it in Internet Explorer.

i. Test each hyperlink in your Web publication in Internet Explorer. Use the Return to Sales News home page hyperlink when appropriate. Click the Back button on the Internet Explorer toolbar to return to the Sales News home page from the New employee orientation page and the Publishers' Weekly Web site. You must be connected to the Internet to view the Publishers' Weekly Web site.

j. Print each of the Web pages you created using the Print button in Internet Explorer. Print only the first slide of the presentation.

k. Close all open files then exit all programs.

Independent Challenge 1

You are a volunteer at The Grapevine, an emergency shelter for families in crisis. The Grapevine would like to advertise its programs and services, including requests for donations, on the Internet. At a recent meeting you volunteered to create a Web site for The Grapevine. You'll use existing files for printed material as the basis for most of your Web pages.

a. Sketch the The Grapevine Web publication. The home page for the publication should include a mission statement, links to other Web pages in the publication, and links to three Internet Web sites devoted to the problem of homelessness. You will create the other Web pages in the publication from existing files: a Word document with information on items sought for donation, an Access table detailing the shelter's programs, an Excel table showing 2003 income and expenses, and a PowerPoint presentation summarizing the shelter's recent activities and immediate goals. Be sure to include the links between the pages in your sketch.

b. Use your favorite search engine to search the Internet for information on homelessness and programs for the homeless. Use the keyword **homeless** to conduct your search. Write down the page titles and URLs of at least three Web pages you find. You will create hyperlinks from your home page to these Web pages later in this exercise. If your search does not result in links to information on homelessness, try looking at the following Web sites:
www.hud.gov
http://nch.ari.net
www.speakeasy.org/nasna

c. Start Word and create a home page for The Grapevine using the Simple Layout template and the Sumi Painting theme. (Select a different theme if Sumi Painting is not available to you). Include the text and formatting shown in Figure D-19 on your home page. (*Hint*: Format the main heading in bold and center it.) For the links listed under the For more information… heading, substitute the page titles of the Internet Web pages you found in Step b.

FIGURE D-19

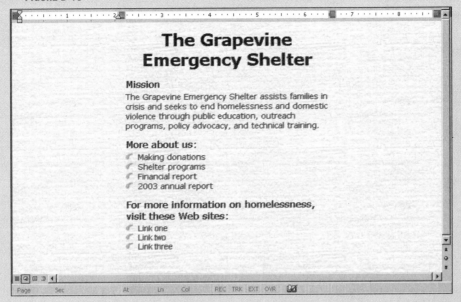

d. Save the Web page with the filename **Grapevine Home** and the page title **The Grapevine Home Page**. (*Hint*: If you want your name on the printed solution, add it to the page title.) Close the Grapevine Home file.

e. Create a Web page from the Project File INT D-9.doc. Save the Web page with the filename **Donations** and the page title **Donations to The Grapevine**. Apply the Sumi Painting theme and format the Web page with styles and bullets.

f. At the bottom of the Web page, insert a hyperlink to the home page file Grapevine Home. Save your changes, preview the Web page in Internet Explorer, make any necessary adjustments to the file in Word, then save and close the file.

g. Start Access and create a formatted HTML document from the Programs table in the Project File INT D-10.mdb. Name the HTML file **Programs**.

h. Exit Access, then open the Programs.html file in Word. Apply the Sumi Painting theme, apply the Table theme style to the table, then autofit the table contents to fit the window. Change the table heading to **Grapevine Programs**, then apply a heading style to the table heading.

i. At the bottom of the Web page, insert a hyperlink back to the home page. Save your changes, preview the Web page in Internet Explorer, make any necessary adjustments to the file in Word, then save and close the file.

j. Start Excel and create a Web page from the range A1:F20 in the Project File INT D-11.xls. Save the Web page with the filename **Financial Report** and page title **Grapevine Financial Report**, then exit Excel without saving changes.

k. Open the Financial Report.htm file in Word. Delete the heading **Grapevine Financial Report**, then apply the Sumi Painting theme. Format the Web page with styles so its look is consistent with the other Web pages and it is easy to read.

l. At the bottom of the Web page, insert a hyperlink back to the home page. Save your changes, clicking Yes to overwrite the file, preview the Web page in Internet Explorer, make any necessary adjustments to the file in Word, then save then close the file.

m. Start PowerPoint and create a Web publication from the Project File INT D-12.ppt. Use the filename **Grapevine Annual Report** and the page title **Grapevine 2003 Annual Report**.

n. At the bottom of the first slide, insert a hyperlink back to the home page. Save your changes, preview the presentation in Internet Explorer, make any necessary adjustments to the file in PowerPoint, save and close the file, then exit PowerPoint.

o. Open the home page file, **Grapevine Home**, in Word. Format the hyperlinks under the More about us heading to link to the to the appropriate Web pages. Format the hyperlinks under the For more information… heading to link the appropriate URLs.

p. Save your changes, then preview the Web publication in Internet Explorer, making sure to test each hyperlink.

q. Use the Print button in Internet Explorer to print each Web page you created and the first page of each Internet Web site you created a hyperlink to.

r. Close Internet Explorer, then exit Word.

Independent Challenge 2

You work in the public relations office at Meed Oil Corporation. Recognizing public concern following recent oil spills by other companies, Meed Oil wants to publicize the steps it is taking to guard against oil-tanker spills. Your supervisor asks you to adapt documents created for print and television ad campaigns to create a Web publication for Meed's Internet site.

a. Sketch the Web publication for Meed Oil. The home page for the publication should include a heading, a graphic that enhances the environmentally-friendly message, links to other Web pages in the publication, and links to two Web sites devoted to oil spill prevention. You will create the other Web pages in the publication from existing files: a press release saved in Word, an Access table detailing Meed's oil spill prevention programs, an Excel table showing a 30-year history of oil spills by major oil companies, and a PowerPoint presentation highlighting Meed's oil spill record and its efforts to prevent future spills. Be sure to include links between the pages in your sketch.

b. Use your favorite search engine to search the Internet for information on oil spill prevention. Use the keywords **oil spill** to conduct your search. Write down the page titles and URLs of at least two Web pages you find. You will create hyperlinks from the home page to these Web sites later in this exercise. If your search does not result in links to information on oil spills, try looking at the following Web sites:
www.epa.gov
www.state.ak.us

c. Start Word and create a home page for the oil spill prevention publication. Apply the Nature theme, and include the text and formatting shown in Figure D-20. For the links under the Research heading, substitute the page titles of the Internet Web pages you found in Step b. Insert the clip art graphic shown in Figure D-20 or use another appropriate clip art image. (*Hint*: Click Insert on the menu bar, point to Picture, then click Clip Art to open the Insert Clip Art task pane. You can search on the keyword **nature** or **environment**. You may need to resize the clip art graphic after you insert it.)

d. Save the Web page with the filename **Oil Spill Home** and the page title **Meed Oil—Oil Spill Prevention Home Page**. (*Hint*: If you want your name on the printed solution, add it to the page title.) Close the Oil Spill Home file.

e. Create a Web page from the Project File INT D-13.doc. Save the Web page with the filename **Press Release** and the page title **Meed Oil Press Release**. Apply the Nature theme and format the Web page so it is attractive and easy to read.

f. At the bottom of the Web page, insert a hyperlink back to the home page. Save your changes, preview the Web page in Internet Explorer, make any necessary adjustments to the file in Word, then save and close the file.

g. Start Access and create a formatted HTML document from the Prevention Programs table in the Project File INT D-14.mdb. Name the HTML file **Prevention Programs**.

h. Exit Access, then open the Prevention Programs.html file in Word. Apply the Nature theme and format the Web page so it is attractive and easy to read. Change the table heading to **Meed Oil – Oil Spill Prevention Programs**.

i. At the bottom of the Web page, insert a hyperlink back to the home page. Save your changes, preview the Web page in Internet Explorer, make any necessary adjustments to the file in Word, then save and close the file.

FIGURE D-20

Inside the Word window shown:

Meed Oil Corporation

A clean record in oil spill prevention

Meed Oil links
- Press release
- Oil spill prevention programs
- 30-year history of oil spills by major oil companies
- Meed's commitment to protecting our environment from future oil spills

Research
- Link one
- Link two

j. Start Excel and create a Web page from the range A1:F8 in the Project File INT D-15.xls. Save the Web page with the filename **Oil Spills by Company** and page title **Oil Spills by Major Oil Companies,** then exit Excel without saving changes.

k. Open the Oil Spills by Company.htm file in Word. Delete the text **Oil Spills,** in the first row of the table, then apply the Nature theme. Format the Web page with styles so that its look is consistent with the other Web pages and it is easy to read.

l. At the bottom of the Web page, insert a hyperlink back to the home page. Save the changes, clicking Yes to overwrite the file, preview the Web page in Internet Explorer, make any necessary adjustments to the file in Word, then save and close the file.

m. Start PowerPoint and create a Web publication from the Project File INT D-16.ppt. Use the filename **Oil Spill Presentation** and the page title **Meed Oil's Commitment to Oil Spill Prevention**.

n. At the bottom of the first slide, insert a hyperlink back to the home page. Save your changes, preview the presentation in Internet Explorer, make any necessary adjustments to the file in PowerPoint, save and close the file, then exit PowerPoint.

o. Open the home page file, **Oil Spill Home**, in Word. Format the hyperlinks to link to the Web pages you created. Format the Research hyperlinks to link to the appropriate URLs.

p. Save your changes, then preview the Web publication in Internet Explorer, making sure to test each hyperlink.

q. Use the Print button in Internet Explorer to print the first page of each Web page you created and the first page of each Internet Web site you created a hyperlink to.

r. Close Internet Explorer, then exit Word.

► Visual Workshop

Create the Web publication shown in Figure D-21. Use the Left-aligned Column Web page template in Word to create the Café home page. (*Hint*: The graphic is included in the Web page template.) Create the **Daily Specials** Web pages by creating a presentation in PowerPoint and converting it to HTML. Create the **Contact** Web page by creating a table in Excel and converting it to a Web page. Use the Sandstone theme for the Web pages you format in Word, and use the Maple Design template for the presentation (select a different theme or template if these are not available to you). If you want your name on the printed solution, add it to the page title for each page. Finally, add links between the Web pages. Preview the Web publication in Internet Explorer, then print the first page of each Web page using Internet Explorer.

FIGURE D-21

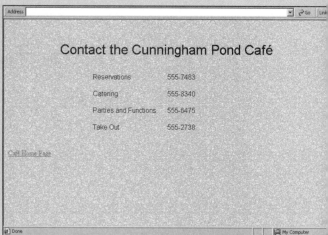

Unit
A

Getting
Started with Outlook 2002

Objectives

► **Understand e-mail**
► **Start Outlook 2002**
► **View the Outlook 2002 window**
► **Add a contact to the Address Book**
► **Create and send new messages**
► **Reply to and forward messages**
► **Send a message with an attachment**
► **Create a distribution list**
► **Send a message to a distribution list**

Microsoft Outlook 2002 is an integrated desktop information management program that lets you manage your personal and business information and communicate with others. Using Outlook, you can manage information such as your electronic messages, appointments, contacts, tasks, and files. In this unit, you will focus on the electronic mail features of Outlook. You are a marketing assistant at MediaLoft, a chain of bookstore cafés that sells books, CDs, and videos. MediaLoft wants to add more international coffee and tea products to their selection. Your manager, Alice Wegman, has asked you to research how to purchase Chai tea products directly from India to sell at MediaLoft. You will use Outlook 2002 to communicate with Alice about your progress.

Understanding E-Mail

E-mail software lets you send and receive electronic messages, e-mail, over a network and the Internet. A **network** is a group of computers connected to each other with cables and software. The Internet is a network that connects millions of computer users around the world. Figure A-1 illustrates how e-mail messages can travel over a network. ✐ MediaLoft employees use e-mail to communicate with each other and with clients because it is fast and easy. E-mail is an effective way to communicate with co-workers or colleagues who are at located in different places.

Details

The following are some of the benefits of using e-mail:

► Provides a convenient and efficient way to communicate

You can send and receive messages whenever you wish; the recipients do not have to be at their computers to receive your message at the same time that you send it. E-mail uses **store and forward technology**. Unlike communication through a telephone call, the senders and recipients don't have to be on their computers at the same time to communicate.

► Allows you to send large amounts of information

Your messages can be as long as you wish, and you can also attach a file (such as a spreadsheet or word processing document) to a message.

► Lets you communicate with several people at once

You can create your own electronic address book, containing the names of the people with whom you frequently communicate. You can then send the same message to multiple individuals at one time.

► Ensures delivery of information

With Outlook, you have the option of receiving a notification message when a recipient receives and reads your e-mail, if you and the recipient of the message are connected to the same network.

► Lets you communicate from a remote place

If you have an Internet connection and communications software, you can connect your computer at home to the computers at your office. This gives you the flexibility to send and receive messages when you are not at the office. You can also sign up with an ISP (Internet service provider) and send e-mail to people on the Internet. You can connect to the Internet using a telephone line or other, faster technologies including, cable, ISDN (Integrated Services Digital Network), T1, T3, or DSL (Digital Subscriber Line).

► Provides a record of communications

You can organize the messages you send and receive in a way that best suits your working style. Organizing your saved messages lets you keep a record of communications, which can be very valuable in managing a project or business.

► Allows you to store information

You can store e-mail messages in folders and refer to them again in the future. Unlike paper mail, which can be lost or damaged, e-mail is safely stored on your computer. Just like any other files you store on your computer, make sure you regularly back up the drive where your Outlook files are stored.

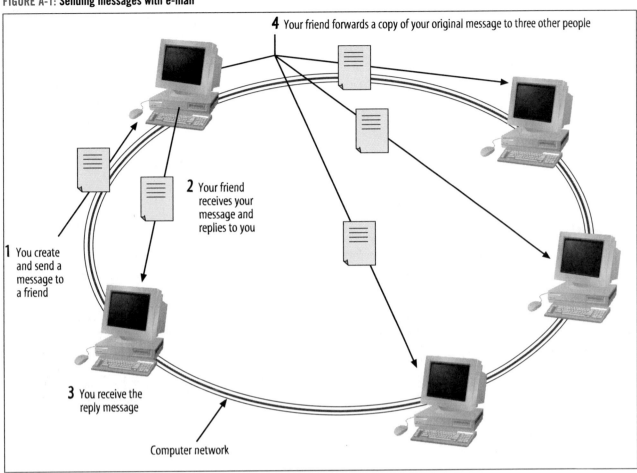

4 Your friend forwards a copy of your original message to three other people

2 Your friend receives your message and replies to you

1 You create and send a message to a friend

3 You receive the reply message

Computer network

CLUES TO USE

Electronic mail etiquette

When you compose a message, take extra care in what you say and how you say it. The recipient of your message doesn't have the benefit of seeing your body language or hearing the tone of your voice to interpret what you are saying. For example, using all capital letters in the text of a message is the e-mail equivalent of shouting and is not appropriate. Carefully consider the content of your messages before you send them, and don't send confidential or sensitive material.

Remember, once you send a message, you may not be able to prevent it from being delivered. If your e-mail account is a company account, it's a good idea to learn whether your company permits the sending of personal messages. All messages you send have been legally interpreted as property of the company for which you work, so don't assume that your messages are private.

Starting Outlook 2002

Before you can read or send messages, you must start Outlook. Depending on how your e-mail system is set up, you may be prompted to choose a profile during the startup process. A **profile** is a set of information used to identify individual e-mail users. Profiles allow more than one user to have individual e-mail accounts on the same computer and are common in classroom environments. You need to start Outlook in order to send an e-mail message to Alice.

Steps

1. Click the Start button 🏁**Start on the taskbar, then point to Programs**
Outlook is on the Programs menu. See Figure A-2.

2. Click Microsoft Outlook
Outlook starts and displays one of its many views. Your installation may or may not be set up to start in the Outlook Today view.

Trouble?
If the Choose Profile dialog box opens, click the Profile Name list arrow to select your profile, then click OK. If you don't know which profile to use, ask your technical support person.

3. Click the Outlook Today shortcut in Outlook Shortcuts on the Outlook Bar
Figure A-3 shows the Outlook Today view. Outlook Today is customizable, so the layout of your Outlook Today may differ. When you have items in the Calendar and Tasks folders, they will appear in this view along with any messages in your Inbox.

QuickTip
You can click the Inbox shortcut on the Outlook Bar to view the Inbox.

4. Click View on the menu bar, point to Go To, then click Inbox
The Inbox folder is the folder in Outlook that stores all incoming e-mail messages.

FIGURE A-2: **Starting Outlook 2002**

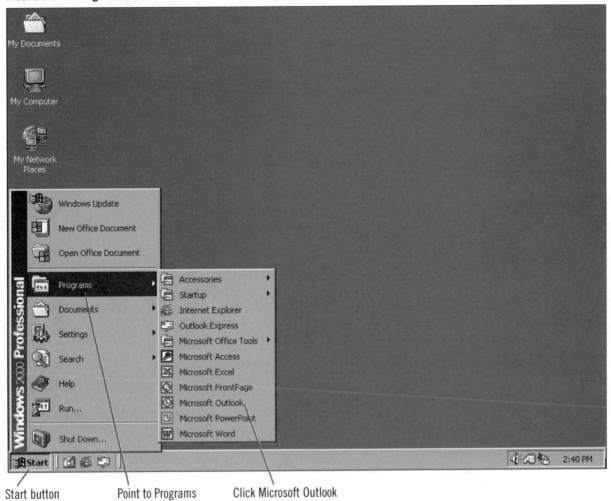

Start button   Point to Programs   Click Microsoft Outlook

FIGURE A-3: **Outlook Today view**

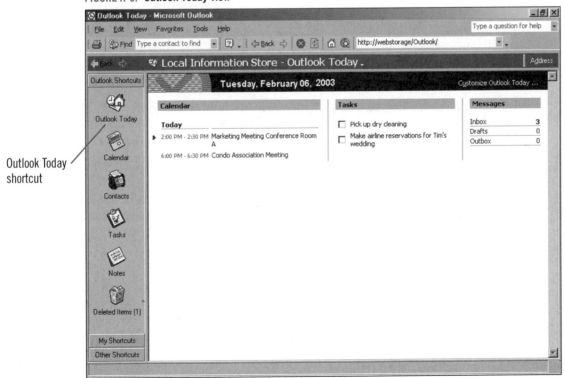

Outlook Today
shortcut

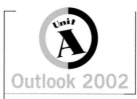

Outlook 2002

Viewing the Outlook 2002 Window

Before you can use the many features of Outlook, you need to understand how each part of the Outlook window works. Figure A-4 shows the Outlook window with the Inbox displayed. Read the details in this lesson to learn about the various elements of the window.

Details

▶ At the top of the window, the **title bar** displays the name of the program, Microsoft Outlook. When you double-click a message to open it in a new window, the subject of the message appears in the title bar.

▶ The **menu bar** (as in all Windows programs) contains the names of the menu items. Clicking a menu item on the menu bar displays a list of related commands. For example, you use the commands on the Edit menu to edit the text of your message.

▶ The **Inbox** shows a list of message headers for the e-mail you have received. Each **message header** identifies the sender of the message, the subject, the date and time the message was received, and the size of the message. Message headers of unread messages appear in boldface. By default, Outlook displays the Inbox with a **preview pane**, the lower pane of the Inbox. You use the preview pane to read and scroll through messages without opening them in a new window.

▶ **Message header icons** to the left of the sender's name identify the attributes of the message. For example, an icon that looks like a closed envelope indicates that the message has not been read. See Table A-1 for a description of the icons that may appear in the Inbox.

▶ **Column headings**, above the message headers, identify the sections of the message header. You can use the column headings to sort and organize your messages, by clicking on the headers.

▶ On the left side of the Outlook window is the **Outlook Bar**. The Outlook Bar contains short-cuts to frequently used folders. The Inbox folder is currently open. To open a different folder, you simply click the folder icon. The Inbox folder contains all the messages other users have sent you. Other shortcuts on the Outlook Bar include Calendar, Contacts, Tasks, Notes, and Deleted Items folders. The Deleted Items folder contains messages you have deleted.

▶ Under the menu bar, the **Standard toolbar** contains buttons that give you quick access to the most frequently used commands, such as Reply, Forward, Print, Find, and Delete. You can access your Address Book from the Standard toolbar and enter a contact name in the Find a Contact text box. Outlook will search for the contact, then display the contact window for that person.

▶ Just below the Standard toolbar, the **folder banner** displays the name of the open folder. The folder banner in Figure A-4 shows that the Inbox folder is currently open. The **status bar** at the bottom of the window indicates the total number of messages that the open folder contains, as well as the number of messages that have not been read.

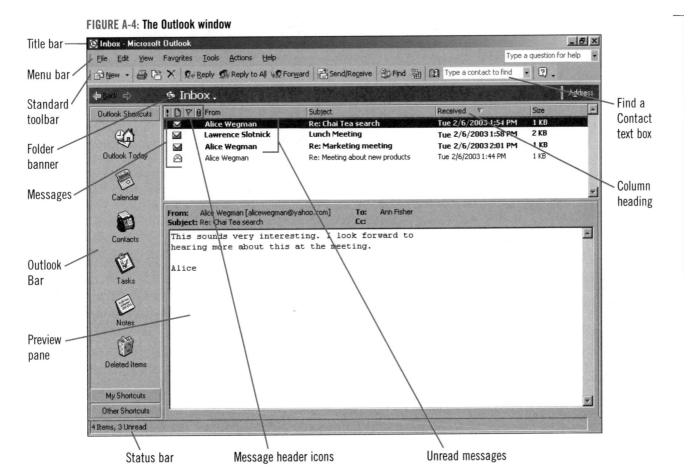

FIGURE A-4: The Outlook window

Title bar

Menu bar

Standard toolbar

Folder banner

Messages

Outlook Bar

Preview pane

Status bar

Message header icons

Unread messages

Find a Contact text box

Column heading

TABLE A-1: Message header icons

icon	description
	High-importance message
	Low importance message
	Unread message
	Read message
	Forwarded message
	Replied to message
	Notification of a delivered message
	Message has an attachment
	Message has been flagged for follow up
	Notification of an undeliverable message

Adding a Contact to the Address Book

You can add the names and e-mail addresses of people to whom you frequently send e-mail messages to the Address Book in Outlook. Outlook refers to your Address Book entries as "contacts," and places them in a folder called Contacts. When you create a new contact, you type the person's full name and e-mail address. You are given the option of entering additional information about that person, including his or her mailing address, telephone number, mobile phone number, and even birthday. Adding a contact to your Address Book saves you from having to type someone's e-mail address each time you want to send a message to him or her. It also reduces the chance that your message will not be sent because you typed someone's e-mail address incorrectly. ✒ Since you'll be corresponding with Alice frequently, you create a contact for her in your Address Book. You also decide to create contacts for Catherine Favreau and Peter DiGirgio, MediaLoft colleagues, since they will eventually be involved in the Chai Tea project.

Steps

Trouble?
If a list appears in your Address Book, someone has already entered contacts.

1. **Click the Address Book button 📖 on the Standard toolbar**
   The Address Book opens, as shown in Figure A-5. Presently the Address Book does not contain any contacts. The Address book is also available if you click Tools on the menu bar, then click Address Book.

2. **Click the New Entry button 🖳 on the Address Book toolbar**
   The New Entry dialog box opens, as shown in Figure A-6.

3. **Make sure New Contact is selected, then click OK**
   The Untitled Contact window opens as shown in Figure A-7. You can see that Outlook can store a lot of information about each contact.

QuickTip
Click the Full Name button 【Full Name...】 in the Contact window to open the Check Full Name dialog box to create a contact with a Title, First name, Middle name, Last name, and Suffix.

4. **Type Alice Wegman in the Full Name text box, click the E-mail text box, type alicewegman@yahoo.com, then press [Tab]**
   Outlook recognizes Alice as the first name and Wegman as the last name, as entered in the Full Name text box. If Outlook had been unsure of the name because of a nontraditional entry, such as just one name, the Check Full Name dialog box would have opened to give you an opportunity to verify the entry. Alice's name and e-mail address appear in the Display as text box, as shown in Figure A-8. You can edit the Display as text box to change the way a name is displayed.

QuickTip
Click the Save and New button 🖫 if you are adding a list of contacts at one time.

5. **Click the Save and Close button 🖫 on the Standard toolbar, click the New Entry Button 🖳 on the Address book toolbar, then click OK**
   Alice Wegman is added as a new contact in the Address book. A new Untitled Contact window opens.

6. **Type Peter DiGiorgio in the Full Name text box, type your e-mail address in the E-mail text box, then click 🖫**
   Peter DiGiorgio is added to the Address Book with your e-mail address.

7. **Click 🖳, click OK, type Catherine Favreau in the Full Name text box, type your e-mail address in the E-mail text box, click the Save and Close button 🖫 on the Address Book toolbar, click the Add this as a new contact anyway option button in the Duplicate Contact Detected dialog box, then click OK**
   Three new contacts are added to your Address Book.

8. **Click the Close button ✖ on the Address Book window title bar**
   The Address Book closes and you return to the Inbox view.

FIGURE A-5: Address book

New Entry
button

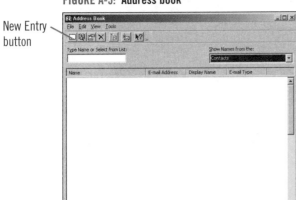

FIGURE A-6: New Entry dialog box

Make sure that
New Contact is
selected

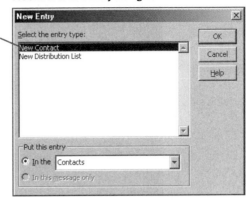

FIGURE A-7: Contact window

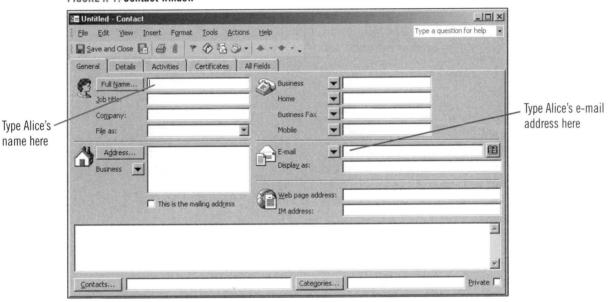

Type Alice's
name here

Type Alice's e-mail
address here

FIGURE A-8: Alice Wegman Contact window

Save and Close
button

Save and
New buttton

Full Name
text box

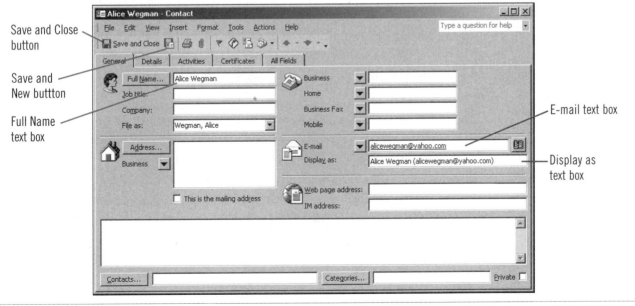

E-mail text box

Display as
text box

Creating and Sending New Messages

When you create an e-mail message, you must indicate for whom the message is intended and specify any other recipients who should receive a copy. You also need to enter a meaningful subject for the message. You write the text of your message in the message body, then send it. Outlook 2002 uses Microsoft Word as the default text editor, which means that you have access to the same text formatting features in Outlook that you use in Word documents. You can change the color of text in your message to place emphasis, you can create a bulleted list within your e-mail message, and you can check the spelling of your message easily. ✐ You are ready to write your message and send it to Alice. You've already invited an international marketing expert, Douglas Willard, to the meeting. You also send him a copy of the message to remind him about it.

Steps 1 2 3 4

1. **Click the New Mail Message button 📧 on the Standard toolbar**
   A new Untitled **Message window** opens, as shown in Figure A-9. You can type the recipient's e-mail address in the To text box, or click the To button 🔳 to select a contact from the Select Names dialog box.

2. **Click the To button 🔳**
   The Select Names dialog box opens. Contacts appears in the Show Names from the text box. You can see the three entries that you added to the Contacts folder.

3. **Click Alice Wegman in the Name list, then click To ->**
   Alice's name is placed in the list of Message Recipients, as shown in Figure A-10. In the Message Recipients box, you can see the Display As name followed by the e-mail address for each contact in the list.

4. **Click OK**
   The Select Names dialog box closes. You can still add recipients to the message through the Message window. You can send e-mail to recipients even if they are not already in your Address Book.

5. **Click the Cc text box, then type dougwillard@yahoo.com**
   Cc stands for courtesy copy. Courtesy copies are typically sent to message recipients who need to be aware of the correspondence between the sender and the recipients. Bcc, or blind courtesy copy, is used when the sender does not want to reveal who he or she has sent courtesy copies to.

6. **Press [Tab], then type Meeting about Chai Tea in the Subject text box**
   The subject text box should be a brief statement that indicates the purpose of your message.

7. **Press [Tab] to place your cursor in the message body, then type the body of the message, as shown in Figure A-11**
   The message is complete. You can see that Word's spelling feature has identified the word "Chai" as a possible spelling error.

8. **Click the Send button 📧 on the Message Standard toolbar**
   The message is sent, the Message window closes, and Outlook stores a copy of the message in your Sent Items folder.

9. **Click the Inbox list arrow 📬 Inbox ▾ in the Folder Banner to show the Folder List, then click the Sent Items folder**
   A copy of the Meeting about Chai Tea message is stored in the Sent Items folder, as shown in Figure A-12.

FIGURE A-9: Message window

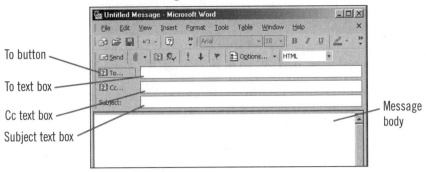

To button
To text box
Cc text box
Subject text box
Message body

FIGURE A-10: Select Names Dialog box

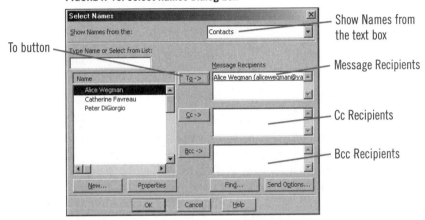

To button

Show Names from the text box
Message Recipients
Cc Recipients
Bcc Recipients

FIGURE A-11: Composing a message

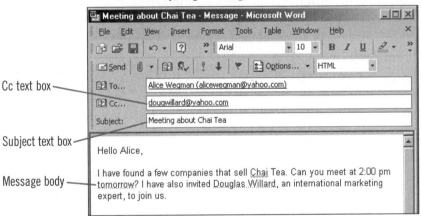

Cc text box
Subject text box
Message body

FIGURE A-12: Viewing the Sent items folder

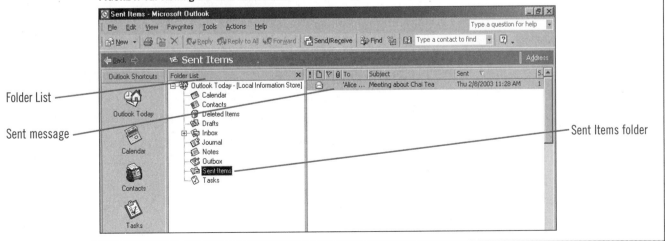

Folder List
Sent message
Sent Items folder

Replying to and Forwarding Messages

To read a message in your Inbox, you can select it and then preview it in the preview pane, or you can double-click anywhere in the message header to open it in its own window. After reading a message, you can delete it, file it in another folder, or keep it in your Inbox. You can also send a response back to the sender of the message by clicking the Reply button on the Standard toolbar. Reply automatically addresses the e-mail to the original sender and includes the text of the original sender's message in the message body. You can send a message that you have received to another person by using the Forward button on the Standard toolbar. ✎ Alice responds that she will be unavailable. You reply to her and forward her message to Douglas, to let him know the meeting is off for now.

Steps

Trouble?

Yahoo! mail only sends one AutoResponse to each sender. Even if you send more than one message to Alice's e-mail address from the same e-mail address, you will only get one Yahoo! AutoResponse message back.

1. **Click the Send/Receive button 🔁 on the Standard toolbar**
   Outlook checks for any messages that need to be sent and delivers messages that have been sent to you.

2. **Click the Inbox shortcut on the Outlook Bar**
   A message from Alice Wegman appears in the Inbox window, as shown in Figure A-13. Alice is out of the office and has set up an automatic response through her e-mail service. Alice uses Yahoo! as her e-mail service. Yahoo! automatically changes the subject line to "Yahoo! Auto Response" for messages sent by the Auto Response system. When you send messages to people who use Outlook, the original subject line will appear preceded by RE: in their response message to you.

3. **Click the Reply button 🔁 on the Standard toolbar**
   A new Message window for replying to Alice's message opens. The message is addressed back to Alice. The subject line: Yahoo! Auto Response is preceded by RE, which indicates that the message is a reply message. Information about the original message, including the sender, date, time, recipient, and subject appear in the Message window above the original message from Alice. The insertion point is at the top of the message, ready for you to type a reply.

QuickTip

You can reply simultaneously to the sender of an e-mail message and everyone that the original message was sent to by clicking the Reply to All button on the Standard toolbar.

4. **Type I will call you next week to reschedule. as shown in Figure A-14**
   You are now ready to send your reply back to Alice.

5. **Click the Send button 📧 on the Standard toolbar**
   The message is sent and a copy of it is stored in your Sent Items folder. The original message from Alice is still selected in the Message window.

6. **Click the Forward button 🔁 on the Standard toolbar**
   A new Message window for forwarding Alice's message opens. The subject line is the same, and it is preceded by FW, which indicates that the message is a forwarded message. There are no addresses in the To or Cc boxes yet.

7. **Type dougwillard@yahoo.com in the To text box, then press [Enter]**
   The message is addressed to Doug. AutoComplete will fill in an address as you type once it recognizes it as unique. You are forwarding a copy of Alice's message to Douglas Willard.

8. **Click the at top of the message body, type Doug, I have to cancel the meeting for now, then click 📧**
   The message is sent to Doug, and a copy of it is stored in your Sent Items folder.

FIGURE A-13: Inbox displaying message from Alice

Inbox folder

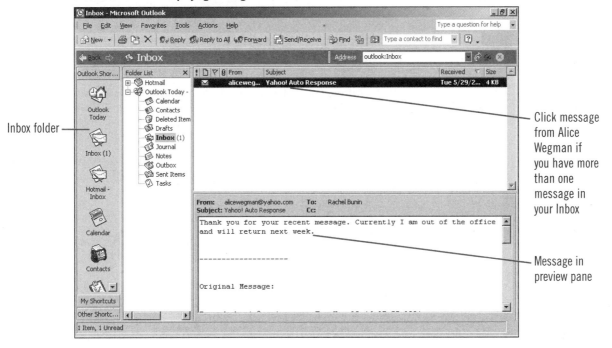

Click message from Alice Wegman if you have more than one message in your Inbox

Message in preview pane

FIGURE A-14: RE: Meeting about Chai Tea message window

Send button

Click here to type message

Details regarding the sender, date, time, recipient, and subject of the message

Alice's original message

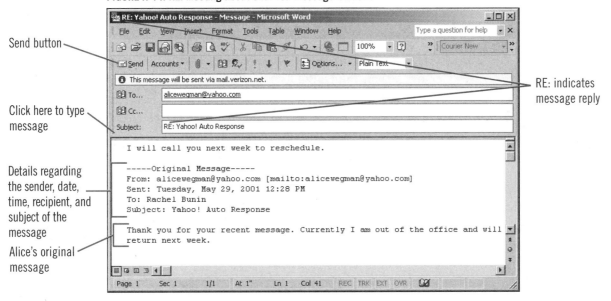

RE: indicates message reply

Emoticons

If you see something like this :-) in an e-mail message, you are looking at an emoticon. Emoticons are faces created by simple keyboard characters—in this example the colon, dash, and end parenthesis—to express an emotion or mood. (Turn the page sideways to see the face.) You can show a sad face by using a left parenthesis, or a wink by replacing the colon with a semicolon. Many people use emoticons humorously in e-mail messages.

Sending a Message with an Attachment

In addition to sending a message to a coworker or friend, you can attach a file to an e-mail message. For example, in an office environment, employees can attach Word or Excel documents to e-mail messages so that other employees can open them, make changes to them, and then return them to the original sender or forward them on. You can attach any type of computer file to an e-mail message, including pictures, video clips, and audio clips. The recipient will need the appropriate software in order to open an attachment. You have compiled some notes about Chai tea that you would like Alice to have when she returns to the office. You send her an e-mail message and attach a text file, called Tea.doc, to it.

1. Click the **New Mail Message button** on the Standard toolbar
A new Untitled Message window opens.

2. Type **Ali** in the To text box
Outlook recognizes the first three letters of the Alice Wegman contact and fills in the rest of her e-mail address.

Trouble?
If you have other contacts that begin with Ali, continue typing Alice's name until Outlook recognizes your entry.

3. Press [Tab] twice, type **Chai Tea Notes** in the Subject text box, as shown in Figure A-15
The subject indicates the purpose of the e-mail message.

4. Click the **Insert File button** on the Message window Standard toolbar
The Insert File dialog box opens.

5. Click the **Look in list arrow**, then locate the drive and folder where your Project Files are stored, as shown in Figure A-16
Your Project Files for this unit appear.

QuickTip
You can attach more than one file to an e-mail message. Attachments such as video clips or picture files may be too large in file size for some e-mail systems to handle.

6. Click **Tea.doc**, then click **Insert**
The Tea.doc file appears in the Attach text box, as shown in Figure A-17. The icon next to the filename indicates that this is a Word document file.

7. Click the **Send button** on the Standard toolbar
The Chai Tea Notes message, along with the Tea.doc file, is sent, and a copy of it is stored in your Sent Items folder.

FIGURE A-15: Chai Tea Notes message window

Insert File
button

FIGURE A-16: Insert File dialog box

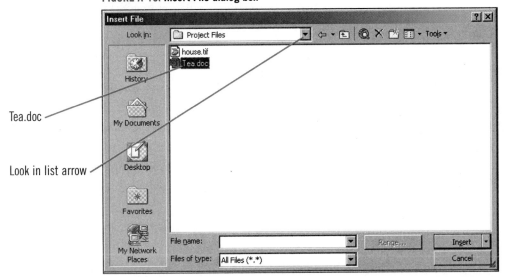

Tea.doc

Look in list arrow

FIGURE A-17: Chai Tea Notes message with Tea.doc attachment

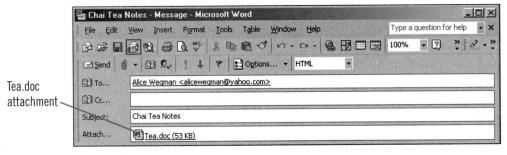

Tea.doc
attachment

Options when sending messages

In Outlook, there are several options that affect how messages are delivered. To change these options, click the Options button 📧 on the Message toolbar to open the Message Options dialog box shown in Figure A-18. You can, for example, assign a level of importance and a level of sensitivity so that the reader can prioritize messages. You can also encrypt the message for privacy. When you want to know when a message has been received or read, you can enable the Request a delivery receipt for this message or the Request a read receipt for this message check box. The sender and receiver must both be using Outlook for the receipt options to work.

FIGURE A-18: Message Options dialog box

Creating a Distribution List

When using Outlook to communicate with friends or coworkers, you may find that you need to send information to the same group of people on a regular basis. If there are many names in the Contacts folder, it can be time-consuming to scroll through all the names to select the ones you want. Fortunately, Outlook provides an easy way to manage the contacts you use most often. You can create a **Distribution List**, which is a collection of contacts to whom you regularly send the same messages. For example, if you send messages reminding your staff of a weekly meeting, you can create a distribution list called "Team" that contains the names of your staff. When you want to send a message to everyone on the team, you simply select "Team" from the Select Names dialog box, instead of selecting each user's name. Distribution lists are automatically added to the Contacts folder. You will be sending a lot of information about Chai tea to Alice, Peter, and Catherine. You decide to create a distribution list containing Alice, Peter, and Catherine's e-mail addresses. You name the distribution list, Marketing.

1. Click the **Address Book button** 🔳 on the Standard toolbar, then click the **New Entry button** 🔲 on the Address Book toolbar

   The New Entry dialog box opens. You can choose New Contact or a New Distribution List from the New Entry dialog box.

2. Click **New Distribution List**, verify that **Contacts** appears in the Put this entry In the text box, as shown in Figure A-19

   The new distribution list will be placed in the Contacts folder, along with your other contacts.

3. Click **OK**

   The Untitled Distribution List window opens. The Members tab is selected.

4. Type **Marketing** in the Name text box, as shown in Figure A-20, then click the **Select Members button** [Select Members...]

   The Select Members dialog box opens. It displays the contacts in your Contacts folder, alphabetically by the first name. From this list, you select the names to include in the Marketing distribution list.

> **QuickTip**
>
> If the names in the Select Members dialog box you want are contiguous, click the first name, press and hold [Shift], then click the last name to select all the names in the list.

5. Click **Alice Wegman**, press and hold [Ctrl], click **Catherine Favreau**, click **Peter DiGiorgio**, then release [Ctrl]

   Your Select Members dialog box should look similar to Figure A-21. The [Ctrl] key lets you select noncontiguous (nontouching) names in the list.

6. Click the **Members button** [Members ->] to move the three names to the Add to distribution list text box, then click **OK**

   The three names appear in the Members tab of the Marketing Distribution List dialog box. You can easily see who will get mail sent to the Marketing distribution list, and you can add new members or remove members. You could also click the Notes tab to write information to help describe the purpose of the list.

7. Click the **Save and Close button** 🔳 on the Distribution list toolbar

   The Marketing distribution list appears alphabetically in the Address Book, as shown in Figure A-22. A Distribution list icon 🔳 precedes the name of each distribution list.

8. Close the Address Book

   The Address Book closes, and you return to the Outlook Inbox.

FIGURE A-19: New Entry dialog box

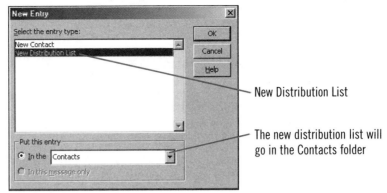

New Distribution List

The new distribution list will go in the Contacts folder

FIGURE A-20: Untitled Distribution List window

Name of distribution list

Select Members button

FIGURE A-21: Select Members dialog box

Contacts that are currently in the Contacts folder

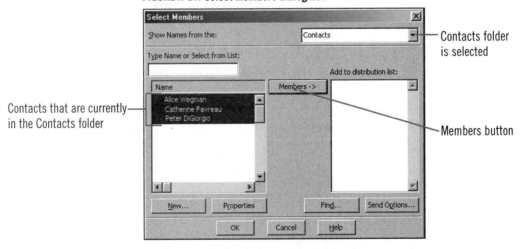

Contacts folder is selected

Members button

FIGURE A-22: Marketing distribution list in Address Book

Marketing distribution list

Distribution list icon

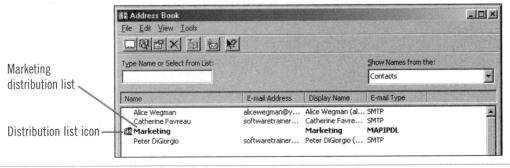

Sending a Message to a Distribution List

Distribution lists make it possible for you to send a message to the same group, without having to select each contact in the group. Once a distribution list is created, you can add new members to it or delete members from it, as necessary. If you change information about a contact who is part of a distribution list, the distribution list is automatically updated. ✎━━ The meeting about Chai tea has been rescheduled. You want to send the agenda for the meeting to everyone who will be attending. You compose a message and send it to the Marketing distribution list.

Steps 1 2 3 4

1. Click the **New Mail Message button** 🖃 on the Standard toolbar

2. Click the **To button** 🕮 in the Message window, then type **m** in the Type Name or Select from List text box, as shown in Figure A-23
   The first entry that starts with M, the Marketing distribution list is highlighted.

3. Double-click **Marketing** to move it to the Message Recipients list, then click **OK**
   The Select Names dialog box closes. The Marketing distribution list is added to the To box in the Message window.

4. Type **Meeting Agenda** in the Subject text box, press [**Tab**], type **9 am–10 am, Overview of Chai Tea products**, press [**Enter**], type **10 am–11 am, Questions and Answers**, then press [**Enter**]
   Your screen should resemble Figure A-24. When you send this message, it will go to all the members on the Marketing distribution list.

5. Type your name below the meeting agenda in the message body, click **File** on the menu bar, click **Print**, verify the settings in the Print dialog box, then click **OK**
   You want to tape the agenda to your bulletin board in your office.

6. Click the **Send button** 🖃, click the **Send/Receive button** 🖄 on the Standard toolbar, then click the **Inbox shortcut** on the Outlook Bar
   The message is sent to the Marketing distribution list. You received your copy. It is important to know how to clear out your Inbox and the various folders in Outlook. You need to delete the messages created in this unit.

7. Click the **first message** in the Inbox, press and hold [**Shift**], click the **last message** in the Inbox, click the **Delete button** ✕ on the Standard toolbar
   The messages in the Inbox are now in the Deleted Items folder. You can access messages in the Deleted Items folder as long as it has not been emptied.

8. Click the **My Shortcuts** group button on the Outlook Bar, click the **Sent Items folder** on the Outlook Bar, select all the messages, then click the **Delete button** ✕ on the Standard toolbar
   The messages in the Sent Items folder are placed in the Deleted Items folder.

9. Click the **Address Book button** 🕮 on the toolbar, press [**Ctrl**], click each name that you created in this unit, click the **Delete button** ✕, then close the Address Book

10. Click **Tools** on the menu bar, click **Empty "Deleted Items" folder** click **Yes**, click **File** on the menu bar, then click **Exit** to exit Outlook
    The Deleted Items folder is emptied and Outlook is closed.

Trouble?
If you have another entry that begins with the letter M and precedes Marketing, click the down arrow on your keyboard until Marketing is selected.

QuickTip
If you have other messages in your Inbox that you haven't read, delete only the messages relating to this unit.

FIGURE A-23: Selecting the Marketing distribution list

Type m to jump to the first entry that begins with the letter M

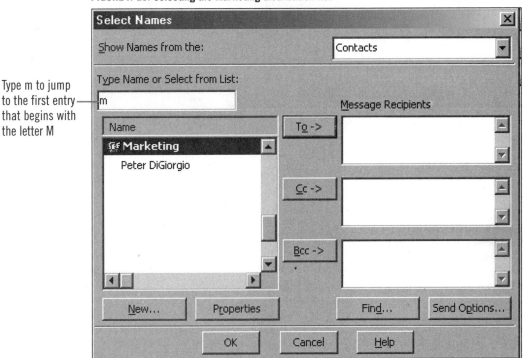

FIGURE A-24: Message addressed to the Marketing group

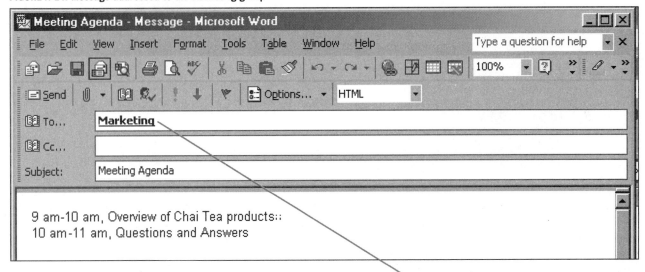

Message is addressed to the Marketing distribution list

What is Microsoft Outlook Express?

Microsoft Outlook Express is a program that you can use to exchange e-mail and join newsgroups. It comes with Windows 2000. It focuses primarily on e-mail, so it does not have the many features of Outlook. Outlook is an integrated desktop information manager that combines the Inbox function with a Calendar, Contacts database, Tasks database, and Notes database. (See the Appendix for more information on the additional features of Outlook.) However, once you learn how to use the e-mail capabilities of Outlook, you will be able to apply those skills to Outlook Express.

Practice

► Concepts Review

Label the elements of the Outlook window shown in Figure A-25.

FIGURE A-25

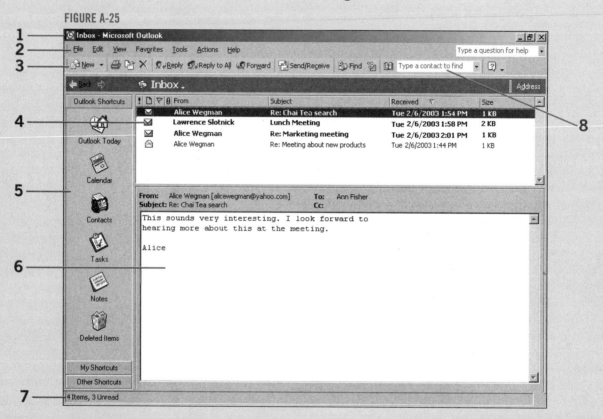

Match each term with the statement that best describes it.

9. E-mail
10. Distribution list
11. Contacts folder
12. Attachment
13. Inbox
14. Message header

a. Stores all of the names of users to whom you can send messages

b. A list of contacts that are grouped together and given a descriptive name

c. A computer file, such as a Word or Excel document, that is sent along with an e-mail message

d. Messages that are sent and received over a computer network

e. Contains messages you have received

f. Identifies the sender, subject, and date of the message

Select the best answer from the list of choices.

15. You can see how many messages are in your Inbox and how many are unread by viewing the:
- **a.** Folder banner.
- **b.** Menu bar.
- **c.** Preview pane.
- **d.** Status bar.

16. Which menu do you use to empty the Deleted Items folder?
- **a.** Tools
- **b.** Edit
- **c.** Actions
- **d.** File

17. Which of the following is *not* a message header icon?
- **a.** !
- **b.**
- **c.**
- **d.**

18. To read a message that arrives in your Inbox, you:
- **a.** Click View on the menu bar, then click Read.
- **b.** Double-click the message.
- **c.** Click the Read button on the Standard toolbar.
- **d.** Click the Inbox folder.

19. To send an attachment with your e-mail message, you:
- **a.** Create a message, then click the Attach File button.
- **b.** Create a message, then click the Insert File button.
- **c.** Click the Insert File button, then click the New Mail Message button on the Standard toolbar.
- **d.** Click the Attach File button, then click the New Mail Message button on the Standard toolbar.

20. To forward a selected message to another user you:
- **a.** Click File on the menu bar, then click Forward.
- **b.** Click the Forward button on the Standard toolbar.
- **c.** Click the Send button in the Message window.
- **d.** Click Tools on the menu bar, then click Forward.

21. To create a new message, you:
- **a.** Click the New Mail Message button.
- **b.** Click the Create button.
- **c.** Click the Mail button.
- **d.** Click the Send button.

22. To send the same message to multiple recipients, which of the following is *not* an option?
- **a.** Dragging the message to each of the recipient names.
- **b.** Selecting multiple names from the Contacts folder in the Select Names dialog box.
- **c.** Entering multiple names in the To text box.
- **d.** Creating a distribution list containing the names of the users.

Skills Review

1. Start Outlook and view the Outlook 2002 window.

a. Click the Start button on the taskbar, point to Programs, then click Outlook.

b. Choose a profile if you are prompted to during the startup of Outlook.

c. Click the Outlook Today shortcut on the Outlook Bar.

d. Click View on the menu bar, point to Go To, then click Inbox.

e. Locate the following items: menu bar, title bar, status bar, preview pane, Standard toolbar, and folder banner.

f. Click the Address Book button on the Standard toolbar.

g. Close the Address Book.

2. Add a contact to the Address Book.

a. Click the Address Book button on the Standard toolbar.

b. Click the New Entry button on the Address Book toolbar.

c. Make sure that New Contact is selected, then click OK.

d. Type **Martha Sevigny** in the Full Name text box, click the E-mail text box, type **martha_sevigny@yahoo.com**, then press [Tab].

e. Click the Save and Close button on the Address Book toolbar.

f. Close the Address Book.

3. Create and Send new messages.

a. Click the New Mail Message button on the Standard toolbar.

b. Click the To button.

c. Verify that Contacts appears in the Show Names from the text box.

d. Double-click Martha Sevigny in the Names list.

e. Click OK to close the Select Names dialog box.

f. Type **alicewegman@yahoo.com** in the Cc text box.

g. Type **Lunch on Tuesday** in the Subject text box, then press [Tab].

h. Type **Martha, I will be near your office on Tuesday. Can you meet me for lunch? I would also like to invite Alice Wegman.**

i. Click the Send button.

4. Reply to and Forward messages.

a. Click the Send/Receive button on the Standard toolbar.

b. Click the Inbox folder on the Folder List.

c. Read the message from Martha in the preview pane.

d. Click the Reply button on the Standard toolbar.

e. Click the message body, then type **Martha, I look forward to hearing about your vacation**. Send the message.

f. Click the Forward button on the Standard toolbar.

g. Type **alicewegman@yahoo.com** in the To text box.

h. Click the top of the message body, then type **Alice, Martha has responded below that she cannot make our lunch meeting. We'll reschedule lunch for another time.**

i. Click the Send button.

5. Send a message with an attachment.

a. Click the New Mail Message button.

b. Click the Address Book button.

c. Select Martha Sevigny as the message recipient.

d. Close the Select Names dialog box.

e. Type **picture of cottage** in the Subject text box.

    f. Type **Martha, here is the picture you requested. Let me know if you would like to rent the house this summer** in the message body.

    g. Click the Insert File button.

    h. Click the Look in list arrow, then click the drive and folder where your Project Files are stored.

    i. Click house.tif, then click Insert.

    j. Click Send.

6. Create a distribution list.

    a. Create three new contacts in the Address Book. You can use your own e-mail address and/or those of your friends.

    b. Click the Address Book button on the Standard toolbar.

    c. Click the New Entry button.

    d. Click New Distribution List, then click OK.

    e. Type **Summer House** in the Name text box.

    f. Click the Select Members button, then select at least three contacts from the Select Members dialog box.

    g. Click OK, then click the Save and Close button.

    h. Close the Address Book.

7. Send a message to a distribution list.

    a. Click the New Mail Message button.

    b. Click the To button in the new mail Message window.

    c. Double-click Summer House in the Select Names dialog box, then click OK.

    d. Type **security deposit** in the Subject text box.

    e. Type **Please turn in your share of the security deposit for the summer house we are renting. Thank you**.

    f. Click the Send button.

    g. Delete all of the messages in the Inbox folder from this exercise.

    h. Delete all of the messages in the Sent Items folder from this exercise.

    i. Delete all of the fictitious addresses in the Address Book.

    j. Click Tools on the menu bar, then click Empty Deleted Items folder.

    k. Exit Outlook.

► Independent Challenge 1

You are a member of the student newspaper at your school. The editor has asked you to organize monthly dinner meetings for the newspaper staff to brainstorm new ideas for the paper. You decide to use Outlook to notify the staff of upcoming dinner meetings. Since you'll be corresponding with the staff frequently, you create a distribution list of the newspaper staff members.

    a. Start Outlook.

    b. Using the e-mail addresses of your friends, create a distribution list called Newspaper.

    c. Be sure to include yourself on the list.

    d. Add at least four contacts to the distribution list.

    e. Create a new message and address it to the Newspaper distribution list.

    f. Type **dinner meeting** in the Subject text box.

    g. Type **This month's meeting will be at the Italian Kitchen on March 3, 2003 at 7:00 pm.** in the message box.

    h. Click the Send button, then click the Send/Receive button. Depending on the speed and type of Internet connection you are using, you may need to click the Send/Receive button again, after waiting a few moments, if you do not receive a response e-mail the first time you click the Send/Receive button.

    i. Read the dinner meeting message, then print it.

    j. Delete all of the messages in the Inbox folder related to this Independent Challenge.

k. Delete all of the messages in the Sent Items folder from this exercise.

l. Delete the Newspaper distribution list, and any fictitious addresses in the Address Book.

m. Empty the Deleted Items folder.

n. Exit Outlook.

▶ Independent Challenge 2

Practice sending an e-mail message with an attachment to a friend, family member, or classmate.

a. Start Outlook.

b. Create a new message and address it to a friend, family member, or classmate.

c. Enter your e-mail address in the Cc text box.

d. Type **picture** in the Subject text box.

e. Attach a picture to the e-mail message. Use a picture stored on your computer or one from your Project Files (*Hint*: Click the Insert File button on the Message window Standard toolbar, click the Look in list arrow in the Insert File dialog box to navigate to the drive and folder where the picture you want is stored, then click Insert.) Graphics files have extensions including .tif, .bmp, .jpg, or .gif.

f. Type a short note to the recipient of the message, telling him or her that you thought they would like this picture.

g. Click the Send button, then click the Send/Receive button. Depending on the speed and type of Internet connection you are using, you may need to click the Send/Receive button again, after waiting a few moments, if you do not receive a response e-mail the first time you click the Send/Receive button.

h. Print a copy of the picture message.

i. Delete all of the messages in your Inbox.

j. Delete all of the messages in the Sent Folder.

k. Empty the Deleted Items folder.

l. Exit Outlook.

Appendix

Beyond E-mail: Understanding Additional Outlook Features

Objectives

► **Manage your appointments and tasks**
► **Manage your contacts**
► **Preview your day**

To effectively use Microsoft Outlook 2002 in managing your business and personal information, it is important to know not only how to use the Inbox to send and receive e-mail, but also how to use the additional components in Outlook. Outlook integrates several tools, including Inbox, Calendar, Contacts, Tasks, Notes, and Outlook Today to provide you with a uniquely comprehensive information manager.

Now that you know how to manage your e-mail with the Inbox, you will learn how Outlook combines e-mail with its other components to create an integrated desktop information manager.

Managing Your Appointments and Tasks

Details

The Calendar and Tasks in Microsoft Outlook provide convenient, effective means to manage your appointments and tasks. **Calendar** is the electronic equivalent of your desk calendar, while **Tasks** is an electronic to-do list. Calendar defines an **appointment** as an activity that does not involve inviting other people or scheduling resources, a **meeting** as an activity you invite people to or reserve resources for, and an **event** as an activity that lasts 24 hours or longer. You can specify the subject and location of the activity, and its start and end times. You can also ensure that you do not forget the activity by having Outlook sound a reminder prior to the start of the activity. Outlook will notify you if the activity conflicts with, or is adjacent to, another scheduled activity. You can view any period of time in Calendar. For example, you can look at and plan activities for next month or even next year.

Review the following features of Calendar and Tasks:

▶ To review your appointments, meetings, and events, open the **Outlook Shortcuts** group on the Outlook Bar, then click the **Calendar shortcut**. The Calendar is shown in Figure AP-1. To make your view match the figure, click View on the menu bar, point to Current View, click Day/Week/Month with AutoPreview, then click the Day button on the toolbar. To create appointments, click the **New Appointment button** 🖼 New ▾ on the Standard toolbar. Recurring appointments are entered once, and then you set a recurrence pattern. The appointments that recur have a special icon.

▶ To facilitate planning your activities, you can choose to view Calendar by day, week, or month, and you can use the **Date Navigator** to quickly view specific dates. Dates displayed in boldface on the Date Navigator indicate days on which you have scheduled appointments.

▶ To schedule a meeting by having the Calendar check the availability of all the invitees and resources, once you have selected a meeting time and location, you can send invitations in meeting requests. If an invitee accepts the invitation, Outlook will post the meeting automatically to the invitee's calendar.

▶ To publish a Calendar over the Web, you save the Calendar as an HTML file. It can then be shared over an **intranet** or over the Internet.

▶ To manage your business and personal to-do list, click the **Tasks shortcut** in the Outlook Shortcuts group on the Outlook Bar. Figure AP-2 shows the Tasks in Simple List view.

Click the **New Task button** ☑ New ▾ to create new tasks. Once you create a task, you can work with that task in several ways. Click the **Organize button** 📊 to organize your tasks by grouping them by **Category**. Outlook provides a list of 20 categories such as Ideas, Personal, and Competition, or you can create your own. View your tasks in several different ways, including by subject, by status, and by due date. You can mark your progress on tasks by percentage complete, and you can have Outlook create status summary reports in e-mail messages and then send the update to anyone on the update list.

Use the **New Task Request** command on the Actions menu to assign tasks to a coworker or assistant and have Outlook automatically update you on the status of the task completion. To help you coordinate your tasks and your appointments, the task list from Tasks can be displayed in the **TaskPad** in Calendar. To schedule time to complete a task, simply drag a task from the TaskPad to a time block in the Calendar. Any changes you make to a task are reflected in both the TaskPad in Calendar and the task list in Tasks.

QuickTip

Notes is the electronic version of the popular colored paper sticky notes.

▶ To quickly write down an idea or a note concerning an appointment or a task, simply click the **Notes shortcut** on the Outlook Bar and click the **New Note button** 📝 New ▾ on the toolbar. Notes can be color-coded as well as organized by Category. See Figure AP-3.

FIGURE AP-1: Calendar

New appointment button

Click to view Calendar

Appointments

Recurring appointment

Reminder is set

Outlook bar

Day button

Date Navigator

TaskPad

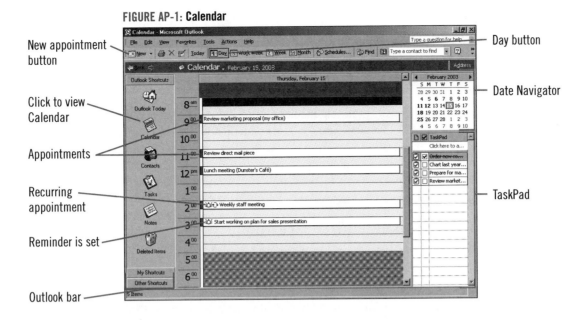

FIGURE AP-2: Tasks

New Task button

Organize button

Click to view Tasks

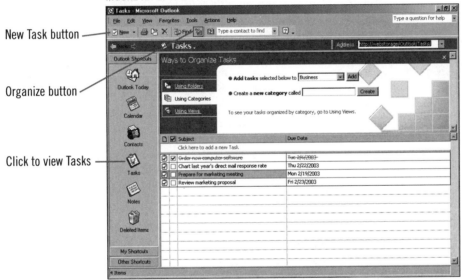

FIGURE AP-3: Notes

New Note button

Three notes

Click to view Notes

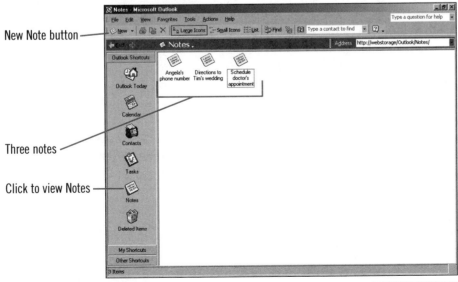

Managing Your Contacts

Details

Contacts in Microsoft Outlook enables you to manage all your business and personal contact information. With Contacts, you can store general and detailed information for the people you want to communicate with. From Contacts, you can quickly send a meeting request, task request, or a simple e-mail message. You can sort, group, and filter contacts by any parts of their name or address to help you manage and stay in touch with your personal and business contacts. You can also easily share contacts within your business or personal community.

Review the following features of Contacts:

▶ To open Contacts, click the **Contacts shortcut** on the Outlook Bar. See Figure AP-4. Click the **New Contact button** on the toolbar to enter information for a new contact.

Type the contact's name in the Name text box. If you do not enter a first and last name, the Check Full Name dialog box will open, allowing you to enter the full name for the contact, including title, first name, middle name, last name, and suffix if appropriate. You can also open the Check Full Name dialog box, by clicking the **Full Name button**. You can filter, sort, and group your contacts by any part of their names.

You can store up to three addresses in the Address text box, by choosing Business, Home, or Other from the Address list, then typing the address in the Address text box. If Outlook can't identify an appropriate street, city, state/province, postal code, and country/region, the Check Address dialog box will open for you to verify or complete the information. You can store more than a dozen telephone and fax numbers, three e-mail addresses, and a Web page address. Click the **Details tab** to store each contact's detailed information, including the department or office, the assistant's or manager's name, the contact's birthday, anniversary, or even the contact's nickname. Figure AP-5 shows the Details tab of Alice Wegman's contact information.

Outlook allows you to file each contact under any name that you choose, including by first name, last name, a company name, or company or job title. Outlook will automatically present you with several File as options. Once you have entered your contacts' information, you can view your contacts in a variety of ways, including as detailed address cards, as a phone list, or by company, category, or location.

▶ Quickly dial a contact telephone number if you have a modem. Click the **Dial button** on the Contacts toolbar, to open the New Call dialog box. After Outlook has dialed the phone number, pick up the phone handset then click **Talk.**

▶ Keep track of all e-mail, tasks, appointments, and documents relating to specific contacts. For example, when you create a new Outlook item, such as a task, you can link it to the contacts to which it relates. You can also link any items, such as meetings, that already exist in folders to the relevant contacts. And, you can link documents and files you create in other Office programs to contacts.

▶ Send contact information over the Internet by using **vCards**, the Internet standard for creating and sharing virtual business cards. To send a vCard to someone via e-mail, click **Contacts**, click the contact you want to send as a vCard, click **Actions** on the menu bar, then click **Forward as vCard**. You can also include your vCard with your e-mail signature.

▶ Create a mailing list that's a subset of your Contacts folder, by filtering the Contacts list, and then using the filtered list to begin a mail merge from Outlook. When you **filter** a list, you search for only specific information—for example, only those contacts that live in New Jersey. You can create a variety of merged documents in Word, then you can begin your mail merge from Outlook. You can create form letters, print mailing labels, or print addresses on envelopes. You can also send bulk e-mail messages or faxes to your contacts. To send a mail merge to a filtered set of your contacts, click **View** on the menu bar in Contacts, point to **Current View**, and then click **Customize Current View.** Click **Filter** and then specify the filter criteria. Once you have filtered the contacts you want for the merge, to start the mail merge, **Tools** on the menu bar, then click **Mail Merge.**

FIGURE AP-4: Contacts displayed in the Contacts window

New Contact button

Dial button

Click to view Contacts

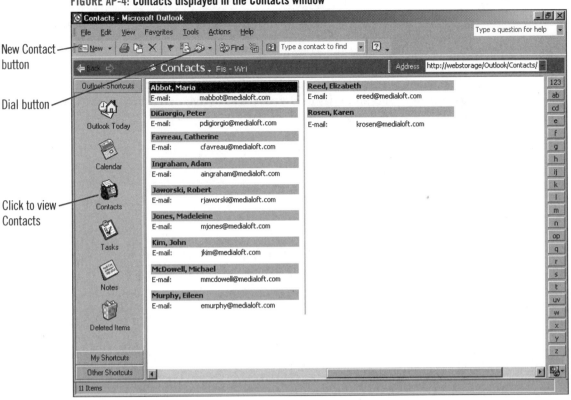

FIGURE AP-5: Details tab of Alice Wegman's Contact window

Details tab

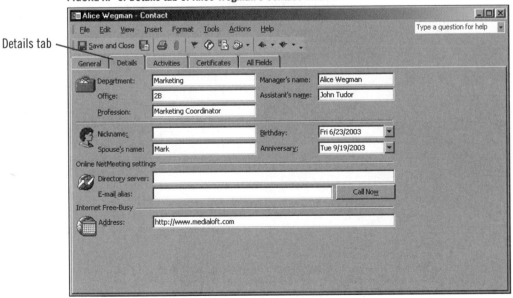

Previewing Your Day

The **Outlook Today page** provides a preview of your day at a glance. It is the electronic version of your day planner book and provides a snapshot view of the current activities, tasks, contacts, notes, and messages in the Outlook folders. Just as with a paper-based daily planner, you can customize how you view Outlook Today to fit your personal style and work habits. See Figure AP-6.

Review the following features of Outlook Today:

► View how many messages are in your Inbox, Outbox, and Drafts folders. The right column of Outlook Today displays your message information. You can customize Outlook Today to show any of your Personal Folders in the Messages column.

► View your appointments over the next few days. These appear in the Calendar section of Outlook Today, which is located in the left column. You can choose to show anywhere from 1–7 days of appointments in your Calendar.

► View your to do list to see what you have to do. Tasks appear in the center column of Outlook Today, allowing you to list all of your tasks in one convenient place. You can customize Outlook Today to show all your tasks or just today's tasks. You can also sort your tasks by Importance, Due Date, Creation Time, or Start Date, and in ascending or descending order. In addition, you can keep track of tasks by clicking the check box to the left of the task to indicate you've completed it. The task list will be updated automatically in the Tasks folder.

► View detailed information on any item in Outlook Today by clicking the task, appointment, or meeting. Clicking the appointment or meeting opens the item's dialog box.

► Customize the Outlook Today page for the way you work by clicking Customize Outlook Today. You can make Outlook Today your default page when you start Outlook. You can change the way tasks appear on the Outlook Today page, change how many days' appointments appear on the Outlook Today page, determine which folders appear so you can see how many messages are in each folder, and change the style of Outlook Today (how it looks). The styles lay out the calendar, messages, and tasks in different column arrangements with special background colors and text effects.

FIGURE AP-6: Outlook Today page

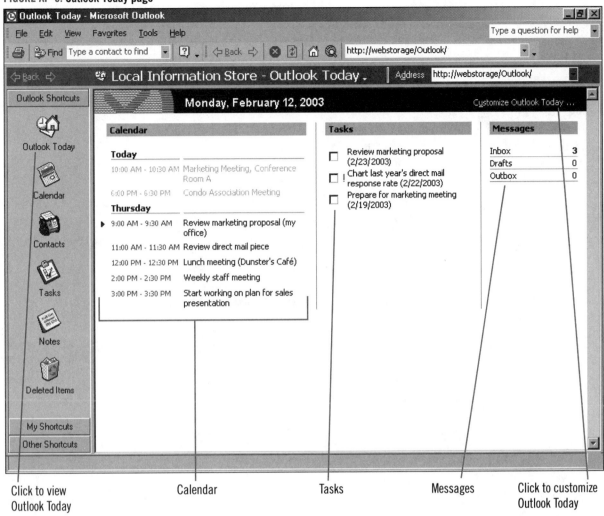

Click to view
Outlook Today

Calendar

Tasks

Messages

Click to customize
Outlook Today

Practice

► Concepts Review

Label the elements of the calendar window shown in Figure AP-7.

FIGURE AP-7

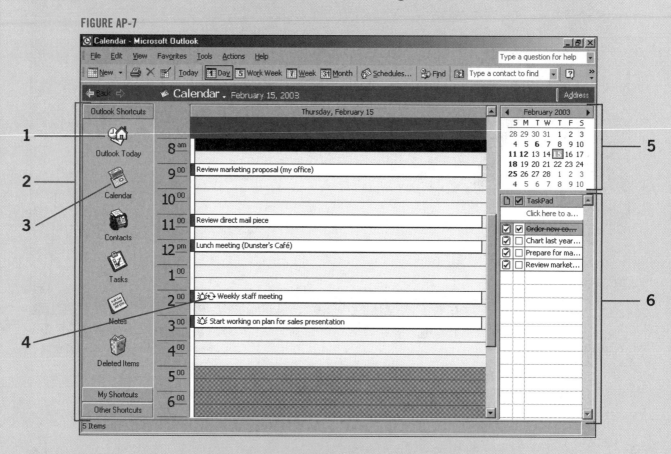

Select the best answer from the list of choices.

7. Which of the following is *not* one of the Outlook folders:
   a. Inbox   **b.** Meeting Planner   **c.** Calendar   **d.** Notes

8. Use the _____ to schedule your appointments, meetings, and events.
   a. Calendar   **b.** Tasks   **c.** Notes   **d.** Contacts

9. Use the _____ to manage your business and personal to-do list.
   a. Calendar   **b.** Tasks   **c.** Notes   **d.** Contacts

10. Use the _____ to supplement the information stored in Calendar and Tasks.
    a. Calendar   **b.** Tasks   **c.** Notes   **d.** Contacts

Formatting
a Disk

A **disk** is a device on which you can store electronic data. Disks come in a variety of sizes and have varying storage capacities. Your computer's **hard disk**, one of its internal devices, can store large amounts of data. **Floppy disks**, on the other hand, are smaller, inexpensive, and portable. Most floppy disks that you buy today are 3½" (the diameter of the inside, circular part of the disk). Disks are sometimes called **drives**, but this term really refers to the name by which the operating system recognizes the disk (or a portion of the disk). The operating system typically assigns a drive letter to a drive (which you can reassign if you want). For example, on most computers the hard disk is identified by the drive letter "C" and the floppy drive by the drive letter "A." The amount of information a disk can hold is called its **capacity**, usually measured in megabytes (Mb). The most common floppy disk capacity is 1.44 Mb. Newer computers come with other disk drives, such as a **Zip drive**, a kind of disk drive made to handle **Zip disks**. These disks are portable like floppy disks, but they can contain 100 Mb, far more than regular floppy disks.  In this appendix, you will prepare a floppy disk for use.

Formatting a Disk

In order for an operating system to be able to store data on a disk, the disk must be formatted. **Formatting** prepares a disk so it can store information. Usually, floppy disks are formatted when you buy them, but if not, you can perform this function yourself using Windows 2000.

To complete the following steps, you need a blank floppy disk or a disk containing data you no longer need. Do not use your Project Disk for this lesson, as all information on the disk will be erased.

Steps 1234

Trouble?

This unit assumes that the drive that will contain your floppy disks is drive A. If not, substitute the correct drive any time you are instructed to use the 3½ Floppy (A:) drive.

1. Start Windows if necessary, then place a 3½" floppy disk in drive A

2. Double-click the **My Computer icon** on the desktop

My Computer opens, as shown in Figure AP-1. This window lists all the drives and printers that you can use on your computer. Because computers have different drives, printers, programs, and other devices installed, your window will probably look different.

3. Right-click the 3½ **Floppy (A:) icon**

When you click with the right mouse button, a pop-up menu of commands that apply to the item you right-clicked appears. Because you right-clicked a drive, the Format command is available.

Trouble?

Windows cannot format a disk if it is write-protected; therefore, you may need to slide the write-protect tab over until it clicks to continue. See Figure AP-3 to locate the write-protect tab on your disk.

4. Click **Format** on the pop-up menu

The Format dialog box opens, as shown in Figure AP-2. In this dialog box, you specify the capacity of the disk you are formatting, the File system, the Allocation unit size, the kind of formatting you want to do, and if you want, a volume label. You are doing a standard format so you will accept the default settings.

5. Click **Start**, then, when you are warned that formatting will erase all data on the disk, click **OK** to continue

Windows formats your disk. After the formatting is complete, you will probably see a summary about the size of the disk; it's okay if you don't.

6. Click **OK** when the message telling you that the format is complete appears, then click **Close** in the Format dialog box

QuickTip

Once a disk is formatted, you do not need to format it again. However, some people use the Quick Format option to erase the contents of a disk quickly, rather than having to select the files and then delete them.

7. Click the **Close button** in the My Computer window

My Computer closes and you return to the desktop.

FIGURE AP-1: My Computer window

Drive containing your disk

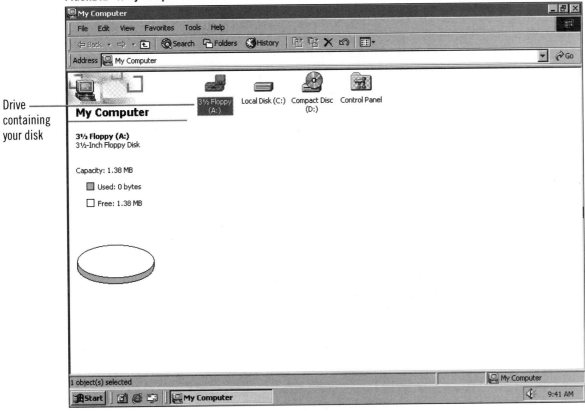

FIGURE AP-2: Format dialog box

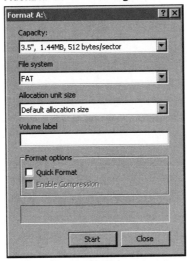

FIGURE P-10: Replicated objects

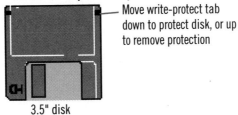

Move write-protect tab down to protect disk, or up to remove protection

3.5" disk

Appendix A:
Formatting a Disk

A **disk** is a device on which you can store electronic data. Disks come in a variety of sizes and have varying storage capacities. Your computer's **hard disk**, one of its internal devices, can store large amounts of data. **Floppy disks**, on the other hand, are smaller, inexpensive, and portable. Most floppy disks that you buy today are 3½" (the diameter of the inside, circular part of the disk). Disks are sometimes called **drives**, but this term really refers to the name by which the operating system recognizes the disk (or a portion of the disk). The operating system typically assigns a drive letter to a drive (which you can reassign if you want). For example, on most computers the hard disk is identified by the drive letter "C" and the floppy drive by the drive letter "A." The amount of information a disk can hold is called its **capacity**, usually measured in megabytes (Mb). The most common floppy disk capacity is 1.44 Mb. Newer computers come with devices, such as a **Zip drive**, a new kind of disk drive made to handle **Zip disks**. These disks are portable like floppy disks, but they can contain 100 Mb, far more than regular floppy disks.

In this appendix, you will prepare a floppy disk for use.

Formatting a Disk

For an operating system to be able to store data on a disk, the disk must be formatted. **Formatting** prepares a disk so it can store information. Usually disks are formatted when you buy them, but if not, you can perform this function yourself using Windows 98. To complete the following steps, you need a blank disk or a disk containing data you no longer need. Do not use your Project Disk for this lesson, as all information will be erased.

1. Start Windows if necessary, then place a 3½" floppy disk in drive A

2. Double-click the **My Computer icon** on the desktop

My Computer opens, as shown in Figure AP-1. This window lists all the drives and printers that you can use on your computer. Because computers have different drives, printers, programs, and so forth installed, your window will probably look different.

3. Right-click the **3½ Floppy (A:) icon**

When you click with the right mouse button, a pop-up menu of commands that apply to the item you right-clicked appears. You right-clicked a drive so the Format command is available.

4. Click **Format** on the pop-up menu

The Format dialog box opens, as shown in Figure AP-2. In this dialog box, you specify the capacity of the disk you are formatting and the kind of formatting you want to do. See Table AP-1 for a description of formatting options.

5. Click the **Full option button**, then click **Start**

Windows formats your disk. By selecting the Full option, you ensure that your computer can read the disk. After the formatting is complete, you will probably see a summary about the size of the disk; it's okay if you don't.

6. Click **Close** in the Format Results dialog box, then click **Close** in the Format dialog box

7. Click the **Close button** in the My Computer window

My Computer closes and you return to the desktop.

Trouble?
This unit assumes that the drive that will contain your floppy disks is drive A. If not, substitute the correct drive any time you are instructed to use the 3½ Floppy (A:) drive.

Trouble?
Windows cannot format a disk if it is write-protected; therefore, you need to move the write-protect tab to continue. See Figure AP-3 to locate the write-protect tab on your disk.

QuickTip
Once a disk is formatted, you do not need to format it again. However, some people use the Quick (erase) option to quickly erase the contents of a disk rather than having to select the files and then delete them.

TABLE AP-1: Options in the Format dialog box

option	description
Capacity	Use to specify the amount of information your disk is made to hold
Quick (erase)	Use for an already-formatted disk that contains files you want to erase; it takes less time than the Full option
Full	Use for a new, unformatted disk; this option initializes the disk, preparing it to receive data and requiring more time to complete than the Quick option
Copy system files only	Use to make an already-formatted disk bootable, meaning you will be able to start your computer with it
Label	Use to give your disk a name to make it easier to identify later
Display summary when finished	Use to see information about the disk after formatting is finished, such as how much space is available on the disk
Copy system files	Use to format the disk and then make it bootable after formatting is complete by copying system files to it

FIGURE AP-1: **My Computer window**

Drive containing your disk

Your icons may look different

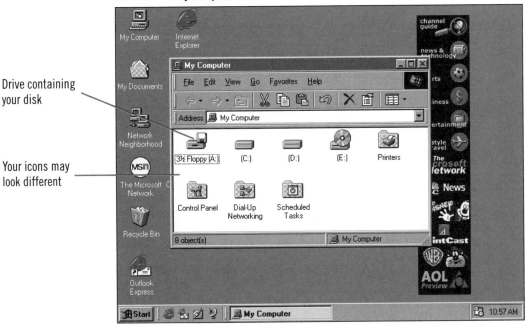

FIGURE AP-2: **Format dialog box**

Click to format a new, unformatted disk

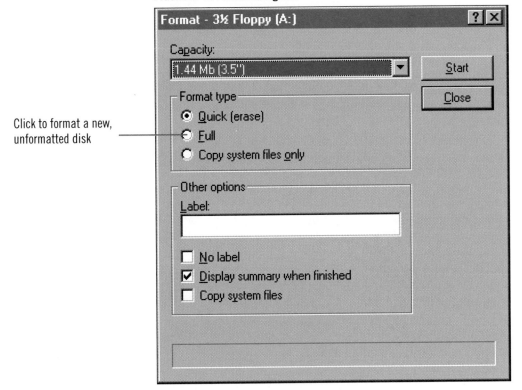

FIGURE AP-3: **Write-protect tab**

Write-protect tab

3.5" disk

Unit
A

Bonus Exercises

for Office XP

► **Word**
► **Excel**
► **Access**
► **PowerPoint**
► **Integration**

This unit contains bonus exercises for Word, Excel, Access, PowerPoint, and Integration. These exercises were created to enhance the Office XP skills you learned in earlier units and to offer further practice. Each exercise is categorized by the industry it focuses on to help provide real-world context for the skills covered.

1. **Start Word XP.**
   a. Start Word using the Programs menu.
   b. Select Print Layout view and the Page Width zoom level.

2. **Explore the Word program window.**
   a. Identify the title bar, the menu bar, the status bar, and the Standard and Formatting toolbars.
   b. Review the contents of each menu and read the ScreenTip for each button on the Standard and Formatting toolbars.
   c. Review the contents of the New Document task pane.
   d. View the blank document in Normal, Web Layout, Print Layout, and Outline view, then return to Print Layout view.

3. **Start a document.**
   a. Close the New Document task pane, then start a memo to inform colleagues about an upcoming company picnic.
   b. Type **MEMORANDUM** at the top of the page, then press [Enter] twice.
   c. Type the following lines of text, pressing [Tab] and [Enter] as indicated:
      To:[Tab]**All Employees**[Enter][Enter]
      From:[Tab]**Your Name**[Enter][Enter]
      Date:[Tab]**Today's Date**[Enter][Enter]
      Re:[Tab]**Company Picnic**[Enter][Enter]
   d. Press [Enter] once more, then type **We'll bring the food and you bring the red ants! All employees of Mason & Associates are invited to our fourth annual picnic at Pacific Spirit Park on July 8 from noon to 4 pm. Bring your families and your swim suits!**
   e. Press [Enter] twice, then type **Please call Doris at Extension 2366 if you plan to attend.**
   f. Using the [Backspace] key, delete **Picnic** in the Re: line, then type **Barbeque**.
   g. Using the [Delete] key, delete **picnic** in the first paragraph, then type **barbeque**.

4. **Save a document.**
   a. Save the document as **Picnic Memo**.
   b. Change the location of the picnic to Jericho Beach Park, then save the changes.

5. **Print a document.**
   a. View the document in Print Preview, zoom in on the memo, then proofread it.
   b. Zoom out on the document, close Print Preview, then correct any errors, if necessary.
   c. Save the document, then print a copy of the memo, using the default print settings.

6. **Use the Help system.**
   a. Use the Office Assistant to search for help using the keywords **printing a document**.
   b. Click the topic Print more than one copy, then read about how to print multiple copies of a document.
   c. Click the Show button at the top of the Help window if necessary, click the Contents tab, double-click the topic Managing Files, then double-click the topic Finding Files.
   d. Click the topic Find a file, then read the topic.
   e. Close the Help window and hide the Office Assistant.

7. **Close a document and exit Word.**
   a. Close the Picnic Memo document, saving your changes if necessary, then exit Word.

Education

Create the document shown in Figure Word-1, substituting your name and your address where indicated. Save the document with the name **College Information Letter**, print a copy of the letter, then close the document and exit Word.

FIGURE WORD-1

[Your Name]
[Your Address]

April 10, 2004

Admissions Officer
Business Administration Program
West Falls College
1600 Birch Avenue
Manchester, NH 03104

Dear Sir/Madam:

I wish to obtain information about the Business Administration Department at West Falls College. At present, I am enrolled in a one-year program in the Department of Applied Business Technology at Wessex College in Bradford. I will graduate in June with an Accounting Assistant certificate.

I would like to receive information about your two-year Marketing program. Specifically, I need information about entrance requirements, course content and prerequisites, tuition costs, and application deadlines.

I would also like to know what financial aid and/or bursaries are available.

I hope to apply for your program this spring for entrance in the fall. Thank you for your attention to my request; I look forward to hearing from you.

Sincerely,

[Your Name]

1. **Open a document.**
   a. Start Word, then open the file BWD-1 from the drive and folder where your Project Files are located and save it with the filename **Dance Classes**.

2. **Select text.**
   a. Select **Fall** in the subtitle and replace it with **Spring**.
   b. Select **September 10** in the first paragraph and replace it with **March 15**, then select **1950s** in the Beginners Swing paragraph and replace it with **1940s**.
   c. Delete **Advanced Country Dancing** and its description at the end of the document, then save your changes.

3. **Cut and paste text.**
   a. Use the Cut and Paste buttons to switch the order of the two sentences in the Advanced Swing Dancing description.
   b. Use the drag method to move **Beginners Latin Dancing** and its accompanying paragraph above **Beginners Country Dancing**. Add line spaces between paragraphs where necessary, then save your changes.

4. **Copy and paste text.**
   a. Use the Copy and Paste buttons to copy **Dancing** in the subtitle so that it appears after **Swing** in the line Beginners Swing.
   b. Use the Paste Options button to change the formatting of the pasted text to match the formatting of the Beginners Swing line.
   c. Use the drag method to copy **ballroom** from the first sentence of the Beginners Ballroom Dancing description and paste it before the word **dancing** in the first sentence of the Advanced Ballroom Dancing description, then save your changes.

5. **Use the Office Clipboard.**
   a. Open the Office Clipboard in the task pane, then cut **Advanced Ballroom Dancing** and its accompanying description and **Beginners Latin Dancing** and its accompanying description to the clipboard.
   b. Use the Office Clipboard to paste the Advanced Ballroom Dancing item under the Beginners Ballroom Dancing item and the Beginners Latin Dancing item as the last item in the document.
   c. Add or remove line breaks where necessary, close the Office Clipboard, then save your changes.

6. **Use the Spelling and Grammar checker and the Thesaurus.**
   a. Using right-click, set Word to ignore the spelling of "pardner" in the Beginners Country Dancing description.
   b. Move the insertion point to the top of the document, then use the Spelling and Grammar command to search for and correct any spelling and grammatical errors in the press release. Note that "Lindy" and "cha cha" are not errors.
   c. Use the Thesaurus to replace **refine** in the Advanced Swing Dancing description with a different suitable word, then save your changes.

7. **Find and replace text.**
   a. Using the Replace command, replace all instances of **basic** with **fundamental**.
   b. Replace all instances of **Music** with **music**, taking care to use the Match case function.
   c. Type your name at the bottom of the document, save your changes, print a copy, then close the document.

8. **Use wizards and templates.**
   a. Use the New command to open the New Documents task pane, then use the General Templates hyperlink to open the Templates dialog box.
   b. Create a new document using the **Professional Fax** template.

c. The name of the company sending the fax is **Ikon Productions** at **44 S.W. Banff Avenue, Calgary, Alberta, T5G 0P6, Phone: (403) 555-4175, Fax: (403) 555-4173**. (*Hint*: Type the address and phone numbers on different lines.)

d. The 1-page fax is sent from you on the current date to **Karl Schrader** at fax number **(604) 555-1222** and phone number **(604) 555-1223** regarding the script for a film called The Jane Morris Story. The fax is urgent.

e. The fax message is **Please send us the latest draft of the script for The Jane Morris Story. We are ready to storyboard the next sequences. If you need to chat about the changes, call me after 4 p.m. today.**

f. Delete any placeholders that do not apply to the fax, save the fax as **Ikon Productions Fax**, print a copy, close the document, then exit Word.

▶ Visual Workshop Word Unit B

Sales

Create the memo shown in Figure Word-2 using the Professional Memo template and substituting your name where indicated. Save the memo as **Holiday Preparations Memo**. Check the memo for spelling and grammar errors, then print a copy.

FIGURE WORD-2

Candlelight Magic

Memo

To: All Employees
From: Your Name
Date: Current Date
Re: Holiday Preparations

Only 50 shopping days are left until the holiday season! I enjoyed meeting all of you at our recent Holiday Prep Party. I especially enjoyed meeting our new part-timers. We look forward to providing all of you with an interesting and worthwhile employment experience.

In this memo, I will discuss the upcoming Aromatherapy Day and our new Online Customer Support procedures.

As I announced at the Holiday Prep Party, we will be holding an Aromatherapy Day on November 15. Joanne Holmes, our licensed Aroma Therapist, will spend all day at the store to answer questions, hold informal seminars, and provide consultation services. Every customer to the store will also receive free samples of some of our best-selling aromatherapy candles.

We are also really trying to push our online ordering service. Whenever possible, talk about the online ordering service to every customer you serve. Ask them if they have a computer and an Internet connection and then tell them how easy online ordering can be. Reassure customers that our online ordering service is completely secure.

Advertising

1. **Format with fonts.**
   a. Start Word, open the file BWD-2 from the drive and folder where your Project Files are located, then save it as **House Advertisement**.
   b. Format the title **House for Rent in Provence** in 20-point Forte (or a different font if Forte is not available to you).
   c. Format each of the following headings in 16-point Forte: **Location**, **House Description**, **Grounds**, **Sightseeing**, **Driving Directions**, and **Rates and Contact**, then save the document.

2. **Change font styles and effects.**
   a. Change the font color of the title, Location heading, and the Rates and Contact heading to Dark Blue.
   b. Change the font color of each of the remaining headings to Orange.
   c. Format the paragraph under Location in italics and small caps.
   d. Under the Grounds heading, format the text **Perfect for a family with children** in bold, italic, and dark blue.
   e. Scroll to the top of the document, change the character scale of the title to 150%, then save your changes.

3. **Change line and paragraph spacing.**
   a. Add 6 points of space before each heading in the advertisement.
   b. Select the last three lines, change the line spacing to 1.5 lines, then save your changes.

4. **Align paragraphs.**
   a. Center the title of the document, then center the Location heading and its accompanying paragraph.
   b. Justify the first paragraph of text under the House Description heading and the paragraph under the Grounds heading.
   c. Center the Rates and Contact heading and the last two lines.
   d. Press [Ctrl][End], press [Enter] once, type **your name**, then right-align it.

5. **Work with tabs.**
   a. Select the text from Age through to Washing Machine under the House Description paragraph.
   b. Set a right tab stop at the 5½" mark.
   c. With the text still selected, open the Tabs dialog box, select the 4 tab leader option, then deselect the text.

6. **Work with indents.**
   a. Select the seven lines of tabbed text under the House Description paragraph and change the left indent to 1".
   b. Indent the paragraph under House Description and the paragraph under Grounds .2" from the left and .2" from the right, then save your changes.

7. **Add bullets and numbering.**
   a. Apply bullets to the list of items under the Sightseeing heading.
   b. Change the bullet style to small squares (or choose another bullet style if small squares are not available).
   c. Change the font color of the bullets to Orange.
   d. Format the list of items under the Driving Directions heading as a numbered list.
   e. Format the numbers in 12-point Forte, change the font color to Orange if necessary, then save your changes.

8. **Add borders and shading.**
   a. Apply 10% Gray shading to the document title.
   b. Apply 10% Gray shading to the House Description heading, then add a 1½-point Dark Blue border below the House Description heading.
   c. Use the Format Painter to copy the formatting of the House Description heading to the Grounds, Sightseeing, and Driving Directions headings.
   d. Save your changes, then print the document.

► Visual Workshop Word Unit C

Fine Arts

Create the price list shown in Figure Word-3 and save it as **Art Supply Specials**. Format the title with the Bauhaus 93 font (or a similar font), 24-point, 150% character scaling, and .3-point expanded spacing. Apply Light Green shading with a 2 ¼-pt Dark Green border and ½" left and right indenting. Format the subtitle with Arial 24-point and 18-point before and after spacing with a 3-pt Green border line top and bottom. Each heading is formatted with the Bauhaus 93 font, 16-point, 150% scaling, .3-point expanded spacing, Light Green shading, a Dark Green 2 ¼-pt border line, and single spacing. The right tab with leaders is set at 5.88" and all the items in the tabbed lists are double-spaced. Add 12-point spacing before the first item in each of the three tabbed lists. Right-align your name at the bottom of the document, then print a copy of the completed price list.

FIGURE WORD-3

Palette and Brush
Art Supplies

September Specials

PAINT AND BRUSHES

Aqua-Hue acrylic paint, titanium white, 40ml $15.00

Svenson acylic paint, ivory black, 60ml $20.00

Aqua-Hue acrylic paint, yellow ochre, 40ml $16.50

Rubens oil paint, cerulean blue, 30ml $26.00

Rubens oil paint, cadmium red, 20ml $20.00

Artworks brushes, fan brush, 4" $18.00

DRAWING SUPPLIES

Leadworks drawing pencils, 2B, B, HB $2.00

Corot Vellum paper, 20lb, watercolor pad $40.00

OTHER SUPPLIES

Artworks outdoor tripod easel $75.00

Lomax mat cutter, 24" $120.00

1. Set document margins.

   a. Start Word, then open the file BWD-3 from the drive and folder where your Project Files are located. Save the document as **Festival Proposal**, change the top margin to 1.2", the bottom margin to .9", and the left and right margins to 1.3", then save your changes.

2. Divide a document into sections.

   a. Insert a continuous section break before the heading **Book Store Information**.

   b. Format the text in section 2 in two columns, then save the changes.

3. Add page breaks.

   a. Insert a hard page break before the heading **Introduction** at the bottom of page 1 of the document.

   b. Insert a hard page break before the heading **Festival Events**, then save the changes.

4. Add page numbers.

   a. Go to the top of the document, insert page numbers in the document but do *not* show page numbers on the first page. Right-align the page number at the bottom of the page.

   b. View the page numbers on pages 2 and 3 in Print Preview, then save your changes to the document.

5. Insert headers and footers.

   a. Show the Header and Footer toolbar, click the Show Next button on the Header and Footer toolbar to move to section 2, then type your name in the Header area.

   b. Press [Tab] twice, then use the Insert Date button on the Header and Footer toolbar to insert the current date.

   c. Move to the Footer area, then type **Festival Proposal** at the left margin.

   d. Format the page number in bold italic, close the Header and Footer toolbar, then save the document.

6. Edit headers and footers.

   a. Open headers and footers, then apply bold italic to the text in the header starting on page 2.

   b. Insert the ✍ symbol (in the Wingdings font) to the left of Festival in the footer, increase the font size of the ✍ to 16-point, insert a space between the symbol and Festival, then enhance Festival Proposal with bold italic.

   c. Preview the header and footer in Print Preview, then save your changes.

7. Format columns.

   a. Click in the two columns of text on page 2 of the document, then open the Columns dialog box.

   b. Change the spacing between the columns to .3" and insert a line between the two columns.

   c. Balance the columns on page 2 by inserting a continuous section break at the bottom of the second column.

   d. Format the text in section 3 in one column, then save your changes to the document.

8. Insert clip art.

   a. On page 1, place the insertion point at the second blank line below the text May 14 to May 22, 2004.

   b. Open the Clip Art task pane and search for clips related to the keyword **writing**.

   c. Select and then insert an appropriate clip art picture.

   d. Drag the sizing handles so that the graphic is approximately 3" in height, then remove any extra hard returns so that all the title page text appears on one page.

   e. On page 3, place the insertion point before **Festival Dates**, then insert a clip art picture of an award.

   f. Open the Format Picture dialog box and apply the Square wrapping style, then move the graphic so that it appears within the paragraph, but at the right side. The first line of the paragraph should appear above the graphic. Resize the graphic so that it fits the space attractively.

   g. Save your changes to the document. Preview the document, print a copy, then close the document and exit Word.

Use the file BWD-4 from the drive and folder where your Project Files are located to create the document shown in Figure Word-4. Change the left and right margins to .5" and the top and bottom margins to .8", and set the between columns spacing at .3". Change the font color of the title and headings to Brown and make the two border lines 3-point and Brown. Select different clip art if the clips shown in the figure are not available to you. The keywords "Eiffel Tower," "mountains," and "dog" were used to find the clips. Type your name at the bottom of column 3, save the document with the filename **Collectible Calendars**, then print a copy.

FIGURE WORD-4

Collectible Calendars
Subject Categories

Attractions

More and more tourists are choosing to select a calendar as an inexpensive commemoration of a visit to an historic landmark or tourist attraction. Our Attractions catalog includes a huge selection of world landmarks—from the Great Wall of China to the castles of Scotland to Mount Rushmore.

The Attractions category also includes works of art. Museum gift shops are finding calendars showing the great art masterpieces of the world can barely be kept in stock.

You can choose to supply images related to specific attractions or art works that are not included in our catalog. For an extra charge of $.50 per calendar, you can include on each calendar the logo or URL of your store or museum.

Landscapes

National and state parks, tourist offices, and souvenir shops report consistently good sales of landscape calendars. The key requirement is photographs that are immediately recognizable as representing a specific region, season, or mood. Tropical scenes lead the list of most popular landscapes for calendars, followed by sunsets, mountains, and historic villages.

You can choose stock images from our extensive catalog, which includes photographs from every state, provincial, and national park in the United States and Canada, along with an extensive selection of landscapes from popular tourist spots around the world. For an extra charge of $.50 per calendar, you can include on each calendar the logo or URL of your store or museum.

Animals

Calendars depicting animals are universally popular. Topping the list are calendars that feature puppies or kittens. Wildlife calendars are also very popular, particularly at gift shops associated with national parks or wildlife refuges. Calendars that feature endangered species just fly out of gift shops attached to natural history and science museums.

You can supply your own photographs of animals relating to a particular theme or choose stock images from our catalog.

For an extra charge of $.50 per calendar, you can include on each calendar the logo or URL of your store or museum.

To place your orders call 1-800-555-2333 or check us out online at www.collectiblecalendars.com.

1. **Start Excel 2002.**
   a. Open Microsoft Excel from the Start menu.

2. **View the Excel window.**
   a. Identify the title bar, the menu bar, and the Standard and Formatting toolbars.
   b. Identify the formula bar, name box, and the active cell.

3. **Open and Save a workbook.**
   a. Open the workbook BEX-1 from the drive and folder where your Project Files are located.
   b. Save the workbook as **Scents Sense Sales** using the Save As command on the File menu.

4. **Enter labels and values.**
   a. Click cell B6, then enter the labels shown in Table EXCEL-1.
   b. Enter the values shown in Table Excel-1.
   c. Clear the contents of cell A4 using the Edit menu, then type **In Millions** in cell A4.
   d. Type **your name** in cell A12.
   e. Save the workbook by clicking the Save button.

TABLE EXCEL-1

	2001	2002	2003	2004
Stress	6	7	5	8
Energy	7	9	3	9
Relax	9	11	15	9
Focus	15	17	12	18

5. **Name and move a sheet.**
   a. Name the Sheet1 tab **Sales**, then name the Sheet2 tab **Charts**.
   b. Move the Sales sheet so that it appears after the Charts sheet.
   c. Change the tab color of the Sales sheet to bright pink (first column, fourth row).
   d. Change the tab color of the Charts sheet to bright green (fourth column, fourth row).
   e. Save the workbook.

6. **Preview and print a worksheet.**
   a. Make the Sales sheet active.
   b. View it in Print Preview. Use the Zoom tool to get a closer look at the worksheet.
   c. Print one copy of the worksheet.

7. **Get Help.**
   a. Display the Office Assistant if it is not already displayed.
   b. Use the Office Assistant to search for the keywords **showing dollar signs**, then click the link to Add a currency symbol.
   c. Print information offered by the Office Assistant using the Print button in the Help window.
   d. Close the Help window.

8. **Close a workbook and exit Excel.**
   a. Close the file using the Close command.
   b. If asked if you want to save the worksheet, click No.
   c. Exit Excel.

► Visual Workshop Excel Unit A

Tourism

Create a worksheet similar to Figure Excel-1 using the skills you learned in this unit. Save the workbook as **Sightseeing Excursions** to the drive and folder where your project files are located. The Long Tours sheet tab is yellow and the Short Tours sheet tab is aqua. Type **your name** in cell A12, then preview and print the worksheet.

FIGURE EXCEL-1

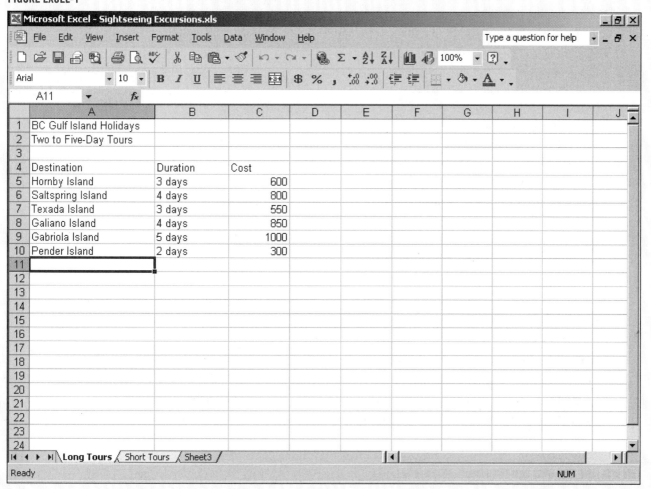

Conservation

1. **Edit cell entries and work with ranges.**
   a. Start Excel, open the workbook BEX-2 from the drive and folder where your Project Files are located, then save it as **Attendance Figures**.
   b. Change the number of adults who visited the Everglades Wildlife Reserve in June to **16000**, change the number of seniors who visited in July to **13000**, and change the number of children who visited in August to **21000**.
   c. Enter **your name** in cell A13, then save the workbook.

2. **Enter formulas.**
   a. In cell B9, use the pointing method to enter the formula **B5+B6+B7**.
   b. In cell C9, use the pointing method to enter the formula **C5+C6+C7**, then click cell D9 and enter the formula **=D5+D6+D7**.
   c. Save your work.

3. **Create complex formulas.**
   a. In cell B11, enter the formula **B9-(B9*.15)** to determine total attendance figures for June if 15% fewer people come to the Everglades Wildlife Reserve.
   b. In cell C11, enter the formula **C9-(C9*.15)**, then enter the formula in cell D11 that will calculate a 15% reduction in attendance for August.
   c. Save your work.

4. **Introduce Excel functions.**
   a. In cell E4, enter the label **Total**.
   b. Select cells B5 through E11, then use the AutoSum button to calculate the totals.
   c. Enter the label **Average** in cell F4.
   d. In cell F9, use the AVERAGE function to determine the average number of people who visited the Everglades Wildlife Reserve in June, July, and August.
   e. Save your work.

5. **Copy and move cell entries.**
   a. Select the range **A1:A2**, then copy the range to cell A2 in the Summer 2005 worksheet.
   b. In the Summer 2005 worksheet, select the range **A4:E9**, then use drag and drop to copy the range so that the first cell is in cell A12.
   c. Move the labels in cells A2:A3 to cell A1, then save your changes.

6. **Copy formulas with relative cell references.**
   a. In the Summer 2005 worksheet, copy the formula in cell B9 to cells C9:D9.
   b. Use the Edit command to fill cells E6:E9 with the formula in cell E5, then delete the **0** in cell E8.
   c. Complete the formulas required for the values in cells B13 through E17. The total in cell E17 will match the total in cell E9.
   d. Save your work.

7. **Copy formulas with absolute cell references.**
   a. Enter the label **Increase** in cell F2, then enter the value **1.1** in cell F3.
   b. In cell B13, enter the formula **=B5*F3** and make F3 an absolute cell reference. You are calculating an increase in attendance figures of 10%.
   c. Copy the formula across to cell D13 and then down to D15.
   d. Change the value in cell F3 to reflect a 25% increase in the cell. (*Hint:* Enter 1.25 in cell F3.)
   e. Enter the label **Projections for Increased Attendance** in cell A11.
   f. Save the workbook, preview both worksheets, print a copy of both worksheets, then close the workbook and exit Excel.

▶ Visual Workshop Excel Unit B

Recreation

Open the workbook BEX-3 from the drive and folder where your Project Files are stored, then save it as **Tour Commissions**. Complete the worksheet so that it appears as shown in Figure Excel-2. You will need to move the label in cell F1 to E1, enter a formula in the Revenue column that multiplies the # of Tours by the Tour Price, then enter a formula in the Commission column that multiplies the Revenue by the commission amount shown in the figure in cell G1. You will also need to calculate the required totals and the average commission earned by the tour guides. Type **your name** in cell A14, then preview and print the worksheet. Change the amount in cell G1 to .15, save the modified workbook as **Tour Commissions 2**, print the worksheet, then close the workbook and exit Excel.

FIGURE EXCEL-2

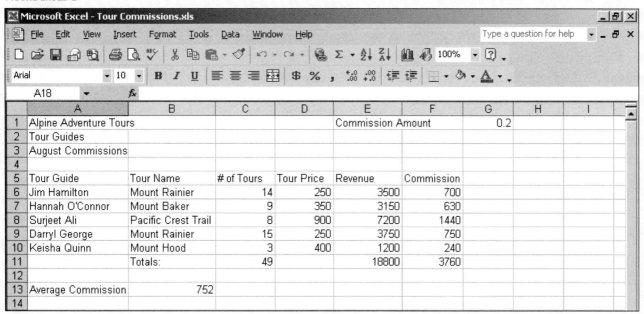

	A	B	C	D	E	F	G	H	I
1	Alpine Adventure Tours				Commission Amount		0.2		
2	Tour Guides								
3	August Commissions								
4									
5	Tour Guide	Tour Name	# of Tours	Tour Price	Revenue	Commission			
6	Jim Hamilton	Mount Rainier	14	250	3500	700			
7	Hannah O'Connor	Mount Baker	9	350	3150	630			
8	Surjeet Ali	Pacific Crest Trail	8	900	7200	1440			
9	Darryl George	Mount Rainier	15	250	3750	750			
10	Keisha Quinn	Mount Hood	3	400	1200	240			
11		Totals:	49		18800	3760			
12									
13	Average Commission	752							
14									

Education

1. **Format values.**
   a. Start Excel, open the workbook BEX-4 from the drive and folder where your Project Files are located, then save it as **Seminar Sales**.
   b. Apply the Comma format to all the values in cells B4:G10.
   c. Apply the italics and bold attributes to each of the year labels (cells B3:G3).
   d. Insert formulas in the Totals row to add the seminar sales for each year.
   e. Apply the Currency format to the Totals data, then save your work.

2. **Use fonts and font sizes.**
   a. Change the font of the worksheet title in cell A1 to Britannic Bold (or another if it is not available).
   b. Change the font size of the worksheet title to 24-point, then change the font size of the worksheet subtitle to 16-point.
   c. Change the font size of the labels in row 3 to 12-point, then save your work.

3. **Change attributes and alignment.**
   a. Use the Bold button to boldface the Seminar Sales, Seminar Name, and Total labels.
   b. Select the worksheet title **Healing Tones Music Therapy** and use the Bold button to boldface it.
   c. Use the Merge and Center button to center the title and the Seminar Sales labels over columns A through G.
   d. Center each of the year labels in cells B3:G3.
   e. Select the range of cells containing the seminar names (cells A4:A10), then apply bold and right alignment.

4. **Adjust column widths.**
   a. Use the Format menu to change the size of each of the year columns to 12.
   b. Use the AutoFit feature to resize column A, then save your changes.

5. **Insert and delete rows and columns.**
   a. Insert a new row between rows 2 and 3.
   b. Insert a new row between rows 5 and 6, then type **Find the Beat** in cell A6.
   c. Enter **2400** in cell B6, copy the formula from cell C5 to cell C6, then copy the formula from C6 across to G6.
   d. Delete the row containing information about the Building Team Tones seminar.
   e. Edit the comment so it reads **Our best-selling seminar!**, then save your changes.

6. **Apply colors, patterns, and borders.**
   a. Add a Top and Double-Bottom border to cells B12:G12.
   b. Apply a dark blue background to the title, then change the color of the font to light yellow.
   c. Apply a light yellow background to the subtitle.
   d. Apply a dark blue background to the labels in row 4, then change the color of the font to light yellow.
   e. Add a light yellow background to the labels in cells A5:A11.

7. **Use conditional formatting.**
   a. Select cells B5:G11, then create conditional formatting that changes the seminar sales data to bold and blue if it is greater than or equal to 12000 and bold and red if it is less than or equal to 8000.
   b. Create a third conditional format that changes the seminar sales data to bold and green if a value is between 8001 and 11999, then save your changes.

8. **Check spelling.**
   a. Use the spell checker to check the spelling in the worksheet and then correct any errors. (*Hint*: Ignore "Nutri".)
   b. Type **your name** in cell A14, save your changes, then preview and print the worksheet. (*Hint*: To print the worksheet on one page, click File on the menu bar, click Page Setup, click the Fit to option button in the Scaling section of the Page tab, then click OK.)

Media Relations

Open the workbook BEX-5 from the drive and folder where your Project Files are stored, then save it as **Media Analysis**. Complete the worksheet so that it appears as shown in Figure Excel-3. You will need to format the worksheet title with Arial Black (or a similar font) and 20-point and the subtitle with 16-point and bold. Create a conditional format in the Per Response column so that entries greater than 2.5 appear in bold and dark red. Type **your name** in cell A19, then save and print the worksheet.

FIGURE EXCEL-3

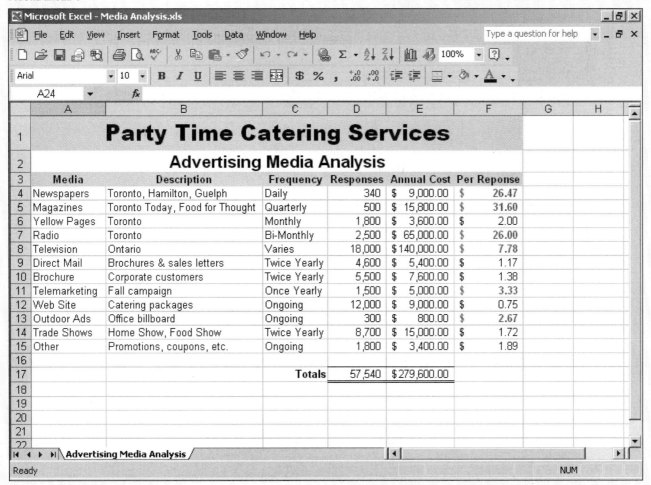

Retail

1. Create a chart.

a. Start Excel, open the workbook BEX-6 from the drive and folder where your Project Files are located, then save it as **Grand Piano Sales**.

b. Select the range A4:F9, then click the Chart Wizard button.

c. In the Chart Wizard, select a Line chart, verify that the series are in rows, add the chart title Grand Piano Sales: 2000 to 2004, then make the chart an object on the worksheet.

d. After the chart appears, save your work.

2. Move and resize a chart.

a. Make sure the chart is still selected, then move it beneath the data so that the left edge of the chart starts in column A.

b. Resize the chart so that its bottom right corner extends to cell K30.

c. Move the legend below the charted data, then save your work.

3. Edit a chart.

a. Note the color of the line representing sales of Steinway pianos, then change the value representing the 2002 sales of Steinway pianos to 13.

b. Change the chart type to Area.

c. Change the chart type to Column, then save the worksheet.

4. Format a chart.

a. Make sure the chart is still selected.

b. Use the Chart Options dialog box to turn off the displayed gridlines.

c. Change the color of the columns representing Petrof pianos to bright pink.

d. Change the font size of the Legend labels to 12-point.

e. Change the font size of the x-axis and y-axis labels to 10-point.

f. Change the font of the chart title to Bauhaus 93 (or choose a different font if Bauhaus 93 is not available), then change the font size to 16-point.

g. Save your work.

5. Enhance a chart.

a. Open the Chart Options dialog box, then click the Titles tab.

b. Enter **Number of Pianos Sold** as the y-axis title.

c. Change the font size of the y-axis title to 10-point.

d. Change the background color of the chart to light yellow. (*Hint*: Right-click a blank area of the chart, click Format Chart Area, click the Patterns tab, then click the light yellow color box in the Area section.)

e. Add a drop shadow to the chart title, then save your work.

6. Annotate and draw on a chart.

a. Make sure the chart is still selected, then create the text annotation **Outstanding Year for Steinway**.

b. Position the text annotation above the plot area, then change the font size of the text to 12-point and bold.

c. Draw an arrow from the text annotation to the 2002 column representing Steinway sales.

d. Save your work.

7. Preview and print a chart.

a. In the worksheet, enter **your name** in cell A33.

b. Preview the chart and data.

c. Change the page orientation to landscape, then center the page contents horizontally and vertically on the page.

d. Print the data and chart from the Print Preview window.

e. Save your work, then close the workbook and exit Excel.

► Visual Workshop Excel Unit D

Music

Open the workbook BEX-7 from the drive and folder where your Project Files are stored, then save it as **Opera Production Costs**. Create the doughnut chart, then change the chart so that it appears as shown in Figure Excel-4. Enter **your name** in cell A22, then save, preview, and print the worksheet.

FIGURE EXCEL-4

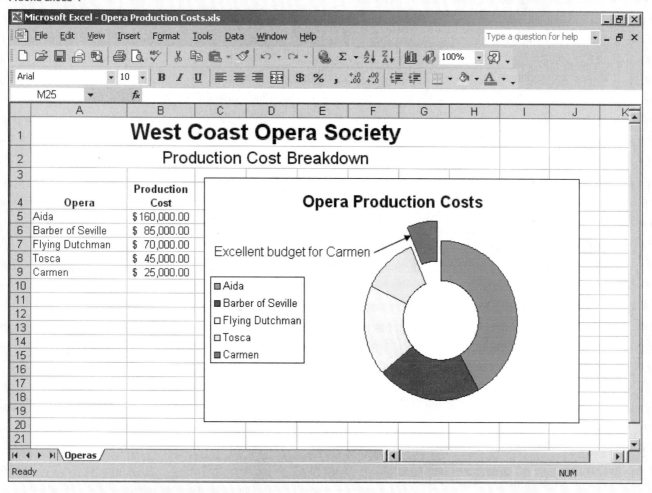

1. **Define database software.**
   a. Start a new document in Word, then save it as **Database Basics**. This document will contain answers to the following questions:
      1. Give an example of how information stored in a database can be viewed and sorted in multiple ways.
      2. What is the significance of the phrase "Access databases are inherently multiuser"?
      3. What is the storage capacity of an Excel workbook and an Access database?
   b. Save the document, but keep it open.

2. **Learn database terminology.**
   a. In the Database Basics document, describe what is meant by the term "relational database"?
   b. Describe the purpose of a table, a query, and a form.
   c. In which Access objects can data be entered?
   d. Save the document, but keep it open.

3. **Start Access and open a database.**
   a. Start Access, then open the **Antiques-A** database from the drive and folder where your Project Files are located.
   b. Press [Print Screen] to capture an image of the screen to the Windows clipboard.
   c. Switch to the Database Basics document, go to a new blank page, then click the Paste button.
   d. Print the page containing the picture of the opening database window, then identify the following elements: Microsoft Access title bar, Menu bar, Objects bar, Antiques-A Database title bar, Antiques-A Database window, and Database toolbar.

4. **View the database window.**
   a. Maximize both the Access window and the Antiques-A Database window.
   b. Click each of the objects on the Objects bar, and view the list of objects and object shortcuts for each object type. Notice how the toolbars change slightly for each type of object.
   c. In the Database Basics document, identify the names of each of the objects in the Antiques-A database.
   d. Type your name at the bottom of the document, save it and print a copy, then close it and exit Word.

5. **Navigate records.**
   a. Open the Customers table.
   b. Press [Tab] or [Enter] to move through the fields of the first record and [Shift][Tab] to move backward through the fields of the first record.
   c. Press [Ctrl][End] to move to the last field of the last record, then press [Ctrl][Home] to move to the first field of the first record.
   d. Click the Last Record navigation button to quickly move to the record for Ronald Storey.

6. **Enter records.**
   a. In the Customers table, click the New Record button, press [Tab], then add the three records from Table Access-1.
   b. Move the LName field so that it precedes the FName field in the datasheet.

   TABLE ACCESS-1

FName	LName	Address	City	State	Zip Code
Marilyn	Crowther	1200 L Street	Washington	DC	20018
Ivan	Zoltov	808 Liberty Avenue	Philadelphia	PA	19146
Harriet	Smith	245 Laurel Street	Atlanta	GA	30481

7. **Edit records.**
   a. Change the LName field in record 10 to **Prentiss**, then change the FName in record 5 to **Patty**.
   b. Change the Address field in record 8 to **345 Broad Street**.
   c. Enter your last name, first name, and address as a new record, then delete the record for Gilliam McKim.

8. **Preview and print a datasheet.**

   a. Preview the Customers table datasheet.

   b. Change the page orientation from portrait to landscape, then print the Customers table datasheet.

9. **Get Help and exit Access.**

   a. Close the Customers table, saving the changes. Close the Antiques-A database, but leave Access open.

   b. Click the Ask a Question box, type **sorting records**, then press [Enter].

   c. Click the link for the About sorting records option.

   d. Click the Show All link, then print a copy of the information related to sorting records.

   e. Close the Microsoft Access Help window, then exit Access.

▶ Visual Workshop Access Unit A

Fitness

Open the **Fitness-A** database from the drive and folder where your Project Files are stored, then open the Classes table datasheet. Modify the records in the existing Classes table to reflect the changes shown in Figure Access-1. The name of the instructor for the first three classes has changed, the name of the instructor for the Yoga class on Monday at 8:00 pm has changed, and three new records have been added. Also, enter a new record using your name as the instructor of a Class ID 42 called Tae Box Cardio that is held on Thursday at 6:00 pm. Print the datasheet, close the Classes table, close the Fitness-A database, then exit Access.

FIGURE ACCESS-1

	ClassID	Class Name	Instructor	Day	Time
+	22	Aerobics	Bev Martin	Monday	9:00 AM
+	23	Aerobics	Bev Martin	Wednesday	9:00 AM
+	24	Aerobics	Bev Martin	Friday	9:00 AM
+	25	Weight Training	Doris Kwan	Tuesday	6:00 PM
+	26	Weight Training	Doris Kwan	Thursday	6:00 PM
+	27	Step Aerobics	Harrison Janzen	Monday	7:00 PM
+	28	Step Aerobics	Harrison Janzen	Wednesday	7:00 PM
+	29	Circuit Training	Yuri Weston	Tuesday	10:00 AM
+	30	Yoga	Grace Lu	Monday	8:00 PM
+	31	Stretching	Tanis Allen	Wednesday	8:00 PM
+	32	Step Aerobics	Gertie Egbert	Tuesday	7:00 PM
+	33	Step Aerobics	Gertie Egbert	Thursday	7:00 PM
+	34	Intense Aerobics	John Bowman	Monday	5:00 PM
+	35	Intense Aerobics	John Bowman	Wednesday	5:00 PM
+	36	Yoga	Tanis Allen	Saturday	10:00 AM
+	37	Yoga	Tanis Allen	Saturday	2:00 PM
+	38	Weight Training	Doris Kwan	Saturday	1:00 PM
+	39	Spin Cycle	Elinor Bartz	Monday	7:00 PM
+	40	Spin Cycle	Jerry Moore	Wednesday	7:00 PM
+	41	Spin Cycle	Elinor Bartz	Friday	7:00 PM
*	0				

Record: 14 ◀ 20 ▶ ▶I ▶* of 20

► Skills Review Access Unit B

1. Plan a database.
a. Plan a database that will contain names, ages, countries, and sports of athletes in the 2006 Winter Olympics.

b. Start a new document in Word, save it as **Using Databases**, then list the field names and data types you could include in the database. Save the document in Word, but keep it open.

2. Create a table.
a. Start Access and use the Blank Access database option to create a database. Save the file as **Athletes** in the drive and folder where your Project Files are stored.

b. Use the Table Wizard to create a new table. Click the Personal option button in the Table Wizard dialog box, then click Authors in the list of Samples Tables.

c. Choose each of the sample fields in the following order: AuthorID, FirstName, LastName, Nationality, Birthdate, and MajorInfluences.

d. Rename the AuthorID field as **AthleteID**, then rename the **MajorInfluences** field as **Sport**.

e. Name the table **Athletes**, and allow Access to set the primary key field.

f. Click the Modify the table design option button in the last Table Wizard dialog box, then click Finish.

3. Modify a table.
a. Add a new field called **Gender** with a Text data type, then change the Field Size property of the Gender field to **1**.

b. Add the description **M or F** to the Gender field, then move the Gender field so that it appears above the Nationality field. (*Hint*: To move a field, click to the left of it, then drag the field to the new location.)

c. Save the Athletes table, display the Athletes datasheet, then enter the information for the two records from Table Access-2.

d. Preview the datasheet, fit it on one page, then print the page.

e. Close the Athletes database.

TABLE ACCESS-2

First Name	Last Name	Gender	Nationality	Birthdate	Sport
Igor	Malavich	M	Russian	03/10/80	Alpine Skiing
Sophia	Clementi	F	Italian	10/28/84	Figure Skating

4. Format a datasheet.
a. Open the **Athletes-B** database from the drive and folder where your Project Files are stored.

b. Open the Athletes datasheet, then change the font of the datasheet to Berlin Sans FB, 12-point.

c. Change the gridline color to Dark Blue and the background color to Yellow.

d. Resize columns, where necessary, so that all the data is visible, change the left and right margins to 2", change the Page Orientation to Landscape, then save and close the datasheet.

5. Understand sorting, filtering, and finding.
a. Open the Athletes datasheet, then in the Using Databases document, list three ways that you might want to sort the Athletes datasheet. Specify both the field you would sort on and the sort order.

b. Identify three ways in which you could filter the Athletes datasheet. Specify both the field you would filter on and the criteria you would use.

c. Save the document, but keep it and the Athletes datasheet open.

6. Sort records and find data.
a. Sort the records in ascending order on the Sport field, then in the Using Databases document, list the first two last names that appear.

b. Use the Find command to find the records in which the Nationality field contains British, then list the last names of the British athletes.

c. Sort the records in ascending order on the AthleteID field.

7. Filter records.

a. Filter the records for all male athletes, press Print Screen to copy the screen, then paste the screen into the Using Databases document.

b. Filter the records for all male athletes from Norway, then paste the screen into the Using Databases document.

c. Remove the filter, then save and close the Athletes table.

8. Create a query.

a. Use the Query Wizard to create a new query based on the Athletes table with the following fields: FirstName, LastName, Nationality, and Sport.

b. Name the query **Skaters**, switch to Query Design view, then add the criteria ***Skating*** to the Sport field. (*Hint*: Include the asterisk (*) before and after so that all records with the word "skating" are shown.)

c. View the query and change the record for Lana Martens so that it shows your name and your nationality. Increase column widths if necessary, then save the query.

9. Modify a query.

a. Modify the Skaters query to include only those athletes who are American, German, and your nationality (if different).

b. Sort the records in ascending order of nationality, then add the AthleteID field as the first field in the datasheet.

c. Save and print the sorted datasheet then close the datasheet.

d. Close the Athletes-B database, then exit Access, type your name at the bottom of the Using Databases document, save it, print a copy, then close the document and exit Word.

▶ Visual Workshop Access Unit B

Multimedia

Open the **Videos-B** database from the drive and folder where your Project Files are located. Create a query based on the Inventory table that displays the datasheet shown in Figure Access-2. Notice that only the Western category is displayed and that the records are sorted in ascending order on the Video Title field. The datasheet is formatted with Violet gridlines and the Comic Sans MS font. Change the Artist or Director of the first record to include your last name, then print the datasheet. Save the query as **Westerns** in the Videos-B database.

FIGURE ACCESS-2

Westerns : Select Query

Video ID	Video Title	Artist or Director	Category	Decade
17	Gunfight at the OK Corral	Your Name	Western	1950
8	High Noon	Gary Cooper, Grace Kelly	Western	1950
2	High Noon	Gary Cooper, Grace Kelly	Western	1950
27	Shane	Alan Ladd, Jean Arthur	Western	1950
13	Stage Coach	John Wayne (Director: John Ford)	Western	1930
34	The Searchers	John Wayne, Jeffrey Hunter	Western	1950
19	Viva Zapata	Marlon Brando, Anthony Quinn	Western	1950
▶ ɔNumber)				

Record: 8 of 8

1. Plan a form.

   a. Plan a form to use for entering the titles of books to be sold at a bookstore.

   b. Start a new document in Word and save it as **Database Forms**.

   c. List the fields and labels required for the form. Also identify what type of control could be used for each field (for example, check boxes, text boxes, list boxes, etc.).

   d. Type your name at the bottom of the document, save it, print a copy, then close Word.

2. Create a form.

   a. Start Access and open the **Gallery-C** database from the drive and folder where your Project Files are located.

   b. Use the wizard to create a new form based on the Paintings table that includes all of the fields.

   c. Use a Columnar layout, the Sumi Painting style, and title the form Art Inventory Form.

3. Move and resize controls.

   a. In Design View, move the Medium text box and corresponding label to the right of the Size text box, so that the label starts at 3.5" on the horizontal ruler.

   b. Move the Price and Commission labels to the right of the Artist Name text boxes. Their left edges should be even with the Medium label.

   c. Increase the size of the Painting Title box to the 4" mark on the horizontal ruler.

   d. Adjust the vertical spacing of all the text boxes and labels in both columns so that equal distance appears between them.

4. Modify labels.

   a. Right-align all of the labels.

   b. Change the caption of the Artist FName label to **Artist First Name**, the Artist LName label to **Artist Last Name**, the Price label to **Gallery Price**, and the Commission label to **Artist Commission**.

5. Modify text boxes.

   a. Add a new text box below the Artist Commission text box.

   b. Replace Unbound with the expression =[Price]-[Commission].

   c. Change the Format property to Currency for the new calculated control, then right-align it.

   d. Change the accompanying label from Text16 to Net Price and right-align it.

   e. Move and resize the new calculated control and label so that they are aligned beneath the Artist Commission control.

6. Modify tab order.

   a. Change the Tab order so that pressing [Tab] moves the focus through the text boxes in the following order: PaintingID, Artist First Name, Artist Last Name, Painting Title, Size, Medium, Gallery Price, Artist Commission, Net Price.

   b. Save your changes, then test the new tab order in Form View.

7. Enter and edit records.

   a. Use the form to enter the new records from Table Access-3.

   b. Find the record for the painting called Beach Classic, enter your first name in the Artist First Name text box and your last name in the Artist Last Name text box, then print the record.

TABLE ACCESS-3

Artist First Name	Artist Last Name	Painting Title	Size	Medium	Gallery Price	Artist Commission
Joanne	Miller	Red Swirl	6'x 5'	Oil on canvas	$6,000.00	$3,000.00
Kevin	Lee	Forest Torn	5'x 4'	Oil on canvas	$8,000.00	$3,500.00

c. Go to record 2, filter for all records with a Gallery Price of $5,000.00, sort the filtered list in ascending order by Painting Title, go to the second filtered record (Arcs of the Sun), replace the artist's first and last name with your name, print the record, then remove the filter.

8. Add an image.

a. In Form Design view, expand the Form Header section to the 1½" mark on the vertical ruler.

b. Use the Image control to insert the BlueIdol.jpg file from the drive and folder where your Project Files are located in the left side of the Form Header.

c. To the right of the image, add the label **Gallery Alpha** in 36-point and the Broadway font (or a similar font).

d. Resize the label so that the text appears on two lines, then add your name as a label in 12-point and Arial.

e. View the form in Form View, then spell check the records. Ignore artist names.

f. Sort the records in ascending order based on the Gallery Price values, then print only the first record.

g. Save and close the form, close the database, then exit Access.

▶ Visual Workshop Access Unit C

Photography

Open the **Photos-C** database from the drive and folder where your Project Files are located, then use the Form Wizard to create the form called **Prehistoric Subjects** based on the Photos table, as shown in Figure Access-3. Select all the fields in the table, then when creating the form, select the Columnar layout and the Stone style. In Form Design view, insert the image called **Menhir.jpg** from the drive and folder where your Project Files are located. The label in the form header is formatted in Century Gothic, Bold, and 24-point. The Net Price text box is a new calculated control containing the expression =[Price]-[Discount]. Note also that some of the labels are changed and many of the controls are moved and resized. In Form View, enter the information for record 10 as shown in Figure Access-3, substituting your name where indicated. Print the form for record 10.

FIGURE ACCESS-3

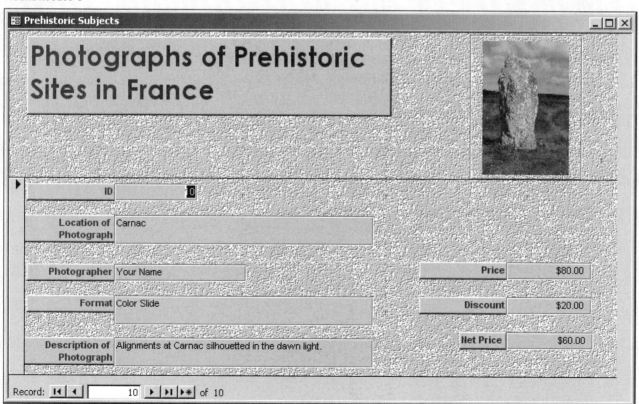

Education

1. **Plan a report.**
   a. Plan a report to use for keeping track of accommodation options for an upcoming vacation to Hawaii. To gather the raw data for your report, find a Web site with hotel listings for Maui, Oahu, and Kauai.
   b. Start a new document in Word and save it as **Database Reports**.
   c. Identify the Report Header, Group Header, and Detail sections for a report that will list accommodation options on three Hawaiian islands.
   d. Type your name at the bottom of the document, save it, print a copy, then close Word.

2. **Create a report.**
   a. Start Access and open the **Seminars-D** database from the drive and folder where your Project Files are located.
   b. Use the Report Wizard to create a report based on the Participants table.
   c. Include the following fields in the following order for the report: FirstName, LastName, PhoneNumber, FeeOwed, FeePaid, SeminarName.
   d. Skip the Grouping and Sorting dialog boxes, select the Tabular layout, Landscape orientation, and the Corporate style, and title the report Seminar Participants.

3. **Group records.**
   a. In Report Design view, open the Sorting and Grouping dialog box, then group the report by the SeminarName field in descending order.
   b. Open both the Group Header and Group Footer sections for the SeminarName field, then close the Sorting and Grouping dialog box.
   c. Move the SeminarName text box in the Detail section up to the left edge of the SeminarName Header section.
   d. Delete the SeminarName label from the page Header.

4. **Change the sort order.**
   a. In Report Design view, open the Sorting and Grouping dialog box, add LastName as a sort field in ascending order below the SeminarName field.
   b. Close the Sorting and Grouping dialog box, then preview the first page of the report.

5. **Add a calculation.**
   a. In Report Design view, add a text box control in the SeminarName Footer section directly below the FeeOwed text box, then delete the label to the left of the unbound text box.
   b. Add another text box control in the SeminarName Footer section below the FeePaid text box, then delete the label to the left of the new unbound text box.
   c. In the unbound text box below FeeOwed, enter the expression **=Sum([FeeOwed])** and in the unbound text box below FeePaid, enter the expression **=Sum([FeePaid])**.

6. **Align controls.**
   a. In Report Design view, right-align the new calculated controls in the SeminarName Footer section, then align them below the appropriate text boxes in the Detail section.
   b. Preview the report, then return to Report Design view to resize and arrange the labels and fields so that all text is visible in the report and the columns in the report appear balanced. Most of the labels and text boxes should move a few inches to the right and their widths should increase. Check Print Preview frequently as you work and make sure the labels in the header are aligned with the fields they represent.

7. **Format controls.**
   a. Change the format of the two calculated controls to Currency.
   b. Change the font size of the text box in the Report Header to 24-point, increase the size of the text box to the 4" mark on the horizontal ruler, then change the Fill/Back color to Turquoise (row 3, column 5).
   c. Change the font size of the SeminarName text box to 14-point, bold the control, then increase the height of the SeminarName Header section to fit the resized text.

d. Add your name as a label to the right of the report header, then save, preview, print, and close the report.

8. Create labels.

a. Use the Label Wizard and the Participants table to create mailing labels using product number C2242, the Times New Roman font, 12-point, Semi-bold, and a blue text color.

b. Organize the prototype label as follows:
> FirstName LastName
> Address
> City, Province
> Code

c. Sort the labels by the City field, name the report **Mailing Labels - Your Name**, print the labels, save and close the report, then exit Access.

► Visual Workshop Access Unit D

Retail

Open the **Pets-D** database from the drive and folder where your Project Files are located to create the report based on the Dog and Cat Sales Query. The report is shown in Figure Access-4. The Report Wizard, Tabular layout, and Soft Gray style were used to create the report. The records are grouped by the Category field in descending order and sorted in ascending order within each group by the Sale Date. A calculated control that totals the sales of each category is displayed in the Category footer. The control is enhanced with bold and the currency format. Add a label with your name to the Report Header section, then save and print the report.

FIGURE ACCESS-4

Dog and Cat Sales   Your Name

Sale Date	Animal	Price
Dog		
9/1/2004	Basset Hound Puppy	$450.00
9/3/2004	Irish Setter	$600.00
9/3/2004	Cocker Spaniel Puppy	$400.00
9/10/2004	Dachsund Puppy	$350.00
9/14/2004	Beagle Puppy	$375.00
9/25/2004	Border Collie	$250.00
9/27/2004	Saint Bernard Puppy	$500.00
		$2,925.00
Cat		
9/2/2004	Siamese Kitten	$230.00
9/3/2004	Persian Kitten	$350.00
9/15/2004	Blue Russian Kitten	$325.00
9/28/2004	Tabby Kitten	$150.00
9/28/2004	Siamese Kitten	$250.00
		$1,305.00

1. **Start PowerPoint and view the PowerPoint window.**
   a. Start PowerPoint.
   b. Study the PowerPoint window and identify the following elements: Title bar, Standard toolbar, Outline tab, Slides tab, slide pane, notes pane, task pane, and view buttons.

2. **Use the AutoContent Wizard.**
   a. Start the AutoContent Wizard, then select the category Sales/Marketing.
   b. Choose Selling a Product or Service as the presentation type and On-screen presentation as the output type.
   c. Enter **Pacific Estates Marketing Plan** as the presentation title, enter your name in the footer, then verify that the Date last updated and Slide number check boxes are selected.
   d. Finish the wizard to show the first slide of the presentation.

3. **View a presentation and run a slide show.**
   a. View each slide in the presentation, then return to Slide 1.
   b. Review the presentation contents in the Outline tab.
   c. Change to Notes Page view, then check if the notes pages contain text.
   d. Return to Normal view, then view the presentation in Slide Sorter view.
   e. View all the slides in Slide Show view, then end the slide show to return to Slide Sorter view.

4. **Save a presentation.**
   a. Open the Save As dialog box, then navigate to the drive and folder where your Project Files are located.
   b. Enter **Marketing** as the presentation filename.
   c. Choose the option from the Tools menu in the Save As dialog box to embed fonts in the presentation.
   d. Save the file.
   e. View the presentation in Normal view, then save the presentation again.

5. **Get Help.**
   a. Type **printing presentations** in the Ask a Question box, then press [Enter].
   b. Click the About handouts hyperlink.
   c. Scroll down, and read the information.
   d. Click the Index tab, search for the keyword **chart**, then click the topic About working on a chart.
   e. Click Show All at the top of the topic, then read about creating charts in PowerPoint.
   f. Click the Contents tab, double-click Microsoft PowerPoint Help, double-click Running Presentations, double-click Setting Up a Presentation, then read about some of the topics listed.
   g. Close the Help window.

6. **Print and close the file, and exit PowerPoint.**
   a. Save your presentation.
   b. Print slides 3 and 4 as slides in pure black and white.
   c. Print all the slides as handouts, 6 slides per page, in Grayscale.
   d. Print the presentation outline.
   e. Save and close the file, then exit PowerPoint.

Create the presentation shown in Figure PowerPoint-1 using the Recommending a Strategy AutoContent Wizard in the General category. Save the presentation as **Trade Show Tips** to your Project Disk. Print slides 2 and 6 in pure black and white. Note that the name of the registered user of the software will appear as the subtitle on the first slide in the presentation and the current date will appear in the footer.

FIGURE POWERPOINT-1

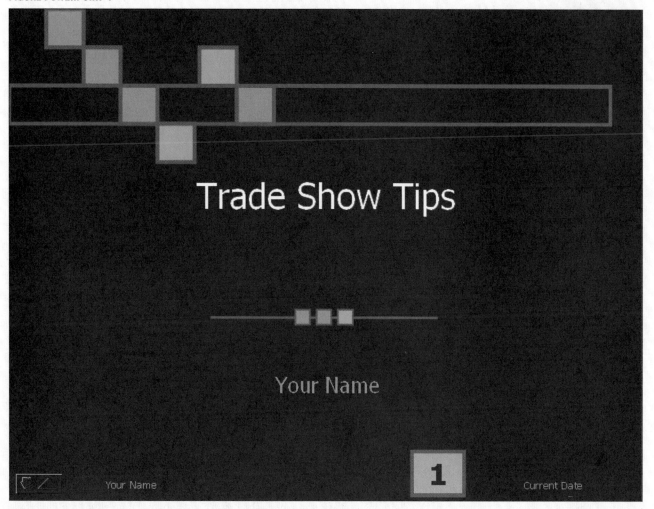

1. **Enter slide text.**
   a. Start PowerPoint. In the slide pane in Normal view, enter the text **Rainforest Cycling** as the title, enter **Company Overview** in the subtitle, then on the next line type your name.
   b. Save the presentation as **Rainforest Cycling** to the drive and folder where your Project Files are located.

2. **Create new slides.**
   a. Create a new Title and Text slide, then enter **Presentation Overview** as the slide title.
   b. Enter each of following four points at the first indent level: **Mission Statement**, **Company Activities**, **Product Categories**, and **Expansion Plans**.
   c. Create a new bulleted list slide, enter **Mission Statement** as the slide title, then at the first indent level enter the text **Our mission is to provide a premium quality bicycle supply and repair service combined with cycle tours and workshops that introduce novices and experts to mountain biking on some of the gnarliest trails in the world.**
   d. Create a new slide using the Title and 2-Column Text layout, enter **Product Categories** as the title, then complete the slide as shown in Table PowerPoint-1.
   e. Save your changes.

   TABLE POWERPOINT-1

Column 1	Column 2
• Sales	• Tours
○ Bicycles	○ Day trips
○ Cycling accessories	○ One- and two-week excursions
• Repair Services	• Workshops
○ On-site	○ Bicycle maintenance
○ Olympic certified	○ Riding tips and tricks

3. **Work in Outline view.**
   a. Click the Outline tab, create a new Title and Text slide, enter **Expansion Plans** as the title, then enter this text:
      • **Offer custom cycling tours**
        ○ **Develop a custom tour-building tool for the Web site**
      • **Develop workshops for teens**
        ○ **Focus on trail riding**
        ○ **Sponsor an international cycling event**
        ○ **Invite local cycling champions**
   b. Move the second bullet point under "Develop workshops for teens" to the first indent position, then save your work.

4. **Add slide headers and footers.**
   a. Open the Header and Footer dialog box, enter the current date into the Fixed text box, add the slide number to the footer, then type your name in the Footer text box.
   b. Click the Notes and Handouts tab in the Header and Footer dialog box, enter your name in the Fixed text box and **Rainforest Cycling** in the Header text box.
   c. Apply the header and footer information to all the slides, then save your work.

5. **Choose a look for a presentation.**
   a. Open the Slide Design task pane, then locate the Watermark template.
   b. Click Color Schemes at the top of the Slide Design task pane, click the green color scheme, then save your changes.

6. **Check spelling in a presentation.**
   a. Spell check the presentation and correct any misspelled words. Ignore words that are correctly spelled but that the spellchecker does not recognize, then save your changes.

7. Evaluate a presentation.

a. View Slide 1 in Slide Show view, then move through the slide show.

b. Evaluate the presentation. Check to ensure that the message is focused and the text is concise, and that the design is simple, easy-to-read, and appropriate to the content.

c. Print the outline of the presentation.

d. Print slides 2 and 4 in grayscale with a frame around each slide.

e. Print the handouts three to a page.

f. Save your changes, close the presentation, and exit PowerPoint.

► Visual Workshop PowerPoint Unit B

Health Sciences

Create the presentation shown in Figures PowerPoint-2 and PowerPoint-3. Add the current date as the date on the title slide. Save the presentation as **Nutrition Tips**. Use the Capsules design template with the color scheme in the second column of the second row in the Color Schemes task pane. Add your name as a footer to the slides, then print the slides in the presentation in grayscale with a frame around each slide.

FIGURE POWERPOINT-2

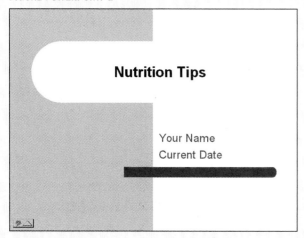

FIGURE POWERPOINT-3

1. **Nutrition Tips**
   Your Name
   Current Date

2. **Basic Principles**
   - Adopt a Heart Healthy Diet:
     - Low Fat
     - Low cholesterol
     - High Fiber
   - Eat Vegetarian a Few Times a Week

3. **Shopping Tips**
   - Buy plenty of fruits and vegetables
   - Buy whole grain breads and cereals
   - Buy low fat dairy products
   - Go easy on snacks
     - Try pretzels!

4. **Cooking Tips**
   - Sauté in water
   - Cut oil, butter or margarine in half
   - Replace whole eggs with bananas or tofu

5. **Eating Out**
   - Healthy choices:
     - Pizza without cheese
     - Stir-fried dinners
     - Steamed vegetables and salads
     - Pasta and tomato sauce
     - Dressings on the side

1. Open an existing presentation.

  a. Open the file BPPT-1 from the drive and folder where your Project Files are stored, then save it as **Business Convention**.

  b. Replace Your Name on the title slide with your name.

2. Draw and modify an object.

  a. On Slide 1, draw a rounded rectangle from the Basic Shapes category on the AutoShapes menu that is approximately 6" wide and 1" high.

  b. Change the fill color to light blue (named Follow Background Scheme Color).

  c. Click the Shadow Style button on the Drawing toolbar, then click the Shadow Style 1 button.

  d. Move the rectangle over the title Home-Based Business Convention, click Draw on the Drawing toolbar, click Order, then click Send to Back.

  e. Size and position the rounded rectangle so that it appears on the title slide as shown in Figure PowerPoint-4.

3. Edit drawing objects.

FIGURE POWERPOINT-4

  a. On Slide 3, press and hold the [Shift] key, then drag the lower-right sizing handle of the hexagon up until the right point of the hexagon is below the "v" in Convention.

  b. Insert the text Seminars in the hexagon, then fill the hexagon with light blue (named Follow Background Scheme Color).

  c. Make three copies of the hexagon and arrange them in a 2-up, 2-across pattern, as shown in the completed slide in Figure PowerPoint-5.

  d. Replace Seminars with the required text as shown in Figure PowerPoint-5.

  e. Select all of the hexagons, format the text with 20-point, bold, then save your changes.

4. Align and group objects.

  a. Use Align and Distribute commands on the Draw menu to align and distribute the four hexagons so that they are positioned as shown in Figure PowerPoint-5.

  b. On Slide 6, distribute the three happy faces horizontally, then group them.

  c. Change the fill color to a very light yellow. (*Hint*: Use the Colors dialog box.)

  d. Using [Shift] to maintain proportions, reduce by half the size of the grouped object, position it so that it appears centered under the slide title, then save your work.

FIGURE POWERPOINT-5

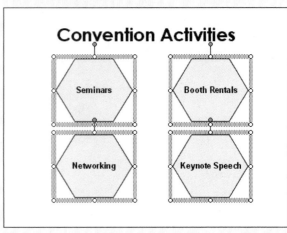

5. Add and arrange text.

  a. Go to Slide 5, then near the bottom of the slide to the left of the graphic, create a text box about 5" wide that contains the text **Government Support for Businesses Home-Based**.

  b. Drag the word **Home-Based** in front of the word **Businesses**, then save your changes.

6. Format text.

  a. On Slide 5, select the entire text object that you added, then change the font to 32-point, Arial Black, italic.

b. Resize the text box so the text appears over two lines (breaking after "for").

c. On Slide 4, align the italicized text in the text box to the right, change the font size to 32-point, the font color to dark blue, and the text box background color to light yellow.

7. Import text from Microsoft Word.

a. Click Slide 4 in the Slides tab, then import the Word file BPPT-2.

b. Check the formatting of each new slide, drag Slide 6 above Slide 5, delete Slide 7, then save your changes.

8. Customize the color scheme and background.

a. Open the Background dialog box, select Fill Effects, then click the Gradient tab.

b. Select the Two colors option, change color 1 to light blue and color 2 to medium blue, select the Diagonal down shading style and the top-right variant, then apply the background to all slides in the presentation.

c. Add your name as a footer on every slide *except* the title slide and on every page of the notes and handouts, then print the slides as handouts (2 slides per page).

▶ Visual Workshop PowerPoint Unit C

Tourism

Create a one-slide presentation that looks like the one shown in Figure PowerPoint-6. Select a similar color of pink to fill each heart and use the Daybreak preset gradient for the background. (*Hint:* In the Gradient tab of the Fill Effects dialog box, click the Preset option button, click the Preset colors list arrow, then select Daybreak.) Add your name as a footer on the slide. Save the presentation as **Romantic Getaways** to the drive and folder where your Project Files are stored, then print the slide.

FIGURE POWERPOINT-6

Hospitality

1. **Insert clip art.**
   a. Open the presentation BPPT-3 from the drive and folder where your Project Files are stored, then save it as **Restaurant Sales**.
   b. From Slide 1, search for clipart using the keyword **lobster**, then insert one of the clips that appears.
   c. Position the clip in the blank area below the slide title. Resize the clip, if necessary.

2. **Insert, crop, and scale a picture.**
   a. Go to Slide 5 and insert the picture file BPPT-4.jpg from the drive and folder where your Project Files are located.
   b. Crop the picture so that only the plate of lobster is visible.
   c. Scale the graphic 30% larger than its original size.
   d. Position the picture in the middle of the slide, then save your changes.

3. **Embed a chart.**
   a. Go to Slide 4 and apply the Title and Content layout.
   b. Start Microsoft Graph, deselect the chart object, then save your changes.

4. **Enter and edit data in the datasheet.**
   a. Open Graph again, then enter the information shown in Table PowerPoint-2 into the datasheet.
   b. Delete any unused rows of default data, then save your changes.

TABLE POWERPOINT-2

	ME	NH	MA	CT
2004	1.2	1.3	2.1	1.8
2005	1.4	1.6	2.5	2.2

5. **Format a chart.**
   a. Close the datasheet, but leave Graph running.
   b. Change the font size of the state names on the X-axis to 22-point.
   c. Apply the Currency Style with one decimal to the values on the vertical axis.
   d. Add the title **In Millions** to the Z-axis, then change the alignment of the label to vertical.
   e. Change the color of the columns representing 2004 sales to yellow, center the chart, enlarge it so that it fills the space attractively, then save your changes.

6. **Create a table.**
   a. Insert a new slide after Slide 4 using the Title and Content slide layout and the slide title **Guidebook Ratings**.
   b. Insert a table with two columns and three rows, then enter text into the table as shown in Table PowerPoint-3.
   c. Change the font size of the table text to 32-point, apply bold, then adjust the column widths so none of the text wraps.
   d. Decrease the height of the table so the top is even with 1 (above 0) on the vertical ruler bar.
   e. Fill the table cells with red, change the font color to white, change the vertical text alignment to middle, then save your changes.

TABLE POWERPOINT-3

Best of New England	4 Lobsters
Gourmet Guide	5 Chefs
Traveler's Choice	3 Stars

7. **Use slide show commands.**
   a. Beginning at Slide 1, proceed through the slide show to Slide 3, select red for the pen color, then use the pen to draw a straight line under the two competitors listed.
   b. Erase the pen annotations.
   c. Use the Go command to go to Slide 5, view the last slide in the presentation, then return to Normal view.

8. **Set slide show timings and transitions.**
   a. In Slide Sorter view, open the Slide Transition task pane, then specify that all slides should advance after four seconds.
   b. Apply the Shape Diamond transition effect to all slides, view the slide show, then save your changes.

9. Set slide animation effects.

a. In Normal view, open the Slide Design—Animation Schemes task pane.

b. Apply the Pinwheel animation effect (in the Exciting section) to Slide 1.

c. Open the Custom Animation task pane, select the lobster clip art, then apply the (Emphasis) Grow/Shrink effect.

d. On Slide 4, apply the (Entrance) Boomerang animation effect to the chart object (*Hint*: Look in the Exciting section after clicking More effects), then on Slide 6, apply the (Entrance) Spiral In animation effect at Medium speed to the picture.

e. Run the slide show from the beginning to check the animation effects.

f. On Slide 1, replace Your Name with yourk name, print the presentation as handouts (6 slides per page), save your changes, close the presentation, then exit PowerPoint.

▶ Visual Workshop PowerPoint Unit D

Accounting

Create a slide that looks like the example in Figure PowerPoint-7. Use the Blends template with the dark purple color scheme. Use the keyword "investment" to find the clip art. To fill the three rows of the table with light purple, change the fill color to the purple color used for the header row, click More Fill Colors, then select a lighter purple in the Custom color dialog box. Add your name as a footer on the slide, then save the presentation as **Key Investments**.

FIGURE POWERPOINT-7

Key Investments

Fund Name	Risk
Pacific Coast Bonds	High
Growth Funds	Medium
Harris Investor Bonds	High

► Skills Review Integration A: Word and Excel

1. **Open multiple programs.**
   a. Start Word, open the file BINT-1.doc from the drive and folder where your Project Files are located, then save it as **Midlands Catering Letter**.
   b. Minimize the Word program window.
   c. Start Excel, open the file BINT-2.xls from the drive and folder where your Project Files are located, then save it as **Midlands Catering Invoice**.
   d. Minimize the Excel program window.
   e. Tile the windows vertically so that both program windows are in view on your screen.

2. **Copy Word data into Excel.**
   a. In Word, enter the current date where indicated at the top of the letter, then enter your name where indicated at the bottom of the letter.
   b. Select the WordArt object Midlands Catering at the top of the letter, press [Ctrl], then drag the WordArt object to cell A1 in the Excel worksheet.
   c. Adjust the position of the WordArt object in Excel, if necessary.
   d. Save the Excel worksheet.

3. **Copy Excel data into Excel.**
   a. In Excel, enter the current date in cell **G11** and your name in cell **G14**.
   b. Click cell **G29**, then use the AutoSum button to calculate the total of cells G24 to G27.
   c. Select cells **A23 to G32** in Excel, then click the Copy button on the Excel Standard toolbar.
   d. In Word, click at the paragraph mark that appears between the second and third paragraphs in the letter. (*Hint*: If paragraph marks are not visible in Word, click the Show/Hide button on the Word Formatting toolbar.)

4. **Create a dynamic link between Excel and Word.**
   a. In Word, click Edit on the menu bar, then click Paste Special.
   b. Click the Paste link option button in the Paste Special dialog box, then click OK.
   c. In Word, scroll right and note the total of **£10,354.18**.
   d. In Excel, change the Unit Price of the dinners (cell F26) to **£18.00**.
   e. Verify that the total of **£9,926.18** appears in cell G32 in Excel and in the pasted worksheet in the Word document.
   f. In Word, remove the extra blank paragraph above and below the pasted worksheet so that just one blank line appears above and below the worksheet.
   g. Save your changes, print a copy of the letter, then close the document and exit Word.
   h. In Excel, save your changes, print a copy of the invoice, then close the workbook and exit Excel.

Child Care

Create the Word document shown in Figure Integration-1. Note that the title is enhanced with 18-point bold and the subtitle is enhanced with 14-point bold. Enter your name below the table, save the document as **Day Camp Activities**, then print a copy. Copy the table in Word, then paste it into cell A3 in a blank Excel worksheet. Format the worksheet so that it appears as shown in Figure Integration-2 . Use the AutoSum command to calculate the total number of hours in cell C9 and change the font to Arial for the table contents. (*Hint*: To reduce row heights, select cells A3 to C9, click Format on the menu bar, point to Row, then click AutoFit.) Enter your name in cell A11, center the worksheet horizontally on the page (use the Margins tab in the Page Setup dialog box), save the workbook as **Day Camp Schedule**, then print a copy.

FIGURE INTEGRATION-1

San Diego Sun Seekers Summer Day Camp
Week 3 Activities

Day	Activity
Monday	Miniature Golf at Beach Acres Fun Land
Tuesday	San Diego Wild Animal Park
Wednesday	Sea World Adventure Park
Thursday	Wet 'n Wild Wonderland
Friday	Legoland California

FIGURE INTEGRATION-2

Microsoft Excel - Day Camp Schedule.xls

File   Edit   View   Insert   Format   Tools   Data   Window   Help   Type a question for help

Arial   10   B I U

A11

San Diego Sun Seekers Day Camp

Week 3 Schedule

Day	Activity	Hours
Monday	Miniature Golf at Beach Acres Fun Land	4
Tuesday	San Diego Wild Animal Park	9
Wednesday	Sea World Adventure Park	9
Thursday	Wet 'n Wild Wonderland	5
Friday	Legoland California	6
	Total Hours	33

Recreation

1. **Merge data between Access and Word.**

   a. Start Access, then open the file BINT-3.mdb from the drive and folder where your Project Files are located.

   b. Click the Participants table (but do not open it), point to Office Links from the Tools menu, select Merge It with Microsoft Word, then click OK to accept an existing Word document as the location to link to.

   c. In the Select Microsoft Word Document dialog box, select the file BINT-4.doc from the drive and folder where your Project Files are located, then maximize the Word program window.

   d. Replace [Current Date] with the current date and [Your Name] at the end of the letter with your name. Save the document as **Conference Letter**.

2. **Use Mail Merge to Create a Form Letter.**

   a. In the Mail Merge task pane, click the **Next: Write your letter hyperlink**.

   b. Position the pointer to the second paragraph mark below the date. (*Hint*: If paragraph marks are not visible, click the Show/Hide button on the Formatting toolbar.)

   c. Click Address block in the Mail Merge task pane, then click OK.

   d. Scroll down to the second paragraph, click at the end of the paragraph (after "workshops:"), press [Spacebar] once, click More items in the Mail Merge task pane, click Workshop1, click Insert, click Close, press [Spacebar] once, type **at**, press [Spacebar] once, click More items again, click Time1, click Insert, then click Close.

   e. Press [Spacebar] once, type **and**, repeat step d above to insert Workshop2 at Time2, insert a period following the Time2 merge field, then preview the letters for all ten recipients.

   f. Click Previous. Write your letter at the bottom of the Mail Merge task pane to return to the form letter so you can add a chart from Excel in the next activity.

3. **Export an Access table to Excel.**

   a. In Access, click Queries on the Objects toolbar, verify the Recreation Areas query is selected, then use the Office Links command to analyze the table in Microsoft Excel.

   b. Click the RecreationArea label in cell C1, then sort the table alphabetically by Recreation Area.

   c. In Excel, click cell **E1**, then enter the labels and values in cells E1 through G2 as shown in Table Integration-1.

   d. Select cells E1 to G2, click the Chart Wizard button, click Next to accept the column chart, click Next, enter Participant Interests as the chart title, remove the Legend (*Hint*: Click the Legend tab, then click the Show legend check box to deselect it), then click Finish.

   e. In Excel, size and position the chart, add the Y-axis title, and change the font size of the labels to 10-point and the font size of the chart title to 18-point as shown in Figure Integration-3.

TABLE INTEGRATION-1

Fitness	Hiking	Kayaking
5	2	3

FIGURE INTEGRATION-3

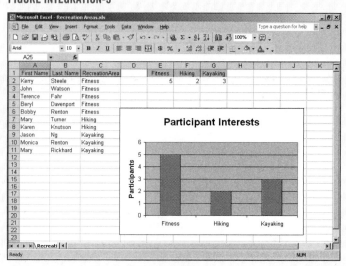

4. **Copy the chart to Word and complete the Merge.**

a. Copy the chart, switch to the Conference Letter in Word, click at the second paragraph mark between the third and fourth paragraphs of the letter, then paste the chart.

b. View the letter in Whole Page view, then, if necessary slightly reduce the size of the chart size so that the letter fits on one page when the merge data is previewed.

c. In the Mail Merge task pane, preview the letters, then click Complete the Merge.

d. Click the Edit individual letters hyperlink in the task pane, click OK in the Merge to New Document dialog box, then save the document as **Merged Conference Letters**.

e. Print a copy of the letters to **Mary Turner**, **Jason Ng**, and **Beryl Davenport**.

f. Close all documents, saving changes when prompted, then exit all applications.

5. **Send a Message with Outlook.**

a. Start Outlook and open a new mail messaging window. *Note: If you are not able to use Microsoft Outlook, go on to the next exercise. If you are able to complete Skills Review 5, you will need to be online to receive the e-mail.*

b. Enter your e-mail address in the To: text box.

c. Enter **Form Letter for Recreation Conference** as the message subject.

d. In the message area, type **Here's a copy of the form letter we're sending to all the people who are attending the Rocky Mountain recreation conference in Calgary.**

e. Press [Enter] twice following the message, then type your name.

f. Attach the Word file **Conference Letter** to the e-mail, then send the e-mail.

g. When you receive the e-mail, print a copy, then exit Outlook.

Graphic Design

In Access, open BINT-5.mdb from the drive and folder where your Project Files are located, select the July Contracts table, then publish it with Word. In Word, open BINT-6, then save it as **Company Profile**. Copy the table in the July Contracts.rtf document and paste it in the Company Profile document after paragraph 2. Modify the table and add clip art so that the completed Word document appears as shown in Figure Integration-4. Format the table with the Table Columns 2 autoformat. Adjust the column widths, then modify the text in row 1 with bold and 12-point. To find the clip art, search for the keyword Internet. Add your name at the bottom of the document, print a copy, then save and close all documents.

FIGURE INTEGRATION-4

Artisan Web Designs

Company Profile

Description

Artisan Web Designs provides Web site design services to small business owners in the Dallas area. At present, few other local Web site design services offer personalized and comprehensive services to individuals and small business owners on a budget. *Artisan Web Designs* specializes in helping small businesses obtain and maintain a presence on the World Wide Web. In addition, *Artisan Web Designs* helps clients add e-commerce capabilities to their sites in order to take advantage of a global market.

Service Overview

The table displayed below lists all the contracts performed by *Artisan Web Designs* in July of 2004.

ID	Date	Client Name	Job Category	Revenue
1	July 2	Karen Watters	New Web Site Design	$400.00
2	July 2	Desert Tours	E-Commerce Preparation	$1,400.00
3	July 6	Texas Rose Books	E-Commerce Preparation	$1,600.00
4	July 7	Larry Quinn	New Web Site Design	$500.00
5	July 8	Dallas Arms Hotel	Web Site Upgrade	$300.00
6	July 11	Tex-Mex Haven Café	Web Site Upgrade	$500.00
7	July 14	Bronco Boot Shop	E-Commerce Preparation	$1,300.00
8	July 15	Sagebrush Day Cay	New Web Site Design	$900.00
9	July 15	Home on the Range Lodge	Flash Animations	$1,500.00
10	July 18	Yani's Bike Repair	Web Site Upgrade	$800.00
11	July 19	Small Planet Whole Foods	Flash Animations	$1,900.00
12	July 22	Dallas Dan's Bistro	Flash Animations	$1,500.00
13	July 28	Western Duds	E-Commerce Preparation	$1,900.00
14	July 29	Sanchez Motors	Flash Animations	$1,100.00
15	July 31	Rodeo Inn	New Web Site Design	$800.00

On average, *Artisan Web Designs* completes two contracts each week for a total of eight contracts each month. In July, *Artisan Web Designs* received orders for an additional seven contracts. At present, its owner completes all contracts accepted by *Artisan Web Designs*. In order to accept new contracts, however, *Artisan Web Design* will need to hire new personnel to assist the owner.

Education

1. Create a Web page.

a. Start Word, then create a new Web page using the Frequently Asked Questions page template.

b. Save the document as a Web page called **FAQ** to the drive and folder where your Project Files are located. Enter **Outdoor School Frequently Asked Questions** as the page title.

c. Apply the Nature theme to the Web page (or a different theme if Nature is not available).

d. Replace the template text with the text shown in Figure Integration-5, delete remaining placeholder text and extra hard returns, then save the changes.

FIGURE INTEGRATION-5

Frequently Asked Questions

Who are the teachers at Juneau Outdoor School?
The Juneau Outdoor School employs four full-time teachers in addition to the director. Click here to learn about our fine team of educators.

What do students have to say about Juneau Outdoor School?
Students love Juneau Outdoor School! Click here to check out their responses to our annual surveys.

What subjects will my child learn at Juneau Outdoor School?
Your child can choose from thirteen activities in six subject categories. Click here to view the activity/subject list.

Do you provide information for group presentations?
We sure do! Click here to view a slide show presentation that you can share with groups of parents and teachers.

2. Format a Web page.

a. Apply the Heading 2 style to all the questions.

b. Insert the file BINT-7.jpg from the drive and folder where your Project Files are located to the right of the Frequently Asked Questions heading. (*Hint*: With the picture selected, open the Format Picture dialog box, click the Layout tab, click Square, then click the Right option button.)

c. Save the changes, then preview the Web page in Internet Explorer.

3. Create a Web page from a Word document.

a. Open the file BINT-8.doc from the drive and folder where your Project Files are located, then save it as a Web page with the page title **Juneau Outdoor School Personnel** and the filename **Personnel**.

b. Apply the Nature theme (or the theme you selected in step 1c) to the page, apply the Heading 1 style to the title and the Heading 2 style to the subtitle (Personnel), then center the title and subtitle.

c. Center the table, save the changes, preview the Web page in Internet Explorer, then close the Personnel file.

4. Create a Web page from an Access table.

a. Start Access, then open the file BINT-9.mdb from the drive and folder where your Project Files are located.

b. Open the Activities table, review the records, close the datasheet, then export the Activities table as a formatted HTML document with the filename **Activities**. If an Outputs Options dialog box appears, click OK.

c. Exit Access, open the Activities file in Word, apply the Nature theme, then apply the Table List 1 style to the table.

d. Apply the Heading 2 style to the table heading (first row), then center the heading.

e. Below the table, press [Enter] once, type **Return to the FAQ page**, save the changes, preview the Web page in Internet Explorer, then close the Activities file.

5. Create a Web page from an Excel workbook.

a. Start Excel, then open the file BINT-10.xls. Select the range A1:E10, then save the range as a Web page with the filename **Feedback** and the title **Juneau Outdoor School Student Feedback**.

b. Exit Excel, open the Feedback file in Word, apply the Nature theme (or the same theme you used previously if Nature is not available to you), enhance the title with the Heading 2 style, then center the title.

c. Save the changes, preview the Web page in Internet Explorer, then close the Feedback file.

6. Create a Web page from a PowerPoint presentation.

a. Start PowerPoint, then open the file BINT-11.ppt. Save the presentation as a Web page with the page title **Juneau Outdoor School Presentation** and the filename **Presentation**.

b. Format the text "Return to the FAQ page." on Slide 1 as a hyperlink to the FAQ.htm page.

c. Preview the presentation in Internet Explorer, close the file, then exit PowerPoint.

7. Add hyperlinks.

a. In the FAQ.htm page, format "here" in the first question as a hyperlink to the **Personnel.htm** file, format "here" in the second question as a hyperlink to the **Feedback.htm** file, format **"here"** in the third question as a hyperlink to the **Activities.html** file, then format "here" in the fourth question as a hyperlink to the **Presentation.htm** file.

b. Type your name at the bottom of the page, then save your changes.

c. In Word, open the Activities.html, Personnel.htm, and Feedback.htm Web pages and format the text **Return to the FAQ page** as a hyperlink to the file FAQ.htm.

d. Preview each page in Internet Explorer, test the hyperlinks, then print each page from Internet Explorer.

e. Preview FAQ.htm in Internet Explorer, test the links, print the page, then close all open files and programs.

 Visual Workshop Integration C: Word, Excel, Access, PowerPoint, Internet Explorer

Human Resources

Create the Web publication shown in Figure Integration-6. Use the Right-aligned Column Web page template in Word to create the home page saved as **Fitness.htm**. Replace the graphic with a fitness-related clip. (*Hint*: Use the keyword "fitness" to find the clip shown.) Create the **Rewards** Web page by creating a table in Excel, converting it to a Web page, then formatting it in Word. Use the Watermark theme for the Web pages formatted in Word. For the presentation, use the BINT-12.ppt file saved as a Web page called **FitnessPresentation**. Include your name on the first slide in the presentation. Add links between the Web pages, preview the Web publication in Internet Explorer, then print the first page of each Web page.

FIGURE INTEGRATION-6

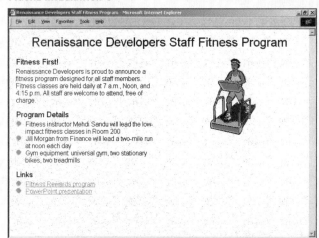
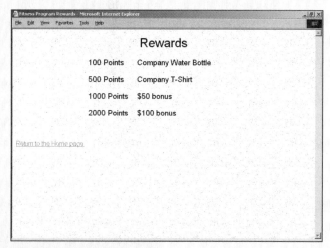
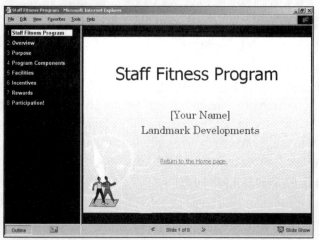

Microsoft Word 2002 Microsoft Office Specialist Certification Objectives

Below is a list of the Microsoft Office Specialist program objectives for the Core Word 2002 skills, showing where each Microsoft Office Specialist objective is covered in the Lessons and Practice. This table lists the Core Microsoft Office Specialist certification skills covered in the units in this book (Units A–D). The core skills without page references are covered in *Microsoft Office* XP*—Illustrated Second Course* (Units E–H). For more information on which Illustrated titles meet Microsoft Office Specialist certification, please see the inside front cover of this book.

Microsoft Office Specialist Standardized Coding Number	Activity	Lesson page where skill is covered	Location in lesson where skill is covered	Practice
W2002-1	**Inserting and Modifying Text**			
W2002-1-1	Insert, modify and move text and symbols	WORD B-4 WORD B-5	Steps 1–8, Clues to Use Table	Skills Review Independent Challenges 1–4 Visual Workshop
		WORD B-6 WORD B-7 WORD B-8 WORD B-9 WORD B-10 WORD B-11 WORD B-14 WORD B-15	Steps 1–7 Clues to Use Steps 1–7, Clues to Use Table Steps 1–9 Clues to Use Steps 1–9 Clues to Use	
		WORD D-12 WORD D-13	Steps 2–3 Clues to Use	Skills Review Independent Challenges 2–3
W2002-1-2	Apply and modify text formats	WORD C-2 WORD C-3 WORD C-4 WORD C-5	Steps 2–9 Clues to Use Steps 1–9 Clues to Use	Skills Review Independent Challenges 1–3 Visual Workshop
W2002-1-3	Correct spelling and grammar usage	WORD B-12	Steps 1–9	Skills Review Independent Challenges 1–3 Visual Workshop
W2002-1-4	Apply font and text effects	WORD C-4	Steps 1–9, Quick Tip	Skills Review Independent Challenges 1–3 Visual Workshop
		WORD C-5 WORD C-16	Clues to Use Clues to Use	
W2002-1-5	Enter and format Date and Time	WORD D-8 WORD D-10 WORD D-11	Clues to Use Steps 2–3, Quick Tip Clues to Use	Skills Review Independent Challenge 3
W2002-1-6	Apply character styles	WORD C-4 WORD C-5 WORD C-7	Steps 1–8 Clues to Use Clues to Use	Independent Challenge 3
W2002-2	**Creating and Modifying Paragraphs**			
W2002-2-1	Modify paragraph formats	WORD C-6 WORD C-7 WORD C-8 WORD C-9 WORD C-10 WORD C-12 WORD C-16	Steps 1–9 Clues to Use Steps 1–9 Clues to Use Steps 1–9 Steps 1–6, Table Steps 1–8, Clues to Use	Skills Review Independent Challenges 1–3 Visual Workshop

Microsoft Office Specialist Standardized Coding Number	Activity	Lesson page where skill is covered	Location in lesson where skill is covered	Practice
W2002-2-2	Set and modify tabs	WORD C-10	Steps 1–9	Skills Review Independent Challenges 1–3
W2002-2-3	Apply bullet, outline, and numbering format to paragraphs	WORD C-14 WORD C-15	Steps 1–8 Clues to Use	Skills Review Independent Challenges 1–3
W2002-2-4	Apply paragraph styles	WORD C-7	Clues to Use	Independent Challenge 3
W2002-3	**Formatting Documents**			
W2002-3-1	Create and modify a header and footer	WORD D-10 WORD D-11 WORD D-12	Steps 1–7, Quick Tips Table Steps 1–8	Skills Review Independent Challenges 1–3
W2002-3-2	Apply and modify column settings	WORD D-4 WORD D-5 WORD D-6 WORD D-14	Steps 4–5 Clues to Use Clues to Use Steps 1–8, Quick Tips	Skills Review Independent Challenges 1, 2 Visual Workshop
W2002-3-3	Modify document layout and Page Setup options	WORD D-2 WORD D-3 WORD D-4 WORD D-5 WORD D-6 WORD D-7 WORD D-8	Steps 1–8 Clues to Use Steps 1–6, Quick Tips, Table Clues to Use Steps 1–5, Clues to Use Table Steps 1–7, Quick Tip	Skills Review, Independent Challenges 1–4 Visual Workshop
W2002-3-4	Create and modify tables	WORD C-11	Clues to Use	
W2002-3-5	Preview and Print documents, envelopes, and labels	WORD A-12	Steps 1–4, 6–7	Skills Review Independent Challenges 1–4 Visual Workshop
W2002-4	**Managing Documents**			
W2002-4-1	Manage files and folders for documents	WORD B-3	Clues to Use	Independent Challenge 3
W2002-4-2	Create documents using templates	WORD B-16	Steps 1–9	Skills Review Independent Challenge 2 Visual Workshop
W2002-4-3	Save documents using different names and file formats	WORD A-10 WORD A-11 WORD B-2 WORD B-3	Steps 1–6, Clues to Use Table Steps 5–6 Clues to Use	Skills Review, Independent Challenges 1–4 Visual Workshop Skills Review Independent Challenges 1–4 Visual Workshop
W2002-5	**Working with Graphics**			
W2002-5-1	Insert images and graphics	WORD D-16	Steps 1–8	Skills Review, Independent Challenges 1, 2 Visual Workshop
W2002-5-2	Create and modify diagrams and charts			
W2002-6	**Workgroup Collaboration**			
W2002-6-1	Compare and Merge documents			
W2002-6-2	Insert, view, and edit comments			
W2002-6-3	Convert documents into Web pages			

Microsoft Excel 2002 Microsoft Office Specialist Certification Objectives

Below is a list of the Microsoft Office Specialist program objectives for the Core Excel 2002 skills, showing where each Microsoft Office Specialist objective is covered in the Lessons and Practice. This table lists the Core Microsoft Office Specialist certification skills covered in the units in this book (Units A–D). The core skills without page references are covered in *Microsoft Office* ^{XP}—*Illustrated Second Course* (Units E–H). For more information on which Illustrated titles meet Microsoft Office Specialist certification, please see the inside front cover of this book.

Microsoft Office Specialist Standardized Coding Number	Activity	Lesson page where skill is covered	Location in lesson where skill is covered	Practice
Ex2002-1	**Working with Cells and Cell Data**			
Ex2002-1-1	Insert, delete and move cells	EXCEL B-12	Step 7	Skills Review
		EXCEL B-19	Clues to Use	Skills Review
		EXCEL C-6	Step 6	Skills Review, Independent Challenge 4
Ex2002-1-2	Enter and edit cell data including text, numbers, and formulas	EXCEL A-10	Steps 1–7 Step 2 Tip	Skills Review, Independent Challenges 2–4
		EXCEL B-4	Steps 2–9	Skills Review
		EXCEL B-6	Steps 1–6	Skills Review, Independent Challenges 1–4
		EXCEL B-8	Steps 1–5, Clues to Use	Skills Review, Independent Challenges 1–4
		EXCEL B-10	Steps 2–9	Skills Review, Independent Challenge 2
		EXCEL C-2	Steps 2–7	Skills Review, Independent Challenges 1–4
		EXCEL C-3	Clues to Use	Skills Review, Independent Challenges 1–4
Ex2002-1-3	Check spelling	EXCEL C-16	Steps 1–5	Skills Review, Independent Challenges 1–4
Ex2002-1-4	Find and replace cell data and formats			
Ex2002-1-5	Work with a subset of data by filtering lists			
Ex2002-2	**Managing Workbooks**			
Ex2002-2-1	Manage workbook files and folders	EXCEL A-8	Steps 1–3, Step 4 Tip	Skills Review
Ex2002-2-2	Create workbooks using templates	EXCEL A-9	Clues to Use	Independent Challenge 3
Ex2002-2-3	Save workbooks using different names and file formats	EXCEL A-8	Step 4 Tip	Skills Review
		EXCEL A-8	Steps 4–5	Skills Review, Independent Challenges 1–4
		EXCEL C-2	Step 1 Tip	Skills Review, Independent Challenges 3–4
Ex2002-3	**Formatting and Printing Worksheets**			
Ex2002-3-1	Apply and modify cell formats	EXCEL C-2	Steps 2–7	Skills Review, Independent Challenges 1–4
		EXCEL C-3	Clues to Use	Skills Review
		EXCEL C-4	Steps 2–5	Skills Review, Independent Challenges 2, Visual Workshop
		EXCEL C-6	Steps 1–7	Skills Review, Independent Challenges 1–4, Visual Workshop
		EXCEL C-12	Steps 1–8	Skills Review, Independent Challenges 1, 2, 4, Visual Workshop
		EXCEL C-14	Steps 2–5	Skills Review, Independent Challenge 1, 2, 4, Visual Workshop

Microsoft Office Specialist Standardized Coding Number	Activity	Lesson page where skill is covered	Location in lesson where skill is covered	Practice
Ex2002-3-2	Modify row and column settings	EXCEL C-10	Steps 1–6	Skills Review, Independent Challenges 1, 2
Ex2002-3-3	Modify row and column formats	EXCEL C-6 EXCEL C-7 EXCEL C-8	Steps 6–7 Table Steps 1–7	Skills Review, Independent Challenges 2–4 Skills Review, Independent Challenges 1–3
		EXCEL C-9	Clues to Use	Independent Challenge 3
Ex2002-3-4	Apply styles			
Ex2002-3-5	Use automated tools to format worksheets	EXCEL C-7	Clues to Use	Independent Challenges 3,4
Ex2002-3-6	Modify Page Setup options	EXCEL C-16 EXCEL D-16	Step 8 Step 4	Independent Challenge 2 Skills Review, Independent Challenges 1–4
Ex2002-3-7	Preview and print worksheets and workbooks	EXCEL A-14	Steps 1–5	Skills Review, Independent Challenges 1–4
Ex2002-4	**Modifying Workbooks**			
Ex2002-4-1	Insert and delete worksheets			
Ex2002-4-2	Modify worksheet names and positions	EXCEL A-12 EXCEL A-12	Step 7 Steps 3–6 Step 3 Tip	Skills Review Skills Review, Independent Challenge 3
Ex2002-4-3	Use 3-D references			
Ex2002-5	**Creating and Revising Formulas**			
Ex2002-5-1	Create and revise formulas	EXCEL B-6	Steps 1–6	Skills Review, Independent Challenges 1, 4, Visual Workshop
		EXCEL B-8	Steps 1–5, Clues to Use	Skills Review, Independent Challenges 1,4, Visual Workshop
		EXCEL B-10 EXCEL B-14	Steps 1–4, 6 (Concept)	Independent Challenge 2 Skills Review Independent Challenges 1, 4
		EXCEL B-16	Steps 1–6	Skills Review, Independent Challenges 1, 4, Visual Workshops
		EXCEL B-18	Steps 4–7	Skills Review, Independent Challenges 1, 4, Visual Workshops
Ex2002-5-2	Use statistical date and time, financial, and logical functions in formulas	EXCEL B-10	Steps 1–4, 6	Independent Challenge 2
		EXCEL B-11	Clues to Use	Skills Review
Ex2002-6	**Creating and Modifying Graphics**			
Ex2002-6-1	Create, modify, position and print charts	EXCEL D-4	Steps 2–7	Skills Review, Independent Challenges 1–4
		EXCEL D-8	Steps 3–6	Skills Review, Independent Challenges 1–4
		EXCEL D-10	Steps 1–6	Skills Review, Independent Challenges 1–4
		EXCEL D-12	Steps 1–8	Skills Review, Independent Challenges 1, 3
		EXCEL D-14	Steps 1–8	Skills Review, Independent Challenges 2, 3, Visual Workshop
		EXCEL D-16	Steps 2–7	Skills Review, Independent Challenges 1–4, Visual Workshop
		EXCEL D-17	Clues	Skills Review, Independent Challenge 1–4, Visual Workshop
Ex2002-6-2	Create, modify and position graphics	EXCEL C-5	Clues to Use	Independent Challenge 3
		EXCEL D-14	Steps 1–8	Skills Review, Independent Challenges 2, 3, Visual Workshop
Ex2002-7	**Workgroup Collaboration**			
Ex2002-7-1	Convert worksheets into web pages			
Ex2002-7-2	Create hyperlinks			
Ex2002-7-3	View and edit comments	EXCEL C-11	Clues to Use	Skills Review

Microsoft Access 2002 Microsoft Office Specialist Certification Objectives

Below is a list of the Microsoft Office Specialist program objectives for the Core Access 2002 skills, showing where each Microsoft Office Specialist objective is covered in the Lessons and Practice. This table lists the Core Microsoft Office Specialist certification skills covered in the units in this book (Units A–D). The core skills without page references are covered in *Microsoft Office XP—Illustrated Second Course* (Units E–H). For more information on which Illustrated titles meet Microsoft Office Specialist certification, please see the inside front cover of this book.

Microsoft Office Specialist Standardized Coding Number	Activity	Lesson page where skill is covered	Location in lesson where skill is covered	Practice
AC2002-1	**Creating and Using Databases**			
AC2002-1-1	Create Access databases	ACCESS B-4	Steps 1–2	Skills Review Independent Challenges 1, 3
AC2002-1-2	Open database objects in multiple views	ACCESS A-4 ACCESS A-10 ACCESS A-16 ACCESS B-6 ACCESS B-16 ACCESS C-6 ACCESS D-6	Table A-2 Step 1 Step 1 Step 7 Steps 5, 7 Steps 1, 7 Steps 1, 7	Skills Review Independent Challenges 2, 3 Visual Workshop (Units B, C, D) Skills Review Independent Challenges 1, 2, 3, 4 Visual Workshop
AC2002-1-3	Move among records	ACCESS A-10 ACCESS A-11 ACCESS C-4 ACCESS C-12	Steps 1–6 Table A-4 Steps 5–6 Steps 5–7	Skills Review Independent Challenges 2, 3 Visual Workshop Skills Review Independent Challenges 1, 2, 3, 4
AC2002-1-4	Format datasheets	ACCESS B-8	Steps 3–5	Skills Review Independent Challenges 2, 3
AC2002-2	**Creating and Modifying Tables**			
AC2002-2-1	Create and modify tables	ACCESS B-2 ACCESS B-3 ACCESS B-4 ACCESS B-6 ACCESS B-7	Clues Table B-1 Steps 3–7 Steps 1–6 Clues	Skills Review Independent Challenges 1, 3
AC2002-2-2	Add a pre-defined input mask to a field				
AC2002-2-3	Create Lookup fields				
AC2002-2-4	Modify field properties	ACCESS B-6 ACCESS B-7	Steps 2–6 Clues	Skills Review Independent Challenge 1
AC2002-3	**Creating and Modifying Queries**			
AC2002-3-1	Create and modify Select queries	ACCESS B-16 ACCESS B-18	Steps 1–7 Steps 1–8	Skills Review Independent Challenges 2, 3 Visual Workshop
AC2002-3-2	Add calculated fields to Select queries				
AC2002-4	**Creating and Modifying Forms**			
AC2002-4-1	Create and display forms	ACCESS C-4 ACCESS C-5 ACCESS C-5	Steps 2–4 Table C-2 Clues	Skills Review Independent Challenges 1, 2, 3, 4 Visual Workshop

Microsoft Office Specialist Standardized Coding Number	Activity	Lesson page where skill is covered	Location in lesson where skill is covered	Practice
AC2002-4-2	Modify form properties	ACCESS C-2	Table C-1	Skills Review
		ACCESS C-6	Steps 1–6	Independent Challenges 1, 2, 3
		ACCESS C-7	Table C-3	Visual Workshop
		ACCESS C-8	Steps 1–6	
		ACCESS C-9	Table C-4	
		ACCESS C-10	Steps 1–7	
		ACCESS C-12	Steps 2–4	
		ACCESS C-13	Table C-5	
		ACCESS C-16	Steps 1–5	
AC2002-5	**Viewing and Organizing Information**			
AC2002-5-1	Enter, edit, and delete records	ACCESS A-12	Steps 2–5	Skills Review
		ACCESS A-14	Steps 1–9	Independent Challenge 3
		ACCESS A-15	Table A-5	Visual Workshop
		ACCESS B-16	Step 4	Skills Review
				Independent Challenges 1, 2, 3, 4
				Visual Workshop
		ACCESS C-12	Steps 1, 5–7	Skills Review
		ACCESS C-14	Steps 1–5	Independent Challenges 1, 2, 3, 4
		ACCESS C-16	Step 6	Visual Workshop
AC2002-5-2	Create queries	ACCESS B-16	Steps 1–8	Skills Review
		ACCESS B-18	Steps 1–7	Independent Challenges 2, 3
		ACCESS B-19	Clues	Visual Workshop
AC2002-5-3	Sort records	ACCESS B-11	Table B-2	Skills Review
		ACCESS B-12	Steps 1–3	Independent Challenges 2, 3
		ACCESS B-13	Clues	Visual Workshop
		ACCESS B-18	Step 4	
		ACCESS C-4	Step 5	Skills Review
				Independent Challenge 2
AC2002-5-4	Filter records	ACCESS B-11	Table B-2	Skills Review
		ACCESS B-14	Steps 1–5	Independent Challenge 2
		ACCESS B-17	Table B-4	
		ACCESS C-4	Step 7	Skills Review
		ACCESS C-14	Steps 6–8	Independent Challenge 3
AC2002-6	**Defining Relationships**			
AC2002-6-1	Create one-to-many relationships			
AC2002-6-2	Enforce referential integrity			
AC2002-7	**Producing Reports**			
AC2002-7-1	Create and format reports	ACCESS D-3	Table D-1	Skills Review
		ACCESS D-4	Steps 2–6	Independent Challenges 1, 2, 3, 4
		ACCESS D-14	Steps 1–6	Visual Workshop
		ACCESS D-15	Table D-3	
		ACCESS D-16	Steps 1–7	
AC2002-7-2	Add calculated controls to reports	ACCESS D-6	Steps 4–6	Skills Review
		ACCESS D-10	Steps 1–3	Independent Challenge 2
				Visual Workshop
AC2002-7-3	Preview and print reports	ACCESS D-8	Steps 3–5	Skills Review
		ACCESS D-14	Steps 6–7	Independent Challenges 1, 2, 3, 4
				Visual Workshop
AC2002-8	**Integrating with Other Applications**			
AC2002-8-1	Import data to Access			
AC2002-8-2	Export data from Access			
AC2002-8-3	Create a simple data access page			

Microsoft PowerPoint 2002 Microsoft Office Specialist Certification Objectives

Below is a list of the Microsoft Office Specialist program objectives for the Comprehensive PowerPoint 2002 skills, showing where each Microsoft Office Specialist objective is covered in the Lessons and Practice. This table lists the Microsoft Office Specialist certification skills covered in the units in this book (Units A–D). The skills without page references are covered in *Microsoft Office^XP—Illustrated Second Course* (Units E–H). For more information on which Illustrated titles meet Microsoft Office Specialist certification, please see the inside front cover of this book.

Microsoft Office Specialist Standardized Coding Number	Activity	Lesson page where skill is covered	Location in lesson where skill is covered	Practice
PP2002-1	**Creating Presentations**			
PP2002-1-1	Create presentations (manually and using automated tools)	POWERPOINT A-8	Steps 1–9	Skills Review Independent Challenges 2, 3 Visual Workshop
		POWERPOINT B-4	Clues to Use	
		POWERPOINT B-4	Steps 1–10	Skills Review
		POWERPOINT B-12	Steps 1–5 QuickTip Step 2	Independent Challenges 1–4 Visual Workshop
		POWERPOINT B-13	Clues to Use	
PP2002-1-2	Add slides to and delete slides from presentations	POWERPOINT B-6	Steps 1–3	Skills Review
		POWERPOINT B-8	Steps 2–6	Independent Challenges 1–4 Visual Workshop
		POWERPOINT C-14	Step 6	Skills Review Independent Challenges 2–4
PP2002-1-3	Modify headers and footers in the Slide Master	POWERPOINT B-10	Steps 1–9	Skills Review Independent Challenges 1–4 Visual Workshop
PP2002-2	**Inserting and Modifying Text**			
PP2002-2-1	Import text from Word	POWERPOINT C-14	Steps 1–3	Skills Review, Independent Challenge 2
PP2002-2-2	Insert, format, and modify text	POWERPOINT B-4	Steps 2–9	Skills Review Independent Challenges 1–4 Visual Workshop
		POWERPOINT B-6	Steps 4–9	
		POWERPOINT B-8	Steps 3–6	
		POWERPOINT B-14	Steps 1–4	
		POWERPOINT C-10	Steps 2–8	Skills Review
		POWERPOINT C-12	Steps 1–10	Independent Challenges 2–4 Visual Workshop
PP2002-3	**Inserting and Modifying Visual Elements**			
PP2002-3-1	Add tables, charts, clip art, and bitmap images to slides	POWERPOINT D-2	Steps 3–5 Clues to Use	Skills Review Independent Challenges 1–4
		POWERPOINT D-4	Steps 1–9 Clues to Use	Visual Workshop
		POWERPOINT D-6	Steps 2–3	
		POWERPOINT D-12	Steps 1–5	
PP2002-3-2	Customize slide backgrounds	POWERPOINT C-16	Steps 1–8	Skills Review Independent Challenges 2–4
		POWERPOINT D-4	Steps 2–3 Clues to Use	Skills Review Independent Challenge 2

Microsoft Office Specialist Standardized Coding Number	Activity	Lesson page where skill is covered	Location in lesson where skill is covered	Practice
PP2002-3-3	Add OfficeArt elements to slides	POWERPOINT C-4 POWERPOINT C-6	Steps 4–8 Steps 1–9	Skills Review Independent Challenges 2, 3 Visual Workshop
PP2002-3-4	Apply custom formats to tables	POWERPOINT D-12	Steps 5–9	Skills Review Independent Challenges 3, 4
PP2002-4	**Modifying Presentation Formats**			
PP2002-4-1	Apply formats to presentations	POWERPOINT B-6 POWERPOINT B-7 POWERPOINT B-8 POWERPOINT B-12 POWERPOINT C-4 POWERPOINT D-2 POWERPOINT D-4 POWERPOINT D-6	Steps 2–3 Table Step 3 Steps 1–5 QuickTip Step 5 Steps 2–3 Step 2 Steps 3–4 Steps 1–2	Skills Review Independent Challenges 1–4 Visual Workshop Skills Review Independent Challenges 2, 4 Independent Challenges 1–4
PP2002-4-2	Apply animation schemes	POWERPOINT D-18	Steps 1–7	Skills Review Independent Challenges 1–3
PP2002-4-3	Apply slide transitions	POWERPOINT D-16	Steps 1–5	Skills Review Independent Challenges 1–3
PP2002-4-4	Customize slide formats	POWERPOINT B-6 POWERPOINT B-8 POWERPOINT C-4 POWERPOINT D-2 POWERPOINT D-4 POWERPOINT D-6	Steps 2–3 Table Step 3 Steps 2–3 Step 2 Step 1 Steps 1–2	Skills Review Independent Challenges 1–4 Visual Workshop Skills Review
PP2002-4-5	Customize slide templates	POWERPOINT B-12 POWERPOINT B-13 POWERPOINT C-16	Steps 1–5 QuickTip Step 2 Clues to Use Steps 1–7	 Skills Review Independent Challenges 1–4
PP2002-4-6	Manage a Slide Masters			
PP2002-4-7	Rehearse timing			
PP2002-4-8	Rearrange slides	POWERPOINT B-8 POWERPOINT B-16	Steps 8–9 Steps 2–3	Skills Review, Independent Challenges 1–4
PP2002-4-9	Modify slide layout	POWERPOINT B-6 POWERPOINT B-7 POWERPOINT B-8 POWERPOINT C-4 POWERPOINT D-4 POWERPOINT D-6	Steps 2–3 Table Step 3 Steps 2–3 Steps 3–4 Steps 1–2	Skills Review Independent Challenges 1–4 Visual Workshop Skills Review, Independent Challenges 1–4
PP2002-4-10	Add links to a presentation			
PP2002-5	**Printing Presentations**			
PP2002-5-1	Preview and print slides, outlines, handouts, and speaker notes	POWERPOINT A-16 POWERPOINT B-11 POWERPOINT B-14	Steps 1–7 Clues to Use QuickTip Step 5	Skills Review Independent Challenges 2, 3 Visual Workshop Skills Review

Microsoft Office Specialist Standardized Coding Number	Activity	Lesson page where skill is covered	Location in lesson where skill is covered	Practice
PP2002-6	**Working with Data from Other Sources**			
PP2002-6-1	Import Excel charts to slides			
PP2002-6-2	Add sound and video to slides	POWERPOINT D-16	Step 5	Independent Challenges 1–3
PP2002-6-3	Insert Word tables on slides			
PP2002-6-4	Export a presentation as an outline			
PP2002-7	**Managing and Delivering Presentations**			
PP2002-7-1	Set up slide shows			
PP2002-7-2	Deliver presentations	POWERPOINT A-10	Steps 6–7	Skills Review Independent Challenge 2
		POWERPOINT B-16	Steps 1–4 Details	Skills Review Independent Challenges 1–4
		POWERPOINT D-14 POWERPOINT D-16 POWERPOINT D-18	Steps 1–9 Steps 1–6 Steps 1–7	Skills Review Independent Challenges 1–4
PP2002-7-3	Manage files and folders for presentations			
PP2002-7-4	Work with embedded fonts	POWERPOINT A-13	Clues to Use	Skills Review
PP2002-7-5	Publish presentations to the Web			
PP2002-7-6	Use Pack and Go			
PP2002-8	**Workgroup Collaboration**			
PP2002-8-1	Set up a review cycle			
PP2002-8-2	Review presentation comments			
PP2002-8-3	Schedule and deliver presentation broadcasts			
PP2002-8-4	Publish presentations to the Web			

Project Files List

Read the following information carefully!

It is very important to organize and keep track of the files you need for this book.

1. **Find out from your instructor the location of the Project Files you need and the location where you will store your files.**

   - To complete many of the units in this book, you need to use Project Files. Your instructor will either provide you with a copy of the Project Files or ask you to make your own copy.

   - If you need to make a copy of the Project Files, you will need to copy a set of files from a file server, stand-alone computer, or the Web to the drive and folder where you will be storing your Project Files.

   - Your instructor will tell you which computer, drive letter, and folders contain the files you need, and where you will store your files.

   - You can also download the files by going to www.course.com. See page PROJECT FILES 19 for instructions on how to download your files.

2. **Copy and organize your Project Files.**

   ### Floppy disk users

   - If you are using floppy disks to store your Project Files, the list on the following pages shows which files you'll need to copy onto your disk(s).

   - Unless noted in the Project Files List, you will need one formatted, high-density disk for each unit. For each unit you are assigned, copy the files listed in the **Project File Supplied column** onto one disk.

   - Make sure you label each disk clearly with the unit name (e.g., Word Unit A).

   - When working through the unit, save all your files to this disk.

   ### Users storing files in other locations

   - If you are using a zip drive, network folder, hard drive, or other storage device, use the Project Files List to organize your files.

   - Create a subfolder for each unit in the location where you are storing your files, and name it according to the unit title (e.g., Word Unit A).

   - For each unit you are assigned, copy the files listed in the **Project File Supplied column** into that unit's folder.

   - Store the files you modify or create for each unit in the unit folder.

3. **Find and keep track of your Project Files and completed files.**

   - Use the **Project File Supplied column** to make sure you have the files you need before starting the unit or exercise indicated in the **Unit and Location column**.

   - Use the **Student Saves File As column** to find out the filename you use when saving your changes to a Project File that was provided.

   - Use the **Student Creates File column** to find out the filename you use when saving a file you create new for the exercise.

Unit and Location	Project File Supplied	Student Saves File As	Student Creates File
Windows 2000 Unit A	(No files provided or created)		
Windows 2000 Unit B			
DISK 1			
Lessons	Win_B-1.bmp		
DISK 2			
Skills Review	Win_B-2.bmp		
Introducing Office XP	(No files provided or created)		
Internet Explorer Unit A	(No files provided or created)		
Word Unit A			
Lessons			Marketing Memo.doc
Skills Review			Lacasse Fax.doc
Independent Challenge 1			Zobel Letter.doc
Independent Challenge 2			Smart Tags Memo.doc
Independent Challenge 3			Komata Letter.doc
Independent Challenge 4			Business Letters.doc
Visual Workshop			Publishing Cover Letter.doc
Word Unit B			
Lessons	WD B-1.doc	NY Press Release.doc	
			NYT Fax.doc
Skills Review	WD B-2.doc	CAOS Press Release.doc	
			CAOS Fax.doc
Independent Challenge 1	WD B-3.doc	Lyric Theatre Letter.doc	
Independent Challenge 2			Global Dynamics Letter.doc
Independent Challenge 3	WD B-4.doc	Computer Memo.doc	
Independent Challenge 4	WD B-5.doc	Web References.doc	
Visual Workshop			Visa Letter.doc
Word Unit C			
Lessons	WD C-1.doc	Chicago Marketing Report.doc	
Skills Review	WD C-2.doc	EDA Report.doc	
Independent Challenge 1	WD C-3.doc	Zakia Construction.doc	
Independent Challenge 2	WD C-4.doc	Membership Flyer.doc	
Independent Challenge 3	WD C-5.doc	Solstice Memo.doc	

Unit and Location	Project File Supplied	Student Saves File As	Student Creates File
Independent Challenge 4	WD C-6.doc	Fonts.doc	
Visual Workshop	WD C-7.doc	Rosebud Specials.doc	
Word Unit D			
Lessons	WD D-1.doc	MediaLoft Buzz.doc	
Skills Review	WD D-2.doc	Amherst Fitness.doc	
Independent Challenge 1	WD D-3.doc	Bon Appetit.doc	
Independent Challenge 2	WD D-4.doc	Parking FAQ.doc	
Independent Challenge 3	WD D-5.doc	Stormwater.doc	
Independent Challenge 4	WD D-6.doc	MLA Style.doc	
			MLA Sample Format.doc
Visual Workshop	WD D-7.doc	Gardener's Corner.doc	
Excel Unit A			
Lessons	EX A-1.xls	MediaLoft Cafe Budget.xls	MediaLoft Balance Sheet.xls
Skills Review	EX A-2.xls	MediaLoft Toronto Cafe.xls	
Independent Challenge 1	(No files provided or created)		
Independent Challenge 2			Sample Payroll.xls
Independent Challenge 3			Training Workbook.xls
			Template Sample.xls
Independent Challenge 4			New Computer Data.xls
Visual Workshop			Carrie's Camera and Darkroom.xls
Excel Unit B			
Lessons	EX B-1.xls	Author Events Forecast.xls	
Skills Review	EX B-2.xls	Office Furnishings.xls	
Independent Challenge 1			Young Brazilians.xls
Independent Challenge 2	EX B-3.xls	Beautiful You Finances.xls	
Independent Challenge 3			Learn-it-All.xls
Independent Challenge 4			Temperature Conversions.xls
Visual Workshop			Annual Budget.xls
Excel Unit C			
Lessons	EX C-1.xls	Ad Expenses.xls	
Skills Review			MediaLoft GB Inventory.xls
	EX C-2.xls	Monthly Operating Expenses.xls	
Independent Challenge 1	EX C-3.xls	BY Inventory.xls	

Unit and Location	Project File Supplied	Student Saves File As	Student Creates File
Independent Challenge 2	EX C-4.xls	Community Action.xls	
Independent Challenge 3			Classic Instruments.xls
Independent Challenge 4			Currency Conversions.xls
Visual Workshop	EX C-5.xls	Projected March Advertising Invoices.xls	
Excel Unit D			
Lessons	EX D-1.xls	MediaLoft Sales - Eastern Division.xls	
Skills Review			MediaLoft Vancouver Software Usage.xls
Independent Challenge 1	EX D-2.xls	Springfield Theater Group.xls	
Independent Challenge 2	EX D-3.xls	BY Expense Charts.xls	
Independent Challenge 3	EX D-4.xls	Bright Light.xls	
Independent Challenge 4			New Location Analysis.xls
Visual Workshop	EX D-5.xls	Quarterly Advertising Budget.xls	
Integration Unit A			
Lessons	INT A-1.doc	Manager Memo.doc	
			Manager Sales.xls
Independent Challenge 1	INT A-2.xls	Chamber Statistics.xls	
	INT A-3.doc	Chamber Consultants.doc	
Independent Challenge 2			Population Projections.xls
			Population Analysis.doc

Note: In Access, the original Project Files are used to complete the exercises. Therefore, it is a good practice to make a backup copy of the supplied Project Files before you use them, in case you need to go back and repeat any of the exercises.

Unit and Location	Project File Supplied	Student Saves File As	Student Creates File
Access Unit A			
Lessons	MediaLoft-A.mdb		
Skills Review	Recycle-A.mdb		
Independent Challenge 1	(No files provided or created)		
Independent Challenge 2	Recycle-A.mdb		
Independent Challenge 3	Recycle-A.mdb		
Independent Challenge 4	(No files provided or created)		
Visual Workshop	Recycle-A.mdb		

Unit and Location	Project File Supplied	Student Saves File As	Student Creates File
Access Unit B*			
DISK 1			
Lessons			MediaLoft.mdb
	MediaLoft-B.mdb		
Skills Review			Doctors.mdb
	Doctors-B.mdb		
Independent Challenge 2	Doctors-B.mdb		
Visual Workshop	MediaLoft-B.mdb		
DISK 2			
Independent Challenge 1			Movies.mdb
Independent Challenge 3			People.mdb
Independent Challenge 4	Baltic-B.mdb		

* Because the files created in this unit are large, you will need to organize the files onto two floppy disks if you are using floppies and completing all the exercises. Copy the files as outlined above, and label each disk clearly (e.g., Access Unit B Disk 1).

Unit and Location	Project File Supplied	Student Saves File As	Student Creates File
Access Unit C			
Lessons	MediaLoft-C.mdb Smallmedia.bmp		
Skills Review	Membership-C.mdb Hand.bmp		
Independent Challenge 1	Clinic-C.mdb		
Independent Challenge 2	Clinic-C.mdb		
Independent Challenge 3	Clinic-C.mdb Medical.bmp		
Independent Challenge 4	Baltic-C.bmp		
Visual Workshop	Clinic-C.mdb Medstaff.bmp		
Access Unit D			
Lessons	MediaLoft-D.mdb		
Skills Review	Club-D.mdb		
Independent Challenge 1	Therapy-D.mdb		
Independent Challenge 2	Therapy-D.mdb		
Independent Challenge 3			Colleges.mdb
Independent Challenge 4	Baltic-D.mdb		
Visual Workshop	Club-D.mdb		

Unit and Location	Project File Supplied	Student Saves File As	Student Creates File
Integration Unit B			
Lessons	MediaLoft-IB.mdb		
	INT B-1.doc		Survey Form Letter.doc
			Survey Letters.doc
			Customers.xls
Independent Challenge 1			Student Records.mdb
			Student Info.xls
			Student Info.doc
Independent Challenge 2	MediaLoft-IB.mdb		
			Funding Letter.doc
			Pleasantown Letters.doc
PowerPoint Unit A			
Lessons			New Ad Campaign.ppt
Skills Review			Practice.ppt
Independent Challenge 1	(No files provided or created)		
Independent Challenge 2			ArtWorks.ppt
Independent Challenge 3			Sales Trainging.ppt
Independent Challenge 4			PowerPoint Productivity Tips.doc
Visual Workshop			Phase 3A.ppt
PowerPoint Unit B			
Lessons			iMedia1.ppt
Skills Review			RouterJet Testing.ppt
Independent Challenge 1			Harvest Proposal.ppt
Independent Challenge 2			Class 1.ppt
Independent Challenge 3			Training Class.ppt
Independent Challenge 4			Presentation Tips.ppt
Visual Workshop			Sales Project.ppt
PowerPoint Unit C			
Lessons	PPT C-1.ppt	iMedia2.ppt	
	PPT C-2.doc		
Skills Review	PPT C-3.ppt	Cafe Report.ppt	
	PPT C-4.doc		
Independent Challenge 1			Arranging Objects.doc

Unit and Location	Project File Supplied	Student Saves File As	Student Creates File
Independent Challenge 2	PPT C-5.ppt		Title Meeting 9-23-03.ppt
	PPT C-6.doc		
Independent Challenge 3			Software Learning.ppt
PowerPoint Unit D			
Lessons	PPT D-1.ppt	IMedia3.ppt	
	PPT D-2.tif		
Skills Review	PPT D-3.ppt	CD Product Report.ppt	
	PPT D-4.bmp		
Independent Challenge 1	PPT D-5.ppt	Fund Seminar.ppt	
Independent Challenge 2			Student Employment.ppt
Independent Challenge 3			JM Design.ppt
Independent Challenge 4	PPT D-6.ppt	Retirement Presentation.ppt	
Visual Workshop			Costs.ppt
Integration Unit C			
Lessons	INT C-1.ppt	Company Status.ppt	
	INT C-2.doc		
	INT C-3.xls		
	Cafe Profit.xls		
			Handouts for Status Meeting.doc
Independent Challenge 1			Office Review.ppt
	INT C-4.doc		
Independent Challenge 2	INT C-5.xls	Statistics.xls	
			Stat Outline.doc
			Bureau.ppt
			Bureau Handouts.doc
Independent Challenge 3	INT C-6.doc	Cover Letter.doc	
	Nomad.tif		
	Customer Data.mdb		
	INT C-7.xls	Tour Type.xls	
			Tour Evaluation.ppt
	INT C-8.doc		
Independent Challenge 4			Rail Tours.doc
			Royal Tours.ppt
			Royal Tours Data.xls

Unit and Location	Project File Supplied	Student Saves File As	Student Creates File
Integration D*			
DISK 1			
Lessons			Welcome.htm Welcome_files folder and related files
	Mloft.jpg		
	INT D-1.doc	Vacation.htm Vacation_files folder and related files	
	INT D-2.mdb	Health Plans.htm Health Plans_files folder and related files	
	INT D-3.xls	Bonus.htm Bonus_files folder and related files	
	INT D-4.ppt	AR Presentation.htm Annual_files	
DISK 2			
Skills Review	Mloft.jpg INT D-5.doc INT D-6.mdb INT D-7.xls INT D-8.ppt TOC.htm Employee.htm	TOC.htm TOC_files folder and related files Survey.htm Survey_files folder and related files Sales Reps.htm Sales_Reps_files folder and related files Division Sales.htm folder and related files Eastern Presentation.htm Eastern_files folder and related files	
DISK 3			
Independent Challenge 1	INT D-9.doc INT D-10.mdb INT D-11.xls INT D-12.ppt	Grapevine Home.htm Gravepine Home_files folder and related files Donations.htm Donations_files folder and related files Programs.htm Programs_files folder and related files Financial Report.htm Financial Report_files folder and related files Grapevine Annual Report.htm Grapevine Annual Report_files folder and related files	

Unit and Location	Project File Supplied	Student Saves File As	Student Creates File
DISK 4			
Independent Challenge 2	INT D-13.doc INT D-14.mdb INT D-15.xls INT D-16.ppt	Oil Spill Home.htm Oil Spill Home_files folder and related files Press Release.htm Press Release_files folder and related files Prevention Programs.htm Prevention Programs_files folder and related files Oil Spills by Company.htm Oil Spills by Company_files folder and related files Oil Spill Presentation.htm Oil Spill Presentation_files folder and related files	
DISK 5			
Visual Workshop			Cafe Home.htm Cafe Home_files folder and related files Daily Specials.htm Daily Specials_files folder and related files Contact.htm Contact_files folder and related files

*Because the files created in this unit are large, you will need to organize the files onto 5 floppy disks if you are completing all the exercises. Copy the files as outlined above, and label each disk clearly (e.g., Integration Unit D Disk 1).

Unit and Location	Project File Supplied	Student Saves File As	Student Creates File
Outlook Unit A			
Lessons	Tea.doc		
Skills Review	House.tif		

Instructions for Downloading the Project Files from the World Wide Web

1. Using your browser, go to the Web site www.course.com. Follow the link to find your Project Files (listed as student files, student downloads, or data disk files).

2. Browse by entering your book's ISBN, then click the link for the project files (listed as data disk files) you want to download.

3. If the File Download dialog box appears, make sure the Save this program to disk option is selected, and then click OK.

4. If the Save As dialog box appears, make sure the location in the Save in box is one chosen by your instructor.

5. The filename of the compressed file appears in the File name text box (e.g. 3500-8.exe). Click either OK or Save.

6. If a dialog box indicates that the download is complete, click OK or Close, then close your browser.

7. Open Windows Explorer and display the contents of the folder to where you downloaded the files. Double-click the downloaded filename on the right side of the Windows Explorer window.

8. In the WinZip Extractor window, specify the drive and folder name to unzip the files to. Click Unzip.

9. When the WinZip Self-Extractor displays the number of files unzipped, click OK, then click Close. You are now ready to access your Project Files.

Office XP

Glossary

Absolute link A hyperlink that contains a fixed Web page address.

Absolute reference A cell reference that contains a dollar sign before the column letter and/or row number to indicate the absolute, or fixed, contents of specific cells. For example, the formula $A$1+$B$1 calculates only the sum of these specific cells no matter where the formula is copied in the workbook.

Active cell A selected cell in a Graph datasheet or an Excel worksheet.

Address The location of a specific cell or range expressed by the column and row coordinates; for example, the address of the cell in column A, row 1, is A1.

Address bar The bar that displays the address of the Web page currently opened in the Web browser window.

Address book A collection of usernames and e-mail addresses you can access to quickly address an e-mail message.

Adjustment handle A small yellow diamond that changes the appearance of an object's most prominent feature.

Align To place objects' edges or centers on the same plane.

Alignment (Access) Commands used in Form or Report Design view to either left-, center-, or right-align a value within its control, or to align the top, bottom, right, or left edge of the control with respect to other controls on the form or report.

Alignment (Excel) The placement of cell contents; for example, left, center, or right.

Alignment (Word) The position of text in a document relative to the margins.

And criteria Criteria placed in the same row of the query design grid. All criteria on the same row must be true in order for a record to appear on the resulting datasheet.

Animation scheme A set of predefined visual effects for a slide transition, title text, and the bullet text of the slides in a PowerPoint presentation.

Annotate A freehand drawing on the screen made by using the Annotation tool. You can annotate only in Slide Show view.

Application See *Program.*

Appointment A scheduled activity that does not involve inviting other people or scheduling resources.

Area chart A line chart in which each area is given a solid color or pattern to emphasize the relationship between the pieces of charted information.

Argument ToolTip A yellow box that appears as you build a function; shows function elements, which you can click to display online help for each one.

Arguments The pieces of information a function needs to create the final answer. In an expression, multiple arguments are separated by commas. All of the arguments are surrounded by a single set of parentheses.

Arithmetic operator A symbol used in a formula (such as + or -, / or *) to perform mathematical operations.

Ascending order A sequence in which information is placed in alphabetical order or arranged from smallest to largest. For a text field, numbers are sorted first, then letters.

Ask a Question box The list box at the right end of the menu bar in which you can type or select questions for the Help system.

Attribute The styling features such as bold, italics, and underlining that can be applied to cell contents.

AutoComplete (Excel) A feature that automatically completes entries based on other entries in the same column.

AutoComplete (Word) A feature that automatically suggests text to insert.

AutoContent Wizard A wizard that helps you get a presentation started by supplying a sample outline and a design template.

AutoCorrect A feature that automatically detects and corrects typing errors, minor spelling errors, and capitalization, and inserts certain typographical symbols as you type.

AutoFill   A feature that creates a series of text entries or numbers when a range is selected using the fill handle.

AutoFit   A feature that automatically adjusts the width of a column to accommodate its widest entry when the boundary to the right of the column selector is double-clicked.

AutoFormat   Preset schemes that can be applied to format a range instantly. Excel comes with 16 AutoFormats that include colors, fonts, and numeric formatting.

AutoNumber   A data type in which Access enters a sequential integer for each record added to the datasheet. Numbers cannot be reused, even if the record is deleted.

AutoReport   A tool used to quickly create a new report based on the selected table or query.

AutoSum   A feature that automatically creates totals using the SUM function when you click the AutoSum button.

AutoText   A feature that stores frequently used text and graphics so they can be easily inserted into a document.

Background   The area behind the text and graphics on a slide.

Background color   The color applied to the background of a cell.

Bar chart   A chart that shows information as a series of horizontal bars.

.bmp   The abbreviation for the bitmap graphics file format.

Body text   Subpoints or bullet points on a slide under the slide title.

Bold   Formatting applied to text to make it thicker and darker.

Border (Excel)   The edge of a cell, an area of a worksheet, or a selected object; you can change its color or line style.

Border (Word)   Lines that can be added above, below, or to the sides of paragraphs, text, and table cells.

Bound control   A control used in either a form or report to display data from the underlying record source; also used to edit and enter new data in a form.

Bound image control   A bound control used to show OLE data such as a picture on a form or report.

Browser   A program used to view the text graphic images and multimedia data on the Web. Also known as a Web browser.

Browser window   The area where the current Web page appears.

Bullet   A small graphic symbol used to identify items in a list.

Business productivity software   Programs, such as word processors, spreadsheets, and databases, that businesses use to accomplish daily tasks and become more productive.

Calculated control   A control that uses information from existing controls to calculate new data such as subtotals, dates, or page numbers; used in either a form or report.

Calculation   A new value that is created by entering an expression in a text box on a form or report.

Calendar   The scheduling component within Outlook that stores appointments, meetings, and scheduled events; it is the electronic equivalent of your daily desk calendar.

Cancel button   The X in the Formula bar; it removes information from the formula bar and restores the previous cell entry.

Caption property   A field property used to override the technical field name with an easy-to-read caption entry when the field name appears on datasheets, forms, and reports.

Categories   A method for organizing items in Outlook.

Cell   The intersection of a column and row in a worksheet, datasheet, or table.

Cell address   The location of a specific cell expressed by the column and row coordinates; for example, the cell address of the cell in column A, row 1, is A1.

Cell pointer   A highlighted rectangle around a cell that indicates the active cell.

Cell reference   The address or name that identifies a cell's position in a worksheet; it consists of a letter that identifies the cell's column and a number that identifies its row; for example, cell B3. Cell references in worksheets can be used in formulas and are relative or absolute.

Cell   The intersection of a column and row within a worksheet, datasheet, or table.

Center   Alignment in which an item is centered between the margins or edges of the cell.

Character spacing   Formatting that changes the width or scale of characters, expands or condenses the amount of space between characters, raises or lowers characters relative to the line of text, and adjusts kerning (the spacing between standard combinations of letters).

Character style   A named set of character format settings that can be applied to text to format it all at once.

Chart   A graphical representation of information from a datasheet or worksheet. Types include 2-D and 3-D column, bar, pie, area, and line charts.

Chart sheet   A separate sheet that contains only a chart linked to worksheet data.

Chart title   The name assigned to a chart.

Chart Wizard   A series of dialog boxes that helps you create or modify a chart.

Check box (Access)   A bound control used to display "yes" or "no" answers for a field. If the box is "checked" it indicates "yes" information in a form or report.

Check box (all applications)   A square box in a dialog box that can be clicked to turn an option on or off.

Clear   A command on the Edit menu used to erase a cell's contents, formatting, or both.

Click and Type pointer   A pointer used to move the insertion point and automatically apply the paragraph formatting necessary to insert text at that location in the document.

Clip art   A collection of graphic images that can be inserted into documents, presentations, Web pages, spread sheets and other Office files.

Clip Organizer   A library of art, pictures, sounds, video clips, and animations that all Office applications share.

Clipboard   A temporary storage area for cut or copied items that are available for pasting. See *Office Clipboard*.

Clipboard task pane   A task pane that shows the contents of the Office Clipboard; contains options for copying and pasting items to and from the Office Clipboard.

Close   A command that closes the file so you can no longer work with it, but keeps the program open so that you can continue to work on other files.

Color scheme   The eight coordinated colors that make up a PowerPoint presentation; a color scheme assigns colors for text, lines, objects, and background color. You can change the color scheme on any presentation at any time.

Column break   A break that forces text following the break to begin at the top of the next column.

Column chart   The default chart type in Excel, which displays information as a series of vertical columns.

Column heading   Gray boxes along the top of a datasheet.

Column headings (Outlook)   Part of the e-mail window that identifies sections of the message header.

Combo box   A bound control used to display a list of possible entries for a field in which you can also type an entry from the keyboard. It is a "combination" of the list box and text box controls.

Command button   An unbound control used to provide an easy way to initiate an action or run a macro.

Comparison operators   Characters such as $>$ and $<$ that allow you to find or filter data based on specific criteria.

Complex formula   An equation that uses more than one type of arithmetic operator.

Computer network   Two or more connected computers that can share information and resources.

Conditional format   A cell format that is based on the cell's value or the outcome of a formula.

Contacts folder   A folder that stores all the e-mail addresses and personal information for your contacts.

Contacts   The Outlook component that enables you to manage all your business and personal contact information.

Control   Any element on a form or report such as a label, text box, line, or combo box. Controls can be bound, unbound, or calculated.

Control menu box   A box in the upper-left corner of a window used to resize or close a window.

Copy To place a copy of an item on the Clipboard without removing it from a file.

Crawl The process by which a Web search engine methodically catalogs the entire Internet to create huge databases with links to Web pages and their URLs.

Criteria The conditions you specify within a database that determine which records to display.

Crop To hide part of a picture or object using the Cropping tool.

Currency A data type used for monetary values.

Current record box See *Specific record box.*

Current record symbol A black triangle symbol that appears in the record select or box to the left of the record that has the focus in either a datasheet or a form.

Custom dictionary Supplemental dictionary to which you add words that are spelled correctly, such as proper names, but which are not already stored in the default dictionary.

Cut To remove an item from a file and place it on the Clipboard.

Cut and paste To move text or graphics using the Cut and Paste commands.

Data The unique information that you enter into the fields of the records.

Data access page See *Page.*

Data label Information that identifies the data in a column or row in a datasheet.

Data marker A graphical representation of a data point, such as a bar or column.

Data point Individual piece of data plotted in a chart.

Data series A column or row in a datasheet; also, the selected range in a worksheet that Excel converts into a graphic and displays as a chart.

Data series marker A graphical representation of a data series, such as a bar or column.

Data source The file that contains the data to be used in a mail merge.

Data type A required property for each field that defines the type of data that can be entered in each field. Valid data types include AutoNumber, Text, Number, Currency, Date/Time, OLE Object, Memo, Yes/No, and Hyperlink.

Database A collection of related information, such as a list of employees.

Database management system A program that organizes data and allows you to link multiple groups of information.

Database software Software used to manage data that can be organized into lists of things such as customers, products, vendors, employees, projects, or sales.

Database window The window that includes common elements such as the Access title bar, menu bar, and toolbar.

Datasheet The component of a chart that contains the numerical data displayed in a chart.

Datasheet (Access) A spreadsheet-like grid that shows fields as columns and records as rows.

Datasheet View A view that lists the records of the object in a datasheet. Table, query, and most form objects have a Datasheet View.

Date ascending order: 1/1/57, 1/1/61, 12/25/61, 5/5/98, 8/20/98, 8/20/99.

Date descending order: 1/1/99, 1/1/98, 12/25/97, 5/5/97, 8/20/61, 8/20/57.

Date Navigator A feature in Calendar that allows you to quickly view days, even nonadjacent days.

Date/Time A data type used for date and time fields.

Delete To permanently remove an item from a file.

Deleted Items folder The folder that contains messages you have deleted. Empty the Deleted Items folder to permanently remove the items from your computer.

Descending order A sequence in which information is placed in reverse alphabetical order or arranged from largest to smallest. For a text field, letters are sorted first, then numbers.

Design templates Predesigned slide designs with formatting and color schemes that you can apply to an open presentation.

Design View A view in which the structure of the object can be manipulated. Every Access object has a Design View.

Desktop publishing program A program for creating publications containing text and graphics.

Destination file The file into which you paste, link, or embed data from another file.

Destination program The program used to create the destination file.

Detail section The section of a form or report that contains the controls that are printed for each record in the underlying query or table.

Details tab A tab in the Contact dialog box used to store each contact's detailed personal information.

Dialog box A window that opens when a program needs more information to carry out a command.

Distribution list A collection of contacts to whom you regularly send the same messages.

Document The electronic file you create using Word.

Document window The workspace in the program window that displays the current document.

Drawing toolbar A toolbar that contains buttons that let you create lines, shapes, and special effects.

Dummy column/row Blank column or row included at the end of a range that enables a formula to adjust when columns or rows are added or deleted.

E-mail Electronic mail messages used in online collaboration.

E-mail software A program that lets you send and receive electronic messages over a network and the Internet.

Edit A change made to the contents of a cell or worksheet.

Edit mode The mode in which Access assumes you are trying to edit a particular field, so keystrokes such as [Ctrl][End], [Ctrl][Home], [←], and [→] move the insertion point *within* the field.

Edit record symbol A pencil-like symbol that appears in the record selector box to the left of the record that is currently being edited in either a datasheet or a form.

Electronic spreadsheet A computer program that performs calculations on data and organizes information into worksheets. A worksheet is divided into columns and rows, which form individual cells.

Embed To paste an object into a file while maintaining a connection to the source file; you can edit an embedded object in the destination file by double-clicking it to open the source program.

Embedded object An object that is created in one application and copied to another. An embedded object remains connected to the original program file in which it was created for easy editing.

Emoticons Simple keyboard characters that are used to express an emotion or mood such as colon and left parenthesis used to create a smiling face ☺ or a colon and a right parenthesis used to create a sad face.

Enter button The check mark in the formula bar used to confirm an entry.

Event An activity defined by Outlook that lasts 24 hours or longer.

Exploding pie slice A slice of a pie chart that has been pulled away from the whole pie to add emphasis.

Explorer Search task pane The left pane of the browser window that opens when you use Internet Explorer's search feature. The Explorer Search task pane contains the Search Assistant.

Expression A combination of values, functions, and operators that calculates to a single value. Access expressions start with an equal sign and are placed in a text box in either Form or Report Design View.

Favorites menu A menu that contains a list of frequently visited Web pages that you can access without having to type the URL.

Field (Access) The smallest piece or category of information in a database such as the customer's name, city, state, or phone number.

Field (Word) A code that serves as a placeholder for data that changes in a document, such as a page number.

Field list   A list of the available fields in a table or the query that it represents.

Field names   The names given to each field in Table Design or Table Datasheet View. Field names can be up to 64 characters long.

Field Property   See *Properties.*

Field Size property   A field property that determines the number of characters or digits allowed for a field.

File   An electronic collection of information that has a unique name, distinguishing it from other files.

File format   A file type, such as .wmf or .gif.

Filename   The name given to a document when it is saved.

Fill color   The cell background color.

Fill Down   A command that duplicates the contents of the selected cells in the range selected below the cell pointer.

Fill handle   A small square in the lower-right corner of the active cell used to copy cell contents.

Fill Right   A command that duplicates the contents of the selected cells in the range selected to the right of the cell pointer.

Filter (verb)   To search for information based on specific criteria.

Filter (Access)   A temporary view of a subset of records. A filter can be saved as a query object if you wish to apply the same filter later without recreating it.

Filter window   A window that appears when you click the Filter By Form button when viewing data in a datasheet or in a form window. The Filter window allows you to define the filter criteria.

Find   A command used to locate information the user specifies.

Find & Replace   A command used to find one set of information and replace it with new information.

First line indent   A type of indent in which the first line of a paragraph is indented more than the subsequent lines.

Fit (print option)   An option that automatically adjusts a preview to display all pages in a report.

Floating graphic   A graphic to which text wrapping has been applied.

Floating toolbar   A toolbar within its own window, not anchored along an edge of the application window.

Focus   The property that indicates which field would be edited if you were to start typing.

Folder   A subdivision of a disk that works like a filing system to help you organize files.

Folder banner   In Outlook, the horizontal bar below the Standard toolbar that indicates the name of the open folder.

Font   The typeface or design of a set of characters (letters, numbers, symbols, and punctuation marks).

Font effects   Font formatting that applies special effects to text, such as shadow, outline, small caps, or superscript.

Font size   The size of characters, measured in units called points (pts).

Footer   Text or graphics that appears at the bottom of every page in a document or a section.

Form   An Access object that provides an easy-to-use data entry screen that generally shows only one record at a time.

Form Design toolbar   The toolbar that appears when working in Form Design View with buttons that help you modify a form's controls.

Form Design View   The view of a form in that you add, delete, and modify the form's properties, sections, and controls.

Form Footer   Section on a form that contains controls that are only printed once, at the bottom of a printout.

Form Header   Section on a form which contains controls that are only printed once, at the top of a printout.

Form View toolbar   The toolbar that appears when your're working in Form view, with buttons that help you print, edit, find, and filter records.

Form Wizard   An interactive tool used to create a new form based on existing tables or queries.

Format The appearance of text and numbers, including color, font, attributes, borders, and shading. See also *Number format*.

Format Painter A feature used to copy the formatting applied to one set of text or in one cell to another.

Formatting marks Nonprinting characters that appear on-screen to indicate the ends of paragraphs, tabs, and other formatting elements.

Formatting toolbar A toolbar that contains buttons for frequently used formatting commands.

Formula A set of instructions used to perform numeric calculations (adding, multiplying, averaging, etc.).

Formula bar The area below the menu bar and above the Excel workspace where you enter and edit data in a worksheet cell. The formula bar becomes active when you start typing or editing cell data. It includes the Enter button and the Cancel button.

Formula prefix An arithmetic symbol, such as the equal sign (=), used to start a formula.

Function A special, predefined formula that provides a shortcut for a commonly used calculation; for example, AVERAGE.

.gif The abbreviation for the graphics interchange format.

Go button A button on the Address bar that activates a search after you enter a keyword or words in the Address bar.

Graphic See *Image*.

Grid Evenly spaced horizontal and vertical lines that appear on a slide when it is being created but not when it is shown or printed.

Gridlines Horizontal and/or vertical lines within a chart that make the chart easier to read.

Group To combine multiple objects into one object.

Group Footer The section of the report that contains controls that print once, at the end of each group of records.

Group Header The section of the report that contains controls that print once, at the beginning of each group of records.

Grouping To sort records in a particular order plus provide a section before and after each group of records.

Groups button In the opening database window, the button that expands or collapses the section of the Objects bar that presents Access groups.

Gutter Extra margin space left for a binding at the top or left side of a document.

Handles See *Sizing handles*.

Hanging indent A type of indent in which the second and subsequent lines of a paragraph are indented more than the first.

Hard page break A page break inserted to force the text following the break to begin at the top of the next page.

Header Text or graphics that appears at the top of every page in a document or a section.

Help system Pages of documentation and examples that are available through the Help menu option, the Microsoft Access Help button on the Database toolbar, or the Office Assistant.

Highlighting Transparent color that can be applied to text to call attention to it.

Hits The result of an Internet keyword search that appears as a list of related sites.

Home page The first Web page that opens every time you start Internet Explorer.

Horizontal ruler A ruler that appears at the top of the document window in Print Layout, Normal, and Web Layout view.

Hyperlink (Access) A data type that stores *World Wide Web* or file address information, such as http://www.course. com or \\Personnel\Employees.mdgb.

Hyperlink Text or a graphic that opens a file, Web page, or other item when clicked. Also known as a link.

Hypertext Markup Language (HTML) The formatting language used to structure Web pages.

I-beam pointer The I pointer, used to move the insertion point and select text.

Image A nontextual piece of information such as a picture, piece of clip art, drawn object, or graph. Because images are graphical (not numbers or letters), they are sometimes referred to as *graphical images*.

Inbox The folder that contains incoming messages.

Indent The space between the edge of a line of text or a paragraph and the margin.

Indent markers Markers on the horizontal ruler that show the indent settings for the active paragraph.

Inline graphic A graphic that is part of a line of text.

Input Information that produces desired results, or output, in a worksheet.

Insertion point (Excel) The blinking vertical line that appears in the formula bar or in a cell during editing.

Insertion point (PowerPoint) A blinking vertical line that indicates where text appears in a text placeholder.

Insertion point (Word) The blinking vertical line that shows where text will appear when you type in a document.

Integration The ability to use data created in one Office program in a file created in another Office program.

Internet A communications system that connects computers and computer networks located around the world using telephone lines, cables, satellites, and other telecommunications media.

Internet Explorer A popular browser from Microsoft.

Intranet A computer network that connects computers in a specific area only, such as the computers in a company's office. An intranet can be accessed internally or through a remote location.

Is Not Null Criterion that finds all records in which any entry has been made in the field.

Is Null Criterion that finds all records in which no entry has been made in the field.

Italic Formatting applied to text to make the characters slanted.

Justify Alignment in which an item is flush with both the left and right margins.

Key field See *Primary key field*.

Key field symbol In table Design View, the symbol that appears as a miniature key in the field indicator box to the left of the field name. It identifies the field that contains unique information for each record.

Keyboard shortcut A combination of keys or a function keys that can be pressed to perform a command.

Keyword A representative word on which the Help system can search to find information on your area of interest.

Label (Access) An unbound control that displays static text on forms and reports.

Label (Excel) Descriptive text or other information that identifies the rows and columns of a worksheet. Labels are not included in calculations.

Label prefix A character, such as the apostrophe, that identifies an entry as a label and controls the way it appears in the cell.

Label Wizard A report–generation tool that helps you create mailing labels.

Landscape orientation Page orientation in which the page is wider than it is tall.

Left indent A type of indent in which the left edge of a paragraph is moved in from the left margin.

Left-align Alignment in which the item is flush with the left margin.

Legend A key explaining how information is represented by colors or patterns in a chart.

Line chart A graph of data that is mapped by a series of lines. Line charts show changes in data or categories of data over time and can be used to document trends.

Line control An unbound control used to draw lines on a form or report that divide it into logical groupings.

Line spacing The amount of space between lines of text.

Link (verb) To paste an object into a file while maintaining a connection to the source file; when you edit the source file, the changes are automatically updated in the destination file.

Link (noun) Text or image within a Web page that takes you to other sites or documents; also known as hyperlinks.

Links bar Located next to the Address bar, it contains links to frequently visited Web pages.

List box A bound control that displays a list of possible choices from which the user can choose, used mainly on forms.

Lookup wizard A wizard that helps link the current table to another table. A field created with the lookup wizard will display data from another table or list.

Macro An Access object that stores a collection of keystrokes or commands such as those for printing several reports in a row or providing a toolbar when a form opens.

Mailing labels Printed labels that are used for many business purposes such as identifying folders in a filing cabinet, labeling products for sale, or providing addresses for mass mailings.

Main document In a mail merge, the document into which you are merging the data source.

Main text placeholder A reserved box on a slide for the main text points.

Margin The blank area between the edge of the text and the edge of a page.

Meeting An activity you invite people to or reserve resources for.

Memo A data type used for lengthy text such as comments or notes. It can hold up to 64,000 characters of information.

Menu bar The bar beneath the title bar that contains the names of menus, that when clicked, open menus from which you choose program commands.

Merge Combining data from one file with data from another file to create a new file.

Merge fields In a mail merge, placeholders in the main document that are replaced with data from the data source during the merge.

Message header icons Icons to the left of the sender's name that identify the attributes of the message.

Message header The area at the top of a message that identifies the sender of the message, the subject, the date and time the message was received, and the size of the message.

Microsoft Graph The program that creates a datasheet and chart to graphically depict numerical information.

Microsoft Outlook Express A program that you can use to exchange e-mail and join newsgroups. Microsoft Outlook Express comes with Windows 2000.

Mirror margins Margins used in documents with facing pages, where the inside and outside margins are mirror images of each other.

Mixed reference A formula containing both a relative and absolute reference.

Mode indicator A box located at the lower-left corner of the status bar that informs you of a program's status. For example, when Excel is performing a task, the word "Wait" appears.

Module An Access object that stores Visual Basic programming code that extends the functions and automated processes of Access.

Mouse pointer A symbol that indicates the current location of the mouse on the desktop. The mouse pointer changes its shape to indicate what you can do next; for example, when you insert data, select a range, position a chart, change the size of a window or a column, or select a topic in Help.

Moving border The dashed line that appears around a cell or range that is copied to the Clipboard.

Multitask The ability to open several programs and files at once and then to switch back and forth among them.

Name box The left-most area in the formula bar that shows the cell reference or name of the active cell. For example, A1 refers to cell A1 of the active worksheet. You can also display a list of names in a workbook using the Name list arrow.

Name property Property of a text box that gives the text box a meaningful name.

Named range A range of cells given a meaningful name; it retains its name when moved and can be referenced in a formula.

Navigation buttons Buttons in the lower-left corner of a datasheet or form that allow you to quickly navigate between the records in the underlying object as well as add a new record.

Navigation mode A mode in which Access assumes that you are trying to move between the fields and records of the datasheet (rather than edit a specific field's contents), so keystrokes such as [Ctrl][Home] and [Ctrl][End] move you to the first and last field of the datasheet, respectively.

Negative indent A type of indent in which the left edge of a paragraph is moved to the left of the left margin.

Network A group of computers connected to each other with cables and software.

New Document task pane A task pane that contains shortcuts for opening documents and for creating new documents.

New Record button A button that, when clicked, displays a new record for data entry. It is found on both the Form View and Datasheet toolbars as well as being one of the Navigation buttons.

New Workbook task pane A task pane that lets you quickly open new or existing workbooks.

Normal view (PowerPoint) A presentation view that divides the presentation window into Outline, Slide, and Notes panes.

Normal view (Word) A view that shows a document without margins, headers and footers, or graphics.

Notes folder The folder that stores the Notes.

Notes Page view A presentation view that displays a reduced image of the current slide above a large text box where you can type notes.

Notes pane The area in Normal view that shows speaker notes for the current slide; also in Notes Page view, the area below the slide image that contains speaker notes.

Notes The component in Outlook used to write short reminders, an idea or a note concerning an appointment or task, it is an electronic version of the popular colored paper sticky notes.

Null The term that refers to a state in which a field is empty. Any entry such as 0 in a numeric field or an invisible space in a text field is *not* null. It is common to search for empty fields by using the criteria "Is Null" in a filter or query. The "Is Not Null" criterion finds all records where there is an entry of any kind.

Number A data type used for numeric information used in calculations, such as quantities.

Number ascending order: 1, 10, 15, 120, 140, 500, 1200, 1500.

Number descending order: 1500, 1400, 1200, 140, 120, 15, 10, 1.

Number format A format applied to values to express numeric concepts, such as currency, date, and percentage.

Object An item that can be moved and resized and that contains handles when selected. Objects can be drawn lines and shapes, text, clip art, imported pictures, and embedded objects.

Object (Access) A table, query, form, report, page, macro, or module.

Object list box In Form Design view and Report Design view, this box is located on the Formatting (Form/Report toolbar) and displays the name or caption for the currently selected control.

Objects bar In the opening database window, the toolbar that presents the seven Access objects and groups. When you click an object button on the Objects bar, options and wizards used to create an object of that type, as well as existing objects of that type, appear in the main portion of the database window.

Objects button In the opening database window, the button that expands or collapses the section of the Objects bar that presents seven the Access objects.

Office Assistant An animated character that offers tips, answers questions, and provides access to the program's Help system.

Office Assistant tip A hint, indicated by the appearance of an onscreen light bulb, about the current action you are performing.

Office Clipboard A temporary storage area shared by all Office programs that can be used to cut, copy and paste multiple items within and between Office programs. The Office Clipboard can hold up to 24 items collected from any Office program. See also *System Clipboard* and *Clipboard task Pane.*

OLE Object (Access) A data type that stores pointers that tie files created in other programs to a record such as pictures, sound clips, word processing documents, or spreadsheets.

Online collaboration Using the Internet to share and review documents, hold online discussions, and send e-mail with business colleagues or friends.

Open A command that retrieves a file from the drive or folder where it is stored and displays it on the screen.

Option button A bound control used to display a limited list of possible choices for a field such as "female" or "male" for a gender field in a form or report.

Or criteria Criteria placed on different rows of the query design grid. A record will appear in the resulting datasheet if it is true for any single row.

Order of precedence The order in which Excel calculates parts of a formula: (1) exponents, (2) multiplication and division, and (3) addition and subtraction.

Outbox folder The folder that contains messages you have sent, but which Outlook has not yet delivered.

Outline tab The area in Normal view that displays your presentation text in the form of an outline, without graphics.

Outline view A view that shows the headings of a document organized as an outline.

Outlook Bar The vertical bar located on the left side of the program window that contains groups and the shortcuts to frequently used folders.

Outlook Shortcuts group A collection of frequently used shortcuts on the Outlook Bar; includes frequently used folders.

Outlook Today page A customizable view within Outlook that provides a preview of your day's tasks, appointments, and messages at a glance.

Output The end result of a worksheet.

Overtype mode A feature that allows you to overwrite existing text as you type.

Page An Access object that creates Web pages from Access objects as well as provides Web page connectivity features to an Access database. Also called data access page.

Page Footer The section of the form or report that contains controls that print once, at the bottom of each page.

Page Header The section of the form or report that contains controls that print once at the top of each page. On the first page of a report, the Page Header section prints below the Report Header section.

Pane A section of the PowerPoint window, such as the Slide or Notes pane.

Paragraph spacing The amount of space between paragraphs.

Paragraph style A named set of paragraph and character format settings that can be applied to a paragraph to format it all at once.

Paste A command that copies information on the Clipboard to a new location. Excel pastes the formula, rather than the result, unless the Paste Special command is used.

Paste Function A series of dialog boxes that helps you build functions; it lists and describes all Excel functions.

Paste Options Button A button that appears after an item is pasted; click its list arrow to keep source formatting, match destination cell formatting or keep the source cell's column widths.

Personal information manager (PIM) A program that includes tools, such as a scheduler and a contact manager, that help you manage a typical business day.

Pie chart A circular chart that represents data as slices of a pie. A pie chart is useful for showing the relationship of parts to a whole; pie slices can be extracted for emphasis. See also *Exploding pie slice.*

Placeholder A dashed line box where you place text or objects.

Plot area The area inside the horizontal and vertical chart axes.

Point A unit of measure used for fonts, the space between paragraphs and characters, and row height. One inch equals 72 points, or a point is equal to 1/72 of an inch.

Pointing method Specifying formula cell references by selecting the desired cell with the mouse instead of typing its cell reference; it eliminates typing errors. Also known as Pointing.

Portrait orientation Page orientation in which the page is taller than it is wide.

PowerPoint Viewer A special application designed to run a PowerPoint slide show on any compatible computer that does not have PowerPoint installed.

PowerPoint window A window that contains the running PowerPoint application. The PowerPoint window includes the PowerPoint menus, toolbars, and Presentation window.

Presentation graphics program A program that is used to develop slides and handouts for visual presentations.

Presentation window The area where you work on and view your presentation. You type text and work with objects in the Presentation window.

Preview pane The lower pane of the Inbox that allows you to read and scroll through your messages without opening them.

Primary key field A field that contains unique information for each record. A primary key field cannot contain a null entry.

Primary sort field In a query grid, the leftmost field that includes sort criteria. It determines the order in which the records will appear and can be specified as "ascending" or "descending."

Print Layout view A view that shows a document as it will look on a printed page.

Print Preview A command you can use to view a file as it will look when printed.

Profile A set of information used to identify individual e-mail users.

Program Task-oriented software (such as Excel or Word) that enables you to perform a certain type of task, such as data calculation or word processing.

Programs menu The Windows Start menu that lists all available programs on your computer.

Properties Characteristics that further define the field, control, section, or object.

Property sheet A window that displays an exhaustive list of properties for the chosen control, section, or object.

Prototype label A sample mailing label used to display how the resulting mailing labels will appear when created using the Label Wizard.

Publish To post Web pages on an intranet or the Web so people can access them using a Web browser.

Query An Access object that provides a spreadsheet-like view of data, similar to tables. It may provide the user with a subset of fields and/or records from one or more tables.

Query design grid The lower portion of the Query Design view window in which you determine the order of fields, add sort orders, and enter limiting criteria.

Query Design View The view of a query in which you can add, delete, or modify the field order, sort order, and limiting criteria saved within the query.

Range A selected group of adjacent cells.

Range finder A feature that outlines an equation's arguments in blue and green.

Range format A format applied to a selected range in a worksheet.

Raw data The individual pieces of information stored in the database in individual fields.

Record A group of related fields, such as all demographic information for one customer.

Record selector box The small square to left of a record in a datasheet that marks the current record or the edit record symbol when the record has the focus or is being edited.

Record source In a form or report, either a table or query object that contains the fields and records that the form will display.

Rectangle control An unbound control used to draw rectangles on the form that divide the other form controls into logical groupings.

Relational database A database in which more than one table, such as the customer, sales, and inventory tables, can share information. The term "relational database" comes from the fact that the tables are linked, or "related", by a common field of information.

Relative cell reference A type of cell reference used to indicate a relative position in the worksheet. It allows you to copy and move formulas from one area to another of the same dimensions. Excel automatically changes the column and row numbers to reflect the new position. Also known as Relative reference.

Relative link A hyperlink that gives another Web page's address in relation to the current page.

Report An Access object that creates a professional printout of data that may contain such enhancements as headers, footers, and calculations on groups of records.

Report Design View View of a report in which you add, delete, and edit the report's properties, sections, and controls.

Report Footer section On a report, a section that contains controls that print once, at the end of the last page of the report.

Report Header section On a report, a section that contains controls that print once, at the top of the first page of the report.

Report Wizard An interactive tool used to create a new report based on a table or query.

Reset usage data An option that allows adapted toolbars and menus to be returned to their default settings.

Right indent A type of indent in which the right edge of a paragraph is moved in from the right margin.

Right-align Alignment in which an item is flush with the right margin.

Rotate handle A green circular handle at the top of a selected object that you can drag to rotate the selected object upside-down, sideways, or to any angle in between.

Row heading The gray box containing the row number to the left of the row.

Row height The vertical dimension of a cell.

Row selector The small square to the left of a field in Table Design view.

Sans serif font A font whose characters do not include serifs, such as Arial.

Save To store a file permanently on a disk or to overwrite the copy of a file that is stored on a disk with the changes made to the file.

Save As Command used to save a file for the first time or to create a new file with a different filename, leaving the original file intact.

Scale To change the size of a graphic a specific percentage of its original size.

ScreenTip A label that appears on the screen to identify a button or provide information about a feature.

Scroll To use the scroll bars or the arrow keys to display different parts of the document in a document window.

Scroll arrows The arrows at the ends of the scroll bars that are clicked to scroll a document one line at a time.

Scroll bars The bars on the right and bottom edges of the document window that are used to display different parts of the document in the document window.

Scroll box The box in the scroll bars that can be dragged to scroll a file and indicates your relative position within the file.

Search Assistant A search feature that displays a list of search categories for finding Web pages, people, businesses, previous searches, or maps.

Search engine An Internet site that lets you enter a keyword or phrase describing the information you want to find and then provides you with a list of related Web sites.

Secondary sort field In a query grid, the second field from the left that includes sort criteria. It determines the order in which the records will appear if there is a "tie" on the primary sort field.

Section (Access) A location on a form or report that contains controls. The section in which a control is placed determines where and how often the control prints.

Section (Word) A portion of a document that is separated from the rest of the document by section breaks.

Section break A formatting mark inserted to divide a document into sections.

Select To click or highlight an item in order to perform some action on it.

Selection box A slanted line border that appears around a text object or placeholder indicating it is ready to accept text.

Selection handles Small boxes appearing along the corners and sides of charts and graphic images that are used for moving and resizing.

Sent Items folder The folder that contains messages you have sent.

Series of labels Preprogrammed series, such as days of the week and months of the year. They are formed by typing the first word of the series, then dragging the fill handle to the desired cell.

Serif font A font whose characters include serifs — small strokes — at the ends, such as Times New Roman.

Shading A background color or pattern that can be applied to text, tables, or graphics.

Sheet A term used for a worksheet.

Sheet tab A description at the bottom of each worksheet that identifies it in a workbook. In an open workbook, move to a worksheet by clicking its sheet tab. Also known as Worksheet tab.

Sheet tab scrolling buttons Buttons that enable you to move among sheets within a workbook.

Shortcut key See *Keyboard shortcut.*

Sizing handles (Access) Small squares at each corner of a selected control in Access. Dragging a handle resizes the control. Also known as *handles.*

Sizing handles The small circles that appear around a selected object. Dragging a handle resizes the object.

Slide A "page" in an on-screen display in a visual presentation.

Slide indicator box A small box that appears when you drag the vertical scroll box in Slide and Notes Page view identifying which slide you are on.

Slide layout This determines how all of the elements on a slides are arranged including text and content placeholders.

Slide pane The area of Normal view that contains the current slide.

Slide show An on-screen display of consecutive images in a presentation.

Slide Show view A view that shows a presentation as an electronic slide show.

Slide Sorter view A view that displays a thumbnail of all slides in the order in which they appear in your presentation; used to rearrange slides and add special effects.

Slide timing The amount of time a slide is visible on the screen during a slide show.

Slide transition The special effect that moves one slide off the screen and the next slide on the screen during a slide show. Each slide can have its own transition effect.

Slides tab The area in Normal View that displays the slides of your presentation as small thumbnails.

Smart tag A purple dotted line that appears under text Word identifies as a date, name, address, or place.

Smart Tag Actions button The button that appears when you point to a smart tag.

Soft page break A page break that is inserted automatically at the bottom of a page.

Sort To place records in a specific order (ascending or descending) based on the values of a particular field.

Source document (Access) The original paper document that records raw data such as an employment application. In some databases, there is no source document because raw data is entered directly into the computer.

Source file The file from which you copy the data you are going to paste, link, or embed in the destination file.

Source program The program used to create the source file.

Specific record box Part of a box in the lower left-hand corner in Datasheet View and Form View. Navigation buttons that indicates the current record number. You can click in the specific record box, then type a record number to quickly move to that record. Also called the current record box or record number box.

Spelling check A command that attempts to match all text in a file with the words in the dictionary.

Spreadsheet A program used to analyze data, perform calculations, and create charts.

Standard toolbar The toolbar containing the buttons that perform some of the most frequently used commands.

Start To open a software program so you can use it.

Status bar (Access) The bar at the bottom of the Access window that provides informational messages and other status information (such as whether the Num Lock is active or not).

Status bar (Excel) The bar at the bottom of the Excel window that provides information about various keys, commands, and processes.

Status bar (Internet Explorer) A bar located at the bottom of the Web browser window that displays information about your connection progress whenever you open a new Web page, notifies you when you connect to another Web site, and identifies the percentage of information transferred from the Web server to your browser. It also displays the Web addresses of any links on the Web page when you move your mouse pointer over them.

Status bar (Outlook) The bar at the bottom of the Outlook window that provides information such as the total number of messages that the open folder contains, the number of those messages that have not been read, whether or not a filter is applied.

Status bar (PowerPoint) The bar at the bottom of the PowerPoint window that contains messages about what you are doing and seeing in PowerPoint, such as the current slide number or a description of a command or button.

Status bar (Word) The bar at the bottom of the Word window that shows the vertical position, section, and page number of the insertion point, the total number of pages in a document, and the on/off status of several Word features.

Status indicator The logo on the toolbar that is animated while a new Web page loads.

Store and forward technology A computer-based communication system in which the senders and recipients don't have to be on their computers at the same time to communicate.

Style A named collection of character and paragraph formats stored together that can be applied to text to format it quickly.

Subscript A font effect in which text is formatted in a smaller font size and placed below the line of text.

Suite A set of programs with similar icons, buttons, and commands that are designed to work together to complete business tasks.

SUM The most frequently used function, this adds columns or rows of cells.

Superscript A font effect in which text is formatted in a smaller font size and placed above the line of text.

Surfing The process of using the Web and navigating to new Web pages and sites.

Symbols Special characters that can be inserted into a document using the Symbol command.

System Clipboard A clipboard that stores only the last item cut or copied from a document.

Tab See *Tab stop*.

Tab control An unbound control used to add a three-dimensional aspect to a form so that other controls can be organized and shown in Form View by clicking the "tabs."

Tab leaders Lines that appear in front of tabbed text.

Tab order The sequence in which the controls on the form receive the focus when the user presses [Tab] or [Enter] in Form view.

Tab stop A location on the horizontal ruler that indicates where to align text.

Table An Access object that is a collection of records for a single subject, such as all of the customer records.

Table   An arrangement of text or data in columns and rows.

Table Datasheet toolbar   The toolbar that appears when you are viewing a table's datasheet.

Table Design View   The view of a table in which you can add, delete, or modify the fields.

Table Wizard   An interactive tool used to create a new table from a list of sample tables and sample fields.

Tags   HTML codes that describe how the elements of a Web page should appear when viewed with a Web browser.

Task pane (Excel)   A window area to the right of the worksheet that provides worksheet options, such as creating a new workbook, opening an existing workbook, conducting a search, inserting Clip Art, and using the Office Clipboard.

Task pane (PowerPoint)   A separate pane seen in all the PowerPoint views except Slide Show view that contains sets of hyperlinks for commonly used commands.

TaskPad   An area in Calendar that displays your task list.

Tasks folder   The folder that stores your business and personal to-do list.

Tasks   The component within Outlook that works as an electronic to-do list. You can view tasks in several different ways, including by subject, by status, and by due date. You can mark your progress on tasks in many ways, and you can assign tasks to colleagues and track completion.

Template (Excel)   An Excel file saved with a special format that lets you open a new file based on an existing workbook's design and/or content.

Template (Word)   A formatted document that contains placeholder text you can replace with your own text.

Text   A data type that allows entry of text information or combinations of text and numbers such as a street address. By default, it is 50 characters.

Text annotations   Labels added to a chart to draw attention to a particular area.

Text ascending order: 123, 3H, 455, 98, 98B, animal, Iowa, New Jersey

Text box (Access)   A common control used on forms and reports to display data bound to an underlying field. A text box can also show calculated controls such as subtotals and dates.

Text box (PowerPoint)   Any text you create using the Text Box button. A word processing box and a text label are both examples of a text box.

Text color   The color applied to text.

Text descending order: Zebra, Victory, Langguth, Bunin, 99A, 9854, 77, 740, 29, 270, 23500, 1.

Text label   A text box you create using the Text Box button where the text does not automatically wrap inside the box.

Text placeholder   A box with a dashed-line border and text that you replace with your own text.

Theme   A set of Web page formats, including backgrounds and styles, that are named and stored together; can be applied to a Web page to format it quickly.

Thumbnail   A small image of a slide. Thumbnails are found on the Slides tab and in Slide Sorter view.

Tick marks   Notations of a scale of measure on a chart axis.

Timing   See *Slide timing*.

Title   The first line or heading on a slide.

Title bar   The bar at the top of the program window that indicates the program name and the name of the current file.

Title placeholder   A box on a slide reserved for the title of a presentation or slide.

Title slide   The first slide in your presentation.

Toggle button   A button that turns a feature on and off.

Toggle button (Access)   A bound control used to indicate "yes" or "no" answers for a field in Access. If the button is "pressed", it displays "yes" information.

Toolbar   A bar that contains buttons that you can click to perform commands.

Toolbar Options button   A button you click on a toolbar to view toolbar buttons not currently visible.

Toolbox toolbar The toolbar that has common controls that you can add to a report or form when working in the report or form's Design View.

Truncate To shorten the display of cell information because a cell is too wide.

Unbound controls Controls that do not change from record to record and exist only to clarify or enhance the appearance of the form, such as labels, lines, and clip art.

Unbound image control An unbound control that is used to display clip art and that doesn't change as you navigate from record to record on a form or report.

Undo To reverse a change by using the Undo button or command.

Uniform Resource Locator (URL) A Web page's address.

Value axis Also known as the y-axis in a 2-dimensional chart, this area often contains numerical values that help you interpret the size of chart elements.

Values Numbers, formulas, or functions used in calculations.

Vertical alignment The position of text in a document relative to the top and bottom margins.

Vertical scroll bar A scroll bar that allows you to move the current Web page up or down in the Web browser window.

View (PowerPoint) A way of displaying a presentation, such as Normal view, Notes Page view, Slide Sorter view, and Slide Show view.

View (Word) A way of displaying a document in the document window; each view provides features useful for editing and formatting different types of documents.

View buttons Buttons on the horizontal scroll bar that are used to change views.

View buttons The buttons at the bottom of the Outline tab and the Slides tab that you click to switch among views.

Voice recognition A program feature that allows you to enter data and give commands verbally using a computer microphone.

Web browser A software program used to access and display Web pages.

Web Layout view A view that shows a document as it will look when viewed with a Web browser.

Web page A file saved in HTML format that can be viewed using a Web browser.

Web server A computer that stores Web pages.

What-if analysis A decision-making feature in which data is changed and formulas based on it are automatically recalculated.

Wildcard characters Special characters used in criteria to find, filter, and query data. The asterisk (*) stands for any group of characters. The question mark (?) wildcard stands for only one character. The pound sign (#) can only be used as a wildcard in a numeric field and stands for a single number.

Window A rectangular area of a screen where you view and work on the open file.

Windows Media Player An Internet Explorer suite component that lets you listen to and/or view live and prerecorded sounds, images, and videos.

Wizard An interactive set of dialog boxes that guides you through a task.

.wmf The abbreviation for the Windows metafile file format, which is the format of much clip art.

Word processing program A software program that includes tools for entering, editing, and formatting text and graphics.

Word program window The window that contains the Word program elements, including the document window, toolbars, menu bar, and status bar.

Word wrap A feature that automatically moves the insertion point to the next line as you type.

Word processing box A text box you create using the Text Box button, where the text automatically wraps inside the box.

Workbook A collection of related worksheets contained within a single file.

Worksheet An electronic spreadsheet containing 256 columns by 65,536 rows.

Worksheet tab See *Sheet tab*.

Worksheet window The worksheet area that includes the tools needed to create and work with worksheets in which data is entered.

World Wide Web (Web or **WWW)** A part of the Internet, containing Web pages linked together with hyperlinks, that brings text, graphics, and multimedia information to your desktop.

X-axis The horizontal axis in a chart; because it often shows data categories, such as months, it is also called the category axis.

X-axis label A label describing a chart's x-axis.

Y-axis The vertical axis in a chart; because it often shows numerical values in a 2 dimensional chart, it is also called the value axis.

Y-axis label A label describing the y-axis of a chart.

Yes/No A data type that stores only one of two values (Yes/No, On/Off, True/False).

Zoom A feature that enables you to focus on a larger or smaller part of the worksheet in Print Preview.

Zoom pointers Mouse pointers displayed in Print Preview that allow you to toggle the zoom magnification of a printout.

Index

Index

Index

Index

Index

Index